DEMOCRACY, DIVERSITY, AND GOOD GOVERNMENT

An Introduction to Politics in Canada

Eric Mintz

SIR WILFRED GRENFELL COLLEGE, MEMORIAL UNIVERSITY OF NEWFOUNDLAND

Livianna Tossutti

BROCK UNIVERSITY

Christopher Dunn

MEMORIAL UNIVERSITY OF NEWFOUNDLAND

Pearson Canada
Toronto

Library and Archives Canada Cataloguing in Publication

Mintz, Eric
  Democracy, diversity, and good government : an introduction to politics in Canada /
  Eric Mintz, Livianna Tossutti, Christopher Dunn.

Includes bibliographical references and index.
ISBN 978-0-13-235061-7

1. Canada—Politics and government—Textbooks. I. Tossutti, Livianna S., 1964– II. Dunn,
Christopher J. C., 1948– III. Title.

JL75.M56 2011   320.971   C2010-900567-8

ISBN 978-0-13-235061-7

Vice-President, Editorial Director: Gary Bennett
Editor-in-Chief: Ky Pruesse
Senior Acquisitions Editor: Laura Pratt
Executive Marketing Manager: Judith Allen
Developmental Editor: Heather Parker
Production Editor: Melissa Hajek
Substantive Editor: Sharon Kirsch
Copy Editor: Lisa Berland
Proofreaders: Kelly Coleman and Susan McNish
Production Coordinator: Sarah Lukaweski
Composition: MPS Limited, A Macmillan Company
Permissions and Photo Research: Rachel Irwin
Art Director: Julia Hall
Cover and Interior Design: Miguel Angel Acevedo
Cover Image: Getty Images

1 2 3 4 5   14 13 12 11 10

Printed and bound in the United States of America.

To Aaron, Diane, and Kaila
The loves of my life

E.M.

To my mother, Therese Gallery Tossutti
*Love is the tide
and she the eternal sea.*

L.T.

To the memory of my mother, Patricia Mary Gracia Dunn,
who introduced me to the study of Canadian politics.

C.D.

BRIEF CONTENTS

CONTENTS

PART III   Public Involvement, Organization, and Influence   137

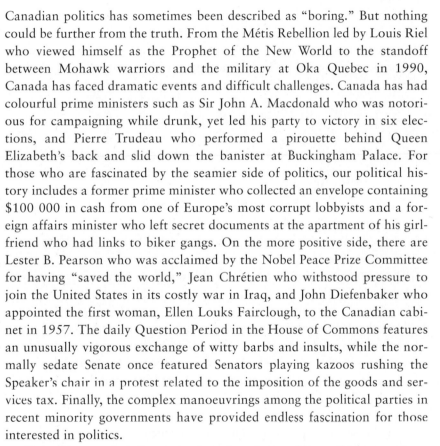

PREFACE

Canadian politics has sometimes been described as "boring." But nothing could be further from the truth. From the Métis Rebellion led by Louis Riel who viewed himself as the Prophet of the New World to the standoff between Mohawk warriors and the military at Oka Quebec in 1990, Canada has faced dramatic events and difficult challenges. Canada has had colourful prime ministers such as Sir John A. Macdonald who was notorious for campaigning while drunk, yet led his party to victory in six elections, and Pierre Trudeau who performed a pirouette behind Queen Elizabeth's back and slid down the banister at Buckingham Palace. For those who are fascinated by the seamier side of politics, our political history includes a former prime minister who collected an envelope containing $100 000 in cash from one of Europe's most corrupt lobbyists and a foreign affairs minister who left secret documents at the apartment of his girlfriend who had links to biker gangs. On the more positive side, there are Lester B. Pearson who was acclaimed by the Nobel Peace Prize Committee for having "saved the world," Jean Chrétien who withstood pressure to join the United States in its costly war in Iraq, and John Diefenbaker who appointed the first woman, Ellen Louks Fairclough, to the Canadian cabinet in 1957. The daily Question Period in the House of Commons features an unusually vigorous exchange of witty barbs and insults, while the normally sedate Senate once featured Senators playing kazoos rushing the Speaker's chair in a protest related to the imposition of the goods and services tax. Finally, the complex manoeuvrings among the political parties in recent minority governments have provided endless fascination for those interested in politics.

Canadians are heavily exposed to American politics, which sometimes adds to the feeling that politics in Canada is less interesting and less important than that of our neighbour. What happens in American politics certainly has a profound effect on Canada and the rest of the world. However, we should not be too modest about Canada's role in the world. Canadians played a major part in defeating the Nazis in the Second World War and were active in creating the United Nations and other international institutions that are of continuing importance. Canada and Canadians took the lead in eliminating the threat to the environment caused by ozone-depleting substances, in creating the International Criminal Court that can bring to justice those accused of crimes against humanity, and in gaining agreement among many countries to ban anti-personnel land mines. While U.S. president Barack Obama gained great attention for his efforts to bring some modest changes to the American health care system, many Canadians are too young to remember the much tougher stance of the premier of Saskatchewan who stood in the face of a doctors strike to bring in Canada's first universal public medicare system.

Of course, politics in Canada is more than interesting stories and events. It affects our lives in many ways, such as the ability of students to afford higher education, the safety of the food we eat, how well the natural environment is protected, whether our opportunities will be limited by high unemployment, and even who we can legally marry. In this book we focus particularly on analyzing how the great diversity of Canada provides important challenges for the practice of democracy and the good government that Canadians expect. By reading this book you should gain a good understanding of such important topics as the workings of the parliamentary system of government, the protection of rights and freedoms, the competition among political parties, the federal system, and the ways in which citizens try to influence government policies. We believe it is the duty and responsibility of all citizens to understand and participate in the political life of their country. It is our hope that this book will contribute to the achievement of that important objective.

There are many features that make this textbook interesting and easy to understand:

- Each chapter opens with a *vignette* that provides an interesting and often provocative story that relates to the content of the chapter. Among the vignettes are the struggle of women to be recognized as "persons," student protests against a new system of student loans, and the challenge to Facebook's weak privacy policy.
- *Boxes* in each chapter provide examples that illustrate the material in the text. These boxes deal with such topics as cyberactivism, same-sex marriage, and the controversy concerning the participation of the leader of the Green party in the 2008 leaders' election debate.
- To guide students in understanding the textbook, each chapter includes *Chapter Objectives* at the start and a *Summary and Conclusion* at the end.
- *Key Terms* are printed in bold in the text, defined in the margin for instant reference, and compiled in the end-of-book glossary.

- The *Discussion Questions* at the end of each chapter are designed to spark critical thought and discussion.
- The *Further Reading* at the end of each chapter provides suggestions for those who would like to explore further the topics in the chapter. *Weblinks* in the margins provide additional research resources.
- The *graphics*—photos, figures, and tables—illustrate concepts discussed in the text and illuminate some features of Canadian politics.

SUPPLEMENTS

The supplements package for this book has been carefully created to enhance the topics discussed in the text.

Instructor's Resource CD-ROM (IRCD). This instructor resource CD includes the Instructor's Manual, Test Item File, and PowerPoint Presentations.

Instructor's Manual. For each chapter of the text, this manual provides sample lecture outlines, clarification of potentially confusing terms and ideas, and a description of the major themes. In addition, it includes sample course outlines and lecture schedules.

PowerPoint Presentations. This instructor resource contains key points and lecture notes to accompany each chapter in the text.

Test Item File. This test bank contains multiple-choice, true/false, short answer, and essay questions.

MyTest. The test bank is also available as a MyTest, a powerful assessment-generation program that helps instructors easily create and print quizzes, tests, exams, as well as homework or practice handouts. Questions and tests can be authored online, allowing instructors ultimate flexibility and the ability to manage assessments efficiently anywhere, anytime. The MyTest can be accessed by visiting **www.pearsonmytest.com**.

Companion Website. This student resource features chapter objectives and study questions, as well as links to interesting material and information from other sites on the Web that reinforce and enhance the content of each chapter. The companion website can be accessed at **www.pearsoned.ca/mintz**.

CourseSmart for Instructors. CourseSmart goes beyond traditional expectations—providing instant, online access to the textbooks and course materials you need at a lower cost for students. And even as students save money, you can save time and hassle with a digital eTextbook that allows you to search for the most relevant content at the very moment you need it. Whether it's evaluating textbooks or creating lecture notes to help students with difficult concepts, CourseSmart can make life a little easier. See how when you visit **www.coursesmart.com/instructors**.

CourseSmart for Students. CourseSmart goes beyond traditional expectations—providing instant, online access to the textbooks and course materials you need at an average savings of 50%. With instant access from any computer and the ability to search your text, you'll find the content you need quickly, no matter where you are. And with online tools like highlighting and note-taking, you can save time and study efficiently. See all the benefits at **www.coursesmart.com/students**.

ACKNOWLEDGMENTS

We would like to thank the many political science professors who provided detailed and helpful suggestions by reviewing the draft chapters of this book. Among these reviewers were the following individuals (in alphabetical order): Mark Blythe, University of Alberta; Ayla Kilic, Okanagan College; Christian Leuprecht, Royal Military College of Canada; Chris Maddocks, Niagara College; David B. MacDonald, University of Guelph; Fiona MacDonald, University of Manitoba; Greg Narbey, Humber College; Ray Pillar, Thompson Rivers University; John Soroski, Grant MacEwan University; Nelson Wiseman, University of Toronto.

Many people at Pearson Education Canada took great care in turning the authors' drafts into a very readable and interesting textbook. In particular, we would like to thank Laura Patterson Pratt, Heather Parker, Melissa Hajek, and Sharon Kirsch.

Eric Mintz would like to thank Aaron Mintz for his excellent legal research that enhances the chapters on the constitution, federalism, Aboriginal rights, and the judicial system. Aaron also read and commented on a number of chapters. Diane Mintz not only put up with the many, many long hours he spent on this book and provided much-needed support and encouragement, but also carefully reviewed all the chapters and made numerous suggestions to ensure the book was clearly written. One of the best chapter-opening vignettes came from discussions with Sam Dinicol while our families enjoyed dinner in Barra de Navidad. Finally, Sir Wilfred Grenfell College provided some necessary time to work on this textbook.

Livianna Tossutti would like to thank her wonderful parents whose love and encouragement have sustained and inspired her across time and distance. Ma, this text is dedicated to your memory and to the countless ways in which you enriched my life. I miss you. Pa, thank you for your strength and wisdom.

Livianna would also like to acknowledge the fine scholars who have been instrumental in shaping her understanding of Canada. A special thank you for the insightful discussions, advice, and friendship of the late Dr. Richard Price and Dr. Ronald Wagenberg, University of Windsor; Dr. Lawrence LeDuc, University of Toronto; Dr. Doreen Barrie and Dr. James Frideres, University of Calgary; and her colleagues in the Metropolis research network. She is also grateful to the wonderful friends who have been the constants in her life: Samantha, Luigi, Michelle, Ian, Ellen and Doug and family, Mary and Lauro and family, Amerina and Roberto, the "gang" at Wellspring Sunnybrook, and Mike.

A Great Way to Learn and Instruct Online

The Pearson Education Canada Companion Website is easy to navigate and is organized
to correspond to the chapters in this textbook. Whether you are a student in the classroom
or a distance learner you will discover helpful resources for in-depth study and research
that empower you in your quest for greater knowledge and maximize your potential for
success in the course.

Companion
Website

[www.pearsoned.ca/Mintz]

PEARSON

Jump to...   http://www.pearsoned.ca/Mintz | Home | Search | Help | Profile | Companion Website

Home >

Companion Website

Democracy, Diversity, and Good Government
by Mintz, Tossutti, and Dunn

Student Resources

The modules in this section provide students with tools for learning
course material. These modules include
- Chapter Objectives
- Chapter Quizzes
- Internet Activites
- Web Destinations

In the quiz modules students can send answers to the grader and
receive instant feedback on their progress through the Results
Reporter. Coaching comments and references to the textbook may
be available to ensure that students take advantage of all available
resources to enhance their learning experience.

INTRODUCTION

INTRODUCTION TO CANADIAN GOVERNMENT AND POLITICS

Chapter 1

PHOTO ABOVE: A huge Canadian flag is passed along a crowd that came to Montreal on October 27, 1995, in support of Canadian unity.

CHAPTER OBJECTIVES

After reading this chapter, you should be able to

1. Define some basic political concepts.
2. Examine and evaluate the basic features of Canadian democracy.
3. Evaluate alternative approaches for enhancing Canadian democracy.
4. Discuss the political significance of Canadian diversity.
5. Outline the criteria for good government.

On October 30, 1995, Jan Gabelic sat transfixed in front of his TV set. Originally from Croatia, the recently minted Canadian citizen was awaiting the results of a referendum posed by the Parti Québécois government: Should the province become sovereign (independent) if a proposal for a new economic and political partnership with Canada was rebuffed? Gabelic spoke fluent French and felt very much at home in Montreal, yet he had moved to Canada for its political stability and economic opportunity. Although he shared the view of many Quebecers that the province deserved greater autonomy, he voted no, fearing the consequences of separation from Canada. Would his fellow Quebecers follow suit? And if not, would the Quebec government be justified in declaring itself sovereign if only a small majority of people voted in favour?

Those promoting Quebec independence argued that the democratic principle of majority rule meant Quebec could declare itself sovereign if more than 50 percent voted for that option. Critics countered that a bare majority was not enough to justify such a drastic change. As well, they argued that democracy involves not only majority rule but also consideration for the rights of minorities, such as the English-speaking minority, Aboriginal peoples, and many ethnic groups who are strongly opposed to Quebec independence.

Quebec nationalists view Quebecers as a people with the right to "self-determination" under international law—that is, they should be able to freely determine their political status. In a democracy, they assert, the people should decide how they wish to be governed through a majority vote. However, international law is vague about what constitutes a "people" and the precise meaning of "self-determination." Further, some claim that the country as a whole should grant approval before a province is allowed to separate.

The distinctiveness of Quebec and the risk that it might seek separation has affected the governing of Canada. Satisfying the demands of the Quebec government (and other provincial governments) for more powers has made it difficult to adopt Canada-wide initiatives such as a national child-care program. Recognizing the distinctiveness of Quebec angers many people in the rest of Canada who believe that all provinces should be equal.

On October 30, 1995, participation in the Quebec referendum was exceptionally high, with 93.52 percent of those eligible casting their vote. And the result was extremely close, with 49.42 percent voting yes and 50.58 percent voting no. Jan Gabelic was content, and Canada had escaped having to deal with a majority yes vote—but the country had come precariously close to breaking up. The narrow victory of the no side highlighted some fundamental issues in Canadian politics and government:

- the challenge of maintaining Canadian unity and a strong Canadian identity in a vast country with different languages and cultures;
- the rival perceptions of Canada as one multicultural nation with equal citizens versus a multinational country including not only a Quebec nation, but also many Aboriginal First Nations; and
- the difficulty of organizing the system of governing so as to accommodate the diversity of peoples, including the sizeable number that is of neither British nor French ancestry.

Overall, accommodating diversity, pursuing the democratic ideal of rule by the people, and providing the good government that people expect is an ongoing challenge for Canadian politics and government. Politicians will have to work hard to meet the challenge of keeping Quebec in Canada while satisfying the wishes of other provinces, ethnic minorities, and Aboriginals. If they do so, citizens like Jan Gabelic will be well satisfied.

POLITICS

The word "politics" may conjure up images of Parliament Hill, federal–provincial squabbles, or even underhanded lobbyists, but what exactly does it mean? **Politics** can be thought of as all of the activity related to influencing, making, and implementing collective decisions.[1] Political activity usually involves controversy because different people have contrasting interests, values, and priorities when collective decisions are at stake. As well, controversy and conflict characterize politics because of the relentless competition for positions of political power.

Politics, particularly in stable, democratic countries like Canada, often also involves activity aimed at resolving conflicts or at least playing down their significance. For example, after Quebec's divisive referendum, the Canadian government made some overtures to appease those Quebecers who voted yes because they craved changes to Canada's federal system but did not necessarily believe in outright independence. The gestures included presenting a resolution to the House of Commons recognizing "that the Québécois form a nation within a united Canada," and providing the Quebec government and any other provincial or territorial government that wished to do so the ability and financial resources to assume responsibility for labour market training.

Power is a key feature in the analysis of politics. Power involves the ability to affect the behaviour of others, particularly by getting them to act in ways that they would not otherwise have done. For example, take a student group that succeeds in pressuring its provincial government to lower tuition fees. If the government would not have taken action without pressure from the students, we can say that the group has exercised its power—and done so effectively.

The collective decisions of a political community mirror, to a large extent, the distribution of political power. Those who have scant political power will likely find that collective decisions do not reflect their interests or values. For example, through much of Canada's political history, Aboriginals, women, and various minority ethnic groups enjoyed almost nothing in the way of political power. It is hardly surprising, then, that Canadian governments barely paid attention to the needs and aspirations of these groups and, indeed, adopted policies that discriminated against or even oppressed these groups. Although the right to vote in elections gives some political power to all citizens, the reality is that some people, groups, and interests are much better

POLITICS
Activity related to influencing, making, and implementing collective decisions.

POWER
The ability to affect the behaviour of others particularly by getting them to act in ways that they would not otherwise have done.

---

[1]*Politics*, like many other terms used in political science, is subject to different contending definitions that often reflect different political perspectives. In particular, some prefer to think about politics in terms of any relationship that involves the use of power. A distinction between public, collective decisions and private decisions, it is argued, obscures the use of power to dominate subordinate groups in society.

equipped to influence government than is the "ordinary" citizen. For example, the Canadian Council of Chief Executives, which represents the leaders of Canada's largest corporations, has demonstrated a very considerable ability to shape government policy on a variety of important issues such as the pursuit of free trade agreements.

GOVERNMENT

Canada is a sovereign (independent) **state** whose governing institutions are able to make and enforce rules that are binding on the people living within its territory. The national and provincial governments that are currently in office act on behalf of the state (legally referred to as the "Crown"). The state also refers to all of the institutions and agencies that act on behalf of the state, including the police and military forces and state-owned (Crown) corporations.

At the centre of political life are **governments:** the sets of institutions that have the authority to make executive decisions; present proposed laws, taxes, and expenditures to the appropriate legislative body; and oversee the implementation of laws and policies. When we talk about the Canadian government (also termed the "national" or "federal" government), we are usually referring to the prime minister and Cabinet. However, the term "government" is sometimes used in a broader sense to include Parliament as well as the variety of departments and agencies that fall under the direction of the prime minister and Cabinet.

In analyzing the power of governments, political scientists often make use of the related concepts of authority and legitimacy. **Authority** refers to the right to exercise power. Those in governing positions in Canada claim the right to make and implement decisions in keeping with the constitution, including the procedures by which those in authority are selected and decisions are made. **Legitimacy** refers to the acceptance by the people that those in positions of authority have the right to govern. Governments can exercise power through their ability to direct the major means of force—the police and military. However, since those in positions of authority have usually been able to establish their legitimacy in the eyes of the public, governments in Canada have rarely needed to rely on the use of force to exercise power. In this respect, Canada contrasts sharply with countries like Iran and China, where authorities often depend on force to maintain their power.

Without free and fair elections to select the governing party, the legitimacy of Canadian governing institutions would be compromised. In addition, the willingness of those in government to abide by constitutional rules helps to preserve the legitimacy of governmental authority while placing some limits on how government acts. However, the legitimacy of a government may weaken among those who feel that the government is systematically unfair to their group or unjust in its policies.

STATE
An independent self-governing country whose governing institutions are able to make and enforce rules that are binding on the people living within a particular territory.

GOVERNMENT
The set of institutions that have the authority to make executive decisions; present proposed laws, taxes, and expenditures to the appropriate legislative body; and oversee the implementation of laws and policies.

AUTHORITY
The right to exercise power.

LEGITIMACY
The acceptance by the people that those in positions of authority have the right to govern.

Legitimacy also comes into play in analyzing the state. If some groups feel the state was forced on them or is controlled by and acts in the interests of others, then the legitimacy of the state may be challenged. For example, some Aboriginal First Nations claim that they never gave up their right to sovereignty (that is, their right to govern themselves and their territory without outside interference). The Canadian state in this view is an illegitimate colonial power. Thus, some First Nations argue, they should not be subject to the laws of Canadian governments. In another example, if Quebecers had voted for independence and the Canadian government had refused to recognize Quebec's sovereignty, the Quebec government might have challenged the legitimacy of the Canadian state.

Governments not only have the power to make and implement decisions, but also have some ability to persuade the society they govern about the desirability of their policies. They may be able to influence society by controlling information, gaining media exposure for their views, and carrying their messages to the public through advertising. For example, in September 2009, the Canadian government spent $34 million on advertising to support the claim that its economic action plan was benefiting the public. Politics thus not only involves the attempts of various groups and individuals to influence government, but also involves a two-way relationship between society and government.

In thinking about the power of government, it is important to keep in mind that Canada has a variety of governments, including federal, provincial, municipal, and Aboriginal. As discussed in Chapter 13, Canada's federal system is characterized by quite a high level of conflict, as well as considerable cooperation, among the federal and provincial governments. The power of the Canadian government is limited because provincial governments enjoy considerable power that they are determined to wield in their dealings with the federal government. Action on a number of topics relies on negotiation and agreement between national and provincial governments.

Although governments and legislatures have the authority to make binding, collective decisions, a variety of other organizations, groups, and individuals also often have a hand in making and implementing decisions. For example, Canadian governments often invite interest groups representing different elements of society or sectors of the economy to help develop policies on topics that affect them. Similarly, businesses and community organizations are sometimes involved as partners with government in developing and carrying out specific programs.

DEMOCRACY

Most Canadians view democracy as the best form of government—much preferable to the authoritarian regimes that exercise an iron grip over many countries. However, the democratic ideal can be understood in different ways, and disagreements arise as to whether Canada should work toward a more vigorous form of democracy.

The term **democracy** originated with two words of ancient Greek that can be interpreted as "rule by the people." In the **direct democracy** of some of the ancient Greek city-states, such as Athens, citizens took charge of the governing decisions, especially by discussing the issues and then voting on laws in an open forum that all citizens could (and were expected to) attend. Democracy was viewed as putting power in the hands of ordinary citizens rather than in the hands of an elite group, particularly the wealthy few. By contemporary standards, however, ancient Greek city-states would not be considered democracies, because women, slaves, and the foreign-born were excluded from participating in political life.

Representative Democracy

In modern times, **representative democracy** has served as the primary method of implementing the democratic ideal. In this system, citizens are not directly involved in making governing decisions. Instead, in representative democracy citizens elect representatives to make governing decisions on their behalf. In electing a representative nominated by a political party, Canadian voters are choosing which political party will form the government—at least in the sense that the successful party's leader will become the prime minister, who then will select cabinet ministers from members of the governing party.

Representative democracy is often viewed as the most practical way of applying the democratic ideal to large, modern, complex societies. Voters may get a sense of what those vying to be elected will do by studying the campaign platforms of political parties, and thus they may be able to influence the general direction of the government by choosing among the competing parties. If citizens are disgruntled with the policies of government or believe that the actions of their representatives do not reflect the wishes of the people, they can vote out their representatives in the next election. Admittedly, the people may have only limited control over those they elect. Yet the desire to get re-elected can lead politicians and governing political parties to act in ways that will help them to achieve that goal, particularly by meeting the expectations of the majority. Further, we can hope that our elected representatives will devote their knowledge, skills, and energies toward deciding what is in the public interest, thus freeing up the rest of the population from much of that responsibility.

Critics of representative democracy point out that elections are imperfect vehicles for ensuring that representatives act according to the wishes of the people. There is the ever-present danger that those we vote in will be preoccupied with their own interests or those of their backers rather than the interests of the public as a whole. As well, those we elect may act on their own perspectives and values, which may diverge from those of the population they

DEMOCRACY
Rule by the people either directly or through the election of representatives.

DIRECT DEMOCRACY
A form of democracy in which citizens are directly involved in making the governing decisions.

REPRESENTATIVE DEMOCRACY
A form of democracy in which citizens elect representatives to make governing decisions on their behalf.

represent. Political parties often do not offer clear choices to voters or spell out exactly how they will act in office. And, those we elect do not always respect the positions taken and fulfill the promises made during election campaigns. For example, during the 2008 Canadian election campaign, Prime Minister Stephen Harper promised that his government would not run a deficit despite the worsening economic climate. Several months later, the Canadian government was headed toward its largest deficit ever.

Liberal Democracy

Elections are an essential feature of representative democracy. However, beyond ensuring that elections are free and fair, we usually think of democracy as meaningful only if people are able to express their views, organize for political action, and access a variety of sources of information and opinions that are not controlled by government (Dahl, 1989). The term **liberal democracy** is often used to refer to a political system in which

LIBERAL DEMOCRACY
A political system in which the powers of government are limited by law, the rights of the people to freely engage in political activity are well established, and fair elections are held to choose those who make governing decisions.

- the powers of government are limited by law,
- the rights of the people to freely engage in political activity are well established, and
- fair elections that involve free competition among all those seeking public office are held to choose those who make governing decisions.

CONSTITUTIONAL GOVERNMENT
A government that consistently acts in keeping with established fundamental rules and principles.

Liberal democracies feature **constitutional government**—that is, a government that consistently acts in keeping with established fundamental rules and principles.

Liberal democracy involves protecting rights and freedoms from both arbitrary governments and their whims and from majorities who might like to curb the rights of unpopular individuals or groups. Liberal democracy does not only guarantee protection of the political rights needed for a meaningful democracy, but also ensures that individuals are entitled to live as they choose, as long as they do not significantly harm others or interfere with their rights. In other words, the "liberal" aspect of liberal democracy means maintaining a substantial area of private activity where government should not intervene. Thus liberal democracy protects diversity within society by allowing people to follow their own values and practise their own beliefs, even if the majority view these practices as undesirable or they clash with the values of most Canadians (see Box 1-1, The Knife-Edge: Private Rights and Public Safety in Schools).

Within liberal democracy, opinion varies widely on the distinction between the private sphere of activity and those public matters in which government legitimately may be involved. Some argue that the proper function of government is to safeguard the freedoms of individuals, thus ensuring a large area of private activity where government does not interfere. For example, the role of government in economic matters should be limited primarily to such measures as upholding contracts and protecting private

BOX 1-1

The Knife-Edge:
Private Rights and Public Safety in Schools

In 2001, twelve-year-old Gurbaj Singh Multani dropped the sheathed steel knife, or *kirpan,* he was wearing at a Montreal elementary school. As required by his Khalsa Sikh faith, he had made a spiritual commitment to carry a *kirpan* (which is only to be used as a weapon of defence) at all times. When Gurbaj dropped the *kirpan* while playing in the schoolyard, the mother of another student complained to school officials ("Timeline: The Quebec Kirpan Case," 2006). Although Gurbaj's family accepted a school board request that the *kirpan* be securely covered, higher school authorities resolved that the *kirpan,* like other weapons, should be banned from schools. When this decision was overturned in a court challenge, some parents picketed the school and refused to send their children to class. Because of the taunts that pursued him, Gurbaj left to attend a private school.

Eventually, the question of whether *kirpans* should be banned in schools went before the Supreme Court of Canada. Its ruling in 2006 allowed Gurbaj to wear the *kirpan,* as long as it was under his clothes and sewn into a sheath. In the court's view, a complete ban could not be justified because of the right to freedom of religion enshrined in the *Charter of Rights and Freedoms.* As well, Justice Louise Charron argued that a ban is "disrespectful to believers in the Sikh religion and does not take into account Canadian values based on multiculturalism."

Many Canadians favoured the banning of *kirpans* in schools. While the Supreme Court decision may

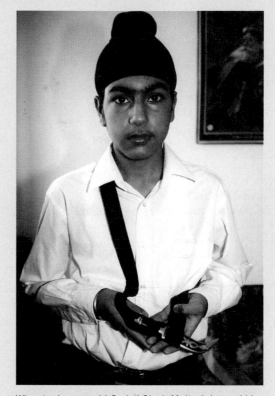

▲ When twelve-year-old Gurbaj Singh Multani dropped his *kirpan* (sheathed steel knife) at school in 2001, he had no idea that he would become central to a Charter case about freedom of religion that would not be decided by the Supreme Court until five years later.

not have reflected the opinion of the majority of Canadians, it did uphold the right of a minority group to follow their religious beliefs while trying to ensure that practices based on those beliefs did not harm or endanger others.

---

property, leaving individuals free to pursue their own interests in the marketplace. Others advocate a more active role for government, particularly to assist the disadvantaged. A variety of **welfare state** programs, including employment insurance, free health care and education, social assistance, and old-age pensions, are viewed as helping to ensure the well-being of all members of society.

WELFARE STATE
A state in which government ensures that all people have a minimum standard of living and receive some protection from hardships resulting from unemployment, sickness, disability, and old age.

Social Democracy

Those who believe that corporations and other privileged elements of society benefit from an undue influence on government often argue that for Canada to be fully democratic, greater social and economic equality is needed. This would allow everyone to have the opportunity to participate more effectively in political life. Government, in the perspective of **social democracy**, should play an active role in reducing or banishing inequalities, furnish a wide range of public services, and ensure that businesses act in the public interest. Contemporary social democrats often advocate a **mixed economy** that combines public and private ownership, along with some government planning and direction of the economy. Although favouring a larger role for government in the economy, social democrats support the basic principles of liberal democracy.

Plebiscitary Democracy

At various times, some Canadians have pushed for modifications to the system of representative democracy to give the people greater control of representatives and the decisions that are made. The Progressives in the 1920s (a farmers-based political party) and the Reform Party in the 1980s advocated **plebiscitary democracy**: the use of referendums, initiatives, and recall procedures as an alternative to what they viewed as the elite-oriented nature of representative democracy. **Referendums** are votes by the people on a particular question asked by the government or a legislative body. The Canadian government has resorted to referendums only three times (for the prohibition of alcohol, the imposition of conscription, and a package of constitutional changes known as the Charlottetown Accord), whereas some provincial and local governments have turned to referendums on a number of occasions. **Initiatives** are proposed new laws or changes to existing laws that are drafted by individuals or groups rather than by a government or a legislature. They are put to vote by the people after enough signatures have been collected. In Canada, only British Columbia has set up a procedure for initiatives. Because the procedures make it challenging to get enough signatures, no initiatives have so far gone to a vote.[2] Finally, **recall** procedures allow citizens to recall their representative and require that a new election be held, as long as sufficient names appear on a petition. Again, British Columbia is the only province that provides this opportunity. No representative has yet been recalled, although one representative resigned rather than face a recall election.

Plebiscitary mechanisms give citizens a chance to vote for more than the election of a representative. However, there are some potential problems. The

---

[2]At least 10 percent of eligible voters in each provincial electoral district have to sign a petition within a ninety-day period and the initiative has to be passed by a majority of voters including a majority in at least two-thirds of the electoral districts.

SOCIAL DEMOCRACY
A perspective that government should play an active role in reducing or eliminating inequalities, provide a wide range of public services, and ensure that businesses act in the public interest.

MIXED ECONOMY
A combination of public and private ownership and control of the economy.

PLEBISCITARY DEMOCRACY
The use of referendums, initiatives, and recall procedures as an alternative to what some view as the elite-oriented nature of representative democracy.

REFERENDUM
A vote by the people on a particular question asked by the government or legislative body.

INITIATIVE
A proposed new law or changes to an existing law drafted by an individual or group rather than by a government or legislature. The proposal is put to a vote by the people after enough signatures have been collected.

RECALL
A procedure that allows citizens to recall their representative and require that a new election be held, provided sufficient names are obtained on a petition.

wording of a referendum question or initiative proposal may be misleading or manipulative. For example, the Canadian government criticized the 1995 Quebec referendum question on the grounds that the phrasing did not provide voters with a clear question about independence. As well, almost all referendums and initiatives allow voters to respond only yes or no to a particular proposition. More nuanced ways of dealing with an issue are not presented. As with elections, those with money or influence may be able to sway voters in referendums.[3] Furthermore, turnout for referendums (and initiatives in the United States) is often low. For example, although a very high proportion of Quebecers voted in the 1995 referendum, the turnout for the 1997 Newfoundland referendum on the elimination of the denominational school system was a scant 53 percent. As well, if voters are called upon to decide on several issues at the same time, they may not pay enough attention to all of the complexities involved. Referendums and initiatives may also be used to trample the rights of unpopular minorities. For example, several American states have held referendums that led to banning same-sex marriage. Finally, the recall procedure does not fit easily into Canada's parliamentary system, in which individual representatives are expected to vote along party lines rather than in keeping with the wishes or interests of their constituents.

Deliberative Democracy

In recent times, political scientists and political philosophers have devoted considerable effort to discussing the possibility of **deliberative democracy**. Unlike plebiscitary democracy, which gives citizens extra opportunities to vote, deliberative democracy involves citizens in deliberating about governing decisions through discussion (Mendelsohn & Parkin, 2001). The underlying idea is that ordinary citizens can make recommendations that are in the public interest, provided they have the opportunity for free and equal discussion and have access to the information, ideas, and time needed for intelligent deliberation. Unlike politicians, whose decisions are often based on seeking advantage in the ongoing struggle for power, ordinary citizens may be able to reach some form of consensus on key issues despite having different interests, values, and viewpoints. Deliberative democracy can, therefore, be a means to accommodate the diversity of society, provided that those actively involved in the deliberation reflect that diversity. As discussed in Chapter 6, citizens' assemblies were used in British Columbia and Ontario to make recommendations about changes to those provinces' electoral systems.

The idea of deliberative democracy faces the hurdle that interest in politics is not generally high and many people may not be willing to devote the time and energy needed to discuss and deliberate about complex issues. However,

DELIBERATIVE DEMOCRACY
A form of democracy in which governing decisions are made based on discussion by citizens.

---

[3]Canada's legislation concerning referendums does place some limits on spending during a referendum campaign.

although many people are not deeply engaged in competitive partisan politics, they are likely to take an interest in those political issues and problems that concern or affect them. Indeed, active participation in politics has increased substantially through participation in interest groups and social movements seeking to influence public policy, bring about social change, or protest the actions of government. Contemporary communications technologies (such as the internet), combined with a more educated population, can facilitate informed discussion of political issues. However, those most likely to actively participate in public deliberations are typically the best-educated people and those with higher social and economic status, as well as spokespersons for particular interests. Unless major efforts are made to involve a wide diversity of people, deliberative democracy can result in recommendations that do not adequately take into account the views and interests of many elements of society.

Canadian Democracy

Having reviewed the myriad forms of democracy, you might reasonably ask, "Which system applies to Canada?" Canada can basically be considered a liberal representative democracy. Over time, the right to vote and seek public office was gradually extended to all adult citizens. Canadian governments respect and follow the provisions of the constitution. The *Charter of Rights and Freedoms* that was adopted in 1982 provides constitutional protection for a variety of rights and freedoms, and the courts have been willing to use the Charter to guarantee these rights. Canadian governments play a fairly active role in the economy. However, although Canada has developed a modest welfare state, it has not moved as far toward social and economic equality as social democrats would like. As mentioned earlier, referendums are used infrequently in Canada. Although governments are making greater use of public consultations, the idea of deliberative democracy has had little impact on the processes of government decision making.

Despite Canada's reputation for democracy, not all features of the Canadian political system fully reflect democratic principles. For example the Senate, one of the two chambers of Parliament, is an appointed rather than an elected body and was established, in part, to serve as a check on democracy. Further, the power of government has become more and more concentrated in a small number of hands, particularly in the hands of the prime minister and the prime minister's advisers, along with a few key cabinet ministers. The result? The role of the House of Commons in representing the people of Canada and holding the government accountable for its actions is not as vigorous as one might expect in a democratic system. The strict party discipline that characterizes the House of Commons curbs the ability of elected Members of Parliament to vote according to the wishes of their constituents. In addition, some argue that our single-member plurality system of elections (discussed in Chapter 9) is not democratic enough, as it often sweeps to power governing parties that do not enjoy the support of the majority of voters. As well, it tends to limit the diversity of perspectives in the House of Commons by making achieving representation very challenging for smaller parties (such as the Green party). The system also contributes to the under-representation of women and various minority groups in the House of Commons.

More generally, some argue that political power in Canada is very unevenly distributed. Elite groups, particularly the corporate elite with global connections, play a leading role in affecting major decisions (Carroll, 2004; Clement, 1977; Olsen, 1980; Porter, 1965). Others, however, suggest that the development of a vast array of interest groups and social movements representing different sectors of society and contrasting political perspectives has provided an avenue for the general public to try to influence public policies—a way to exercise power beyond the choices made in an election.

DIVERSITY

A key characteristic of Canada that carries great political weight is the diversity of its peoples. Precisely how to accommodate Quebec's distinct society within the Canadian federal system has often commanded considerable attention in Canadian politics. Other provinces and territories also vary in their economic characteristics, their historical experiences, the cultural and linguistic characteristics of their populations, and the identities, values, and political perspectives that are widely held by their residents. Aboriginal First Nations have been searching for a new relationship that respects what they view as their inherent right to self-government; that is, the ability to govern their own people and lands. Immigrants from many parts of the world have added greatly to the diversity of Canada by bringing assorted values, beliefs, identities, and political perspectives. Furthermore, differences in interests, values, and practices are found among those in different social classes, genders, and sexual orientations, as well as those with contrasting religious beliefs and political ideologies.

The diversity of Canada not only raises questions about how to accommodate different cultures, values, perspectives, and practices, but also how to deal with the problems and injustices that different groups have experienced or continue to experience. Aboriginals, women, gays and lesbians, immigrants, and various cultural, ethnic, and religious groups have suffered discrimination and often face continuing social and economic barriers to full equality. As well, many provincial governments have emphasized real or perceived unfair treatment of their province at the hands of the national government.

BOX 1-2

"Just Quiet Down, Baby": Should Equal Representation for Women and Men Be Guaranteed?

Sheila Copps was elected to the House of Commons in 1984 and became a member of the Liberal "Rat Pack"—a group notorious for its fierce attacks on the Progressive Conservative (PC) government. In response, PC Members of Parliament often heckled Copps with sexist comments such as John Crosbie's "just quiet down, baby," to which she responded, "I'm nobody's baby."

Even though women gained the right to vote in Canadian elections in 1918, scarcely any women were elected until recent decades (see Figure 1-1). Even today, only about one-fifth of those elected to Parliament and provincial legislatures are women. As discussed in Chapter 8, political parties, notably the Liberals and the New Democratic Party, have taken measures to try to increase the number of women nominated for election. However, their efforts have not significantly improved the representation of women. Parliament has tended to remain a male domain.

Some groups promoting equal representation for women have suggested that voters in each electoral district elect one female and one male representative. This system was proposed for the new, largely Inuit territory of Nunavut. However, in 1997, 57 percent of Nunavut voters rejected the system in a referendum, although with a turnout of only 39 percent (Young, 1999). Despite the support of Inuit political leaders for gender equality, some Inuit questioned whether separate elections for men and women representatives violated the idea that men and women should have equal rights, while others contended that the proposal was inconsistent with traditional Inuit values (Dahl, 1997).

Supporters of gender parity argue for mandatory methods to overcome the barriers that women face in getting nominated and elected, and they maintain that a stronger female presence in legislative bodies would improve the quality and tone of debate and discussion. Gender parity would also make it more likely that the concerns of the 52 percent of the population that is female would be addressed. However, some critics beg to differ. They argue that gender does not necessarily determine how a person will act in a legislative body, and that electing people on the basis of their gender would not necessarily yield the "best" representatives. Others argue that women are by no means the only group that is under-represented in legislative bodies; other groups whose voices are not often heard in politics, such as racial and ethnic minorities and those in working- and lower-class positions, are also inade-

Accommodating diversity can occur in a variety of ways. Protecting individual freedoms is essential to ensuring that those with contrasting beliefs, cultures, and values can live according to their own convictions. Providing equal rights and benefits for those with different characteristics or lifestyles is important in accommodating diversity. For example, legalizing same-sex marriages has accommodated gays and lesbians. The *Charter of Rights and Freedoms* and human rights codes prohibit various forms of discrimination based

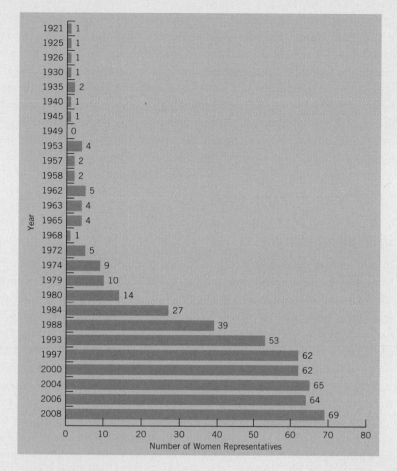

FIGURE 1-1

THE REPRESENTATION OF WOMEN IN THE HOUSE OF COMMONS

Source: *Compiled from Parliament of Canada, 2008, "Women Candidates in General Elections—1921 to Date." Retrieved from http://www2.parl.gc.ca/ Sites/LOP/HFER/hfer.asp?Language= E&Search= WomenElection*

quately represented. It would, nevertheless, be difficult to ensure that a legislative body accurately represented the characteristics of the population at large.

Sheila Copps ran for the leadership of the Liberal party in 2003 but was trounced by Paul Martin. Several months later, she lost a battle for re-nomination in her district—a defeat she chalked up to Martin's efforts to remove women, as well as his opponents, from the party's caucus.

on such characteristics as race, ethnic origin, religion, sex, age, and disability. A more active approach involves adopting policies to ensure diversity in different jobs and political positions (see Box 1-2, "Just Quiet Down, Baby": Should Equal Representation for Women and Men Be Guaranteed?).

Providing rights, freedoms, and opportunities for individuals does not necessarily take into account the importance of the community in shaping how we live our lives. At the collective level, allowing a community that differs from the mainstream to govern itself affords a way of accommodating diversity. By that means, the values and interests of a group of people can lay the foundation for the policies and laws of their community. However, even when a group has common characteristics or lives in a common geographical area, they will not necessarily share values and interests. For example, the government of Quebec views itself as representing the entire Quebec community, yet the English-speaking minority in that province has fought against the government's measures to make French the sole public language. Aboriginal governments, although based on a people with common ancestry and culture, have come in for criticism by organizations of Aboriginal women for being male dominated.

Diversity and Unity

In the past, diversity often triggered negative thoughts and feelings. People from foreign or minority cultures were expected to assimilate to the dominant Canadian culture by adopting the language, customs, and values of the majority. Those who did not "fit in" and looked or acted differently from the majority were often scorned, discriminated against, and shut out of positions of political power. Although many people continue to believe that assimilation is necessary to create a unified country, diversity has met with growing acceptance in recent decades. Indeed, repressing diversity may be more likely to create fragmentation and disunity than embracing diversity.

However, unity likely requires a feeling of solidarity among the diverse groups making up the country and a consensus about the basic political values by which the country is governed. Generally, the various groups that make up Canadian society share a sense of solidarity, even though some people identify more strongly with their province or ethnic group than with Canada. There is also a broad consensus on the desirability of democracy, even though individuals have different takes on what democracy entails and to what extent democratic principles should be applied. For example, many associate democracy with the belief in the equal rights and responsibilities of all citizens, expecting that no special privileges should exist for selected individuals and groups. Others argue that provisions for those with different cultures, values, and identities recognize and respect the contribution of diverse peoples to Canada and are consistent with democratic principles.

GOOD GOVERNMENT

We cannot assume that governments, even in a democratic country, will necessarily act in the public interest. Because of the competitive struggle for power, those in governing positions may be more preoccupied with staying in power than with doing what best serves the country and its people. The

◄ The diversity of Canada's population has great political significance. Those of different social classes, ethnic groups, genders, and sexual orientations as well as those with different religious beliefs often have different political interests, values, and ideological perspectives.

governing party may act in ways that are designed to discredit the opposition, dupe the public, or provide perks and benefits to those expected to support them in the next election. Furthermore, those in governing positions may be tempted to act in ways that personally reward themselves and their families. Although recent efforts have tried to ensure that public office holders act ethically, some individuals inevitably will abuse their positions of authority.

Even if most of those in governing positions are dedicated to serving the public interest, competing views exist as to what the public interest entails. Different interests, values, and ideological perspectives shape perceptions of the public interest. For example, some people argue that "the government that governs best governs least," while others believe that government should supply a wide variety of services, play an active role in economic development, and reduce inequalities.

Many people assess the actions of government in terms of their particular interests, values, and identities. That is, they may focus more on the well-being of their province, local community, cultural group, social class, or gender than on the well-being of the country as a whole. It is natural to be concerned with our own well-being and that of our family, friends, and groups with which we identify. But in a diverse country like Canada, this tendency to judge the broader effects of government primarily in terms of those groups or localities we identify with seems firmly entrenched; it may be stronger than in countries with a more homogenous population and a stronger sense of being part of a single national community. Canada's federal system, which divides governing authority between national and provincial governments, tends to reinforce or heighten tendencies to assess the actions of governments in terms of the benefits or costs for particular provinces.

Even if we set aside the interests of the groups we identify with, there remains the issue of whether we should evaluate government actions primarily in terms of the public interest of Canada or that of the world as a whole. For example, government policies that encourage the conversion of land from growing food crops to growing crops for biofuel may benefit Canadian farmers and the Canadian economy, but may contribute to higher food prices, food shortages, and even starvation in other parts of the world. Should we assess good government only in terms of what's advantageous for Canadians? Or should good government also involve actions and initiatives like protecting the global environment, assisting the development of poorer countries, promoting human rights, and working toward a peaceful world?

Finally, there is the issue of the relative importance of the public interests of Canadians in the present and the interests of Canadians in the future. For example, degradation of Canada's natural environment may fuel prosperity in the present while harming opportunities for future generations to enjoy and benefit from the natural environment.

Criteria of Good Government

There are a variety of criteria by which good government can be assessed.[4]

ACCOUNTABILITY   To begin with, governments should be *accountable* for their actions. This involves

- providing valid justifications for the actions and policies of government,
- responding to criticisms, and
- moving swiftly to remedy problems resulting from government actions and policies.

For accountability to be effective, legislators, the media, and interested members of the public should be able to investigate and scrutinize the activities of government. Public inquiries headed by independent individuals, as well as independent court systems, are also key to dealing with allegations of illegal or improper behaviour by government. Likewise, independent review and investigative processes are needed to ensure that various state agencies operating somewhat independently of government—such as the RCMP and other police, military, and national security agencies—do not abuse the power invested in them.

---

[4]These criteria are based, in part, on the Canadian Democratic Audit. The UBC Press published a series of books about Canadian politics and government based on this audit. See also "What Is Good Governance?" prepared by the United Nations Economic and Social Commission for Asia and the Pacific, 2009, available at www.unescap.org.

PARTICIPATION   The informed *participation* of the public, including groups that represent all sectors of society, helps those in governing positions to grasp the needs, wishes, and perspectives of those being governed. Of particular importance is participation by marginalized groups in society whose views and interests are often ignored because of their limited power and organizational capabilities. Likewise, the *inclusiveness* within governing, legislative, and administrative organizations of diverse elements of society allows different voices with contrasting needs and values to be taken into account. Developing a broad consensus based on participation and inclusiveness helps to shore up the legitimacy of the state and its governing institutions among all elements of society.

TRANSPARENCY   To allow the community an effective voice in public decision making, hold government accountable for its actions, and prevent corruption, government must be as *transparent* (open) as possible. Governments often have a strong tendency to withhold information that may reflect negatively on them, but hiding information can hinder government from using constructive criticism to correct its mistakes and better its performance. Transparency also matters in allowing the public a chance to participate in an informed manner in political life. Access to information (also known as freedom of information) legislation, backed up by the ability of the courts or an independent body to require that information be released in a timely manner, is important in making transparency more than mere rhetoric. However, some limits on transparency are needed to protect national security, individual privacy, ongoing negotiations, and the functioning of Cabinet.

RESPONSIVENESS   Government should be *responsive* to the needs and wishes of the people it governs. Governments can easily lose touch with ordinary people, and elections every few years may not be enough to ensure responsiveness. Governments do frequently use public opinion polls, although on occasion more to craft messages for electoral advantage than to respond to public opinion and concerns. Opposition parties are quick to exploit opportunities in the House of Commons to raise awareness of the problems people face. However, governments are often reluctant to act on issues raised by opposition parties (Docherty, 2005).

Does good governing simply entail doing what the majority of people want government to do? We often expect government to provide leadership, which may involve creating a vision for the country and trying to convince people that a certain course of action will, in the long run, achieve important, widely shared values. Nevertheless, leadership should ideally be based on the hopes and aspirations of the people and include the public in a dialogue about where the country should be going. However, responsiveness to the wishes of the majority needs to be balanced by protections for the rights of minorities and individuals.

EFFICIENCY AND EFFECTIVENESS   Government should also be *efficient* and *effective*. Governments in Canada (national, provincial, and local) spend about two-fifths of the country's gross national product either directly by providing services or indirectly by transferring money to other levels of government and to individuals. It is crucial that these large sums of money be spent efficiently. Further, we expect public policies to be effective in the sense of achieving their goals. Governments have often fallen far short of meeting their stated objectives (for example, eliminating child poverty and reducing greenhouse gas emissions) not only because they lack firm commitment to them, but also because of the complexities involved. Developing effective policies requires extensive research and the willingness to consider a variety of approaches.

ACHIEVING IMPORTANT GOALS   The procedural criteria discussed above are not the only way of evaluating good government. Good government can also be assessed using substantive criteria—that is, the values and goals that are being pursued. Here we would include the protection of rights and freedoms; the elimination of various forms of injustice in society; the adoption of policies for achieving full employment and a decent standard of living for all; and the promotion of a healthy, active, and well-educated population. Furthermore, good government should be oriented to sustainability, so that the quality of life and the quality of the natural environment are at least as good for future generations as they are today. Finally, good government should include a genuine commitment to the pursuit of peace, development, human rights, and protection of the environment for the world as a whole.

Overall, it is unrealistic to expect all of the criteria of good government to be completely fulfilled. Indeed, some of the criteria can be viewed as contradictory. For example, high public participation may reduce the efficiency of governing processes, while responsiveness to a wide variety of public views may lead to compromises that are limited in their effectiveness. Nevertheless, by enhancing the legitimacy of the system, public participation and responsiveness can be viewed as achieving important objectives.

LOOKING AHEAD

Throughout this book, we will return to the themes of democracy, diversity, and good government in Canada as we examine the myriad aspects of politics and government. Chapters 2 to 5 provide the context for understanding Canadian politics and government by looking at Canada's political history, the nature of its economy and society, and the political ideas, values, and identities that affect how Canadians relate to politics. Chapters 6 to 9 consider the various ways in which individuals and groups can affect the governments of the country and the decisions that are made. Chapters 10 to 17 focus on the constitution and the institutions and processes of governing. Finally, Chapter 18 considers Canada's international presence—its place in the world.

Summary and Conclusion

Politics, an activity related to making collective decisions for political communities, involves controversy and conflict because of the different interests, values, and priorities that exist within any political community. Controversy and conflict also result from the competition to exercise political power. The distribution of power is important in determining what collective decisions are made.

The Canadian political system can be classified as basically a liberal representative democracy. Voters elect representatives to make decisions on their behalf, and people are free to express their concerns, organize for political action, and try to influence the decisions of government. Clearly, each Canadian citizen has some potential political power through the ability to cast a vote in elections. Yet questions arise as to whether some powerful groups are in a strong position to influence government for their own advantage. As well, government decisions often are a product of interactions among governments and within government rather than the influence of the public. Some people favour a fuller realization of the democratic ideal of rule by the people through greater involvement by all members of the public in political debate and decision making, as well as through greater social and economic equality.

Canadian politics is strongly affected by the diversity of the country, and in particular, the different ethnic, cultural, and linguistic communities and the distinctive provincial societies. The diversity of Canadian society has meant that many Canadians do not have an overriding or exclusive Canadian political identity. Treating all Canadians similarly, as equal citizens, is but one perspective in Canada; controversy has arisen over whether distinctive groups or distinctive provinces should enjoy a different status, powers, and laws to protect and develop their own identities. Good government requires governing institutions and policy-making processes that are directed to achieving the public interest of the political community. However, given the diversity of Canada, a tendency often exists to evaluate the public interest in terms of the interests of one's group or province rather than in terms of the country as a whole.

Discussion Questions

1. Should a province have the right to secede from Canada if a majority of its population votes in favour of secession?

2. Do you think that political power is widely dispersed or highly concentrated in Canada?

3. Should the Canadian government try to promote a common set of values?

4. Should Canada move in the direction of greater democracy?

5. Should special measures be adopted to guarantee greater representation of women and minorities in legislative and governing institutions?

Further Reading

Bickerton, J., & Gagnon, A.-G. (Eds.). (2004). *Canadian politics* (4th ed.). Peterborough, ON: Broadview Press.

Broadbent, E. (Ed.). (2001). *Democratic equality: What went wrong?* Toronto, ON: University of Toronto Press.

Carmichael, D., Pocklington, T., & Pyrcz, G. (1991). *Democracy and rights in Canada.* Toronto, ON: Harcourt Brace Jovanovich Canada.

Charlton, M., & Barker, P. (Eds.). (2009). *Crosscurrents: Contemporary political issues* (6th ed.). Scarborough, ON: Thomson Nelson.

Dahl, R. A. (1998). *On democracy.* New Haven, CT: Yale University Press.

Grace, J. & Sheldrick (Eds.). (2006). *Canadian politics. Democracy and dissent.* Toronto, ON: Pearson Prentice Hall.

McRoberts, K. (1997). *Misconceiving Canada. The struggle for national unity.* Toronto, ON: Oxford University Press.

Michelmann, H. J., Story, D. C., & Steeves, J. S. (Eds.). (2007). *Political leadership and representation in Canada: Essays in honour of John C. Courtney.* Toronto, ON: University of Toronto Press.

Resnick, P. (1997). *Twenty-first century democracy.* Montreal, QC: McGill-Queen's University Press.

Saul, J. R. (2008). *A fair country: Telling truths about Canada.* Toronto, ON: Viking Canada.

Whittington, M., & Williams, G. (Eds.). (2008). *Canadian politics in the 21st century* (7th ed.). Scarborough, ON: Thomson Nelson.

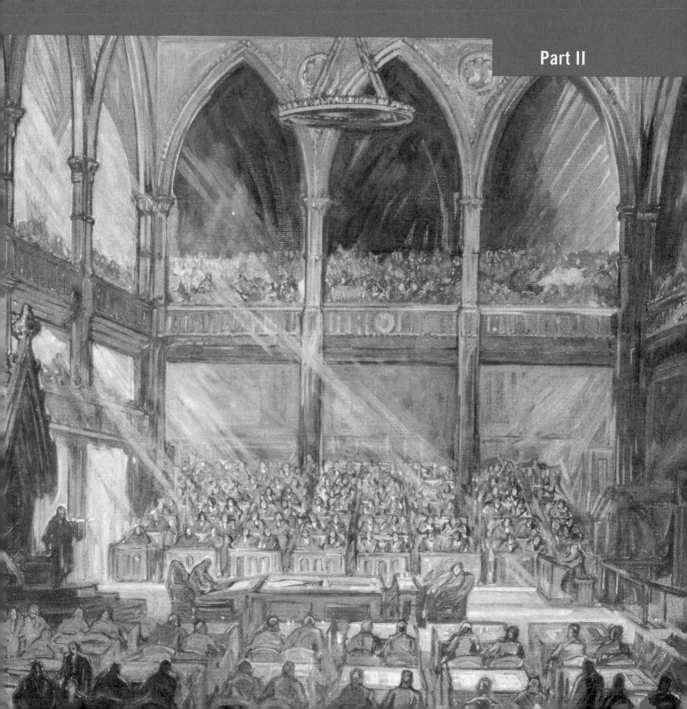

THE CONTEXT OF CANADIAN POLITICS

Part II

Chapter 2

THE HISTORICAL CONTEXT

PHOTO ABOVE: Delegates from the legislatures of Canada, New Brunswick, Nova Scotia, and Prince Edward Island pose for a photo during the September 1864 convention in Charlottetown at which it was agreed to consider the union of the British North American colonies.

CHAPTER OBJECTIVES

After reading this chapter, you should be able to

1. Outline the key political events in Canada prior to Confederation.
2. Explain the significance of responsible government.
3. Discuss the reasons for Confederation.
4. Examine the opposition to Confederation.
5. Discuss the major challenges faced by Canada since 1867.

On July 1, 1867, many flags were flown at half-mast in Nova Scotia. Buildings were draped in black crepe. Premier Charles Tupper was burned in effigy alongside a rat. A newspaper described "young and fair Nova Scotia" being forced into an "unhappy union" by "an old, crabbed and almost bankrupt" Canadian suitor, while her numerous friends "intend shortly to take prompt and decided steps to procure a divorce" (quoted in "Married," 1867/2005).

Although Ontarians greeted the formation of Canada in 1867 with enthusiasm, this was not the case in other parts of the new country, particularly in Nova Scotia and New Brunswick. The Nova Scotia government agreed to join Canada against the wishes of the majority of its population. In the first Canadian election, the Anti-Confederate Party, advocating seceding from Canada, won eighteen of Nova Scotia's nineteen seats in the Canadian Parliament. Likewise, in November 1867, the anti-Confederates won thirty-six of the thirty-eight seats in the Nova Scotia legislature. Thirty-one thousand Nova Scotians signed a petition in favour of separation (almost as many as voted in the 1867 election), and in 1868 the Nova Scotia legislature passed a motion to secede from Canada. The British government refused to accept this request. Bowing to the inevitable, Joseph Howe, leader of the anti-Confederates, accepted a position in the Canadian Cabinet after having been given a promise of "better terms" for Nova Scotia by Sir John A. Macdonald, Canada's first prime minister.

In neighbouring New Brunswick, there was also considerable opposition to Confederation. In 1865, the government of Samuel Tilly, which supported joining Canada, was defeated by the anti-Confederates, who claimed that Tilly had sold the province for eighty cents a person—the customs revenues the province would receive for joining Canada (Morton, 2006). However, the British government was determined to persuade New Brunswick to join Canada.

The British-appointed governor forced an election in 1866 to oust Premier Albert J. Smith, who opposed the terms of the Confederation, and Tilly's pro-Confederation party was returned to power. A raid on New Brunswick by the Fenians (Irish Americans opposed to British rule in Ireland) helped to convince many New Brunswickers that union with Canada was necessary for their security, as the British government claimed that they were unwilling to continue to provide military protection indefinitely (Conrad & Finkel, 2007).

In Quebec, there was also significant opposition to Confederation. However, the defeat of the Rebellion of 1837–38 had resulted in political apathy and passivity among much of the population. With the powerful Catholic Church preaching that legitimate authority had to be obeyed, the Conservative Bleus who supported Confederation decisively beat the anti-Confederate Rouges in the first Canadian election. Nevertheless, except among the English-speaking business community in Montreal, there was not much enthusiasm for the new country.

Now a country of more than 33 million, Canada had a precarious start in 1867. Nevertheless, Canada has successfully developed a stable and peaceful political system. Of course, survival over a period of nearly a century and a half does not guarantee a smooth path for the future of Canada. Indeed, some of the tensions that Canada struggled with in the past are reflected in the political challenges of the present.

EARLY SETTLEMENT AND HISTORY

Canada was first settled more than 10 000 years ago by the ancestors of contemporary First Nations (misleadingly termed "Indians" by European explorers) who crossed from Asia. Much later, about 1000 years ago, the ancestors of the Inuit spread from Western Alaska to the Canadian Arctic. These various Aboriginal groups developed a variety of different languages and cultures. While some had hunter-gatherer economies, others established settled communities based on agriculture and fishing and developed intricate cultures and governing systems prior to European settlement.

European settlement began in the seventeenth century, when the colony of New France developed along the St. Lawrence River and the smaller French colony of Acadia was established in what are now the Maritime provinces. Britain set up colonies in what is now the Atlantic region of the United States. There were also small British and French colonies in Newfoundland, and the Hudson's Bay Company, which was granted a British royal charter in 1670 covering the vast territory known as Rupert's Land, had a few trading posts in the North.

Britain and France vied for control over Canada. Wars between the two countries resulted in British control of Newfoundland and parts of the Maritimes in 1713. In 1755, Britain expelled several thousand French-speaking Acadians who refused to swear allegiance to the British Crown. From 1756 to 1763, during the global Seven Years War between Britain and France and their European allies, the British army captured the remaining parts of Acadia, along with Quebec City, the capital of New France (1759), and Montreal (1760). By the Treaty of Paris (1763), New France and Acadia were ceded to Britain.[1]

British Rule

ROYAL PROCLAMATION, 1763
Established British rule over the former French colonies and placed "Indians" under the protection of the British Crown.

THE FATE OF THE "INDIANS" AND THE FRENCH   The **Royal Proclamation, 1763**, established British rule over the former French colonies. It placed "Indians" under the protection of the British Crown, stated that they were to be left undisturbed, established their exclusive hunting rights over a vast territory, and provided that their lands could not be sold without the approval of authorized representatives of the monarch. Although the Royal Proclamation is often cited today as recognition of Aboriginal rights, its protection of Aboriginals from the inroads of settlers was often not enforced by the colonial governments (Dickason, 2009). Nevertheless, the British, like the French, claimed sovereignty, but not ownership, of the territories inhabited by Aboriginal peoples. Aboriginal peoples in Canada were never conquered by the European powers. Historically, they were not subject to

[1]France retained the islands of St. Pierre and Miquelon off the south coast of Newfoundland and, until 1904, had fishing rights along the "French Shore" of Newfoundland.

British or French laws and government policies, except in areas settled by those of European ancestry and in their relations with non-Native persons (Bumsted, 2003a).

Britain hoped that settlers from the American colonies and from Britain would turn Quebec into a colony composed largely of people of British ancestry. In fact, after 1763 Quebec remained primarily French-speaking and Catholic, with the exception of several hundred American merchants who followed in the wake of the British conquest. Thus, although the British legal system was introduced, in practice the British governors recognized the need to be conciliatory to the leaders of the French-speaking Catholic population and left most laws and practices from the French regime intact. The **Quebec Act, 1774**, passed by the British Parliament formalized this arrangement with guarantees that Catholics would be able to freely practise their religion, the privileges of the Catholic Church would be maintained, and the French system of civil (private) law would be used alongside British criminal law.

AN INFLUX OF IMMIGRANTS   Support in Quebec and the other northern colonies for the American War of Independence (1775–83) was limited, and an American invasion of Quebec in 1775–76 was eventually repulsed by the British army. The success of the American revolutionaries in gaining independence from Britain resulted in many Americans who had remained loyal to the British Crown (the **Loyalists**), along with those who had fought in the British army and Indians who had fought against the Americans, seeking refuge in the British North American colonies. The British authorities provided land and subsidies for the Loyalists and former soldiers to settle in the colonies of Nova Scotia (particularly in the area that later became New Brunswick) and Quebec (including what is now southern and eastern Ontario).

The newcomers to British North America added not only a substantial population to the colonies but also a somewhat greater diversity. Among the Loyalists and former soldiers were substantial numbers of Scots, Germans, and people of other nationalities. A significant proportion of the new settlers came from a variety of Protestant groups other than the Church of England (Anglican). As well, a sizeable number of Black Americans settled in Nova Scotia, although discriminatory treatment by that colony soon resulted in about one-half leaving for Sierra Leone. In addition, because Britain had awarded large areas of Indian lands south and southwest of the Great Lakes to the United States at the end of the war, the Iroquois and some other Indian nations that had fought against the Americans were resettled in what is now southern Ontario. The settlement of refugees from the United States was followed in subsequent decades by other Americans, some of whom were Loyalists, while others simply sought to take advantage of the available lands in British North America.

QUEBEC ACT, 1774
An act of the British Parliament that guaranteed that Catholics would be able to freely practise their religion, the privileges of the Catholic Church would be maintained, and the French system of civil (private) law would be used alongside British criminal law.

LOYALISTS
Americans who remained loyal to the British Crown at the time of the War of Independence. Subsequently, many Loyalists migrated to the British North American colonies.

The influx of new settlers led to important changes in the politics of the British North American colonies. In response to Loyalist demands, New Brunswick was separated from Nova Scotia in 1784. In the same year Cape Breton also became a separate colony (although it rejoined Nova Scotia in 1820). The settlement of a large number of English-speakers created problems for the colony of Quebec. In particular, the settlers expected to be governed by British laws and to have an elected representative assembly as had been established in the other British North American colonies (except Newfoundland, which did not have an assembly until 1832). To some extent this was resolved when the British Parliament passed the **Constitution Act, 1791,** dividing Quebec into two colonies: Upper Canada (the forerunner of Ontario) and Lower Canada (Quebec), with each having its own elected representative assembly.

THE WAR OF 1812   Tensions between Britain and the United States did not end with the Treaty of Paris (1783) in which Britain accepted American independence. In 1812, the United States declared war on Britain as a result of the British blockade of European ports during the Napoleonic Wars that cut off American trade with Europe, the actions of the British navy in boarding American ships in international waters, and British support of the First Nations in the territories that Britain had ceded to the United States. As well, some members of the U.S. Congress in areas bordering British North America wanted to annex the British colonies (Bumsted, 2003b). British soldiers, militiamen from Upper and Lower Canada, and First Nations warriors successfully resisted the American invasions into Upper and Lower Canada. The War of 1812 ended in 1814 without a clear victory for either side.

Rebellions and Unification

Despite having elected assemblies, the British North American colonies were far from democratic. The British governors of the colonies were expected to follow the orders of the British government. Appointed councils composed of powerful local elites provided advice to the governor, and had the right to reject any legislation proposed by the elected representatives in the assembly. Elections of the unpaid representatives were often marked by the buying of votes fostered by the lack of a secret ballot (Bumsted, 2003b). Democratic reform movements developed to challenge the powers of the elites that dominated the colonies and to increase the power of the assembly. Ultimately this led to rebellions in both Canadian colonies in 1837. The rebellion in Upper Canada was small, lacked broad support, and was quickly suppressed. The rebellion in Lower Canada was more serious, as it not only involved a struggle for greater democracy but also reflected tensions between the English-speaking minority who controlled most of the economic and political power in the colony and the French-Canadian majority who had come to dominate the Quebec Assembly. Nevertheless, after a few bloody clashes, the rebellion in Lower Canada was quashed in 1838.

CONSTITUTION ACT, 1791
Divided Quebec into two separate colonies: Upper Canada and Lower Canada.

As a result of the rebellions, the British government sent Lord Durham to investigate the causes of the conflicts in the Canadian colonies. His report was telling: "I expected to find a contest between a government and a people. I found two nations warring in the bosom of a single state." To end "the deadly animosity that now separates the inhabitants of Lower Canada into the hostile divisions of French and English," he recommended that Upper and Lower Canada be reunited (quoted in Bumsted, 2003b, p. 349). This, he hoped, would lead to the gradual assimilation of the French-speaking population and their acceptance of "superior" English values. In addition, the **Durham Report, 1839** (*Report on the Affairs in British North America*), recommended that a more democratic system, known as **responsible government,**be adopted. In a system of responsible government, the executive (Cabinet) is responsible to an elected, representative legislative body, and can only remain in office as long as it maintains the support of a majority of that body.

Based on Durham's recommendation, the British Parliament passed the **Act of Union, 1840,** creating the United Province of Canada. Each of the two parts, termed "Canada East" (Quebec) and "Canada West" (Ontario), was awarded equal representation in the Province of Canada's elected Legislative Assembly (despite the larger population of Canada East at the time). English was made the language of the assembly, although later the right to use French in the assembly was added. This recognition of two official languages was a significant feature in the subsequent Confederation agreement.

With Canada East and Canada West each electing half of the assembly, power was shared between English and French. Joint leaders, an English-speaking politician from Canada West and a French-speaking politician from Canada East, governed the colony. As well, although Canada East and Canada West had no separate governing structures, ministers from each part were responsible for matters within their half of Canada. Indeed, Canada East and Canada West continued to have different legal and educational systems. Further, the practice developed that laws were expected to be passed by a "double majority"—that is, by majorities of representatives in each of the two regions. Thus the governance of the Union reflected, to a considerable extent, the distinctiveness of its two components and could be viewed as a forerunner of the federal system adopted in 1867.

Durham's recommendation concerning responsible government did not come into effect with the Act of Union. The British governor was not prepared to surrender his power. He continued to reject bills (proposed legislation) passed by the Legislative Assembly, interfered in elections to the assembly, and decided upon appointments to the Executive Council. This caused tensions with the reformers in the elected assembly who pressed for the adoption of responsible government. The principle of responsible government was accepted in Nova Scotia in 1848 after a vigorous campaign by Joseph Howe and shortly thereafter in New Brunswick (1848) and the Province of Canada (see Box 2-1, The Struggle for Responsible Government in Canada). A few

Report of Lord Durham:
**http://faculty.marianopolis.edu/
c.belanger/quebechistory/docs/
durham**

DURHAM REPORT
A report of the British governor that recommended the union of Upper and Lower Canada and the adoption of responsible government.

RESPONSIBLE GOVERNMENT
A governing system in which the executive is responsible to an elected, representative legislative body and must retain its support to remain in office.

ACT OF UNION, 1840
United Upper and Lower Canada creating the United Province of Canada.

BOX 2-1

The Struggle for Responsible Government in Canada

Governor General Lord Elgin is often associated with the struggle for responsible government in Canada. In 1848, Lord Elgin, on instructions from the British government, appointed a cabinet nominated by the majority grouping of Reformers in the Legislative Assembly, which was led by Robert Baldwin and Sir Louis-Hippolyte LaFontaine. Both men were key advocates of responsible government.

In 1849, the principle of responsible government was tested and then confirmed when Lord Elgin did not veto the highly controversial *Rebellion Losses Bill* that had been passed by the Legislative Assembly and the Legislative Council. The objective of the bill was to compensate those individuals, including most of the rebels, who had suffered property losses in the 1837–38 Rebellion in Lower Canada. The "Tories" (conservatives), supported by many prominent members of the English-speaking community in Lower Canada, demanded that Lord Elgin refuse to give royal assent. Although Lord Elgin had his misgivings about the bill, he did not yield to their demands. Royal assent was granted.

Infuriated by the decision, a crowd of English Montrealers pelted Lord Elgin's carriage with rotten eggs and burned down the Parliament buildings. Some English Montreal merchants, already dismayed by the lack of a free-trade agreement with the United States, circulated a petition demanding the annexation of Lower Canada to the U.S. Curiously they found some support among radical French Canadians who believed they, too, would be better treated by their neighbour to the south (Gillmore & Turgeon, 2000).

After the burning of the Montreal Parliament buildings, later sessions of the Legislative Assembly had to be held in Toronto and Quebec City, with the final session in 1866 held in Ottawa, the new capital. Despite the controversy over the *Rebellion Losses Bill*, the principle of responsible government became the cornerstone of the governing system in Canada—one that has survived into the twenty-first century.

years later responsible government was adopted in Prince Edward Island (1851) and Newfoundland (1858).

The shared governing of the Province of Canada brought a number of successes, including involvement in negotiating a partial free-trade treaty (Reciprocity Treaty, 1854) with the United States, reform of the school system in Canada West, modernization of the land tenure system in Canada East, and the building of a railway system. Less satisfactorily, the shifting coalitions of political factions meant frequent changes of government, and the need for a "double majority" often led to a stalemate that made legislative decisions difficult to achieve.

Differences between Canada West and Canada East were heightened as the population of Canada West surpassed that of Canada East. The Clear Grits, a radical reform movement in Canada West, demanded representation by population rather than the equal representation of West and East. In addition, reflecting their evangelical Protestant beliefs, the Clear Grits favoured the separation of church and state and opposed the privileges granted to the Anglican Church. Further, they tended to express negative views about French Canadians (Bumsted, 2003b).

CONFEDERATION

The political problems of governing the colony of Canada encouraged some, particularly in Canada West, to look to a larger union to avoid the problems of the Province of Canada. Economic concerns, too, helped to pave the way for Confederation; the uniting of the British North American colonies was seen as economically advantageous, as it would create a larger domestic market. This became particularly important when the United States, a key market for Canadian exports, cancelled the Reciprocity Treaty that had allowed unprocessed goods to trade freely without customs duties between the two countries.

Myriad other issues also contributed to the drive for unification. A union of the colonies was viewed as important in creating a government able to finance a railway link between the Maritimes and central Canada. A larger union was also seen as facilitating the opening up of the West to settlement. Nor were security concerns negligible. Some worried that the large army mobilized in the American Civil War would be turned against Canada. Threats also came from the Fenians, an Irish-American group that conducted raids on the colonies as part of their nationalist campaign to free Ireland from British rule. A union of the British North American colonies was seen as allowing the colonies to better provide for their own defence against potential American invasion.

The idea of uniting the British North American colonies had been talked about for a long time and was supported by the British government. However, it took a proposal by George Brown, leader of the Reformers, to get the process under way. Brown suggested forming a "Grand Coalition" with the Conservatives, led by John A. Macdonald, and the Bleus, the major political grouping in Canada East, led by George-Étienne Cartier. The objective? To achieve a federal union of the colonies.

From the start, the politicians put forward different models for the union. Macdonald preferred a legislative union (that is, a single legislature) rather than a federal union (one in which each province would have its own legislature in addition to the Canadian Parliament). In Macdonald's view the American federal system had failed because each state had sovereign powers. However, Macdonald realized that a legislative union would not gain the support of Quebec and the Maritime colonies, and thus he looked to the establishment of a strong Parliament having all of the major legislative powers needed to develop a great nation while provincial legislatures dealt with local matters (LaSelva, 1996). His ally Cartier had a somewhat different view. He believed that maintaining ethnic and religious diversity would benefit the new country. Canadians would create a "political nationality," rather than one based on a

CHARLOTTETOWN
CONFERENCE, 1864
A meeting of the leaders of
Canada and the Maritimes at
which it was decided to hold
further discussions about uniting
the British North American
colonies.

BRITISH NORTH
AMERICA ACT, 1867
An act of the Parliament of the
United Kingdom establishing the
Dominion of Canada. In 1982 it
was renamed the Constitution
Act, 1867.

particular ancestry or religion. A federal system in which provincial governments had substantial powers, along with protection for minority rights, was, in Cartier's view, essential for the formation of Canada (LaSelva, 2009).

In September 1864, delegates from Canada attended a conference of Maritime leaders who had planned to discuss uniting the Maritime colonies. The Canadian delegation was able to convince the Maritime leaders at this **Charlottetown Conference (1864)** to put aside the idea of a regional union in favour of discussing a broader union of all the British North American colonies. A month later at a closed-door conference in Quebec City, seventy-two resolutions were adopted "to establish a federal union under the Crown of Great Britain, provided such union can be effected on principles just to the several provinces" (quoted in McNaught, 1969). The delegations from Prince Edward Island and Newfoundland, however, did not think that the terms of union provided them with sufficient benefits. After further discussion in London, England, in 1866 by delegates from Canada, Nova Scotia, and New Brunswick, the British Parliament passed the **British North America Act, 1867**, based on the resolutions of the colonial leaders and the Dominion of Canada was established (see Figure 2-1).

The union of the British North American colonies did not enjoy widespread popularity. As discussed in the opening vignette, the majority of the public in Nova Scotia opposed the union and considerable opposition surfaced

FIGURE 2-1
CANADA IN 1867

New Brunswick, Nova Scotia and
Canada are united in a federal state,
the Dominion of Canada, by the British
North America Act (July 1, 1867). The
province of Canada is divided into
Ontario and Quebec. The United States
of America proclaims the purchase of
Alaska from Russia (June 20).

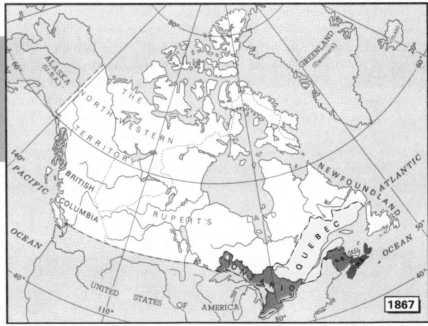

Source: *Natural Resources Canada, 2004, "Territorial Evolution 1867,"* Atlas of Canada.

among French Quebecers as well. For Maritimers, the fear was domination by Canada, meaning Ontario and Quebec, and loss of their own identities. For French Quebecers, the worry was that their culture, language, and religion would be threatened by their minority status in the newly expanded Canada. As for Canada's first inhabitants, the Aboriginal population of British North America was neither consulted nor considered in the establishment of the new country.

EXPANSION OF CANADA

From this contentious beginning, Canada grew over time "from sea to sea to sea." In 1868, to expand westward and northward, the Canadian government negotiated an agreement to purchase Rupert's Land (the large Hudson's Bay drainage area) and the North-Western Territory from the Hudson's Bay Company.[2] The residents and governing council of the Red River settlement (in what is now southern Manitoba) were not consulted about this annexation, which took effect in 1870. A Métis rebellion led by Louis Riel forced the Canadian government in 1870 to agree to the establishment of the Manitoba provincial government initially in the area around the Red River Valley (see Box 2-2, The Métis Rise Up: Louis Riel and the Rebellion of 1869–70).

Soon after, in 1871, British Columbia (which had been created by a merger of the colonies of Vancouver Island and British Columbia in 1866) became a Canadian province. Opposition to joining Canada was overcome when favourable terms were negotiated; these included a large subsidy and the assumption of the impoverished colony's debts, as well as the promise of a railway to link the province with the rest of the country within fifteen years (completed in 1885), and the adoption of responsible government for the province. As elsewhere, the Aboriginal peoples who formed a large majority of the population at the time were neither considered nor consulted in the negotiations.

Although Charlottetown is often viewed as the birthplace of Confederation, Prince Edward Island refused to join Canada in 1867. However, after a costly railroad in the colony created an unsupportable debt, the colony decided to join Canada in 1873 in return for the assumption of the debt by Canada, a buyout of British absentee landlords who controlled much of the land, and a commitment to maintain a year-round ferry service to the island.

Newfoundland joined Canada long after Manitoba, British Columbia, and Prince Edward Island. The Newfoundland government did not find the terms for joining Canada in 1867 to be adequate. More acceptable terms were

---

[2]These vast territories became the North-West Territories (now Northwest Territories) in 1870.

BOX 2-2

The Métis Rise Up:
Louis Riel and the Rebellion of 1869–70

French Quebecers were not the only minority who feared for their language and culture. Further west, in the Red River Valley, lived many Métis, descendants of French fur traders and Aboriginal women. When the Métis learned that Canada planned to annex the North-Western Territory, including the Red River Valley, they began to mobilize. Above all, they wanted to prevent the loss of their land and the large-scale immigration that would threaten their language, culture, and Catholic religion.

To prepare for the formal annexation of the North-Western Territory, the Canadian government appointed William McDougall, an Ontario Member of Parliament with notoriously anti-French views, as governor-designate. The Métis banished McDougall from their settlement and formed a provisional government with Louis Riel as its president. Their goal was to negotiate with the Canadian government to create a provincial government in southern Manitoba (rather than being administered by the Canadian government as part of a territory) and to gain protection for their rights.

Opponents of the provisional government who threatened to take up arms were arrested, and Thomas Scott, convicted of insubordination, was executed by a Métis firing squad. In 1870, the Canadian government agreed to establish the provincial government of Manitoba, and a military force was sent to Manitoba to enforce Canadian authority. Fearing for his life, Louis Riel fled to the United States.

He was subsequently elected three times to Canadian Parliament but prevented by the Canadian government from assuming his seat in Parliament.

▲ Louis Riel and the members of his provisional government (1869–70) wished to create a provincial government in southern Manitoba and to gain protection from the Canadian government for their rights.

After returning to Canada in 1885 to lead the North-West Rebellion (discussed later in this chapter), Riel was captured and tried for treason. Although the jury that convicted him recommended mercy, Riel was sentenced to be hanged. While Quebec Catholics pleaded for the prime minister to spare Riel from the noose, Ontario Protestants demanded his execution. In the end, Prime Minister Macdonald refused to commute the sentence, saying, "He shall hang though every dog in Quebec bark in his favour."

Over time, Riel has come to be seen by many Canadians as a defender of his people rather than a murderous traitor. Manitobans now have a holiday in February to celebrate Louis Riel Day, and there have been attempts to have the Canadian Parliament overturn Riel's conviction. Although Riel was hanged more than a century ago, his defence of minority rights resonates with many Canadians today.

negotiated in 1869. However, reflecting the sentiments of the popular anti-Confederate song ("Come near at your peril, Canadian Wolf!"), Newfoundland voters decisively defeated the pro-Confederation government in 1869. Some seven decades later, during the Great Depression, the government of Newfoundland faced bankruptcy. Based on the recommendation of a royal commission, the Newfoundland legislature agreed to suspend responsible government until self-sufficiency was restored. In 1934, an appointed Commission of Government was formed with three commissioners from the United Kingdom and three from Newfoundland. In effect, Newfoundland reverted to the status of a British colony.

The building of large American and Canadian bases during World War II brought an element of prosperity to Newfoundland. At the end of the war, the British government decided that an elected national convention should consider options for the future of Newfoundland, with the people to choose between those options in a referendum. Although the Newfoundland National Convention rejected putting confederation with Canada as an option on the ballot, the British government, which favoured confederation, insisted that it be included in the referendum. On June 3, 1948, a return to responsible government (that is, independence) received 44.6 percent of the vote, confederation with Canada 41.1 percent, and continuation of Commission of Government 14.3 percent. A second referendum held on July 22, 1948, resulted in 52.3 percent voting for confederation and 47.7 percent for responsible government. Negotiations with the Canadian government on the terms of union (including the assumption of the Newfoundland government's debt, subsidies, and the guarantee of steamship service to Nova Scotia) succeeded, and on March 31, 1949, Newfoundland became Canada's tenth province.[3]

The British Arctic Territories (islands in the High Arctic) were ceded to Canada in 1880 and became part of the North-West Territories. As a result of its growth during the Klondike Gold Rush, the Yukon became a separate territory in 1898. The provinces of Alberta and Saskatchewan were created out of the North-West Territories in 1905. The territory of Nunavut was separated from the Northwest Territories in 1999, reflecting the wishes of Nunavut's mainly Inuit population.

Canada has not only grown in territorial size, but also in population (see Figure 2-2). Canada's population today is almost ten times its population in 1867. In the decades after Confederation more people emigrated from Canada (primarily to the United States) than immigrated to Canada. However, since the beginning of the twentieth century, immigration has substantially exceeded emigration (except during the Great Depression of the 1930s). Indeed, in recent years, immigration has contributed to more than one-half of Canada's total population growth.

---

[3]In 2001, the province's name officially changed to Newfoundland and Labrador.

FIGURE 2-2
**POPULATION GROWTH,
1871–2009**

Note: 2009 is an estimate as of
August 12, 2009.

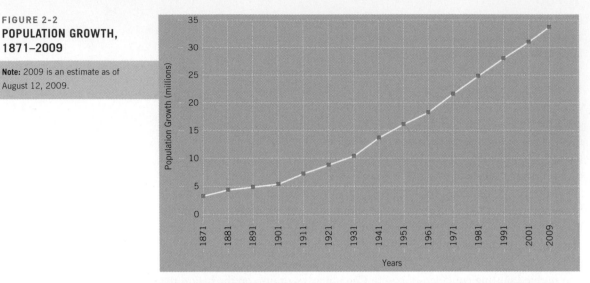

Sources: *Statistics Canada, 2005,* Census of Population. Population and Growth Components (1851–2001
Censuses), *retrieved from http://www40.statcan.gc.ca/l01/cst01/demo03-eng.htm?sdi=population; Statistics
Canada, 2009,* Canada's Population Clock, *retrieved from http://www.statcan.gc.ca/edu/clock-horloge/
edu06f_0001-eng.htm*

POLITICAL INDEPENDENCE

Canada did not become a completely sovereign (independent, self-governing) country in 1867. The British government retained important controls, including the right to overturn Canadian legislation, extend British laws to Canada, and control Canada's foreign policy. The British government's involvement in Canadian affairs was not always in Canada's interests. For example, in 1903, the British representative on a tribunal to settle the dispute over the boundary between Alaska and British Columbia sided with the Americans, depriving Canada of coastline for northern British Columbia.

The major contribution of Canada to the British effort in World War I and the heavy sacrifices of Canadian soldiers helped to make the case for greater Canadian independence. Canada (along with other British dominions) signed the peace treaties that ended the war, participated in the Paris Peace Conference, and became a member of the League of Nations (the forerunner of the United Nations). In 1926, an Imperial Conference recognized Canada (along with the other dominions) as having complete autonomy and equality in status with the United Kingdom. The governor general was no longer an agent of the British government, but rather a representative of the Crown. The ending of British imperial control of Canada was formalized in the **Statute of Westminster,** passed by the Parliament of the United Kingdom in 1931. However, due to disagreements between the Canadian and provincial governments about the procedures for formal constitutional amendments, the Constitution did not come entirely under Canadian control until 1982 (see Chapter 10). As well, the

**STATUTE OF
WESTMINSTER, 1931**
An Act of the Parliament of the
United Kingdom ending British
control of Canada.

Judicial Committee of the Privy Council (consisting of British law lords) continued to be the highest court of appeal for some Canadian cases until 1949.

In addition, although Canada was, in effect, independent from 1926, Canada was slow to adopt all of the symbolism of a sovereign country because of the continuing strength of many Canadians' emotional ties to Britain. Canadians remained "British subjects" until Canadian citizenship was adopted in 1947. A distinctive Canadian flag was adopted in 1965 only after very considerable controversy among those who wanted to retain the British Union Jack. In 1967, "O Canada" replaced "God Save the Queen" as the national anthem (although it was not officially recognized until 1980). And, Canada continues to use the British monarch as the formal symbolic head of state.

POLITICAL CONFLICT IN POST-CONFEDERATION CANADA

The Provinces and the Canadian Government

As noted in the introductory vignette, the new Dominion of Canada faced an immediate challenge from a separatist movement in Nova Scotia. However, despite the election victories of the anti-Confederation forces in the first Nova Scotian elections, the British government refused to entertain a petition for separation. In 1886, Premier W. S. Fielding won a Nova Scotia election on a promise to lead the three Maritime provinces out of Confederation, but he did not carry out his promise.

The Maritime provinces did not fully share in the growth of the Canadian economy. The shift from cross-Atlantic trade with Britain to north–south trade with the United States placed the Maritime provinces on the periphery of Canada. Further, the sale of many leading Maritime businesses to central Canadians reduced Maritimers' control of their own economies and contributed to the out-migration of skilled personnel. As well, the development and expansion of Ontario and Quebec and the rapid growth of the West reduced the political influence of the Maritime provinces.

Dissatisfaction with the declining economic and political position of the Maritimes in Canada resulted in a **Maritime Rights Movement** in the 1920s, which sought better terms for the Maritimes within Canada. However, the historical differences and competing interests of the Maritime provinces made unified political action difficult. Although the Canadian government implemented some of the recommendations of the Royal Commission on Maritime Claims (1926) that was established in response to the demands of the Maritime Rights Movement, these measures were insufficient to reverse the decline of the region.

MARITIME RIGHTS MOVEMENT A political movement in the 1920s that sought better terms for the Maritime provinces within Canada.

PROVINCIAL RIGHTS   Macdonald's vision of a strong central government was reflected, to a considerable extent, in the Constitution that was approved by the Parliament of the United Kingdom in 1867 (as discussed in Chapter 10).

The expansion of Canada to the Pacific coast, the massive undertaking to build a transcontinental railroad, actions taken to encourage manufacturing to locate in Canada, and recruitment of immigrants to settle the West reflected his vision of creating a great country matching the growth of the United States, but based on different values.

The idea of the Canadian government leading the development of a centralized Canadian nation was opposed by some provincial governments seeking to protect and promote provincial rights. The Liberal government in Ontario of Sir Oliver Mowat (1872–96) challenged the centralizing orientation of Conservative Prime Minister Sir John A. Macdonald (1867–73 and 1878–91). The hanging of Riel stirred nationalist feelings in Quebec, contributing to the election victory of the Parti National led by Honoré Mercier in 1887. Premier Mercier called an interprovincial conference (attended by representatives of the governments of Ontario, New Brunswick, and Nova Scotia, but not Prince Edward Island or British Columbia), which he hoped would "safeguard the autonomy of every province in the federation by guaranteeing their independence" (quoted in Ryan, 2003). Although there was agreement about provincial autonomy among those attending, the conference was not followed by subsequent meetings. Nevertheless, tensions between various provincial governments and the Canadian government have been and still are a regular and prominent feature of Canadian politics (as discussed in Chapter 13).

DISSATISFACTION IN THE WEST AND NEWFOUNDLAND AND LABRADOR   Western alienation has also been and continues to be a significant theme in Canadian politics. In the first decades of the Prairie provinces' existence, the Canadian government treated them somewhat like colonies to be exploited. Unlike other provincial governments, the Alberta, Saskatchewan, and Manitoba governments did not gain control of their natural resources until 1930. Macdonald's **National Policy** (1879), which involved placing high **tariffs** on manufactured goods coming into Canada so as to encourage the development of industry located primarily in Ontario and Quebec, did little to assist Westerners who had to sell their products on international markets. Subsequently, many Western Canadians demanded that the Canadian government pursue a free trade agreement with the United States. Further, the Canadian government's regulation of railway freight rates tended to discourage the location of manufacturing and processing in Western Canada. When in 1980 the Canadian government incensed Albertans (and some other Western Canadians) by adopting the **National Energy Program,** the government was thus exacerbating long-established resentment in the West.

The National Energy Program, adopted at a time of high international oil prices and concerns about energy shortages, included keeping oil prices below the international level, increasing the Canadian government's share of oil revenues, establishing a federal Crown corporation to be involved in the oil industry, and encouraging and subsidizing oil exploration on federal lands in the Arctic and offshore Newfoundland to reduce dependence on Alberta oil.

NATIONAL POLICY
A Canadian government policy adopted in 1879 that included a high tariff on the import of manufactured products, railway construction, and the encouragement of immigration to Western Canada.

TARIFF
A tax or customs duty on imported goods.

NATIONAL ENERGY PROGRAM
A Canadian government program adopted in 1980 that included keeping oil prices below the international level, increasing the Canadian government's share of oil revenues, establishing a federal Crown corporation to be involved in the oil industry, and encouraging and subsidizing oil exploration on federal lands in the Arctic and offshore Newfoundland.

Although the National Energy Program was scrapped a few years later, it has continued to symbolize Ottawa's catering to the manufacturing interests of Ontario and Quebec (that benefited from lower energy costs) at the expense of the oil-producing provinces.

In Newfoundland and Labrador, the mismanagement by the Canadian government of cod stocks and disputes concerning offshore oil revenues have led to considerable dissatisfaction with the Canadian government. In addition, the unwillingness of the Canadian government to require Quebec to allow Labrador power to be transmitted through Quebec led to the sale of Labrador power to Quebec Hydro. This provides a benefit to Quebec of between one and two billion dollars per year, while the province of Newfoundland and Labrador receives minimal revenues from its hydro power (Feehan, 2009). Indeed, there is a strong sense of Newfoundland nationalism that emphasizes the province's unique identity, is critical of the "giveaways" of the province's resources, and questions whether the province has benefited from joining Canada. At times, the government of Newfoundland and Labrador has echoed the demands of Quebec governments for greater autonomy. However, unlike Quebec, a significant independence movement has not been formed. Likewise, an attempt to elect the equivalent of the Bloc Québécois to represent the interests of Newfoundland in Parliament (the "Newfoundland First" party) gained little support in the 2008 Canadian election.

English–French Relations

The Constitution that was adopted in 1867 included only limited provisions protecting the rights of the French-Canadian minority. English or French may be used in the Canadian Parliament and courts established by Parliament. The records and acts of Parliament must be published in both languages. Similar provisions in the Constitution for the use of English and French in the Quebec legislature and courts were designed to protect the English minority in that province. Catholic and Protestant denominational school systems in provinces where they had been established in law at the time of Confederation were also protected by the Constitution. Although the Constitution made education the exclusive responsibility of provincial legislatures, the Canadian Parliament was given the right to pass remedial legislation if those denominational rights were violated.

The establishment of new provinces raised controversial issues about language and education. The *Manitoba Act,* 1870, made both English and French the languages of the provincial legislature and the province's courts. However, as the English-speaking population swelled (primarily with Protestants from Ontario), the Manitoba legislature in 1890 passed the *Official Language Act* making English the sole language of the legislature and courts.[4] As well, the *Manitoba Schools Act,* 1890, eliminated public funding

---

[4]Although various courts ruled the *Official Language Act* as unconstitutional, it was not until the 1980s that the Manitoba government began to take action to translate its acts into French.

BOX 2-3

Minorities and Education: The Manitoba Schools Question

In the 1880s, fears among the French-Catholic minority about their fate in Canada were heightened, in part as a result of the decision to hang Louis Riel. Anti-Catholic and anti-French sentiments were expressed by some politicians and newspapers, and newly developed political movements promoted the idea of an exclusively English-speaking British Canada. French Canadians lobbied Parliament to use its constitutional authority to pass remedial legislation ensuring that the constitutional right to denominational schools in Manitoba was restored.

The issue of remedial legislation was highly controversial because it would interfere with provincial control of education. As a result, both the Conservative and Liberal parties in the House of Commons were divided on the issue. The federal Conservative government, which had strong representation from Quebec, eventually introduced remedial legislation. Yet the opponents of the legislation, and in particular a group of Conservatives from Ontario who had very negative attitudes toward French-Canadian Catholics, were able to block the legislation from passing.

The Liberal leader Wilfrid Laurier opposed the remedial legislation because it interfered with provincial control of education. He promised that he would find a way to resolve the issue.

When he won the 1896 Canadian election, he took action. With Thomas Greenway, the premier of Manitoba, Laurier worked out a compromise that avoided the use of remedial legislation. Some religious education after hours in public schools was allowed, and parents were given the right to have their children educated in English and another language. However, in 1916, the right to educate children in a language other than English was lost due to wartime animosity toward Germans and those of some other continental European ancestries.

The controversy over the *Manitoba Schools Act* foreshadowed later disputes about the language of instruction in other provinces. In 1912 Ontario's Ministry of Education adopted Regulation 17, which made English the language of instruction in all Ontario schools (modified slightly in 1913 to allow some limited teaching of French). This regulation was dropped in 1927, although the right to a French-language education was not guaranteed in Ontario until 1968.

More recently, in 1977, the Quebec government passed Bill 101, which included provisions preventing most children from enrolling in a publicly funded English-language school unless at least one of their parents had been educated in English in Quebec (as discussed further in Chapter 4).

for denominational schools (including French-language Catholic schools) and established a public school system with English as the language of instruction (see Box 2-3, Minorities and Education: The Manitoba Schools Question).

THE BOER WAR, THE NAVY, AND THE CONSCRIPTION CRISIS   In the late nineteenth and early twentieth centuries, Canadians struggled to define themselves in relation to the British Empire. English-Canadian imperialists promoted the idea that Canada and the other former colonies settled by those of British ancestry should unite with Great Britain in an Imperial Federation. This would allow Canada "its proper place in the councils of the Empire and in the destiny of the world" (Stephen Leacock, quoted in Bumsted, 2008, p. 162). Others looked to the development of a fully independent Canada. For example, Henri Bourassa, founder of the newspaper *Le Devoir*, promoted an independent bilingual and bicultural Canada based on the mutual respect of English and French Canadians. Still others viewed closer ties or some sort of union with the United States as desirable and inevitable (Bumsted, 2008).

While many English Canadians favoured Canadian participation in Britain's imperialistic war against the Boers (Dutch-speaking settlers) in South Africa (1899–1902), French Canadians were generally opposed to involvement in this British war against a threatened minority in a distant land. Faced with strong divisions in his Liberal party on the issue, Prime Minister Laurier avoided taking the issue to Parliament. Instead he arranged for Canadian volunteers to be organized, equipped, and sent to South Africa with their pay covered by the British government (Morton, 2007). A privately funded cavalry unit, Lord Strathcona's Horse, commanded by Sam Steele (a veteran of the North-West Mounted Police) won high praise for its effectiveness during the Boer War.

Several years later, Laurier was less successful in finding a compromise regarding demands for a Canadian contribution to the British Royal Navy (as discussed in Box 2-4, The Naval Services Bill: A Divisive Issue for a Young Country).

WORLD WARS   Canada's entry into the First World War was widely supported, even by French-Canadian nationalists in the House of Commons. However, the lengthy war eventually resulted in controversial calls for conscription despite the large number of volunteers that had enlisted. Many French Canadians, as well as many people of other non-British

▶ When he was recommended as "the best man in Canada" to lead a unit in South Africa, Sam Steele had just commanded the North-West Mounted Police contingent that kept the peace during the Yukon gold rush. He had joined in the militia during the 1866 Fenian Raids, participated in the Red River Expedition in 1870, and enlisted in the NWMP when it formed in 1873. His NWMP career, including command of Steele's Scouts in the Northwest Campaign of 1885, reads like a history of the opening of the Canadian West. Not surprisingly, under Lt.-Col. Steele the Strathcona Horse won high praise for its effectiveness during the Boer War (1899–1902), even though the militia's participation was under some question at home.

BOX 2-4

The Naval Services Bill:
A Divisive Issue for a Young Country

As Germany began to challenge British naval supremacy in the early twentieth century, the British government pressured its colonies for contributions to the Royal Navy. Prime Minister Laurier rejected the request; instead, in 1910, his government introduced the *Naval Services Bill,* which proposed building a small Canadian navy. With support from English Canadians, the Conservative opposition criticized what they described as a "tin-pot navy" and demanded that Canada provide two dreadnoughts (large battleships) to the Royal Navy. Nationalists in Quebec, led by Henri Bourassa, strongly opposed the *Naval Services Bill*, arguing that it would lead to unwarranted Canadian participation in British wars (Beck, 1968).

In spite of their deep differences about whether Canada should contribute to the Royal Navy and, more generally, about Canada's role in the Empire, the Conservatives and the Quebec Nationalists joined forces in the 1911 Canadian election, ousting the Liberals. The victorious Conservatives, to the disgust of their Quebec nationalist allies, subsequently proposed to contribute $35 million to Britain to build three dreadnaughts. Although closure (cutting off debate) was used to push the legislation through the House of Commons, the Liberal majority in the Senate defeated the bill to aid the British navy (Morton, 2007). The *Naval Services Bill* presented a divisive issue for a young country, underscoring differences between French Quebecers and English Canadians.

---

ancestries, opposed compulsory military service.[5] Violent anti-conscription demonstrations in Quebec City resulted in Canadian troops being sent to that city, and four people were killed when the troops opened fire (Torrance, 1986). Nevertheless, conscription was imposed by a Union government composed of Conservatives, along with most of the Liberal Members of Parliament from English Canada. The Union government won the 1917 election by a substantial margin, although Quebecers elected anti-conscription Liberals in every area that had a French-speaking majority. To help ensure a solid victory, the Union government extended the right to vote to women serving overseas as nurses in the army and to women with close relatives fighting in the war. The **conscription crisis** reinforced the negative feelings that many English Canadians harboured toward French Canadians. It also had a long-term effect on Canada's party system, contributing to the difficulties the Conservative party experienced in appealing to Quebecers for decades afterwards.

The conscription issue arose again during the Second World War. To gain support from French Canadians for the war effort, Liberal Prime Minister

CONSCRIPTION CRISIS
The imposition of compulsory military service during the First World War that sharply divided many English and French Canadians.

---

[5]A large proportion of volunteers were immigrants to Canada. There was also considerable opposition to conscription among some groups of English Canadians when various exemptions from compulsory military service (such as the exemption for farmers' sons) were removed in 1918.

Mackenzie King promised that there would be no conscription for overseas service. Conscription for Home Guard duty was introduced in 1940. Then in 1942 the Canadian government held a national referendum asking to be released from its promise not to impose conscription. The cautious prime minister promised "conscription if necessary but not necessarily conscription." Outside Quebec 72.8 percent voted in favour of allowing conscription, while in Quebec only 27.9 percent voted in favour. Nevertheless, conscription for overseas service was not implemented until November 1944,[6] and a relatively small number of conscripts ended up on the front lines before the end of the war. Despite the controversy over conscription, the Liberals managed to get re-elected shortly after Victory in Europe Day, albeit with a substantially reduced popular vote. The Bloc Populaire, which was formed by Quebec's anti-conscriptionists, managed to win only two seats and disappeared soon afterwards.

Overall, tensions between English and French Canadians brought to the fore a conservative form of nationalism in Quebec that sought to isolate French Quebecers from modern influences and enforce the authority of the traditionalist Catholic Church. As discussed in Chapter 4, this form of Quebec nationalism was, to a considerable extent, superseded by a secular form of Quebec nationalism in the early 1960s.

ABORIGINALS   Until recent decades, Aboriginals were generally ignored in the visible arenas of Canadian politics. In the decades after Confederation, there was a flurry of activity as the Canadian government signed treaties with First Nations in order to open up vast areas of land for settlement by those of European ancestry. Shunted off to reserves and subjected to repressive Canadian government control by the *Indian Act*, 1876, Aboriginals were generally excluded from political life (although participating in Canada's wars). Furthermore, diseases brought by European settlers (for which Aboriginals had no immunity) continued to weaken and decimate the Aboriginal population. Starvation became a serious problem for Aboriginals on the Prairies as the introduction of firearms and the reduction of habitat by European settlement resulted in the near extinction of the buffalo herds on which Aboriginals relied for food (as well as skins used for clothing and shelter).

Post-Confederation Canada did not experience the series of wars and massacres that the United States had with Indian tribes, which continued throughout the nineteenth century. Indeed, some American tribes took refuge in Canada. Nevertheless, Canada was not immune from serious conflict, as discussed in Box 2-5, Aboriginal Unrest: The North-West Rebellion of 1885.

---

[6]Some Home Guard conscripts were sent to Alaska's Aleutian Islands in 1943 to fight the Japanese, who had captured two islands. However, this was not considered overseas service.

BOX 2-5

Aboriginal Unrest: The North-West Rebellion of 1885

Faced with starvation and the destruction of their traditional way of life in the 1870s and early 1880s, Prairie Cree leaders, including Big Bear and Poundmaker, reluctantly agreed to sign treaties with the Canadian government and moved to reserves. The Department of Indian Affairs provided little assistance, even after Cree leaders wrote to Prime Minister Macdonald about their desperate situation. Tensions developed as some starving Aboriginals stole cattle from settlers, while others considered protest actions including armed rebellion (Bumsted, 2008; Conrad & Finkel, 2007).

Many Métis moved to what is now Saskatchewan after being denied title to the lands they had been promised in the Red River area. Here, the Métis (as well as white settlers) faced problems concerning land grants, assistance for farming, and services such as schools and local police (Conrad & Finkel, 2007). When the Canadian government ignored their petitions, the Métis invited Louis Riel to return from the United States to take up their cause. Believing he had a divine mission to save God's chosen people, the Métis, Riel consented.

Riel's peaceful attempts to persuade the Canadian government to improve the plight of the people in the region were unsuccessful. He and his Métis supporters set up a provisional government of Saskatchewan with Gabriel Dumont as military leader. After the Métis had some success in a clash with the North-West Mounted Police at Duck Lake, Cree warriors, upset about broken treaty promises, attacked the community of Frog Lake, killing nine settlers including the Indian agent. The Canadian government quickly sent a military force over the newly built Canadian Pacific Railway. In the final Battle of Batoche, the Métis were easily defeated by the larger Canadian force. Riel was arrested and Dumont fled to the United States where he became a star performer in the Wild West Show. A few weeks later the Cree were defeated in the Battle of Loon Lake. Eight Cree were hanged and many others were imprisoned, including Big Bear and Poundmaker who had opposed the armed uprising.

Although the North-West Rebellion was short-lived, the Rebellion challenges the popular myth that the Canadian West was settled peacefully with respectful relations between the Mounted Police and Aboriginals.

Racial and Ethnic Minorities

Canada is often thought of as a county that is tolerant of racial, ethnic, and religious diversity. However, a review of Canadian history challenges this outlook. A significant number of Black people were used as slaves in British North America. Although Upper Canada passed a *Slave Act* in 1793 preventing the importation of new slaves, slavery continued until it was abolished in the British Empire in 1834. In the nineteenth century, sympathetic Canadians assisted thousands of African-American slaves who fled to Canada from the United States on the "Underground Railroad." However, after settling in

Canada, African-Americans often faced discrimination and social exclusion. For example, in 1946 Viola Desmond, a Nova Scotia businesswoman, was forcibly removed from a movie theatre in New Glasgow, Nova Scotia, and arrested when she refused to move from the white section rather than sit in the Black balcony, where, she said, she could not see the film.[7] This incident led to a lengthy political struggle to end Nova Scotia's segregation law, which was finally revoked in 1954.

Prejudice against Asian immigrants was common, particularly as other workers feared the loss of jobs to those willing to accept low wages. As discussed in Chapter 4, a "head tax" was imposed on Chinese immigrants after the Canadian Pacific Railroad, to which Chinese workers had made a major contribution, was completed. In 1907, the Asiatic Exclusion League was formed in Vancouver to try to stop Asian immigration. Riots occurred as thousands of members and supporters of the racist league marched through Chinatown and Japantown, smashing windows. The areas were placed under martial law, and for days fearful Chinese and Japanese residents avoided going into the streets.

In the 1920s, the Ku Klux Klan, notorious for their violence against Blacks and their hatred of Catholics, established "klans" in various Canadian communities, with particular strength in Saskatchewan. In 1929 they campaigned against Liberal Premier Jimmy Gardiner, burning crosses at his rallies among other activities. The Liberals were defeated, although the accusation that the Klan was connected to the victorious Conservatives has been questioned.

Anti-Semitism has also had a significant presence in Canada, with Jews suffering various forms of discrimination. In 1933, a riot occurred at the Christie Pits Park in Toronto after an anti-Semitic club displayed a large Nazi swastika at a softball game. Many people were injured as thousands swarmed to the park to participate in the ensuing brawl. As Jews fled Nazi oppression and extermination in Europe, the Canadian government was willing to accept only a tiny number of Jewish refugees—even forcing a boat carrying refugees to return to Europe in 1939.

Women

Women were largely invisible in Canadian politics until recent decades, although active in charitable, social, religious, and community organizations. Women did not receive the vote in federal elections until 1918, and only a handful had been elected to Parliament until recent decades. Women were often prevented from becoming members of various professions. They were

---

[7]Because Viola Desmond had paid for a ticket in the balcony, she was convicted and jailed for defrauding the Canadian government of one cent—the difference in the amusement tax between the Black and white seats.

expected to be responsible for home and family, while leaving the "dirty" business of politics to men.

Women have, of course, entered the paid labour force, professions, and business in large numbers in recent decades. The rights of women are constitutionally protected through the *Charter of Rights and Freedoms*. Nevertheless, as discussed in Chapter 3, women face various hurdles in the pursuit of full equality. And women continue to be greatly under-represented in Parliament, provincial legislatures, and many senior political positions.

Farmers and Workers

The struggle of farmers and workers to improve their position has played a key role in Canada's political history. In the pre-Confederation British North American colonies, reformers with support based in farming communities struggled against the wealthy, privileged elite who dominated government, the economy, and society. In the first decades of the twentieth century, farmers' movements developed throughout Canada, with particular strength on the Prairies and in rural Ontario. Both major political parties, the Conservatives and the Liberals, were seen as beholden to the interests of big business. Many in the farmers' movement were critical of representative democracy and favoured arrangements in which the people had direct control over their representatives and the policies adopted by governments.

Following World War I, the farmers' movement entered the arena of electoral politics, with farmers nominating candidates who pledged to act on the wishes of their constituents. The collection of farmers' representatives achieved considerable success (in combination with a small number of independent labour representatives), forming the United Farmers governments of Alberta, Manitoba, and Ontario and, under the label National Progressives, becoming the second-largest party in the Canadian Parliament for a short time.

In early Canada, criminal laws concerning conspiracy were used to lay charges against those involved in organizing workers and taking strike action. George Brown, a prominent Liberal politician and publisher of *The Globe* newspaper, provoked a large demonstration against this law after he used it to arrest striking printers. Subsequently, Conservative Prime Minister Sir John A. Macdonald presented legislation to Parliament to legalize unions. Nevertheless there have been, on a number of occasions, bitter confrontations between employers and workers, with governments often siding with employers (see Box 2-6, Labour Asserts Itself: The Winnipeg General Strike, the On-to-Ottawa Trek, and the GM Strike).

Socialist parties and groups seeking, in some cases, radical or revolutionary changes to Canada's capitalist economic system developed in some parts of Canada (notably British Columbia) in the late nineteenth century. Like the farmers, the socialists believed that the Conservative and Liberal parties,

BOX 2-6

Labour Asserts Itself:
The Winnipeg General Strike, the
On-to-Ottawa Trek, and the GM Strike

THE WINNIPEG GENERAL STRIKE

During World War I, industrial employment and union membership increased substantially. Some individuals in the divided labour movement were striving to create One Big Union that would fundamentally transform the capitalist system. In 1919, building and metal trades workers in Winnipeg went on strike when their employers rejected collective bargaining. As an act of solidarity, the Winnipeg Trades and Labour Council (as well as workers in various other Western communities) decided to strike as well. With socialism on the rise and the Bolshevik (Communist) revolution having recently occurred in Russia, governments and business leaders raised the fear of revolution in Canada led by non-British "aliens." Although the General Strike was non-violent, the city police who showed some sympathy for the strikers were replaced and the militia and RCMP were called in. When the strike supporters held a peaceful march in defiance of the city's ban on parades, the RCMP and militia broke up the march, killing one spectator and wounding others. The strike leaders were thrown in jail and charged with seditious conspiracy (McNaught, 1969).

THE ON-TO-OTTAWA TREK

During the Great Depression of the 1930s, the federal government established work camps for the desperate, hungry unemployed men who were paid twenty cents a day for hard labour. A communist-led Worker's Relief Camp Union was established to protest the conditions at the camps. Four thousand men left the relief camps in B.C. and went on strike in Vancouver (Gillmor, Michaud, & Turgeon, 2001). One thousand left Vancouver on boxcars, and many others joined the "On-to-Ottawa Trek" en route. Among the demands were first aid equipment for the camps, coverage by workers' compensation, and the right of the relief workers to vote.

After a bitter, unsuccessful meeting between the strike leaders and Conservative Prime Minister R. B. Bennett, the trekkers held a public meeting in Regina. RCMP riot squads battled with the strikers and their supporters for four hours. Many were wounded, and one plainclothes policeman and one striker died. The protestors were encircled with barbed wire and denied food and water. The premier of Saskatchewan accused the RCMP of instigating the riot. Subsequently, the prime minister and his party were decisively defeated in a general election, the federal work camps disbanded, and wages for workers on relief slightly increased.

THE GM STRIKE

In 1937, a strike began at the General Motors automobile plant in Oshawa, Ontario, when the company refused to recognize the United Auto Workers as the bargaining agent for the workers. Ontario Premier Mitch Hepburn, an opponent of industrial unions, organized a special force of 400 men with plans to set up machine guns and instructions to shoot strikers at the knees, if ordered. "I'd rather walk with the workers than ride with General Motors," retorted David Croll, an Ontario cabinet minister. Later he and another cabinet minister resigned in protest. Fortunately, a compromise was reached and a contract was signed between General Motors and the union local.

As a result of the determined actions of workers, the right to organize, bargain collectively, and take strike action has become well established. Nevertheless, labour is often at odds with business and government, not only about wages and working conditions but also about what social and economic policies should be adopted.

which dominated politics and government, represented the interests of big business. By the late nineteenth and early twentieth centuries, a variety of labour representatives were elected provincially and nationally. In Ontario, the Independent Labour Party participated in a coalition government led by the United Farmers of Ontario. The democratic socialist Co-operative Commonwealth Federation was formed in 1933 and elected to govern Saskatchewan in 1944. The New Democratic Party, still a force in Canadian politics today, was formed in 1961 as "the political voice of labour."

Canada–U.S. Relations: The Free Trade Issue

Some concerns about American expansion into Canada persisted in the decades following Confederation. However, American expansionism and imperialism in the nineteenth and early twentieth centuries was directed at the Caribbean, Mexico, Central America, Hawaii, and the Philippines rather than Canada. Instead, debate raged in Canada about the identity and future of the country. Influential British-born intellectual Goldwin Smith, in his book *Canada and the Canadian Question* (1891), argued that Canada was an "unnatural country" with no real reason to exist, and that it should unite with the United States because there were no major differences between Canadians and Americans. However, no significant movement for a political union between Canada and the United States developed. Instead, the negotiation of free trade with the United States became, at times, a focal point for intense political controversy.

In the decade after Confederation, both the Conservative and Liberal governments tried to persuade the American government to re-establish the Reciprocity Treaty that had allowed unprocessed goods to trade freely without customs duties between the two countries. However, the United States, which established high tariffs to encourage the development of its industries, was uninterested in reciprocity. In 1879 as a major component of the National Policy, the Conservative Prime Minister Sir John A. Macdonald placed a high tariff on manufactured products (averaging 30 percent) coming into Canada from the United States. While the tariff promoted the development of industries in Canada, it also increased American economic influence in the country as American companies set up branch plants in Canada to avoid the tariff barrier.

In 1888, with a global recession hurting Canada, and the United States proposing to increase tariffs on some important Canadian exports, Wilfrid Laurier's Liberal party advocated unrestricted reciprocity (that is, free trade) with the United States. This became the centrepiece of the 1891 election campaign. With his government plagued by scandals, tensions between English and French, and opposition from provincial governments, Prime Minister Macdonald accused the Liberals of "veiled treason" and taking part in a "deliberate conspiracy . . . to force Canada into the American Union" (quoted in Beck, 1968, p. 64). Further, he played to the loyalist sentiments of many English Canadians by proclaiming that "A British subject I was born—a British subject I will die." Although the Conservatives lost some seats in central Canada, the nationalistic appeal helped to ensure a final election victory for Macdonald.

The issue of free trade with the United States was also central to the 1911 election. Prime Minister Laurier and U.S. President William Howard Taft reached an agreement regarding free trade in many natural products and lower tariffs on some manufactured products (Conrad & Finkel, 2007). When the House of Commons failed to approve the agreement because of a Conservative filibuster (a tactic to prevent proposed legislation coming to a vote, usually with long, drawn-out speeches), Laurier requested an election. A group of eighteen prominent businessmen, the Canadian Manufacturers Association, and some Liberal Members of Parliament bolstered Conservative opposition to the agreement. In addition to the self-interest of those Canadian businesses that had benefited from the National Policy, opponents raised nationalist concerns about the possibility of being absorbed by the United States. "No truck or trade with the Yankees" was a popular slogan in the campaign. Fears about the intentions of the United States were reinforced by Champ Clark, the Speaker of the U.S. House of Representatives, who asserted in the American debate that "I hope to see the day when the American flag will float over every square foot of the British North American possessions, clear to the North Pole" (quoted in Beck, 1968, p. 125). In the end, the Conservatives defeated the Liberals in the 1911 election and the agreement was not signed.

In 1935, however, Liberal Prime Minister Mackenzie King signed a Canada–United States trade agreement that had been initiated by R. B. Bennett, his Conservative predecessor. This agreement reduced Canadian tariffs on a variety of American manufactured products in return for the free entry of most Canadian fish, forest, and farm products into the United States. Because of the harsh economic times of the Great Depression, this agreement faced virtually no opposition in either country (Conrad & Finkel, 2007). In 1947, Canada proposed a comprehensive free trade agreement with the United States that would eliminate nearly all tariffs. Secret negotiations produced a rough draft of the agreement. However, after reflecting on the fate of the Liberals in the 1911 election and how his legacy would be perceived, Mackenzie King decided not to proceed with the proposed agreement.

The Canada–United States Free Trade Agreement reached in 1987 under the direction of Progressive Conservative (PC) Prime Minister Brian Mulroney and U.S. President Ronald Reagan was extremely controversial. The 1988 election was fought almost exclusively on this issue, with Liberal leader John Turner promising to tear up the agreement which, Liberals claimed, would, in effect, wipe out the border between the two countries. Although slightly less

**NORTH AMERICAN
FREE TRADE AGREEMENT**
A 1992 agreement between
Canada, the United States, and
Mexico that established a high
level of economic integration in
North America.

than one-half of Canadians supported the free trade agreement, the PCs won the election and implemented the agreement. In 1992 a broader **North American Free Trade Agreement** (NAFTA) including Canada, the United States, and Mexico was negotiated. Like the Canada–United States Free Trade Agreement, NAFTA (discussed further in Chapter 3) goes beyond the removal of tariffs to provide for quite a high level of economic integration in North America, including provisions for the sharing of Canada's petroleum resources in times of shortage. The Liberal party led by Jean Chrétien promised to renegotiate the NAFTA agreement that the previous PC government had negotiated. However, after an election victory in 1993, the Liberals put the agreement into effect with only minor face-saving modifications.

Canadian nationalists (such as the Council of Canadians) view NAFTA as a major step in the promotion of the "deep integration" of the North American continent that would undermine the sovereignty of Canada, making this country, in effect, a colony of the United States.

Summary and Conclusion

The story of Canada's past can take many forms. Some describe Canadian historical development as the evolution from colony to independent nation. Others view the development of a close relationship with the United States as limiting the independence of contemporary Canada or even making Canada, in effect, a colony of the United States. Still others look at Canadian history as the continuing struggles for democracy, equality, respect, and justice by diverse groups including women, Aboriginals, French Canadians, ethnic and racial minorities, and those in disadvantaged social classes.

Canadian politics has often focused on the tense relations between English and French Canadians and the conflicts between the Canadian government and various provincial governments. These tensions are frequently seen as creating challenges to "national unity."

Concerns about American domination and possible absorption or annexation by the United States have also been, at times, an important element of Canadian politics. The question "Can Canada survive?" has often been raised by Canadian academics, literary figures, and journalists.

This chapter has highlighted some serious political conflicts that have threatened Canadian unity. However, Canada has, for the most part, enjoyed a peaceful existence and developed as a widely respected country since 1867. Like other countries, it has faced and will continue to face various problems and challenges. While maintaining Canadian unity and sovereignty continue to be relevant concerns, other issues, including environmental degradation, Aboriginal self-government, equality for women, and the accommodation of those with different cultures and religious practices, have become increasingly important in recent decades.

Discussion Questions

1. If you had lived in British North America in the 1860s, do you think you would have supported or opposed Confederation?

2. What have been the most serious challenges Canada has faced? What challenges do you think will be most important in the coming years?

3. Are all of the political conflicts discussed in this chapter still relevant in contemporary Canadian politics? Have other conflicts become more important?

4. Should the Métis leader Louis Riel be considered a Canadian hero?

5. Was it a mistake to impose conscription during World War I and World War II?

Further Reading

Ajzenstat, J., Romney, P., Gentles, I., & Gairdner, W. D. (Eds.). (2003). *Canada's founding debates*. Toronto, ON: University of Toronto Press.

Bumsted, J. M. (2003). *The peoples of Canada. A pre-Confederation history* (2nd ed.). Don Mills, ON: Oxford University Press.

Bumsted, J. M. (2008). *The peoples of Canada. A post-Confederation history* (3rd ed.). Don Mills, ON: Oxford University Press.

Conrad, M., & Finkel, A. (2007). *Canada: A national history*. Toronto, ON: Pearson Longman.

Dickason, O. P. (with McNab, D. T.). (2009). *Canada's first nations: A history of founding peoples from earliest times* (4th ed.). Don Mills, ON: Oxford University Press.

Gillmor, D., & Turgeon, P. (2000). *Canada: A people's history* (Vol. 1). Toronto, ON: McClelland & Stewart.

Gillmor, D., Menaud, A., & Turgeon, P. (2001). *Canada: A people's history* (Vol. 2). Toronto, ON: McClelland & Stewart.

Morton, D. (2006). *A short history of Canada* (6th ed.). Toronto, ON: McClelland & Stewart.

Palmer, B. D. (1992). *Working class experience: Rethinking the history of Canadian labour, 1800–1991*. Toronto, ON: McClelland & Stewart.

Strong-Boag, V., & Feldman, A. C. (1997). *Rethinking Canada: The promise of women's history* (3rd ed.). Toronto, ON: Oxford University Press.

Chapter 3

POLITICS AND THE ECONOMY

PHOTO ABOVE: Kimberly Rogers, pregnant, died in 2001 after being confined to her stifling apartment as a result of a conviction for welfare fraud. The circumstances of her death drew national attention and raised questions about the availability of financial and political resources for all.

1. Outline the basic features of the Canadian economy.
2. Discuss the issues relating to foreign ownership.
3. Evaluate the North American Free Trade Agreement.
4. Examine the changing role of government in the economy.

5. Explain the significance of economic inequalities for Canadian politics.
6. Discuss the issues related to the role of women in the workforce.

On a very hot summer day in 2001, Kimberly Rogers was found dead in her stifling Sudbury apartment as a result of an overdose of an antidepressant. Rogers was eight months pregnant and on medications for a variety of illnesses that prevented her from working. She had been confined to her apartment after being convicted of welfare fraud and was allowed out only three hours a week. Her crime: collecting social assistance while receiving a student loan needed to pay for her four years of college education.

Several months earlier, Rogers' social assistance benefits had been automatically suspended as a result of the conviction. She challenged this suspension as "cruel and unusual punishment" that violated the *Charter of Rights and Freedoms* as well as violating Charter protections of life, liberty, and security of the person and equality rights. Judge Epstein of the Ontario Superior Court granted a temporary injunction reinstating Rogers' benefits while the case was being considered. In her judgment, Epstein stated, "There is overwhelming public interest in protecting a pregnant woman in our community from being destitute." Nevertheless, Kimberly Rogers' social assistance payment amounted to $468 a month while her rent for a tiny rundown apartment was $450 a month. She relied on food banks to avoid starvation, but did not have available the food needed for a healthy pregnancy.

The most vulnerable elements of society with few political resources, including single mothers and those with disabilities, often find that governments are not sympathetic to their plight. Indeed, despite the publicity surrounding Kimberly Rogers' death, the Progressive Conservative government led by Premier Mike Harris ignored the recommendations of the coroner's jury and implemented a law that established a lifetime ban on receiving social assistance for anyone who had abused the welfare system. The law establishing a lifetime ban was repealed shortly after the Ontario Liberals won the 2003 election.

In the 1990s many governments in Canada cut welfare benefits, leaving the poor in dire straits. Assistance for single parents in Ontario was cut 31.7 percent from 1994 to 2003, while somewhat smaller cuts occurred in other provinces, such as British Columbia (12.3 percent) and Quebec (9.3 percent).

Only Newfoundland and New Brunswick bucked this trend by slightly increasing payments. In addition, Ontario and Alberta cut the number of people eligible for welfare through work requirements and various administrative procedures that created more barriers to receiving assistance (Kneebone & White, 2009). A British Columbia law introduced in 2002 that limited those considered "employable" to only two years of assistance in a five-year period was abandoned as a result of strenuous opposition from a wide variety of groups, including city councils, school boards, religious groups, and anti-poverty organizations.

In part, the cutbacks in welfare resulted from the Canadian government's decision to end the cost sharing of social assistance with provincial governments and to greatly reduce the money it transferred to provincial governments in the mid-1990s. The attack on welfare in some provinces also reflected an ideological perspective (often referred to as "neoliberalism") that favoured clawing back the role of government, slashing taxes, and leaving individuals responsible for their own well-being in a free-market economic system. This approach can, however, lead to dire consequences for the less fortunate members of society.

Discussions of the Canadian economy often focus on the question of how to stimulate economic growth. However, the quality of life of Canadians depends not only on the total production of goods and services, but also on how the country's wealth is distributed. The continued existence of inequalities in our rich country, as well as Canada's close economic ties to the United States, raises important political issues.

THE CANADIAN ECONOMY

Economic historians often describe Canada as a country whose financial well-being has relied on the export of a few resource staples: the near-unparalleled riches of its seas, forests, mountains, and plains. Europeans first became interested in what is now Canada for the abundant cod as well as whale oil for lamps. Next, the export of furs to Europe—beaver, silver fox, muskrat, ermine—became a leading source of revenues from the early seventeenth century until the early nineteenth century. In the nineteenth century, timber from New Brunswick and Quebec, as well as wheat from Ontario, became major export commodities. Early in the twentieth century Prairie wheat came to the fore as a major export. More recently, oil and natural gas have become Canada's leading exports.

Canada's dependence on a few staples has often been viewed as undesirable for long-term economic development. Resource commodities are subject to sharp fluctuations in world demand and prices leading to cycles of "boom" and "bust." Exporting unprocessed or lightly processed materials does not create many long-lasting jobs, particularly with the development of labour-saving modern technology. As well, some natural resources (such as oil and minerals) are non-renewable and thus of declining importance over time. Some renewable resources (such as fish and forest products) have become depleted due to over-exploitation. Natural resource exploitation can also damage the environment. For example, Alberta's huge oil sands developments are damaging one of the world's major freshwater river systems, as well as being a major source of greenhouse gas emissions.

Canada's economy began to diversify in the latter part of the nineteenth century with the production of consumer goods such as clothing and shoes. Toward the end of the nineteenth century and in the first decades of the twentieth century, "heavy industries" such as iron and steel, pulp and paper plants, machinery, and chemical plants were established (Conrad & Finkel, 2007). In the last decades of the twentieth century, Canada's manufacturing sector, aided by a low exchange rate for the Canadian dollar (allowing goods to be produced more cheaply than in the United States), flourished in areas such as automobile production and telecommunications.[1] Canada's exports of manufactured products exceeded its imports of such products (Stanford, 2008). Throughout the twentieth century and into the twenty-first, the service sector of the economy has exploded. As Table 3-1 indicates, the bulk of employment is now in the broadly defined service sector.

However, with some notable exceptions such as the development of Waterloo-based Research in Motion's BlackBerry, Canada lags behind most other leading countries in terms of innovation and advanced technology.

---

[1]The high cost of providing health insurance to employees has also made manufacturing more expensive for many companies in the United States.

TABLE 3-1
**EMPLOYMENT BY
INDUSTRY, 2007
(IN THOUSANDS)**

ALL INDUSTRIES	16 866.4
Goods-producing sector	**3 993.0**
Agriculture	337.2
Forestry, fishing, mining, oil and gas	339.3
Utilities	138.0
Construction	1 133.5
Manufacturing	2 044.9
Services-producing sector	**12 873.5**
Trade	2 682.4
Transportation and warehousing	822.8
Finance, insurance, real estate and leasing	1 060.4
Professional, scientific and technical services	1 136.9
Business, building and other support services	702.1
Educational services	1 183.2
Health care and social assistance	1 846.1
Information, culture and recreation	782.0
Accommodation and food services	1 069.4
Other services	723.5
Public administration	864.6

Source: *Statistics Canada, 2009,* Employment by Industry *(Catalogue no. 71F0004XCB). Retrieved from
http://www40.statcan.gc.ca/l01/cst01/econ40-eng.htm?sdi=industry*

Indeed, research and development spending relative to the size of the economy has dropped significantly in recent times, threatening the competitiveness of Canadian industry (Council of Canadian Academies, 2009). The bankruptcy of Canada's telecommunications giant, Nortel Networks, and the controversial sale of its assets to foreign companies in 2009 caused great concern about the loss of Canada's major developer of leading-edge technology.

The "de-industrialization" of the Canadian economy in the first decade of the twenty-first century has triggered anxiety. Even before the recession that began in 2008, Canada had lost several hundred thousand manufacturing jobs and become a net importer of manufactured goods. Skyrocketing oil and mineral prices buoyed the Canadian dollar, making Canadian manufactured goods less competitive. More importantly, China and other low-cost countries became major sources of manufactured products. The overall effect of a decline in manufacturing was somewhat offset by the prices received for the export of oil and other natural resources. Nevertheless, the shifting economic trends raised questions as to whether the Canadian government should be actively implementing an industrial strategy rather than relying on market forces to determine the nature of the economy (Stanford, 2008).

Overall, the Canadian economy has always relied heavily on exports. Before the United Kingdom adopted free trade policies in the 1840s, Canadian exports benefited from the preferential treatment given to British colonies. After British preferential treatment ended, Canadian trade shifted toward the

TABLE 3-2
**EXPORT OF GOODS ON A
BALANCE-OF-PAYMENTS
BASIS BY PRODUCT, 2008**

Energy products	25.7%
Industrial goods and materials	22.8
Machinery and equipment	19.0
Automobile products	12.5
Agricultural and fishing products	8.3
Forestry products	5.2
Other consumer goods	3.7

Source: *Calculated from Statistics Canada, 2009, Export of goods on a balance-of-payments basis, by product. Retrieved from http://www40.statcan.gc.ca/l01/cst01/gblec04-eng.htm*

United States, which became, by far, Canada's largest trading partner. In 2008, for example, 75.5 percent of Canada's nearly $490 billion of goods exported went to the United States (Statistics Canada, 2009c). As Table 3-2 indicates, energy is the largest category of goods exported, with industrial goods and materials (including minerals and metals, chemicals, plastics, and fertilizer) the second-largest category. Automobile products, although they and their makers are much in the news, rank only fourth, after the less media-friendly category of machinery and equipment.

FOREIGN INVESTMENT AND OWNERSHIP

Canada's economy has relied heavily on foreign investment. In the nineteenth century, Canadian governments borrowed intensively through bond issues to finance the building of canals, railways, and other infrastructure essential to the growth of the new country. British financiers were a key source of loans for Canadian governments and businesses. With the development of **branch plants** of American companies beginning late in the nineteenth century, along with American companies setting up operations to obtain the raw materials needed for American industry, American companies became owners of many larger Canadian businesses.

Foreign ownership of Canadian business has, at times, been a hotly contested political issue. Although Canadian governments have generally welcomed foreign investment, they have placed limitations on foreign ownership in certain key sectors of the economy such as banking and insurance, the mass media, airlines, and telecommunications. In the 1960s concerns were raised about the high level of American ownership of the Canadian economy. At the time, about one-half of Canada's manufacturing, mining, and petroleum industries were foreign (largely American) owned. Significantly, the proportion of Canada's economy that was foreign owned far exceeded that of any other country. Some saw foreign investment as desirable, arguing that it brought increased economic activity and employment to Canada, access to modern technology, access to markets outside Canada, and increased competitiveness for Canadian industry leading to greater efficiency and lower prices. Yet critics were numerous—and vocal.

BRANCH PLANT
A term that usually refers to a factory set up by an American company to produce and sell products for the Canadian market similar to the company's plant in the United States.

Critics argued that the American branch plants often purchased their parts and supplies in the United States, concentrated their research and development activities as well as their management functions in the United States, and were often limited by their American parent companies to producing only for the Canadian market. Further, they noted that most of the funds to buy out Canadian companies or to establish new enterprises came from Canadian financial institutions, while foreign ownership led to an outflow of profits, dividends, and management fees from Canada. As well, critics registered concerns that American-owned companies operating in Canada were subject to American laws. For example, the American *Trading with the Enemy Act* prevents American-owned companies and executives from trading with Cuba. More generally, Canadian nationalists feared that the high level of American ownership limited Canadian independence by increasing American political and cultural influence on Canada.

In 1973, the Canadian government established the **Foreign Investment Review Agency** (FIRA). This allowed the Canadian government to reject proposals by foreigners to take over Canadian businesses or set up new businesses that were not of significant benefit to Canada. Although few investment proposals were rejected outright, the agency gave the Canadian government some ability to negotiate with foreign firms to achieve more benefits for Canada. The Canadian government also established Petro-Canada as a Crown corporation in 1975 to give Canada a stake in the highly profitable petroleum industry (Clarkson & McCall, 1994). As well, the Liberal government (prompted by the New Democratic Party) believed that controlling a state-owned oil company would provide government with the knowledge needed to develop energy policies that promoted Canadian interests. The National Energy Program (1980) gave Petro-Canada the right to acquire a share in Arctic and offshore oil developments. However, these nationalist economic policies were sharply criticized by the American government (as well as by the Alberta government and the oil companies), and the Liberal government of Pierre Trudeau backed down from its plan to apply additional rules for stricter screening of foreign investment proposals. Nevertheless, the proportion of foreign ownership of Canadian business declined substantially from its peak in the early 1970s and the issue declined in political importance.

In 1984, Progressive Conservative Prime Minister Brian Mulroney came to office committed to restoring harmonious relations with the United States. The National Energy Program was scrapped and Petro-Canada privatized.[2] The 1989 Canada–United States Free Trade Agreement and the 1994 North American Free Trade Agreement (NAFTA) limited the ability of the Canadian

FOREIGN INVESTMENT REVIEW AGENCY (FIRA)
A Canadian government agency established in 1973 to review proposals from foreigners to take over Canadian businesses or to set up new businesses.

---

[2]In 2009 Petro-Canada merged with Suncor Energy, which retained the Petro-Canada brand for the former company's gas stations.

government to screen American investment or to adopt policies that give preferential treatment to Canadian-owned companies. In 1985, FIRA was converted to **Investment Canada** with a mandate to attract foreign investment (although with the power to recommend that proposals that do not provide a "net benefit" to Canada be rejected). By the end of 2007, about 16 500 foreign investment proposals had been submitted and not one rejected. It is noteworthy that 97.2 percent of the proposals reviewed by Investment Canada were for takeovers of existing companies rather than for investments in new businesses (Hurtig, 2008).

INVESTMENT CANADA
A Canadian government agency established in 1985 with a mandate to attract foreign investment.

The level of foreign ownership of Canadian business has increased in recent years.[3] In 2006 and 2007 Canada surrendered ownership of some of its largest companies during a wave of foreign takeovers. Following are just a few examples:

- Inco was bought out by Vale (Brazil)
- Noranda and Falconbridge by Xstrata (Switzerland)
- Alcan by Rio Tinto (British-Australian)
- Dofasco by ArcelorMittel (Luxembourg)
- Stelco by U.S. Steel
- Algoma Steel by the Essar Group (India)
- PrimeWest Energy by Abu Dhabi State Energy
- Fairmont Hotels by Colony Capital (U.S.) and Kingdom Holding (Saudi Arabia)
- ATI Technologies by AMD (U.S.)

Even the venerable Hudson's Bay Company, Canada's longest running corporation dating back to the days of the fur trade, was taken over by American-owned NRDC Equity. The rash of takeovers prompted Dominic D'Alessandro, chief executive officer of Manulife Financial, to tell shareholders, "I worry sometimes that we may all wake up one day and find that as a nation, we have lost control of our affairs" (quoted on CBC, May 3, 2007).

Only once since 1985 has the Canadian government intervened to keep a home-grown company in Canadian hands. In 2008, the government rejected a proposal by Alliant Techsystems, an American firm specializing in military equipment, to purchase the space technology division of MacDonald Dettwiler & Associates. Critics of the proposed sale noted that the division had developed the Radarsat-2 observation satellite with $400 million in government subsidies, and that information gathered by the satellite about foreign vessels in the Canadian Arctic might no longer be available to the Canadian government. Concerns existed, too, that the sale would help the United States to weaponize space, an initiative that many Canadians oppose.

---

[3]Canadian companies have also greatly increased their direct investments in foreign countries.

THE NORTH AMERICAN FREE TRADE AGREEMENT

In the past, Canada was often described as having a "branch plant" economy. The National Policy (1879) that established substantial tariffs on imported manufactured goods encouraged many American companies to set up subsidiaries in Canada. By making similar products in Canada for the Canadian market, the American subsidiaries could escape the tariffs. This arrangement benefited Canadians, too, by creating jobs for Canadian workers and helping to build a manufacturing base in Canada. However, the Canadian plants tended to be less efficient than the American ones because of the smaller market for their products.

To overcome the inefficiencies resulting from separate production facilities in the two countries, an integrated system of production for automobiles in Canada and the United States was created by the **Canada–United States Automotive Agreement, 1965.** The "Auto Pact," as the agreement became known, eliminated tariffs between the two countries on new automobiles, trucks, buses, and original vehicle parts, while providing guarantees about the level of production in Canada. The agreement benefited the "Big Three" American automobile manufacturers because of the removal of tariffs and the rationalization of production. As well, the high level of productivity of the Canadian plants led to substantial increases in automobile production in Canada as the American auto companies located new assembly plants in Canada to produce cars and trucks for the North American market. The production guarantees proved to be unnecessary.[4]

The Auto Pact can be considered, to some extent, the forerunner of more recent (but broader) free trade agreements involving Canada and the United States. In the 1980s, Canada and the United States enjoyed a high level of trade, and the majority of goods were traded without tariffs. Nevertheless, Canadian businesses worried that Americans could apply their trade remedy laws (and proposals for even tougher laws were being considered) to protect their own producers against imports from Canada by levying punitive duties on imported goods. Specifically, American trade remedy laws allow **countervailing duties** to be imposed when a country subsidizes its exports in a way that harms the American producers of a competing product. Similarly, **anti-dumping duties** can be imposed when a foreign producer sells a product in the United States for less than its "fair value" (that is, below its cost of production or at a lower price than the price in the exporting country). While trade remedy laws are allowed under the rules of the World Trade Organization (of which Canada and the

CANADA–UNITED STATES AUTOMOTIVE AGREEMENT, 1965 ("AUTO PACT"). An agreement that eliminated tariffs between the two countries on new automobiles, trucks, buses, and original vehicle parts, while providing guarantees about the level of production in Canada.

COUNTERVAILING DUTIES Duties imposed on imports of a particular product that have been subsidized by the exporting country in a way that harms the home producers of that same product.

ANTI-DUMPING DUTIES Duties imposed on imports of a particular product when a foreign producer sells the product in the importing country for less than its "fair value."

---

[4]The "Auto Pact" was essentially folded into the Canada–U.S. and North American Free Trade Agreements. However, the preferential treatment provided for the "Big Three" American auto makers was challenged by Japan and Europe, resulting in a 1991 ruling of the World Trade Organization that ended that preferential treatment.

United States are members), the U.S. government has often been aggressive in using its rules, at the instigation of powerful American industries, to harass imports to the United States. Moreover, Canadian businesses have argued that American law goes further than international trading rules by, for example, not requiring conclusive proof of serious injury to domestic producers.

Thus a major goal of the Canadian government (and the strong business lobby that pressured the Canadian government for an agreement) in negotiating a free trade agreement with the United States[5] was to be exempted from the application of American trade remedy laws, or at least to subject their use to a binding, impartial means of settling trade disputes. The U.S. government, on the other hand, wanted a comprehensive agreement that would cover all aspects of trading in goods and services, investment, and access to natural resources. However, the U.S. government did not want to give up its sovereign powers, in particular its power to legislate and enforce its own trade remedy laws.

The provisions of NAFTA include

- eliminating tariffs on goods traded among the three countries;
- eliminating restrictions on the export of almost all goods;
- forbidding new laws and regulations to protect service industries;
- requiring that investments from the other countries be treated the same as domestic investments (although allowing the screening of proposed takeovers of large domestically owned companies);
- forbidding Canada from placing higher taxes on energy exported to the U.S. than it levies on energy consumed in Canada (and prohibiting the Canadian government from imposing restrictions that reduce American imports of Canadian energy);
- allowing the retention of agricultural marketing boards that set production quotas to protect farmers; and
- allowing Canada to continue its existing protection of its cultural industries, with the United States retaining the right to retaliate against new cultural protection measures.

Although Canada had hoped to be exempted from American trade remedy laws, the Americans refused this concession, and no agreement was reached on what constituted an "unfair subsidy" that could result in special duties. A decision to impose special countervailing or anti-dumping duties can be appealed to a binational dispute settlement tribunal made up of representatives chosen by the countries involved in the dispute. However, the tribunal's powers are limited. It can determine only whether the rules of the country

---

[5]This refers particularly to the Canada–United States Free Trade Agreement. The Canadian government decided to participate in subsequent negotiations leading to the North American Free Trade Agreement for fear that a bilateral agreement between the United States and Mexico would be detrimental to Canada's interests.

BOX 3-1

Competing Interests:
The Softwood Lumber Dispute

Softwood lumber, used primarily for building houses, is one of Canada's leading exports. In particular, Canadian companies annually export billions of dollars' worth of softwood lumber to the United States. The export is not popular with American lumber producers, who claim that the stumpage fees provincial governments charge for harvesting wood on Crown lands is less than American companies pay in their free market system. From the American vantage point, the lower fees constitute an unfair subsidy. Further, the American producers argue that Canadian lumber is sold in the United States for less than its total cost of production (McKinney, 2004).

As the Canada–United States Free Trade Agreement (FTA) was being negotiated, American lumber producers lobbied Congress and the president, urging them not to sign on unless the issue was resolved. At the same time, they launched an action to have a countervailing duty imposed on Canadian lumber exports. To salvage negotiations and to avoid the imposition of a duty, the Canadian government modified its position: It agreed to impose a 15 percent export tax on softwood lumber (other than lumber from the Maritime provinces where the stumpage issue is not relevant) until provincial governments had changed their stumpage fees and forest management policies. In

1981 the Canadian government ended the export tax based on the changes the provincial governments had made. This did not, however, satisfy the American lumber companies, who launched actions under the provisions of the FTA and later NAFTA, as well as through the procedures of the World Trade Organization (WTO). Canada won almost all the cases. Yet the United States rejected the decisions of tribunals, continually challenging them. As well, the U.S. government changed its laws to try to justify imposing new duties on Canadian lumber. Despite the judgments of the NAFTA and WTO panels, the U.S. government refused to give back the duties it had improperly collected from Canadian lumber companies (Clarkson, 2008).

At last, in 2006, the government of Stephen Harper retrieved $4.5 billion of the duties withheld by the United States—the majority, but not all, of the money owed. As part of the deal, both countries agreed to settle future disputes through arbitration.

Although the softwood lumber case is unusual, it highlights the limitations of trade agreements and the challenges of enforcing them. A powerful country like the United States may refuse to be bound by international rules and procedures when its interests (or those of powerful groups within the country) are at stake.

levying the duty were correctly applied using the judicial review standards and precedents of that country. Although the provision has helped to resolve some trade disputes, the United States was unwilling to accept the tribunal's verdict in the important softwood lumber case (as discussed in Box 3-1, Competing Interests: The Softwood Lumber Dispute), and there is little evidence that it has reduced unfair trade law actions (Blonigen, 2005).

A particularly controversial provision of NAFTA is its investor-state dispute resolution mechanism, contained in Chapter 11 of the agreement. This section allows foreign companies to sue governments that they allege are harming their investments through expropriation or actions "tantamount to expropriation." Claims for compensation may be based on government actions that affect "the company's future profitability or opportunities for growth" (Boyd, 2003, p. 257). Many of the actions launched by corporations under Chapter 11 have sought compensation for government actions to protect the environment. For example, a Canadian government order preventing PCBs (a cancer-causing chemical) from being shipped to the United States triggered a lawsuit against the Canadian government by S.D. Myers, an American waste disposal company. Even though the Canadian government pointed out that it was acting in accordance with the Basel Convention on the Transboundary Movement of Hazardous Wastes and Their Disposal (a treaty recognized in NAFTA as taking precedence over trade rules), a tribunal ruled that Canada had violated Chapter 11. To make amends, Canada was ordered to pay the company US$6 million in damages (Clarkson, 2008).

In general, the North American Free Trade Agreement tends to reflect the interests of big business—the major corporations that lobbied governments to negotiate the agreement and that were consulted by governments throughout the negotiations. NAFTA's Chapter 11, in particular, gives corporations unprecedented powers to challenge governments through binding international arbitration (Boyd, 2003). The labour and environmental "side agreements" that American President Bill Clinton wanted before signing the agreement that was negotiated by his predecessor, George Bush, Sr., are largely toothless.

Despite its significance in integrating the economies of Canada, the United States, and Mexico, NAFTA, unlike the European Union, is not a "supranational" government (Clarkson, 2008). NAFTA has not led to the establishment of any meaningful governing institutions to develop, oversee, and enforce rules for North America. Unlike the European Union, it offers no guidelines for social policies and human rights and barely addresses the environment or the mobility of workers across national borders. Reflecting a business agenda that seeks to limit the ability of governments to adopt policies that interfere with trade and investment, NAFTA can be viewed as restricting the scope of democracy. Further, with tribunals that typically conduct their business in secret and committees that are generally invisible to the public, NAFTA cannot be characterized as a transparent and accountable organization (Clarkson, 2008).

The Economic System and the Role of Government

Canada has a basically free market capitalist economy. People are free to start and operate businesses in most sectors of the economy. Governments generally do not direct businesses as to what they should produce, where they should locate, and what prices they should charge for their goods and services. Instead, investors and businesspeople seeking profits are primarily responsible for making decisions that affect the economy and prosperity of different communities.

GOVERNMENT PARTICIPATION IN THE FREE MARKET ECONOMY

The Canadian state has played a significant role in helping to shape the Canadian economy. The formation of Canada was an act of faith—a belief that a country could be built across northern North America despite the costs involved. To build links across a sparsely populated country, very substantial Canadian government subsidization of the railway system was required. For example, the Canadian Pacific Railway Company was awarded ten million hectares of land, a twenty-year monopoly, exemption from tariffs on imported materials, and a twenty-year exemption from taxation, as well as substantial government cash grants and loans guarantees (Conrad & Finkel, 2007). Later, the Canadian government got directly involved by consolidating various bankrupt rail companies into the government-owned Canadian National Railways (CNR). Likewise, the Canadian government owned and operated a major airline, Trans-Canada Air Lines. Originally a subsidiary of CNR, Trans-Canada is familiar to us in its more recent incarnation: Air Canada (1964). Air Canada was privatized in 1985 and the CNR in 1995 (although the passenger rail service, VIA Rail, remains a Crown corporation). Canada's first national radio and television network, the Canadian Broadcasting Corporation, continues to be a Crown (state-owned) corporation. A number of provincial and local governments have established major power-generating and electrical distribution facilities and other utilities. In many cases, government involvement proved essential because private business did not have the capability to provide the service or because the service was not likely to turn a profit.

As noted in Chapter 2, the impetus behind the adoption of the National Policy in 1879 was to encourage the development of manufacturing in Canada. Similarly, the National Energy Policy in 1980 was designed to keep manufacturing industries competitive at a time of high oil prices. As with CNR, Canadian governments have also bailed out or taken over major companies facing bankruptcy; for example, the Canadian government assisted Massey Ferguson, a leading manufacturer of agricultural machinery, in 1981. In the mid-1980s, the Canadian government took part in restructuring the ailing east coast fisheries industry, including establishing and temporarily acting as the majority shareholder in Fisheries Products International (now a division of High Liner Foods). At the provincial level, the Nova Scotia government took over the failing coal mining and steel industries in Cape Breton in 1967. To help maintain the Canadian offshoots of two of the bankrupt North American automobile companies, the Canadian and Ontario governments in

2009 contributed $10.6 billion to the bailout of General Motors and $3.8 billion to Chrysler. In return for their contribution to the bailout of GM, the Canadian and Ontario governments received 11.7 percent ownership of the company, one of the thirteen seats on the board of directors, and promises to retain a portion of the company's auto production in Canada.

Generally, the Canadian government has participated in the economy to try to foster economic growth by providing assistance to business. Although we often think of business as being opposed to government intervention, in fact business interests (or at least some sectors of the business community) have often sought government assistance. For instance, manufacturing interests that benefited from the high tariffs on manufactured products supported John A. Macdonald's National Policy. Likewise, business interests supported the Ontario government's establishment of the Hydro-Electric Commission of Ontario in 1906 to supply low-cost electricity to the province.

THE GREAT DEPRESSION   The Great Depression of the 1930s created a shift in thinking about the role of government. With millions of Canadians unable to find work and earn the necessities of life, private charities and local governments struggled to meet the problems of the needy. Instead of viewing those who were unable to provide for themselves and their families as lazy and irresponsible, many people began to believe that the economic system was responsible for widespread poverty and unemployment. They looked to government to become more hands-on in regulating the economy and helping those in need. More radical ideas that condemned the banking and financial institutions or the entire capitalist system gained support.

The Conservative government of Prime Minister R. B. Bennett seemed ineffectual in addressing the devastating problems of the Depression. Bennett had initially looked to higher tariffs, but finally announced proposals (somewhat similar to those of the **New Deal** in the United States) to remedy "social and economic injustice" and "ensure to all classes a greater degree of equality in the distribution of the capitalistic system" (quoted in Beck, 1968, p. 209). Bennett's proposals were too little and too late to avoid defeat in the 1935 election. Moreover, social security proposals such as the introduction of unemployment insurance were struck down by the Judicial Committee of the Privy Council as an unconstitutional interference with provincial legislative powers.[6]

WORLD WAR II AND ITS AFTERMATH   World War II resolved the problem of unemployment as Canadian industry expanded rapidly to produce materials for the war effort. Indeed, a shortage of labour prompted efforts to

NEW DEAL
A package of programs adopted by U.S. President Franklin Delano Roosevelt that included relief to those suffering from the Great Depression of the 1930s and reforms of the banking system.

---

[6]This obstacle was remedied by a constitutional amendment in 1940 giving the Canadian Parliament legislative authority over unemployment insurance. Unemployment insurance legislation was passed by Parliament in 1941.

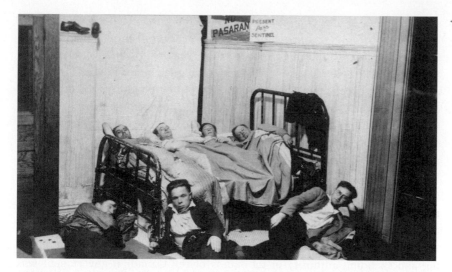

During the Great Depression in the 1930s, the idea developed that the economic system was responsible for widespread poverty and unemployment. Many people, such as these unemployed workers, began to look to government to become more active in regulating the economy and helping those in need.

recruit women into the labour force. As well, faced with burgeoning member-ship in labour unions and numerous strikes and work slowdowns, govern-ments responded to the growing power of workers by ending many unfair labour practices and guaranteeing the right of workers to organize and bar-gain collectively (Conrad & Finkel, 2007). The Canadian government, coop-erating with business leaders, tightly controlled the economy through such measures as wage and price controls and rationing. Concern about finding work for returning soldiers at the end of the war and providing support to the families of those killed or injured encouraged national and provincial govern-ments to consider adopting new or expanded social security programs, such as family allowances and old age pensions. In 1943 Leonard Marsh, research director for the Canadian government's Advisory Committee on Post-War Reconstruction, published the *Report on Social Security for Canada,* which called on government to guarantee a "social minimum" to protect the disad-vantaged. Although the wide-ranging reforms were not fully accepted at the time, Marsh's recommendations were gradually implemented in the following decades, creating what is referred to as a **"welfare state."** Politically, support was growing for the socialist Co-operative Commonwealth Federation (CCF), particularly in Ontario, and in Saskatchewan, where the CCF triumphed in the 1944 provincial election. The popularity of the CCF platform encouraged the Liberal and Progressive Conservative parties to promise a comprehensive social security system.

A more active role for government also resulted from the acceptance of the ideas of British economist John Maynard Keynes. In contrast to classical lib-eral economic views that government should involve itself as little as possible in the economy, Keynes argued that government policies should be used to

WELFARE STATE
A country whose governments ensure that all people have a minimum standard of living and are provided protection from hardships, including those caused by unemployment, sickness, disability, and old age.

smooth out the tendencies of a free market economy to go through cycles of boom and bust. Government could maintain nearly full employment by stimulating the economy (through spending, tax cuts, or lowering interest rates) when business investment was weak. By taking the opposite measures, government could cool down the economy when inflation was rampant. Keynes did not advocate "**balanced budgets**" for government, the practice of spending no more than the government revenues collected annually. Instead, he argued that governments should run a deficit when economic stimulus was needed and a surplus when cooling down was needed.

The Canadian government's *White Paper on Employment and Incomes* (1945) echoed the themes of **Keynesian economics**, with its call for government to ensure a "high and stable level of employment" by incurring deficits to promote job creation when unemployment threatens (quoted in Bothwell, Drummond, & English, 1989, p. 57). To achieve this, a centralization of taxing and spending authority in the hands of the Canadian government was needed. Keynesian economics played an important role in the thinking of government and public servants in the post–World War II era.

Generally, in the prosperous decades following World War II, there was a broad consensus in support of Keynesian economic policies and a modest welfare state. Key ministers, particularly those ministers in the Liberal governments that held power until 1957, were attentive to business interests. Workers and the general public were generally pleased with the protections provided by the development of social security programs. Expansion of the post-secondary education system created opportunities for those who did not come from wealthy families, and helped to provide business with a more skilled workforce. In fact, many of the benefits that Canadians value today date from this postwar era.

In Quebec, however, some opposed the leading role taken by the Canadian government in developing social security policies. In the view of the Quebec government, this centralization was inconsistent with the constitutional powers of provincial governments. Quebec was not alone in its dissatisfaction. In the 1960s the Ontario government also raised objections to Canadian government involvement in the social policy field. In particular, the Progressive Conservative government of Ontario criticized the federal medical care program that replaced the medical care insurance from private insurance companies.

A SHIFT TO THE NEO-LIBERAL RIGHT   In the 1970s the Keynesian economic doctrines that had guided policy in Canada and other Western countries were challenged. A combination of economic stagnation and inflation (termed "stagflation") ended the long period of economic growth. Prominent economists blamed government spending that "crowded out" private investment. High taxes and welfare state programs were reducing the incentives for hard work and investment. A return to the classic free market with the role of government limited to its basic functions would be the harsh medicine

BALANCED BUDGET
The practice of government spending no more than the revenues it collects annually.

KEYNESIAN ECONOMICS
A perspective on managing the economy through government stimulation of the economy when business investment is weak and cooling the economy when inflation is rampant.

needed—a cure for the inefficiencies created by the growth of government. During this era, leading politicians, including British Prime Minister Margaret Thatcher and U.S. President Ronald Reagan, successfully challenged the power of the unions. The Reagan administration adopted **supply-side economics,** which views reducing taxes on businesses that supply (produce) goods and services as the most effective way to achieve economic growth. The Keynesian belief that helping the poor is the best way to create demand for the goods that industry could produce (as the poor tend to spend any money received) was discarded. Instead, cutting taxes on the rich and on large corporations was seen as creating a trickle-down effect from which all, affluent and poor alike, would eventually benefit. Further, in the optimistic view of the Reagan administration, the effect of sharp cuts in taxes on government revenues would be offset by an increase in revenues from the economic growth generated by the private sector. In Canada, as elsewhere, business groups demanded reductions in taxes and government regulations in order to allow Canadian business to be more competitive internationally.

To some extent the Progressive Conservative government of Brian Mulroney (1984–93) adopted the ideology of **neo-liberalism**—a perspective based on a strong belief in a free market system that advocates a major reduction in the role of government in regulating business, the dismantling of the welfare state, a substantial reduction in taxes, and global free trade. Consistent with this influential perspective that was promoted by Thatcher and Reagan, the Mulroney Government negotiated the Canada–United States and North American Free Trade Agreements, privatized a number of Crown corporations, and reduced government regulation of business. Even so, Canadian government spending and some taxes increased. Disillusionment with the Mulroney Government led many conservative Westerners to support the new Reform party, which advocated hefty cuts in taxes and government spending. In the mid-1990s, the Liberal government of Jean Chrétien slashed government spending in response to a perceived financial crisis, as discussed in Box 3-2, Bankrupt Canada?

Overall, Canada's total government spending as a proportion of Canada's gross national product has declined since the mid-1990s and is now among the lowest of the thirty high-income countries with free market economies that make up the Organization for Economic Co-operation and Development (OECD). Similarly, the average tax burden on Canadians is slightly lower than the average for the OECD countries (Organization for Economic Co-operation and Development [OECD], 2009).

Inequality and Politics

Defenders of the free market capitalist system typically argue that inequalities in income and wealth are fair and just. Investors and businesses should be rewarded for the risks they take. People need incentives to encourage them to

SUPPLY-SIDE ECONOMICS
The perspective that reducing taxes on those who supply goods and services is the most effective way to achieve economic growth.

NEO-LIBERALISM
A perspective based on a strong belief in a free market system that advocates such measures as a major reduction in the role of government, including the dismantling of the welfare state, substantial reduction in taxes, and global free trade.

Bankrupt Canada?

From the fiscal years 1970–71 to 1996–97, the Canadian government was a stranger to balanced budgets, running a deficit (expenses greater than revenues) every year. The annual deficit skyrocketed, reaching a peak of $49.4 billion in the 1995–96 fiscal year. The accumulated deficit (the debt of the Canadian government) reached its maximum, $562.881 billion, the following fiscal year (Public Works and Government Services Canada, 2008).

Not surprisingly, in January 1995, the *Wall Street Journal* ran an editorial entitled "Bankrupt Canada?" "Mexico isn't the only U.S. neighbour flirting with the financial abyss," said the *Journal.* "Turn around and check out Canada which has now become an honorary member of the Third World" (quoted by Lynch, 2007). The next month, Moody's Investment Services announced it was putting the Canadian government's debt "on review for a possible downgrade" (which occurred in May 1995), reflecting the government's ballooning deficit. Liberal Finance Minister Paul Martin angrily responded, "Who the hell are they to pass judgment on us" (quoted by Klein, 2004, p. A01). His words fell on deaf ears. The Canadian dollar dropped and foreign investors dumped government bonds.

Faced with a potential financial crisis, Martin, in his March 1995 budget, announced severe cuts in government spending, major reductions to the public service, reduced eligibility for unemployment insurance, an end to the Canada Assistance Plan, and drastic cuts to the money transferred to provincial governments to pay for health, post-secondary education, and social assistance. In turn, most provincial governments slashed their spending, particularly for social assistance and post-secondary education. Martin's budget cuts had the desired effect. From 1997–98 through 2007–08 the Canadian government ran surpluses each year. More importantly, the debt, as a proportion of Canada's gross national product (GNP), dropped to the lowest debt ratio of the G7 countries, the exclusive club of the world's leading economies (See Figure 3-1). In 2002, Moody's restored the Canadian government's Triple A investment rating (the highest rating).

With the economy improving and government revenues increasing, the Liberal government of

work hard. In a competitive free market, argue its supporters, rewards are determined by the impersonal workings of the marketplace rather than by privileges granted by the state or by a person's social status. Overall, supporters of the free market economy insist that this economic system, with minimum government involvement, yields maximum prosperity for society.

Yet the free market has its critics. They argue that the capitalist system leads to an unjustifiable and undesirable level of inequality. The capitalist system is not really all that free and competitive, but rather some firms are able to dominate major sectors of the economy. Extensive power rests in the hands of large corporations, which are able to exploit workers and consumers and extract special benefits from government. Furthermore, those who want government to reduce the uneven distribution of income and wealth argue that substantial inequalities are inherently undesirable in a democratic society. The benefits of the prosperity of a country should be used to guarantee that everyone enjoys a decent standard of living, rather than providing extreme wealth for just a few.

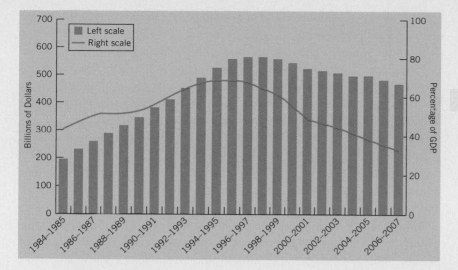

FIGURE 3-1

THE ACCUMULATED DEFICIT (DEBT) OF THE GOVERNMENT OF CANADA, 1984–2007

Note: GDP = gross domestic product.

Source: Receiver General for Canada, 2008, *Public accounts of Canada 2008: Vol. 1. Summary Report and Financial Statements,* Financial Statements Discussion and Analysis Section 1 1.7. Retrieved from http://www.tpsgc-pwgsc.gc.ca/recgen/pdf/49-eng.pdf

Paul Martin and the Conservative government of Stephen Harper were able to lower taxes despite increased government spending. But 2008 brought the onset of a serious recession, and the Harper Government began sliding into deficit. For 2009–10 the Canadian government projected a record deficit in excess of $50 billion as it ratcheted up spending on infrastructure building programs to stimulate the economy. With government deficits projected to continue for several years, Harper's 2008 election promise not to run a deficit seems destined for the dustbin of history. Nevertheless, Canada's government debt load is much lower than that of other countries. Thus, no one is likely to "cry wolf" about the possibility of Canada going bankrupt.

Opposition to or defence of inequalities is an important aspect of political life. Members of groups who believe their opportunities are limited because of discrimination or oppression may act politically to challenge perceived injustices. The groups suffering from economic inequalities are diverse, including those in the working or lower class, those in disadvantaged regions, and women. Kimberly Rogers, described in the opening vignette, faced a uniquely female problem: She was pregnant and lacked the proper means to nourish her unborn child. Similar economic inequalities also have serious effects among immigrants and racial minorities (see Chapter 4) and Aboriginals (see Chapter 12).

SOCIAL CLASS

Social class refers to a large category of people who hold a similar position in the hierarchy of society. Class is often analyzed in terms of different positions

SOCIAL CLASS
A large category of people who hold a similar position in the hierarchy of society.

MARXIST THEORY
The theory that a fundamental feature of capitalist societies is an antagonistic and exploitative relationship between the capitalist class and the working class that leads to class conflict.

CLASS CONSCIOUSNESS
The awareness within a social class of their common interests and a willingness to collectively act on those interests.

SOCIO-ECONOMIC STATUS
A combination of income (or wealth), education, and occupational status.

related to the production and exchange of goods. In particular, **Marxist theory** characterizes capitalist societies as featuring an antagonistic relationship between the capitalist class (bourgeoisie), who own and control the means of production, and the working class (proletariat), who sell their labour power to earn a living but are exploited by the capitalist class to gain an undeserved profit. In between are the old middle class, or petite bourgeoisie—small business owners, small farm owners, and independent professionals, such as doctors and lawyers—and a new middle class of salaried professionals such as teachers, nurses, managers, technicians, and civil servants, who have some control over their working conditions. The working class, Marx argued, would develop a **class consciousness,** that is, an awareness of their common interests and a willingness to collectively organize to transform the capitalist system.

Others define class (or **socio-economic status**) in terms of a combination of income (or wealth), education, and occupational status. Sometimes a distinction is made between upper, middle, and lower classes, but often further distinctions are made, such as upper middle and lower middle classes. Those who define class in this way generally do not view the struggle between the working class and the capitalist class as the dominant characteristic of society and politics.

Many argue that Canada is not a class-based society and that class divisions do not have great political significance. Following are some of the most common arguments that support this position:

- Canadians enjoy a considerable degree of social mobility (Wanner, 2009). Many people of working-class backgrounds take advantage of educational opportunities to move into middle class professional positions, and some people of modest backgrounds break into the once-closed circles of the economic elite.
- People of different social classes are often not easily identifiable from the dialect they speak, the clothes they wear, or the leisure activities they enjoy. Canada does not have a working-class culture to the same extent as do England and other European countries.
- The level of class consciousness is not generally strong. Other identities, such as those based on province, ethnicity, religion, and gender, are often stronger than class-based identities.
- The general affluence of Canada has resulted in many working-class people viewing themselves as middle class based on incomes that provide a comfortable lifestyle. In other words, the distinction between the working class and the middle class has been somewhat blurred, at least in times of prosperity.
- Employment in manufacturing and resource-extraction industries, often considered the basis of the working class, has sharply declined, while service and information-based activities are now the largest source of employment.

The relatively low level of working-class consciousness in Canada is sometimes also attributed to the weakness of political organization of the working class (Brodie & Jenson, 1988). Although about 30 percent of the non-agricultural workforce is organized into labour unions, these organizations tend to devote more of their efforts to collective bargaining than to promoting class consciousness. Further, a substantial proportion of union members are now middle-class public sector employees rather than working-class wage earners. Although the New Democratic Party (NDP) is often viewed as a working-class political party because of its social democratic ideology and its formal links to the Canadian Labour Congress, it has tended to focus on electoral politics rather than raising the consciousness of workers.

Nevertheless, the image of Canada as a classless society can be questioned. A close look at Canada reveals significant inequalities in the distribution of wealth and income. For a time, in the decades after World War II, the gaps in income and wealth lessened in Canada as the various government social programs provided assistance to the less well-off. As well, income taxes helped somewhat to redistribute wealth by taxing the rich more heavily than those with lower incomes. However, inequality began to increase in the 1990s as governments cut back on programs such as social assistance (welfare) and unemployment insurance, and the income tax system took on a somewhat less redistributive character. In particular, higher-income people are more likely to use a variety of tax breaks (such as registered retirement savings plans) than middle- or lower-income people. On the other hand, some tax benefits, such as the child tax credit, have been directed toward those with lower incomes.

Canada has a somewhat higher degree of income inequality than the majority of comparable high-income countries, as noted in Box 3-3, Income Inequality and Poverty in Canada. According to the OECD, inequality in recent times has accelerated faster in Canada than in all but one of the thirty economically developed countries. Income inequality in Canada was above the OECD average in 2005, contrasting sharply with the previous two decades when Canada demonstrated below-average inequality (OECD, 2008).

A key factor in the growing inequality has been the astronomical rise in the compensation for corporation executives. For example, the total compensation for the chief executive officers (CEOs) of corporations in 2007 was 259 times that of the average wage earner, compared with 85 times in 1995. The top one hundred CEOs averaged over $10 million each in total compensation in 2007. Most of the compensation is in the form of stock options, which are only taxed on one-half of the value of the capital gains (Mackenzie, 2009). In contrast, the average wages of workers have been generally stagnant in recent decades (when the effect of inflation is taken into account), although family incomes increased as two-income families rather than one-income families became the norm. Furthermore, Canada is one of the only developed countries without an estate tax, thus allowing inequalities in wealth to be passed on from generation to generation.

Income Inequality and Poverty in Canada

On a scale from A to D, the Conference Board of Canada (2008) has graded Canada's performance on a number of indicators compared with the performance of other high-income countries.

A GRADE:

Level of poverty among the elderly (second of seventeen countries)

Intergenerational class mobility (fifth of eleven countries)

Income of disabled persons (seventh of sixteen countries).

B GRADE:

Joblessness among youth (fifth of eleven countries).

C GRADE:

Income inequality (tenth of seventeen)
Unemployment (eleventh of seventeen)
Child poverty (twelfth of seventeen)
Working age poor (thirteenth of seventeen)
Gender inequality (fourteenth of fifteen)

Although Canada did not earn a D or flunking grade for any of the criteria, its results are hardly distinguished. Canada has much work to do in banishing inequality and restoring dignity and affluence to some of its most vulnerable citizens.

At the opposite end of the spectrum from the corporate executives is Canada's sizeable lower class (sometimes referred to as the "underclass"), which includes many Aboriginals, single mothers, unemployed and part-time workers, those who work in minimum-wage jobs, and people with limited education. This diverse group tends to depend on government assistance for a basic standard of living and is generally less likely to be politically active.

Like Canada's rate of inequality, Canada's rate of poverty is higher than the OECD average (OECD, 2008). In the 2006 census, 11.4 percent of Canadians were considered low income.[7] Extreme poverty has become more visible as the number of homeless people and the use of food banks have burgeoned in recent decades. A survey of food banks found that 704 414 people received food in March 2008 (Food Banks Canada, 2008). Those on social assistance (welfare), as well as those working for minimum wages, generally have incomes well below the poverty line. Furthermore, although the proportion of people living in poverty had declined according to the statistics available at the time this textbook was written, in periods of high unemployment and economic recession or depression the incidence of poverty soars.

Food Banks Canada:
www.foodbankscanada.ca

Canada Without Poverty:
www.napo-onap.ca

---

[7]Low income is defined by Statistics Canada as spending 20 percentage points more of one's income than average on food, clothing, and shelter. The proportion of people living in poverty is calculated after the effects of various government payments and taxes are taken into account.

◀ Do you know where your next meal is coming from? Extreme poverty has become more visible as the number of homeless people and the use of food banks have increased in Canada in recent decades.

Regional Disparities

Canada is renowned for the distinctiveness of its regions. Geographically vast, and with an extraordinary array of physical features and climates, the country varies, too, in ethnic, cultural, and linguistic characteristics from one region to another. Further, there are substantial differences in the economies of different regions, which lead to inequalities in wealth, income, and employment opportunities.

Canada's uneven economic development has resulted in regional economic disparities and contributed to dissatisfaction with the Canadian government in various provinces. Control of Canada's industrial, commercial, financial, and cultural activities is largely concentrated in southern Ontario and in the Montreal region. In addition to the economic power resulting from the location of corporate head offices in this region, the concentration of Canada's population in Ontario and Quebec provides considerable political power to these provinces (see Table 3-3). In contrast, other provinces (as well as the northern areas of Ontario and Quebec) have depended heavily upon the extraction and export of commodities such as forest and agricultural products, minerals, petroleum, and fish. Such commodities tend to fluctuate sharply in demand and price, and generally provide less employment than other economic activities. As Table 3-4 indicates, fairly substantial income differences exist among the residents of different provinces. Likewise, inequality exists among different regions within provinces. For example, in January 2009 the unemployment rate in northern Manitoba was 26.3 percent compared with 4.5 percent in Winnipeg (Human Resources and Social Development Canada, 2009). The dependence of hinterland areas on resource extraction industries tends to make

TABLE 3-3

POPULATION BY PROVINCE AND TERRITORY

Note: Total estimated population as of July 1, 2008: 33 311 400.

CANADA	100.0%
Newfoundland and Labrador	1.5
Prince Edward Island	0.4
Nova Scotia	2.8
New Brunswick	2.2
Quebec	23.3
Ontario	38.8
Manitoba	3.6
Saskatchewan	3.0
Alberta	10.8
British Columbia	13.2
Yukon	0.1
Northwest Territories	0.1
Nunavut	0.1

Source: *Statistics Canada, 2009,* Population by year, by province and territory. *Retrieved from http://www40.statcan.gc.ca/l01/cst01/demo02d-eng.htm*

TABLE 3-4

MEDIAN TOTAL FAMILY INCOME (2005) AND RATE OF UNEMPLOYMENT (JUNE 2009) BY PROVINCE AND TERRITORY

Notes: Income (from 2006 census) from all sources before taxes. Unemployment rates (from Labour Force Survey) for provinces are seasonally adjusted. Unemployment rates for the territories use a different methodology including a three-month unadjusted moving average.

	INCOME	PERCENTAGE OF NATIONAL AVERAGE	PERCENTAGE UNEMPLOYED
Newfoundland/Labrador	$51 791	78.1	15.6
Prince Edward Island	$56 207	84.7	12.2
Nova Scotia	$57 078	86.0	9.4
New Brunswick	$54 520	82.2	9.2
Quebec	$59 734	90.0	8.7
Ontario	$72 734	109.6	9.6
Manitoba	$60 754	91.6	5.2
Saskatchewan	$59 998	90.4	4.6
Alberta	$76 526	115.3	6.8
British Columbia	$65 787	99.2	8.1
Yukon	$78 583	118.4	7.7
Northwest Territories	$90 865	137.0	6.6
Nunavut	$62 592	94.3	14.5
Canada	$66 343	100.0	8.6

Sources: *Calculated from Statistics Canada, 2008,* Median total income, in 2005 constant dollars, of economic families, Canada, provinces and territories, 2000 and 2005 *(Catalogue no. 97-563-XWE2006002). Retrieved from http:/www12.statcan.ca/english/census06/analysis/income/tables/table12.htm; Statistics Canada, 2009,* Labour force characteristics, seasonally adjusted, by province *(Catalogue no. 71-001-XIE). Retrieved from http://www40.statcan.gc.ca/l01/cst01/lfss01a-eng.htm and http://www40.statcan.gc.ca/l01/cst01/lfss06-eng.htm?sdi=unemployment%soterritory*

them more vulnerable to downturns in the economy and they more easily fall prey to high unemployment. However, Ontario's manufacturing centres were also hard hit by the recession that began in 2008.

Canadian governments have devoted considerable attention to regional economic disparities. Beginning in 1957, the Canadian government provided equalization payments to the governments of the poorer provinces to enable them to provide their populations with a comparable level of services to that of the richer provinces (discussed in Chapter 13). In the 1960s, the Canadian government set up various programs to promote rural regional economic development, most notably through the establishment in 1969 of the Department of Regional Economic Expansion, which focused on Atlantic Canada and eastern Quebec. However, the success of these programs in promoting economic development was limited. In 1987 a somewhat more decentralized approach was adopted, with the establishment of agencies to galvanize economic development in Atlantic Canada, Western Canada, northern Ontario, and, beginning in 1991, Quebec. More recently, the 2009 federal budget announced the establishment of a development agency for southern Ontario, a region that traditionally boasted a robust economy. Thus, there has been a movement away from the original focus on bolstering development in the poorest areas of the country.

Overall, over the past few decades, the incomes of people in the poorer provinces have moved closer to the national average. However, regional differences in unemployment rates have proved hard to budge. A resident of Newfoundland and Labrador is still much more likely to be unemployed than a resident of Alberta.

Gender

Canada has experienced major changes in the status of women in recent decades, particularly as legions of women have entered the paid workforce, including nearly 70 percent of women with young children (Statistics Canada, 2006). This change has raised issues about male–female inequalities in wages, discrimination in hiring and promotion, and the provision of affordable, quality child care. Moreover, the women's movement has challenged traditional attitudes to male–female relationships, raised issues about violence against women, lobbied for women to have access to abortion, and demanded greater representation of women in legislative and other governing bodies.

Labour trends for men and women continue to differ, however. A somewhat higher proportion of men than women are in the paid labour force, and women are more likely to work part-time than men. Interestingly, men in the labour force are more likely to be unemployed than women (Statistics Canada, 2008a). Young women are now more likely than young men to obtain a university degree, and many are pursuing careers in professions such as medicine, law, and business. Nevertheless, university-educated women are more likely to pursue careers in lower-paid female-dominated occupations such as nursing, education, and social work than in higher-paid male-dominated occupations such as engineering and computer science.

In spite of the drive for equality, average earnings for women remain significantly lower than for men. As Table 3-5 indicates, this inequality between

TABLE 3-5

AVERAGE EARNINGS BY SEX AND WORK PATTERN

FULL-YEAR, FULL-TIME WORKERS			
YEAR	WOMEN $ CONSTANT 2007	MEN	EARNINGS RATIO %
1998	39 500	55 000	71.9
1999	38 000	55 600	68.4
2000	39 300	55 600	70.6
2001	39 600	56 700	69.9
2002	39 900	56 800	70.2
2003	39 700	56 600	70.2
2004	41 000	58 700	69.9
2005	40 900	58 000	70.5
2006	42 200	58 700	71.9
2007	43 000	60 300	71.4

Source: *Statistics Canada, (2009),* Average earnings by sex and work pattern, *CANSIM Table 202-0102.* Retrieved from http://www40.statcan.gc.ca/l01/cst01/labor01b-eng.htm

males and females has not changed significantly in recent years.[8] Male–female inequality is particularly strong among those without a university education. To a considerable extent, earning differences result from lower pay in occupations that have a high proportion of female employees, the tendency of women to have greater family responsibilities and thus fewer years of job experience, and the effects of lower levels of education for older women.

For decades, national and provincial laws have required that employers pay men and women equal wages for carrying out the same or substantially similar work (although differences can be based on such factors as experience, qualifications, and merit). This requirement does not, however, remedy the overall inequality between men and women because women tend to be employed in lower-paying occupations. To overcome gender-based economic inequalities, women's groups have sought government action to pass and enforce **pay equity** laws. Pay equity requires that equal pay be given for work of *equal value*. Specifically this involves a business or government organization increasing the pay of those working in occupations that are staffed primarily by women to the level of pay of equivalent occupations that are primarily staffed by men. The equivalency of different occupations is determined by a combination of the skill, effort, responsibility, and working conditions involved in each occupation. For example, if the occupation of school secretaries was determined to be equivalent to that of school janitors, then pay equity would require that a school board raise the salary of school secretaries to match that of school janitors. Most jurisdictions in Canada have

PAY EQUITY

Laws or policies that require that equal pay be given for work of equal value.

Status of Women Canada: www.swc-cfc.gc.ca

---

[8]In 2009, women earned an average of 85.3 percent of the hourly wages of men (Statistics Canada, Labour Force Survey, May 2009).

adopted some form of pay equity legislation (usually with exceptions for smaller businesses), although many question whether pay equity legislation is effectively applied and enforced. Many business leaders have been concerned about the cost of pay equity, and argue that wages and salaries should be determined by the market.

Women's groups have also advocated that **employment equity** (affirmative action) programs be established to encourage or require the hiring and promotion of women for positions in which they are under-represented. For example, the Canadian government requires that government departments set targets to increase the proportion of women (as well as Aboriginals, visible minorities, and people with disabilities) in senior positions. Federally regulated companies and companies seeking substantial contracts from the Canadian government are also required to set up employment equity programs. Most universities and colleges have adopted employment equity policies, and many professional programs have adopted measures to try to heighten the diversity of their student body. Still, despite major increases in the proportion of women in some traditionally male occupations, gender segregation remains surprisingly evident. Further, although many more women now hold managerial positions in business, top-level executives are still predominantly male.

EMPLOYMENT EQUITY
Programs that encourage or require the hiring and promotion of women (or other groups) for positions in which they are under-represented.

Summary and Conclusion

Canada is fortunate in being a prosperous country. However, Canada depends on natural resources for more of its wealth than most other developed countries. The Canadian economy also relies heavily on trade with the United States, and a substantial proportion of the country's major industries is owned by foreign, and particularly American, companies. The North American Free Trade Agreement (1994) reinforced the already close ties between the Canadian and U.S. economies. Not without its opponents, the agreement has resulted in a high level of economic integration in North America and has tended to enhance the power of corporations.

Canadian governments have often played an active role in developing the Canadian economy. The adoption of various social and health care programs in the decades after the Second World War helped to improve the quality of life of all Canadians.

Nevertheless, the development of a "welfare state" was partly reversed in the 1990s because of concerns about government deficits, as well as an ideological shift toward free markets and away from an active role for government in ensuring the welfare of all its citizens. Ideology thus shapes how citizens and politicians alike define good government from one era to the next.

Although Canada is often viewed as a "classless society," the distribution of income and wealth continues to be unequal—and to grow even more so—and significant poverty is not uncommon. A free market economy with limited government involvement may be efficient in maximizing the wealth of the country.

However, some citizens worry about the tendency for power and wealth to be concentrated in the hands of those who own and control large corporations. They question whether this result is consistent with the view that a democratic society should strive toward the equality of all its citizens.

Discussion Questions

1. Is reliance on natural resources desirable?
2. Should Canada try to limit foreign ownership of Canadian businesses?
3. Should the North American Free Trade Agreement be renegotiated?
4. Was the Canadian government's bailout of GM and Chrysler a wise decision?
5. Are regional divisions more important than class divisions?
6. Should governments be more active in pursuing greater social and economic equality? If so, what policies should be adopted?

Further Reading

Clarkson, S. (2008). *Does North America exist? Governing the continent after NAFTA and 9/11*. Toronto, ON: University of Toronto Press.

Grabb, E., & Guppy, N. (Eds.). (2009). *Social inequality in Canada: Patterns, problems and policies* (5th ed.). Toronto, ON: Pearson Education Canada.

Hale, G. (2006). *Uneasy partnership: The politics of business and government in Canada*. Peterborough, ON: Broadview Press.

Hamilton, R. (2005). *Gendering the vertical mosaic: Feminist perspectives on Canadian society* (2nd ed.). Toronto, ON: Pearson Education Canada.

Howlett, M., & Brownsey, K. (Eds.). (2008). *Canada's resource economy in transition: The past, present, and future of Canadian staples industries*. Toronto, ON: Emond Montgomery.

Hurtig, M. (2008). *The truth about Canada: Some important, some astonishing, and some truly appalling things all Canadians should know about our country*. Toronto, ON: McClelland & Stewart.

McDougall, J. M. (2006). *Drifting together: The political economy of Canada-US integration*. Peterborough, ON: Broadview.

Raphael, D. (2007). *Poverty and policy in Canada: Implications for health and quality of life*. Toronto, ON: Canadian Scholars' Press.

Rice, J. J., & Prince, M. J. (2000). *Changing politics of Canadian social policy*. Toronto, ON: University of Toronto Press.

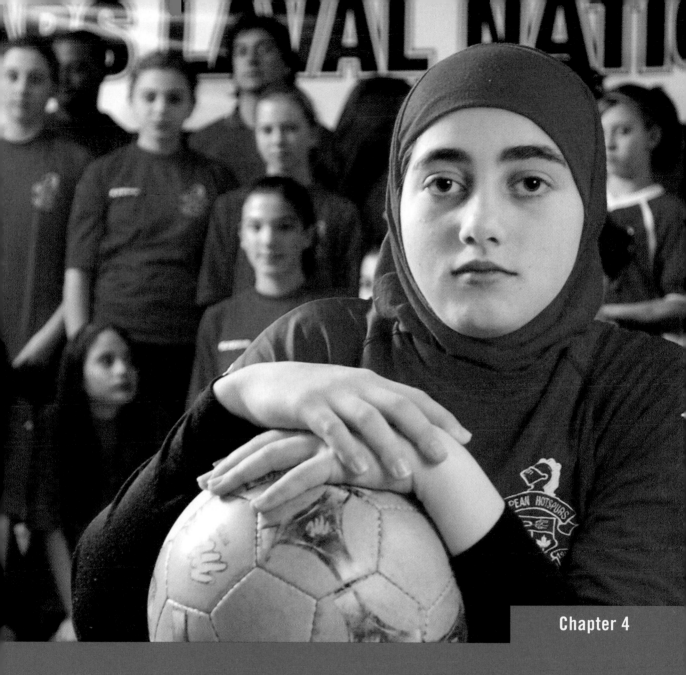

Chapter 4

THE CANADIAN NATION, IDENTITY, AND THE CHALLENGE OF CULTURAL DIVERSITY

PHOTO ABOVE: Asmahan Mansour of the Nepean Hotspurs Select sparked a debate about the accommodation of religious minorities when she was ordered off the pitch in 2007 for wearing hijab during a soccer tournament in Quebec.

CHAPTER OBJECTIVES

After reading this chapter, you should be able to

1. Define and distinguish between an ethnic nation and a civic nation.
2. Discuss the significance of identities and the different ways of understanding the Canadian identity.
3. Discuss the contribution of multinationalism and immigration to cultural diversity in Canada.
4. Define and distinguish between a national minority and an ethnic group.
5. Discuss the trajectory of French-Canadian and Québécois nationalism, and how Canada has responded to the challenge of minority nationalism.
6. Discuss Canada's response to polyethnicity, as shown by its immigration and integration policies.

In February 2007, a referee ejected an eleven-year-old soccer player from a tournament in Laval, Quebec, because she was wearing hijab, a head scarf worn by many Muslim women. The referee, a Muslim himself, ruled that the hijab violated a no-headgear rule set down for safety reasons by the Fédération Internationale de Football Association (FIFA), the sport's governing body. A spokesperson for the Quebec Soccer Federation defended the referee's decision, saying that Asmahan Mansour had been given the choice of removing her hijab or not playing in the tournament. Mansour had worn the head scarf during games she played in Ontario, where it is permitted by the provincial soccer association. After Mansour was ordered off the soccer pitch, her team promptly quit the tournament in protest, saying it would not come back until the rules are changed.

The incident highlighted the controversial and delicate nature of debates about the accommodation of ethnic and religious minorities in Canadian society. Quebec Premier Jean Charest weighed in on the incident, noting that the referee was only applying the rules of the Quebec Soccer Federation. But others slammed the referee's decision, saying that it was another example of how Quebec is trying to get immigrants to toe a cultural line. The Muslim Council of Montreal urged the province's soccer federation to respect the religious rights of its players. A director with the Canadian Arab Federation maintained that traditional headgear such as hijab, turbans, and yarmulkes are worn by soccer players in Canada and around the world. Others questioned how a tucked-in hijab could be seen as dangerous when many girls run around soccer pitches with loose ponytails.

FIFA was asked to consider Mansour's case, and after a "heated discussion" between board members, the governing body responsible for international soccer rules upheld the Quebec Soccer Federation's ban on the hijab. The FIFA board reiterated current regulations, which state that a player "must not use equipment or wear anything that is dangerous to himself or another player (including any kind of jewellery)," and that the referee has the discretion to make decisions that concern the safety of the athlete and others. While the FIFA list of items that a player is entitled to wear does not mention head scarves, it does not explicitly ban headgear, including the hijab (Blatchford, 2007; Wyatt, 2007). A FIFA board member commented, "It's absolutely right to be sensitive to people's thoughts and philosophies, but equally, there has to be a set of laws that are adhered to" ("Religious Accommodation," 2007).

The controversy that first erupted on a Canadian soccer pitch and spilled over into the premier's office and then across the Atlantic Ocean into the boardroom of soccer's international governing body illustrates the dilemma faced by decision makers in multicultural societies when a potential conflict exists between the traditions of cultural minorities and prevailing institutions and practices. It raises the thorny question of whether societies should adapt their institutions to respond to the requirements of ethnic and religious minorities. In your view, did the referee make the right decision when he ordered Mansour off the pitch after she refused to play without the hijab? If you had been officiating the match and had the discretion to allow her to play or not, what would you have done?

CANADA'S EXPANDING CULTURAL DIVERSITY

If you used Google Earth to zoom in over Canada, you would notice the country's distinctive physical features: a huge land mass bounded by three oceans and traversed by long rivers, lakes and bays as vast as small seas, and numerous mountain ranges. If you could use a different Google engine to observe the country's social features, you would notice that Canadians come from myriad cultural backgrounds. In 2006, Canadians reported more than 200 different ethnic origins and more than 150 different languages. Close to one-fifth of the total population was born in another country. It is this astounding cultural diversity that defines Canada as much as the country's spectacular landscape.

Cultural diversity is both a source of pride for many Canadians and a challenge for public officials who are striving to build a cohesive political community. Canada's Aboriginal peoples have pressed for more power in governing their affairs, as well as territorial, economic, and resource rights. The predominantly francophone province of Quebec has held two referendums on whether it should establish an independent state. Canadians across the country are debating whether and to what extent public institutions should be adapted to accommodate the different traditions of increasingly multicultural, multilingual, and multifaith local populations.

Many states are confronting the challenge of building a nation out of territories inhabited by people from different backgrounds. In the early 1970s, only 10 percent of the world's states could be considered **nation-states,** in the sense that the total population of the state shared a single ethnic culture (Connor, 1972). By the early 1990s, 160 countries were home to an estimated 862 ethnic groups (Fearon, 2003). The implications are significant: the territorial boundaries of the state rarely incorporate people who are drawn from a single ethnic group.

NATION-STATE
A state in which the population shares a single ethnic culture.

The vast majority of Canadians express pride in their country, but they also identify with, or feel a sense of belonging to, their language group, ethnic ancestry, province, region, and other affiliations. The persistence of linguistic, ethnic, and regional identities in Canada and other advanced capitalist states has surprised integrationist theorists, who expected these allegiances to weaken as societies modernized (Deutsch & Foltz, 1963; Tilly, 1975). They predicted, prematurely, that scientific and technological progress, the spread of mass education and communications, the geographic concentration of economic activities, urbanization, and secularism would narrow differences between people and encourage cultural uniformity. To the contrary, since World War II, indigenous movements and regional languages and cultures have enjoyed a renaissance in many liberal democratic states. This has led to the growth of nationalist or regional movements making separatist claims or clamouring for more political autonomy.

The persistence of cultural differences raises the question of how liberal societies should go about building a unified political community out of

CLASSICAL LIBERALISM
An intellectual tradition based on a belief in a minimal role for government, leaving individuals free to pursue their interests and follow their own beliefs as long as they do not seriously harm others.

disparate parts. **Classical liberalism** is based on the idea that the state should remain neutral in cultural and religious matters, and concentrate on protecting individual rights and freedoms and the life, liberty, and property of its citizens. A second brand of liberalism allows for a state to encourage the survival and flourishing of a particular national, cultural, or religious group, as long as the basic rights of citizens who do not belong to that particular group, or who do not share its goals, are protected (Walzer, 1992). In Canada, supporters of these contrasting liberal traditions debate whether the state should grant special rights to cultural minorities or whether it should treat all Canadians the same, regardless of their ancestry. Political philosopher Charles Taylor (1992) has argued that the recognition of group identities and differences is consistent with liberal principles, providing the state protects the basic rights of all citizens. In practice, this would entitle members of certain cultural groups to specific rights and powers that are not enjoyed by other Canadians. In contrast, former Prime Minister Pierre Trudeau (1968), a supporter of the classical liberal tradition, adamantly opposed the organization of any political society along ethnic lines.

A LOOK AHEAD   This chapter begins with an exploration of the nature of Canada's nationhood and identity. Is Canada a nation, and does it have a single and distinct identity? The chapter then takes a closer look at how Canada has dealt with two important sources of cultural diversity within its borders: the existence of more than one nation and polyethnicity. Canada could be considered a **multination state** because its historical development involved the English, French, and Aboriginal **nations**.[1] In this context, the term "nation" refers to a historical community with its own institutions, occupying a given territory, and sharing a distinct language and culture. Canada is also a **polyethnic state** because it is composed of many ethnic groups formed by immigrants who left their countries of origin to live in another society (Kymlicka, 1995).

MULTINATION STATE
A state that contains more than one nation.

NATION
A historical community with its own institutions, occupying a given territory or homeland, and sharing a distinct language and culture.

POLYETHNIC STATE
A state that contains many ethnic groups.

When discussing Canada's approach to building one political community out of a multination state, we will focus on how it has responded to the claims of the French-Canadian, and subsequently, Québécois national minority for language rights and self-government. The chapter will also examine the decisions Canada has made with respect to admitting immigrants to the country and integrating members of ethnic groups into broader society. Since Canada's policy responses have changed over time, the project of building the Canadian political community is best viewed as an interesting work in progress.

---

[1]The Canadian constitution recognizes three distinct groups of Aboriginal peoples: Indians (commonly referred to as First Nations), Métis, and Inuit, each with their own histories, languages, cultural practices, and spiritual beliefs. The First Nations people alone represent more than fifty nations or cultural groups.

CANADA AND NATIONHOOD

Is Canada a nation? The answer to this provocative question depends on how one defines this concept. Anthony Smith (1976, 1999) distinguishes between two types of nations: ethnic and civic. An **ethnic nation** describes a community with a distinctive culture and history, which operates solely for the benefit of that cultural group. Members of the ethnic nation can trace their roots to common ancestry, language, customs, and traditions. The **civic nation** is not based on a homogeneous population but on the common territory in which its members live and are governed. The civic nation is thus identified with the territory, a community of laws and institutions, and legal equality among the members of the community.

Canada is not, and never was, an ethnic nation. When European settlers made first contact with the original inhabitants of North America, they met indigenous peoples from many cultural backgrounds. Each Aboriginal group had a unique economic organization, language, religion, and set of values. The Aboriginal peoples were in turn confronted with predominantly French and British settlers who imported their unique political and legal structures and cultural traditions. The migration of forty to fifty thousand Loyalist settlers from the Thirteen Colonies during the 1780s further diversified the cultural mix in the British North American colonies.

Between 1815 and 1867, a massive exodus of emigrants from the British Isles escaping Old World poverty sought new opportunities in British North America. From Confederation until the first decade of the twentieth century, the Canadian government heavily promoted immigration from the United States, Central and Eastern Europe, and Scandinavia to develop the fledgling state's economy and population base. As early as 1901, the census recorded about twenty-five ethnic groups living in Canada. People who reported Aboriginal ancestries and British and French origins comprised the lion's share of the population at the time, although German, Ukrainian, Polish, Japanese, Chinese, and other ethnic groups formed sizeable communities. They were joined in the latter half of the twentieth and early twenty-first centuries by large numbers of immigrants from across Europe, Asia and the Middle East, South America, and Africa (see Table 4-1). A growing number of mixed marriages or common-law unions between people from different cultural backgrounds have heightened awareness of family heritage and have boosted the number of Canadians reporting multiple ethnic origins. In 2006, 41.4 percent of the population reported more than one ethnic origin, compared with 35.8 percent in 1996 (Statistics Canada, 2006).

Canada is also home to the fifth-largest foreign-born population among the countries in the Organization for Economic Co-operation and Development (OECD), after Luxembourg, Australia, Switzerland, and New Zealand (Lemaitre, 2005). Few of the 6.2 million immigrants (about one-fifth of Canada's population) share the same national origins, languages, cultures,

ETHNIC NATION
A community with a distinctive culture and history, which operates solely for the benefit of that cultural group. Members of the ethnic nation share common ancestry, language, customs, and traditions.

CIVIC NATION
A community based on the common territory in which its members live and are governed.

TABLE 4-1
ETHNIC ORIGINS OF CANADIANS, 2006 (PERCENTAGE)

Notes: Includes both single and multiple responses to a question concerning ethnic origin and thus total exceeds 100%. Ethnic origin is derived from a question concerning the ethnic or cultural origins of one's ancestors.

British Isles	36.8
Canadian	32.2
European	31.8
French	16.0
East/South East Asian	7.1
Aboriginal	5.4
South Asian	4.2
Caribbean	1.8
Other North American	1.6
Arab	1.5
African	1.3
Latin, Central and South American	1.2
West Asian	1.0
Oceania	0.2

Source: *Calculated from Statistics Canada, 2008,* Ethnocultural portrait of Canada highlight tables, 2006 census *(Catalogue number 97-562-XWE2006002). Retrieved from http://www12.statcan.ca/english/census06/ data/highlights/ethnic/index.cfm?Lang=E*

and religious traditions. The trend toward an increasingly heterogeneous society is expected to continue, as the foreign-born population grew at four times the rate of the Canadian-born population between 2001 and 2006 (Chui, Tran, & Maheux, 2007).

Asia and the Middle East have replaced Europe and the United States as the principal source regions for immigration (see Figure 4-1). In 1971, 61.6 percent of newcomers to Canada were from Europe, while only 12.1 percent of newcomers who arrived in the late 1960s were Asian-born. Among the more than 1.1 million immigrants who arrived in the country between 2001 and 2006, almost six in ten were born in Asia and the Middle East (Chui, Tran, & Maheux, 2007).

FIGURE 4-1
REGION OF BIRTH OF RECENT IMMIGRANTS TO CANADA, 1971–2006

Notes: "Recent immigrants" refers to landed immigrants who arrived in Canada within five years prior to a given census. "Other" includes Greenland, St Pierre and Miquelon, the category "other country," as well as a small number of immigrants born in Canada.

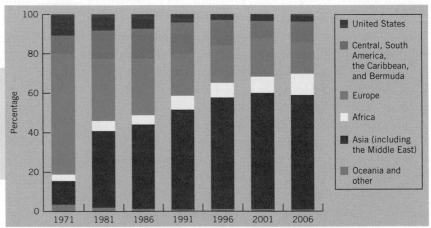

Source: T. Chui, K. Tran, & H. Maheux, 2007, *2006 Census: Immigration in Canada: A Portrait of the Foreign-born Population, 2006 Census: Findings* (Catalogue No. 97-557-XIE2006001). Retrieved from http://www12.statcan.ca/census-recensement/2006/as-sa/97-557/figures/c2-eng.cfm

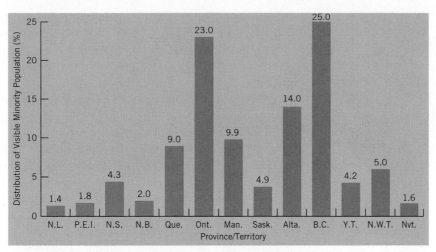

FIGURE 4-2
PERCENTAGE DISTRIBUTION OF VISIBLE MINORITY GROUPS, BY PROVINCE AND TERRITORY (2006)

Source: Statistics Canada, 2008, *Ethnocultural Portrait of Canada Highlight Tables, 2006 Census.* Retrieved from http://www12.statcan.ca/english/census06/data/highlights/ethnic/index.cfm?Lang=E

The dramatic changes in the source countries of immigration have reinforced the multiracial character of Canadian society (see Figure 4-2). In 2006, visible minorities accounted for 16.2 percent of the population, up from 11.2 percent in 1996.[2] The number of visible minority Canadians, like the immigrant population, is also growing rapidly. Between 2001 and 2006, Canada's visible minority population grew five times faster than the average population growth rate (Statistics Canada, 2006).

Multilingualism and religious pluralism also contribute to Canada's social diversity. In 2006, more than 20 percent of Canadians reported that their mother tongue is neither English nor French, up from 16 percent in 1991. This linguistic diversity does not mean that people cannot converse in one of the two official languages. In fact, only 8 percent of allophones—or Canadians whose mother tongue is neither English nor French—cannot carry on a conversation in one of the official languages (Jantzen, 2008). Moreover, followers of religions other than Christianity are projected to increase from 6.3 percent of the total population in 2001, to between 9.2 and 11.2 percent by 2017. The Muslim population, for example, more than doubled between 1991 and 2001 (Winnemore & Biles, 2006).

This demographic portrait of the Canadian population illustrates that Canada cannot be described as an ethnic nation. Canada does, however, exhibit characteristics of the civic nation, although some Aboriginals and Québécois might not consider themselves part of the civic nation. Canadians

---

[2]Under the *Employment Equity Act*, visible minorities are defined as "persons, other than Aboriginal persons, who are non-Caucasian in race or non-white in colour." They include individuals who are Chinese, South Asian, Black, Arab, West Asian, Filipino, Southeast Asian, Latin American, Japanese, Korean, and members of other groups, such as Pacific Islanders.

▶ These dancers waiting to audition for the hit television show *So You Think You Can Dance Canada* reflect the country's cultural diversity.

share a common territory, live in a political community where the principle of the legal equality of its members is entrenched in the Constitution, and are governed by a community of laws and institutions.

THE ELUSIVE AND EVOLVING CANADIAN IDENTITY

IDENTITIES
Individual and group self-understandings of their traits and characteristics.

Individuals and groups possess **identities**, or self-understandings of their traits and characteristics. A country may also be associated with a unique identity that is understood by the people who live within and outside its borders. Identities are crucial because they affect how people interpret the world; how they interpret the past, present, and future; how they understand other groups and states; and how they perceive their political and economic interests (Abdelal, Herrera, Johnston, & McDermott, 2005).

Some commentators view loyalty to the larger political community as a form of national identity. If this is the case, then we can confirm that a Canadian identity exists. In 2006, almost 96 percent of Canadians saw themselves as citizens of their country. Others have linked the Canadian national identity to the land, its people, and its history. For celebrated author Pierre Berton (1994), an essential part of the Canadian identity can be found in the way many Canadians revel in the harshness of the northern winter. The Canadian identity has also been linked to symbols such as the flag and anthem (the Maple Leaf and "O Canada") or to the accomplishments of the country's authors and artists (e.g., Farley Mowat, Alice Munro, the Group of Seven, Norval Morrisseau), musicians (e.g., Joni Mitchell, Celine Dion, Great Big Sea), and athletes (e.g., Cindy Klassen, Wayne Gretzky, Terry Fox, Gilles Villeneuve).

Others feel the Canadian identity is rooted in important events, institutions, laws, and public policies (e.g., Vimy Ridge, the *Charter of Rights and Freedoms,* universal medicare, and official bilingualism). For some Canadians, cultural diversity is a defining attribute of their country. In a poll taken in 2003, 85 percent of Canadians felt that multiculturalism was important to the Canadian identity (Kymlicka, 2009). Canadians often define themselves in terms of their differences from Americans (Lipset, 1990). As discussed in Chapter 5, Canadians view their country as less violent and more compassionate to the less fortunate. Canadians are also more likely to hold more liberal attitudes on the abolition of the death penalty, access to abortion, gay marriage, and the legalization of marijuana (Resnick, 2005). One thing, above all, is indisputable—the elements of the Canadian identity are as multifaceted and wide-ranging as the country's inhabitants. You can no doubt think of other characteristics that make Canada a country unlike any other.

Multiple and Overlapping Identities

The quest to describe the elusive Canadian identity is complicated by the fact that Canadians also identify with their province, region, class, gender, religion, and sexual orientation, among other affiliations. In 2006, almost 96 percent of Canadians saw themselves as citizens of their country *and* their provinces or regions (World Values Survey, 2006). These identities have a political impact because they influence perceptions of the role the regions play in the broader Canadian political community. Western Canada has long harboured resentment toward the federal government, and a belief that federal politicians have been preoccupied with the concerns of Ontario and Quebec (Cooper, 1984; Gibbins & Arrison, 1995). Leaders in the Maritime provinces have also criticized what they have seen as unjust treatment by Ottawa.

Globalization theorists have argued that we live in an era in which identities are no longer inherited at birth but can take shape as a result of the deliberate choices that people make during their lives (Castells, 1997; Giddens, 1994). This opens up possibilities for the flourishing of more identities based on political struggles to achieve major social and cultural changes. For example, union activism and farmers' movements have created and reinforced class and occupational identities. During the 1960s, a wave of new social movements, including the women's, environmental, and lesbian and gay movements, contributed to the growth of identities based on gender, environmentalism, and sexual orientation (Smith, 2005).

Changing English- and French-Canadian Identities

Finally, it is important to note that identities can change over time. Both the English- and French-Canadian identities—essential components of the Canadian identity—have shifted from a model of nationhood based on common ancestry to a more inclusive civic model (Resnick, 2005). After control over New France was transferred to the British in 1763, French-Canadian society promoted a collective identity based on Roman Catholicism, the French language and ancestry, and agricultural vocations. This ethnic-based identity extended beyond the borders of the new colony of Quebec to include everyone of French-Canadian ancestry.

On the English-Canadian side, the British connection was the primary source of identity for people of British Isles ancestry. During the interwar period in English Canada, a stronger brand of Canadian nationalism emerged as the country became more autonomous from Great Britain. After the Second World War, the economic and military prestige of Great Britain declined and Canada became a major industrial and diplomatic player on the world stage (Bumstead, 2004). Correspondingly, the British roots of the English-Canadian identity also began to wither. The government set up a legally separate Canadian citizenship in 1947, ended appeals to the British Judicial Committee of the Privy Council in 1949, replaced British-born with Canadian-born governors general, and adopted the Maple Leaf flag in 1965 in place of the red ensign with the Union Jack. In 1967, the federal government put a stop to the discriminatory elements of an immigrant selection system that favoured British and other Caucasian immigrants over immigrants from Asia, Africa, and the Middle East. The move away from the British connection was reinforced by the adoption of a policy of official bilingualism in 1969 and **official multiculturalism** in 1971 (discussed later in this chapter).

Resnick (2005) argues that the French-Canadian identity has also evolved from an ethnic-based model into a more civic and inclusive identity that can be embraced by all Quebecers, regardless of their ancestral origins. Supporters of Quebec sovereignty insist that the Quebec nation includes people of any ethnic, racial, or religious origin, as long as they conform to the common public language of French. Sovereignists thus contend that Québécois society includes francophone Blacks with roots in Haiti, francophone Jews and Muslims with roots in Egypt or Morocco, bilingual anglophones, and immigrants whose first language is neither English nor French (Howard, 1998). This interpretation of the modern Quebec identity competes with the views of some who argue that the Quebec identity remains rooted in ethnicity.

CANADA: A MULTINATION AND POLYETHNIC STATE

Political philosopher William Kymlicka (1995) has described Canada as a multination state built on a federation of three distinct national groups: English, French, and Aboriginal. Aboriginal Canadians and the Québécois are considered **national minorities** because they constitute nations—or historical communities with their own institutions, occupying a given territory, and sharing a distinct language and culture—that have been incorporated into a

OFFICIAL MULTICULTURALISM
A policy introduced in 1971 that encouraged individuals to embrace the culture and tradition of their choice while retaining Canadian citizenship.

NATIONAL MINORITY
A culturally distinct and potentially self-governing society that has been incorporated into a larger state.

larger state. Canada is also a polyethnic state composed of many **ethnic groups,** which Kymlicka defines as groups of immigrants who have left their countries of origin to enter another society. Although such groups establish their own religious, commercial, cultural, and educational institutions (e.g., churches or mosques, specialty food shops, community centres, and schools), they are not considered "nations" because they do not occupy a separate territory. Furthermore, their members participate within the public institutions of the dominant culture, and most of them speak English or French, although some may speak their own language within their own communities.

Canada, like other multination and polyethnic states, has been confronted with the challenge of responding appropriately to the claims of national minorities and ethnic groups for recognition of their cultural distinctiveness. One way to meet such demands is by extending legal protections for civil and political rights to individuals. Guarantees of rights of freedom of association, religion, speech, mobility, and political organization allow individual members of national minorities and ethnic groups to protect and promote their rights and interests (Kymlicka, 1995, p. 26). Another approach is to grant special group-based legal or constitutional rights to national minorities and ethnic groups, or what Iris Young (1989) has referred to as **differentiated citizenship.** Kymlicka has identified at least three forms of group-based measures for accommodating national and ethnic differences: **self-government rights, polyethnic rights,** and **special representation rights.**

Self-Government Rights

Many multination states have met the demands of national minorities for recognition by giving them some kind of territorial jurisdiction or autonomy over their political and cultural affairs. One way of achieving this is through federalism, an institutional arrangement that divides powers between the central and regional or provincial governments. Federalism can effectively provide self-government for a national minority if the national minority is geographically concentrated. For example, the federal division of powers in Canada gives the provinces, including Quebec, control over issues such as education, language, and social services that are crucial to the survival of minority cultures.

States may also redraw territorial boundaries so that national minorities living within a particular geographic area can acquire self-government. This is what occurred in 1999, when the Northwest Territories was divided into two and the territory of Nunavut was created in its eastern half. This arrangement effectively gave the Inuit the right of self-government. As discussed in Chapter 12, several First Nations have also concluded self-government agreements with the federal government, and more control over health, education, family law, policing, criminal justice, and resource development matters has been handed over to First Nations councils on reserves.

ETHNIC GROUPS
Groups of immigrants who have left their countries of origin to enter another society, but who do not occupy a separate territory in their new homeland.

DIFFERENTIATED CITIZENSHIP
The granting of special group-based legal or constitutional rights to national minorities and ethnic groups.

SELF-GOVERNMENT RIGHT
A group-based right that grants a national minority some kind of territorial jurisdiction or autonomy over its political and cultural affairs.

POLYETHNIC RIGHT
A group-based right that allows ethnic groups and religious minorities to express their cultural distinctiveness without discrimination.

SPECIAL REPRESENTATION RIGHTS
The provision of guaranteed representation for particular groups in legislative bodies or other political institutions.

Polyethnic Rights

Polyethnic rights give ethnic groups and religious minorities the right to express their cultural distinctiveness without discrimination. These rights would include public funding of ethnic cultural practices and the teaching of immigrant languages, as well as exemptions from laws that disadvantage minorities (Kymlicka, 1995). Following the introduction of official multiculturalism in 1971, the federal government established a multiculturalism program that was oriented toward helping ethnic groups maintain their cultural traditions and languages (see the discussion of official multiculturalism later in this chapter). Many federal institutions have also implemented policies that exempt minorities from dress codes that offend their religious traditions. For example, the Canadian Air Transport Security Authority, which employs screening officers at airports across the country, has a policy that recognizes its duty to respond to individual uniform requests by respecting the need for accommodation based on, but not limited to, race, national or ethnic origin, colour, religion, age, sex, or disability. The *Employment Equity Act,* 1995, and the *Charter of Rights and Freedoms,* 1982, provide the basis for the extension of some group-based rights for members of ethnic groups, as discussed later in this chapter.

Special Representation Rights

Special representation rights may also be given to national minorities and immigrant groups so that they can participate in the political process. However, unlike New Zealand, which has established electoral districts in which only the indigenous Maori population can vote, Canada does not reserve seats for the representation of national minorities in the House of Commons and Senate. One of the proposals in the ill-fated 1992 Charlottetown Accord to amend the constitution included guarantees for the representation of Aboriginals in the Senate.

MINORITY NATIONALISM AND THE CANADIAN STATE

In the 2006 census, more than five million people or 16 percent of the total population reported a French ancestry. Canadians of French ancestry share a common linguistic, religious, and historical heritage. They live in communities across Canada but are largely concentrated in Quebec, northern New Brunswick, and Ontario. Ninety percent of all Canadian francophones live in Quebec, where more than 80 percent of the population claims French as a mother tongue. Quebec's distinctive cultural makeup explains why the province has vied for more control over matters that it considers vital to the preservation of the French language and its social institutions.

Conquest and the Will to Survive

The Conquest of New France in 1759 marked a tragedy for French-speakers and the central event in the history of Canadians of French ancestry. British governors replaced French officials, and English-speaking merchants from Britain and the American colonies quickly assumed control of Quebec's economic affairs (Cook, 1977). The Roman Catholic Church was the only important institution in Quebec to remain outside of British control and it became the principal defender of the French-Canadian way of life. French-Canadian clerical and political leaders urged their people to resist **assimilation** into the anglophone culture through a strategy of *la survivance,* or survival. The French-Canadian nation was to be preserved by resisting the anglicizing pressures of Protestantism, liberal democracy, and commercial occupations, and by remaining fiercely loyal to the Catholic religion, the French language, and the traditional mores of rural life. Supporters of traditional nationalism portrayed French Canada as an ethnic nation whose boundaries reached beyond Quebec to include all French Canadians.

As discussed in Chapter 2, British colonial authorities passed the *Quebec Act* in 1774 in order to secure the allegiance of French-Canadian clerical and civil leaders to the British Crown. The *Quebec Act* granted formal protection to the status of the Roman Catholic religion and the system of civil law. In the meantime, the French Canadians found a means of strengthening their ranks that involved neither military manoeuvres nor government proclamations— the high fertility rate among French Canadians enabled them to continue to outnumber English-speaking colonists, even after the immigration of Loyalists from the United States and English speakers from the British Isles.

The strategy of *la survivance* ensured the cultural survival of the French nation in Quebec, but it also contributed to the relative dearth of French Canadians in industry and finance. Discrimination against francophones was also a recognizable feature of the Quebec economy until the 1960s (McRoberts, 1988). Some francophones ran small- and medium-sized businesses, but anglophones controlled most of the province's wealth and high-paying managerial and technical jobs. The processes of economic and social modernization that unfolded from the early to mid-twentieth century placed increasing pressure on traditional French-Canadian nationalism. By 1921, Quebec's urban population had surpassed the rural population, and manufacturing workers outnumbered farm workers by the mid-century (McRoberts, 1993). Quebec's economic modernization prompted groups representing cultural, academic, labour, and other interests to challenge the monopoly on power held by clerical elites, English-Canadian and foreign business interests, and Maurice Duplessis' Union Nationale government that ruled in 1936–39 and 1944–59. The goal of these groups was to bring Quebec's society, economy, and government up to date—a goal that became known as *rattrapage,* or catching up.

ASSIMILATION
The process through which groups of individuals with a different culture learn and adopt the values and norms of the host society.

Modern Quebec Nationalism and the Role of Language

The early 1960s marked a turning point in the province's history. The election of the provincial Liberals under Jean Lesage in 1960 ushered in a series of political, institutional, and social reforms referred to as the **Quiet Revolution**. The modern nationalism of the Quiet Revolution identified the French-Canadian nation with the territory of Quebec. Instead of defining the nation in terms of language and religion, modern nationalism promoted the idea that the Québécois should assume control of their own affairs through the government of Quebec. The province replaced church authority in the areas of education, health, and social services, and took over a broader range of economic functions. It established a ministry of education; nationalized privately owned hydroelectric companies; created Crown corporations such as the Caisse de dépôt et placement, which manages public pensions and insurance funds; set up a Quebec Pension Plan; and provided career opportunities for the growing number of francophones. The provincial government also succeeded in persuading the federal government to give it more powers over social policy and immigration.

QUIET REVOLUTION
A series of political, institutional, and social reforms ushered in under the Quebec Liberal leader Jean Lesage beginning in 1960.

LINGUISTIC CLAIMS   In the face of declining birth rates and the tendency for immigrants to adopt English as their home language, several Quebec governments introduced language policies aimed at ensuring that francophones would not become a linguistic minority in the province. The *Official Language Act* of 1974 (*Loi sur la langue officielle*), also known as Bill 22, made French the sole official language of Quebec. It was eventually replaced by the *Charter of the French Language* (also known as Bill 101) in 1977. Several provisions of Bill 101 had its opponents up in arms. The bill's main features stated that

- French would be the sole official language in Quebec, the exclusive official language for proceedings of the provincial legislature and the courts, and the main language for public administration;
- businesses with fifty or more employees would need to receive a "francisation certificate" as a condition of doing business in the province;
- commercial signs and advertisements would be in French only; and
- children could enrol in English school if one of three conditions were met: the child's parents had been educated in English in Quebec and the child had a sibling already going to an English school; the child's parents were educated in English outside of Quebec but were living in the province when the law was passed; or the child was already enrolled in an English school when the law came into effect.

Three of these provisions prompted court challenges from organizations in the anglophone community that strenuously objected to the restrictions on the use of English in the province. In 1979, the Supreme Court of Canada ruled that the provision making French the sole official language of the provincial legislature and the courts violated Section 133 of the *British North America Act,* 1867, which guaranteed the equality of both languages in the Quebec National Assembly and in the courts of Quebec. The provisions concerning the language of commercial signage (modified in 1983 to make an exception for bilingual advertising by "ethnic businesses") were also challenged in court. In 1988, the Supreme Court of Canada ruled that the prohibition of all languages other than French in public signs, posters, and commercial advertising violated the right to freedom of expression guaranteed in the Canadian and Quebec Charters of Human Rights and Freedoms.

In response to the Court's decision, the government of Quebec passed Bill 178, which invoked the "notwithstanding" clause of the Canadian Charter.[3] It reaffirmed the ban on languages other than French for commercial signs outside a business while permitting the use of other languages on interior signs, providing the French language was more prominently displayed. Just as the five-year limit on the application of the notwithstanding clause was set to expire, a less controversial law was put in place. In 1993, Bill 86 was passed, stating that other languages can be used on commercial outdoor signs as long as French is "markedly predominant."

Bill 101's provisions concerning access to English-language education generated the most opposition from anglophones and immigrant groups who were upset that they could not send their children to English-language public schools and who were worried about the long-term viability of English-language schools in the province. In 1984, the Supreme Court ruled that Bill 101's provision that guaranteed access to English-language education only to those children of Canadian citizens who had been educated in English in Quebec was unconstitutional because it violated the *Charter of Rights and Freedoms.* The Charter guarantees the right of Canadian citizens to have their children receive primary and secondary school instruction in English, providing they received their primary school instruction in English in Canada, or they have a child who has received or is receiving primary or secondary school instruction in English in Canada.[4] This right applies wherever in the province there is sufficient demand to warrant the provision of minority language instruction out of public funds. In 1993, the education provisions of Bill 101 were brought in line with the Charter.

THE CANADIAN STATE AND LANGUAGE RIGHTS   In contrast to the unilingual approach of the Quebec government, Canada has dealt with the

---

[3]As discussed in Chapter 11, the "notwithstanding" clause allows federal or provincial governments to pass legislation that infringes on fundamental freedoms, legal rights, and equality rights.

[4]Except in Quebec, this Charter right also applies to Canadian citizens "whose first language learned and still understood is that of the English or French linguistic minority of the province in which they reside."

issue of language claims by embedding the principle of linguistic duality in the country's constitution, laws, and policies. Section 133 of the *Constitution Act, 1867,* states that English and French have equality of status in the federal Parliament and the Quebec National Assembly, and in any court of Canada, including Quebec. Language rights were extended in the 1982 *Charter of Rights and Freedoms,* enshrining English and French as the two official languages of all of the institutions of Parliament and the Canadian government. At the provincial level, the Charter contains the same provision enshrining the equality of the two official languages in New Brunswick. As noted above, Canadian citizens also have the right to have their children educated in their own official language where numbers warrant. These provisions help to protect and preserve both English and French and the cultures associated with them throughout Canada.

The principle of linguistic duality can also be seen in the federal government's policy response to the rising tide of Quebec nationalism in the 1960s. In 1963, the Liberal government of Lester B. Pearson established the Royal Commission on Bilingualism and Biculturalism to inquire into and report on the state of bilingualism and biculturalism in the country and to recommend what steps should be taken to develop Canada on the basis of an equal partnership between the English and French, taking into account the contributions made by the other ethnic groups. The government followed up on the Commission's recommendations by passing the *Official Languages Act* (OLA) in 1969, which regulates bilingualism in the federal public service and federally regulated industries in the private sector. The act was designed to address the issue of francophone under-representation in the public service and to transform the language of the public service, which was, in most parts of the country, English. It reflects a philosophy of a Canada in which language rights are guaranteed to individuals and are safeguarded by national institutions.

The OLA gives individual members of the public the right to be served by the federal government in English or French, it requires the equitable representation of francophones and anglophones in the public service, and it guarantees the ability of public servants from both language groups to work in the language of their choice. To strengthen the bilingual character of the federal bureaucracy, language training has been provided for public servants, and an increasing share of positions have been designated as bilingual. Approximately 40 percent of positions in the public service require knowledge of both official languages (Treasury Board of Canada Secretariat, 2007).

The federal government has also promoted bilingualism through the financial assistance it provides for minority language education and second language instruction delivered by the provincial and territorial school boards. Although the goal of encouraging bilingualism across the country has yet to be realized, rates of bilingualism have grown among anglophones in every province and territory since 2001 (Corbeil & Blaser, 2007).

Public opinion seems to favour continuing support for minority French- and English-language communities and bilingualism. A 2006 poll found that slightly more than 63 percent of Canadians felt that federal institutions should support the development of the official language minority community in their province, an increase of 17 percent over 2002 (Canadian Heritage/ Decima, 2006). A strong majority of Canadians (72 percent) favour bilingual- ism for all of Canada, with support increasing in all parts of the country between 1988 and 2006 (Office of the Commissioner of Official Languages, 2006). Quebecers, francophones, young Canadians, and women tend to be the greatest supporters of bilingualism (see Figure 4-3 and Figure 4-4).

Self-Government and Sovereignty Claims

ORIGINS   During the Confederation debates, most English-Canadian leaders from the province of Canada favoured a unitary system of government that would assign all legislative powers to a national parliament. Yet French-Canadian representatives from Canada East wanted a federal system that would give the provinces jurisdiction over linguistic and cultural matters. Politicians from the Maritimes also preferred the federal option because they had developed strong local identities, and some politicians from Canada West felt that the conflict between English Protestant and French Catholic commu- nities, which had led to government instability in Canada, would subside if local affairs were assigned to the provinces.

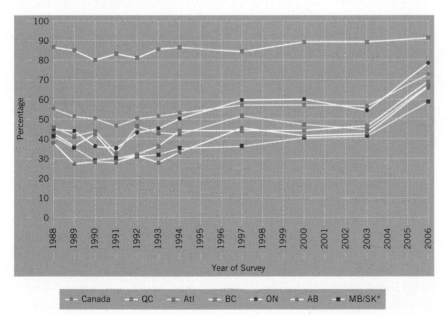

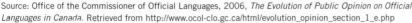

FIGURE 4-3
SUPPORT FOR BILINGUALISM IN 2006* (PERCENTAGE)

Source: Office of the Commissioner of Official Languages, 2006, *The Evolution of Public Opinion on Official Languages in Canada*. Retrieved from http://www.ocol-clo.gc.ca/html/evolution_opinion_section_1_e.php

FIGURE 4-4
**SUPPORT FOR
BILINGUALISM IN 2006*
(PERCENTAGE)**

*Respondents were asked, "Are you
personally in favour of bilingualism
for all of Canada?"

**Second column is Canada outside
Quebec.

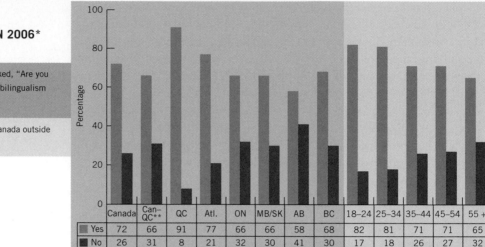

	Canada	Can–QC**	QC	Atl.	ON	MB/SK	AB	BC	18–24	25–34	35–44	45–54	55 +
Yes	72	66	91	77	66	66	58	68	82	81	71	71	65
No	26	31	8	21	32	30	41	30	17	18	26	27	32

Source: Office of the Commissioner of Official Languages, 2006, *The Evolution of Public Opinion on Official Languages in Canada*. Retrieved from http://www.ocol-clo.gc.ca/html/evolution_opinion_section_1_e.php

The *Constitution Act,* 1867, established a federal system in which the authority to make laws and to tax was divided between a national government and provincial governments. Provincial governments were given exclusive jurisdiction over matters such as hospitals, municipal institutions, and property and civil rights, as well as shared jurisdiction over immigration. Each province could also make laws in relation to education, providing they did not overstep the existing religious education rights of the Protestant or Roman Catholic minority communities in their provinces. By the middle of the twentieth century, the federal government had become more and more involved in provincial affairs through its power to initiate programs and spend money in policy areas under provincial jurisdiction. At the same time, successive Quebec governments became more protective of what they argued were their exclusive powers under the constitution.

THE QUEST FOR INDEPENDENCE   Before the mid-1960s, the idea of Quebec independence did not enjoy broad support. Quebec's quest for independence, or "sovereignty," became a crucial issue with the victory of the Parti Québécois (PQ) in the 1976 provincial election—a victory that sparked the exodus of many anglophones from the province. In May 1980, Quebecers were asked to vote yes or no—*oui ou non*—on a proposal that would give the province a mandate to negotiate a new agreement with Canada; the agreement would "enable Quebec to acquire the exclusive power to make its laws, levy its taxes and establish relations abroad—in other words, sovereignty—and at the same time, to maintain an economic association with Canada, including a common currency" (LeDuc, 2003). It was defeated by 59.6 percent of provincial voters, with a majority of francophones voting against independence.

Some fifteen years later, on June 12, 1995, leaders of the PQ, the federal Bloc Québécois, and the provincial Action Démocratique du Québec signed an agreement on how Quebec would assume independence, what would be contained in a treaty between Canada and Quebec, and the joint institutions that the two would share. The agreement stated that after a Yes victory in a provincial referendum, the provincial government would propose to Canada a treaty on a new economic and political partnership (Government of Canada, 2000). If negotiations succeeded, the treaty would provide for a customs union, shared monetary policy, Quebec citizenship, and the mobility of people, capital, and services. If negotiations failed, the stalemate would empower the National Assembly to declare sovereignty.

In September 1995, the government of Quebec publicized the wording of the referendum question: "Do you agree that Québec should become sovereign, after having made a formal offer to Canada for a new Economic and Political Partnership, within the scope of the Bill respecting the future of Québec and of the agreement signed on June 12, 1995?" Ninety-four percent of eligible voters turned out to vote, and they narrowly defeated the proposal by a 50.6 percent to 49.4 percent margin. However, Quebec's PQ Premier Jacques Parizeau declared that the separatists had not really lost because more than 60 percent of francophones had voted for independence. To the consternation of many, he added that the sovereignist forces had been defeated by money and the ethnic vote, raising the spectre that Quebec nationalism was not civic in character.

In the wake of the second referendum, many of the sovereignist movement's more charismatic leaders abandoned politics. The 2003 provincial election then returned the Liberals to power, meaning that debates about independence no longer dominated Quebec politics. Nevertheless, it would be a mistake to underestimate the appeal of minority nationalism. The separatist Bloc Québécois, which elected 49 Members of Parliament in the 2008 federal election, still commands considerable support in the province. As the controversy that broke out in early 2009 over the mock restaging of the Battle of the Plains of Abraham shows, sensitivities about historic conflicts are as real in the twenty-first century as they were centuries ago (see Box 4-1, The Plains of Abraham, Round 2)

Canada's Response to Claims for Self-Government and Sovereignty

During the 1980 Quebec referendum campaign, Prime Minister Pierre Trudeau promised that his government would begin the process of renewing the federal system if Quebec voted no to the sovereignty-association proposal. As discussed in Chapter 10, the federal government and nine provinces reached an agreement in 1981 on constitutional reform that would become the *Constitution Act,* 1982. The act included formal procedures for amending

BOX 4-1

The Plains of Abraham, Round 2

In February 2009, the National Battlefields Commission cancelled a planned re-enactment of the 1759 Battle of the Plains of Abraham in Quebec City. It was to have been the final chapter in a series of mock battles that have been staged in Canada and the United States since 2004 to mark the North American portion of the Seven Years War. Nationalist groups in Quebec criticized what they consider a celebration of the British conquest of their ancestors for the entertainment of tourists. Some sovereignist groups threatened to disrupt an event that would have involved 2000 costumed participants and was expected to draw more than 100 000 tourists.

Defenders of the plan argued that re-enactments are about honouring the people who were there, not about glorifying the triumph of one group over another. One of the members of the British militia unit commented that Southerners and Northerners in the United States have re-enacted the bloody Battle of Gettysburg and "when it's all over they sit down, have a few drinks and have a good time" (Perreaux, 2009). However, the American South no longer harbours serious plans to secede from the North, whereas the partnership between French and English Canada remains an uneasy one.

The flare-up over the restaging of a seminal event in Canadian history highlights the longevity of nationalist sensitivities on both sides. How would you have handled this controversy? Was it a good idea to use public funds to restage the British Conquest of New France? Should the event have been allowed to go on as planned? Did the proposed re-enactment revive the sovereignty movement in Quebec to any significant degree?

the constitution and a *Charter of Rights and Freedoms,* but did little to satisfy the requests for change that Quebec governments, both federalist and separatist, had presented since the Quiet Revolution. Specifically, the PQ government of René Lévesque refused to sign the 1981 agreement on the grounds that it failed to meet the following conditions:

- It did not recognize the character of Quebec as a distinct society.
- It restricted the provinces' exclusive rights in linguistic matters.
- The amending formula removed what Quebec considered its traditional veto over constitutional changes.
- The amending formula did not guarantee financial compensation for provinces that chose not to participate in a transfer of provincial legislative power to the Canadian Parliament other than on matters related to education and culture.

Despite Quebec's refusal to sign the 1981 agreement, the *Constitution Act, 1982,* applies to the province. Subsequently, the prime minister and all provincial leaders reached agreements on constitutional changes—the Meech Lake Accord, 1987, and the Charlottetown Accord, 1992—that included recognition of Quebec as a distinct society. However, as discussed in Chapter 10, both accords failed to be approved, ending efforts to achieve comprehensive constitutional reform.

FEDERAL PLANS A AND B   The razor-thin victory for the federalist side in Quebec's 1995 sovereignty referendum led the federal government to develop two strategies to defuse Quebec nationalism. The first approach, dubbed "Plan A," was designed to convince Quebecers about the benefits of staying in Canada. It consisted of non-constitutional initiatives that responded to some of Quebec's traditional demands. In 1996, the House of Commons passed a resolution recognizing the distinct character of Quebec's unique culture, civil law tradition, and French-speaking majority in the province. The 1996 *Constitutional Amendments Act* gave Quebec a form of veto over future constitutional changes. This law affirmed that any changes approved by Parliament would require consent from Ontario, Quebec, and British Columbia, as well as two of the four Atlantic provinces and two of the Prairie provinces. However, since it is an act of Parliament and not a constitutional amendment, it can be revoked by Parliament without the approval of Quebec.

Intergovernmental agreements that decentralized powers to the provinces were also part of the federal government's strategy following the Quebec referendum (Russell, 2006). Beginning in 1996, more powers over forestry, mining, recreation, tourism, social housing, and labour market training were devolved to the provinces. The 1999 Social Union Framework Agreement (SUFA), discussed in Chapter 13, placed some limitations on the use of federal government powers. Although agreed to by the federal government and the other provincial and territorial governments, the Quebec government did not sign SUFA because it did not go far enough in restricting federal spending in areas of provincial jurisdiction.

The second thrust of Ottawa's post-referendum strategy, dubbed "Plan B," was aimed at clarifying the terms for secession in order to make it very difficult for future referendums on Quebec's sovereignty to succeed. In April 1996, the federal government sought a ruling from the Supreme Court on three questions:

- Under the Constitution of Canada, can the National Assembly, legislature, or government of Quebec effect the secession of Quebec from Canada unilaterally?
- Does international law give the National Assembly, legislature, or government of Quebec the right to effect the secession of Quebec unilaterally? Is there a right to self-determination under international law that would give the National Assembly, legislature, or government of Quebec the right to effect the secession of Quebec from Canada unilaterally?
- In the event of a conflict between domestic and international law, which would take precedence?

The Court ruled in 1998 (*Secession Reference*, 1998) that while Quebec did not enjoy a right under international or domestic law to unilateral secession, the federal government would be obligated to negotiate with Quebec if a clear majority of Quebecers responded to a clear question that they no longer wished to remain in Canada.

In response to the ruling, in 2000 Parliament passed the *Clarity Act,* proposed by the Liberal government of Jean Chrétien. The *Clarity Act* sets out the rules by which the government and Parliament would react to future referendums. It states that the government will not negotiate the terms of separation with a province unless the House of Commons has determined that the question is clear and that a clear expression of will has been obtained by a clear majority of the population. Negotiations would have to include the division of assets and liabilities, changes to the borders of the province, the "rights, interests and claims" of Aboriginals, and the protection of minority rights. Finally, a constitutional amendment approved by all provincial governments would have to be passed before separation could occur. This would, undoubtedly, make it extremely difficult for a province to separate from Canada. The Quebec government retaliated with its own act respecting the exercise of the fundamental rights and prerogatives of the Québec people and the Québec state. It states that "the Québec people has the inalienable right to freely decide the political regime and legal status of Québec," and that a simple majority of 50 percent plus one of the valid votes cast in a referendum counts as an expression of the people's will (Statutes of Quebec, 2000, ch. 46).

Since 2006, the Conservative government of Stephen Harper has also pursued non-constitutional measures in a bid to temper support for Quebec independence. These have included allowing Quebec to take a formal role at the United Nations Educational, Scientific and Cultural Organization (UNESCO), and persuading the House of Commons to support a motion recognizing "that the Québécois form a nation within a united Canada." Supporters of the motion argued that it would help defuse Quebec nationalism by recognizing that Quebec is a distinct sociological nation within the united civic nation of Canada. Others worried that the recognition of nationhood might legitimize future claims for sovereignty.

SUPPORT FOR INDEPENDENCE   Public opinion polls over the past several decades have rarely found that a clear majority of Quebecers support independence.[5] Instead, many Quebecers support increased powers for their provincial government while remaining within Canada. For example, in June 2009, an online poll of Quebecers found that 32 percent felt that Quebec had enough sovereignty and should remain a part of Canada, 30 percent felt Quebec needed greater sovereignty but should remain a part of Canada, while 28 percent felt that Quebec should be a separate, independent country (Angus Reid Strategies, 2009).

---

[5]Support for independence peaked at 70 percent in 1990 after the defeat of the Meech Lake Accord.

POLYETHNICITY AND THE CANADIAN STATE

Wave after wave of immigration has made Canada a polyethnic state that is home to hundreds of ethnic groups with different cultural traditions and practices. Contemporary immigrants are overwhelmingly attracted to Canadian cities, where 95 percent of the country's foreign-born population has settled. The urban character of Canadian immigration extends beyond Toronto, Montreal, and Vancouver, as large numbers of immigrants and their families have settled in Edmonton, Calgary, Winnipeg, Ottawa, and Halifax. More and more newcomers are also immigrating to smaller urban centres such as Abbotsford, Saskatoon, Sherbrooke, and Moncton. Communities that were until recently unilingual and culturally homogeneous now see Chinese, Pakistanis, South Africans, Jamaicans, and many others living and working side by side.

How has Canada responded to the challenge of admitting and integrating newcomers from around the world into a new homeland? The following discussion of immigration and citizenship legislation, and the country's approach to helping immigrants adapt after their arrival, shows there have been significant shifts in official views about the desirability of cultural diversity. It also demonstrates that Canada's multicultural model of integrating immigrants into the broader political community expresses support for cultural pluralism, within a constitutional and legislative framework that grants rights and protections primarily to individuals. Some group-based polyethnic rights are guaranteed in certain laws and policies. The most significant laws and policies that support the multicultural model of integration—the shift from an assimilationist to a multicultural integration model in 1971, the *Human Rights Act* (1977), the *Canadian Charter of Rights and Freedoms* (1982), the *Multiculturalism Act* (1988), and the *Employment Equity Act* (1995)—are discussed below.

Immigration

From Confederation until the 1960s, Canada's immigration policy was not designed to change the primarily white, European character of the population. Until the early twentieth century, Asian immigrants were imported as cheap labour for the railways, mines, and forest industries of Western Canada (Li, 1998). Between 1880 and 1884, when the transcontinental Canadian Pacific Railway was being constructed, Chinese labourers were recruited to work on the most dangerous and worst-paid jobs. Once the railway was completed, the federal government tried to discourage the labourers from settling permanently in Canada. It passed the *Chinese Immigration Act, 1885*, which introduced the "head tax" system through which Chinese admission to Canada was made more expensive. The 1923 *Chinese Exclusion Act* later banned all but a trickle of Chinese immigration.

In the early twentieth century, the Liberal government of Prime Minister Wilfrid Laurier (1896–1911) embarked upon a plan to recruit Eastern Europeans to populate and develop the agricultural potential of the Prairie provinces. Clifford Sifton, the minister of the Interior, described the Eastern European, "a stalwart peasant in a sheepskin coat . . . with a stout wife and a half dozen children," as the ideal immigrant (quoted in Knowles, 1992). In the same era, the government put measures in place to discourage Black Americans and South Asians from entering Canada. During the two world wars and the Depression era, immigration to Canada was greatly reduced in response to these crises. Following the end of the Second World War, an economic boom favoured the opening up of Canadian immigration policy. In 1947, Prime Minister Mackenzie King stated that the government would encourage population growth through immigration, but that immigration was not to change the fundamental demographic character of the community—an aspiration far removed from today's policy of promoting diversity. The 1952 *Immigration Act* continued to give preferential status to immigrants from Western European and some Commonwealth countries. The act empowered the Cabinet to limit the admission of people on the basis of their

- nationality, citizenship, ethnic group, occupation, class or geographical area of origin,
- peculiar customs, habits, modes of life . . . unsuitability having regard to the climatic, economic, social industrial, educational, labour, health or other conditions existing . . . in Canada . . . or
- probable inability to become readily assimilated or to assume the duties and responsibilities of Canadian citizenship. (Kelley & Trebilcock, 1998, p. 324)

Several developments led to a more open and inclusive immigrant selection system in the 1960s. These included the country's postwar participation in international organizations and agreements committed to the protection of human rights, the need for labour in a rapidly expanding economy, and a decline in applications from traditional regions as European economies recovered from wartime upheaval. In 1962, the Progressive Conservative government of John Diefenbaker issued new regulations that eliminated the provisions for preferred countries for **independent immigrants,** or people with specific occupational skills, experience, and personal qualifications who are selected on the basis of criteria that assess their ability to adapt and to contribute to the country. For the first time in the history of Canada's immigration policy, the admission criteria would be based solely on factors such as education, work experience, and other skills, rather than on a candidate's race or nationality. In 1967, a new points system for independent immigrants was adopted. The points system assigned no weight to country of origin, but rather assessed prospective immigrants on their occupational experience and

INDEPENDENT IMMIGRANTS
People with specific occupational skills, experience, and personal qualifications who are selected on the basis of criteria that assess their ability to adapt and to contribute to the country.

training, educational background, knowledge of the official languages, and related criteria.

The 2002 *Immigration and Refugee Protection Act* amended the points system to give more weight to formal education and knowledge of English or French. Additional changes made to the immigration process in 2008 have given the immigration minister powers to identify which occupations deserve precedence in the selection of skilled workers for admission to Canada. The minister can also personally decide who should be selected or rejected. Critics say these changes inflate the power of the minister, could exclude worthy candidates, or could assign a lower priority to applications from sponsored family members and **refugees**. Refugees are people living in or outside Canada who fear persecution in their home country or whose removal from Canada to their country of origin would subject them to torture, a risk to their life, or a risk of cruel and unusual treatment (Citizenship and Immigration Canada, 2008).

Immigration can be a divisive issue and is especially so in many European countries with long traditions of cultural and linguistic uniformity. In Canada, public opinion about ideal levels of immigration varies between surveys and can be affected by the response options that are provided and by the timing of the survey. For example, it is widely believed that prevailing economic conditions and significant news events have shaped opinions about immigration. In general, polls conducted between 1998 and 2007 that asked respondents whether they felt there were too many, too few, or about the right number of immigrants coming to Canada indicate a greater acceptance of immigrants (Figure 4-5).

REFUGEES

People living in or outside Canada who fear persecution in their home country or whose removal from Canada to their country of origin would subject them to torture, a risk to their life, or a risk of cruel and unusual treatment.

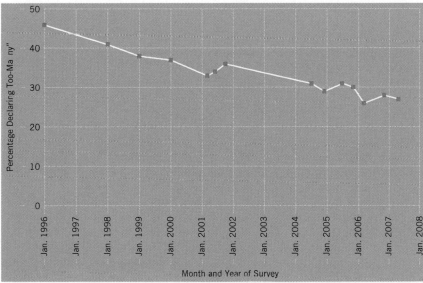

FIGURE 4-5
ATTITUDES TOWARD IMMIGRATION LEVELS, 1998–2007*

*Question: In your opinion, do you feel that there are too many, too few, or about the right number of immigrants coming to Canada?

Source: Jack Jedwab, 2008, "Receiving and Giving: How Does the Canadian Public Feel about Immigration and Integration?" in J. Biles, M. Burstein, and J. Frideres (Eds.), *Immigration and Integration in Canada in the Twenty-first Century* (211–230), Montreal, QC, and Kingston, ON: McGill-Queen's University Press.

Citizenship

Canadian citizenship means having legal status, sharing equally in the rights and responsibilities that belong to each Canadian, and taking an active part in Canadian society. Citizens possess important rights that are not enjoyed by **permanent residents**, such as the right to vote and to run for political office in federal and provincial elections, the right to hold certain public offices, and the right to hold a Canadian passport. Canada's current citizenship laws embody the principles of diversity and equality. Citizenship is relatively open and accessible to people from different national origins, and all citizens have equal rights and responsibilities.

Permanent residents must live in the country for at least three of the four years before their application for Canadian citizenship. Applicants must be at least eighteen and parents may apply on behalf of their minor children. They must also be able to speak English or French and demonstrate knowledge of Canada and the rights and responsibilities of citizenship. This knowledge is evaluated in a written test or oral interview with a citizenship judge. People over fifty-five years of age are exempt from the language and knowledge requirements, and minors are exempt from the residency, language, or knowledge requirements. People may be denied citizenship if they were charged or convicted of certain crimes. The final step in becoming a citizen is to take the oath of citizenship at a ceremony where a citizenship judge administers the oath and presents each new Canadian with a Certificate of Canadian Citizenship (Garcea, 2003).

Canadian citizenship is a surprisingly recent phenomenon. Prior to 1947 and the introduction of the first *Citizenship Act,* there was legally no such thing as Canadian citizenship. Both native-born and naturalized citizens were

PERMANENT RESIDENTS
Immigrants who are allowed to live in Canada and receive certain rights and privileges, while remaining a citizen of their home country. Permanent residents must pay taxes and respect all Canadian laws.

▶ At a citizenship ceremony, people are welcomed into the Canadian family and accept the rights and responsibilities of Canadian citizenship.

The Dual Citizenship Dilemma

At Confederation, Members of Parliament came mostly from Ireland, England, and Scotland, with a few from the United States and France. More than a century later, the seats are being filled with people born in Uganda, India, and China, among many other countries. Many of these elected representatives are eligible for dual citizenship and a second passport.

The practice of dual citizenship was called into question when former Liberal leader Stéphane Dion said he would keep his French citizenship, which he automatically acquired because his mother was born in France. Some pundits criticized his decision to retain dual citizenship, claiming that the leader would be unduly influenced by a foreign country. Dion refused to renounce his French citizenship, responding that he was proud of his heritage and loyal to Canada. A similar debate arose in 2005 over the dual citizenship status of Governor General–designate Michaëlle Jean. As she prepared to take up her post, Jean renounced her French citizenship, which she acquired when she married her French-born husband. Jean said at the time that it would have felt "kind of strange" to remain a French national, given the duties she would be assuming, including the title of commander-in-chief of the Canadian Forces.

What is your opinion about dual citizenship? Does it represent Canada's cultural diversity or a conflict of interest? Should the same rules governing dual citizenship apply to political and military leaders as to ordinary citizens?

British subjects. In 1977, the current *Citizenship Act* came into force. An important change allowed Canadians to take on citizenship in another country without automatically losing their Canadian citizenship. Thus, the current act makes it possible to hold two or more citizenships at the same time, for an indefinite period.

The practice of dual citizenship came to the fore in a public debate when Israel launched retaliatory air strikes on Hezbollah militants based in Lebanon in 2006. The Canadian government evacuated an estimated 14 000 Canadian citizens who had been visiting or residing in Lebanon from the conflict zone (Standing Senate Committee on Foreign Affairs and International Trade, 2007). Some commentators wondered whether the Canadian government should help citizens who had not lived in Canada for years. Others questioned whether allegiance to more than one country is genuinely possible. Former Liberal leader Stéphane Dion and Governor General Michaëlle Jean both had their loyalty to Canada questioned when it was revealed that they held dual citizenship (see Box 4-2, The Dual Citizenship Dilemma).

Immigrant Integration

Since the 1970s, governments have grappled with the major issue of how to integrate immigrants into Canadian society (Frideres, 2008). The concept of **integration** can be understood as both an outcome and process. Integration may

INTEGRATION
The multidimensional process through which an immigrant becomes a member of the host society.

imply a desirable result that is reflected in low levels of conflict between native-born and immigrant Canadians based on mutual respect and understanding between these groups (Ruspini, 2005). Integration can also describe the process through which an immigrant becomes a member of the host society. Moreover, within these two broad definitions, there are different types of integration. For example, social integration describes the participation of immigrants in Canadian institutions. Cultural integration describes the processes of learning about the host culture, its values and norms (Heckmann, 1997). Economic integration refers to the process of finding a job and earning an income that matches one's educational and experiential background. Political integration refers to participation in electoral processes and other forms of political engagement.

Until 1971, Canada generally encouraged immigrants to assimilate into the dominant, usually anglophone, culture. Since Canada adopted a policy of official multiculturalism (discussed later in this chapter), recognizing cultural diversity has become a cornerstone of the Canadian identity and the model for integrating members of cultural groups into the political community.

Until the mid-twentieth century, immigrants to Canada were considered responsible for their own integration. Today, prospective immigrants and newcomers benefit from settlement and integration programs and services before and after their arrival in Canada. Three main programs provide the foundation for the federal government's settlement and integration services (Winnemore & Biles, 2006). The Immigrant Settlement and Adaptation Program (ISAP) provides funding for the following:

- translation, interpretation, and job search services;
- pre- and post-arrival orientation sessions;
- settlement support in schools for teachers, immigrant children, and their parents;
- Enhanced Language Training that provides more advanced language training in English or French; and
- mentoring, work placement, and other help for immigrants to find employment.

Second is the volunteer-based Host program, which matches newcomers with a Canadian host who will help orient them to their new community, help them practise new language skills, and introduce them to other Canadians. Third, the Language Instruction for Newcomers Program (LINC) funds language instruction and assessment for adult newcomers in English or French. Also, through the educational system, provincial governments offer English as a Second Language (ESL) programs for newcomer children.

Immigration presents economic, demographic, and cultural development opportunities for countries, but it also challenges their capacity to come up with the best mix of programs and services that will help newcomers adjust to a new homeland. Despite the programs discussed above, injustices persist in Canadian society. For example, members of certain visible minority groups feel that they are more likely to be the target of discriminatory or unfair treatment than white Canadians. According to a Statistics Canada survey, 32 percent of Black Canadians report that they have been discriminated against or treated unfairly by others because of their ethnocultural characteristics, compared with 21 percent of South Asians and 18 percent of Chinese Canadians (Government of Canada, 2003). A related tension that surfaces frequently in public discourse is the question of racial profiling used by police and security agencies. Studies have shown that members of the Black community are both subject to greater police surveillance and more likely to get caught when they do break the law (Wortley & Tanner, 2004). Muslim Canadians also feel they are often subject to tighter-than-justified security surveillance (Kahn & Saloojee, 2003).

The economic integration of newcomers is another source of strain. Critics argue that Canada needs to do more to inform newcomers about labour market conditions and society before people make the decision to migrate. Questions arise, too, about the emphasis that the points system places on selecting immigrants with high levels of formal education and language skills. Supporters of the points system argue that it offers a more objective and non-discriminatory method of selecting potential citizens and ensures that Canada has a highly educated and skilled labour pool. Critics feel that the new system favours wealthier immigrants who can pay for education and training. Others are increasingly concerned about the emphasis on selecting highly educated and skilled immigrants, only to see many of them underemployed in low-wage jobs following their arrival because their foreign education credentials and work experiences are not recognized (Grant & Sweetman, 2004; Picot & Hou, 2003).

"REASONABLE ACCOMMODATION"   Conflicts between established members of a community and newcomers are not uncommon in polyethnic societies. They have occurred in federal politics (see Box 4-3, Veiled Voters) and they occur in the provinces and local communities. Recent debates in Quebec about how to accommodate the requests of cultural and religious minorities for differential treatment illustrate how easily these tensions may be ignited. Beginning in 2006, sometimes incendiary or exaggerated media reports of "excessive" accommodations prompted calls from the public for a tougher approach to immigrants and minorities. Part of the population felt that some minority group practices threatened Quebec's core values. In response to perceptions of a growing crisis, Premier Jean Charest appointed the Bouchard-Taylor Commission in 2007 to examine accommodation practices in Quebec and other societies, to conduct public consultations, and to recommend accommodation practices that conformed to Quebec's values.

The commission examined several controversies that had arisen over the place of religion in public space and the accommodation of minority religious practices. In September 1994, a Quebec student who had converted to Islam was expelled from school because she wore a head scarf, thus violating a dress code that prohibited all head coverings. In February 1995, her behaviour was

BOX 4-3

Veiled Voters

In 2007, the Conservative government and Elections Canada, an independent electoral agency, became embroiled in a debate over the issue of forcing veiled women to show their faces if they want to vote in federal elections. Prime Minister Harper lambasted Elections Canada after it refused to require veiled voters in three federal by-elections in Quebec to show their faces at polling stations. Just a few months earlier, the House of Commons had adopted legislation that voters be required to prove their identity and residential address before being given a ballot.

Chief Electoral Officer Marc Mayrand responded that the law passed by Parliament did not require women voters wearing veils to take them off to be identified, and that a fresh vote by Parliament would be needed to change those procedures. Voters had several means of identifying themselves:

They could either provide a government-issued photo identification that included the voter's photo, name, and address, or two pieces of identification containing the voter's name, with one of them containing the residential address; or they could be vouched for by another voter whose name is on the voters' list at the same polling station. Mayrand also noted that people who vote by mail are not called upon to provide visual proof of their identity.

In June 2009, the Conservative government quietly announced that it did not intend to proceed with proposed legislation requiring veiled voters to uncover their faces.

How do you think Canada should deal with the question of veiled voters? Should all Canadians, regardless of their cultural background or religious beliefs, be required to provide visual proof of their identity?

---

vindicated when the *Commission des droits de la personne et des droits de la jeunesse* handed down an opinion that approved the wearing of the head scarf in public schools. In March 2006, a spat broke out between members of a Montreal YMCA and leaders of a neighbouring Hasidic Jewish congregation. The trigger was the YMCA management's decision to install frosted glass windows in place of the regular glass in the windows of its exercise room. The congregation had requested and paid for the new windows because it was concerned that its younger male members were able to view "scantily clad" women exercising. After members of the YMCA complained about the frosted glass, the YMCA replaced it with regular glass and equipped the windows with blinds.

The Bouchard-Taylor Commission concluded that Quebec society had made significant strides in accommodating cultural diversity, and that there was no indication of a crisis in public institutions. Nevertheless, it noted the need for improved intercultural understanding and pointed out the existence of xenophobic and even racist sentiments against Muslims and Jews. It made recommendations for providing cultural sensitivity training for journalists and the staff of all public institutions, encouraging state and partly state-controlled institutions to adopt policies on accommodating cultural and religious diversity, adding an interpretive clause to the Quebec Charter establishing gender equality as a core value of Quebec society, and reinforcing the principle of state neutrality and the separation of church and state. In late 2008, the Quebec government announced that all new immigrants to the province must sign a pledge to "respect the common values of Québécois society." These include gender equality, the rule of law, and the separation of church and state.

MULTICULTURALISM   In 1971, Canada became the first country in the world to adopt a policy of official multiculturalism. The policy marked a new approach to nation-building that encouraged individuals to embrace the culture and tradition of their choice while retaining Canadian citizenship. The landmark policy was introduced in response to the recommendation from the Royal Commission on Bilingualism and Biculturalism that Canada adopt an official policy of multiculturalism and multilingualism as a means of integrating immigrants into Canadian society. Prime Minister Trudeau instead chose to promote a policy of multiculturalism within a bilingual framework. The main objectives of the policy were to

- assist cultural groups to retain and foster their identity;
- assist members of all cultural groups to overcome cultural barriers to their full participation in Canadian society;
- promote creative exchanges among all Canadian cultural groups; and
- assist immigrants in learning at least one of Canada's official languages.

The government followed through by providing financial grants to ethnic and immigrant organizations, funding ethnic studies programs at universities, official language training, and initiatives to help ethnic minorities in the areas of human rights, racial discrimination, citizenship, and cross-cultural understanding (Mahtani, 2002). Until 1990, the federal government also provided modest support to ethnocultural organizations to offer **heritage language** instruction in German, Italian, Ukrainian, and other languages. The policy gained further momentum after ethnic groups successfully lobbied for the inclusion of a clause in the *Charter of Rights and Freedoms* (section 27) recognizing Canada's multicultural heritage. In 1988, the Conservative government passed the *Multiculturalism Act,* which included the objectives of assisting in the preservation of culture and language, reducing discrimination, enhancing cultural awareness and understanding, and promoting culturally sensitive institutional change at the federal level.

Funding for multicultural programs was cut back in the 1990s as part of the government's overall debt and deficit reduction strategy—and in response to criticisms that the existing program was undermining the development of immigrant attachments to Canada. Beginning in the 1990s, the program's focus shifted to removing discriminatory barriers for the growing number of visible minority immigrants whose main concerns were finding employment, housing, and education, and fighting discrimination (Dewing & Leman, 2006). New program objectives place more emphasis on promoting what the

HERITAGE LANGUAGE
All languages other than the Aboriginal languages of the First Nations and Inuit peoples and the official languages of English and French.

government refers to as Canadian values: democracy, freedom, human rights, and rule of law (Citizenship and Immigration Canada, 2009).

Since the adoption of multiculturalism, Canadians have debated its impact on the integration of immigrants and their children. Supporters have argued that multiculturalism helps newcomers feel more welcome, leading to a stronger sense of belonging in Canada. Critics have countered that it has weakened national identity and could lead to the possible infringement of human rights, and in particular, women's rights (Jedwab, 2005). In his book *Selling Illusions: The Cult of Multiculturalism in Canada*, Trinidad-born novelist Neil Bissoondath (1994) argued that the government's policy of encouraging ethnic differences encouraged immigrants to isolate themselves in distinct enclaves and away from "mainstream" culture. Quebecers have also expressed uneasiness about federal multiculturalism policy since its beginnings. Many have viewed multiculturalism as an attempt to dilute the French fact in Canada and to weaken the status of francophones.

Various publications and polls suggest that Canadians generally support a multicultural society, at least in principle. In fact, a growing body of research suggests that the process of immigrant and minority integration is working better in Canada than in other countries and that multiculturalism policy has played a role in this success (Kymlicka, 2009). Immigrants and minorities express high levels of pride in Canada and praise the country's freedom, democracy, and multiculturalism (Adams, 2007). Immigrants to Canada and visible and religious minorities also fare better than most, if not all, foreign-born populations in other Western democracies. For example, the children of immigrants have better educational outcomes in Canada than in other countries (OECD, 2006 cited in Kymlicka, 2009) and earn more than other Canadians (Corak, 2008). Canadian neighbourhoods with a high concentration of immigrants are not characterized by the same levels of poverty and social isolation that can be found in the "ghettos" of major American or European cities (Hiebert, Schuurman, & Smith, 2007).

In terms of political integration, immigrants in Canada are much more likely to become citizens than are immigrants in other Western democracies (Bloemraad, 2006). Furthermore, more foreign-born citizens are elected to Parliament than in any other country (Adams, 2007). Political parties run minority candidates in competitive ridings, and once they are nominated, there is no evidence that voters discriminate against these candidates, although minorities are still under-represented in the House of Commons (Black & Erikson, 2006; Tossutti & Najem, 2002). Compared with other countries, Canada has been less affected by the global surge in anti-Muslim sentiments. According to a survey conducted in 2006, 83 percent of Canadians agree that Muslims make a positive contribution to Canada (Focus Canada, 2006).

In March 2009, the minister of Citizenship and Immigration announced that the Conservative government would like to move the country away from a multicultural model of integration that encourages newcomers to retain their ethnic ancestral identities (Martin, 2009). If the government adopts this approach, it will signal a major shift in self-perceptions of the Canadian identity and how others in the world see us.

Protection of Minorities under the Law

HUMAN RIGHTS ACT   The *Human Rights Act, 1977,* is a key piece of federal legislation that supports multiculturalism by granting rights to individuals. It prohibits discriminatory practices against individuals based on their race, national or ethnic origin, colour, religion, age, sex, sexual orientation, marital status, family status, disability, or conviction for an offence for which a pardon has been granted. The law applies to the employment, business, and service delivery practices of the federal government and federally regulated industries such as the airlines, banks, television and radio stations, inter-provincial communications, telephone and transportation companies, and First Nations. Throughout the 1960s and 1970s, the provinces also put in place human rights codes or charters to protect individuals from various forms of discrimination by a business, non-business organization, government department, public agency or institution (e.g., school board), or individual.

EMPLOYMENT EQUITY   The origins of employment equity legislation can be traced to the establishment of the Royal Commission on the Status of Women in 1967, which challenged the federal government to tackle the under-representation of women in the public service. In 1983, the Royal Commission on Equality in Employment (the Abella Commission) called for legislated employment equity to provide employment opportunities not just for women, but also for visible minorities, people with disabilities, and Aboriginal people. This led to the passage of the first *Employment Equity Act* in 1986.

The 1995 *Employment Equity Act,* which still applies today, aims to achieve equality in the workforce so that no one is denied employment opportunities for reasons that are not linked to ability. It covers several types of employers: the federal public service; federally regulated employers in the private sector and Crown corporations with more than 100 employees; other public sector employers with 100 or more employees (e.g., Canadian Forces, Royal Canadian Mounted Police, Canada Revenue Agency); and large organizations that bid on or receive substantial contracts to supply goods and services to the federal government. The act's principal goal is to correct the disadvantage in employment experienced by women, Aboriginal peoples, people with disabilities, and members of visible minorities. Employment equity requires employers to eliminate employment barriers against people in designated groups and to institute policies to ensure that people in the designated groups achieve a degree of representation in the employer's workforce that reflects their representation in the Canadian workforce. Employment equity does not require that the employer hire or promote people who are not qualified for the work (Department of Justice, 2009).

Employers have to produce an employment equity plan, including goals and a timetable, as well as progress reports detailing the measures they have undertaken to improve the workforce representation of the four designated groups. The reports are forwarded to the Canadian Human Rights Commission and a fine can be imposed on employers for failure to file. The commission tracks progress in the private and public sectors in the representation of the four designated groups. In 2007–2008, visible minorities were underrepresented in the public service (9.2 percent), compared to their share of the Canadian workforce in 2001 (10.4 percent). They fared better in the private sector banking and communications organizations covered by the act, where their representation in 2007 exceeded their share of the workforce in 2001 (Canadian Human Rights Commission, 2009).

THE CHARTER OF RIGHTS AND FREEDOMS, 1982   The *Charter of Rights and Freedoms* supports Canada's multicultural model of integration by granting rights to individuals and groups. As discussed in Chapter 12, Section 15 of the Charter guarantees individual equality while allowing for affirmative action to assist individuals and groups that have been disadvantaged because of their characteristics. In addition, the Charter's recognition of Canada's multicultural heritage has been used by the Supreme Court to uphold legislation aimed at preventing the expression of hatred against religious and racial minorities.

Summary and Conclusion

Canada has never been an ethnic nation made up of people from a single linguistic or cultural group, and this trend will continue as international migration and intercultural relationships expand the country's longstanding cultural diversity. In general, Canada is best described as a civic nation based on a common territory, a community of laws and institutions, and the legal equality of its members. Canadians attach different meanings to the Canadian identity and express multiple and often overlapping allegiances to other identities. For these and other reasons discussed in this chapter, characterizing the Canadian identity is an elusive endeavour. That may satisfy Canadians who are comfortable with ambivalence, while others will desire more clarity on the question.

The challenge of building a unified political community in a state that is home to a multinational and polyethnic population is closely tied to questions of democracy and good government. Each day, public officials must determine whether the principles of freedom and equality that underpin democratic values are best served by treating all citizens in the same way, regardless of their cultural background, or whether cultural minorities should enjoy special group rights so that they may fully participate in broader society. Their decisions reflect whether Canadians agree that good government includes the accommodation of the requirements of minorities.

Canada's response to fulfilling the lofty goals of democracy and good government in a multinational and polyethnic state has been to grant a combination of group-based and individual rights to national minorities and ethnic groups. Official attitudes about the desirability of cultural diversity have undergone fundamental shifts throughout Canadian history. The Canadian nation-building project has evolved from relying on racially exclusionary immigrant selection criteria and an assimilationist integration model to adopting more open immigration and citizenship policies, and a multicultural approach to admitting and accommodating newcomers. Right now, Canada is under strain as it struggles to respond to ever-growing diversity in a way that upholds liberal traditions. How Canadians resolve these tensions will be fascinating to behold, and will be watched closely both at home and abroad in other states facing similar challenges.

Discussion Questions

1. Is Canada a nation? If not, why not? If so, is it an ethnic or civic nation?

2. Are the Québécois an ethnic or civic nation?

3. Should Canada grant group-specific rights to national minorities and to ethnic groups? Why or why not?

4. Should Canada change its laws, institutions, or policies to accommodate the cultural and religious needs of ethnic groups? Why or why not?

5. Does multiculturalism strengthen or undermine the Canadian identity? Should Canada move away from a multicultural model of integration, as suggested by the minister of Citizenship and Immigration in March 2009?

Further Reading

Adams, M. (2007). *Unlikely Utopia: The surprising triumph of Canadian pluralism.* Toronto, ON: Penguin Group Canada.

Beheils, M. (Ed.). (2000). *Quebec since 1945: Selected readings.* Toronto, ON: Copp Clark Pitman.

Biles, J., Burstein, M., & Frideres, J. (Eds). (2008). *Immigration and integration in Canada in the twenty-first century* (Queen's Policy Series #52). Kingston, ON: McGill-Queen's University Press.

Gagnon, A., & Iacovino, R. (2007). *Federalism, citizenship and Quebec: Debating multinationalism.* Toronto, ON: University of Toronto Press.

Keating, M. (1996). *Nations against the state: The new politics of nationalism in Quebec, Catalonia and Scotland.* Basingstoke, UK: Macmillan.

Kelley, N., & Trebilcock, M. (1998). *The making of the mosaic: A history of Canadian immigration policy.* Toronto, ON: University of Toronto Press.

Kernerman, G. (2005). *Multicultural nationalism: Civilizing difference, constituting community.* Vancouver, BC: UBC Press.

McRoberts, K. (1997). *Misconceiving Canada: The struggle for national unity.* Toronto, ON: Oxford University Press.

Taylor, C. (1994). *Multiculturalism: Examining the politics of recognition.* Edited and introduced by Amy Gutmann. Princeton, NJ: Princeton University Press.

Young, R. (1999). *The struggle for Quebec.* Montreal. QC: McGill-Queen's University Press.

Chapter 5

POLITICAL CULTURE

PHOTO ABOVE: Tommy Douglas, the "father of medicare," in Ottawa in 1983. Chosen as the "Greatest Canadian" during a 2004 CBC contest, he was devoted to social causes that improved the lives of all Canadians.

After reading this chapter, you should be able to

1. Explain the meaning of political culture and how it is analyzed.
2. Discuss how founding fragments theory has been applied to understanding Canadian political culture.
3. Examine the usefulness of formative events theory in assessing the differences between the Canadian and American political cultures.
4. Explain post-materialist theory.
5. Discuss whether there is a single Canadian political culture.

In 2004, CBC Television held a contest to select the "Greatest Canadian." The response was tremendous as Canadians nominated thousands of individuals for this honour. The names of the top one hundred nominees were posted on a CBC website. Each week an advocate for one of the top ten nominees presented his or her nominee's case in an hour-long show. Finally, after over 1.2 million votes were cast through a website and by telephone, Tommy Douglas was declared the "Greatest Canadian"—beating out runners-up Terry Fox, Pierre Trudeau, Frederick Banting, David Suzuki, Lester B. Pearson, Don Cherry, Sir John A. Macdonald, Alexander Graham Bell, and Wayne Gretzky.

Just who was this man Canadians rated more highly than eminent inventors and hockey legends? As a young boy growing up in a family that could not afford proper medical care, Tommy Douglas would have lost his right leg as a result of osteomyelitis if not for the compassion of a visiting doctor who treated him for free. As premier of Saskatchewan from 1944 to 1961, Douglas fought tirelessly to bring free public medical care to the people of his province. Later, as leader of the New Democratic Party (NDP), he successfully persuaded the minority Liberal government of Lester B. Pearson to institute a national medicare system in 1966. Finally, in 1971, his lifelong campaign for free medical care for all residents of Canada was fully achieved.

As President Barack Obama faced a difficult battle in 2009 to gain support for efforts to provide health insurance coverage for the more than fifty million uninsured Americans, Canadians were astonished by criticisms of Canada's medicare system from opponents of Obama's reform proposals. Medicare has become a source of pride for most Canadians and is often referred to when Canadians describe their country as having superior values to those of the United States. Despite some problems with Canada's health care system (such as wait times for some treatments), most Canadians react negatively when basic changes to the system are suggested, such as allowing patients to pay for faster diagnosis and treatment in privately run clinics.

Do the contrasting health care systems in the United States and Canada indicate that the neighbouring countries have different political cultures based on different fundamental political values, beliefs, and orientations to politics? As is often the case in political analysis, there is no easy answer. Many Americans are unhappy with their health care system, although misleading portrayals of the Canadian system have created confusion about alternatives. In Canada, as well, many people were strongly opposed to the introduction of medicare in the 1960s; private insurance companies fought against the loss of their lucrative business and doctors in Saskatchewan went on a lengthy strike in protest against medicare. Furthermore, although medicare in Canada has become a "sacred trust" in which politicians of all political persuasions hasten to proclaim their belief, other elements of the Canadian welfare state (such as social assistance and employment insurance) have suffered from criticism and cutbacks.

Despite being voted the "Greatest Canadian," Tommy Douglas, as national leader of the NDP, did not succeed in gaining widespread electoral support, and he twice lost his seat in federal elections. However, his contribution to the well-being of Canadians won him enduring respect and admiration.

WHAT IS POLITICAL CULTURE?

POLITICAL CULTURE
The fundamental political values, beliefs, and orientations that are widely held within a political community.

The term **political culture** refers to the fundamental political values, beliefs, and orientations that are widely held within a political community.[1] Some analysts view political culture as a collective attribute of a political community (Stewart, 2002). Others focus on individual citizens by measuring the proportion of people in a country who hold particular political attitudes and orientations to political objects (Almond & Verba, 1963).

In Canada, medicare, the Peace Tower on Parliament Hill, the *Charter of Rights and Freedoms,* and the Mountie in uniform are all associated with a political culture. They are among the various symbols, myths, meanings attached to widely used terms, and interpretations of important events that help to shape **political discourse**—the ways in which politics is discussed and the rhetoric that is used in political persuasion. Political culture affects politics of a political community and the general kinds of policies that are adopted by setting some broad limits to the actions governments consider desirable and what the public is willing to accept. It helps to explain why similar political institutions (such as a parliamentary system of government) may operate in quite different ways in countries with different political cultures (Bell, 1992).

POLITICAL DISCOURSE
The ways in which politics is discussed and the rhetoric that is used in political persuasion.

Through a process called **political socialization**, new generations and immigrants are socialized into the political culture through the educational system; the media; exposure to the ideas of parents, friends, and associates; and various organizations such as religious institutions, political parties, community groups, and labour unions. A political culture usually evolves gradually as new circumstances or important events lead to changes in political thinking.

POLITICAL SOCIALIZATION
The process by which new generations and immigrants are socialized into the political culture.

Key to political culture are the dominant values of a society—for example, views concerning freedom, equality, order, security, justice, and prosperity. Such values serve as popular buzzwords and influence our thinking about politics, but which are most important and influential when different values conflict? For example, when faced with the possibility of terrorism, should we place more emphasis on maintaining everyone's civil liberties or take tough measures to protect our safety and security, even if those measures involve curbing individual rights and freedoms? As well, we have to be aware that certain terms, however popular, may be interpreted in different ways. For example, equality may represent a popular value, but its meanings are many and diverse: an equal sharing of wealth and income, ensuring that every individual has an equal opportunity to get ahead in life, protecting the equal legal rights of everyone, or creating equality among differing groups of people.

It is often assumed that each country has its own distinct political culture based on such factors as its historical political experiences, the characteristics of

---

[1]Political culture should be distinguished from the broader cultural characteristics of a society, such as the television and movies we watch, the music we listen to, the books we read, the food we eat, the sports we enjoy, and the ways in which we interact with other people.

its population, its economy, and its geographical characteristics. However, broad similarities often exist among different countries. Canada's political culture bears general similarities to that of other Western liberal democracies and, in particular, countries originally colonized by the United Kingdom (Inglehart, 2009). Furthermore, the political values, beliefs, and orientations of a particular country do not usually develop in a void, isolated from the political ideas of other countries. American political values, in particular, are often thought to have an important influence on Canadian thinking because of the close ties between the two countries and the tremendous influence of the American mass media.

The assumption that each country has its own political culture can also be questioned because genuine differences often exist within a single country. Different groups or areas of a country may hold contrasting—even clashing—values and beliefs. Most countries have **subcultures** that are variations on the national political culture. However in some countries, differences in basic values and beliefs among different groups or regions may be so large and fundamental that we cannot consider the country to have a single unified political culture.

SUBCULTURES
Variations on the national political culture.

ANALYZING POLITICAL CULTURE

There are two major approaches to analyzing political culture. The first involves examining a country's historical experiences, its constitution and governing institutions, the general policies that governments adopt, and the writings of its leading thinkers, political figures, and political observers. In Canada, then, analyzing the effects of the British conquest of New France, the Confederation debates, the operation of the parliamentary system, Macdonald's National Policy, or the writings of Margaret Atwood, John Ralston Saul, and Pierre Trudeau could reveal something about the country's political culture. Yet this approach has limitations—it may depict the political culture of the past rather than the present. For example, the Canadian constitution was written at a time when democratic values were not fully accepted, and thus Canada's governing institutions (particularly the Senate) do not reflect the democratic political values of contemporary Canada. There may be significant differences between the political values, beliefs, and orientations characteristic of those most deeply committed to political life and the political thinking of the general public. The public policies adopted by governments may tend to reflect the views of the more powerful and politically engaged elements of society. This does not mean, however, that all of those who are politically powerful necessarily share a common perspective. For example, substantial differences have been found among the attitudes of Members of Parliament representing different political parties, experienced lawyers (used as a proxy for the judicial elite), and top public officials (Sniderman, Fletcher, Russell, & Tetlock, 1996).

The second major approach to analyzing political culture involves the use of sample surveys of the public. Well-designed surveys can quite accurately capture the views of a population at a given moment, even though only one or two thousand people are normally sampled. However, it is not always clear whether the responses to surveys reveal the deeply held values of the population or fleeting and hasty opinions in response to a battery of questions. Public opinion on particular issues may reflect, to some extent, deeply held values and beliefs, but it may also yield no more than a temporary or knee-jerk reaction to current events.

THEORETICAL APPROACHES TO UNDERSTANDING POLITICAL CULTURE

POLITICAL IDEOLOGY
A set of ideas, values, and beliefs about politics, society, and the economic system based on assumptions about human nature.

LIBERALISM
An ideological perspective that emphasizes the value of individual freedom based on a belief that individuals are generally capable of using reason in pursuit of their own interests.

CONSERVATISM
An ideological perspective that generally looks to laws based on traditional (religious) moral values and established institutions to maintain an orderly society.

SOCIALISM
An ideological perspective that emphasizes the value of social and economic equality and generally advocates social ownership of the major means of production.

FOUNDING FRAGMENTS THEORY
The theory that in the founding of new societies, only a fragment of the political culture of the "mother country" formed the basis for the political culture of the new society.

A **political ideology** is a set of ideas, values, and beliefs about politics, society, and the economic system based on assumptions about human nature. Of particular importance in understanding the political culture of Canada and other Western democracies are the ideologies of **liberalism**, **conservatism**, and **socialism** (see Box 5-1, The Major Political Ideologies: Liberalism, Conservatism, and Socialism). Two major theoretical approaches to understanding Canadian political culture—founding fragments theory and formative events theory—focus on the historical development of ideological perspectives.

Founding Fragments Theory

American political scientist Louis Hartz (1955) pointed out that each of the major political ideologies became an important element of European political cultures. Liberalism developed to challenge the traditional conservative ideas often associated with the feudal era. Socialism provided a synthesis of liberal ideas about individual freedom and traditional conservative ideas about the collective good of society.

Hartz argued in his **founding fragments theory** that in the founding of new societies, such as Canada, the United States, and Australia, only a fragment of the "mother country" formed the basis for the political culture of the new society. The leading ideological perspective in the mother country at the time of colonization tended to become the dominant or sole ideology of the new society. In particular, Hartz characterized the United States as being a classical liberal fragment. Without a significant presence of traditional conservative ideas, the interaction of liberalism and conservatism that he viewed as necessary for the development of socialist ideas could not occur. Instead, ideological development would only take place within the framework of the liberal perspective. Indeed, Hartz claimed that classical liberal ideas had become the unthinking dogma of the United States, the basis for nationalistic views of American superiority, and that they had created a lack of tolerance for those daring to express different views.

As applied to Canada, Hartz's founding fragments theory suggests that the Canadian political culture should be analyzed in terms of two separate

BOX 5-1

The Major Political Ideologies: Liberalism, Conservatism, and Socialism

Liberalism, conservatism, and socialism represent the three major political ideologies that developed in Western societies. The brief descriptions that follow trace only the broad outlines of each ideology.

LIBERALISM

Liberalism emphasizes the value of individual freedom based on a belief that individuals are generally capable of using reason in pursuit of their own interests. Classical liberals in the eighteenth and nineteenth centuries challenged government restrictions on business activity, the privileged position of the aristocracy, and state support for established religions. Government, they argued, should be concerned only with protecting life, liberty, and property, leaving individuals otherwise free to pursue their own interests and follow their own beliefs as long as they do not seriously harm others.

CONSERVATISM

Conservatism holds a less positive view of individual capabilities, and thus places less emphasis on the rights and freedoms of individuals than liberalism. Instead it generally looks to laws based on traditional (religious) moral values and to established institutions to maintain an orderly society. Traditional conservatives typically view the elites of society as having a responsibility to maintain the civilized values of the community, and seek to avoid radical changes that could threaten the collective good of society.

SOCIALISM

Socialism places high value on social and economic equality. Believers in the idea that human beings are naturally social and cooperative, socialists are critical of what they view as the excessive competition associated with the capitalist system. In place of the inequality and exploitation of the capitalist system, socialists have traditionally looked to the establishment of some form of social ownership of the major means of production. In addition, to move toward equality of condition, socialists generally look to government to provide a wide variety of services freely to all and to reduce inequality by redistributing wealth and income.

Each of the ideological perspectives has evolved over time, and many variations exist. For example, many liberals now favour an active role for government in ensuring that all individuals have the means to develop their capabilities (a perspective often labelled "social welfare liberalism"). Neo-liberals (also known as economic liberals), in contrast, retain the classical liberal belief in economic freedom exemplified in the free market system, with minimal government involvement in the economy. Many contemporary conservatives (often referred to as "neo-conservatives") also tend to support the free market system and stress individual responsibility instead of welfare state programs. Nevertheless, many contemporary conservatives favour restrictions on individual freedom to fight crime and terrorism and to discourage what they perceive as immoral behaviour. Many socialists no longer advocate the creation of a socialist economic system. Instead, those who term themselves "social democrats" advocate reforms of the capitalist system that they believe will lead to the common good.

Furthermore, other ideologies, notably feminism and environmentalism, have provided important new perspectives on ending the subordination of women and tackling human exploitation of the natural environment.

"fragments"—French and English Canada.[2] French Canada was established in the seventeenth and eighteenth centuries when authoritarian conservative values still dominated in France, although questions have been raised about whether Quebec was ever really a "feudal fragment" (Forbes, 1987). English Canada was viewed by Hartz and Kenneth McRae (1964) as very similar to the United States in terms of being a classical liberal fragment. Yet Canada showed signs of a **"tory touch"** or "tory streak"—that is, an element of traditional conservatism that includes the defence of a hierarchical rule by a privileged elite on behalf of the collective good of the nation.

The depiction of the political culture of English Canada as very similar to that of the United States, each being a liberal fragment, has been controversial. The Loyalists who fled the American Revolution because of their ties to the British government and their opposition to American independence are often viewed as major founders of English Canada. Some consider the Loyalists to differ little from other Americans in sharing fundamentally liberal views. Indeed, many Americans came to Canada during and after the American Revolution to take advantage of economic benefits (such as free land), rather than because of their political views (Grabb & Curtis, 2005).

Other analysts, however, view the "tory touch" brought by the Loyalists (and others with British ancestry) as having an important impact on the development of the Canadian political culture. In particular, Gad Horowitz (1966) argues that socialist ideas have gained some acceptance in Canada (unlike the United States) because the idea that government should act for the welfare of society as a whole (an important aspect of socialist thought) has not been rejected as an "alien" perspective. The presence of some conservative ideas can be viewed as laying the foundation for some degree of acceptance of the socialist ideas that were brought to Canada by British immigrants (and Canadians studying in British universities). Canadian political culture, in this perspective, is more diverse than the American political culture. Liberalism is the leading ideology, but conservative and socialist ideas also contribute to the diversity of the political culture.

One problem with Horowitz's analysis is that socialist ideas found acceptance in those areas of the country where the "tory touch" is weak or nonexistent. Socialist ideas have played a more significant role in the political culture in parts of Western Canada than in Ontario and the Maritimes, where the Loyalist influence is most strongly felt (see Box 5-2, Saskatchewan and Alberta: Rival Ideologies). As well, it has been pointed out that the version of socialism that has gained popular support in Canada is not that different from what is sometimes labelled "social welfare liberalism"—the version of liberalism that is characteristic of the "left wing" of the Liberal party (Forbes, 1987).

TORY TOUCH
An element of traditional conservatism that includes the defence of a hierarchical rule by a privileged elite on behalf of the collective good of the nation.

---

[2]Hartz does take note of Aboriginal peoples, the original founders of Canada, but does not view them as significant in the development of Canadian political culture.

Saskatchewan and Alberta: Rival Ideologies

To an outside observer, Saskatchewan and Alberta flow one into the other. Driving across the Prairies, one would hardly notice the border between the two provinces. However, their political cultures have differed radically.

In 1944, the socialist Co-operative Commonwealth Federation (CCF) swept forty-seven of Saskatchewan's fifty-three seats. Saskatchewan had elected a socialist government—the first ever in Canada. Over the next twenty years the CCF government instituted free public hospital and health care, established many government-owned corporations, and promoted the idea of a constitutional bill of rights. The New Democratic Party (NDP), the successor to the CCF, has continued to rank as a major player in Saskatchewan politics.

In neighbouring Alberta, the Progressive Conservative party has dominated politics since it was first elected in 1971, and prior to 1971, a fundamentalist conservative Social Credit party dominated political life in the province. The policies adopted by Alberta governments have generally reflected a strong free-enterprise orientation. The CCF and NDP have had little success in Alberta. The political values of Albertans are often described as strongly individualistic, with opposition to a substantial role for government. In contrast, the political values of residents of Saskatchewan have been more favourable to cooperative and collective action.

Nelson Wiseman's analysis of immigration patterns can help to explain the striking differences between Saskatchewan's political culture and that of its neighbour, Alberta. Many people from Britain who had been influenced by the British labour movement and the British Labour Party settled in Saskatchewan's farms and small towns in the first part of the twentieth century. They provided much of the leadership of the radical Farmers' Union, which favoured the compulsory collective marketing of wheat (viewed as part of a transition to socialism). They also encouraged the formation of the Farmer-Labour party in Saskatchewan, which was incorporated into the CCF (Wiseman, 2007). In contrast, many immigrants to Alberta from the 1890s onward came from the United States.[3] These settlers tended to bring populist-liberal and conservative evangelical Christian perspectives rather than socialist perspectives (Wiseman, 2007).

Despite Saskatchewan's reputation as the heartland of Canadian socialism, support for the NDP in that province has declined in recent years (although still greater than in Alberta) as many voters have shifted their support to conservative parties. Nevertheless, the political culture of Saskatchewan continues to differ from that of its Prairie neighbour.

Nelson Wiseman (2007) argues that fundamental features of political culture did not become fixed at the time of early settlement. Rather, wave after wave of immigration brought new ideas to Canada that became incorporated into the political culture. After the first wave of immigrants from France

---

[3]Saskatchewan also had a significant population of immigrants from the United States but, according to Wiseman, they were more likely to be of continental European ancestry and less likely to have English as their mother tongue. Thus they were less influenced by the American political culture than Alberta's large proportion of American immigrants.

prior to 1760 and the second wave of Loyalists in the 1780s, a third wave of immigrants from 1815 to 1851 brought reform-minded workers and artisans from Britain who pushed for responsible government (that is, a government in which the executive is responsible to elected representatives). A fourth wave of immigrants from the 1890s to the 1920s, who settled primarily in the West and Ontario, included socialists influenced by the development of the British Labour Party, populists from the United States who favoured more direct control by ordinary people over government, and continental Europeans. Finally, a fifth wave of immigration since the end of the Second World War has brought people from many parts of the world. People in this diverse fifth wave (who have settled primarily in cities) have enriched Canada with a variety of different perspectives.

Formative Events Theory

FORMATIVE EVENTS THEORY
A theory that emphasizes the importance of a crucial formative event in establishing the basic character of a country's political culture.

Formative events theory, associated with American political scientist and sociologist Seymour Martin Lipset, emphasizes the importance of a crucial formative event in establishing the basic character of a country's political culture. The American political culture was shaped by its revolutionary experience, while Canadian political culture was shaped by its counter-revolutionary stance in reaction to the American Revolution. Similarly, French Canada under the influence of the Catholic Church rejected the radicalism of the French Revolution of 1789 (Lipset, 1996).

The revolutionary experience of the United States resulted, in Lipset's view, in a political culture that emphasized the values of individual freedom, minimal government, and equality of opportunity associated with classical liberalism. In contrast, Canada's counter-revolutionary experience gave rise to a traditional conservative ("tory") political culture that emphasized the rule by an elite, deference to those in positions of authority, and a strong state (Lipset, 1990). Both political cultures have since evolved. The Canadian political culture has adopted some of the individualistic and democratic values of the American political culture. In addition, the Canadian political culture has become more egalitarian in that Canadians have become favourable to the use of government to create greater social and economic equality. To some extent, the American political culture also has come to accept a role for government in dealing with social and economic problems and to support some group-oriented policies, such as affirmative action for minorities. Nevertheless, Lipset argued that there continue to be "fundamental distinctions" between the two countries resulting from the American Revolution; these have been "reinforced by variations in literature, religious traditions, political and legal institutions, and socioeconomic structures" (Lipset, 1990, p. 8).

Lipset tended to view the Canadian political culture as more conservative (in the traditional sense of that term) because of its counter-revolutionary past. However, like Horowitz, he saw the collectivist orientation of traditional conservatism as contributing to the development of a socialist strain within the Canadian political culture. For example, he views the substantially higher level of unionization in Canada than in the United States (other than in the 1930s) as a reflection of the collectivist element in the Canadian political culture. In turn, the union movement has been important in pressuring governments to develop welfare state policies and in supporting democratic socialist parties that have, at times, governed various provinces.

Lipset argued that the tendency of Canadians to take more liberal positions on moral and social issues (such as abortion and homosexual rights) can be explained, at least in part, by long-standing differences in the religious makeup of the two countries. Many of the founders of the United States were members of dissenting and nonconformist Protestant sects that focused on the individual's relationship with God and opposed the establishment of state-supported religious authorities. In contrast, Canada has had conservative, established religions (Catholic and Anglican), along with a variety of Protestant groups that came together in the United Church in 1925. In modern times, the leading religious organizations in Canada have promoted social justice as advocates for the disadvantaged and, particularly in the case of the United Church, have shown themselves to be more liberal on moral issues. In the United States, however, the influential fundamentalist and evangelical movements that take a literal view of the Bible as the word of God hold a strongly moralistic view of the need to eradicate evil. Furthermore, Canada has become a much more secular society than the United States in that religious observance and belief play a less important role in the lives of many Canadians, and Canadians are also less likely to favour religious influence in political life (see Table 5-1). In its largely secular, rather than religious, approach to politics, the Canadian political culture has come to resemble that of a number of countries in Western Europe.

Overall, Lipset likened Canada and the United States to two trains "that have moved thousands of miles along parallel railway tracks. They are far from where they started, but they are still separated" (1990, p. 212). Questions can be raised, however, about Lipset's claim that Canada is "still Tory"

TABLE 5-1

THE IMPORTANCE OF RELIGION IN CANADA AND THE UNITED STATES

VALUE	CANADA	UNITED STATES
Religious leaders should not influence government	70.9%	49.4%
Politicians who don't believe in God are unfit for public office	17.3	32.0
Better if more people with strong religious beliefs in public office	22.8	31.8
Religious leaders should not influence how people vote	77.6	60.5
Attend religious services at least once a month	34.2	48.9

Source: *World Values Survey, 2006.*

▶ The Canada–United States border: Does this line separate two countries that have different political cultures?

(1990, p. 212). For example, some surveys indicate that Canadians are now less deferential to authority than Americans and more critical of government than Americans (Nevitte, 1996). As well, with Canadians having become more liberal than Americans on social issues such as male–female relations (Adams, 2003) and more favourable to egalitarianism, the "tory" label does not seem as useful as it was in the past.

Post-Materialist Theory

POST-MATERIALIST THEORY
A theory that those who have grown up in relative security and affluence are more likely to give priority to post-materialist values rather than materialist values.

POST-MATERIALIST VALUES
Values such as self-expression, participation in economic and political decisions, emphasis on the quality of life, tolerance of diversity, and concern for environmental protection.

Ronald Inglehart (1977, 1990) developed a **post-materialist theory** about changes in political culture related, in part, to the economic changes of recent decades. His theory contends that those who have grown up in relative security and affluence (as has been the case for Canada and other Western countries since the Second World War) are more likely to give priority to **post-materialist values** such as self-expression, participation in economic and political decisions, emphasis on the quality of life, tolerance of diversity, and concern for environmental protection. Earlier generations tend to have materialistic values such as a concern for economic growth, order, and physical security.

Inglehart and his colleagues argue that post-materialism, combined with the development of a post-industrial, knowledge-based economy, greater access to higher education, and more effective means of mass communications, has led to a number of significant trends: greater citizen activism, the questioning of authority, the development of new political parties and new social movements, the raising of new types of issues (such as issues related to the environment and gender equality), and the development of more liberal

	1982 (N = 1186)	1990 (N = 1647)	2000 (N = 1882)	2006 (N = 2164)
Materialist	22.3%	11.9%	8.6%	10.3%
Mixed	61.8	62.5	62.9	58.5
Post-materialist	16.0	25.6	29.4	31.2

Source: *Calculated from World Values Survey, 2006.*

TABLE 5-2
POST-MATERIALISM INDEX

Note: The index is based on responses to two questions: "If you had to choose, which one of the things on this card would you say is most important? and which would be the next most important?"
1. Maintaining order in the nation.
2. Giving people more say in important government decisions.
3. Fighting rising prices.
4. Protecting freedom of expression.
Those responding #1 and #3 were classified as "materialist"; #2 and #4 "post-materialist," and other combinations "mixed."

social values (Dalton, 2006). For example, there has been a substantial decline in recent decades in moral traditionalism (particularly reflecting a greater acceptance of homosexuality) in Canada. Feminist and environmentalist perspectives have also become increasingly important.

At the same time, the extent of value change should not be exaggerated. Although a growing number of Canadians can now be considered post-materialist in their value priorities while a smaller minority is basically materialist, the majority of the population exhibits a mixture of materialist and post-materialist values (see Table 5-2). Nevertheless, when faced with a hypothetical choice between giving priority to protecting the environment even if it caused slow economic growth and some job loss or making economic growth and job creation the top priority even if the environment suffered, 72.2 percent of Canadians chose the environmental priority over the more materialist one (World Values Survey, 2006).

Overall, post-materialist theory does not focus on the distinctiveness of particular political cultures. Instead, it highlights and explains trends in many contemporary societies.

Democratic Values

Canadian political culture is often described in terms of the values of **liberal democracy**. Liberal democracy includes the ideas of a free society, tolerance of different viewpoints, competitive elections, limited government, and the rule of law. Combined with these values associated with liberalism is the democratic ideal that power should ultimately rest with the people, with each citizen being of equal political significance. As Table 5-3 indicates, almost all Canadians view liberal democratic values as highly important.

Support for Democracy

A key component of the Canadian political culture is the view, shared by about seven-eighths of Canadians, that democracy is the best form of government (Dalton, 2006; Perez, 2008). Likewise most Canadians consider it very important to live in a country that is governed democratically (see Figure 5-1). Over three-quarters of Canadians said that "having a strong leader who does not have to bother with Parliament and elections" was a bad or very bad idea (World Values Survey, 2006).

LIBERAL DEMOCRACY
A political system that includes the ideas of a free society, tolerance of different viewpoints, competitive elections, limited government, and the rule of law associated with liberalism combined with the democratic ideal that power should ultimately rest with the people, with each citizen being of equal political significance.

TABLE 5-3
CANADIAN VIEWS OF THE ESSENTIAL CHARACTERISTICS OF DEMOCRACY

Note: Respondents were asked to rank each characteristic on a scale from 1 (not essential) to 10 (essential). Mean scores for American respondents in brackets.

CHARACTERISTIC	NOT ESSENTIAL (1)	ESSENTIAL (10)	MEAN
Women have the same rights as men	1.1%	66.2%	9.1 (8.5)
People choose their leaders in a free election	1.4	50.2	8.7 (8.3)
Civil rights protect people's liberty against oppression	0.9	32.6	8.1 (8.0)
People receive state aid for unemployment	1.4	19.8	7.4 (5.8)
People can change the laws in a referendum	4.0	20.7	7.2 (7.4)
Criminals are severely punished	5.0	23.2	7.1 (6.6)
The economy is prosperous	2.9	17.3	7.1 (6.9)
Governments tax the rich and subsidize the poor	4.1	6.7	6.1 (5.0)
The army takes over when the government is incompetent	29.9	5.1	4.0 (3.9)
Religious authorities interpret the law	33.6	1.1	3.0 (3.2)

Source: *Calculated from World Values Survey, 2006.*

About two-thirds of Canadians are at least somewhat satisfied with the way democracy works in general (Nadeau, 2002; World Values Survey, 2000). However, the general satisfaction with democracy does not extend to positive evaluations of government, politicians, and political parties. About three-fifths of Canadians do not express much confidence in government (World Values Survey, 2006) and only one-fifth of Canadians indicate that they trust

FIGURE 5-1
IMPORTANCE OF DEMOCRACY

V162: Question: How important is it for you to live in a country that is governed democratically? On this scale where 1 means it is not at all important and 10 means absolutely important, what position would you choose?

Number of respondents: 2165.
Mean: 9.0

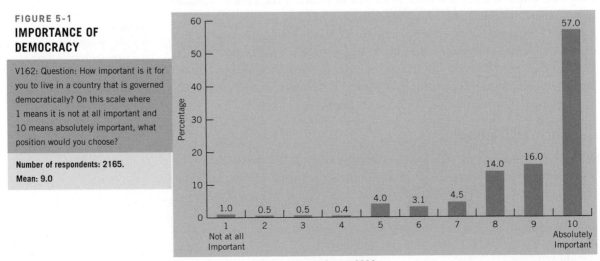

Source: *Data for Canada, World Values Survey, 2006.*

the government in Ottawa to do what is right always or most of the time (Docherty, 2002). While 93 percent of Canadians rated firefighters and 87 percent rated nurses as trustworthy, only 12 percent rated local politicians and 7 percent rated national politicians as trustworthy (Galt, 2007; IPSOS-Reid poll quoted in *Globe and Mail Online*, 2007). About three-quarters of Canadians give political leaders a low or very low rating on ethics and honesty, with a similar proportion feeling that political leaders do not tell the truth or keep their promises (Centre for Research and Information on Canada, 2002). Similarly, 59 percent of those polled said that they thought that most politicians are mainly in politics "because they want to advance their own ambitions" rather than "because they want to do something good for the country" (Canadian Broadcasting Corporation, 2004). Associated with the low level of confidence and trust in government and politicians, the majority of people do not have a strong sense of **political efficacy**—that is, a belief that government is responsive to the people and that they can influence what government does (see Table 5-4).

How have we reached a point where the general distrust of government and politicians runs so deep and is so widespread? In some cases, political scandals and broken promises have sparked negative attitudes toward politicians. As well, the mass media has tended to become more critical of politicians and the failures of government. A more educated and informed public is also a factor; such a public has higher expectations of government, which leads to disappointment when those expectations are not fulfilled. In addition, the decline in trust and confidence in politicians and political institutions may be part of a general decline in deference toward authority in various forms.

Overall, the combination of a general belief in the value of democracy, along with a critical attitude toward government, political parties, and politicians, characterizes not only Canada, but also other Western democratic countries. This combination may be viewed positively. Citizen demands for a greater voice in decision making and expectations that politicians

POLITICAL EFFICACY
A belief that government is responsive to the people and that they can influence what government does.

TABLE 5-4
POLITICAL EFFICACY

	PERCENTAGE AGREEING WITH STATEMENT	
	1965	2004
Elected officials soon lose touch with the people	68	74.0
Government doesn't care much about what people like me think	48	60.7
Sometimes politics and government seem so complicated	71	54.5
People like me don't have any say in what government does	51	51.6

Sources: *Clarke, H.D., Jenson, J., LeDuc, L., & Pammett, J.H. (1991), pp. 42–43; Clarke, H.D., A. Kornberg, A., & J. Scotto, T. J. (2006), p. 26.*

should be more responsive and accountable to the public indicate that the political culture of the Canadian population has become more democratic than in the past.

RIGHTS AND FREEDOMS

There is a very strong consensus among Canadians about the desirability of democratic rights and freedoms. For example, 98 percent of Canadians agreed with the statement, "No matter what a person's political beliefs are, he or she is entitled to the same legal rights and protections as everyone else." However, when asked "whether members of extreme political groups should be allowed to hold a public rally," the proportion agreeing dropped to 61 percent. When asked whether a specific group that respondents indicated they disliked the most (such as communists or fascists) should be allowed to hold a public rally, support for freedom of that group dropped to 35 percent (Sniderman et al., 1996, pp. 20–22). Generally, the majority of Canadians do not take the libertarian position that advocates very few restrictions on individual freedom. Instead, the majority of Canadians tend to favour controls on the rights and freedoms of those they view as promoting hatred, advocating the revolutionary overthrow of government, or posing a potential threat to public safety and national security.

TOLERANCE

As discussed in Chapter 4, the Canadian government has adopted a policy of multiculturalism and has ended discrimination against those of non-European ancestry in its immigration policies. Fortunately, Canada has not experienced the serious violence that has exploded in recent years in some European countries. Nevertheless, issues have arisen surrounding the accommodation of the different religious beliefs and cultural practices of newcomers to Canada from various parts of the world. As Box 5-3 (A Test of Tolerance: Accommodating Religious and Cultural Minorities) suggests, Canadian tolerance of different minorities is not as widespread as is generally believed.

Equality

There is little doubt that Canadians today favour political equality in the sense of all citizens having the right to vote and hold office. Likewise, the vast majority support equal rights for women and men. Overall, however, when asked to choose whether personal freedom ("that is, everyone can live in freedom and develop without hindrance") or equality ("that is, nobody is underprivileged and that class differences are not so strong") is more important, only about one-third of Canadians chose equality (World Values Survey, 1982, 1990).

BOX 5-3

A Test of Tolerance: Accommodating Religious and Cultural Minorities

In 2007 the municipal council of the Quebec town of Hérouxville attracted major media attention after it adopted a non-binding code of conduct for newcomers:

> We wish to inform these new arrivals that the way of life which they abandoned when they left their countries of origin cannot be recreated here. . . . we consider as undesirable and prohibit any action [such as] killing women by lapidation [stoning] or burning them alive in public places, burning them with acid, excising them, infibulating them or treating them as slaves. . . . We listen to music, we drink alcoholic beverages in public or private places, we dance, and at the end of every year we decorate a tree. . . . The only time you may mask or cover your face is during Halloween . . . (Municipalité Hérouxville, n.d.).

Although this town of about 1200 people was home to only one immigrant family, there was little doubt that the code reflected a negative perception of Muslims. As discussed in Chapter 4, a variety of issues related to religious minorities led the Quebec government in 2007 to appoint the Bouchard-Taylor Commission to examine the issue of "reasonable accommodation" of cultural differences. An online survey of 1023 Canadians conducted the same year found that support for accommodation was limited (MacDonald, 2007):

"It is reasonable to accommodate religious and cultural minorities" 18.0%
or "Immigrants should adapt fully to culture in Canada" 53.1
Agree with neither statement 21.3
Unsure 7.6

"Do you support, somewhat support, somewhat oppose or oppose prayer spaces being provided free of charge in public facilities to accommodate religious minorities?"
support: 10.2%
somewhat support: 21.2
somewhat oppose 20.5
oppose 38.1

Respondents who were older or less educated were more likely to oppose the accommodation of minorities. Not surprisingly, given the publicity surrounding various incidents in their province, the two hundred and ninety-five Quebecers who were included in the survey were also more likely to oppose accommodation. As well, because of their minority position in Canada and North America, French Quebecers were more likely to want to enforce the dominance of their cultural values in Quebec. Overall, the responses nationwide challenge the commonly held belief that Canadians accept—and perhaps even nurture—the diversity in their midst.

The question of whether government should try to reduce economic inequalities through redistributing income and wealth or by providing substantial assistance to the disadvantaged is controversial. The public is divided on this question. For example, in 2006, 43.8 percent of Canadians agreed at least to some extent that "incomes should be made more equal" while 56.2 percent took the opposite position that "we need large income differences as incentives." On the other hand, 42 percent took the position that "people should take more responsibility to provide for themselves," while 58 percent took the position that "government should take more responsibility to ensure everyone is provided for" (World Values Survey, 2006).

Laws and policies awarding special treatment to disadvantaged groups to promote equality are also controversial. One survey found that Canadians were almost evenly divided on the question of whether Aboriginals should have "special rights," and about two-thirds opposed the idea that "large companies should have quotas to ensure a fixed percentage of women are hired."[4] A small majority supported the idea that the government in Ottawa should make sure that a certain proportion of the top jobs in government go to women, although only about one-quarter of English-speaking Canadians favoured such a policy for French Canadians (Sniderman et al., 1996).

DIVERSITY AND POLITICAL CULTURE

Accounts of political culture often assume that there is a single political culture in the country. Subcultures may exist among different groups, but these are considered as variations on the national political culture. However, given Canada's diversity, is there a single Canadian political culture with subcultural variations, or do several distinctive political cultures thrive in Canada?

Aboriginals

Studies of Canadian political culture have generally focused on the values of those of European ancestry (particularly British and French ancestry) who have dominated political life. In the past, various groups of Aboriginals have been marginalized or excluded from the mainstream of political life. Now that Aboriginals are taking on a significant role in contemporary Canadian political life, it is important to note that their political values may contrast with those of the "settler" communities. Many Aboriginals have different histories, cultures, languages, experiences, economic and social circumstances, and ways of life than other Canadians.[5] Aboriginal traditions generally involve thinking about politics in terms of seeking a consensus, rather than the adversarial and competitive view of politics that is incorporated in Canadian political institutions and practices. For example, in the Northwest Territories and Nunavut, where Aboriginals make up a substantial proportion of the population, political parties are absent from territorial politics and government. As well, First Nations and

---

[4]However, the use of terms such as "special rights" and "quotas" in the questions might lead to more negative responses than would the use of different terms.

[5]It should be noted that there are major cultural and historical differences among different Aboriginal peoples.

◀ Governor General Michaëlle Jean, middle, uses an ulu to skin a seal during a community feast in Rankin Inlet, Nunavut, on May 25, 2009.

Inuit tend to have a collectivist rather than an individualistic orientation, reflecting both their traditional practices and the system of collective ownership of land and resources that has been maintained through the system of "reserves." Although Canadian governments and Christian missionaries have tried to coax or force Aboriginals to adopt Western values, beliefs, and practices, Aboriginals have often crafted unique combinations of Christian religious and Aboriginal spiritual beliefs, and have retained or re-established various traditional practices. Politically, First Nations often combine the election of community leaders with traditional practices of drawing on the wisdom of community elders to guide decision making.

Quebec

The political culture of French Quebecers can also be considered markedly different from that of the rest of Canada. Not only did French settlers bring different ideas to the New World from those of settlers from Britain and the United States, but also the Catholic Church was influential in persuading many French Canadians that they had a mission to protect their culture and avoid the dominant individualistic, materialistic, and capitalist ideas of English-speaking North Americans. However, the influence of conservative, religious ideas was challenged, particularly during the Quiet Revolution of the early 1960s, by liberal and socialist ideas, and the significance of religion among French Quebecers has declined sharply.

French Quebecers are quite similar to other Canadians in their levels of education and economic status. However, linguistic differences play an important part in maintaining the distinctiveness of the political culture of Quebec. Language is a crucial aspect of culture, as the words we use affect our understanding of the world we live in. People in diverse language groups tend to think about and discuss politics somewhat differently. For example, discussion between English- and French-speakers about whether Quebec is a "nation" can be difficult because the word "nation" has different connotations in the two languages. For English-speaking Canadians, a nation is often thought of in terms of the people of a sovereign country; for French-speakers, it may refer to the culture and identity of people living in a particular area. Controversy thus arises when Quebec is termed a "distinct nation" (Bell, 1992).

As discussed in Chapter 4, the development of a secular form of Quebec nationalism focused on building a strong Quebec "state" has also helped to ensure that the Québécois political culture differs from that of the rest of the country. The Quebec government's efforts to rectify historic inequalities between French and English Quebecers and to steer the social and economic development of the province have given a somewhat greater collectivist character to Quebec politics than is the case in the rest of the country. Quebecers have also tended to become more liberal than English Canadians in their social and moral attitudes. Indeed, in their analysis of survey data, Grabb and Curtis (2005) found that differences between Quebecers and English Canadians tended to be greater than differences between English Canadians and Americans.[6] For example, they found that Quebecers tended to be more liberal than English Canadians (and Americans) in the proportion favouring the equality of women, same-sex marriage and gay rights, and less harsh treatment of criminal behaviour.

Provincial Political Cultures

Although analysts of Canadian political culture have tended to focus on the differences between Quebec and the rest of Canada, it can be misleading to

---

[6]Grabb and Curtis (2005) view Canada and the United States as consisting of "four societies," arguing that just as Quebec has a different political culture from the rest of Canada, the southern states have a political culture that makes them distinct from the rest of the United States.

assume that a single distinctive political culture typifies "English Canada." Immigration and settlement patterns have meant that the characteristics of the population of each province are quite different. Similarly, the historic political experiences of each province vary considerably. For example, the Maritime provinces had a rich political history prior to joining Canada. Likewise, the political culture of Newfoundland and Labrador is still affected by its political experiences prior to joining Canada in 1949 and the controversy surrounding its decision to become the tenth province.

As discussed in Chapter 13, Canada's federal system is quite decentralized, with provincial governments enjoying considerable autonomy and power. Because educational systems are under provincial control, the shaping of young people's understanding of the political world can vary from province to province. Not only is the portrayal of Canada's political history considerably different in Quebec from that in other provinces, but some provincial educational systems, such as that of Newfoundland and Labrador, focus largely on their own province's culture and history.

Although Canada's federal system contributes to the development of somewhat distinctive provincial political cultures, important regional differences often exist within provinces. For example, the political culture of Cape Breton differs significantly from that of "mainland" Nova Scotia; Labrador contrasts sharply with the island portion of Newfoundland; and northern Ontario is distinct from southern Ontario.

Ethnic Cultures

Canada is often described as a multicultural "mosaic" in which diverse cultures have been able to retain their identity. In contrast, the United States has often been characterized as a "melting pot" in which various groups have been encouraged to adopt a common American identity and culture.[7] To some extent this distinction is misleading because the policy of multiculturalism is relatively recent; governments in the past often tried to persuade immigrants to assimilate into the Canadian mainstream. Likewise, many immigrants to Canada and their descendants have adopted the official languages and the customs of their new country.

But to what extent, if any, do different ethnic groups have different politically relevant values? Answering this question is not easy given the great diversity among the many different ethnic groups. To generalize, many individuals of various European origins who moved to Canada before the Second World War adopted the values of the Canadian mainstream. Some of the more

---

[7]The depiction of the United States as a "melting pot" can be misleading. African-Americans were largely excluded from political, social, and economic life until recent decades, and along with Hispanic and other minority groups have, to varying extents, retained distinctive cultures.

recent immigrants of non-European origin tend to have more traditional, morally conservative attitudes toward family, sexuality, and religion, while looking to government to promote equality of opportunity and to protect their rights and freedoms.

Social Class

Many countries are said to have subcultures based on marked differences among social classes. Canada and the United States, however, are sometimes referred to as "classless societies." As discussed in Chapter 3, social class divisions are not as sharp and rigid in Canada as in many other countries, and there is more interaction among those of different classes. Nevertheless, surveys have found that class differences on a number of political attitudes (including ideological perspectives, views on civil liberties, the role of government in the economy, and social welfare policy) tend to be greater than differences among those of different regions and ethnic backgrounds (Ornstein & Stevenson, 1999).

Gender

There are also tendencies for women to think about politics in somewhat different ways than men based on differences in socialization, circumstances, and experiences. Brenda O'Neill suggests that a women's political culture "is distinctive in its political priorities and the degree to which an ethic of care and concern for responsibility permeate it" (2002, p. 52). This is apparent, for example, in a less favourable attitude toward the use of military force, a less positive attitude toward the competitive capitalist system, and a more favourable attitude toward an active role for government in providing assistance to the disadvantaged. Younger women in particular, reflecting the influence of the feminist ideology, are more likely to be critical of traditional views about the role of women in the family, society, and politics.

Other Subcultures

People often talk about a "youth culture," although this tends to refer more to lifestyle than political orientations. However, there are significant differences between different generations in politically relevant values. In particular, recent generations tend to be more liberal in their values on moral issues than older generations, and are more likely to have post-materialist value priorities. As well, the political culture of large cities tends to differ from that of small towns and rural areas, with residents of the latter often having a stronger sense of attachment and involvement in their local community.

Summary and Conclusion

The study of political culture provides a useful antidote to a commonly expressed view that ideas, beliefs, and values are not relevant to understanding Canadian politics. The struggle for power, position, and privilege is important, but politics also involves a contest of ideas and values among those who hold different ideological perspectives.

Both Louis Hartz's founding fragments theory and Seymour Martin Lipset's formative events theory look to the distant past for the foundations of political culture. However, there are differences as to how the past has shaped Canadian political culture. Hartz views English Canada as having a basically liberal political culture similar to that of the United States. In contrast, Lipset sees opposition to the American Revolution as setting Canada in a somewhat more "tory" conservative direction, although with the later development of some liberal and socialist elements. Post-materialist theory offers yet another point of view. It sees Canada as undergoing major changes in value priorities in recent decades, which has resulted in the Canadian political culture becoming less traditionalist, less deferential to authority, and more geared to self-expression and tolerance of diversity.

Nelson Wiseman (2007) argues that there is no "single unifying thread in contemporary Canadian political culture" because "the country is too complex, its regions and peoples too varied, and its history too contentious to unequivocally assert the existence of a singular Canadian identity" (p. 264).

Although the political culture of diverse groups of Canadians differs markedly, some political values and orientations are widely held. In common with other Western countries, the Canadian political culture has as its basis the values of liberal democracy. Nevertheless, there are many ways of interpreting the values of liberal democracy and different priorities may be given to these values. Furthermore, the political cultures of Aboriginal peoples and the Québécois have developed in substantially different ways than, and continue to be distinctive from, the political culture of the Canadian majority. Moreover, the immigration of many people of non-European origin has added considerably to the diversity of Canadian political culture or cultures.

Many Canadians (and, in particular, English-speaking Canadians) share a common heritage with Americans, interact with Americans, and are influenced by the culture of our powerful neighbour. Still, Canadians often view themselves as differing from Americans and consider Canadian values superior to those of the Americans. Canada is sometimes described as a "kinder and gentler" society than the United States, even though some negative attitudes persist toward those of different religious beliefs and racial characteristics. Canadians, like Americans, tend to lean in an individualist direction that gives priority to individual freedom over equality. However, Canadians are somewhat more likely than Americans to believe that governments should play an active role in social and economic affairs to help the disadvantaged, provide public services, and act for the collective good. Although they share much, Canadians and Americans may part ways in an important respect: how they define good government.

Discussion Questions

1. How would you describe your basic political values and beliefs? Are they similar to or different from those of your family, your friends, and other influences on your life?

2. How different are the political cultures of Canada and the United States? How can the similarities and differences best be explained? Is the Canadian political culture becoming more similar to that of the United States?

3. Is the political culture of your province substantially different from that of other areas of Canada?

4. Does Quebec have a distinct political culture and, if so, what are the implications for Canadian politics?

5. How do the political cultures of Aboriginal peoples differ from that of the rest of Canada?

6. Is the Canadian political culture changing rapidly or does it still basically reflect its historic roots?

Further Reading

Ball, T., Dagger, R., Christian, W., & Campbell, C. (2010). *Political Ideologies and the democratic ideal* (2nd Canadian ed.). Toronto, ON: Pearson Education Canada.

Bell, D.V.J. (1992). *The roots of disunity. A study of Canadian political culture* (rev. ed.). Toronto, ON: Oxford University Press.

Fierlbeck, K. (2006). *Political thought in Canada. An intellectual history.* Peterborough, ON: Broadview.

Forbes, H. D. (1987). Hartz-Horowitz at twenty: Nationalism, toryism, and socialism in Canada and the United States. *Canadian Journal of Political Science, 20*(2), 287–315.

Grabb, E.; & Curtis, J. (2005). *Regions apart. The four societies of Canada and the United States.* Toronto, ON: Oxford University Press.

Hartz, L. et al. (1964). *The founding of new societies.* New York, NY: Harcourt Brace.

Horowitz, G. (1966). Conservatism, liberalism, and socialism in Canada: An interpretation. *Canadian Journal of Economics and Political Science, 32,* 143–171.

Kaufman, J. (2009). *The origins of Canadian and American political differences.* Cambridge, MA: Harvard University Press.

Lipset, S. M. (1990). *Continental divide: The values and institutions of the United States and Canada.* New York, NY: Routledge.

Nevitte, N. (1996). *The decline of deference.* Peterborough, ON: Broadview Press.

Wiseman, N. (2007). *In search of Canadian political culture.* Vancouver: UBC Press.

Conservative

Green

Bloc Québécois

New Democrat

Liberal

Chapter 6

POLITICAL PARTICIPATION AND CIVIC ENGAGEMENT

PHOTO ABOVE: A female mallard duck gets its bill cleaned of oil at the Wildlife Rehabilitation Society of Edmonton on April 30, 2008, after being transported from the Syncrude tailings pond at its tar sands site near Fort McMurray, Alberta.

CHAPTER OBJECTIVES

After reading this chapter, you should be able to

1. Define and distinguish between political participation and civic engagement.
2. Identify the different ways Canadians can get involved in political and civic affairs.
3. Describe levels of political participation and civic engagement in Canada, and how they compare with other democracies.
4. Discuss which Canadians are more likely to participate in political and civic affairs, and why.
5. Discuss the significance of political participation and civic engagement to Canadian democracy and to individual Canadians.

In April 2008, two black-clad Greenpeace protesters disrupted Alberta Premier Ed Stelmach's fundraising dinner when they dropped down from the ceiling in climbing harnesses and unfurled a large banner that read, "$telmach, the best premier oil money can buy. Stop the Tar Sands." Stelmach continued his speech as his supporters heckled the activists, who were dangling from the ceiling. As security officers escorted the protesters out of the conference centre, journalists holding microphones and television cameras rushed to record the dramatic turn of events. A Greenpeace organizer said the stunt was aimed at getting his group's message across: "We want the government of Alberta to start listening to the general public and put an end to the Alberta tar sands," he told CBC News ("Greenpeace Stunt," 2008). The daring protest is an example of how a small minority of Canadians express their views about an important political issue, in a bid to influence public policy.

Other groups of Canadians have used more conventional methods—lobbying politicians, issuing statements to the press—to communicate their opinions about the future development of the oil deposits in northeastern Alberta. Oil companies have touted that they contain the second-largest reserves of oil in the world, provide jobs for thousands of Canadians, and are important to the economies of Alberta and Canada. Environmentalists and Aboriginal groups have called for a slowdown or even a halt to development. They argue that the oil sands are a major source of greenhouse gas and other emissions, and pose a health risk to human and non-human life forms.

Shortly after the Greenpeace protest, more than 1600 migrating ducks died when they landed on and sank to the bottom of a tailings pond that is used to process the heavy crude oil in the Athabasca oil sands deposit near Fort McMurray, Alberta. Provincial government investigators said the deaths were caused by the failure of the oil company that operated the pond site to deploy the air cannons it uses to frighten birds away. Syncrude ran full-page ads in major newspapers across Canada apologizing for the tragic incident. Images and stories about the dying waterfowl appeared on news outlets and blogs around the world, renewing an ongoing public debate about the future of the oil sands.

In February 2009, the Alberta government charged Syncrude for failing to provide appropriate wildfowl deterrents. The maximum penalty for violating this section of the Alberta *Environmental Protection and Enhancement Act* is $500 000. Syncrude was also facing a charge under the federal *Migratory Birds Convention Act* for allegedly depositing or permitting the deposit of a substance harmful to migratory birds in waters or in an area frequented by birds. The maximum penalty for the federal charge is a $300 000 fine and/or six months' imprisonment.

Different groups of Canadians have strong opinions about how development of oil deposits that are the size of the state of Florida should proceed. They make their views known through unconventional methods, such as protest activities, and more conventional methods involving lobbying decision makers and communicating their views to the press and the broader public. The intense conflict over how to manage these resources illustrates how and why some Canadians are driven to take political action.

UNDERSTANDING POLITICAL PARTICIPATION AND CIVIC ENGAGEMENT

In the run-up to the presidential and provincial elections held in Afghanistan in 2009, opponents of the governing regime employed rockets, suicide bombings, and roadside explosive devices in an attempt to discourage Afghans from casting a vote. Unlike people living in unstable democracies, Canadians can participate in political affairs without risking their personal security. They enjoy the right to freely express their views about political issues and to pursue their political goals through various means. Canadians may also participate in civic affairs by contributing to community life in some way. This chapter is concerned with the extent to which Canadians exercise these rights.

Political participation refers to the actions people take to raise awareness about political issues, influence the selection of government personnel, and shape the laws and policies that affect their lives. Political participation can assume both conventional and unconventional forms. Conventional political acts can take place during election campaigns, when people vote, attend political meetings or rallies, work for a party, make a donation to a party or candidate, or run for public office. They can also occur outside an election period through personalized contacting, communicating, and interest group activity (Milbrath & Goel, 1977; Verba & Nie, 1972; Verba, Nie, & Kim, 1971; Woodward & Roper, 1950).

People personally contact a government official because they are concerned about an issue that affects them directly. Communication activities involve following and discussing politics, and expressing opinions about issues to public officials and the media. **Cyberactivism**, or political activism that employs online communication tools such as websites, emails, blogs, Facebook, and Twitter, is becoming an increasingly popular way for people to express their opinions and to mobilize other like-minded people to act too. Interest group activity can involve raising awareness of an issue and communicating the group's views to government officials in a bid to influence their decisions.

Canadians can also pursue their political goals through so-called unconventional **protest activities**. Protests in Canada typically involve the use of non-violent methods such as signing a petition, boycotts, sit-ins at government offices, and peaceful marches, demonstrations, or strikes. Some protesters use violent methods such as damaging property or harming the opponents of the cause.

Civic engagement, or participation in community affairs, refers to actions such as joining and/or helping a local voluntary organization, helping other individuals directly, or giving financial donations to charitable causes. There are many categories of voluntary or civic organizations. Examples include youth groups, sports and recreation clubs, religious-based groups, ethnocultural

POLITICAL PARTICIPATION
Actions people take to raise awareness about issues, to influence the choice of government personnel, and to shape the content of legislation and public policies.

CYBERACTIVISM
Political activism that employs online communications tools such as websites, emails, blogs, and social networking services.

PROTEST ACTIVITIES
Political acts that include non-violent actions such as signing a petition, boycotts, peaceful marches, demonstrations, and strikes. They may sometimes involve the use of violence to damage property or harm the opponents of the cause.

CIVIC ENGAGEMENT
A set of activities in the community, such as joining a voluntary organization, volunteering for the organization, helping others directly, or giving financial donations to charitable causes.

associations, service clubs such as the Lions Clubs International, environmental and human rights groups, and business or professional associations. Although voluntary organizations focus their efforts on improving the quality of community life or serving members' social, educational, cultural, recreational, or economic needs, some organizations also take part in political processes. For example, a local environmental group may have been established to clean up a neighbourhood park or beach, but it may also lobby politicians for changes to municipal bylaws or provincial environmental legislation. Although a youth group may be formed to organize social and recreational events for members, it may take political action when a particular issue affects its interests. For example, the youth group may try to persuade municipal officials to fund and build a skateboard park or provide extra basketball courts in the community. In other words, voluntary organizations can take part in political processes, although participation in the political process is not necessarily their central task.

Canadian and International Trends in Public Affairs Involvement

Canadians who are busy with school, jobs, families, and hobbies get involved in political affairs for different reasons. One of the principal reasons is that they have been touched by an issue. They may feel strongly about a particular subject—job creation, environmental protection, poverty, fair trade, gun control, gay marriage, or taxation, for instance—and want to express their opinion about it, or influence the decisions that public officials make. They get involved in civic affairs by volunteering at a local food bank, helping coach a children's soccer team, or giving money to support cancer research, because they want to give back to their communities or because they know someone who needs assistance. Because Canada is a democratic country, citizens may also choose not to get involved in political and civic life. The myriad and complex reasons for citizen disengagement will also be discussed in this chapter.

The extent to which Canadians participate in political and civic affairs, and the ways in which they get involved, paints a telling portrait of the nature of Canadian democracy. Are Canadians activists or apathetic? How do we compare with citizens living in other democratic states? To answer these questions, this chapter tracks long-term trends in political participation and civic engagement, as well as how many Canadians get involved in these activities, whether some of us are more likely than others to participate, and whether Canadians are more or less active than people living in other established democracies.

In general, most of us do not get involved in conventional political activities beyond voting, and only a small minority takes part in the most demanding activities that require extra time, skills, and knowledge, such as joining a party, working on a campaign, or participating in interest group activities.

This makes Canadians very much like citizens living in other democratic countries. Furthermore, people who are active in political affairs do not represent the broader Canadian society; they are generally older, better educated, and better off than non-participants—more likely to be school principals or CEOs than squeegee kids or holders of McJobs.

However, as more people turn away from voting and party involvements in Canada, the United States, much of Europe, Australia, New Zealand, and Japan, protest activity has grown in some of these very same countries. In particular, Canada, the United States, Great Britain, and France have seen more and more protest activity over the past few decades. Cyberactivism is also gaining in popularity as a form of political participation in Canada and around the world. Since the late 1980s, counter-globalization and social justice groups have relied heavily on the World Wide Web to raise awareness about issues and to mobilize members to take online and offline action.

Despite declining or low levels of conventional political participation, as we discuss further later in this chapter, a large number of Canadians take part in community life. In fact, the country boasts one of the highest rates of participation in voluntary organizations in the Americas, and more than 80 percent of Canadians have volunteered to help others directly or have given money to charitable causes. As with political activities, certain types of Canadians are more engaged in civic affairs than others. The people who join voluntary groups tend to be middle-aged, university educated, and affluent. Furthermore, although many Canadians give at least some time and money to others, a relatively small proportion are responsible for the vast majority of volunteer hours and financial donations that are contributed each year.

The trends summarized above inspire questions about the meaning of democratic citizenship in contemporary Canada. Is it necessary for a large number of people to get involved in politics to make democracy work, or can a democracy still thrive if relatively few people are engaged? Does it matter if certain types of Canadians are more likely to participate in political and community life than others? What, if anything, should the state do about plummeting levels of involvement in certain activities?

POLITICAL PARTICIPATION AND DEMOCRACY

Classical Democratic Theory

What level of political participation is ideal in a democracy? Who should try to influence the decisions of public officials? Two broad perspectives exist on these questions. **Classical democratic theory** is based on the idea that it is desirable to have a large number of citizens from different backgrounds participating in political affairs. In *Considerations on Representative Government*, philosopher John Stuart Mill argues that broad citizen participation guarantees that everyone's interests are protected from arbitrary rule. He also

CLASSICAL DEMOCRATIC THEORY
The belief that it is desirable to have a large number of citizens from different backgrounds participating in political affairs.

suggests that political participation changes citizens for the better. It gives them a sense of political efficacy, or control over their own lives. It makes them less likely to devote all their energies to private life, it broadens their interests, and it makes them better informed (Mill, 1872/1991; Thompson, 1976). When individuals join in, they gain skills and knowledge about public affairs so that they can make good decisions. Participation is also said to promote tolerance. When individuals join a group to achieve a political goal, they are exposed to the opinions of others and must respect the decision of the majority, even if they do not agree with the outcome.

Classical theorists are optimistic about the potential for individuals from diverse backgrounds to participate in politics. They assume that citizens are the best judges of their own interests and that political activity is the best way to express those interests and to judge how public officials respond to them. Classical democrats also generally feel that there should be equal levels of participation between members of different social and economic groups.

Over the past decade, governments and private organizations in Canada and around the world have become more and more interested in deliberative democracy, discussed in Chapter 1. **Deliberative democracy** involves citizens deliberating about government decisions through "fair and open" community discussion of the merits of competing political arguments (Uhr, 1998). Interest in forums that encourage people to participate in all stages of the policy-making process has been renewed for several reasons. As citizens express weaker attachments to political parties and less confidence in politicians, governments are looking for new ways to reinvigorate public involvement in political affairs. Internet technology has also made it easier to hold discussions between people in far-flung locations about political ideas. The citizens' assemblies set up by the provincial governments of British Columbia and Ontario to examine the question of electoral reform are examples of deliberative democracy. (See Box 6-1, Citizens Decide: Deliberative Democracy in the Provinces.)

DELIBERATIVE DEMOCRACY
A form of democracy in which governing decisions are made based on fair and open discussion by citizens.

Classical Elite Theory

In contrast to classical democratic theory, **classical elite theory** is based on the idea that a small minority of individuals with more education and political experience is better positioned to decide what is in the public interest than the relatively uninformed, apathetic, and less tolerant electorate (Michels, 1915; Mosca, 1965). Elite democratic theorists feel that widespread participation by members of the public could trigger a conflict between social groups and political instability. Because they believe that not everyone possesses the virtues to make sound decisions about politics, they are more willing than classical democratic theorists to tolerate vast differences in the political involvement of people from different social and economic backgrounds (Mishler, 1979). Some scholars have argued that Mill himself was often skeptical about the benefits of

CLASSICAL ELITE THEORY
The belief that only a small ruling class has the knowledge and skills to decide what is in the public interest, and that mass political participation is undesirable.

BOX 6-1

Citizens Decide:
Deliberative Democracy in the Provinces

In 2003 the government of British Columbia undertook a bold new experiment: letting ordinary citizens decide whether the province should retain the single member plurality electoral system (SMP) or replace it with a new one that would be proposed by the assembly (see "Voting" later in this chapter and also Chapter 9 for an explanation of different electoral systems). Nowhere else in the world had such power over the development of an electoral system been given to unelected citizens.

The Citizens' Assembly on Electoral Reform had 161 members, one man and one woman from each of B.C.'s 79 electoral districts, plus two Aboriginal members and a chairperson. Members were picked at random, by a computer, from the province's voters list. The assembly was diverse in its demographic makeup, with gender, age, and regional representation being reflected. Those who agreed to serve received an honorarium of $150 for each meeting day, plus any expenses associated with their work for the assembly.

Participation in the assembly was not for slackers: the members began their task by studying the pros and cons of different electoral systems used throughout the world. In 2004 they attended fifty public hearings held across the province, where they listened to British Columbians' views on electoral reform. More than 1600 written submissions from members of the public were also made available to the assembly participants for their consideration. After the hearings were over, the assembly members considered what they had studied and what British Columbians had told them, and discussed different options.

The assembly ultimately recommended that British Columbia switch to the single transferable vote system (a system in which voters rank candidates in multimember districts in order of preference, with votes not needed by one candidate transferred to the next preferred candidate). This recommendation was brought to the public for approval in a province-wide referendum on May 17, 2005. Although supported by 58 percent of voters, it failed to reach the required 60 percent level of approval. A second referendum on electoral reform was held together with the 2009 provincial general election. This time, the proposal received only 39 percent support.

In 2006, Ontario set up a similar citizens' assembly to evaluate whether the province should replace its electoral system with a form of proportional representation. It was made up of a chairperson and 103 randomly selected citizens—one from each of the province's electoral districts. The assembly membership was evenly divided between males and females, and at least one member was Aboriginal. Once again, the task was arduous. The members spent an entire year studying various election systems, talking to people in their communities, holding public consultation meetings, reading public submissions, and using online forums to discuss the issues between meetings. In spite of their efforts, the issue received relatively little attention from the media, and ordinary citizens struggled to grasp the concepts. The final recommendation to replace SMP with a mixed member proportional system (MMP) was rejected in a referendum held in October 2007: just under 37 percent of those who cast a vote supported MMP.

Although the reform proposals were rejected in both provinces, the assembly participants agreed they benefited enormously from their personal involvement in the process (Turnbull & Aucoin, 2006). How do you feel about the idea of citizen involvement in the policy-making process? Should important political decisions be left only to professional politicians and bureaucrats? Do the examples from British Columbia and Ontario suggest that deliberative democracy is a viable way of engaging the broader public in politics?

public participation. In *On Liberty*, he worried about the tendency of the majority to impose its own ideas and practices on those who dissent from them. He thought that democracy would encourage mass conformity and intolerance, and inflame factional rivalries (Zakaras, 2007).

In their groundbreaking study of political cultures in five contemporary democracies, Gabriel Almond and Sidney Verba (1963) argued that the majority of citizens expressed only a weak commitment to democratic norms and that their active involvement in politics could lead to political instability and the emergence of authoritarian politics. They favoured a civic culture— a society in which only a small group of well-educated citizens participates actively in politics and where most citizens leave politics to the experts. As discussed in Chapter 5, Canadians strongly support democratic values, and there is little indication that political elites are much more committed to liberal democratic values than the rest of the population.

Which of these two perspectives on the number and types of individuals who participate in political decision making best describes democratic life in Canada? The following section tackles this question by examining trends in political participation, as well as the personal characteristics and attitudes of the Canadians who get involved and those who do not. Since a certain level of political interest is necessary for political action, the section also considers whether Canadians are interested in, and knowledgeable about, politics.

CANADA: A NATION OF POLITICAL ACTIVISTS?

Canada, like many other democracies, is not a nation of political activists. By international standards, Canadians are moderately interested in politics, as we discuss later in the chapter, but not very knowledgeable about it. Only a small minority of people get involved in conventional political acts beyond voting and signing petitions. However, a growing number of Canadians are turning to public interest groups, protest activities, and/or cyberactivism in order to raise awareness about new or neglected issues and to change public policies. Young Canadians and the disadvantaged are an integral part of this phenomenon, although they still do not constitute the majority of participants in protest activities.

Political Interest and Knowledge

People who are interested in political affairs are motivated to spend the time and energy to keep themselves informed so that they can discover what they want, evaluate the government's performance and the options presented by the opposition, and act upon that information. In general, Canadians are only moderately interested in politics and only occasionally discuss politics with their family and friends. When compared with people living in other established Western democracies, however, Canadians actually are more interested in politics and discuss it more frequently than average. As in other countries, television is the leading source of political information for Canadians. Certain Canadians—men, university graduates, and the affluent—are more likely to express interest in politics and in media coverage about policies (Gidengil, Blais, Nevitte, & Nadeau, 2004).

Canada is one of the Anglo-American countries that political scientist Henry Milner has diagnosed as suffering from relatively low levels of political knowledge, in contrast to the Netherlands, Sweden, Norway, Denmark, and Germany, where "civic literacy" is more robust (quoted in Howe, 2006). Significant numbers of Canadians do not know the names of the prime minister, opposition party leaders, prominent cabinet ministers, or the premiers; and cannot identify political parties with their issue positions and whether the federal parties occupy the ideological left, right, or centre (Gidengil et al., 2004). Whereas many Canadians may recognize Bono and Paris Hilton, they may be tongue-tied when asked about Jim Flaherty or Gilles Duceppe. Political knowledge is also not distributed evenly across the population. University graduates, older Canadians, and the affluent know more about politics than Canadians with less formal education, the young, and the less well-off (Gidengil et al., 2004).

Voting

The right to vote is the cornerstone of democracy. When you cast a ballot, you have an opportunity to hold your elected representative accountable and to support or reject a political party's policies. Voting also symbolizes your connection to the political community. Virtually all citizens aged eighteen years and over have the right to vote. However, this was not always the case in Canadian history. At the time of Confederation, only male property owners aged twenty-one years and over, and who were British subjects by birth or naturalization, could vote. Women, racial minorities, most Aboriginals, and the poor were excluded from voting. These laws reflected commonly held views based on the British tradition that certain groups were unsuited to participate in democratic affairs (Courtney, 2004).

The First World War and the suffragette movement led to the doubling of the electorate by 1918. In 1917, Parliament passed the *War-time Elections Act* and the *Military Voters Act*. These laws were designed to increase the number of voters who would support conscription and disqualify those who were opposed to it. The *Military Voters Act* extended the right to vote to all British subjects, male or female, who were active or retired members of the Canadian Forces. Some two thousand military nurses—the "Bluebirds"—became the first women to get the vote. The *War-time Elections Act* gave the vote to close female relatives of people serving in the armed forces. It also took away the vote from likely opponents of conscription: conscientious objectors, pacifist religious minorities, individuals born in an enemy country who became naturalized

British subjects after March 31, 1902 (with the exception of those born in France, Italy, or Denmark and who arrived in Canada before the date on which their country of origin was annexed by Germany or Austria), and British subjects naturalized after March 31, 1902, whose mother tongue was that of an enemy country (Elections Canada, 1997).

Some women of property were able to vote in the colonies until pre-Confederation legislatures passed laws (1849 in the Province of Canada) explicitly preventing women from voting—a restriction that was reiterated in the *British North America Act,* 1867 (Elections Canada, 1997). Within a decade after Confederation, a woman's suffrage movement had taken root in most of the former colonies. In 1916 and 1917, Canada's suffragists and their allies successfully petitioned provincial governments in British Columbia, the Prairies, and Ontario to allow them to vote in provincial elections. The broadening of the provincial **franchise** and the extension of the municipal franchise to propertied women created pressure for change at the federal level. In 1918, women twenty-one years of age and over were given the right to vote, provided they met the same property requirements that applied to male electors. The property requirement was dropped in 1920 (Elections Canada, 1997).

FRANCHISE
The right to vote.

Following the Second World War, racial and religious restrictions on voting were lifted as social attitudes toward minority groups began to change (Elections Canada, 1997). In 1950, Canada restored the vote to the Inuit, who had been disenfranchised in 1934. This was one of several measures taken to protect the country's sovereignty in the Arctic following the onset of the Cold War. In 1960, Status Indians[1] were allowed to vote without having to give up their status and the benefits associated with it. By 1948, the last vestiges of property qualifications and laws excluding the Chinese, Japanese, and South Asians from voting had been removed. In 1955, all remaining voting restrictions against certain religious minorities were dropped. In 1970, Parliament lowered the voting age from twenty-one years to eighteen years in order to discourage the student strikes and unrest that had been taking place in the United States and parts of Europe. Ironically, close to four decades later, voter participation among young people in that age group is low—evidence of how many younger citizens have given up on conventional politics. (See "Who Votes?" and "Young Canadians and Federal Elections" later in this chapter.)

The electorate grew once more with the adoption of the Canadian *Charter of Rights and Freedoms* in 1982. Section 3 of the Charter states that "every citizen of Canada has the right to vote in an election of members of the House of Commons or of a legislative assembly and to be qualified for membership

---

[1]Status Indians are members of First Nations who are listed on the official registry maintained by the Canadian government, and who are entitled to a range of programs and services offered by federal agencies, provincial governments, and the private sector. These benefits do not extend to the Métis, Inuit, or several hundred thousand "non-status" persons who trace their ancestry to a First Nation.

therein." This provision opened the door to a series of successful court challenges that resulted in the extension of the vote to people who had been previously denied it: federally appointed judges, people with mental disabilities, and inmates serving sentences of two years or more.

Although in the past Canadians have fought tirelessly for the right to vote, many Canadians today are more complacent about this hard-won right. In countries such as Afghanistan, Iraq, and Zimbabwe, people have died or have risked their lives in order to vote. Although Canadian citizens do not have these worries, turnout in national elections has not been high by international standards. Between 1945 and 2001, an average 73.9 percent of registered voters cast a ballot, placing Canada's turnout eighty-third out of 169 countries (López Pintor, Gratschew, & Sullivan, 2002).

Some observers argue that Canada's single member plurality (SMP) electoral system accounts for the country's mediocre ranking. Election turnout tends to be lower in SMP systems than in systems based on proportional representation (Blais & Carty, 1990). With SMP, the victorious party often wins more seats in the legislature than the popular support it receives in the election. In proportional representation (PR) systems, a party's representation corresponds more closely to its popular support. For example, if a party wins 20 percent of the vote in a PR system, it will receive about 20 percent of the seats to be distributed. Some experts have argued that turnout is higher in countries that use PR because voters are more likely to think that every vote counts and that their votes will not be "wasted" (LeDuc, 2005). Another institutional factor that has been associated with higher turnout is compulsory voting. In twenty-nine countries, voting is compulsory and is regulated by the constitution or electoral laws. Some of these countries impose sanctions on non-voters, ranging from fines and the removal of civil and social rights, to disenfranchisement and prison time. Countries with enforced compulsory voting have, on average, turnout rates that are fifteen points higher than countries such as Canada, where individuals make up their own minds about whether or not to go to the polls (Gratschew, 2002).

Although nearly every Canadian citizen aged eighteen years and over can vote in federal elections, turnout rates have plummeted over the past two decades (Elections Canada, 2008). Between 1945 and 1988, turnout rates averaged 75.4 percent. By the 2008 general election, they had fallen dramatically to a historic low of 58.8 percent (see Figure 6-1). These trends are not unique to Canada. Between 1990 and 2000, the median average turnout for fifteen Anglo-American, Nordic, and West European countries was 77 percent, down 9.2 percentage points compared with the 1945 to 1989 period.

Since 1990, turnout has typically been higher in provincial elections than in federal elections, although not in Ontario, Alberta, Manitoba, and British Columbia. And while turnout in federal elections has dropped since 1988, turnout trends in provincial elections are not uniform across the country. Turnout has increased in Prince Edward Island and Alberta since the late

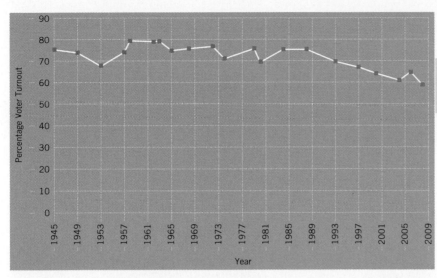

FIGURE 6-1
**TURNOUT RATE IN FEDERAL
ELECTIONS, 1945–2008***

*Official turnout in Canada is based on
the number of electors on the final lists
of electors.

Sources: Elections Canada, 2008a, *Estimation of Voter Turnout by Age Group at the 39th Federal General Election, January 23, 2006*, p. 2, retrieved from http://www.elections.ca/loi/res/rep39ge/estimation39ge_e.pdf; and Elections Canada, 2008b, Fortieth General Election 2008: Official Voting Results, retrieved from http://www.elections.ca/content.asp?section=pas&document=index&dir=40ge&lang=e

1980s, but it has been declining steadily in New Brunswick, Nova Scotia, Manitoba, and Saskatchewan (Gidengil et al., 2004). Participation rates in municipal elections are even lower than federal or provincial elections, despite the fact that local governments are responsible for essential services that touch our daily lives—policing and emergency services, public health, parks and recreation, roads and sewers, garbage collection, and recycling.

The average turnout in the 1990s for some of Canada's largest cities—Vancouver, Edmonton, Winnipeg, Hamilton, Toronto, Ottawa, and Montreal—was 43.2 percent (Gidengil et al., 2004). Municipal turnout may be higher in smaller towns than larger cities because politics is less complicated and impersonal; citizens know each other and how politics works, and know who to contact when they have a problem (Verba & Nie, 1972). This has been shown to be true in Ontario, where turnout in towns with fewer than 10 000 people was, on average, higher than in cities with a population over 100 000. But even in those smaller towns, turnout was still lower than in national and provincial elections (Kushner, Siegel, & Stanwick, 1997).

WHO VOTES?   Although legal restrictions on voting have been virtually eliminated for adult citizens, participation rates in federal elections are lower in the early twenty-first century than in historical periods when fewer Canadians had access to the franchise. The sharp declines witnessed since the late 1980s raise questions about who is voting and who is not. **Generational replacement** has been pinpointed as the main reason for the decline in turnout over the past two decades. Canadians born since 1970 are less likely to vote than their parents or grandparents were when they were the same age

GENERATIONAL REPLACEMENT
The process through which younger-age cohorts enter the electorate and replace their older predecessors.

TABLE 6-1

YOUTH VOTER TURNOUT IN SELECTED DEMOCRATIC STATES (PERCENTAGE)

Note: Calculations by the author based on data from the first round of the European Social Survey (Centre for Comparative Social Surveys, 2003).

COUNTRY	VOTED—TOTAL	VOTED—BORN IN 1980 OR LATER
Austria	88.46	74.6
Belgium	85.23	53.5
Czech Republic	65.93	61.4
Denmark	93.67	78.9
Finland	81.7	54.5
Germany	85.3	72.8
Greece	90.56	59.8
Hungary	80.93	69.2
Ireland	75.87	41.8
Israel	78.66	38.4
Italy	89.45	76.4
Luxembourg	64.74	12.8
Netherlands	86.33	74.8
Norway	83.66	50
Poland	66.16	48.2
Portugal	72.49	41.3
Slovenia	80.21	42
Spain	77.67	27.4
Sweden	86.96	81.4
Switzerland	68.98	17.6
United Kingdom	72.35	41
Average	80.30	52.7

Source: *Henry Milner, "Are Young Canadians Becoming Political Dropouts? A Comparative Perspective," Choices 11(3) (Montreal: Institute for Research on Public Policy, 2005), p. 4.*

(Blais et al., 2004). Furthermore, younger generations of voters are also less likely than their predecessors to start voting as they grow older (Elections Canada, 2008a). This generational pattern is not confined to Canada. In twenty-one democratic countries, young people born in 1980 or later voted at lower rates than the national average (Milner, 2005; see Table 6-1).

Several demographic characteristics influence electoral participation. Age is the most important factor, as young Canadians are less likely to vote than older citizens. In 2006, just 43.8 percent of young adults aged 18 to 24 voted, compared with 61.6 percent of those aged 35 to 44, and 77.5 percent of those aged 65 to 74 (see Figure 6-2). Voters also tend to be wealthier and more educated than non-voters. People with higher household incomes may be more likely to vote because the poor have less time and energy for politics, or because they feel that the political system does not address their concerns (Blais, 2000). People with more formal education may be more likely to vote because it is easier for them to understand complex political messages. Interestingly, gender and immigrant status are not related to turnout. There are no significant differences in the turnout rates of females and males (Gidengil et al., 2004), and citizens

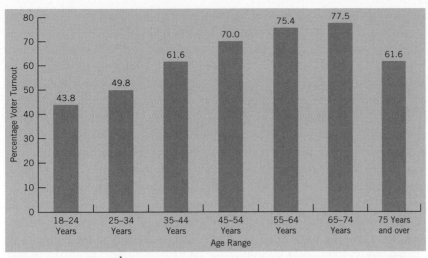

FIGURE 6-2
TURNOUT IN THE 2006 CANADIAN FEDERAL ELECTION BY AGE GROUP

Source: Elections Canada, 2008a, *Estimation of Voter Turnout by Age Group at the 39th Federal General Election, January 23, 2006*, p.5. Retrieved from http://www.elections.ca/ loi/res/rep39ge/estimation39ge_e.pdf

who were born abroad vote at the same rates as Canadian-born citizens. Nevertheless, immigrants who arrived in Canada since 1991 and who were eligible to vote were less likely to vote than more established immigrants in the 2000 election. This may be because relative newcomers have to attend to their most pressing needs—finding employment, housing, and schools for their children and learning a new language—before they can get involved in the political life of their new country (Tossutti, 2007).

Attitudes are also linked to electoral participation. Canadians who are more interested in and knowledgeable about politics vote at higher rates than citizens with less interest and knowledge (Blais, Gidengil, Nadeau, & Nevitte, 2002; Gidengil, Blais, Everitt, Fournier, & Nevitte, 2005; Howe, 2003; Pammett & LeDuc, 2006). This is because awareness of the issues, where the parties stand, and who their leaders are makes it easier to decide how to vote. Voters are also more likely than non-voters to express trust in their elected representatives, a sense of civic duty, or moral obligation to vote, and to believe that their vote would affect the outcome (LeDuc, Pammett, & Bastedo, 2008). Lifestyle circumstances also make a difference. During the 2006 election, many non-voters reported they were too busy with work, school, or family obligations to make time to vote (Pammett & LeDuc, 2006).

YOUNG CANADIANS AND FEDERAL ELECTIONS Political scientists have been preoccupied with explaining why young Canadians are not as likely to turn up at the polls as older Canadians. **Life-cycle effects** partly account for this phenomenon. As people move from their twenties to their thirties and forties, they tend to vote at higher rates (Baum, 2002). This is because as they settle down with a partner, become parents, and find a job, they become more aware of how political issues such as taxes, economic development, and access to social

LIFE-CYCLE EFFECTS The tendency for people to vote at higher rates as they age.

and health services affect their lives. Young people also possess several traits that are associated with lower turnout: they are less well-off, less religious, and less likely to be married (Rubenson, Blais, Fournier, Gidengil, & Nevitte, 2004).

Young Canadians also have attitudes that do not encourage voting. They are less likely than Canadians aged thirty years and over to agree they have a duty to vote, and are less interested in and knowledgeable about politics (Blais et al., 2002; Gidengil et al., 2005; Howe, 2003). Political scientist Henry Milner (2002, 2005) has argued that low levels of political knowledge are linked to declining newspaper readership and watching too much television, and that young Canadians are less likely to read newspapers. During the 2004 election, only 60 percent of Canadians in their twenties could name Paul Martin as Liberal party leader, only 47 percent of young Canadians could name Stephen Harper as leader of the Conservative party, and just 34 percent correctly identified Jack Layton as leader of the NDP (Gidengil, Blais, Everitt, Fournier, & Nevitte, 2005). One international survey asked young adults in nine countries to identify countries on a map. Americans, Canadians, and Mexicans posted the lowest scores, far behind the Swedish, Germans, and Italians (Milner, 2005).

Another survey (Milner, 2008) found that young Canadians were slightly more knowledgeable about politics than young Americans. The biggest difference was on international matters: 55 percent of young Americans were unable to name one permanent member country of the UN Security Council (including the United States), compared with only 30 percent in Canada. People were also ignorant about domestic matters. Fifty-six percent of young Americans were unable to identify citizens as the category of people having the right to vote, compared with 43 percent in Canada. Young Canadians did not score as well as youth in Finland, where fourteen- and fifteen-year-olds in the last year of compulsory school must complete a full-year civic education course in order to graduate. Many then go on to complete upper secondary school, where they are given two compulsory and two optional civic education courses (Milner, 2008).

Finally, political parties play an important role in mobilizing citizens to vote, but they are less likely to contact young Canadians at election time. Voters whose names are on the permanent National Register of Electors are also more likely to cast a ballot. Yet once again, younger Canadians are more likely to report that they did not receive a voter information card and were not on the voters list (Pammett & LeDuc, 2003, 2006).

ABORIGINAL CANADIANS AND FEDERAL ELECTIONS Although turnout rates vary dramatically between on-reserve Aboriginals living in different regions of the country (Guérin, 2003), several studies have shown that on-reserve Aboriginals vote at lower rates than the broader population. In the 2004 general election, 52 percent of Aboriginals living on a reserve cast a ballot, compared with the national turnout rate of 60.9 percent (Elections Canada, 2005). Three broad perspectives have been used to explain the gap in participation rates.

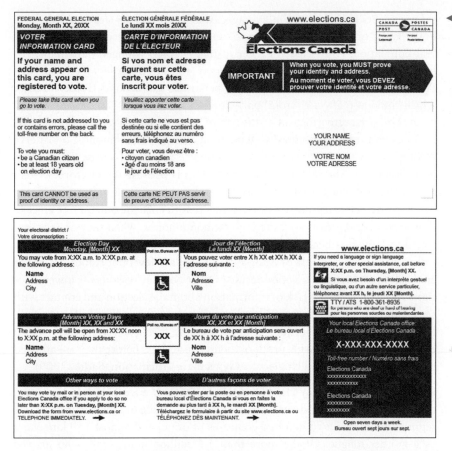

Are you on the voters list? People whose names are on the permanent National Register of Electors receive a voter information card like this one during an election campaign. Receiving this reminder about where and when to vote may be one reason they are more likely to cast a ballot.

The first explanation is that many Aboriginals question the legitimacy of the Canadian state. Some observers have argued that Aboriginals do not trust Canada's electoral system because the federal government used it to try to assimilate them (Cairns, 2003; Ladner, 2003). Before 1960, the government's enfranchisement policy gave Indians (as defined under the *Indian Act*) the right to vote, but only if they gave up their Indian status and the benefits associated with it. For some treaty nations who see themselves as sovereign nations, voting and Canadian citizenship conflict with their desire to deal with Canadian governments on a nation-to-nation basis. They may also feel that non-Aboriginals cannot represent their interests and identities (Cairns, 2003; Ladner, 2003). In fact, turnout does increase when Aboriginal candidates are running and/or political issues are raised that resonate with Aboriginal communities (Guérin, 2003). Aboriginal voting rates are also higher in band or territorial elections, suggesting that these elections are perceived as more legitimate or relevant to Aboriginal interests than federal or provincial elections (Bedford, 2003; Henderson, 2007).

A second view attributes much of the voting gap to differences in the social profile and living conditions of Aboriginal and non-Aboriginal Canadians

(Howe & Bedford, 2009). On average, Aboriginal peoples are younger, have lower levels of income and education, and are in poorer health than the general population. As discussed earlier in this chapter, younger Canadians, the less well-off, and those without a university education are less likely to vote. Poor health can make it harder for a person to get around (Prince, 2007), which could also affect electoral participation.

A third perspective focuses on the role of institutions, laws, and political parties. The nature of the electoral system, along with the fact that most on-reserve Aboriginals live in thinly populated communities scattered across the country, may discourage Aboriginals from voting. This is because the electoral system favours federal ridings that are densely populated by a single cultural group; in other words, cultural groups are better able to influence the outcome of an election or to elect representatives from their communities when they are concentrated in large numbers within a federal riding (Barsh, 1994). Since very few ridings have large numbers of Aboriginals, they have few opportunities to influence riding and national election results. Other possible reasons for lower Aboriginal turnout include a lack of information about the election and contact with the candidates, as well as general feelings of being left out (Barsh, Fraser, Bull, Provost, & Smith, 1997). Changes to the *Canada Elections Act* in 2007, which require that electors provide proof of their civic address before they are allowed to vote, have also created barriers to Aboriginal participation (Sadik, 2009).

ETHNOCULTURAL DIVERSITY AND FEDERAL ELECTIONS   In 2006, close to one in five Canadians were born abroad. These 6.2 million immigrants reported more than two hundred countries of origin and almost 150 languages as a mother tongue. Of the more than 1.1 million immigrants who arrived between 2001 and 2006, almost six in ten were born in Asian countries, including the Middle East. By 2006, 16.2 percent of Canada's population belonged to a visible minority group.[2] Immigration from countries that were not traditionally a source of immigrants has also fuelled the growth of Canada's non-Christian population (Chui, Tran, & Maheux, 2007). In other countries such as the United States, the United Kingdom, and the Netherlands, there are differences in the turnout rates of members of different ethnic groups (Clark, 2003; Electoral Commission, 2005). Is the same also true in Canada?

Although there are no differences in the turnout rates of foreign-born and Canadian-born citizens, recent immigrants are less likely to vote than native-born Canadians and immigrants who have lived here for more than ten years (Tossutti, 2007). As discussed earlier, this can be partly explained by the fact that newcomers devote their first years in Canada to meeting their basic survival needs. Immigrants who are under thirty, single, and earning less than $50 000 also vote at lower rates than older, wealthier immigrants who are

---

[2]The *Employment Equity Act* defines visible minorities as "persons, other than Aboriginal peoples, who are non-Caucasian in race or non-white in colour."

married or involved in common-law relationships. Visible minorities generally vote at lower rates than Canadians of European origin. Among Canadian-born voters, Blacks reported the lowest turnout rates in the 2000 federal election. Among foreign-born voters, the Chinese voted at a lower rate than South Asians, Blacks, and Canadians of European ancestry. However, the differences in the electoral participation of members of different ethnocultural groups disappear when other demographic factors are taken into account (Tossutti, 2007). The lower turnout rates that have been reported by Canadians of East Asian ancestry have been attributed to a history of discriminatory state policies against the Chinese (Li, 1998), discussed in Chapter 4; community orientations that do not place a high priority on voting (Lapp, 1999); language barriers; a lack of awareness of democratic rights or the electoral process; negative attitudes about politics; and the relative recency of mass immigration from East Asia (Elections BC, 2005).

Turnout also differs among citizens who have emigrated from different parts of the world and who belong to different religious denominations (Tossutti, 2007). Canadian citizens who were born in the United States and Europe were more likely to have cast a ballot in the 2000 election than eligible voters born in Africa, Central and South America, the Caribbean, Bermuda, the Middle East, and Asia. Part of the reason for this may be that many immigrants from outside the United States and Europe emigrated from countries that are caught up in violent civil conflicts or that have been ruled by authoritarian regimes. These life experiences may have left voters from those countries less exposed to democratic practices or with negative views about politics. In 2000, Canadians from the Judeo-Christian religious traditions voted at higher rates than Hindus and Sikhs, while the latter voted at higher rates than Muslims and Buddhists (Tossutti, 2007; see Figure 6-3).

Political Party Membership and Campaign Activism

Political parties play a key role in Canadian democracy. They develop positions on issues and dominate political debates in Parliament and in the media. Party members also choose the leaders and candidates in each electoral district who run for the House of Commons. If elected, they may decide whether Canada should send armed forces to participate in a war or peacekeeping missions; how much should be spent on job creation, foreign aid, the environment, health, and other important policy areas; and how much Canadians should pay in taxes. Parties offer their supporters several incentives to join and get involved. These include opportunities for socializing, access to jobs, and political education. They may also give their members a role in party decision making or introduce them to public officials who can help them when they have a problem.

There are few barriers to joining a political party; non-citizens and people who are at least fourteen years old can join, and membership fees are quite low. Nevertheless, parties have not attracted large numbers of Canadians to

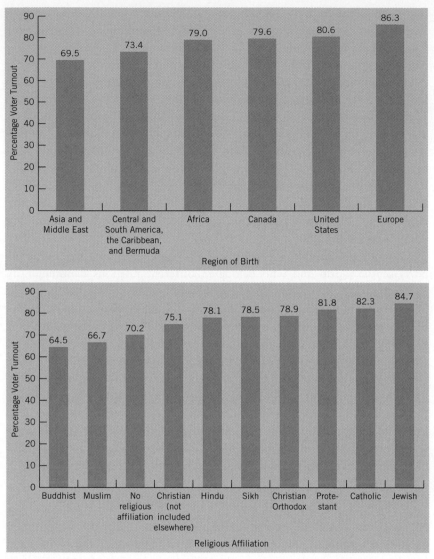

Source: Livianna Tossutti, 2007, *The Electoral Participation of Ethnocultural Communities* (Ottawa: Elections Canada), p. 39.

FIGURE 6-3
TURNOUT IN 2000 FEDERAL ELECTION BY REGION OF BIRTH AND RELIGIOUS DENOMINATION

their fold. Only an estimated 1 to 2 percent of Canadians belong to parties between elections (Cross, 2004). In other countries, too, party membership is becoming a less appealing form of political participation for citizens. Between the mid-twentieth century and the 1990s, party membership declined in twelve of fifteen democracies (Scarrow, 2000). While there is some debate as to whether fewer people are joining the federal political parties than fifty years ago, it is clear that Canadian parties do not have strong membership bases and do not inspire much confidence. In 2006, more than

58 percent of Canadians said they did not have very much confidence in parties, while another 17.9 percent said they had none at all (World Values Survey, 2006).

The small minority of Canadians who do join parties are not typical of broader society. In 2000, just 3 percent of members were between the ages of eighteen and twenty-five (Cross & Young, 2004). Young Canadians in particular are more likely to commit to interest groups, voluntary organizations, and/or protest activities. This "greying" trend in political parties has also been observed in Denmark, Ireland, and Great Britain. The Canadians who do join parties are also more likely to be well-educated, male, native-born, and of European ancestry (Cross, 2004). This profile resembles party membership patterns in the United States, the United Kingdom, and Ireland.

Federal election campaigns in Canada are relatively short and low-budget affairs when compared with elections in the United States. Because of this, political parties need to attract volunteers to attend campaign events, ask for donations, contact voters at their homes, drive voters to the polls on election day, and perform other campaign tasks. In Canada and other countries, most party members are not active. In the 1960s and 1970s, between 20 and 40 percent of Canadians reported that they had worked on a campaign activity (Mishler, 1979). In 2006, only 16.1 percent of Canadians reported that they had ever volunteered for a party (Canadian Election Study, 2006). These low levels mirror declining trends in campaign involvement in Australia, the United States, and six European countries (Dalton, McAllister, & Wattenberg, 2000).

It is widely believed that fewer people are volunteering to help candidates and parties because campaign styles have changed (Gidengil et al., 2004). Since the 1960s, parties have relied more and more on professional public relations consultants, pollsters, advertising agencies, and media specialists to run their campaigns, and on automated dialing software to contact voters. The professionalization and centralization of campaigns has meant that local party members are left with menial tasks. Because members of political parties do not generally have a great influence on policies and laws, many people try to exert influence by joining and becoming active in interest groups or social movements, or by engaging in protest activity and cyberactivism.

Interest Group and Social Movement Involvement

Interest groups are organizations that offer Canadians another avenue to influence the making and implementation of public policies by raising issue awareness, communicating their members' views to the government, and in some cases, negotiating the details of policies with public officials. In both the United Kingdom and Canada, more people belong to interest groups than to political parties (Farrell & Webb, 2000; Maloney, 2006). In 2004, about 14 percent of Canadians reported that they had joined an interest group at some point in their lives (Canadian Election Study, 2004). More Canadians, particularly younger Canadians, feel they have a better chance to influence public policy by joining an interest group rather than a political party (Howe & Northrup, 2000).

As with other vehicles of political participation, interest group membership does not represent society as a whole. Older, affluent university graduates and Canadians of European ancestry are most likely to belong to these groups (Gidengil et al., 2004). Social movements, or networks of groups and individuals that seek major social and political changes, often by acting outside established political institutions, are also gaining in popularity. Some examples include the women's, environmental, lesbian and gay rights, human rights, and animal rights movements. Ronald Inglehart (1971, 1990) has attributed their growth in many advanced capitalist democracies since the Second World War to changes in cultural values. For a fuller discussion of interest groups and social movements in Canada, see Chapter 7.

Protest Activities

While some forms of conventional political participation have been withering, so-called unconventional protest activities have been growing over the past few decades in Canada, Great Britain, the United States, and France (Hall, 2002; Maloney, 2006; Putnam, 2000; Worms, 2002,). Political scientist Neil Nevitte (1996) has attributed this cross-national phenomenon to the shift to a post-industrial economy and the rise of post-materialist values that have produced a growing number of citizens who possess the skills, knowledge, and information to challenge public authorities.

When Canadians protest, they tend to engage in actions that do not require a lot of time and effort. According to the 2006 World Values Survey (2006), 72.5 percent of Canadians had signed a petition at some point in their lives. In comparison, 23.5 percent had joined a boycott and about 26 percent had attended a lawful/peaceful demonstration. Although relatively few Canadians participate in more time-consuming protest activities, even modest efforts can have a major impact on public opinion or business practices. In the 1970s, thousands of Canadians took part in mass demonstrations against the war in Vietnam and nuclear testing off the coast of Alaska. During the 1990s, protests and blockades set up by environmental groups and First Nations drew the world's attention to industrial logging in British Columbia's ancient temperate rainforests, while information campaigns alerted consumers to the cost of buying wood and paper products from this ecosystem.

In the early twenty-first century, boisterous rallies were held across the country to protest the U.S.-led war in Iraq. A boycott of Kentucky Fried Chicken (KFC) outlets, spearheaded by the People for the Ethical Treatment of Animals (PETA), helped persuade the restaurant chain in Canada to buy poultry from suppliers who use a more humane method to slaughter chickens. In the spring of 2009, thousands of Tamil Canadians blocked a major expressway in Toronto to protest the civil war in Sri Lanka that has claimed the lives of many of their relatives and friends. As is the case with conventional political participation, certain types of people are more likely to engage in political protest. They include middle-aged, university-educated Canadians, the relatively affluent, public sector employees, and people from union households (Gidengil et al., 2004).

By international standards, Canadians rarely join in illegal protest activity. In 2004, just 6 percent said they have ever taken part in an illegal strike and just 1 percent reported that they have ever illegally occupied a building or factory (Canadian Election Study, 2004). Although illegal demonstrations or violent protests are not common, they have had a significant impact on Canadian history. In 1837 and 1838, an estimated 40 000 to 200 000 French Canadians participated in the Lower Canada rebellions. In 1869, Louis Riel, the leader of about 10 000 Métis in the Red River area, seized Fort Garry and established a provisional government of Manitoba. More than 15 000 Canadians took part in the conscription riots of 1917, and another 30 000 workers left their jobs in support of the Winnipeg General Strike in 1919. The 1960s and early 1970s saw the Front de Libération du Québec (FLQ), a Quebec secessionist group, carry out bombings and kidnappings that culminated in the deaths of at least five people.

The last two decades have seen many protest activities organized by the indigenous and anti-globalization movements. In 1990, Mohawks near the town of Oka, Quebec, organized a peaceful blockade to oppose the development of a

◀ For more than five hours on May 10, 2009, thousands of Tamil Canadians protested on Toronto's Gardiner Expressway, one of Canada's busiest highways, to demand that the federal government do more to help end the civil war in their native Sri Lanka.

golf course on sacred land. The protest escalated into a seventy-eight-day armed siege at Kanesatake and Kahnawake between Mohawks, the Quebec police, and the Canadian army. In 1991, members of the Peigan nation engaged in an armed standoff with the RCMP. They wanted to halt development of the Oldman Dam in southern Alberta, a project that would flood parts of their homeland and inflict ecological damage in the area. The Six Nations of the Grand River Territory in Caledonia, Ontario, have used protests and blockades to stop commercial development on what they claim are their lands. The Summit of the Americas, held in Quebec City in 2001 to inaugurate the Free Trade Area of the Americas, also saw violent clashes between security forces and activists. When ten thousand activists, many of them young, stormed barriers that had been set up around the meeting site, police unleashed tear gas, plastic bullets, and water cannons to fend off the protesters.

Cyberactivism

The growth of computers and connectivity since the early 1980s has paved the way for another form of political involvement dubbed "cyberactivism," or online activism. New information technologies have radically altered how Canadians learn about political events and how groups raise awareness about issues that are not reported or under-reported in the mainstream media. They have also changed how activists circulate information, organize campaigns, and mobilize their members to take online or offline action.

In Canada and elsewhere, the global social justice movement has relied heavily on websites and email lists to contest trade and investment liberalization, the privatization and deregulation of public health care and other welfare state institutions, and "sweatshop" practices by major clothing companies, among many other issues. The internet was used to alert people to the protests at the Summit of the Americas in 2001. People who could not travel to Quebec City were invited to participate in a virtual walk on a website (Vegh, 2003). Online activism also played an integral role in the international campaign to defeat the Multilateral Agreement on Investment (MAI) in the late 1990s. The Facebook social networking site figured prominently in a 2008 online protest against proposed changes to laws affecting young drivers in Ontario (see Box 6-2, Canadian Cyberactivists). Organizers of the Tamil Canadian protests relied on traditional electronic media, as well as Facebook and text messaging, to mobilize thousands to attend mass rallies against the Sinhalese government (Mathieu & Taylor, 2009).

There are different perspectives on whether the interactive setting of the internet and World Wide Web will revitalize political participation. Optimists argue that "chatrooms, radio and video streaming, personalized websites, as well as access to databases, government documents and unfiltered news sources" give people the freedom to create and interpret information in their own way (Deibert, 2002). The internet can also connect people in isolated

BOX 6-2

Canadian Cyberactivists

The battle against the Multilateral Agreement on Investment (MAI) was the first international campaign in which activists took full advantage of the internet to criticize the agreement, attract mainstream media coverage, and quickly broadcast information about the negotiations to sympathetic activists around the world. Negotiated by members of the Organization of Economic Co-operation and Development (OECD) between 1995 and 1998, the proposed agreement contained much that was controversial. It aimed to limit the powers of governments to support domestic industries, fund public services, or protect the environment if these measures hurt the interests of foreign investors. The mainstream media had not given the negotiations much coverage, and public interest groups had not been consulted about it. However, non-governmental organizations in Canada and abroad were determined to expose the agreement. Using a variety of websites, they mobilized a diverse coalition of consumer advocates and human rights, labour, and environmental groups against the treaty. As public opposition and skepticism about the MAI increased, governments began to withdraw from the negotiations, effectively killing the agreement (Dyer-Witheford, 2005).

In another example of cyberactivism, more than 150 000 Facebook users forced the government of Ontario to back down from proposed changes to the *Highway Traffic Act*. Introduced in late 2008, Bill 126 had been designed to help curb the number of fatalities and injuries sustained by young drivers. When first announced, it included provisions for a zero-tolerance alcohol policy for drivers twenty-one years and under, and restrictions on novice teenage drivers from carrying more than one young passenger aged nineteen and under at any time during the first year of their G2 licence. The bill generated a strong backlash on social networking sites such as Facebook, particularly from young drivers and rural families who objected to the passenger limits. Under pressure from the online campaign, the government cancelled the daytime passenger limits for novice teenage drivers.

The battle against the MAI and the protest against the *Highway Traffic Act* are but two examples of the growing trend of cyberactivism. In the future, the greater sophistication and availability of new information technologies, along with innovations in how to apply them, could make these already powerful tools for political change even more effective.

communities to the outside world. Chief Albert Mercredi, whose band lives downstream from oil sands operations in northern Alberta, says the recent arrival of the internet in his community has done just that ("Finding Their Voice," 2008).

However, there are concerns that the lack of face-to-face interaction in a virtual environment and the ease with which identities can be forged will undermine trust between people (Barney, 2000). There are also inequalities in internet access and usage in Canada. In addition to the fact that the internet remains a minor source of information about politics and elections, a narrow spectrum of Canadian society—university graduates, the affluent, and the young—are more likely to rely on it for information than Canadians who are older, less educated, and less well-off. The "digital divide," whereby wealthier individuals in urban areas are more likely to live in households with internet connections than the poor and residents of rural communities (Dyer-Witheford, 2005, p. 273), mirrors the participation gap between the affluent and less well-off that has been observed in many conventional political activities.

CIVIL SOCIETY, CIVIC ENGAGEMENT, AND DEMOCRACY

CIVIL SOCIETY
The voluntary associations and non-governmental organizations that bring people together to achieve a common goal.

Civil society consists of the voluntary associations and non-governmental organizations that bring people together to achieve a common goal. Some examples of voluntary organizations include the following:

- sports and recreation clubs
- religious associations
- student or campus clubs
- community/service organizations (e.g., Kiwanis, Lions, Canadian Legion)
- ethnocultural associations
- environmental groups
- human rights organizations
- business and professional associations, and labour unions

Although most voluntary associations are not primarily political in nature, many of them become involved in political actions while representing their members' interests. Some examples include student associations that lobby post-secondary institutions and provincial governments for lower tuition and ancillary fees, religious groups that take public stands on controversial moral issues such as abortion and euthanasia, and ethnocultural organizations that lobby the federal government on foreign policy and immigration matters. Canada's civil society sector is the second largest in the world and makes a significant contribution to the national economy and employment (Hall, Barr, Easwaramoothy, Sokolowski, & Salamon, 2005).

Democracy, as Alexis de Tocqueville (1900/1969) argued in his observations of nineteenth-century America, requires civic associations that are not specifically political, but that provide meaning for people and opportunities for them to become involved in their communities. He concluded that voluntary organizations strengthened democracy because they encouraged people to cooperate with each other to achieve the common good. Political scientist Robert Putnam (2000) has argued that voluntary associations provide modern democracies with a crucial supply of **social capital**. Social capital refers to the social networks, norms of generalized reciprocity, and interpersonal trust that foster coordination and cooperation for mutual benefit. Generalized reciprocity refers to the understanding that "I will do this favour for you now without expecting anything specific back from you, in the expectation that someone else will do something for me down the road" (pp. 20–21). This idea was captured in the movie *Pay It Forward,* in which a young boy is asked in

SOCIAL CAPITAL
The networks, norms of generalized reciprocity, and trust that foster coordination and cooperation for mutual benefit.

his social studies assignment to propose an idea that will improve humankind. The boy decides to do good deeds for three new people. If they can also do good deeds for others, or "pay it forward," then positive changes should and do occur.

According to social capital theorists, mutual cooperation and trust between individuals living in the same society are necessary for democracies to thrive. Others are skeptical about the potential for social capital to support democracy. For example, members of groups that promote racial hatred or youth gangs may also trust and cooperate with each other, but they can hardly be described as supporting democracy and tolerance.

Why do many people believe that it is a good thing for a country to have a strong civil society in which many people participate in voluntary groups? One reason is that people who get involved in these associations are more likely to get involved in political activities. This happens because people meet new friends in these groups. They may end up talking about politics or asking new acquaintances to attend a political party meeting, to help out on a campaign, or to join a protest. Furthermore, members of voluntary groups take an interest in community affairs, and often learn how to plan a meeting, cooperate with others to achieve a common goal, and acquire the attitudes and leadership and social skills that are necessary to participate in politics. In Italy, regions with dense networks of amateur soccer clubs, choral societies, community service organizations, and the like, were found to be more prosperous and better governed (Putnam, 1993). In the United States, youths are better off and healthier in states with more voluntary organizations, higher rates of participation in them, and higher rates of volunteering (Putnam, 2000). These states are also safer, more tolerant of civil liberties, and more committed to racial and gender equality. Income gaps between the rich and poor in these states are also lower than in states with fewer civic groups.

CIVIC ENGAGEMENT IN CANADA

Civic engagement refers to different forms of community involvement such as joining a voluntary or civic organization; **volunteering,** or providing unpaid service to help others; and **philanthropy,** or charitable giving. While relatively few Canadians participate in most types of political activities, the country's civic life is healthier. A large percentage of Canadians join and volunteer for civic associations, help others directly, and/or give money to charities and non-profit organizations. Civic engagement, unlike voting and campaign involvement, has not declined over time. The amount of time that Canadians spend on civic acts such as attending community, political, church, or trade union meetings; tutoring; coaching; and/or organizing community events held steady between 1971 and 1998 (Andersen, Curtis, & Grabb, 2006). The percentage of Canadians aged fifteen and over who gave money to a charitable or non-profit organization and who volunteered also remained stable between 2004 and 2007. Despite these

VOLUNTEERING
Providing unpaid service to help others.

PHILANTHROPY
Charitable giving.

positive signs, civic life is also characterized by inequalities. Older, university-educated, and relatively affluent Canadians are more likely to belong to voluntary groups. Furthermore, a small minority of Canadians are responsible for most of the volunteer hours and financial donations (Hall, Lasby, Ayer, & Gibbons, 2009; Hall, Lasby, Gumulka, & Tryon, 2006).

Membership in Voluntary Organizations

Canadians believe that voluntary organizations and volunteers contribute to a better quality of life. People who join voluntary organizations can pursue their own interests and work with others to address issues in their communities. In 2004, two-thirds of Canadians aged fifteen and over reported belonging to a group or organization. Canadians were most likely to belong to sports and recreation organizations, followed by professional associations and unions, religious organizations or groups, and cultural, education, or hobby organizations (Hall, Lasby, Gumulka, & Tryon, 2006). People aged thirty-five to fifty-four who are university-educated and relatively affluent were most likely to belong to these groups. Participation rates also varied across the country. For example, residents of Saskatchewan, Prince Edward Island, Ontario, Alberta, and Manitoba were more likely to belong to civic organizations than residents of Quebec, Newfoundland and Labrador, and New Brunswick.

Volunteering

In 2007, 12.5 million Canadians or 46 percent of the population aged fifteen and older volunteered through a civic organization. Their 2.1 billion hours of unpaid service amounted to the equivalent of more than one million full-time jobs. A typical volunteer contributes 166 hours of his or her time each year to sports and recreation, social services, education and research, and religious organizations, among other areas. Volunteers organized, supervised, or coordinated events and fundraising; they helped teach, coach, and mentor others; or they served on committees. Although close to half of all Canadians volunteered for an organization, the top quarter of volunteers was responsible for contributing 78 percent of all volunteer hours (Hall, Lasby, Ayer, & Gibbons, 2009).

Canadians report some of the highest levels of participation in voluntary organizations in North, Central, and South America (Córdova Guillén, 2008). In 2006, slightly more than 72 percent of Canadians participated in meetings of at least one of the following secular civic organizations: a parents' association at school, a committee or council for community improvement, a professional association, a merchants or farmers association, or meetings of a political party or movement. Although civil society participation in the United States is high (67.5 percent), the country was not at the top of the list (Figure 6-4). As with other forms of political participation and civic engagement, certain types of Canadians were more likely to volunteer for an organization: the young, the

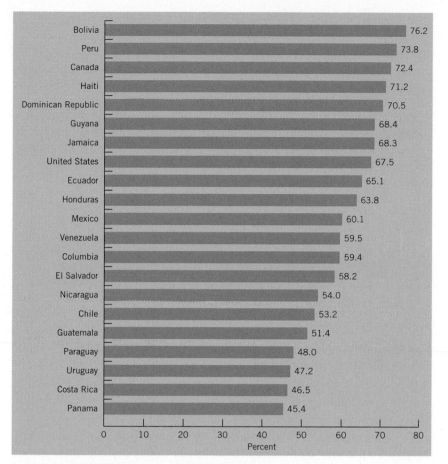

FIGURE 6-4
CIVIC PARTICIPATION IN THE AMERICAS: PERCENTAGE WHO PARTICIPATE IN AT LEAST ONE CIVIC ORGANIZATION

Country	Percent
Bolivia	76.2
Peru	73.8
Canada	72.4
Haiti	71.2
Dominican Republic	70.5
Guyana	68.4
Jamaica	68.3
United States	67.5
Ecuador	65.1
Honduras	63.8
Mexico	60.1
Venezuela	59.5
Columbia	59.4
El Salvador	58.2
Nicaragua	54.0
Chile	53.2
Guatemala	51.4
Paraguay	48.0
Uruguay	47.2
Costa Rica	46.5
Panama	45.4

Source: Based on data from The Americas Barometer by the Latin American Public Opinion Project (LAPOP). Abby B. Córdova Guillén, 2008, "Social Trust, Economic Inequality, and Democracy in the Americas," in Mitchell Seligsen (Ed.) *Challenges to democracy in Latin America and the Caribbean: Evidence from the Americas Barometer 2006–07* (pp. 153–54), Nashville TN: Vanderbilt University.

religiously active, and people with higher incomes, a university education, and school-aged children in the household. Immigrants were less likely than native-born Canadians to volunteer, but those immigrants who did volunteer contributed slightly more hours. Volunteer rates varied across the country because of differences in the economic conditions of provinces and territories, as well as the social and cultural values of the people who make up subnational populations. Saskatchewan had the highest volunteer rate, followed by the Yukon, Prince Edward Island, and Nova Scotia. The lowest volunteer rate was found in Quebec (see Table 6-2).

Canadians say they volunteer because they want to give back to their communities and use their skills and experience, and because they were personally affected by the cause supported by the organization. Many Canadians performed community service in response to requests by schools, employers, or non-profit and charitable organizations. Young Canadians and individuals

TABLE 6-2
VOLUNTEER AND DONATION RATES BY PROVINCE AND TERRITORY (PERCENTAGE)

PROVINCE/TERRITORY	DONATION RATE	VOLUNTEERING FOR ORGANIZATIONS	HELPING OTHERS DIRECTLY
Canada	84	46	84
British Columbia	79	47	83
Alberta	85	52	86
Saskatchewan	84	59	85
Manitoba	87	54	86
Ontario	86	47	83
Quebec	84	37	83
New Brunswick	88	48	85
Nova Scotia	87	55	87
Prince Edward Island	89	56	86
Newfoundland and Labrador	91	46	87
Yukon	78	58	85
Northwest Territories	68	46	67
Nunavut	66	43	83

Source: *M. Hall, D. Lasby, S. Ayer, & W. D. Gibbons, 2009,* Caring Canadians, involved Canadians: Highlights from the 2007 Canada Survey of Giving, Volunteering and Participating *(Ottawa: Minister of Industry), pp. 28, 46, and 56.*

with less formal education were most likely to perform mandatory community service (Hall et al., 2009). The provinces of British Columbia and Ontario are among those jurisdictions that require high school students to perform community service in order to graduate (see Box 6-3, Students at Work: Mandatory Community Service in High Schools).

A large majority of Canadians also help others directly, without working through a voluntary organization (Hall et al., 2009). In 2007, 84 percent reported that they had helped out with household tasks; provided health or personal care, counselling, and advice to someone in need; visited the elderly; or helped care for children. Young people aged fifteen to twenty-four were the most likely to help others directly, as were people with higher incomes and a post-secondary education. The provinces with the highest rates of one-on-one volunteering were Nova Scotia and Newfoundland and Labrador. The lowest rates of helping others directly were reported in the Northwest Territories. See Table 6-2.

Philanthropy

About 23 million Canadians, or 84 percent of the population aged fifteen and over, gave money to a charitable or other non-profit organization in 2007 (Hall et al., 2009). They donated a total $10 billion, with average donations of $437. Religious organizations were the most frequent recipients, followed by health and social service organizations. As with volunteering, charities rely on a relatively small group of donors for most of their support. The top one-quarter of donors provided 82 percent of all donations.

Students at Work:
Mandatory Community Service in High Schools

In response to declining levels of youth engagement in political or civic activities, educational institutions around the world have introduced community service requirements. Their goal is to help students develop an understanding of civic responsibility and the contribution they can make to their communities. In British Columbia, students must participate in thirty hours of work or community service in order to graduate from secondary school (B.C. Ministry of Education, 2008). The Ontario requirements are slightly more demanding. Since 1999, high school students in Ontario must take a civics class and complete a minimum of forty hours of community involvement activities in order to graduate (Ontario Ministry of Education and Training, 1999). Service can involve activities such as cleaning up a local park, volunteering at a local hospital or animal shelter, coaching a young athlete, or any other activity that is not done for pay and that improves the quality of community life.

These curriculum changes were introduced because research has shown that community service can lead to improvements in political knowledge and political efficacy (Niemi, Hepburn, & Chapman, 2000); higher levels of volunteering during high school (Henderson, Brown, Pancer, & Ellis-Hale, 2007); and volunteering involvements later in life (Jasnoski, Musick, & Wilson, 1998). But not everyone agrees that mandatory community service is a good idea. Shortly after the requirement was introduced in Ontario, one principal commented that it "ticks off those students who had no intent of volunteering before, who will act out in defiance of being told what to do and say they're not going to volunteer, possibly putting their graduation prospects at risk" (Volunteer Canada, 2006). Students who are forced to volunteer may also come to view community service as an activity that should be done only when it is required or rewarded (Batson, Jasnoski, & Hanson, 1978). The effectiveness of community service programs also depends on whether students have meaningful placements, are well supervised, and have the opportunity to share their experiences in the classroom (Meinhard & Foster, 1999, 2000).

If you were designing the high school curriculum in your province, would you require that students perform community service in order to graduate? What are the benefits of mandatory community service? Are there any drawbacks?

Donors were more likely to be older, well-off, highly educated, married or widowed, and religiously active. Interestingly, although wealthier individuals gave more money in absolute terms, donors with the lowest incomes gave a higher percentage of their incomes (Hall et al., 2009). Immigrants were slightly less likely to make a donation than native-born Canadians, but gave larger amounts when they did contribute. Charitable giving also varied across the country because it is affected by differences in provincial and territorial economic conditions, social and cultural values, and the personal attributes of the individuals living in the provinces and territories. The donor rate was highest in Newfoundland, followed by Prince Edward Island and New Brunswick, and lowest in Nunavut (Hall et al., 2009). See Table 6-2.

Summary and Conclusion

This chapter has drawn a portrait of democratic life in Canada by examining levels of political participation and civic engagement, how Canadians choose to get involved in these activities, and whether some people are more likely than others to participate. Although there are numerous opportunities to get involved on a local, provincial, national, and international scale, we found that Canadians are not fervent political activists, and that several forms of conventional political involvement are in decline. In this respect, Canadians have much in common with citizens living in other democratic states. Furthermore, the individuals who take part in most types of political and civic activities do not reflect the country's diverse social makeup. A small core of individuals tend to dominate political and civic affairs. The attitudes, personal characteristics, and living conditions of Canadians explain these differences. With some exceptions, voice, power, and influence tend to be concentrated among those who are better off, well educated, and older.

There are some bright spots in this portrait of individual and group participation in democratic life. A large majority of Canadians give back to their communities through volunteering and donations to their favourite causes, and growing numbers are finding new ways to become engaged in politics through interest groups, social movements, protest activity, and cyber-activism. Thus, as Canadians become more disillusioned with their elected representatives and wonder, increasingly, whether good government is an achievable goal, they are developing alternative ways of bringing their ideals and values into the public arena. These vehicles of participation have not replaced and are not likely to replace conventional political activism and more traditional means of communication, but they have already changed public opinion, policies, laws, and the ways Canadians learn about issues, express their views, and take action.

Discussion Questions

1. Classical democratic theorists argue that high levels of political participation by a broad cross-section of society are desirable in a democracy. Elitist theories are based on the premise that participation should be limited to those who have the education and resources to understand complex political issues. Where do you stand?

2. What is your opinion about deliberative democracy? Should citizens play a larger role in the policy-making process?

3. Why are young people less interested in voting than older citizens?

4. What can be done to revitalize youth engagement in conventional political activities such as voting and party membership?

5. Is voting a civic duty?

6. Has the spread of the internet bolstered or undermined democracy?

7. Can violent protest activity ever be justified?

8. Should high schools or colleges and universities institute mandatory civics courses in order for students to graduate?

Further Reading

Almond, G., & Verba, S. (1965). *The civic culture: Political attitudes and democracy in five nations.* Boston, MA: Little, Brown and Company.

Everitt, J., & O'Neill, B. (Eds.). (2002). *Citizen politics: Research and theory in Canadian political behaviour.* Toronto, ON: Oxford University Press.

Gidengil, E., Blais, A., Nevitte, N., & Nadeau, R. (2004). *Citizens.* Vancouver, BC: University of British Columbia Press.

Howe, P. (2007). *The electoral participation of young Canadians.* Ottawa, ON: Elections Canada.

Ladner, K., & McCrossan, M. (2007). *The electoral participation of Aboriginal people.* Ottawa, ON: Elections Canada.

Mishler, W. (1979). *Political participation in Canada: Prospects for democratic citizenship.* Toronto, ON: Macmillan Canada.

Pammett, J. H., & Dornan, C. (Eds.). (2006). *The Canadian federal election of 2006.* Toronto, ON: Dundurn.

Putnam, R. D. (Ed.). (2002). *Democracies in flux: The evolution of social capital in contemporary societies.* New York, NY: Oxford University Press.

Putnam, R. D. (2000). *Bowling alone: The collapse and revival of American community.* New York, NY: Simon & Schuster.

Smith, M. (2008). *Group politics and social movements in Canada.* Peterborough, ON: Broadview Press.

Tossutti, L. (2007). *The electoral participation of ethnocultural communities.* Ottawa, ON: Elections Canada.

Verba, S., Lehman Schlozman, K., & Brady, H. E. (1995). *Voice and equality: Civic voluntarism in American politics.* Cambridge, MA: Harvard University Press.

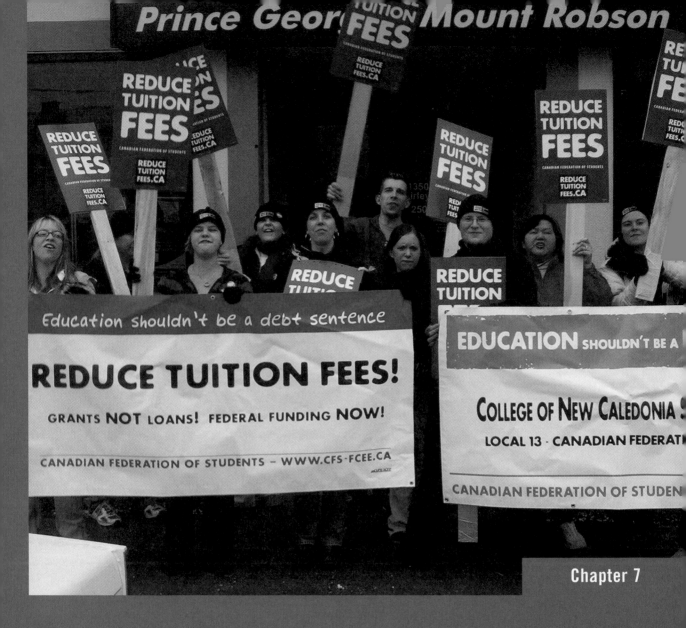

Chapter 7

INTEREST GROUPS, SOCIAL MOVEMENTS, AND LOBBYISTS

PHOTO ABOVE: Students attending B.C.'s College of New Caledonia protest during the 2007 Canadian Federation of Students' National Day of Action.

CHAPTER OBJECTIVES

After reading this chapter, you should be able to

1. Discuss the importance of interest groups.
2. Compare and contrast theoretical perspectives concerning interest groups.
3. Distinguish between the types of interest groups.
4. Discuss the methods by which interest groups try to influence public policy.
5. Explain the significance of social movements.
6. Discuss whether lobbying should be strictly regulated.

Lloyd Axworthy is a passionate reformer. As a long-time Liberal cabinet minister, he often stirred up controversy with bold policy proposals. However, he met his match when he tried to change Canada's student loan system.

As Human Resources Minister, Axworthy promoted the idea of an income contingent repayment plan in which students repay their loans based on the income they earn after graduation. The Canadian Federation of Students (CFS) was sharply critical of the proposal, arguing that it would lead to a lifetime of debt for graduates who did not command high incomes and discourage students from poorer families from pursuing higher education.

The CFS raised their objections at public consultations about the proposal held by a House of Commons committee and in meetings with Minister Axworthy. At a demonstration organized by the CFS on Parliament Hill, Axworthy was pelted with Kraft Dinner and hit by a raw egg (Greenspon & Wilson-Smith, 1996). However, the minister remained committed to the proposal. The CFS then came up with a plan—strike action.

On January 25, 1995, tens of thousands of university, college, and high school students participated in the "National Day of Strike and Action" organized by the CFS. In communities across Canada, students "boycotted class, marched, demonstrated, rallied, organized forums, leafleted, blocked highways and in some cases conducted full-fledged strikes" (Temelini, 2008, p. 234).

Many interest groups, including the Action Canada Network, the Council of Canadians, the National Anti-Poverty Organization, senior citizens groups, women's groups, and labour unions, supported the protest (Temelini, 2008). By building a large coalition of groups in support of their cause, as well as gaining extensive media coverage of their protest action, the CFS succeeded in persuading the government to drop the proposal. However, the 1995 federal government's budget slashed the transfer payments to provincial governments that help to fund post-secondary education as well as health and social programs. As a result, many provincial governments raised tuition fees. Did the CFS win the battle but lose the war?

Interest groups, such as the Canadian Federation of Students, can and do influence the policies that governments adopt. However, it often takes determined and skilful action to achieve their objectives. Also, they may find it difficult to shift the basic direction of government, such as the Canadian government's decision in 1995 to deal with its financial difficulties by cutting the money it transfers to provincial governments. Nevertheless, interest groups persist in taking on government, despite the odds.

The CFS has continued to organize an annual day of action to try to persuade governments to increase funding for post-secondary education and to lower tuition fees. As for Lloyd Axworthy, he now deals with students as president of the University of Winnipeg.

PLURALIST THEORY

In examining the politics of democratic countries a key question is, to what extent are the public and various segments of society able to affect public policies? Is it only through elections that we can have a general say in how our country is governed? Or can we exert influence through the multitude of interest groups that strive to affect public policies? **Interest groups** (also known as pressure groups[1] or advocacy groups) are organizations that pursue the common interests of groups of people, particularly by trying to influence the making and implementation of public policies.

Pluralist theory contends that interest groups are a key aspect of the political process in democratic countries and have a strong effect on the policies governments adopt. Because individuals are free to engage in political activity in a liberal democracy, they will form and join groups to pursue their interests. Interest groups articulate the demands of various interests in society, allowing citizens to make their voices heard by joining an organized group that is able to influence government. Because individuals have differing interests (including those based on region, ethnicity, class, and gender), each person may join or be represented by many groups. A group formed to promote a particular interest or position on an issue will stimulate the creation of other groups to promote different interests or other positions on the same issue. In this way, competing interest groups can represent the diversity of interests present in society.

Pluralist theory also assumes that government will be influenced by pressure from varied interest groups. Politicians will try to find compromises among the positions brought forward by competing interest groups in order to satisfy as many groups as possible. Government, in the pluralist view, is not biased toward a particular interest, but rather reacts to the pressures placed on it by different groups. Of course some interest groups are more powerful than others because of the resources they possess. While some groups may have plentiful financial resources that help them to exert influence, other groups may be able to make use of the voices of their large membership or the expertise they possess. Furthermore, the pattern of group influence will vary from one policy area to another. For example, business groups may be particularly influential when it comes to economic policy, but may be less influential than other groups when government is considering education or health care policies.

Overall, then, pluralist theory suggests that no one group or interest has a dominant influence over public policy. As long as people are free to form and join groups, it is assumed that the differing interests in society will be able to shape public policy. Thus interest groups play a major role in creating a

INTEREST GROUPS
Organizations that pursue the common interests of groups of people, particularly by trying to influence the making and implementation of public policies.

PLURALIST THEORY
The theory that the freedom of individuals to establish and join groups that are not controlled by the government results in a variety of groups having an ability to influence the decisions of government, with no group having a dominant influence.

---

[1]The term "pressure group" is sometimes used to distinguish groups that are primarily devoted to influencing government from the broader category of "interest groups" that share a common interest or goal but do not necessarily devote much attention to political action.

democratic political system in which power is widely dispersed. Further, it is assumed that free competition among the groups, each promoting a particular set of interests, will generally result in policies that are in the public interest.

Pluralist theory is not without critics. Other theories contend that power is concentrated in a small number of hands, and that the major policies adopted by governments do not reflect the views and interests of a wide variety of groups. In this chapter, we will consider the validity of pluralist theory, and examine some alternative theories, as we review the organization and activities of those striving to influence government and public policies.

INTEREST GROUPS

Types of Interest Groups

Some interest groups, termed **self-interest groups**, are primarily concerned with gaining **selective benefits** from government for their members. For example, the twenty corporations that belong to the Forest Products Association of Canada are concerned about government regulations that might block mergers in their industry. They also advocate public policies that facilitate their exports and promote investment in their industry. Likewise, most professionals, such as lawyers, doctors, social workers, and teachers, are organized into interest groups primarily to promote the interests of their profession.

Other groups are concerned with advancing the interests and gaining recognition for the identity of a particular sector of society (for example, the Assembly of First Nations, the Chinese Canadian National Council, and the Canadian Association for the Fifty-Plus). Such groups are not generally focused on gaining specific, selective benefits for their dues-paying members, but rather often seek changes in public policies that reflect the concerns and values of the sector of society that they represent. For example, interest groups representing ethnic groups seek to affect Canada's multicultural and immigration policies, while the issues pursued by the Canadian Association for the Fifty-Plus include health care reform and pension improvements.

Finally, many interest groups (termed **public interest groups** or citizens groups) pursue goals that can be viewed as being for the public good and do not benefit group members exclusively. Examples include the Sierra Club, which campaigns for environmental protection, and the Council of Canadians, which fights to protect Canadian independence. Although the policies championed by various public interest groups may be controversial, public interest groups believe the policies will provide **collective benefits** for society. Groups that seek to influence Canadian public policies to improve conditions in other parts of the world may also be considered public interest groups. For example, the Canadian Council for International Cooperation, a coalition of about one hundred Canadian organizations, aims to "end global poverty and to promote social justice and human dignity for all."

SELF-INTEREST GROUPS
Interest groups that are primarily concerned with selective benefits that are directed toward their members.

SELECTIVE BENEFIT
A particular benefit that is made available to the members of an interest group but is not available to the public as a whole.

PUBLIC INTEREST GROUP
A group that pursues goals that can be viewed as being for the public good and do not benefit members of the group exclusively.

COLLECTIVE BENEFITS
Benefits to society as a whole.

Canadian Council for International Co-operation:
www.ccic.ca

The distinction between types of interest groups can be contentious. For example, a group trying to affect public policies directed at a particular industry will argue that such policies are in the public interest because of the employment their industry creates and its contributions to national prosperity. Nevertheless, industry groups are primarily concerned with selective benefits to members, even though the policies they seek may provide some benefits to the country as a whole. In contrast, the benefits sought by groups that promote the interests of broad sectors of society are not limited to their dues-paying members, but rather the category of people they claim to represent. And particularly for equality-seeking groups such as women's groups and poor people's groups, it can be argued that they are focused on winning similar rights and benefits for their sector of society as are enjoyed by other members of society. For example, gay and lesbian groups have sought the same rights for same-sex couples as for heterosexual couples. Overall, distinctions between self-interest groups, sectoral groups, and public interest groups are useful. Yet claims that the policies sought by any group, company, or individual are in the public interest are often controversial and need to be examined carefully to assess their validity (as discussed in Box 7-1, A Giant Bailout for the Auto Giants).

Political activity is often only one aspect of the activities of interest groups. For example, in addition to pursuing the interests of their profession through political activity, many professional associations also devote considerable attention to activities such as the following:

- educating and informing their members,
- arranging conferences for their members,
- assessing the qualifications of those who seek accreditation to practise their profession, and
- determining whether members should be disciplined for violating the ethics and rules of their profession.

Similarly, business associations may be involved in helping members find export markets, developing certification standards for products, and working with community colleges to ensure potential workers are properly trained. Labour unions, although often active in politics, are primarily concerned with collective bargaining and ensuring that employers honour collective agreements. The Royal Canadian Legion provides social gathering places for veterans, is involved in community activities, and reminds Canadians of the sacrifices made in times of war, as well as lobbying government to improve the pensions and benefits for veterans.

Interest groups also vary in whether they seek to influence the policies adopted by governments on one particular issue or a range of issues. For example, pro-life and pro-choice groups focus on whether abortion should be legal or illegal. The Canadian Council of Chief Executives and the Canadian Labour

A Giant Bailout for the Auto Giants: Public Interest or Self-Interest?

Charles E. Wilson (a former chairman of General Motors) is often quoted as saying, "What's good for General Motors is good for America." As Canadian and U.S. governments were pressured in 2009 by the North American auto industry and the autoworkers unions to provide tens of billions of dollars to bail out the North American automakers that faced bankruptcy, controversy raged as to whether the bailout was in the public interest. The collapse of General Motors (GM) and Chrysler would result in the loss of hundreds of thousands of jobs. Long-time workers would be faced with the loss of company pensions, and many companies supplying parts would fold if the automakers went bankrupt. With the auto industry being an important component of the Canadian economy, the collapse of one or more auto manufacturers could have had devastating effects on the economy in a time of a serious recession.

Others argued that spending large amounts of public money ($10.6 billion for GM by the Canadian and Ontario governments) to invest in companies that had become inefficient and uncompetitive was not in the public interest, but rather reflected the self-interest of the companies and unions. The major automakers had contributed to their own demise through their failure to recognize the growing demand for fuel-efficient cars and by the extravagant compensation of top executives. As well, they had higher labour costs than their Japanese-owned competitors. Selecting one set of companies for assistance was unfair to other people and companies who might need assistance in difficult times. Bailing out failing companies, critics argued, may also lead other companies to make risky decisions knowing that government would protect them from failure.

The decision to provide large sums of public money to restructure two leading companies indicates that determining what is in the public interest is often controversial.

Congress, on the other hand, try to influence government on issues that relate directly or indirectly to the interests of big business and labour unions.

Often, several organizations claim to represent the same interest. For example, both the Canadian Federation of Students (CFS) and the Canadian Association of Student Associations (CASA) claim to represent the interests of students. Not only do the organizations differ in the tactics they use (the CFS is more likely to engage in protest activity, while the CASA focuses on developing good relations with Conservative and Liberal politicians), but also in their general ideological perspective—the CFS leans to the left while the CASA is more conservative. Francophone students in Quebec are represented by yet other student organizations. Similarly, both the Canadian Federation of Agriculture and the National Farmers Union claim to represent Canadian farmers, with the Farmers Union being stronger supporters of agricultural marketing boards and more critical of government policies.

Why Do People Join Interest Groups?

Pluralist theory assumes that individuals join with like-minded people to form groups to influence politics in order to advance their interests (Smith, 2005). As Table 7-1 indicates, a significant proportion of Canadians say that they are members of voluntary groups, although organizations that are not primarily political (such as religious and recreational groups) attract larger numbers of members than those that are more likely to be formed to take up a political cause. Even so, the limited data available indicates that some types of politically active groups, such as environmental organizations, may attract larger memberships than political parties.

Questions have been raised, particularly by **rational choice theory**, as to why individuals would find it in their interest to join and be active in an interest group. Rational choice theory (also known as public choice theory) works from the assumption that individuals rationally pursue their own self-interest. This theory, borrowed from the discipline of economics, analyzes interest groups in terms of the implications of individuals seeking to maximize selective benefits for themselves from political action. Just as individuals and businesses try to maximize their income, wealth, or profits in the marketplace by weighing the costs and benefits of a particular course of action, so too is it assumed that individuals will try to maximize the benefits for themselves through involvement in political activity.

Working from the rational choice perspective, Mancur Olson (1965) noted that individuals acting in their own self-interest may not find it worthwhile to devote time and money to join and be active in a group if they know

RATIONAL CHOICE THEORY
A theory based on the assumption that individuals rationally pursue their own self-interest.

TABLE 7-1
PERCENTAGE OF CANADIANS INVOLVED IN PARTICULAR TYPES OF INTEREST GROUPS

Note: The 2000 survey did not ask respondents if they were active or inactive members.

ORGANIZATION	INACTIVE MEMBER	ACTIVE MEMBER	TOTAL
2000 SURVEY			
Human rights			5.1
Women's group			8.1
Peace group			2.1
2006 SURVEY			
Environmental	9.9	6.6	16.5
Professional association	10.1	18.7	28.8
Charitable/humanitarian	11.7	23.2	34.9
Consumer	7.4	4.5	11.9
Church/religious	22.2	27.9	50.5
Sports/recreational	14.2	29.1	43.3
Art/music/educational	12.6	23.2	35.8
Labour union	12.5	13.6	26.1
Any other voluntary	6.9	4.8	11.7

Sources: *World Values Survey, 2000, 2006.* Retrieved from *http://www.worldvaluessurvey.org*

that they can benefit from the actions of other group members. Why bother to be active in a student organization demanding lower tuition fees if thousands of others will do the work for you? Instead, you can be a "**free rider**" on their activity. Thus "rational, self-interested individuals will not act to achieve their common or group interests" (Olson, 1965, p. 2).

In Olson's analysis, situations arise in which groups form and have the membership needed to pursue collective action. First, coercion may be used to ensure that those benefiting from group action act in their common interest. This is particularly the case where membership is compulsory. Unions, including student unions and associations, generally have compulsory membership, or at least compulsory dues-paying, once a majority of workers or students have voted to form a union. Likewise, to practise many professions, a person must become a member of the professional association. Second, groups that represent the interests of small numbers of individuals or individual companies will find it easier to form and maintain an active membership. In this case, individuals realize that if they do not support the group that aims to represent their interest, the group will fail and they will not gain the benefit they seek. In a small group (particularly one in which members have regular personal contact), peer pressure can help to sustain it. Third, a group may be able to provide some selective incentives to its members that are not available to non-members. For example, many interest groups provide useful information to members and arrange for member discounts on insurance, travel, and other purchases. Although such benefits can help to maintain support, they are in many cases not sufficiently enticing to motivate individuals to join and pay dues to an interest group.

Since Olson wrote his book the number and membership of public interest groups has increased considerably, and most groups do not have much in the way of direct material benefits for members. For example, it has been estimated that between fifteen hundred and two thousand environmental groups exist in Canada (Wilson, 2002). To some extent, people may join an interest group for social reasons, such as the opportunities to attend meetings and interact with others (termed **solidary incentives**). A more compelling reason is the sense of satisfaction that people gain by joining or supporting a group that gives voice to their values or promoting a cause in which they believe (termed **purposive incentives**).

Overall, Olson's analysis seems hard to sustain in an era in which public interest groups as well as groups that represent broad sectors of society have flourished. However, such groups can face problems in keeping up their membership and support base. While business and professional groups that provide material incentives to members can maintain a strong membership and financial base over time, public interest groups often suffer from sharply fluctuating membership and support. For example, when public interest and concern about environmental problems flourished in the late 1980s as a

FREE RIDER
An individual who enjoys the benefits of group action without contributing.

SOLIDARY INCENTIVES
Incentives to join a group for social reasons, such as the opportunities to attend meetings and interact with others.

PURPOSIVE INCENTIVES
Incentives to join a group based on the satisfaction that is gained by expressing one's values or promoting a cause in which one believes.

result of well-publicized environmental disasters, membership in environmental organizations soared. But, as economic concerns increased in the early 1990s, membership in environmental organizations declined substantially. In addition, those joining groups to express their values may move from one cause to another.

Are All Sectors of Society Adequately Represented by Interest Groups?

The growing array of interest groups has meant that almost every conceivable interest has one or more groups claiming to represent it. Interest groups have been formed to represent those elements of society that have in the past been marginalized or excluded from politics—for example, Aboriginals, women, and the poor. Nevertheless, taking the interest group system as a whole, some sectors of society are better represented than others. In particular, those with higher incomes and higher education are more likely to join interest groups (Young & Everitt, 2004). Business interest groups have always been well represented in Canadian politics, while groups representing the less privileged elements of society often struggle to survive.

Interest groups need money and expertise to be effective. It takes considerable financial resources to keep an organization running smoothly, keep its members informed, and develop the expertise needed to sway policy-makers. A Canadian interest group may need to have provincial offices if it wants to affect the many policy areas in which provincial governments play a key role. Further, the bilingual character of Canada means that expensive translation services may be necessary to operate in both official languages. In addition, the increasing use of the courts to advance or protect interests results in expensive legal costs. Indeed, some environmental groups have found themselves the target of lawsuits intended to stifle their criticism of particular businesses deemed to be environmentally unfriendly. For example, the Friends of the Lubicon, a Toronto group that supports the small Cree nation of northern Alberta, faced a lawsuit in 1991, when it launched a boycott against a company that was clear-cutting trees on Lubicon territory. Although an Ontario court ordered the Friends not to ask the public to support the boycott, in 1998 another court ruled that the boycott was a legitimate form of freedom of expression. Subsequently a settlement was reached to end the costly legal battle. Because most public interest groups have meagre financial resources, they often have to rely on unpaid volunteers. In some cases, public interest groups have accepted funds from large corporations. For example, some environmental groups have received corporate donations and have corporate executives on their board of directors, despite the environmental harm that may be caused by these corporations (Dewar, 1995).

One specific challenge to fundraising is that Canadian tax laws limit the ability of interest groups to raise funds. If a group wishes to have charitable status so that it can give donors a deduction on their income tax, the group cannot spend more than 10 percent of its budget on political advocacy. Thus some groups may be discouraged from taking political action so as to not threaten their charitable status. Others work around this provision by setting up a separate organization to undertake activities that are considered charitable rather than political. For example, the Sierra Club Foundation is a charitable organization that funds the educational and scientific research activities of the Sierra Club, which engages in environmental activism. In contrast, when a business undertakes an effort to lobby government or contributes to an interest group that acts on behalf of business, it is considered a tax-deductible business expense.

Sierra Club Canada:
www.sierraclub.ca

Government Sponsorship and Support

Unlike pluralist theory, **state-centred theory** views the state (all the institutions involved in governing) as largely independent of social forces, and thus relatively free to act on its own values and interests. Instead of viewing the state as simply responding to the demands placed on it by groups and individuals, state-centred theory sees the state as trying to shape the political context in which it operates. This can include encouraging and supporting certain interest groups, selecting which interest groups to include in the policy-making process, and using interest groups as a means to persuade the public of the merits of the policies government plans to adopt. Applied to the Canadian context, state-centred theory does not assume that the state is a single-minded actor, but rather sees public policy as largely the outcome of the interaction between, or conflict among, governing institutions (such as the competing interests of national and provincial governments and of different government departments and agencies). In state-centred theory, then, interest groups are not viewed as having a major effect on public policy.

STATE-CENTRED THEORY
The theory that the state is largely independent of social forces and thus state actors are relatively free to act on their own values and interests.

The close ties between government and interest groups that we take for granted today are a relatively recent phenomenon. Until the mid-1960s, Canadian governments generally assumed that interest groups and government should be strictly separate (Pal, 1993). The development and activities of interest groups were considered a private matter, although governments did grant some professional groups (such as doctors and lawyers) the right to regulate their own professions. Governments were also often involved in controversies concerning the right of unions to organize, engage in collective bargaining, and take strike action.

In the mid-1960s the Canadian government, through the Secretary of State Department, began to provide support and encouragement for official language minority groups as part of its campaign to promote bilingualism (and counter Quebec nationalism). Prime Minister Trudeau's interest in the concept of "participatory democracy" and his view that "counterweights" were needed to offset the power of the dominant interests

BOX 7-2

Government and Environmental Groups: An Uneasy Alliance

Since its beginnings in 1971, Environment Canada (the Department of the Environment) has been involved in funding environmental groups. Early on, Environment Canada and other government agencies supported the development of environmental groups to advise the Canadian government at the Stockholm Conference on the Human Environment, 1972. Likewise, Environment Canada has given considerable funding to Canadian environmental groups to participate in subsequent international environmental conferences. One group, the Coalition on Acid Rain, was established at the prompting of the Minister of the Environment in the late 1980s as a vehicle for lobbying the U.S. government to limit acid rain emissions that were affecting Canada. The Department of the Environment also encouraged and funded the development of the Canadian Environmental Network (and its provincial counterparts) to assist it in developing relationships with environmental interest groups. It also provides some funding for a large number of projects carried out by environmental groups.

Environment Canada's commitment to funding hundreds of projects and supporting national and regional environmental organizations is not purely altruistic. In part, the support and funding have resulted from cutbacks in Environment Canada's own personnel. Interest groups now sometimes take charge of activities that used to be the responsibility of government; for example, some environmental groups receive grants to carry out pollution monitoring for the government. Moreover, funding and support can be politically motivated. For instance, to implement the philosophy of sustainable development, Environment Canada has felt that it needs "support from the rest of government and all sectors of society." As government's environmental policy thinking has shifted away from regulation of industries toward pollution prevention, environmental groups have been seen as an effective means of educating and persuading the public. Overall, Environment Canada has increasingly relied on "partnership and joint funding" and developing "more complex networks" to persuade the Canadian government to adopt environmentally friendly policies (Doern, 2002, pp. 107–9). In effect, Environment Canada, like other government departments and agencies, acts, to some degree, in combination with interest groups as a lobbyist within government for the interests it serves.

(such as business interests) that influenced government policy also resulted in other changes; namely, the Canadian government began to support the development of groups representing various sectors of society and viewpoints that had previously enjoyed little or no influence, such as Aboriginal groups, equality-seeking women's organizations, and environmental groups (Pal, 1993). Eventually, most Canadian government departments developed programs to fund interest groups related to their areas of policy-making either in the form of sustaining grants (core funding) or, more typically, grants for specific projects (see Box 7-2, Government and Environmental Groups: An Uneasy Alliance, for the origins of government involvement in environmental groups). Indeed, in a few cases, the Canadian government could actually take credit for establishing interest groups. For example, the Canadian government set up the National Council of Welfare Organizations in 1970 to advise the government on welfare and poverty issues, even though its membership was largely composed of middle-class professionals (Haddow, 1990).

Providing support for interest groups can be useful to government. Interest groups can be a source of information and policy advice. Government officials may be better able to gain an understanding of the views of an element of society, and thereby develop policies less likely to be criticized by that group. Interest groups can also be a channel of communication to the public for government proposals and policies. If an interest group publicly supports the policy and carries the government's message to its members and to the public, effective criticism of the policy is less likely. Interest groups can also be useful in providing support for the positions of government in international politics. Many international conferences include forums for non-governmental organizations. In the context of such forums, support from interest groups that take positions favoured by the Canadian government can increase Canada's international influence.

Interest groups can also be useful for particular departments and agencies. An interest group may further departmental or agency objectives by mobilizing public support for more resources and by supporting the efforts of that department to be granted higher priority in policy-making. For example, interest groups advocating the need for greater military spending have helped the Department of National Defence to gain support for new equipment. Further, interest groups can assist government in achieving its objectives through undertaking voluntary, non-governmental measures, and by building consensus among different or conflicting "stakeholders."

However, providing support to interest groups carries risks to the government by mobilizing the demands, grievances, and criticisms of various segments of society. Because interest groups may not want to accept compromises, they will often be critical of government policies. Equality-seeking groups, for example, have often criticized what they consider to be very limited measures to improve the situation of disadvantaged elements of society.

Government funding of interest groups has been controversial. Critics argue that governments should not be funding "special interests" that may be demanding benefits that increase the costs of government and increase the role of government in the society and economy. Criticisms have also been raised about the choice of groups that have received funding. In the past the Canadian government awarded substantial funding to the National Action Committee on the Status of Women (NAC), which represented a large number of women's groups, while usually denying funding to REAL (Realistic, Equal, Active, for Life) Women, a group that promotes traditional family values and is opposed to such feminist goals as pay equity, affirmative action, and government-subsidized child care. However, the tendency of NAC to become more confrontational in its relations with government led to funding cuts by various governments. Notably, the Harper Government eliminated core funding to NAC (and some other advocacy groups). Without regular government funding, and weakened by internal divisions related to differences concerning race, ethnicity, and sexual orientation, the once-influential NAC has largely faded from the political scene (Dobrowolsky, 2008).

Overall, government participation in encouraging, supporting, and involving groups points to a limitation of pluralist theory. Groups are not necessarily an autonomous product of concerns among different interests in society. Rather, interest groups may be connected in various ways to government, may be involved in carrying out the agendas of government, and may be used by one agency of government in its struggles with other agencies. The danger for interest groups is that they may lose their outspokenness if they depend too heavily on government (or business) for financing. Worries that government may reduce or cut off funding may lead a group to moderate its proposals or avoid criticism of government policies.

Does Competition among Interest Groups Lead to the Public Interest?

Pluralist theory views the activity of interest groups as resulting in policies that are in the public interest. Because numerous interest groups reflect differing interests and perspectives, their influence on policy-makers will likely lead to compromises that take into account the views of those who are interested in a particular policy area. This positive view of interest group activity is not shared by those who favour other theoretical approaches.

Rational choice theorists argue that because small groups are better able to organize, small groups are able to exploit the public as a whole to gain benefits for themselves. For example, dairy farmers have organized themselves and pressured government to create marketing boards that limit production and make it difficult for new operations to be established. Higher prices for consumers are the result. However, consumers are difficult to organize into a strong interest group. The higher costs of dairy products are spread over a large number of people and thus only amount to a small cost for each consumer. In contrast, each dairy farmer benefits substantially from supporting his or her own interest group. As various small groups ("special interests") gain benefits for themselves, the general good is undermined.

Rational choice theorists generally assume that the competitive free market is ultimately in the public interest because its efficiency leads to the maximization of wealth. The actions of interest groups in seeking selective benefits tend to result in special undeserved benefits for some at the expense of maximizing the wealth of all. The political "marketplace" of competing interest groups (unlike the economic free market) is viewed as inefficient.

As discussed in Chapter 3, Marxist theory views capitalist societies, such as Canada, as sharply divided into social classes based on conflicting positions in the processes of production. In this perspective, the state and the public policies that governments adopt are inherently biased toward the interests of capitalism and the capitalist class. Those who take this perspective note that there are often strong personal connections between members of the capitalist class and the political elite. Further, some of the major decisions taken by Canadian governments in recent decades—for example, free trade agreements, deregulation of business, privatization of government-owned Crown corporations, and reductions in corporate taxes—have been promoted by and reflect the interests of business groups and leading corporate executives.

In some contemporary versions of Marxism (termed "neo-Marxism"), government is viewed as playing an active role in trying to ensure that the capitalist system maintains profitability. However, neo-Marxists point out that government also tries to shore up the legitimacy of the capitalist system by providing some benefits to workers so that the working class accepts, or at least is unlikely to mount a serious challenge to, the capitalist system. Further, in the neo-Marxist perspective, government involves itself in trying to reconcile the interests of the different elements of the capitalist class (Clancy, 2008).

In Marxist theory, it is the capitalist system (viewed as the underlying structure of society) rather than the actions of interest groups or political parties that largely determines the basic functioning of society and government. Marxists view the capitalist system as contrary to the interests of a large majority of society, and believe that fundamental change can be achieved only by mobilizing the working class to challenge the capitalist system. However, unlike pluralist theory, which assumes individuals know and act on what is in their interests, Marxist theory argues that the ideas of people are shaped by social forces related to the capitalist system (Smith, 2005). Contemporary Marxists argue that it is not enough to establish organizations to represent the working class, as this will not necessarily result in workers knowing what is in their "true interests." In addition, the dominant ideas of society that legitimize the capitalist system need to be challenged.

State-centred theorists, like Marxist theorists, are critical of the assumption that the state is neutral in responding to the pressure of interest groups. In the state-centred perspective, public officials and politicians are active in pursuing their own interests, or their own views as to what is good for the country. Competition among organizations within government and between levels of government may have some positive results, and public officials may have the knowledge and experience useful in assessing what is in the public interest. On the other hand, if the state is relatively independent of societal influence, policies may not reflect the interests and concerns of all elements of society.

Both Marxist and state-centred theorists make the contentious assumption that governments are not very responsive to societal interests. Even though governments have a strong orientation to maintaining the profitability of business, other groups in society have been able to persuade governments to provide a variety of social programs, often over the objections of business interests. For example, in 1998, the Council of Canadians successfully mobilized opposition to defeat the government's plan, backed by big business, to ratify the Multilateral Agreement on Investment (as discussed in Chapter 6). Various non-business groups have had some degree of success in being regularly consulted during policy development. In addition, politicians need to be responsive to various social interests if they are to succeed. Even though governments do not always act as the majority of people want and do not always act in keeping with the wishes of many interest groups, it would be misleading to assume that Canadian governments ignore a variety of interests or that the interests of business always prevail (Young & Everitt, 2004).

The Organization of Interest Groups

The organizational structure of interest groups is as varied as the groups themselves. A group of neighbours who attempt to get their city to fix the potholes on their street have a quite different organization than the Canadian Manufacturers & Exporters Association or the Canadian Medical Association. The neighbours will not likely bother setting up a formal organization, other than perhaps deciding on a spokesperson, and will probably be temporary. In contrast, **institutionalized interest groups** such as the Canadian Medical Association have a formal organizational structure, a well-established membership base, paid professional staff, executive officers, and permanent offices. This provides the capability for an institutionalized group to respond to members' interests by developing policy positions and pursuing the goals of the group through regular contact with government policy-makers (Pross, 1992). Institutionalized interest groups are typically concerned with promoting their views and proposals on various issues, surviving for the long term, and, often, developing close working relationships with key government policy-makers. Of course, many groups fall between the example of an informal group of neighbours and the well-established institutional groups. Some of these, such as the pro-life and pro-choice groups that developed around the abortion issue, have successfully developed long-lasting organizations and membership bases while focusing on a particular issue.

Although information is not available on the vast array of interest groups in Canada, most major groups appear to have adopted a democratic structure with procedures for members to elect a board of directors to oversee the operations of the group, an annual meeting, and the provision of information to members about the organization's activities. Beyond this, member involvement is often limited to paying dues, while the professional staff runs the organization with some oversight by the board of directors. Some organizations, such as the Canadian Federation of Independent Business, poll their members on particular issues, while others encourage members and supporters to sign petitions to back their causes. A few interest groups set up local chapters so that members can discuss issues regularly. For example, the

INSTITUTIONALIZED INTEREST GROUP

A group that has a formal organizational structure, a well-established membership base, paid professional staff, executive officers, permanent offices, and the capability to respond to the interests of its members by developing policy positions and promoting them through regular contact with government policy-makers.

Canadian Federation of Independent Business:
www.cfib.ca

▲ Institutionalized interest groups, such as the Vanier Institute of the Family (shown in picture), often monitor government policies and work to promote their members' interests to key government policy-makers.

Council of Canadians, which claims to be "Canada's largest public advocacy group" with 100 000 members, features "over seventy" local chapters.

Some groups, such as Greenpeace and the Canadian Taxpayers Federation, have "supporters" rather than members (Young & Everitt, 2004). In such cases the staff or the leaders of the organization are not directly responsible to supporters. Instead, the organization's functioning depends on its ability to raise funds from its supporters for their causes. By purchasing mailing lists and keeping track of past donors, some groups are able to raise substantial amounts of money through direct mailings or email appeals for funds.

To what extent does an interest group actually represent the interests and views of its members or supporters? Groups that focus on interacting with government officials risk losing touch with members. Of course, sharp declines in membership or financial support will likely encourage a group to be more responsive to members. However, the need of some groups to devote great efforts to fundraising may detract from their ability to pursue the interests of their members and supporters. Furthermore, appeals used to raise funds do not always reflect the group's major goals. Groups that mobilize members around their causes through such activities as petitions, letter-writing campaigns, and demonstrations are more likely to be attentive to the views of their members and supporters. Yet groups that have a guaranteed membership may take positions that do not reflect members' views, unless organizers are worried about a campaign to oust the leadership or to break from the association or union. Likewise, groups that people join primarily for non-political reasons (such as religious and recreational groups) may be able to take some political positions that are at odds with the views of the majority

Council of Canadians:
www.canadians.org

Greenpeace Canada:
www.greenpeace.ca

Canadian Taxpayers Federation:
www.taxpayer.com

of members. However, their ability to influence government officials may be compromised if those officials question the credibility of the group's leaders in representing their members' political views.

Canada's federal system has important implications for interest group organization. Because many decisions are made by provincial governments, interest groups often want to influence provincial governments as well as the federal government. This may involve setting up offices in some or all provincial capitals. Moreover, some interest groups are established as federations of provincial associations, for example, the Canadian Association of Social Workers. Further, given the distinctiveness of Quebec and the concentration of the francophone population in that province, there is often a special relationship between the Quebec branch of the interest group and the interest group in the rest of the country. In some cases, Quebec-based groups take a very different position on issues than their counterparts in the rest of Canada. For example, Quebec-based women's groups generally supported the controversial Meech Lake Accord (discussed in Chapter 10) while the National Action Committee on the Status of Women in the rest of Canada was critical of the proposals for constitutional changes.

INFLUENCING PUBLIC POLICY

Interest groups can try to affect the policies that governments develop and implement in many ways. The most effective is to influence those responsible for developing public policies. It is generally thought that "getting in on the ground floor"—that is, exerting influence at the early stages of developing a policy—is most effective. At the early stages of policy development, government officials may be looking for information about a problem and examining possible alternatives. An interest group that is able to interact with key policy developers, typically within the public service, may be able to supply the information and policy ideas that will be considered.

Influencing a cabinet minister who is responsible for the relevant policy area can also be useful because the minister will likely encourage or instruct departmental personnel to give priority to a particular problem and set out the goals to be achieved. As well, the minister will be involved in assessing the alternate policies that may be provided by public servants, and will present recommendations to the relevant cabinet committee and, if necessary, to the Cabinet as a whole. Even so, influencing departmental policy developers and persuading the cabinet minister who heads the department may not be enough to achieve the interest group's objectives. As discussed in Chapter 16, various central agencies (such as the Privy Council Office) play a key role in determining what government does. In addition, the prime minister, along with the central agencies, sets the overall direction of the government. Access to the prime minister is tightly controlled, however, and central agencies are often less open to influence than departments.

Generally, interest groups receive a more sympathetic hearing, and will find it easier to develop a close working relationship with key people, in the department that most closely matches their interests. Although public servants are often thought to be insensitive to political considerations and thus largely free of outside influence, this is not entirely the case. As noted above, public servants often value contact with key interest groups because such groups provide information and ideas that can be useful in developing policy proposals. By interacting with people representing major interests, public servants can benefit in several ways: They can gauge the potential reaction to new policies and try to avoid potential criticism from these interests by involving them in the formulation of policies. As well, consultation with major interest groups can add legitimacy to government decisions.

Political scientists have found that **policy communities**,[2] government officials responsible for a particular policy area and relevant institutionalized interest groups, often collaborate regularly in developing public policies (Coleman & Skogstad, 1990; Pross, 1992). In this situation, interest groups not only promote the interests of their members, but also draw on their information and expertise to engage in deliberation with groups representing different interests and with government officials to develop policies acceptable to the policy community (Montpetit, 2004).

In some cases, the interactions between interest groups and key policy-makers have been formalized through the establishment of advisory councils or committees that include representatives of those interest groups or individuals that the government department or agency considers important. However, in 1992, the Progressive Conservative government eliminated many advisory councils, as well as various policy research organizations that operated at arms length from government (see Box 7-3, Think Tanks: Public Policy Up for Grabs?). Since then, some new advisory councils have been formed, such as the Economic Advisory Council established by the Harper Government in 2008. However, unlike earlier advisory councils, this advisory council does not include representatives of particular interest groups, but instead consists of some of the leading businesspeople in Canada with no representation for other interests, such as labour. Royal commissions and government task forces set up to examine issue areas and make recommendations often include people associated with various interests. For example, the Task Force on Spam established in 2004 and chaired by an assistant deputy minister of Industry Canada included representatives of the Canadian Cable Television Association, the Canadian Association of Internet Providers, the Canadian Marketing Association, the Information Technology Association, and the Coalition Against Unsolicited Commercial Email Canada. Despite the many groups consulted, the task force's

POLICY COMMUNITY
Government officials responsible for a particular policy area and relevant institutionalized interest groups that collaborate regularly in developing public policies.

Government of Canada, Consulting With Canadians:
www.consultingcanadians.gc.ca

---

[2]Policy communities are also often referred to as policy networks, with policy communities sometimes analyzed as a particular type of policy network.

Think Tanks:
Public Policy Up for Grabs?

In 1992, the Progressive Conservatives led by Brian Mulroney shut down five organizations that provided independent policy analysis and advice operating at "arm's length" from government. The reasons given were the need to reduce the government's deficit and that advice was available from universities and think tanks. Some critics argued that the government's disagreement with the policy advice received from these organizations was the real reason for their demise (Dobuzinskis, 2007). The organizations to be axed included the Economic Council of Canada, the Science Council, and the Law Reform Commission.[3]

"Think tanks" have become an important source for public policy discussion. However, a number of think tanks have a strong ideological bias and are more concerned with advocacy than with analysis. For example, the Fraser Institute and the Atlantic Institute for Market Studies take a strongly free market perspective, while the union-backed Canadian Centre for Policy Alternatives promotes policies oriented to social and economic equality. A number of leading think tanks (such as the C.D. Howe Institute) are funded primarily by corporations, although their research is often conducted by academics. Think tanks provide a potential source of business influence on public policy, although how far their influence extends is unclear (Abelson, 2007).

The disappearance of organizations providing independent policy analysis and advice to government opened the way for greater influence from think tanks. Some individuals might argue that think tanks represent a range of interests, thereby offering a balanced influence on public policy. Others, however, fear that the most powerful think tanks promote the views of their corporate backers, enabling conservative business interests to shape government strategy. Is public policy now up for grabs by the rich and powerful?

recommendations were not implemented. Nevertheless, royal commissions, such as the one on bilingualism and biculturalism and the one on the status of women, have often had an important long-term effect on public policy.

Many interest groups take part in the public consultations organized by the Canadian government to discuss various proposals.[4] At their best, these can serve as a useful public forum for interest groups to state their views. However, if government has already committed itself to a proposed policy, it appears unlikely that interest group representation will result in major changes to the proposal. As in the case of changes to student loans discussed at the start of the chapter, convincing the government to change its mind may take strong action and the support of a variety of interests.

---

[3]Subsequently, the Chrétien Government closed the Advisory Council on the Status of Women and some other advisory organizations.

[4]However, in its consultations on democratic reform, the explicit goal of the Harper Government was to avoid "vested interests, entrenched institutions, and powerful lobbyists" by holding citizens forums across the country (Government of Canada, 2007).

Members of Parliament

The most powerful institutionalized interest groups generally devote little attention to trying to influence ordinary Members of Parliament (MPs). As discussed in Chapter 15, MPs play a limited role in policy development. MPs are involved primarily in the passage of legislation presented to Parliament by the government, although they do propose generally minor modifications to legislative proposals in House of Commons committees. As well, parliamentary committee members do involve themselves, to some degree, in developing policy recommendations that are, on occasion, picked up by policy-makers in government. However, party discipline restricts the ability of individual MPs, or groups of MPs, to take an independent role in policy-making. John Bulloch, founder of the Canadian Federation of Independent Business, noted that he was initially "very naive" in trying to influence MPs, but came to the conclusion that it was generally a waste of time "to talk to people who have no influence" (quoted in Pross, 1992). Nevertheless, interest groups do present their cases to MPs and participate in the public hearings of parliamentary committees. As well, there have been situations in which influencing MPs has proved effective. For example, in 1996 the Insurance Bureau of Canada (an interest group representing insurance companies) successfully mounted a campaign against a government proposal to allow the major banks to enter the insurance business. By mobilizing insurance agents in each electoral district to contact their MP, the Insurance Bureau was able to convince the governing Liberal party caucus to oppose the plan promoted by the Canadian Bankers Association (Clancy, 2008). Likewise, in 2009, Canada's 33 000 insurance agents lobbied MPs, particularly those of the governing Conservative party, to prevent banks from marketing insurance policies on their websites. The lobbying campaign was successful, and Finance Minister Jim Flaherty banned the banks from website marketing (Chase & Perkins, 2009). Similarly, the ability of the Canadian Federation of Independent Business to mobilize small business owners to influence Liberal MPs played a significant role (along with opposition from other interest groups) in blocking government approval of a merger of the Royal Bank and the Bank of Montreal into a "superbank" in 1988 (Williams, 2004).

Influencing the Public

Interest groups often take their case to the public as an indirect way of influencing government. They may get the word out through press releases, advertising, websites, and participating in public forums. Petitions and mass emails to politicians may be used to show that a group enjoys substantial support for their positions on particular issues. Public interest groups, in particular, sometimes come up with protest techniques to attract media attention. More than most, Greenpeace is known for its dramatic protest activities. For example, in July 2009 Greenpeace activists chained themselves to the front door of the Quebec Ministry of Natural Resources, set up a banner proclaiming "Boreal

Forest: The Destruction Starts Here," and dumped a load of lumber at the building's entrance. Similarly, President Obama was greeted on his first visit to Ottawa with a large banner, "Stop American imports of tar sands oil." Public techniques are often the only way of trying to influence public policy for the many groups that lack effective access to policy-makers. However, institutionalized groups influential in the policy process sometimes also take their case to the public to try to counter the influence of other groups in the public eye, and to try to demonstrate to politicians that they have public support.

Political Parties and Elections

Canadian interest groups have generally avoided direct involvement in political parties. Interest groups hope to influence whichever political party is in power, and thus most interest groups do not want to be perceived as being "in bed" with one political party. A key exception is the Canadian Labour Congress (CLC), which was involved in the formation of the New Democratic Party. Although the Canadian Labour Congress is not formally affiliated with the NDP, individual CLC unions that are affiliated with the NDP have a voice in party decisions. The relationship between labour unions and the NDP is not always harmonious. For example, Buzz Hargrove, then president of the Canadian Auto Workers union (CAW), was expelled from the NDP after he publicly advised CAW members to vote for the Liberal candidates in districts where the NDP had little chance of winning in the 2006 election, and appeared to publicly endorse Liberal leader Paul Martin. After his expulsion, the CAW ended its affiliation with the NDP.

Interest groups have not generally been significant donors to political parties. Instead, individual corporations were, in the past, the major contributors to the leading political parties. However, as discussed in Chapter 9, contributions from corporations, unions, and associations (including interest groups) to political parties are now banned at the national level and in some provinces. Nevertheless, many interest groups have jumped into election campaigns to publicize their views and to support or oppose specific candidates or parties (see Box 7-4, A Comic-Book Campaign: Interest Groups and Elections, for a case study of the 1988 Canadian election).

The effectiveness of interest group involvement in election campaigns has been questioned by researchers. For example, a study of campaigns conducted by interest groups in the 1997 election did not find a significant effect. Indeed, candidates that the National Citizens Coalition tried to defeat appeared to benefit from the campaign against them (Tanguay & Kay, 1998).

Legal Action

Increasingly, interest groups have used legal action to promote their causes. Historically, some individual businesses used the courts to challenge Canadian government laws that affected their operations, arguing that these laws were

BOX 7-4

A Comic-Book Campaign: Interest Groups and Elections

The 1988 Canadian election focused on an intense controversy—whether or not the Canadian government should ratify the Canada–United States Free Trade Agreement that had been signed by the Progressive Conservative government in Canada and Republican President Ronald Reagan. The Business Council on National Issues, an interest group representing the largest corporations (now called the Canadian Council of Chief Executives), was instrumental in establishing the Canadian Alliance for Trade and Job Opportunities to promote passage of the free trade agreement. This group is estimated to have spent $3 000 000 in the run-up to the election (Doern & Tomlin, 1991) and later spent $2 307 650 on advertising during the election campaign. The Canadian Manufacturers Association was also active in encouraging its members to promote the free trade agreement. In the opposite camp, the Liberal and New Democratic Parties argued vehemently against the agreement. They won the support of the Pro-Canada Network, a coalition of nationalist, labour, women's, and other social groups that spent $752 247 on advertising during the election campaign (Hiebert, 1991). Particularly effective was a widely distributed comic book that included a Q & A dialogue, along with a variety of anti–free trade cartoons. Late in the campaign, the pro–free trade group countered with their own comic book inserted into many newspapers and magazines (Ayers, 1998).

The 1988 election was unusual in attracting major participation from interest groups. Concern about the extent of involvement of interest groups in election campaigns led to legislation to limit the amount that non-party groups can spend during elections (as discussed in Chapter 9). In the 2008 election campaign, fifty-six interest groups, eight individuals, and one provincial political party reported spending at least $500 on campaign-related advertising. Among the leading spenders were the Canadian Labour Congress ($179 135), the Tourism Industry Association of Canada ($167 067), the Professional Institute of the Public Service of Canada ($112 789), the PC party of Newfoundland and Labrador for its "Anything But Conservative" campaign ($81 389), Make Poverty History ($44 775), and the International Fund for Animal Welfare ($30 521).

Canadian interest groups are usually much less involved in election campaigns than their American counterparts (Boatright, 2009). Critics of the American system argue that the ability of various groups to buy influence undermines the democratic process. As we have seen, however, interest groups use a multitude of ways to wield influence, most of which do not depend on election campaigns.

not within the constitutional powers of the national government. The *Charter of Rights and Freedoms* has stimulated the use of the courts by interest groups. Feminist groups have challenged a range of laws and policies that they view as violating the protection of female–male equality entrenched in the Charter. Aboriginal groups have made major advances over time through gaining legal recognition of Aboriginal rights. In turn, their actions have encouraged or forced governments to negotiate with them. Gay and lesbian groups have used the courts to gain the same rights and benefits for same-sex

FIGURE 7-1
**ORGANIZED INTERESTS IN
COURT, 1988–1998**

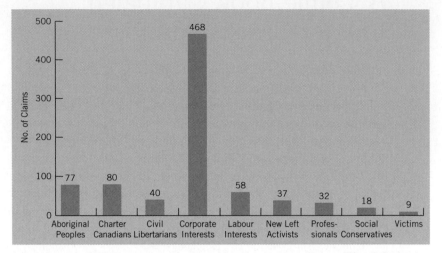

Source: Greg Hein, 2000, Interest group litigation and Canadian democracy, *Choices*, *6*(2), p. 9. Retrieved from http://www.irpp.org/choices/archive/vol6no2.pdf

couples as heterosexual couples. And, environmental groups have forced governments to undertake some environmental reviews of projects in accordance with environmental laws and regulations. Overall, however, corporate interests have been the largest users of the court system to pursue their agendas, as illustrated by Figure 7-1.

In addition to initiating legal actions, interest groups frequently present briefs in cases before higher-level courts. For example, in 2006, non-governmental interveners participated in over two-fifths of the cases before the Supreme Court of Canada. Particularly active as interveners have been the Women's Legal Education and Action Fund (LEAF) and the Canadian Civil Liberties Association, although many other groups have also presented briefs to the Supreme Court (Hausegger, Hennigar, & Riddell, 2009).

A drawback of using the courts to pursue group causes is the high cost of legal action. To help, the Canadian government established the **Court Challenges Program,** which provided some money for individuals and groups seeking to challenge Canadian laws and government actions that violated equality rights and minority language rights. However, the Conservative government shut down this program in 2006[5] (see Box 7-5, Gone but Not Forgotten: The Court Challenges Program).

The Potential for Successful Influence

Interest groups vary in their potential ability to influence public policy in part because of differences in resources. Well-financed groups are able to employ

**COURT CHALLENGES
PROGRAM**
A federal government program that provided some money for individuals and groups seeking to challenge Canadian laws and government actions that violate equality rights and minority language rights.

---

[5]In 2008 the Canadian government established the Program to Support Linguistic Rights to deal with constitutional rights of official language minorities. This program has a mandate to pursue compulsory mediation if those rights are not being respected, with recourse to legal action only if mediation fails.

BOX 7-5

Gone but Not Forgotten: The Court Challenges Program

The Court Challenges Program (CCP) was set up in 1978 to help those trying to pursue cases linked to language rights. With the adoption of the Canadian *Charter of Rights and Freedoms* in 1982 and the implementation of the equality rights provision of the Charter in 1985, the CCP was expanded—the program began to assist in cases involving the equality rights of historically disadvantaged groups, as well as the rights of official language minorities.

The CCP was run by a non-profit organization under the direction of a volunteer board. Independent panels of experts decided which test cases were of national significance in terms of clarifying the equality rights provisions of the Charter and the Charter's guarantee of the language rights of French- and English-language minorities (see Table 7-2). The program's modest budget did not provide full funding for court cases. Instead the CCP relied on lawyers willing to work for less than the standard legal rates.

The Court Challenges Program was first shut down in 1992 by the Progressive Conservative government of Brian Mulroney, which argued that it was no longer needed and that the Department of Justice could fund challenges on an ad hoc basis. However, a lobbying effort by various groups during the 1993 election led to the resurrection of the

TABLE 7-2

TYPES OF CASES FUNDED BY THE COURT CHALLENGES PROGRAM, 1994–2006

Equality Rights including:	416
Aboriginal rights	97
Disabled persons rights	61
Sexual orientation	45
Female equality	41
Poverty	28
Age discrimination	17
Language rights, including:	160
Language of education	89
Language of work, communication, and services	23

Source: *Compiled from Court Challenges Program of Canada (2007),* Annual Report 2006 2007. *Retrieved from http://www.ccppcj.ca/documents/CCPC-AR2007*

program by the Liberal government of Jean Chrétien in 1994. After the Harper Government was elected in 2006, the program was cancelled once again—this time based on the claim that the program was "wasteful, ineffective and did not achieve results" (Court Challenges Program of Canada, 2007). Critics disagreed. They argued that the cancellation reflected a lack of interest by the Conservative government in promoting equality for women.

Despite appearances, the CCP may not be dead and buried: The Liberal party has promised to restore the program if elected.

qualified people, or pay consultants, who can monitor government activities, provide detailed policy analyses and proposals, develop ongoing relationships with key government officials, maintain an effective organization, and mount public relations campaigns. Group members can be useful in persuading politicians and government officials to consider the policies the group is advocating. What matters here is not only the number of members, but also the group's ability to mobilize members in support of its positions. Credibility is also important. For example, professional associations, such as the Canadian

Medical Association and the Canadian Bar Association are usually taken seriously when they speak out on issues related to their profession.

A group's success in influencing government is also affected by its ability to develop close relationships with key officials. It is important for a group to be viewed as the legitimate representative of a particular element of society. If other groups claim to represent the same interest and put forward different policy proposals, the group's influence may be undermined. Further, a group whose perspective is similar to that of the governing party, and whose proposals fit in with the government's agenda and plans, is more likely to be effective than groups looking for government to move in a different direction. For example, feminist and environmentalist groups have found that the Harper Government is not generally responsive to their policy proposals.

For groups that have trouble gaining effective access to policy-makers, attracting the attention of the media and receiving favourable coverage for their cause is important. Groups that cultivate relationships with sympathizers in the media can sometimes gain free publicity for their views. However, the media generally focus on dramatic events, particularly those that have a strong visual component for television. This can make it difficult for a group to provide the information needed to explain their viewpoint.

Finally, if a group can form coalitions with other groups to advance its causes, particularly groups representing different interests or different elements of the population, this can be very useful in successfully influencing policy-makers. By gaining support from other groups, the interest group may no longer appear to be pursuing benefits only for its own members or reflecting a particular point of view. Indeed, some interest groups consist of a coalition of groups. For example, the National Action Committee on the Status of Women was established as a coalition that at its peak represented about 700 groups. Less formally, many environmental groups are members of national and provincial environmental networks.

SOCIAL MOVEMENTS

SOCIAL MOVEMENT
A network of groups and individuals that seeks major social and political changes, particularly by acting outside of established political institutions.

A **social movement** can be thought of as a network of groups and individuals that seeks major social and political changes, particularly by acting outside established political institutions (Martell, 1994). It is not always easy to distinguish between interest groups and organizations based on social movements. However, interest groups tend to focus on affecting a range of specific public policies. In contrast, social movements embrace broader goals, such as challenging and transforming the values, power relationships, and institutions of society and politics. For example, the environmental movement is not only concerned with spurring government to act on environmental problems. It also aims to persuade individuals to change their lifestyles and relationship to nature and to convince businesses to change their practices to reduce their impact on the natural environment. Likewise, the women's movement has challenged traditional male–female relationships, pressured business and government to create more opportunities for women, and tried to raise women's consciousness, pride, and assertiveness. Social movements also often try to forge a sense of collective identity and solidarity among supporters.

Social movements have always played a significant role in Canadian politics. For example, the women's suffrage movement that began in the late nineteenth century eventually succeeded in achieving the right of women to vote and hold public office, as well as changing laws that gave women an inferior legal status. Its tactics included circulating petitions as well as holding mock parliamentary debates to illustrate the political competence of women. The Canadian suffrage movement had connections to other influential early social movements: the temperance movement, which promoted abstinence from alcoholic beverages and advocated banning the making and sale of alcohol, and the social purity movement, which emphasized traditional moral and family values (Smith, 2005).

In the late nineteenth century and early twentieth century a vigorous farmer's movement also developed in Canada. Inspired by populist ideas in the United States, the farmers' movement advocated direct democracy in which elected representatives would be held directly responsible to their constituents and would not be bound by party discipline. The movement was also deeply critical of Eastern Canadian big business and the Liberal and Conservative parties that were connected to business interests. After World War I, the farmer's movement elected many farmer's representatives nationally and formed the government in Alberta, Manitoba, and (for a few years) Ontario.

A labour movement also developed in the late nineteenth century. The labour movement has been involved in some bitter confrontations with businesses and governments (as noted in Chapter 2). However, the developing labour movement suffered from its own internal rifts—between conservative craft unions and more radical industrial unions, between international unions based in the United States and Canadian unions, and between unions formed in Quebec under the guidance of the Catholic Church and unions in other parts of Canada.

The labour movement spawned an array of socialist and labour political parties in the early twentieth century, although some in the labour movement focused on improving rights and benefits in the workplace rather than on engaging in political action. The creation of the Co-operative Commonwealth Federation in 1932, based on a coalition of farmer, labour, and socialist groups and individuals, did not receive strong support from labour unions. However the merging of craft and industrial unions into the Canadian Labour Congress (CLC) in 1956 contributed to the formation of the New Democratic Party in 1961 as "the political arm of labour." Nevertheless, the labour movement is still divided, with the majority of Quebec unions affiliated with the

Confédération des syndicats nationaux (CSN) rather than the CLC. The CSN dropped its connection to the Catholic Church in 1960, and in the 1970s was noted for its strong critique of the capitalist system. It generally supports the Parti Québécois and the Bloc Québécois and encouraged its members to vote yes in the referendums on Quebec independence.

New Social Movements

Beginning in the late 1960s, a number of social movements developed in Canada (and other Western democracies). Among these **new social movements** were the women's movement, the environmental movement, the Aboriginal movement, and the gay and lesbian rights movement. More recently, many Canadians (including students, union members, social activists, and Canadian nationalists) have been involved in the global social justice movement (often labelled the "anti-globalization" movement). These new movements tend to have different goals, values, organizational structures, and types of members from the social movements developed in earlier times (termed "old social movements"). In particular, the new social movements are often characterized as being concerned particularly with developing a collective sense of identity among those who are deemed to suffer from oppression (such as women, Aboriginals, and minority nationalities), along with adopting new cultural values and lifestyles rather than pursuing material interests.

New social movements have tended to avoid involvement with conventional political institutions such as political parties. Because those involved in

NEW SOCIAL MOVEMENT
A social movement concerned particularly with developing a collective sense of identity among those who are deemed to suffer from oppression, along with adopting new cultural values and lifestyles rather than pursuing material interests.

▶ Members and supporters of the Québec Native Women Inc. rally in Montreal in 2007 in support of the United Nations Declaration on the Rights of Indigenous Peoples. Québec Native Women Inc. is part of the new social movements developed during the past few decades.

Save Our Forest: Civil Disobedience

In 1993, protestors at Clayoquot Sound on Vancouver Island stood in front of logging trucks every morning for several months to block loggers from entering the old-growth forest—this despite a court injunction banning the action.

As early as 1979, residents of Tofino, B.C., had begun to protest against clear-cut logging of the old-growth forests at Clayoquot Sound. Yet in 1993 the British Columbia government decided to allow MacMillan Bloedel, a major forestry company, to raze over half the forest. The protestors who gathered in response came from various elements of the environmental movement. About 12 000 people were involved overall, and 857 protestors were arrested, with some sentenced to forty-five days in jail and $1500 in fines. The protest attracted global attention, with Hollywood celebrities such as Barbra Streisand, Robert Redford, Martin Sheen, and Oliver Stone supporting the action and the Australian band Midnight Oil putting on a concert at the protest camp (Bantjes, 2007).

Later, environmental groups, including Greenpeace, the Rainforest Action Network, and the Sierra Club, launched a boycott of companies selling products made from the old-growth forests of British Columbia. The boycott's success eventually persuaded MacMillan Bloedel to agree to a compromise involving a joint venture with the local Nuu-chah-nulth First Nation to harvest parts of the old-growth forest in a more ecologically sound manner. In 1999, MacMillan Bloedel handed over the timber rights to the First Nation, which continued to harvest the forest while leaving pristine valleys untouched. However, with declining wood supply, in 2006 the First Nation and the B.C. government approved plans to allow logging in the remaining pristine valleys of Clayoquot Sound (Friends of Clayoquot Sound, 2006).

The blockade at Clayoquot Sound was one of the largest acts of civil disobedience in Canadian history. Although environmental groups succeeded in raising public awareness about threats to old-growth forests and pressuring companies and governments to change forest management practices, conflicts between the environmental movement and forest companies continue to raise controversial issues concerning the future of Canada's forests.

new social movements have often criticized the hierarchy, bureaucracy, and power politics of conventional political organizations, they have sought to create an alternative—more informal organizations or networks based on grassroots participation by those who share the movement's goals. This trend, along with the exclusion of new social movement activists from the policy-making process, has meant that various forms of public protest have served as an important tool for new social movements to draw attention to their causes. Included in the repertoire of some new social movements has been **civil disobedience**—the deliberate and public breaking of a law in order to draw attention to injustice (see Box 7-6, Save Our Forest: Civil Disobedience). Taking their cue from the successful use of non-violent civil disobedience by the

CIVIL DISOBEDIENCE
The deliberate and public breaking of a law in order to draw attention to injustice.

BOX 7-7

Agents Provocateurs: Protests and Violence

Anti-globalization protests (including the large protest at the Summit of the Americas in Quebec City in 1991) have sometimes featured clashes between masked rock-throwing protestors and police forces that have retaliated with tear gas, pepper spray, and sometimes rubber bullets. Although it is often protesters who initiate the violence, this is not always the case. For example, some of those peacefully protesting the presence of the Indonesian dictator at the 1997 Asia-Pacific Economic Cooperation summit held on the University of British Columbia campus were pepper sprayed by the RCMP.

In 2007 protesters congregated at Montebello, Quebec, where the Canadian prime minister and the American and Mexican presidents were discussing the Security and Prosperity Partnership. Protest organizers tried to stop three young men carrying rocks whose faces were covered, because organizers suspected that the men were *agents provocateurs*. The men refused to uncover themselves, instead pushing through the police line where they were forced to the ground and "arrested." A video of the incident revealed something odd—the "protesters" were wearing the same boots as the police! The video was posted on YouTube and then broadcast on television. The Sûreté du Québec (Quebec's provincial police) admitted that the three "protesters" were in fact police officers. Although the Sûreté denied that they were trying to instigate violence, there have been other instances (particularly involving labour disputes) where police or security forces have sought to stir up violence in order to discredit the protestors.

Although most Canadians do not view violence as a legitimate form of political action, it is not always clear who is responsible for initiating violence.

---

civil rights movement in the United States in the 1960s, Aboriginal groups have used civil disobedience to blockade highways and rail lines to bolster their claims to lands that they view as having been unjustly taken from them; women's groups have organized sit-ins at government offices to protest cutbacks to women's programs; and anti-poverty protestors have jammed traffic in Toronto's financial district.

Although civil disobedience is usually non-violent, clashes between protestors and police or between protestors and affected members of the public have occurred in some cases. Because new social movements involve a range of groups and individuals without a disciplined organization, some individuals and small groups who prefer throwing stones at police, smashing windows, and other violent acts have drawn attention away from the message of the protest (see Box 7-7, *Agents Provocateurs*: Protests and Violence).

New social movement theory argues that the industrial capitalist society, which featured conflict between business and labour, has been transformed into a post-industrial society in which service and knowledge-based

NEW SOCIAL MOVEMENT THEORY
A theory that in post-industrial society new social movements have developed, particularly among the new middle class that is interested in post-materialist values such as a concern for the quality of life, identity, participation, and individual freedom.

employment has become more important than manufacturing. New social movements, in this view, reflect an attempt to form new collective identities as older forms of collective identity, such as that based on class, become less important. New social movements have developed particularly among the new middle class that is interested in post-materialist values (discussed in Chapter 5) such as a concern for the quality of life, identity, participation, and individual freedom.

The distinction between old and new social movements is sometimes exaggerated. Some of the old social movements used various means of protest, including civil disobedience, and some tried to avoid rigid organizational structures. Some early Canadian social movements, such as the temperance and moral purity movements, were middle-class movements focused on values and lifestyles, albeit of a traditional, conventional nature. Moreover, some new social movements, such as the Aboriginal and women's movement, are concerned about material goals such as improving the conditions of Aboriginals and women, as well as seeking recognition for their identities.

As the new social movements mature, they have tended to move away from their unstructured origins to become more conventional, institutionalized organizations. This allows them a better chance of influencing specific policies, while potentially alienating their more idealistic activists. For example, most of the larger organizations associated with the Canadian environmental movement have become institutionalized interest groups with professional staff and a conventional organizational structure. This has allowed them to become a regular part of the policy communities that interact with government officials and business and other interest groups in policy development. However, the environmental movement also encompasses many local and regional groups that are less institutionalized (Wilson, 2002). As well, the movement includes groups like Greenpeace that resist being co-opted by government. While some criticize the more "radical" groups for giving the movement a negative image, such groups can be useful in encouraging government to work with the more "moderate" groups. Also, the radical groups are more likely to be able to mobilize activists in support of the cause, keep issues in the public eye, and prevent moderate groups from straying too far and compromising the movement's goals.

Although the new social movements have not achieved all their goals, they have affected Canadian politics. In particular, they have raised awareness of important problems and issues that have often been ignored. For example, awareness of Canada's environmental problems, the inequalities between women and men, and the rights of Aboriginals has greatly increased as a result of movements that have highlighted those issues. Even if effective policies to deal with many of the issues raised by the new social movements are often still lacking, both the public and government have recognized that these issues are important and need to be resolved.

LOBBYISTS

Lobbying has been defined as "the practice of communication, usually privately, with government officials to try to influence a government decision" (Young & Everitt, 2004, p. 88). The term originated from the historic practice of contacting Members of Parliament in the lobby of the British House of Commons by those seeking benefits from government. Lobbying has become a widespread practice engaged in sporadically, or regularly, by many interest groups and corporations.

The practice of lobbying has become professionalized to a considerable degree. Many institutionalized interest groups, as well as the larger business corporations, employ people who specialize in developing contacts within government so as to represent the interests of their group or corporation on a regular basis. In addition, a number of companies (as well as individuals) provide lobbying services for a hefty fee. The services provided by lobbyists include trying to persuade government officials on a particular topic, and monitoring government activities that may affect an interest group or corporation. Moreover, lobbyists typically provide advice on whom to contact in government, what approach to take if the group or corporation wishes to lobby itself, and how to win public support for the group and the positions it wishes to promote.

Many professional lobbyists have held important positions in government or have been key political "insiders" who have a close relationship with important political figures. Senior government officials and aides to cabinet ministers have often been hired by lobbying firms. Although some lobbying firms have developed a close relationship with one political party, they usually try to ensure that they employ individuals with connections to both leading political parties, so that they are guaranteed to have the appropriate contacts whichever party is in power. As well, lobbying firms have often obtained contracts from government to develop the government's communications strategy, to conduct public opinion research, and to carry the government's message to various audiences.

Lobbying activities have frequently aroused suspicion and sparked debate. Seeking selective benefits from government behind closed doors raises questions about whether the public interest is being ignored. Treating government officials and politicians to expensive dinners, inviting them on expense-paid holidays, and, until recently, making substantial contributions to the governing party's campaign funds creates the impression of unfair or illegal influence. The "sponsorship scandal" that contributed to the defeat of the Liberal government in 2006 included evidence that advertising agencies connected to the Liberal party paid lobbyists (including the former public servant who had been in charge of the sponsorship program intended to promote Canadian unity at various events) to seek contracts for which little work was actually done. In return, substantial sums of money were given to those involved in the Quebec branch of the Liberal Party of Canada.

The practice of senior public officials and cabinet ministers leaving government and becoming lobbyists also creates legitimate concerns. Not only do such people enjoy unfair advantages in influencing their former colleagues, but also their decisions while in public office might be influenced by the hopes for subsequent employment or contracts. For example, shortly after he stepped down as prime minister in 1993, Brian Mulroney received three cash payments totalling at least $225 000 from lobbyist Karlheinz Schreiber. Mulroney has admitted that he received money from Schreiber, including an envelope containing $100 000 in cash, which he pocketed in a New York City hotel room. Accusations were made that the money related to lobbying efforts to persuade Air Canada (then a Crown corporation) to purchase Airbus jets. However, Mulroney claimed that he had accepted the money to help Schreiber (who has been charged in Germany with bribery, fraud, and tax evasion) to promote the sale of German armoured vehicles to foreign governments.

Lobbyist Regulation

Efforts have been made to clean up the process of lobbying. Most recently, the *Lobbyist Act, 2008*, requires that those who are paid to communicate with government officials on various matters or who arrange a meeting with a public office are required to file reports indicating the following:

- whom they are acting on behalf of,
- the name of the department or other government institution that they are communicating with, and
- the subject matter of the communication.

As well, paid lobbyists who ask the public to communicate directly with public office holders must file reports on this activity. Lobbyists are not allowed to receive contingency payments from their clients based on the outcome of their persuasive efforts. In addition, cabinet ministers, their staff, and top public servants (such as deputy ministers and assistant deputy ministers) are forbidden to act as paid lobbyists for five years after leaving their office. The *Lobbying Act* is overseen by a Commissioner of Lobbying, an officer of Parliament. The commissioner is responsible for developing a code of conduct for lobbyists, and can grant exceptions to the rules in certain circumstances.

Although the *Lobbying Act* is stricter than previous laws, the public interest group Democracy Watch (2008) has pointed out that some loopholes still exist. For example, unpaid lobbyists, and lobbyists who spend less than 20 percent of their time lobbying on behalf of corporations, are not required to register as lobbyists. Members of Parliament who are not in the Cabinet can become lobbyists immediately after leaving office, and lobbyists can become cabinet ministers immediately after being elected to Parliament. Lobbyists can also take leading positions in the election campaigns of political parties.

Democracy Watch:
www.dwatch.ca

Summary and Conclusion

Interest groups offer an important way for people to influence public policies. Generally, well-organized groups that are able to cultivate ongoing relationships with key policy-makers are most likely to affect government decisions. Nevertheless, groups not involved in the policy-making process can make a difference if they can mobilize strong public support behind their cause and win the support of other influential groups. Likewise, social movements may achieve a long-term effect by shaping the thinking of society as a whole and by raising issues that would otherwise be ignored.

From the perspective of pluralist theory, the growth of interest groups representing a variety of interests and causes suggests that the decisions and policies adopted by governments are likely to reflect the diverse interests of Canadians, rather than the interests of a small group of powerful people inside or outside government. Critics of pluralist theory argue that business interests continue to have a privileged position despite the development of many groups representing other interests. Because of their economic clout, large corporations have a "guaranteed access" to key government decision makers that empowers them to influence governments (Macdonald, 2007, p. 181). However, business interests do not always get what they want. Public interest groups that can effectively mobilize public support sometimes succeed in persuading government to adopt the policies they favour despite opposition from business interests.

Critics of pluralist theory also argue that governments do not simply respond to the pressures placed on them. Whether as a result of their view of what is in the public interest, a calculation of what is needed to win the next election, or a desire to maintain their power in federal–provincial or international relations, governments do, at times, adopt policies that cannot be explained in terms of the pressures of interest groups.

Interest groups are sometimes viewed as a threat to democracy and good government. Because many interest groups pursue the particular interests of their members, or of one narrow segment of society, there is a risk that powerful interest groups could achieve benefits for some elements of society at the expense of the general public interest.

Further, it is sometimes argued that interest groups can undermine national unity by pursuing the specific interests of particular groups.

On the other hand, the development of groups representing diverse interests, as well as groups concerned with the public interest, can be viewed as a positive feature of political life—one that contributes to the quality of public policies by providing policy-makers with multiple sources of information and ideas. Furthermore, the development of groups representing disadvantaged elements of society that have previously been largely ignored in politics can stimulate the development of a more just society in which diversity is respected. However, despite the development of groups representing the disadvantaged elements of society, interest groups tend to attract their members and supporters from the better-off members of society. The poor and other disadvantaged groups are not adequately represented among those who are able to influence policy-makers. Cutbacks in government funding for equality-seeking groups add to the imbalance of influence and perhaps make the quest for a fully democratic society a more elusive goal.

Social movements may also be viewed as enhancing the quality of democracy. Unlike interest groups that do not necessarily involve their members, social movements often mobilize masses of people to participate in collective actions intended to better society, and the world at large. By challenging embedded structures of social as well as political power, social movements can encourage debate about fundamental issues and values, and voice the concerns of disadvantaged and marginalized groups (Phillips, 2004). However, like interest groups, social movements tend to attract middle-class participants. Further, the strident positions and disruptive actions taken by some of those active in social movements may alienate potential supporters and make it difficult for social movements to influence public policy decision makers.

The activities of lobbyists tend to advance the interests of large corporations and some well-funded interest groups. Despite the passage of laws regulating some of the activities of lobbyists, lobbying activity will likely continue to raise concerns about unfair influence, secret backroom deals, and the need for greater transparency in the policy-making process.

Discussion Questions

1. Are interest groups an essential feature of democracy?

2. Are you active in an interest group? Why or why not?

3. Does your student union or student association effectively represent your interests?

4. Should governments fund interest groups?

5. What are the strengths and weaknesses of the different theoretical perspectives concerning interest groups?

6. Are social movement activists justified in engaging in civil disobedience to advance their cause?

7. Should government officials and elected politicians be prevented from being lobbyists for a considerable length of time after leaving public office?

Further Reading

Ayers, J. M. (1998). *Defying conventional wisdom: Political movements and popular contention against North American free trade.* Toronto, ON: University of Toronto Press.

Carroll, W. K. (Ed.). (1997). *Organizing dissent: Contemporary social movements in theory and practice* (2nd ed.). Toronto, ON: Garamond Press.

Coleman, W. (1988). *Business and politics: A study of collective action.* Montreal, QC: McGill-Queen's University Press.

Hale, G. (2006). *Uneasy partnership: The politics of business and government.* Toronto, ON: University of Toronto Press.

Hammond-Callaghan, M., & Hayday, M. (Eds.). (2008). *Mobilizations, protests & engagements: Canadian perspectives on social movements.* Halifax, NS: Fernwood.

Macdonald, D. (2007). *Business and environmental politics in Canada.* Peterborough, ON: Broadview Press.

Pal, L.A. (1993). *Interests of state: The politics of language, multiculturalism, and feminism in Canada.* Montreal, QC: McGill-Queen's University Press.

Pross, A. P. (1992). *Group politics and public policy* (2nd ed.). Toronto, ON: Oxford University Press.

Smith, M. (2005). *A civil society? Collective actors in Canadian political life.* Peterborough, ON: Broadview Press, 2005.

Smith, M. (Ed.). (2008). *Group politics and social movements in Canada.* Peterborough, ON: Broadview Press.

Young, L., & Everitt, J. (2004). *Advocacy groups.* Vancouver: UBC Press.

Chapter 8

POLITICAL PARTIES

PHOTO ABOVE: NDP leader Jack Layton, Liberal leader Stéphane Dion, and Bloc Québécois leader Gilles Duceppe present their coalition agreement to the national press corps in December 2008. The agreement to form a Liberal-NDP coalition government supported by the Bloc was short-lived.

1. Describe the role of political parties in Canadian democracy.

2. Discuss different types of party systems and their impact on government formation, accountability, and the representation of diverse interests.

3. Understand changing patterns of party competition.

4. Review the ideas and policies of the most significant parties in federal politics.

5. Discuss how much influence party members have over party platforms and the selection and removal of their leaders and local candidates.

On December 1, 2008, the Liberals and New Democratic Party (NDP) signed a historic accord to form a coalition government to replace the Conservative minority government. The separatist Bloc Québécois guaranteed its support to the coalition for eighteen months. The threat to defeat the government came after Finance Minister Jim Flaherty delivered a controversial economic and fiscal update to the House of Commons on November 27. The opposition parties argued that the government had lost the confidence of the House because the update did not include measures to stimulate Canada's faltering economy. They were also opposed to proposals to ban strikes by federal government workers for two years and to eliminate a form of public subsidy that all political parties receive to pay for staff and expenses. This subsidy gives parties $1.95 for every vote they win in a federal election, provided they win at least 2 percent of the nationwide vote, or at least 5 percent of the votes cast in the districts in which they run a candidate.

The political drama prompted a strong reaction from Canadians, who expressed their views about the coalition and the government's proposals in letters to newspapers, online postings, phone-in radio talk shows, and rallies. Facing the prospect that his fledgling government would be toppled by a vote on a non-confidence motion scheduled for December 8, Prime Minister Stephen Harper made a televised appeal to Canadians on December 3. In his address, he referred to the agreement as a backroom deal with the "separatists," and argued that the bid to force the government from office was undemocratic.

On December 4, Harper asked Governor General Michaëlle Jean for permission to prorogue, or suspend Parliament before the vote on the non-confidence motion could take place. Constitutional experts and political pundits took to the airwaves to debate whether the governor general should consent to suspend a Parliament that had conducted no legislative business. Pro- and anti-coalition supporters held rallies in Ottawa and other cities. As Canadians waited to see whether they would be returning to the polls or would witness the country's first coalition government in more than ninety years, Harper emerged from the governor general's residence to announce that Jean had agreed to prorogue Parliament until January 26, 2009. Her precedent-setting decision prevented the defeat of the Conservative government on December 8 and triggered the resignation of Liberal party leader Stéphane Dion.

POLITICAL PARTIES AND CANADIAN DEMOCRACY

Federal election campaigns are brief, intense events that provide most Canadians with their primary exposure to political parties. During the 2008 campaign, about three million Canadians watched the two-hour televised English-language debates between the leaders of five parties (CTV, 2008). Millions more saw party messages and candidates featured in newspapers, television ads, blogs, YouTube videos, or election signs in their neighbourhoods. The nineteen political parties vying for voter support ranged from established organizations to less well-known parties such as the NeoRhinos, who promised to offer free university education, legalize marijuana, and dispatch "Love and Tenderness" squads to hug Canadians.

Parties are the cornerstone of representative democracy in Canada. They compete for your support and the right to form a government and implement their policies. They recruit local candidates and potential leaders for public office, organize campaigns, and encourage citizens to identify with them and to vote. The *Canada Elections Act* underscores their primary role as electoral machines. Under Canadian law, a **political party** is "an organization one of whose fundamental purposes is to participate in public affairs by endorsing one or more of its members as candidates and supporting their election."

POLITICAL PARTY
An organization that endorses one or more of its members as candidates and supports their election.

Their high-profile role at election time tends to overshadow other party functions that sustain democratic life. When elections are not underway, parties are expected to develop fresh policies and to provide their members with meaningful opportunities to craft party platforms and select their leaders and local candidates. Since the largest parties have local organizations in communities across the country, they have also been expected to promote national unity and represent the country's diversity by ensuring that the interests of Canadians from different territorial, linguistic, socio-economic, ethnocultural, and gender backgrounds are reflected in their policies, organizational structures, and personnel.

How much political parties have lived up to their promise as agents of representative democracy and nation-building has been debated since Confederation. Some have argued that Canadian parties, unlike their European counterparts, have never offered voters distinct policy choices (Siegfried, 1966). Since the 1970s, their role as policy innovators has been largely usurped by other institutions, including the Prime Minister's Office, the bureaucracy, royal commissions, the courts, interest groups, and think tanks (Meisel & Mendelsohn, 2001). In the late 1980s and early 1990s, the ability of the country's more established parties to knit the country together was challenged by new organizations such as the Reform and Bloc Québécois parties that championed regional rather than national causes.

The ability of political parties to inspire Canadians to participate in democratic life also seems to have weakened. A tiny minority of Canadians belong to a party between elections (Cross, 2004), and those who do join are dissatisfied with the influence they have on policy development (Cross & Young, 2006). Canadians believe they need political parties, but they do not like or trust them (Howe & Northrup, 2000; World Values Survey, 2006). The public is also becoming less attached to these organizations; between the mid-1960s and late 1990s, fewer and fewer Canadians said they identified with a particular party (Dalton, 2000). About two-thirds of voters changed their federal party identification, or identified with different parties in federal and provincial elections, or voiced weak attachments to parties (Clarke et al., 1979, 1991).

This chapter examines the role of political parties in Canadian democracy. It discusses why some parties have thrived while others have failed, the policies they have championed, and whether they have given their members a say in who should represent them. It will show that party competition has changed over time and that the federal parties have also adapted to changing circumstances. Whether they have evolved sufficiently to meet the expectations of citizens in the twenty-first century will be for you to judge.

CLASSIFYING POLITICAL PARTIES AND PARTY SYSTEMS

Political Parties

Parties may be classified on the basis of how they try to appeal to voters. **Brokerage theory** maintains that Canadian parties do not have clear and coherent ideological programs, but rather act in a pragmatic and opportunistic fashion. According to this perspective, brokerage parties such as the Liberals and Progressive Conservatives adopted similar middle-of-the-road programs and shifted their policy positions routinely in order to appeal to the maximum number of voters at election time. Rather than crafting messages that would appeal to a single region, language group, religious community, or economic class, these brokerage or catch-all parties struck policy compromises between different social groups in the name of national unity (Brodie & Jenson, 1980; Clarke et al., 1984, 1991, 1996; Siegfried, 1966). Other scholars contend that Canadian parties have represented diverse ideological traditions (Christian & Campbell, 1990), particularly **programmatic parties** such as the New Democratic Party (NDP), the Bloc Québécois, and the Reform party (Carty, Cross, & Young, 2000).

BROKERAGE THEORY
A perspective that maintains that parties do not have clear and coherent ideological programs, and that they act pragmatically in order to appeal to the greatest number of voters at election time.

PROGRAMMATIC PARTIES
Parties that articulate distinct, consistent, and coherent ideological agendas.

Party Systems

Almost every democracy has a **party system**, or a pattern of electoral competition that emerges between two or more parties. The simplest method for classifying party systems involves counting the number of parties that compete for office (Duverger, 1954). If there are two or primarily two parties, we

PARTY SYSTEM
A pattern of electoral competition that emerges between two or more parties.

TWO-PARTY SYSTEM
A pattern of competition in
which there are two, or primarily
two, parties.

TWO-AND-A-HALF PARTY SYSTEM
Pattern of competition whereby
two major parties win at least
three-quarters of the vote, and
a third party receives a much
smaller share of the vote.

**MULTI-PARTY SYSTEM WITH
A DOMINANT PARTY**
One large party receives about
40 percent of the vote, and the
two largest parties together win
about two-thirds of voter support.

**MULTI-PARTY SYSTEM
WITHOUT A DOMINANT PARTY**
Competition where there is no
dominant party and three or four
parties are well placed to form
coalitions.

can speak of a **two-party system.** If there are three or more parties, Duverger speaks of a multi-party system.

Two-party systems such as those in the United States, in the United Kingdom between 1945 and 1979, and in most of the former British colonies of the Caribbean typically produce single-party governments (Siaroff, 2005). The party that wins a majority of seats in a legislature following an election forms a single-party government. Single-party governments tend to enhance government accountability because it is easier for voters to identify which party is responsible for public policies. Alternation in power between two relevant parties is also more common in two-party systems. If electors are unhappy with the performance of the governing party, they can vote for its rival in the next election. Parties in two-party competitive environments also tend to adopt moderate, centrist policies (Mair, 2002).

Multi-party systems have been associated with coalition governments in many democratic countries, including Germany, the Netherlands, Italy, Australia, and New Zealand. This is because when three or more parties compete, it is less likely that a single party will win a majority of legislative power. If no single party wins a majority of seats in the legislature, the parties that won the most support may enter into post-election negotiations to decide which parties will share power. Multi-party systems have been praised for allowing for a more diverse range of voices to be heard. Critics of multi-party systems say they may undermine government accountability and the possibility of alternation in government, since the parties that share power often do not change from election to election. Extreme, ideological political parties with narrow bases of support are also more likely to thrive in multi-party systems.

Other classifications of party systems not only consider the number of parties in competition, but also their strength, their relative size, their place on the ideological spectrum, and/or the nature of their support (Blondel, 1968; Lipset & Rokkan, 1967; Sartori, 1976). Jean Blondel identified four distinct patterns of party competition (1968). In two-party systems, two major parties win 90 percent or more of the popular vote and the gap between their vote share is small. In the **two-and-a-half party system,** there are two major parties that win 75–80 percent of the vote, and a much smaller third party. Multi-party systems in which four or more parties play a significant part in the political process may be subdivided into two types. In a **multi-party system with a dominant party,** there is one very large party that receives about 40 percent of the vote, and the two largest parties together win about two-thirds of voter support. In **multi-party systems without a dominant party,** there is no dominant party and three or four parties are well placed to form coalitions.

Party competition in Canada has evolved from a two-party contest to a multi-party system that is more commonly found in European democracies (see Figure 8-1). Until 1917, Canada had a two-party system in which the Liberals and Conservatives dominated party politics. Between 1921 and 1993, Canada had a two-and-a-half party system where the two leading

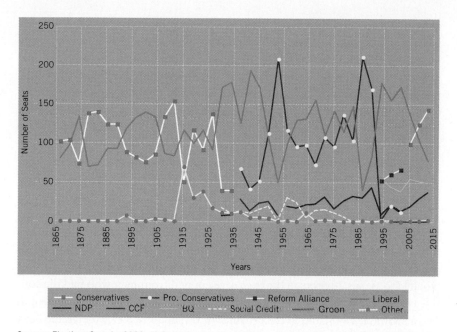

FIGURE 8-1
VALID VOTES CAST (%) FOR CANADIAN POLITICAL PARTIES, 1867–2008

Sources: Elections Canada, 2009, "Information from Past Elections," retrieved from http://www.elections.ca/intro.asp?section=pas&document=index&lang=e; Parliament of Canada, "Electoral Results by Party," 2009, retrieved from http://www2.parl.gc.ca/Parlinfo/compilations/ElectionsAndRidings/ResultsParty.aspx?Language=E

parties regularly combined to win over three-quarters of the popular vote. The remainder went to smaller parties that had no realistic chance of forming a government on their own. Since 1993, electoral competition has adopted the characteristics of a multi-party system. Between 1993 and 2000, the system could be described as multi-party dominant, with the Liberals as the dominant party winning an average 40 percent of the vote. Their principal competitors were divided among four smaller parties. The elections held between 2004 and 2008 produced three minority governments in which no single party won 40 percent of the vote and three parties were in a position to form an alternative governing coalition. For this reason, this period conforms to a multi-party system with no dominant party.

THE EVOLUTION OF PARTY COMPETITION IN CANADA

The Roots

The origins of party competition date back to the early nineteenth century and the struggle to achieve responsible government in British North America. From 1791, the colonies in Upper and Lower Canada and the Maritimes had a system of government that limited popular control over those in charge. The executive consisted of a governor sent by Britain and an executive council appointed by the governor to advise him. The executive council was made up of economic and social elites from the colonies—judges, military officers, businessmen, colonial administrators, and politicians. They were largely British-born men who, together with the governor, held all real political power. The legislative branch consisted of an appointed legislative council, populated by many of the same individuals in the executive council, and an elected legislative assembly to represent the people. However, the assembly was something of a sham—it had little power, and the governor or legislative council could refuse to approve laws passed by the assembly.

Two political tendencies gradually emerged in the colonies. The privileged members of the executive and legislative councils led the conservative or Tory element. Tories believed in the need for a strong executive authority that could check democratic assemblies and promote economic development. Their rivals were the Reformers, who aimed to make the government more democratic and responsive to the popular will (Thorburn, 2001). They planned to achieve their ideal through responsible government, whereby the governor would choose his advisers in the executive council from men who had the confidence of the elected assembly. The achievement of responsible government in Nova Scotia in 1848, and in the Province of Canada in 1849, created the need for more well-organized parties to support or oppose the governor's policy.

After the adoption of responsible government, loose alliances of politicians sharing similar tendencies gradually coalesced into parties. By 1854, John A. Macdonald and Georges Étienne Cartier had forged an alliance of commercial and industrial interests from English-speaking Canada East, conservative French Canadians from Canada East, Tories and moderate Reformers from Canada West, and members of the Family Compact and Château Clique elites,[1] which became the Liberal-Conservative party. After Confederation, the Liberal-Conservative party lost its Liberal elements and by 1878 became known as the Conservative party. English- and French-speaking Reformers from Canada West and Rouges from Canada East opposed the Conservatives. After Confederation this loose coalition welcomed allies from the Maritime provinces, but did not coalesce into a united Liberal party until 1887. The modern-day Liberals are the successors of these nineteenth-century politicians who advocated responsible government (Cook, 1977; Pickersgill, 1962).

The Birth and Collapse of the Two-Party System

Political scientists have identified four eras of party competition, each distinguished from the previous era in terms of the number of parties competing for power, their social and regional bases of support, their policy orientation, and party organization structures (Carty et al., 2000). Between 1878 and 1917,

---

[1]The Family Compact and the Château Clique comprised members of wealthy families in Upper Canada and Lower Canada, respectively. They controlled the government through their roles as members of the Executive Council and Legislative Council.

Canada had a two-party system, with the Conservatives and Liberals winning 95 percent of the vote between them (see Figure 8-1). As two-party systems tend to do, Canada's produced a series of stable majority governments. Power alternated between the Conservatives and the Liberals, and both parties won similar shares of the popular vote in most provinces. However, Canadian society was changing rapidly in the early twentieth century and the parties came under pressure to respond to the demands of people who felt shut out from decision-making processes. Ethnolinguistic rifts over conscription in the First World War led to an important shift in voter loyalties after 1917. Most French Canadians felt that Canada's contribution to the war effort should be a voluntary one, while most English Canadians, particularly urban dwellers, favoured a policy of compulsory enlistment. In particular, francophone Quebecers opposed the pro-conscription position of the Unionist coalition government, which Conservatives and English-speaking Liberals had formed in October 1917. Wilfrid Laurier, the French-Canadian leader of the Liberals, refused to join the coalition. Before conscription was enforced, an election was called for December 1917. The Unionists swept English-speaking Canada, but won only three seats in Quebec. The Liberals won eighty-two seats, all but twenty of which were in Quebec. The election left Quebec almost completely isolated from the rest of Canada, and contributed to the Conservatives' electoral weakness in that province for most of the twentieth century.

Party competition was transformed during the second era (1921–62), as the classic two-party system evolved into a two-and-a-half party system. New parties were created to give voice to emerging regional and class grievances, and the combined vote share for the Liberals and Conservatives slipped to between 70 and 90 percent (see Figure 8-1 and Table 8-1). The Liberals dominated electoral competition and won a plurality of support in every province for most of the period. The smaller parties elected MPs, but had no realistic chance of forming a government on their own.

THE NEW PARTIES   The Progressives were formed in 1920 as the expression of a farmers' protest movement. They represented both a regional protest against the domination of the national economy by central Canada, and a rural protest against urban domination of national politics. The party opposed the National Policy of high tariffs that increased the cost of agricultural implements for farmers, as well as freight rates that made it cheaper to transport manufactured goods from central Canada than ship grain from Western Canada. The Progressives also fought for political reforms such as citizen initiatives, referendums, and recall elections that would weaken the traditional parties that they viewed as dominated by big business interests and give citizens a greater voice in the lawmaking process (Morton, 1950).

While the core of the Progressives' support came from Western Canada, they also won significant support in rural Ontario and some in the Maritimes. The Progressives made a surprising breakthrough in the 1921 election, winning

TABLE 8-1

VALID VOTES CAST (%) AND CANDIDATES ELECTED (N) BY POLITICAL PARTY IN CANADIAN GENERAL ELECTIONS, 1945–2008

YEAR (N)	CONS.	PROG. CONS.	REFORM/ ALLIANCE	LIBERAL	NDP	CCF	BQ	SOCIAL CREDIT	GREEN	OTHER
1945		27.7		41.4		15.7		4.1		11.1
(245)		(67)		(125)		(28)		(13)		(12)
1949		29.7		50.1		13.4		2.4		4.4
(262)		(41)		(190)		(13)		(10)		(8)
1953		31		50		11.3		5.4		2.3
(265)		(51)		(171)		(23)		(15)		(5)
1957		38.9		40.9		10.7		6.6		2.8
(265)		(112)		(105)		(25)		(19)		(4)
1958		53.7		33.6		9.5		2.6		0.6
(265)		(208)		(48)		(8)		(0)		(1)
1962		37.3		37.4	13.4			11.7		0.2
(265)		(116)		(99)	(19)			(30)		(1)
1963		32.9		41.7	13.1			11.9		0.4
(265)		(95)		(129)	(17)			(24)		(0)
1965		32.4		40.2	17.9			3.7		5.8
(265)		(97)		(131)	(21)			(5)		(11)
1968		31.4		45.5	17			0.9		5.2
(264)		(72)		(155)	(22)			(0)		(15)
1972		35		38.5	17.7			7.6		1.2
(264)		(107)		(109)	(31)			(15)		(2)
1974		35.4		43.2	15.4			5.1		0.9
(264)		(95)		(141)	(16)			(11)		(1)
1979		35.9		40.1	17.9			4.6		1.5
(282)		(136)		(114)	(26)			(6)		(0)
1980		32.5		44.3	19.8			1.7		1.7
(282)		(103)		(147)	(32)			(0)		(0)
1984		50		28	18.8			0.1		3
(282)		(211)		(40)	(30)			(0)		(1)
1988		43		31.9	20.4			0.03		4.7
(295)		(169)		(83)	(43)			(0)		(0)
1993		16	18.7	41.3	6.9		13.5			3.6
(295)		(2)	(52)	(177)	(9)		(54)			(1)
1997		18.8	19.4	38.5	11		10.7		0.4	1.2
(301)		(20)	(60)	(155)	(21)		(44)		(0)	(1)
2000		12.2	25.5	40.8	8.5		10.7		0.8	1.5
(301)		(12)	(66)	(172)	(13)		(38)		(0)	(0)
2004	29.6			36.7	15.7		12.4		4.3	1.3
(308)	(99)			(135)	(19)		(54)		(0)	(1)
2006	36.3			30.2	17.5		10.5		4.5	1
(308)	(124)			(103)	(29)		(51)		(0)	(1)
2008	37.7			26.3	18.2		10		6.8	1
(308)	(143)			(77)	(37)		(49)		(0)	(2)

Source: *Elections Canada, n.d.; Parliament of Canada, 2009.*

the second largest number of seats behind the Liberals. Prime Minister Mackenzie King spent the next four years trying to woo the Progressives, whom he regarded as "Liberals in a hurry." Internal divisions between the party's moderate and more radical wings also weakened it. By 1930, most of the Progressives had been absorbed by the Liberals, while others became involved in the formation of the Co-operative Commonwealth Federation.

The Social Credit party first emerged in Alberta during the Great Depression with a critique of the national banking and financial system. It argued that the traditional parties were instruments for eastern banking interests who mercilessly foreclosed on farmers' mortgages, seized their land, and insisted on full payments for debt charges (Irving, 1959). Social Credit proposed to distribute financial dividends to residents. In a province where thousands were unemployed or on the verge of starvation, the party offered a simplistic and immediate solution to calm the anxieties of people who were facing ruin. Another significant element of Social Credit's appeal was the charismatic leadership of Alberta premier William Aberhart, who linked the Social Credit philosophy to Christian fundamentalism by selling Social Credit as a Divine Plan to save society (Macpherson, 1953).

In elections held between 1935 and 1957, the national Social Credit party won 4–6 percent of the vote, drawing most of its support in Alberta and British Columbia (see Figure 8-1 and Table 8-1). In the early 1960s the party's newly formed Quebec wing, the Ralliement des Créditistes, had considerable success representing the rural, Catholic, and traditional values that were threatened by the liberalism and secularism of the Quiet Revolution. The Social Credit party won its last seats in Quebec in 1979 and eventually disbanded. However, some of the ideas of the Progressives and the Social Credit party influenced the founders of the Reform party in 1987.

The Co-operative Commonwealth Federation   The Co-operative Commonwealth Federation (CCF), the forerunner of today's New Democratic Party, had a more lasting impact on Canadian politics. The CCF represented an ideological protest against the major parties. Established in 1932 by Fabian socialists, Marxists, farmers, and workers under the leadership of J. S. Woodsworth, it advocated a democratic socialist program of public ownership of key industries and a planned economy; as well, the CCF argued for universal pensions, universal health care, and unemployment insurance. Nationally, the CCF never attracted more than 16 percent of the popular vote (see Figure 8-1 and Table 8-1). Although its electoral strength came mostly from Saskatchewan, Manitoba, and British Columbia, it also won substantial support in Ontario in some elections. The Cold War and the Liberals' adoption of some of the more popular CCF policies led to a decline in CCF support after the Second World War. By the end of the 1950s, its vote share had dwindled to less than 10 percent. In 1961, the CCF, with the support of the Canadian Labour Congress, transformed itself into the New Democratic

Party (NDP) and adopted a social democratic platform. The formation of the NDP was an attempt to transform the party's image as a regional Western party and broaden its appeal in urban industrial Canada by aligning with organized labour.

Moving to a Multi-party System

The two-and-a-half party system persisted during the third era (1963–93), with the Liberals holding a competitive advantage over the Progressive Conservatives (PC). Although the NDP improved upon the CCF's performance by growing its appeal among trade unionists and the poor, and in northern and urban Ontario, it never placed higher than third in federal elections (see Table 8-1). Liberal dominance of the third era ended when the Progressive Conservatives (PC) won consecutive majorities in 1984 and 1988. By the early 1990s, voter dissatisfaction with the PCs' approach to constitutional reform, the Free Trade Agreement it negotiated with the United States, the unpopular goods and services tax, and a recessionary economy left the field open for new protest parties to challenge the traditional parties.

Since 1993, the federal party system has undergone dramatic changes. The beginning of the fourth era of party competition has seen new regional parties win significant representation in the House, and a controversial merger between two parties that culminated in the dissolution of Canada's oldest party and the creation of a new national party that is challenging Liberal dominance. A growing number of voters are also responding to the environmental appeals of the Green party. The fragmentation of electoral competition across more parties has made it increasingly difficult for any single party to win a majority built on a strong base of support across the country (see Table 8-1).

THE LIBERALS IN CHARGE   The "electoral earthquake" of 1993 dramatically reshaped party competition. The Liberals were returned to power with a majority and the distinction of being the only party that was able to elect members from every province and territory. Two parties that were mainstays of the third era of party competition were nearly decimated. Neither the Progressive Conservatives nor the NDP elected enough MPs to qualify for official party status.[2] The election was also remarkable for the breakthrough made by new regional parties. The Bloc Québécois, created in 1990 by the defections of Progressive Conservative and Liberal MPs who were unhappy with the failure of the Meech Lake Accord, won fifty-four seats and became the official opposition. Bloc leader Lucien Bouchard campaigned on a platform of

---

[2]Recognition of official party status in Parliament allows parties certain privileges. In the House of Commons, a party must have at least twelve seats to be recognized as an official party. Recognition means that the party will get time to ask questions during question period in the House and money for research and staff.

Quebec sovereignty and ran candidates only in Quebec. The Bloc won more than 49 percent of the provincial vote and stripped the Progressive Conservatives of their status as the leading party in the province. Astoundingly, Canada had an official opposition whose goal was to take the country apart. The West, too, was raising its voice in protest against the established system. The Reform party, formed in 1987 to express feelings of political and economic alienation in the West, won fifty-one of its fifty-two seats in Western Canada.

The newcomers challenged the brokerage politics practised by the Liberals and Progressive Conservatives. The leadership of the older parties had generally supported the growth of the social welfare state, an active role for government in managing the economy, official bilingualism and multiculturalism, and the constitutional reform initiatives in the 1980s and early 1990s. However, this public consensus wore thin in the 1980s, as issues such as deficit reduction, welfare reform, and lower taxation began to attract more support within state institutions and the general public. The Reform party benefited from voter dissatisfaction with parties that were perceived to be giving in too much to Quebec's constitutional demands. In contrast, the Bloc capitalized on anger about the failure of constitutional reform efforts to recognize Quebec's distinctiveness and transfer more powers to the provinces.

The Liberals continued to draw on their strength in Ontario and Atlantic Canada to win majority governments in 1997 and 2000. Liberal dominance was assured by the splitting of the right-of-centre vote between Reform and the Progressive Conservatives. The Bloc Québécois remained the leading party in Quebec and the Reform party continued to dominate the West. After Reform's failure to win a single seat east of the Manitoba–Ontario border in the 1997 election, party leader Preston Manning proposed that the PCs and Reform run joint candidates in the next election. Progressive Conservative leader Joe Clark rejected this proposal, as well as Manning's invitation to form a new party that would unite "right-wing" forces and mount a stronger opposition to the Liberals. In 1998, Manning launched the United Alternative (UA) movement with the support of some members of the national and provincial Progressive Conservative parties. At a UA convention in 2000, Reform dissolved itself to create a new party called the Canadian Conservative Reform Alliance.

Attempts to unseat the Liberals seemed destined for failure. The Liberals were re-elected in 2000 with an even larger majority and the Canadian Alliance managed to win just two seats in Ontario, bolstering the perception that the Alliance was yet another Western Canadian protest party. After facing an internal party revolt, Alliance leader Stockwell Day called a leadership race for 2002. Stephen Harper, a former Reform MP and president of the National Citizens Coalition, defeated Day to become the new leader of the Alliance. Some Alliance and Progressive Conservative MPs dreamt of merging the two parties. Together, they believed, they might defeat the Liberals. However, many PCs opposed a merger because they felt that the Alliance shunned the pragmatic and more moderate positions of the Progressive Conservatives. Moreover, new Progressive Conservative leader Peter MacKay had promised a rival candidate during the 2003 PC leadership convention that in exchange for his support on the final ballot to select the leader, no merger with the Alliance would take place. MacKay did not keep his word. In 2003, Harper and MacKay agreed to a merger that would create a united Conservative party.

THE LIBERALS LOSE GROUND   In the three elections held between 2004 and 2008, Liberal support steadily eroded and no single party was able to form a majority government. The Conservatives made significant gains in rural and suburban Ontario at the expense of the Liberals, and had a modest breakthrough in 2006 in ridings that were formerly held by the Bloc in the Quebec City region. The Bloc hung on to its status as the leading party in Quebec and the NDP enjoyed a steady rise in its popular support and parliamentary representation.

The immediate origins of the Liberals' decline in this period can be traced to the release in 2004 of the Auditor General's report on the misallocation of public funds on federal government advertising in Quebec. The scandal severely damaged the Liberals' reputation and they were scaled back to a minority government following the 2004 election. The Conservatives made gains in Ontario but remained weak in Atlantic Canada and elected no members from Quebec. In November 2005, the Liberal minority government was defeated on a non-confidence motion and voters headed back to the polls in January 2006.

During the 2006 campaign, the three opposition parties continued to attack Liberal corruption. The Conservatives set the election agenda in the early weeks by announcing new policies each day, including a cut to the GST, a modest child-care allowance for parents, and a promise to introduce new legislation on government accountability. Right in the middle of the campaign, the Royal Canadian Mounted Police announced a criminal investigation into Finance Minister Ralph Goodale's office for potentially engaging in insider trading before making an announcement on the taxation of income trusts. The probe later cleared Goodale's office of wrongdoing, but the allegations distracted attention from the Liberals' policy announcements and allowed the Conservatives to mount further attacks on Liberal corruption. On January 23, 2006, Canadians elected a Conservative minority government, ending thirteen years of consecutive Liberal rule.

THE BATTLE FOR A MAJORITY GOVERNMENT   The next election was not scheduled to take place until October 2009.[3] However, as discussed in Chapter 9, Harper made a controversial request to the governor general on

---

[3]In November 2006, Parliament passed a law to hold elections on the third Monday in October every four years, starting in October 2009. At the time, Harper argued that the law would prevent governing parties from calling snap elections when public opinion polls favoured them.

September 7, 2008, to dissolve Parliament and call another election for October 14, hoping to secure a majority mandate.

During the first weeks of the 2008 election campaign, the Liberal, NDP, Bloc, and Green parties criticized the government for backing out of Canada's commitments under the Kyoto Protocol to cut greenhouse gas emissions. The Conservatives responded that the Liberals' "green shift" plan to reduce personal and corporate income taxes and shift the tax burden to polluting industries would raise the cost of consumer goods, trigger a recession, and lead to job losses. Public opinion polls indicated low levels of support for Liberal leader Stéphane Dion and the "green shift." However, they also showed that Conservative prospects in Quebec were hurt by Harper's announcements about tougher sentences for young offenders convicted of murder, and cuts to the funding of arts and cultural institutions.

The televised English- and French-language debates held in mid-campaign marked the first time in Canadian history that the leader of the Green party was allowed to participate (see Box 8-1, For or Against: The Green Party's Controversial Debut in the Leaders' Debates). During the English-language debates, NDP leader Jack Layton attacked Harper for doing little to stem the loss of manufacturing jobs, while Dion and Bloc leader Gilles Duceppe compared Harper's "laissez-faire" philosophy to that of U.S. President George W. Bush. Harper responded that the Canadian economy was on sound footing and that the NDP's proposed rollback of corporate tax cuts and the Liberals' "green shift" would stifle growth.

In the final weeks of the campaign, the economy emerged as the most important issue as a financial crisis that had begun in the United States spread to Canadian and world stock markets. Stock market indices plummeted and Canadians became increasingly anxious about their investments, pension plans, and the possibility of an impending recession. On October 14, the Conservatives won a second minority government with 143 seats—19 more than they had won in 2006. They consolidated their hold on the West and displaced the Liberals as the leading party in Ontario. However, they fell short of their bid for a majority and failed to improve upon their 2006 showing in Quebec. The Liberals held on to official opposition status, but were reduced to seventy-seven seats. In a multi-party competitive environment, their national vote dropped to a historic low of 26 percent and their support dropped in most regions of Canada, save for Quebec. The results of the 2008 election indicated that the party's electoral base had shrunk to Atlantic Canada and Canada's three largest cities.

The Bloc's support in Quebec declined four points between 2006 and 2008, but this translated into a loss of just two seats. The NDP improved its representation to thirty-seven seats, largely due to gains in northern Ontario at the Liberals' expense, but failed to improve upon its performance in 1988, when it won forty-three seats. Green party support increased to 7 percent, but the party did not elect a single MP with Elizabeth May failing in her bid to defeat MacKay.

BOX 8-1

For or Against:
The Green Party's Controversial Debut
in the Leaders' Debates

The televised leaders' debates are a highlight of Canadian elections. Although every party leader covets a place in the debate, not every leader is welcome. The question of which parties should participate is determined through negotiations between a consortium of television networks and parties with representation in the House of Commons. This system came under scrutiny in 2008 when the consortium and the leaders of the Conservatives and NDP decided to exclude Green party leader Elizabeth May, the past head of the Sierra Club of Canada, from the debates.

Green party leader Elizabeth May made a historic debut in the 2008 televised federal leaders' debate with Prime Minister Stephen Harper and the opposition leaders.

The Green party had no MPs in the previous session in the House, but public opinion polls showed that it commanded significant support among voters. The Greens champion environmental causes and endorse the central ideas of "new politics" with an emphasis on social justice, pacifism, and decentralized democracy (Brown, 2009).

Opponents of May's participation argued that she should not be included because she had struck a deal with Dion not to run a Green Party candidate in his riding. In turn, the Liberals agreed not to field a candidate against May in the Central Nova riding where she was hoping to unseat Conservative incumbent, Peter MacKay. May countered that the Green party was a national party and that Canadians had a right to hear its message. She also vowed that she would fight the decision in court. Thousands of Canadians protested the decision to exclude the Greens, flooding the leaders with electronic and other messages. Within days of the outcry, the parties and consortium agreed to allow May to take her place in the televised debates, a decision that undoubtedly raised the Greens' profile in the eyes of Canadian voters.

POLITICAL PARTIES AND THE REPRESENTATION OF INTERESTS

Progressive Conservative Party

The Progressive Conservatives ranked as the country's oldest party until they merged with the Canadian Alliance in 2003. Early Conservatives dominated the electoral contests of the nineteenth century, but the twentieth century belonged to the Liberals; between 1921 and their demise, the Progressive

Conservatives formed the government on just eight occasions. As patterns of party competition evolve over time, so do individual political parties. Whereas early Canadian conservatism was based on support for a strong central government, close ties with Britain, and protectionist trade policies, by the late twentieth century, the PCs championed the decentralization of powers to the provinces and free trade with the United States. The party's failure to manage the resurgence of Western alienation and Quebec nationalism in the late 1980s and early 1990s ultimately led to its disappearance from the federal scene.

Canada's first government was formed by the Liberal-Conservative party headed by John A. Macdonald, the leading instigator of Confederation. Its "National Policy" favoured a protective tariff for Canadian industry, government support for railway building, immigration, and Western settlement. The Conservatives' success in the first party system hinged on Macdonald's skills as a builder of a stable coalition of French and English, and Protestant and Catholic, interests. However, his decision not to commute the death sentence of Louis Riel—the Catholic, French-speaking leader of the Métis uprising of 1885—eroded the party's popularity in Quebec (see Chapter 2). The party's appeal in Quebec was further undermined by its support for compulsory enlistment during World War I. By the early 1920s, the Conservatives' high tariff policy had also alienated Western farmers.

The Great Depression, a severe economic depression that originated in the United States and spread worldwide, struck in 1929. The Conservatives, led by New Brunswick–born self-made millionaire R. B. Bennett, demanded that the Liberal government raise tariffs to kick-start Canadian industry and provide jobs to unemployed Canadians through public works projects. These arguments convinced enough Canadians that the Conservatives could solve the country's economic hardships, and the Conservatives were elected to office in 1930. The Bennett government drew on the power of government to battle the depression, but many Canadians thought the government had done too little too late, and re-elected the Liberals in 1935.

The Conservatives remained shut out of power until 1957. During two decades of Liberal dominance, the Conservatives had six leaders and underwent three name changes (National Conservative, National Government, and Progressive Conservative). In 1956, the Progressive Conservatives chose John Diefenbaker, a firebrand prairie populist from Saskatchewan, as their leader. In the 1957 election, Diefenbaker campaigned on a platform attacking Liberal arrogance and insensitivity to the economic problems of Western and Atlantic Canada. The strategy paid off and he won a minority government. He followed this up in 1958 with the largest landslide victory in Canadian history.

During the Diefenbaker era (1957–63), the government increased old-age pensions, extended and enlarged unemployment insurance benefits, provided financial assistance to regions outside central Canada, and helped boost Western Canadian agriculture by arranging wheat sales to China. While in office, his government passed a statutory Bill of Rights, granted the vote to First Nations Canadians, and helped force South Africa out of the Commonwealth for its system of racial apartheid. However, a series of fumbles in nuclear and defence policy and a faltering economy eroded Diefenbaker's popularity, and the Progressive Conservatives' brief interlude in power ended with a Liberal minority victory in 1963. Political analysts have suggested three main reasons that the PCs failed to displace the Liberals as the "natural governing party":

1. The Liberals succeeded in regaining their dominance in Quebec.
2. The Conservatives proved unable to expand their base in the rapidly industrializing and more multicultural regions of Ontario.
3. Divisive internal disputes about the leadership question undermined party unity until the mid-1980s.

After sixteen years of Liberal rule, the Progressive Conservatives led by Joe Clark were elected with a minority government in 1979. Just nine months later, the PC government was defeated on a budget vote and the ensuing 1980 election produced another majority Liberal government. The retirement of Liberal Prime Minister Pierre Trudeau in early 1984 signalled another change in Canadian politics—the "Trudeau era" was over and the "Mulroney years" were about to begin.

In 1984, Brian Mulroney, the fluently bilingual, self-styled "Boy from Baie Comeau," led the PCs to a crushing victory over their rivals, winning 211 out of 282 seats in the House. Mulroney's personal popularity, and tactical errors by Liberal leader John Turner, helped assure the impressive victory. In a recessionary economy, Mulroney's campaign rallying cry of "Jobs! Jobs! Jobs!" was well received by voters eager for a change (Clarke, Kornberg, & Wearing, 2000).

During the Mulroney era (1984–93), the government pursued an ambitious agenda of economic and political reform. It launched two ill-fated attempts at constitutional change designed to meet Quebec's conditions for signing the *Constitution Act, 1982*, and to address provincial demands for the decentralization of powers (see Chapter 10). It also abandoned its historic resistance to closer ties with the United States after a royal commission appointed by the previous Liberal government recommended that Canada seek a free trade agreement. Although Mulroney had opposed the idea when he was vying for his party's leadership, he changed his mind and campaigned for a free trade agreement (FTA) with the United States during the 1988 federal election. In the end, more Canadians voted for parties that opposed the FTA, but the Tories won the largest number of seats and a second consecutive majority. Mulroney's electoral success relied heavily on support from a coalition of pro–free trade Western populists, farmers, business liberals, and Quebec nationalists.

By the early 1990s, a recession, unpopular policies such as the goods and services tax and free trade, and widespread dissatisfaction with the government's approach to constitutional reform contributed to mounting voter discontent. Although all three federal parties supported the constitutional overtures that had been made to Quebec and the other provinces through the Meech Lake Accord, many English-speaking Canadians objected to Quebec as a distinct society. Meech ran into opposition in the Manitoba and Newfoundland legislatures and was not ratified by the 1990 deadline. The Conservative government's next attempt at constitutional reform—the Charlottetown Accord—was defeated in a national referendum in 1992. Mulroney resigned in the spring of 1993 and was succeeded by Kim Campbell, Canada's first—and to date, only—female prime minister.

In the 1993 election, the PCs suffered the worst electoral defeat for a governing party in Canadian history. The results could not have been more humiliating: they were reduced to two MPs and lost official party status, and Campbell lost her own seat. Campbell resigned and was replaced by Quebecer Jean Charest in 1995. The PCs improved their showing in the 1997 election, but Charest resigned shortly thereafter to assume the leadership of the Quebec Liberal Party.

In 2000, the Tories, now led by former Prime Minister Joe Clark, won only twelve seats, splitting the right-of-centre vote with the Canadian Alliance in several Ontario ridings. Clark stepped down as leader in 2003 and, later that same year, his successor Peter MacKay negotiated with Stephen Harper, the leader of the Canadian Alliance, to dissolve the Progressive Conservatives and merge with the Alliance to form a new conservative party.

The Reform Party and the Canadian Reform Conservative Alliance

Since the Diefenbaker era, many Western Canadians had supported the Progressive Conservatives, expecting that the Mulroney Government would address their grievances. Although the PCs dismantled the hated National Energy Program, to many Westerners it seemed that the party was more concerned with pleasing Quebec nationalists (Flanagan, 2001). To give voice to these feelings of economic and political alienation from the traditional parties, Preston Manning, the son of a former Social Credit premier of Alberta, founded the Reform party in 1987.

Reform's populist program called for more public input into policymaking through citizen initiatives, referendums, recall, and free votes in the House. It also supported a "Triple-E Senate": elected, equal, and effective. Reform pushed for a free market over government intervention, deficit reduction, and reduced spending on social programs. It also opposed collective or group rights in favour of individual rights. The party rejected any kind of special status for Quebec, official bilingualism and multiculturalism, affirmative action and preferential programs for minorities, and Aboriginal self-government. The party positions that family and marriage are for heterosexuals exclusively, that a referendum should be held on restricting abortion, and that there should be a reinstatement of capital punishment reflected its ideology of **social conservatism.**

SOCIAL CONSERVATISM
An ideology based on a commitment to traditional ideas about the family and morality.

In the 1988 election, the Reform party fielded seventy-two candidates in Western Canada but did not elect any MPs. It achieved a breakthrough in 1993, winning fifty-two seats and status as the third-largest party in the House of Commons. However, it remained a regional party, fielding no candidates in Quebec and electing just one member from Ontario and none in Atlantic Canada. The party consolidated its western base in the 1997 election but failed to make inroads in central and Atlantic Canada.

Reform's decision to dissolve itself and create the Canadian Conservative Reform Alliance in 2000 was part of its bid to unite Reformers and PCs under one party tent. Within a matter of days, however, the party changed its official name to the Canadian Reform Conservative Alliance after media covering the convention pointed out that if the word "party" was added to its name, it would be referred to as the Conservative Reform Alliance Party, or CRAP. In the 2000 election, the Alliance increased its support, but managed to win just two seats in Ontario.

The Conservative Party

Conservative Party of Canada:
www.conservative.ca

The Conservative party was formed as a result of a merger between the Progressive Conservatives and Canadian Alliance in October 2003. Canada's oldest party and the Alliance were dissolved in an effort to end the vote-splitting on the right that helped the Liberals win three majority governments in 1993, 1997, and 2000. In the 2004 election, the Conservative party campaigned on a platform of government accountability, lower taxes, increased funding for the military, and stiffer sentences for serious crimes. The absence of campaign themes related to abortion, euthanasia, family values, or multiculturalism showed that the party was trying to present a moderate image for centrist voters. The Conservatives did not win the election and remained marginal in Quebec, but they made gains in Ontario, winning 24 of the province's 106 seats.

In 2005, the Conservatives eliminated the populist and regionally oriented parts of its platform that had been popular with Reform-Alliance supporters: a Triple-E Senate, citizens' initiatives, recall, and opposition to "unaccountable judges and human rights bureaucrats." They also eliminated most of the social conservative positions on issues such as abortion, and reached out to Quebec voters by supporting official bilingualism, limiting federal spending powers, and resolving to address what they considered a fiscal imbalance between the revenues of the Canadian government and those of provincial governments (see Chapter 13).

The party's campaign platform for the 2006 election emphasized government accountability, tax cuts, and modest spending initiatives for middle-class voters. The 2008 platform highlighted the accomplishments of the previous

Conservative government, sound economic management, and criminal justice reform as campaign themes. Voter anger with the Liberals over the "sponsorship scandal" and the jettisoning of the populist and social conservative elements of its platform likely helped the Conservatives win minority governments in 2006 and 2008, and achieve electoral gains in Quebec and in suburban and rural Ontario. In the fall of 2009, public opinion polls pegged Conservative support at nearly 40 percent, putting the party within reach of the majority it had sought in 2008.

The Liberal Party

In the post-Confederation period, the Liberal opposition was so fragmented that its members could not even agree among themselves what they opposed. From this inauspicious beginning, the party rose to dominate federal politics in the twentieth century. The self-styled "natural governing party" has been one of the most successful liberal parties in the world, forming the government in twenty-two of forty elections held since Confederation. Its electoral dominance was built on its shrewd adoption of pragmatic and flexible policy positions and skill in bridging social divides between French and English, Catholic and Protestant, and business and labour interests. By the mid-1980s, the Liberals had lost their once-solid electoral bastion of Quebec, and at the turn of the twenty-first century, the Conservatives were challenging their electoral dominance.

Liberal Party of Canada:
www.liberal.ca

As with their main rivals, the Liberals have shifted their stance on key issues over the course of their history. For example, the party was initially a strong proponent of provincial rights and free trade policies. By the 1940s, the war effort and the spread of Keynesian economic theory, which urged governments to help stabilize economic cycles of "boom and bust" by spending money during bad times and cutting back during good times, transformed the Liberals into a proponents of a strong central government. In the 1988 election, the Liberals campaigned against free trade. After their defeat, they returned to their free trade roots and later endorsed the North American Free Trade Agreement with the United States and Mexico.

Alexander Mackenzie formed Canada's first Liberal administration following the downfall of Macdonald's Conservative government in late 1873, triggered by the Pacific railway scandal. Macdonald had been forced to resign after the Liberal opposition revealed that a lucrative contract to build a railway to the Pacific coast had been awarded to a firm headed by a major contributor to the Conservative election campaign in 1872. The Liberals thus prevailed in the 1874 election, but were ousted from office four years later. They returned to power in 1896 under the leadership of the francophone Roman Catholic Wilfrid Laurier.

Laurier went on to win the next three elections by taking a cue from Conservative leader Macdonald's formula for success—build a nationwide coalition of supporters, support an expansionary role for government, and accommodate French and English interests. Some of Laurier's major policy initiatives included backing an aggressive immigration policy and supporting the transcontinental railway—the very initiatives that the Liberals had opposed in the 1880s (Clarkson, 2001). The Laurier Liberals negotiated a reciprocity agreement with the United States, but were defeated in the 1911 election after the Conservatives accused them of being too close to the Americans. Their anti-conscription stance in the 1917 election, while popular in Quebec, cost them votes in English Canada, and they were reduced to a small Quebec-based caucus.

When William Lyon Mackenzie King succeeded Laurier as leader in 1919, he inherited a party divided by race and language. Despite these obstacles, he went on to become the longest-serving prime minister from 1921 to 1948, except for two periods in opposition: briefly in 1926, and between 1930 and 1935. King's success has been credited to his legendary skills in reconciling different interests. He rebuilt the Liberals as an alliance of English and French and accommodated the interests of ideologically opposed groups such as the Western free trade farmers and protectionist manufacturers from central Canada. His governments straddled the ideological centre by combining responsiveness to business concerns with social welfare policies such as the *Old Age Pensions Act* (1927), the unemployment insurance program (1940), and the universal family allowance benefits program (1944).

Liberal Prime Minister Louis St. Laurent (1948–57) maintained the King Government's mix of social welfare policies and a commitment to close economic ties with the United States. After the Progressive Conservatives defeated the Liberals in 1957, the Liberals remained in opposition until 1963, when Lester Pearson, the Nobel prize–winning "inventor" of United Nations peacekeeping, defeated the increasingly unpopular Diefenbaker. During Pearson's time in office (1963–68), the Liberal government passed legislation establishing the Canada Pension Plan (1965) and public medical insurance (1966), and negotiated the Auto Pact, an agreement that removed duties on trucks, cars, and automotive parts moving between Canada and the United States.

After Pearson's retirement, Pierre Trudeau, who had served as minister of justice, won a hard-fought leadership contest in 1968 to become the new leader of the Liberal party. Educated at prestigious institutions in the United States, France, and England, Trudeau had backpacked and hitchhiked around the world as a young man. Suave and free-spirited, Trudeau seemed to capture the spirit of the 1960s, and he swept into office on a wave of "Trudeaumania" in the 1968 election.

Trudeau's approach to constitutional reform and French Canada's place in Confederation was inspired by the principles of liberal individualism and hostility toward the granting of special constitutional status to Quebec. His approach to governance was based on progressive social policies and interventionist economic policies such as regional economic development programs, the National Energy Program, and the Foreign Investment Review Agency, as discussed in Chapter 3.

As the 1970s came to a close, the Liberal government was dealing with large budget deficits, high inflation, and soaring unemployment. The expansion of costly social welfare programs in the postwar period, an economic slowdown, and shrinking government revenues limited its ability to launch new programs to stimulate the economy. The Progressive Conservatives defeated the Liberals in 1979, and Trudeau subsequently announced his intention to resign. However, before another leadership convention could be held, Joe Clark's minority government was defeated on a non-confidence motion and Trudeau was asked to stay on and fight a new election in 1980. The Liberals were re-elected with a majority, but did not win a single seat west of Manitoba.

The last Trudeau Government helped defeat the separatist forces in the 1980 Quebec referendum on sovereignty-association. It also negotiated an agreement with nine provincial premiers to patriate the Constitution, with an entrenched amending formula and *Charter of Rights and Freedoms*. After fifteen years as prime minister, Trudeau resigned in early 1984 and was succeeded by John Turner. Turner called an election shortly thereafter and announced seventeen patronage appointments that Trudeau had made just before he retired from office. The appointments irked the electorate and the Liberals were defeated, having attracted just 28 percent of the popular vote.

Jean Chrétien, a former cabinet minister with a folksy, populist speaking style, succeeded Turner as leader of the Liberal party in 1990. In 1993, he campaigned on the "Red Book" platform, which balanced pro-business policies with concerns for Aboriginal peoples, women, and universal medicare. Widespread public dissatisfaction with the policies of the Mulroney Government and the collapse of the New Democrats helped Chrétien win a strong majority with representation from every province. The Chrétien Governments of the 1990s cut social spending, arguing that a large foreign debt and the need for deficit and debt reduction required fiscally conservative policies. The government also reversed its position on axing the goods and services tax and withdrawing from the North American Free Trade Agreement, and did not implement a promised national child-care program. The policy reversals did not seem to hurt the party's electoral fortunes. An upbeat economic picture and a political opposition that was split among four parties helped the Liberals win another majority government in 1997.

The spending cuts imposed in the 1990s, a decline in interest rates, and a growing economy had created welcome budgetary surpluses for the Liberal government. The Liberals won a third consecutive majority in 2000, but before Chrétien finished his term, he was pressured to resign by his former finance minister Paul Martin and his supporters. Martin had long coveted the office of prime minister, and although he had served successfully under

Chrétien, the two men were rivals. Martin became Liberal leader in 2003, but his tenure was dogged by the sponsorship scandal discussed earlier in this chapter. The Liberals were reduced to a minority government in 2004 and lost the 2006 election to the Conservatives.

Stéphane Dion, a former cabinet minister in the Chrétien and Martin governments, surprised many when he was chosen as the next leader at a party convention in December 2006. In 2008, Dion campaigned on a platform to cut income and corporate income taxes and shift the tax burden to polluting industries. Voters did not warm to Dion, a former academic who lacked the common touch, or to the "green shift" environmental policy. The Liberals emerged from the election with a historic low of 26 percent of the popular vote, hemorrhaging support in most regions of the country. As discussed in the opening vignette, the failure of the Liberal-led coalition to replace the minority Conservative government in December 2008 triggered Dion's resignation and his replacement by Michael Ignatieff.

Under Ignatieff's leadership, the Liberals initially supported the minority Conservative government. In the fall of 2009, they decided they could no longer support the government and introduced a non-confidence motion in Parliament. While the Bloc supported the motion, the NDP decided not to help defeat the Conservatives, at least until the passage of the government's proposed enhancements to the employment insurance program. The NDP's move averted what would have been the country's fourth election in five years.

The New Democratic Party

New Democratic Party of Canada:
www.ndp.ca

The New Democratic Party has achieved more electoral success than its CCF predecessor, winning an average 15.5 percent of the popular vote between 1962 and 2008. Although the party has formed the government in five Canadian provinces and the Yukon Territory, to its frustration, it has never achieved the same feat at the federal level. Since it was founded in 1961, the NDP has held the balance of power in several minority governments, but has never placed higher than third in federal elections.

The NDP's roots can be traced to the struggle of farmers and labourers for better working conditions in the early twentieth century. Labour unrest following World War I gave impetus to the trade union movement and the development of smaller labour parties. Cooperation between more ideologically inclined members of the farmer-led Progressives and independent Labour MPs inspired the formation of the Co-operative Commonwealth Federation—farmer, labour, socialist—in 1932. The Regina Manifesto of 1933, the most important statement of CCF principles, advocated government planning of the economy through the nationalization of the railways, banks, insurance companies, and other industries of large-scale economic importance. The CCF attracted about 11 percent of the national vote, but never formed a government. The staunchest loyalty to the party was in Western Canada, where it drew rural support in Saskatchewan and urban support in Winnipeg and Vancouver.

In 1961, the NDP was formed as a partnership between the CCF and the Canadian Labour Congress in order to broaden the party's appeal to urban central Canada, francophone Quebec, and the labour movement. Its first leader was Tommy Douglas, a former Baptist minister and CCF premier of Saskatchewan who launched medicare. The NDP has pressed for a moderate form of social democracy through government regulation, some public ownership, more generous social programs, and redistributive taxation (Whitehorn, 2001, 2007).

The NDP played a key role in the minority Parliament of 1972–74, when it pressured the governing Liberals into passing election finance reforms and increasing old-age pensions and family allowances. It saw its best results in 1988, when it won forty-three seats and 20 percent of the national vote under Ed Broadbent's leadership. The 1990s proved a difficult decade for the party. After Broadbent resigned, he was replaced by Audrey McLaughlin, the first female leader of a major federal party. In the 1993 election in which regional parties achieved a major breakthrough, the NDP elected only nine MPs and lost official party status. The party's next leader, Alexa McDonough, moved the party closer to the centre, winning twenty-one and thirteen seats in the 1997 and 2000 elections, respectively. After McDonough's resignation, Jack Layton, who had served as a Toronto city councillor and president of the Canadian Federation of Municipalities, defeated five rivals to win the 2003 party leadership race. Under Layton, the NDP has improved its popular support and legislative representation.

During the 2004–05 Liberal minority government, the NDP pressured the Liberals into accepting an amendment to the 2005 budget that promised more government spending for infrastructure and social programs. It also voted with the Conservatives and Bloc to defeat the Liberals on the non-confidence motion that precipitated the 2006 election. During the 2006 election, the NDP directed its attacks against Liberal corruption. The party campaigned on a platform that combined fiscally conservative policies, such as balanced budgets and no new taxes, with social democratic promises to set up a national prescription drug plan and child-care program. In 2006, the NDP increased its vote share to 17.5 percent. In the 2008 campaign, Layton argued that the governing Conservatives had not done nearly enough to stimulate job growth, address climate change, and reform the employment insurance system. Although the party won eight additional seats in 2008, its vote share increased by less than 1 percent.

Some analysts have attributed the NDP's failure to win elections or even form the official opposition to its leftist principles, which fell out of favour during the 1990s when an increasing number of Canadians became concerned that government spending was a more pressing problem than limiting the power of big business. The electoral system has also hurt NDP fortunes, since it has always received a smaller percentage of seats in Parliament than its percentage of the popular vote, as discussed in Chapter 9. Finally, the party has never managed to build a strong following in Quebec. This can be partly attributed to its support for a major role for the federal government—a position that is not widely shared by many Quebecers. The emergence of the Bloc as a protest party with a generally social democratic platform has also undercut potential support for the NDP in the province (Whitehorn, 2001, 2007).

The Bloc Québécois

Bloc Québécois:
www.blocquebecois.org

In 1990, former PC cabinet minister Lucien Bouchard and a handful of dissident Conservative and Liberal MPs founded the Bloc Québécois following the defeat of the Meech Lake Accord. The demise of Meech persuaded Bouchard that attempts at constitutional reform were futile and that a new federal party should be established to achieve an independent Quebec. The Bloc stunned political observers in 1993 when it emerged with 49 percent of the Quebec vote and fifty-four of the province's seventy-five seats—enough to guarantee it the role of the official opposition. While in opposition in the 1990s, the Bloc had three goals: to protect Quebec's interests, to promote the idea of deficit reduction, and to oppose the reduction of benefits paid to the unemployed and others hurt by the recession (Crête & Lachapelle, 2001).

Following the 1995 referendum on Quebec sovereignty, Parti Québécois leader Jacques Parizeau resigned, and Bouchard left federal politics in January 1996 to become the premier of Quebec. The party elite chose Michel Gauthier as Bouchard's successor, but he was replaced a year later by Gilles Duceppe. After a period of relative decline in the 1997 and 2000 elections, the party rebounded in 2004 to elect fifty-four MPs. The Bloc's comeback was linked to rising support for sovereignty after the disclosure of corruption in the federal sponsorship program the Liberal government had set up following the 1995 referendum. The Bloc's popular support declined eleven percentage points in Quebec between 2004 and 2008. Nevertheless, it remains a significant political force in the province by diverting support from the federalist parties.

The Green Party

Green Party of Canada:
www.greenparty.ca

The Green Party of Canada was founded in 1983 and is part of the global environmental movement. It has fielded at least a partial slate of candidates in every subsequent federal election and since 2004 has run candidates in all or nearly all ridings across Canada. Between 2000 and 2008, its electoral support grew from less than 1 percent to about 7 percent. Although Green parties in many other countries have elected representatives to national legislatures, this has not been the case in Canada. The Greens' relative lack of success can be partly attributed to the single-member plurality electoral system, which does not reward parties with seats proportionate to their electoral strength. The party is also dogged by an image as a "fringe" party, and, until recently, has been ignored by the media (Harada, 2006).

As with its more established counterparts, the Green party's platform has evolved. Between 1997 and 2001, the Greens broadened their platform beyond ecological activism to include human rights, poverty, health care, and globalization issues. The party's 2006 platform placed a stronger emphasis on the environment, reaffirming support for the Kyoto targets and promising to enshrine the right of Canadians to a healthy environment in the *Charter of Rights and Freedoms* (Harada, 2006). U.S.–born lawyer, writer, and activist Elizabeth May led the party to its best-ever showing in the 2008 election. While her participation in the televised leadership debates increased the Greens' profile, the party failed to elect a single MP.

PARTY ORGANIZATIONS AND THEIR MEMBERS

Historically, methods of selecting party leaders and candidates, along with procedures for accommodating regional demands, were a far cry from what we would now consider to be democratic. In the 1860s and 1870s, there were no extensive party organizations outside Parliament, and parliamentarians and local elites carried out most party business. Party leaders were selected by the parliamentary caucus or by the governor general in consultation with party leaders (Courtney, 1973). The cabinet or party leaders worked out broad accommodations of diverse regional demands between them. In the electoral districts, locally prominent individuals selected candidates and offered party supporters jobs and public works contracts (Carty, 1991). After World War I, parties gradually expanded their organizations beyond Parliament and a small number of local notables.

Today's party organizations are far more elaborate. They consist of a parliamentary wing composed of the party leader and caucus, and an extraparliamentary wing, which consists of an executive and permanent office, the national convention, and local electoral district associations. **Party conventions** are held to elect party officials and debate policy and amendments to the party's constitution. Until recently, parties also held **leadership conventions** at which selected delegates chose the party leader.

Although a significant number of party members join a party because they believe in its policies (Cross & Young, 2002), party conventions have not evolved into forums where members can influence those policies. That role is jealously guarded by professional pollsters, advertising agencies, media consultants, and the leader's personal staff. The work of party members in debating and adopting policies at these conventions is often forgotten once they are over, and governing parties have traditionally been less open to providing grassroots members with a say. For example, the first Trudeau Government (1968–72) promised that policy positions adopted at the Liberal party convention would be included in the next election platform, but this did not happen (Clarkson, 1979). True to tradition, in 2008, Conservative party members

PARTY CONVENTIONS
Meetings of party members that are held to elect party officials and debate policy and amendments to the party's constitution.

LEADERSHIP CONVENTION
A meeting of party members to select a new leader.

had no say in Prime Minister Harper's campaign announcement about the withdrawal of Canadian troops from Afghanistan by 2011.

Party members have been more successful in influencing policy when their parties have been in opposition. The Liberal party used the period between 1958 and 1962, when it was in opposition, to develop a platform for its return to government. Much of the policy agenda the party pursued in the first years of the Pearson Government originated with these consultations on social, economic, and foreign policy.

ELECTORAL DISTRICT ASSOCIATION

An association of members of a political party in a territorial area that is represented by a member in the House of Commons.

An **electoral district association** is the local organization of political party members. It recruits members and volunteers, raises campaign funds, elects convention delegates who will debate party policies, and nominates the candidates who will represent the party in the riding. Although party membership fees are low and non-citizens and people as young as fourteen years old can join a party, only 1 to 2 percent of Canadians belong to parties between elections. Furthermore, party members do not reflect the broader population. They are disproportionately male, university educated, over the age of forty, and Canadian-born individuals of European ancestry (Cross, 2004).

Canada's federal system has influenced both the structure of party organizations and the parties that Canadians can support at election time. Some federal parties do not have provincial counterparts of the same name, and some provincial parties do not have federal counterparts. This is why some voters may belong to the same party at both levels, others may belong to a party at just one level, and others may belong to different parties at the provincial and federal levels (Carty, 2006). See Box 8-2, Worlds Apart: Federal and Provincial Party Politics.

How Do Parties Choose Their Leaders?

One of the most important powers held by party members is the right to select their leader. As discussed earlier, during the first party system, party leaders were chosen by a small, elite group of elected politicians and appointed officials. The parties' desire to broaden their support base, as well as membership demands for a greater say in party affairs, have gradually led to the adoption of more inclusive and democratic leadership selection processes. In the early twenty-first century, all party members have a direct say in choosing the next prime minister and prime minister in waiting.

Until 1919, Canada adopted the British model of choosing party leaders. Members of the parliamentary caucus and the retiring leader selected the new leader, usually with the agreement of the governor general. Party supporters outside Parliament did not have a direct say in leadership selection. The first major change to this process occurred in 1919, when the Liberals chose King to succeed Laurier at a convention attended by thousands of delegates from across the country. In 1927, the Conservatives followed the precedent set by the Liberals, electing R. B. Bennett at a national convention.

Worlds Apart:
Federal and Provincial Party Politics

When federal elections are called, Canadians begin the process of weighing the pros and cons of all the parties before they decide how to vote. One of the factors that might affect their choice is their allegiance to a provincial political party. But how should they vote if their favourite provincial party does not exist at the federal level? This is the dilemma facing, for example, supporters of the Saskatchewan Party and the Action démocratique du Québec (ADQ).

The Liberals and New Democrats are the only two parliamentary parties that operate at both the federal and provincial levels. The federal Conservatives are organizationally separate from the provincial Progressive Conservative parties in Atlantic Canada, Ontario, Manitoba, Alberta, and Saskatchewan. Furthermore, although the Bloc works closely with the provincial Parti Québécois to promote Quebec sovereignty, there are no formal links between them.

The distinctive nature of federal and provincial party systems is reinforced by the fact that parties with the same name often operate independently of one another in federal and provincial arenas. In the Atlantic provinces and Saskatchewan, people who join the provincial Liberal party automatically become members of the federal Liberal party, and vice versa. The same is not true in Ontario, British Columbia, Alberta, Quebec, or Manitoba, where the provincial Liberal parties are organizationally separate from the federal Liberals. The NDP is the sole party that is integrated across the federal–provincial divide.[*] Members join the party only at the provincial level, and in the process, become federal party members.

These structural divisions tend to minimize cooperation between parties of the same name, and make it easier for political leaders to cross partisan boundaries (Carty, 2006). During the 2008 federal election, the PC Premier of Newfoundland and Labrador, Danny Williams, exhorted voters across Canada to vote "ABC"—"Anything But Conservative." While the "different worlds" of federal and provincial politics reflect the diversity of provincial political cultures, they have also contributed to fractious regionalism.

---

*There has been no provincial New Democratic Party in Quebec since 1994.

Between 1927 and 1956, leadership conventions expanded to include a larger number of delegates elected by party members in each district. While these delegate conventions allowed more party members to select their leaders, the delegates did not mirror the general population. In fact, convention delegates were mostly older males drawn from the middle and upper classes (Courtney, 1995). By the 1960s, party members began to demand more open and representative conventions that would give grassroots supporters a stronger voice in leadership selection and party decision making. The trend toward larger conventions with designated youth, female, and Aboriginal delegates continued through the 1970s and 1980s (Cross, 2004).

As conventions became more inclusive, leadership campaigns became increasingly expensive because the contenders needed to mobilize a larger number of supporters. This meant that fewer leadership candidates could afford to mount a competitive campaign. When the Liberals met in Calgary in 1990 to select a leader, only two candidates—Jean Chrétien and Paul Martin—had a realistic chance of winning. Chrétien spent more than $2.5 million on his campaign and emerged the victor. The Reform party and the Bloc were the first federal parties to eschew large delegate conventions and use the one member, one vote method of leadership selection, which allows every party member to participate directly in the selection of the leader. In response to criticisms about problems with the selection of delegates and the inability of many ordinary party members to afford the fees to attend conventions, the major parties have also adopted the one member, one vote system.

The Conservative party used a modified one member, one vote method for the 2004 leadership contest between former Ontario Progressive Conservative cabinet minister Tony Clement, Stephen Harper, and Belinda Stronach, a businesswoman and philanthropist. Under this system, every party member could vote directly for the leader and rank the candidates in order of preference on the ballot. Leadership candidates were assigned a number of points based on the percentage of the popular vote they received from party members in each riding. However, each vote did not have the same value, because each electoral district was assigned 100 points, regardless of the number of members voting in that district. To win the leadership, a candidate had to obtain a majority of points from across the country.

Members could vote in person or by fax, and the results of the vote were announced at a convention in which the three candidates delivered their final speeches. If no candidate won a majority of support on the first count, then the candidate with the lowest number of votes would be dropped from the competition and the second place preferences on those ballots would be redistributed among the remaining candidates. Because Harper obtained 56 percent support after the first count of the ballots, no additional rounds of counting were needed.

The Liberals used a combination of the one member, one vote and delegate convention methods to select Stéphane Dion at the December 2006 leadership convention. Prior to the convention, party members in each riding cast a direct ballot for one of the eight candidates in the leadership race. They also voted to send delegates to the national leadership convention, proportional to the support won by each candidate in the riding association. Once at the convention, the delegates were required to vote according to the wishes of their constituency on the first ballot. If no candidate garnered a majority on the first ballot, then the candidate with the lowest number of votes was dropped off the next ballot until a winner emerged.

Former NDP Ontario Premier Bob Rae and Michael Ignatieff, a Harvard professor and author, were the front-runners in the race. However, Dion, who had entered the convention as an "underdog" candidate and was in third place on the first ballot, ultimately prevailed over Ignatieff on the fourth and final ballot, with 54.7 percent of the convention vote. In a bid to make their party more open and inclusive after its defeat in 2008, delegates at the party's 2009 leadership and biennial convention voted to adopt the one member, one vote leadership selection process. Like the Conservative party, a weighted vote system with each district given the same number of points regardless of the number of members voting was adopted (Liberal Party of Canada, 2009). Giving every party member a direct vote brings the Liberals in line with all other federal parties.

The NDP's leadership selection process combines the one member, one vote system with a "plus labour" format. Under the one member, one vote principle, each party member has a direct vote in the leadership selection process. Under the "plus labour" principle, affiliated unions elect representative delegates to attend the leadership convention and vote on behalf of their union members. Ballots cast by party members account for 75 percent of the weight in the total result and ballots cast by union delegates account for the remaining 25 percent of the weight. In 2003, party members could vote by mail, through the internet, or at the leadership convention. The mail votes were cast in advance of the convention and counted on convention day. Internet voting was done in advance and in real time on convention day through the NDP website. Under party rules, if no candidate receives enough support on the first ballot to be declared the winner, then consecutive rounds of voting are held. Any candidate receiving less than 1 percent of the vote, in addition to the candidate receiving the lowest percentage of votes, is dropped from the next ballot. Consecutive ballots are held until one candidate receives enough votes to be declared the winner. Because Jack Layton won 53 percent on the first ballot, no additional ballots were required.

How Do Parties Replace Their Leaders?

Until the mid-1960s, party members were stuck with unpopular leaders. There were no formal rules allowing party members to oust them, and leaders were replaced only upon their retirement or their death. This changed when the Liberals and Progressive Conservatives adopted procedures that would allow the party convention to review their leaders' performance. In addition to these formal rules that are discussed below, members of the parliamentary wing can place informal pressure on a sitting leader to leave.

Such was the fate of Stéphane Dion following the disappointing results of the 2008 election. When it appeared that he did not have enough support from his caucus to continue, Dion announced his intention to step down after the selection of a new leader at the party's next convention in May 2009. In the end, he surrendered his leadership long before the convention. The failure of the Liberal–NDP coalition arrangement to prevent the prorogation of Parliament in December 2008 increased caucus pressure on Dion to resign immediately. Shortly after Dion's resignation, Bob Rae and Dominic LeBlanc, a New Brunswick MP, bowed out of the leadership race with Ignatieff so that the parliamentary caucus could select Ignatieff as interim leader to replace Dion. At the party's 2009 leadership and biennial convention, delegates voted to confirm the uncontested Ignatieff as leader.

The parliamentary caucus also wields informal power to oust a sitting prime minister. In 2003, Liberal Prime Minister Jean Chrétien was pressured to resign by supporters of his rival, Paul Martin. Chrétien initially argued that his leadership could be challenged only by a vote of the party membership scheduled for late 2003. When it appeared that he might not win the leadership review, Chrétien announced his intention to resign five months before the scheduled vote.

LEADERSHIP REVIEW
The formal process that sets out the procedures for evaluating and possibly replacing a party leader.

The formal procedures for removing a party leader are laid out in party constitutions. The Conservatives' **leadership review** process is set into motion at the first national party convention following an election loss (thus a Conservative prime minister cannot be removed as party leader). Delegates vote by secret ballot on whether they wish to set a leadership selection process in motion. If more than 50 percent agree, a leadership race is called. The NDP's constitution allows delegates at its biennial convention to determine whether there will be a leadership election (New Democratic Party, 2001). It opens nominations for the position of leader, but if there is no challenger, no vote is required. No incumbent NDP leader has ever been defeated. Since 1992, all Liberal party members have had a direct say in reviewing the leader's performance. This vote takes place in every electoral district at meetings to select delegates to attend the first biennial convention following an election loss. If the leader obtains less than a majority of support, then the leader is not endorsed (Liberal Party of Canada, 2009). No incumbent leader has ever been defeated in a leadership endorsement ballot.

How Do Parties Select Their Local Candidates?

Candidate nomination processes take place in each federal election district, often before the drop of the election writ. The electoral district associations accept nominations from would-be candidates and organize the contests. There are few formal barriers to becoming a candidate. Nomination is open to all citizens aged eighteen and over, and candidates are often not required to live in the electoral district they want to represent. The candidates try to convince the party's supporters to attend a nomination meeting and vote for them. On the day of the nomination contest, local party members generally meet in schools or community centres to listen to the candidates' speeches and vote for their preferred candidates. The individual who wins a majority of support from those present is chosen as the party's candidate.

Although district associations choose the local candidates, their nominees are subject to the approval of party leaders. This has been the case since 1972, when the *Canada Elections Act* was amended to provide for the inclusion of

◀ Political parties can demonstrate their openness and diversity through their candidate selection. Gender and ethnic diversity are especially valuable. Leona Aglukkaq, shown here during question period in April 2009, is Canada's first Inuit cabinet minister.

party affiliation next to local candidates' names on the ballot. Since then, a candidate who wants to be listed on the ballot with the party affiliation must have his or her nomination papers signed by the party leader. However, party leaders will sometimes bypass local nominations and appoint "star" candidates to ridings because they are expected to attract support. In some circumstances, leaders have used their powers to reject candidates whom they perceive as undesirable. This is what happened to Mark Warner, who was acclaimed in 2007 as the Conservative party candidate for Toronto Centre, an urban district with a high population of poor, gay, and immigrant residents. The party replaced Warner because he had emphasized housing, health care, AIDS, and urban issues during his nomination campaign—issues that central party officials did not want to highlight in the election.

Parties sometimes intervene in local nomination processes in order to show they are open to under-represented groups such as women and visible minorities.

TABLE 8-2
FEMALE CANDIDATES AND MPS IN FEDERAL ELECTIONS, 1980–2008

	WOMEN AS PERCENTAGE OF CANDIDATES (N)	WOMEN AS PERCENTAGE OF ELECTED MPS (N)	PERCENTAGE OF FEMALE CANDIDATES ELECTED
1980	14.5 (218)	5 (14)	6.4
1984	14.7 (214)	9.6 (27)	12.6
1988	19.2 (302)	13 (39)	12.9
1993	22.1 (476)	18 (53)	11.1
1997	24.4 (408)	20.6 (62)	15.2
2000	20.6 (373)	20.6 (62)	16.6
2004	23.2 (391)	21.1 (65)	16.6
2006	23.3 (380)	20.8 (64)	16.8
2008	27.8 (445)	22.1 (69)	15.5

Sources: *Elections Canada, 2003, 2006, 2009, n.d.; Parliament of Canada, n.d.*

While there have been gains in the representation of females in electoral politics—twice as many women ran for office in 2008 as did in 1980, and the number who were elected increased fivefold over the same period—their presence in the House does not reflect their share of the population. In the 2008 election, just 28 percent of all candidates and 22 percent of MPs were female (see Table 8-2). The parliamentary representation of visible minorities has also lagged behind their share of the population, despite growth in the number of candidates and MPs from visible minority groups between 1993 and 2006 (Black, 2008; Black & Hicks, 2006; Tossutti & Najem, 2002). See Figure 8-2.

FIGURE 8-2
VISIBLE MINORITY CANDIDATES AND MPS IN FEDERAL ELECTIONS, 1993–2006

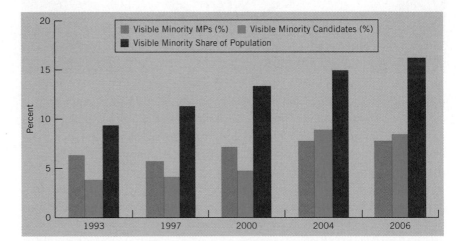

Source: Livianna Tossutti & Tom Najem, 2002, Minority representation in the fourth party system: Macro and micro constraints and opportunities, *Canadian Ethnic Studies/études ethniques au Canada,34* (1), 85–111; Jerome Black & Bruce Hicks, 2006, Visible minority candidates in the 2004 election, *Canadian Parliamentary Review, 29*(2): 26–31; Jerome Black, 2008, The 2006 Federal election and visible minority candidates: More of the same? *Canadian Parliamentary Review, 31*(3), 30–36.

Electing a Diverse House of Commons: Have the Parties Delivered?

Of all the parties, the NDP has introduced the most clear-cut affirmative action measures. Since 1991, it has required that the party field female candidates in a minimum of 60 percent of ridings where it has a chance of winning. Moreover, in at least 15 percent of ridings where the NDP has a reasonable chance of winning, it must run candidates who reflect Canada's diversity. These include members of affirmative action groups such as women, visible minorities, Aboriginals, and people with disabilities (Tossutti & Najem, 2002). In addition to these measures, the party also offers financial support to affirmative action candidates for nomination contests and training for women considering seeking a nomination (New Democratic Party, 2000).

Other parties have adopted less hands-on approaches to electing a more diverse House. Liberal strategies to improve female representation have involved identifying and encouraging promising candidates to run for office, as well as providing training sessions and financial assistance for campaigns (Erickson, 1998). In 1984, the Liberals set up the Judy LaMarsh Fund, which provides financial support to female candidates. In 1993, the Liberals changed party rules to allow the leader to bypass a nomination meeting and appoint a local candidate. Chrétien took advantage of this freedom to appoint female or visible minority candidates in certain ridings. The party also set a target that 25 percent of its candidates would be female. In 2008, Dion established a 33 percent target for female candidacies. In contrast, the Conservative party does not make use of special initiatives to increase the number of candidates from under-represented groups.

The different approaches raise questions about how to build a House that better reflects the Canadian population. Should party leaders use their power to appoint candidates from under-represented groups, or should nomination decisions be left up to party members in the electoral district? So far, the more proactive strategies have failed to create a House of Commons that fully reflects Canada's diversity. If these initiatives don't work, what else might?

The representation of females and visible minorities varies across the political parties. The NDP and Liberals have fielded a higher proportion of female candidates than the Progressive Conservatives, Reform party, Canadian Alliance (Young, 2003), and the Conservative party. Between 1993 and 2000, the Progressive Conservatives and Bloc lagged behind the Liberals, Reform, Canadian Alliance, and NDP in terms of the percentage of visible minority candidates they nominated (Tossutti & Najem, 2002). By 2006, the Liberals had a small edge in visible minority candidates over the Conservatives and NDP (Black, 2008). Canadian parties have responded in different ways to the question of whether any special measures should be undertaken to improve the representation of females and visible minorities in the House of Commons (see Box 8-3, Electing a Diverse House of Commons: Have the Parties Delivered?).

Summary and Conclusion

Political parties perform vital electoral and non-electoral functions in a representative democracy. They have largely succeeded in organizing campaigns and recruiting candidates and leaders, albeit individuals who do not reflect Canada's social diversity. They have evolved into more inclusive and democratic organizations that provide their members with opportunities to select key officials and influence policies. However, falling rates of voter turnout and party identification, along with low rates of party membership, suggest that their power to engage Canadians in the political life of the country is limited. As well, how much parties offer their members meaningful opportunities to influence policies and the selection of key personnel is debatable. Party leaders, their advisers, or the parliamentary caucus still wield the ultimate authority over the content of campaign platforms, the suitability of local candidates, and the timing of the departure of unpopular leaders.

Canadians have formed new parties when they have felt that established parties were neglecting their interests. This behaviour has contributed to the shift of party competition from a two-party to multi-party system. It is clear that Canadians have more party choices, if not more distinct options. It was proposed at the beginning of this chapter that party organizations are not static, and that they resemble living organisms. There is no doubt that their ideas and internal practices have changed over time. Their continued survival will partly hinge on their ability to meet the expectations of a diverse population for democracy and good governance.

Discussion Questions

1. Are parties necessary in a democracy?
2. What is the difference between a brokerage and programmatic party? Which parties may be classified as brokerage or programmatic?
3. Are the diverse interests of Canadians best represented by programmatic or brokerage parties?
4. Have political parties promoted the cause of national unity? If so, how? If not, why not?
5. Have the parties adequately represented Canada's diversity?
6. Just 3 percent of party members in 2000 were between the ages of eighteen and twenty-five. Why are younger Canadians not attracted to political parties? What should parties do to appeal to young people?
7. Who should have the final say in removing an unpopular party leader—the parliamentary caucus or party members?
8. Should political parties strive to increase the presence of under-represented groups such as females and visible minorities in Parliament? If so, how should they go about it? If not, why not?

Further Reading

Archer, K., & Whitehorn, A. (1997). *Political activists: The NDP in convention.* Toronto, ON: Oxford University Press.

Brodie, J., & Jenson, J. (1988). *Crisis, challenge and change: Party and class in Canada revisited.* Ottawa, ON: Carleton University Press.

Carty, R. K. (1992). *Canadian political party systems, 1978–1984.* Peterborough, ON: Broadview Press.

Carty, R. K., Cross, W., & Young, L. (2000). *Rebuilding Canadian party politics.* Vancouver: UBC Press.

Christian, W., & Campbell, C. (1990). *Political parties and ideologies in Canada* (3rd ed.). Toronto, ON: McGraw-Hill Ryerson.

Cornellier, M. (1995). *The Bloc.* Toronto, ON: Lorimer.

Courtney, J. C. (1995). *Do conventions matter? Choosing national party leaders in Canada.* Montreal, QC: McGill-Queen's University Press.

Cross, W. (2004). *Political parties.* Vancouver: UBC Press.

Gagnon, A., & Tanguay, B. G. (Eds). (2007). *Canadian parties in transition* (3rd ed.). Toronto, ON: Nelson Canada.

Laycock, D. (2002). *The new right and democracy in Canada: Understanding Reform and the Canadian Alliance.* Don Mills, ON: Oxford University Press.

Tremblay, M., & Trimble, L. (Eds.). (2003). *Women and electoral politics in Canada.* Don Mills, ON: Oxford University Press.

Wearing, J. (1981). *The L-shaped party: The Liberal Party of Canada 1958–1980.* Toronto, ON: McGraw-Hill Ryerson.

Whitaker, R. (1977). *The government party: Organizing and financing the Liberal Party of Canada, 1930–1958.* Toronto, ON: University of Toronto Press.

Young, W. (1969). *The anatomy of a party: The National CCF, 1932–1961.* Toronto, ON: University of Toronto Press.

Chapter 9

ELECTIONS AND THE ELECTORAL SYSTEM

PHOTO ABOVE: These two young teens protesting against debt clearly demonstrate their interest in the political process. Should this earn them the right to vote earlier than age eighteen?

CHAPTER OBJECTIVES

After reading this chapter, you should be able to

1. Outline the rules and procedures for conducting elections.
2. Discuss the strengths and weaknesses of Canada's single-member plurality electoral system.
3. Evaluate whether election campaigns help to inform the electorate.
4. Outline the provisions for financing political parties and their election campaigns.
5. Examine the explanations of the choices made by voters.

For many Canadians, the very mention of jail conjures up images of barred windows, barbed wire, sullen inmates, and snarling German shepherds. Less common is the image of prisoners casting their (mail-in) ballots to elect Members of Parliament.

In the past, prisoners were indeed stripped of the right to vote. Yet in 1992, court rulings struck down this provision. Parliament afterwards amended the *Canada Elections Act* to ban voting by prisoners who were serving a sentence of two or more years. Then in 2002, the Supreme Court of Canada struck down this provision in a narrow 5–4 vote. Some would argue that those who committed serious criminal offences have proved that they are not responsible citizens, and thus have forfeited the right to vote. In the opinion of the majority of Supreme Court Justices, however, "to deny prisoners the right to vote is to lose an important means of teaching them democratic values and social responsibility . . . Denial of the right to vote on the basis of attributed moral unworthiness is inconsistent with the respect for the dignity of every person that lies at the heart of Canadian democracy and the Charter." (*Sauvé v. Canada,* 2000, quoted in Courtney, 2004, p. 38). One political party, the Conservatives, questioned the wisdom of the Supreme Court ruling. In the 2006 election, the Conservative platform included a promise that the party would "work for a constitutional amendment to forbid prisoners in federal institutions from voting." At the time this textbook was written, the initiative had gone no farther than the election promise.

At what age individuals deserve the right to vote is another hotly disputed topic. Canada, like most other countries, has adopted eighteen as the minimum age to vote. However there has been some discussion about lowering the voting age to sixteen. Advocates argue that this would help to encourage young people to get involved in the political process, that youth are affected by the decisions of government, and that many young people are interested in and knowledgeable about politics. After all, they point out, fourteen-year-olds can become members of political parties and vote for their party's leader, and seventeen-year-olds can join the Armed Forces. In contrast, critics point to the lack of maturity and the low level of interest in and knowledge about politics and government that seems rampant among young people. They question whether teenagers who are below the legal drinking age and who tend to be more focused on designer runners than political runners-up are ready to vote. In 2005, a private member's bill in the House of Commons that proposed lowering the voting age to sixteen was defeated. So far, youth under eighteen have remained on the voting sidelines.

The right of all citizens to vote is a fundamental principle of democracy. Are any exceptions to this principle justified? Is a violent criminal who is politically aware more deserving of this right than a politically apathetic sixteen-year-old with a clean record?

THE IMPORTANCE OF ELECTIONS

Elections are a cornerstone of Canadian democracy. When we cast our ballot, we are exercising a hard-won right: the ability to participate in the selection of an individual to represent our electoral district in the House of Commons. Since nearly all of those elected represent a political party, our vote also matters to the overall outcome of the election in terms of which party will take charge of governing the country and which party leader will assume the office of prime minister. Voters can play a role in shaping the future direction of the country by choosing the party whose ideological perspective, policy proposals, or election promises they view as most desirable. Elections also create an opportunity for a variety of parties to raise issues and present policy proposals, and for individuals and groups to try to influence those seeking to be elected. Furthermore, voters can hold the governing party accountable for its actions (or inactions). Finally, if an election is perceived as being fair, it will help to establish the legitimacy of government; even those voters who hoped for a different outcome will be more likely to accept the winning party and to respect its right to govern.

In this chapter we examine how elections are conducted and the **electoral system** that translates the votes we cast into the representation of political parties in the House of Commons. As well, we discuss the campaigns organized by parties and candidates as they try to sway voters. Finally, some of the research revealing why people vote the way they do is summarized. As you read this chapter, consider the extent to which Canadian elections are effective in implementing the democratic ideal of rule by the people.

ELECTORAL SYSTEM
The system by which the votes that people cast are translated into the representation of political parties in the House of Commons.

ELECTION RULES AND PROCEDURES

Ideally, an election can be considered fair and fully democratic if a number of conditions are met:

- All adult citizens can vote and measures are taken to ensure that all citizens have a reasonable opportunity to cast their ballot.
- All adult citizens have the right to run for office with no financial or other obstacles limiting the effective exercise of this right.
- All political parties are free to nominate candidates and campaign on their behalf.
- Voting is done by a secret ballot so that voters cannot be bribed or intimidated at the polling station.
- Each voter can cast only one vote and each vote counts equally.
- An impartial organization oversees the process of elections and the counting of votes.
- Candidates and parties are able to witness the casting of votes and the counting of ballots with the right to demand a recount.
- The electoral process is used to fill all of the seats in the legislative body.

- Parties and candidates have a reasonable opportunity to carry their message to voters.
- The information needed to make an intelligent choice is easily available to voters.
- Elections are required to be held every few years.

Voting

In the past, as discussed in Chapter 6, women, those who did not own a certain amount of property, Aboriginals, and various ethnic, racial, and religious minority groups were denied the right to vote and to seek public office. Almost all restrictions were removed by 1960, and in 1970 the minimum voting age was dropped from twenty-one to eighteen. The right to vote is guaranteed constitutionally through the *Charter of Rights and Freedoms* (1982), which provides that "every citizen of Canada has the right to vote in

◄ Civic participation is vital to democracy. By completing her ballot, this B.C. voter exercises her rights and duties as a citizen.

an election of members of the House of Commons or of a legislative assembly and to be qualified for membership therein" (sec. 3). In practice, however, requirements for identification, including an address, occasionally create problems for the homeless, some Aboriginals and students, and those in long-term care facilities.

Most votes are cast at polling stations in easy-to-get-to local venues. Voting is by secret ballot, which helps to prevent the selling of votes and intimidation of voters. People hired and trained by Elections Canada are responsible for the voting procedures, and representatives of each candidate are entitled to observe the process of casting and counting votes. A National Register of Electors is maintained with updated information collected from such sources as income tax returns, postal change of address forms, and motor vehicle registrations. To vote (or to be registered at the polling station), an individual must present valid identification, or another registered voter who lives in the same polling division must vouch for the person's eligibility.[1] For those who will be away on election day, the option exists to vote through advance polls and mail-in ballots. Likewise, provisions are made for those who are ill, disabled, or in jail. Employers must ensure that voters have three consecutive hours off during voting hours. To further encourage voting, some people have suggested that voting by internet and cellphones should be introduced (as discussed in Box 9-1, Wired Democracy: Voting by Internet and Cellphone).

Canadian elections are run by an independent, non-partisan agency of Parliament, Elections Canada. The Chief Electoral Officer is appointed through a resolution of the House of Commons, holds office until age sixty-five, and can be removed only for cause by the governor general after a joint address of the House of Commons and Senate. Indeed, the Chief Electoral Officer has launched investigations of potential violation of election laws by the governing party as well as violations by opposition parties and candidates.

Elections Canada:
www.elections.ca

Running for Office

Any citizen who is at least eighteen years old can be a candidate for elected office, even if that citizen does not live in the electoral district. For elections to the House of Commons, several requirements exist:

- A minimum of one hundred eligible electors must sign the nomination papers (fifty in certain remote areas).
- An official agent and auditor must be appointed.
- A deposit of $1000 must be paid (this is reimbursed after an audited statement of expenses is submitted).

---

[1]A registered voter can vouch for only one person.

Wired Democracy: Voting by Internet and Cellphone

In Canada's first elections, a voter had to stand on a platform to publicly announce his choice of candidate to the cheers and jeers of the audience that gathered to observe this event. Today, in our electronic age, our system of casting paper ballots in polling stations may also seem like an archaic procedure. Indeed, Elections Canada has recommended that a system of online voting be tested by 2013 ("Elections Canada Advocates," 2009). By making voting easier, the trend of declining voter turnout might be reversed.

However, elections are crucial to the struggle for power, and the temptation is always there for contenders or their supporters to use "dirty tricks" to increase their chances of success. Inevitably, newer technology could open the way to previously unknown threats to the integrity of the system. The security of the vote could be compromised if internet browsers or the host operating system were infected with viruses and spyware.

The anonymity of the vote could be compromised if votes, along with identification, were recorded in a central database. As well, attempts to bribe or intimidate voters would be easier if voting were done at home rather than in a public place. Also, denial of service attacks on election day (as apparently occurred when Estonia used internet voting in 2007) might interfere with the voting process. Further, it can be argued that voting alongside one's neighbours in a polling station creates a sense that voting is an expression of being part of a political community rather than simply a private action.

Although our system of voting is costly and requires extensive organization, it has been conducted in a fair and efficient manner in modern times. Line-ups at polling stations are rarely long and, unlike in countries where electronic voting machines are used, serious questions have not arisen about the validity of the outcome.

However, unless a person is a candidate for one of the major political parties, the likelihood of being elected is very low. To have a party affiliation alongside the candidate's name on the ballot, the leader of a registered political party or the leader's representative must confirm that the candidate has been accepted as the party's nominee for that electoral district.

To become a registered political party, a party must meet several criteria:

- Two hundred and fifty eligible voters must support the party's application.
- The party must run at least one candidate in each general election.
- The party must have a leader, three officers, an auditor, and a chief agent.

Some people have argued that the Bloc Québécois should not be allowed to participate in elections and hold seats in the House of Commons because one of its goals is to promote the independence of Quebec. However, any attempt to ban a political party because of its views would likely be struck down as a violation of the *Charter of Rights and Freedoms*.[2]

Representation in the House of Commons

Canada uses a single-member plurality electoral system (SMP). This involves electing one representative from each electoral district, also known as a constituency or riding. The candidate who attracts the most votes (regardless of whether or not the candidate has a majority of votes) is elected. Dividing the country into electoral districts is a complex and sometimes contentious process.

The House of Commons is based, in part, on the principle of representation by population such that each electoral district will have a similar number of people. The Constitution requires that readjustments of electoral districts occur after the comprehensive census that is conducted every ten years to take account of population changes. The number of seats allocated to each province is generally in proportion to its population. However, the Constitution modifies this principle by specifying that no province can have fewer seats in the House than its number of senators. As a result, Prince Edward Island elects four members to the House, even though its population would only justify a single member. As well, the *Representation Act* (1985) guarantees that a province will have no fewer seats than it had in 1976, or in the period between 1984 and 1988, even if its population dwindles or does not grow as fast as that of the rest of the country. The three territories are guaranteed one seat each. Although guarantees of minimum representation for certain provinces and each territory might be considered a violation of the principle of equal representation by population, it can be argued that in a federal system it is important that each province receives adequate representation in Parliament (Courtney, 2004).

Legislation was introduced in the House of Commons in 2007 to move closer to representation by population by increasing the total number of representatives. It was projected that the new formula would give British Columbia seven additional seats, Alberta five, and Ontario ten after the 2011 census. However, the Ontario government strongly objected to the formula, arguing that Ontario would not move closer to having a share of seats

---

[2]At various times after its founding in 1921, the Communist Party of Canada was banned, although members of that party were elected under the banners of the Progressive Unity Party and the Labour Progressive party. The Communist party successfully fought against the deregistration of the party and the seizure of its assets in 2003, when it failed to nominate fifty candidates in that year's election (the requirement at that time). The Supreme Court of Canada ruled in favour of the registration of small parties, arguing the Charter protected the right of every citizen to participate in politics (*Figueroa v. Canada*).

proportionate to its growing population. The Quebec government also protested, noting that although Quebec's number of seats would remain the same, its proportion of seats would decrease so that it would be slightly under-represented. In December 2008, Prime Minister Harper agreed to give Ontario the twenty-one additional seats that would make its share of seats proportionate. Nevertheless, the legislation to achieve this objective had not been introduced at the time this textbook was written, and Quebec's protest had met with no response.

Until 1964, the design of electoral districts was the responsibility of Parliament. This frequently resulted in **gerrymandering**—the drawing of boundaries for partisan advantage, particularly for the advantage of the governing party (Courtney, 2004). It is now carried out by a three-member independent boundary readjustment commission for each province, chaired by a judge, with the other members (often political scientists) chosen by the Speaker of the House of Commons. Both the public and Members of Parliament have an opportunity to voice their opinion about proposed changes to the electoral districts. However, the commission makes the final decision.

Each commission is expected to draw the boundaries of electoral districts so as to take into account existing communities and territorially based "communities of interest." They are also expected to draw the boundaries so that each electoral district in the province is as close as possible to having the same number of residents, with no electoral district being more than 25 percent above or below the average number of residents in that province, other than in exceptional circumstances. In practice, remote districts with low population density tend to have smaller populations than urban districts. Although this might be considered to violate the principle of equal representation, the Supreme Court of Canada has ruled that the desirability of "effective representation" may justify some deviation from the absolute equal voting power of individuals (Courtney, 2004).

GERRYMANDERING
The drawing of boundaries for partisan advantage, particularly for the advantage of the governing party.

The Timing of Elections

The Canadian Constitution requires that the House of Commons (and provincial and territorial legislatures) cannot continue for more than five years without holding a general election. An exception is allowed in times of real or apprehended war, invasion, or insurrection if no more than one-third of the members disagree with the extension. The prime minister recommends to the governor general when an election is to be called. When the governing party loses the confidence of a majority in the House of Commons (for example, if the opposition parties pass a non-confidence motion, or if a major piece of government legislation such as a budget is defeated), the prime minister will ask the governor general to dissolve Parliament and call an election. A prime minister can also ask the governor general to call an election at a time that the

Fixed Election Dates or a Fixed Election?

In the 2006 election campaign the Conservative party, as part of a platform of democratic reforms, promised that it would institute a system of fixed election dates. Elections would "be held every four years except when a government loses the confidence of the House." Accordingly, in 2007, Parliament passed an amendment to the *Canada Elections Act* requiring that elections be held on the third Monday in October every four years, with the first election to be held in October 2009. In pushing for fixed election dates, Prime Minister Harper had criticized former Liberal Prime Minister Jean Chrétien for calling an early election in 2000 that had caught the new leader of the Canadian Alliance, Stockwell Day, unprepared. Fixed election dates, Harper said, would stop leaders from trying to manipulate the election calendar and level the playing field for all parties ("Harper Wants Fixed Dates," 2006).

The 2007 amendment to the *Canada Elections Act* contained one exception: A provision safeguarded "the power of the governor general to dissolve parliament at the governor general's discretion." On September 7, 2008, Prime Minister Stephen Harper asked Governor General Michaëlle Jean to dissolve Parliament and hold an election on October 14, even though his government had not been defeated in the House of Commons. Amid a storm of controversy over Harper's request, she granted him permission.

The opposition parties complained bitterly that Harper had ignored his government's own fixed-date election law in hopes of catching the other parties unprepared for the election campaign. In turn, Harper claimed that he asked for an early election because Parliament had become "dysfunctional." In particular, he argued that his thirty-one-month-old minority government could no longer govern in a fractious Parliament. The opposition parties argued that the governing party itself had made Parliament dysfunctional and pointed out that Parliament had passed much of the legislation presented to it by the government.

Certainly, the ability of a prime minister to choose the timing of an election can be viewed as giving an unfair advantage to the governing party—a means to fix the election. For example, it allows the prime minister to call an election when his party leads in public opinion polls, and it gives the governing party the ability to plan its election campaign in advance. It also makes the running of an election more difficult for Elections Canada. Should the prime minister be able, in effect, to hold an election whenever he or she feels that it is necessary? Or should an election only be held at four-year intervals unless a motion is passed in the House of Commons indicating that the majority of members do not have confidence in the government?

prime minister chooses.[3] In recent years, the procedure for calling elections has been modified by the adoption of fixed election dates at the national level and in the provinces of British Columbia, Ontario, New Brunswick, Prince Edward Island, and Newfoundland and Labrador (see Box 9-2, Fixed Election Dates or a Fixed Election?).

---

[3]The governor general has the right to refuse the prime minister's request for an election and to call on another Member of Parliament to form a government. However, this power has been used only once (known as the "King-Byng dispute," 1926) and in that case there was considerable criticism of the governor general's decision. It is unlikely that a governor general would refuse a request for an election except in unusual circumstances such as a request for an election within a year of a previous election.

THE SINGLE-MEMBER PLURALITY ELECTORAL SYSTEM

Canada's method of electing members to the House of Commons and provincial legislatures, the **single-member plurality electoral system** (SMP), has provoked considerable criticism and many proposals for change. The SMP system (also known as "first-past-the-post") does not accurately translate the votes that are cast for each party into the representation each party receives in a legislative body. Typically, the party that receives the most votes ends up with a larger proportion of seats than the proportion of the vote it received. This can result in a **majority government** (that is, one with a majority of seats) even when the majority of votes went to other parties. For example, in the 1993, 1997, and 2000 elections, the Liberal party led by Jean Chrétien only received about 40 percent of the votes cast, yet emerged with a comfortable majority of seats in the House of Commons. In a few cases, the effect of over-representing the leading party can be so strong that the other parties receive few seats. For example, in the 1987 New Brunswick election, the Liberal party, with 60.4 percent of the vote, won all fifty-eight seats (see Table 9-1). Supporters of the SMP electoral system argue that its potential to create majority governments that can govern for a full term of office provides more stability than systems that more accurately reflect the preferences of voters.

Occasionally, the party that received the most votes does not win the most seats. This can occur when the second most popular party wins a substantial number of seats by a small margin, while the most popular party "wastes" some of its votes by winning some seats by large margins. For example, in the 1979 Canadian election the Progressive Conservative (PC) party won 136 seats with 35.9 percent of the vote, while the Liberals won only 114 seats with 40.1 percent of the vote. Despite receiving nearly one million votes fewer than the Liberals, the PCs became the governing party, just six seats short of a majority. This pattern has repeated itself several times in provincial politics. For example, in 1998 the Parti Québécois won a large majority of seats

SINGLE-MEMBER PLURALITY ELECTORAL SYSTEM
An electoral system in which voters in each district elect a single representative. The candidate with the most votes is elected, regardless of whether that candidate received the majority of votes.

MAJORITY GOVERNMENT
A governing party that has a majority of seats in the House of Commons regardless of whether it received a majority of votes in an election.

TABLE 9-1
THE DISTORTING EFFECTS OF THE SINGLE-MEMBER PLURALITY SYSTEM

This hypothetical result of voting in five electoral districts illustrates the distorting effects that can arise from the SMP electoral system. Party A would win all five districts despite having the support of less than two-fifths of the voters. A substantial proportion of the population would not be represented by the party they chose.

| | PERCENTAGE VOTES RECEIVED | | | | | |
	DISTRICT #1	DISTRICT #2	DISTRICT #3	DISTRICT #4	DISTRICT #5	TOTAL
Party A	37	35	38	34	39	37
Party B	35	33	30	31	37	33
Party C	20	22	21	25	18	21
Party D	8	0	11	10	6	9
Total	100	100	100	100	100	100

PARTY	VOTE %	SEATS %
Conservative	37.7	46.4
Liberal	26.3	25.0
NDP	18.2	12.0
Bloc	10.0	15.9
Green	6.8	0.0
Other	1.0	0.6

Source: *Adapted from Tables 7 and 9, Elections Canada, Official Voting Results, 2008. Retrieved from www.elections.ca*

despite having slightly fewer votes than the Liberal party. Similarly, the PC party in New Brunswick lost the 2006 election to the Liberal party despite winning slightly more votes.

The SMP system discriminates against smaller parties, particularly those whose support is spread relatively evenly across the country (see Table 9-2). For example, since its founding, the New Democratic Party has received a substantially smaller proportion of seats in the House of Commons than its proportion of the vote in every election.

The SMP electoral system also tends to exaggerate the regional character of political parties, and can be viewed as an important factor in the development of the regionalization of parties discussed in the previous chapter. For example, winning just over one-half of the vote in Western Canada gave the Conservative party seventy-one of the region's ninety-two seats in the 2008 election. The Liberal party received almost half of its seats in Ontario (thirty-eight of seventy-seven), even though about two-thirds of its votes came from outside that province. More significantly, the Bloc Québécois, with 38.1 percent of the votes of Quebecers, won forty-nine of that province's seventy-five seats. This created the impression that Quebecers supported the separatist party, even though a sizeable majority of Quebec voters favoured other political parties. Thus the SMP system can benefit regional parties while discriminating against parties that have a Canada-wide perspective.

These regionalizing effects can also leave national parties without an effective voice in their parliamentary caucus for certain regions of the country. For example, Conservative parties have often lacked significant representation from Quebec, while the Liberal party has had very few representatives from Western Canada in the past half century. People in certain regions may feel alienated from the Canadian government if they lack effective representation in the Cabinet, and believe that this results in policies that harm their region or province. As well, parties have a strong incentive to concentrate their efforts and appeals on those areas of the country where a small shift in support may yield a large number of seats. Areas where a party is weak may be "written off" (Cairns, 1968),[4] while areas where it is strong might be taken for granted.

Because the SMP system generally discriminates against political parties with lower levels of support across the country, it typically results in fewer parties being represented in legislative bodies. Although it does not necessarily produce a two-party system as was once argued (Duverger, 1959), it does tend to create, at most, a limited version of a multi-party system. For example, the near collapse of the Progressive Conservative (PC) party in 1993 enabled the Reform party (aided by the workings of the electoral system) to gain a high proportion of the seats in Western Canada with a platform that appealed strongly to many residents of that region. However, as it tried to gain support to become a serious challenger for national power, the party (and its successor, the Canadian Alliance) found that splitting the right-wing vote with the PC party in Ontario was a serious obstacle. Each party attracted about 20 percent of the votes, meaning that the Liberals won almost every seat in the province. This set the stage for Liberal party dominance in Canadian elections for a decade, and led to pressure for the two right-wing parties to merge into the Conservative party in 2003. If Canada's electoral system more accurately translated the strength of each party into representation, it is unlikely that these two parties, quite different in their perspectives, would have united.

ELECTORAL SYSTEM REFORM

Much discussion and debate have been devoted to changing Canada's single-member plurality electoral system (SMP). Many of those advocating reform favour some version of a **proportional representation system**, particularly the **mixed member proportional system**. Unlike SMP, proportional representation (PR) systems feature a close relationship between the proportion of votes received by a party and the proportion of legislative seats it obtains. Voter turnout tends to be somewhat higher in countries with PR systems because every vote counts toward the number of representatives a party gains. As well, countries with PR systems are generally home to a number of significant parties representing different interests and viewpoints, thus giving more meaningful choices to voters. Those who favour a PR system also point out that countries with this system often feature a higher proportion of women and minority group members in their legislative bodies. Because each party draws up a list of its potential legislative members, each party will likely find it advantageous to ensure that its list represents the diversity of the country.

PROPORTIONAL REPRESENTATION SYSTEM
An electoral system in which the proportion of seats a party receives in the legislative body reflects the proportion of votes the party obtained.

MIXED MEMBER PROPORTIONAL SYSTEM
An electoral system in which voters cast one vote for the party they prefer and one vote for the candidate they prefer. Some legislators represent the district in which they received the most votes, while other legislators are selected based on the proportion of votes received by their party.

---

[4]An exception to this strategy occurred in the 1984 election, when the PC party led by Brian Mulroney successfully appealed to Quebecers (particularly Quebec nationalists) and greatly increased his party's representation from Quebec, despite the party's traditional weakness in that province.

Countries with PR systems almost always feature governments based on a coalition of parties. It is unusual for one party to win a majority of votes when a number of significant parties compete in an election. Without the distortion that can allow an SMP system to create an "artificial" majority for one party, parties in countries with PR systems have usually found that coalitions in which two or more parties share in governing are needed to provide stable and effective government. In practice, this often succeeds (for example, in Germany and Scandinavia), although in some cases it can lead to instability (for example, in Israel and, in the past, Italy). Considerable bargaining among political parties is usually needed to decide on the composition and policies of the government.

In a mixed member proportional system (MMP) used, for example, in Germany, New Zealand, and Scotland, voters cast two ballots: one for the candidate they prefer and one for the party they prefer. Candidates who get the most votes in their electoral district are elected, but others are selected (based on their position on their party's list) so as to make the overall representation of the parties in the legislature reasonably proportional to the votes received by each party in the election.[5] As discussed in Chapter 6, a proposal by the Ontario Citizens' Assembly to adopt an MMP system was rejected by voters in a 2007 provincial referendum. Prince Edward Island voters also rejected an MMP system in 2005. Nevertheless, the many advocates of electoral system reform continue to promote the MMP system as preferable to Canada's single-member plurality electoral system.

ELECTION CAMPAIGNS

The formal election campaign at the national level lasts at least thirty-six days. In reality, however, political campaigning can be never-ending as parties regularly promote themselves or castigate their opponents with an eye to the eventual election. A substantial "permanent campaign" can be run by parties with large financial resources (Flanigan & Jansen, 2009). For example, one month after Stéphane Dion was selected as Liberal party leader in December 2006, the Conservative party ran a series of television ads ridiculing Dion with the tag line "Dion is not a leader." The negative image that the ads created proved difficult for Dion to shake and likely contributed to his party's poor showing in the 2008 election.

Election campaigns have become highly professionalized, with expert campaign managers, advertising agencies, and pollsters responsible for designing and running the campaigns of the major political parties. At the same time, campaigns have become highly centralized, with the national party campaign office trying (not always with complete success) to tightly control

---

[5]Most countries with PR or MMP systems set a minimum percentage that a party must obtain in order to receive representation.

the message that the campaign seeks to deliver. Each party's candidates are expected to echo their party's message in their electoral district and to avoid any straying from the message that might be seized upon by the other parties or the media as evidence of disagreement within the party. However, due to language differences and the distinct political culture and interests of Quebec, the campaign themes and advertising strategies created to appeal to francophone Quebecers often differ dramatically from those for the rest of the country. For example, the 2008 Conservative campaign in Quebec appealed to Québécois nationalism by emphasizing that Stéphane Dion was responsible for the adoption of the *Clarity Act* (an act that made it difficult for a province to separate)—a fact that was not mentioned in the Conservative campaign in the rest of the country, where the act was popular.

Campaigns are highly leader-oriented with a focus on the leader's tour. The leaders criss-cross the country accompanied by a large media contingent. From one day to another, the leaders can be spotted flipping burgers, kissing

◀ During an election campaign, "photo ops" allow party leaders to target the mass media and the public, and share their message with party supporters in particular electoral districts or regions.

babies, swaying to a reggae beat, or even riding a Sea-Doo. In the past, leaders typically spoke at large rallies in the major cities. They also greeted supporters and interested spectators at quick stops in smaller communities while travelling by train (a practice revived by Elizabeth May, the leader of the Green party, in the 2008 election). In modern elections, however, the leaders jet from province to province, stopping for carefully planned "photo ops." These are usually linked to a specific daily campaign promise targeted to the mass media. Although the leaders of the national political parties usually visit every province during the election campaign, the visits are also strategically designed to mobilize party supporters in particular electoral districts or regions (Belanger, Carty, & Eagles, 2003; Mintz, 1985).

CAMPAIGN DEBATES

Although we now take them for granted, nationally televised leaders' debates were first held in 1968 and 1979. Beginning in 1984, debates among the leaders of parties represented in the House of Commons (with English and French debates on separate days) have been central to every election. The French-language debates have sometimes provided the embarrassing spectacle of several anglophone party leaders struggling to make themselves understood in French—and sometimes unable to do so. Some Canadians outside Quebec have been critical of the inclusion of the Bloc Québécois leader in the English-language debate (although the Reform party leader participated in the French-language debate in 1993, even though the party ran no candidates in Quebec). As discussed in Chapter 8, the leader of the Green party was also included in the 2008 debate after considerable outcry about her exclusion, even though no members of her party had been elected to the House.[6]

The debate format has varied from election to election, with some debates including one-on-one sparring between pairs of leaders, while others have been a "free-for-all" among the leaders. In the past, questions were directed to the leaders by a panel of journalists (although questions from the audience were also used in 1997). Some of these questions have put the leaders on the spot. For example in the 1997 French-language debate, Liberal Prime Minister Chrétien was asked if he would accept a popular verdict in favour of Quebec independence if 50.6 percent voted yes to independence in a referendum. Fortunately for Chrétien, the moderator suddenly fell ill and the debate was suspended before he was forced to respond to this controversial question. In the 2006 and 2008 debates, journalists selected questions sent in by the public, whose questions were then videotaped. Although the debates have

---

[6]One Liberal MP had switched allegiance to the Green party just before the 2008 election. In 1979, the leader of the Social Credit party was excluded from the debate despite his party's eleven seats in the House; in 1968 the Social Credit leader was invited to participate only in the last part of the debate.

BOX 9-3

Lies and Recriminations: The Lost Civility of Campaign Debates

Canadian campaign debates are not merely a discussion of major issues. At times, the leaders have aggressively (and sometimes underhandedly) attacked each other and accused each other of lying.

Particularly notable was a severe attack by PC leader Brian Mulroney on Liberal leader John Turner in the 1984 debate. The issue concerned various appointments to public office that Turner had made at the request of retiring Prime Minister Pierre Trudeau. When Turner replied that he had had "no option," Mulroney pointed his finger at Turner and retorted, "You had an option, sir. You could have said, 'I'm not going to do it. This is wrong for Canada. I'm not going to ask Canadians to pay the price.' You had an option, sir, to say no and you chose to say yes—yes to the old attitudes and the old stories of the Liberal party." A clip of the exchange in which Turner had trouble fending off the attack was shown repeatedly in subsequent news broadcasts and set the tone for the remainder of the campaign. However, public opinion surveys did not indicate that Turner's performance in the debate was the cause of the poor showing of his party in the election (LeDuc, 1990). In the 1988 rematch, Turner performed better with a powerful attack on Mulroney for "selling out Canada" by signing the Canada–United States Free Trade Agreement.

In the 2000 election, Canadian Alliance leader Stockwell Day was often accused by the other parties of favouring the replacement of the public health care system with a two-tier system that would give better health care to the rich than the poor. To counter this accusation, Day broke the debate rules by displaying a large handwritten sign during the debate: "No 2-tier healthcare." This did not stop the other party leaders from repeating the accusation. Likewise, the 2004 election debate turned into a shouting match among the four leaders, with viewers hard-pressed at times to understand what was being said. And one of the exchanges during the 2008 debate involved Liberal leader Stéphane Dion accusing Conservative leader Stephen Harper of lying when Harper claimed that the Liberal "green shift" proposal would take twice as much in carbon taxes as would be returned in reduced taxes.

Overall, the debates (which attract impressive numbers of viewers) can provide some useful information for voters as long as appropriate rules are enforced to ensure a respectful airing of the differences among the party leaders.

given the party leaders the opportunity to explain the major elements of their party's platform, they have also featured some sharp exchanges between the leaders (as discussed in Box 9-3, Lies and Recriminations: The Lost Civility of Campaign Debates).

There have been suggestions that holding several debates during the course of the campaign would allow for a more thorough discussion of issues and party positions. Recent U.S. presidential elections, for example, have featured three presidential debates, as well as debates between the vice-presidential candidates. In Canada, the campaign for the 2006 election included two sets of leadership debates. As well, the 1984 election included a separate debate by the three male party leaders on issues of concern to women. In the 1988 election, just one party leader (Alexa McDonough, NDP) decided to participate in the debate on women's issues, which was carried only by CPAC, the Parliamentary channel.

CAMPAIGN PLATFORMS

Historically, political parties would issue a campaign platform that included a variety of promises, usually with specific commitments to appeal to each province or region and to various interests (Carrigan, 1968). The Liberal and PC parties largely abandoned this practice in the 1970s and 1980s, preferring instead to have their leaders announce promises day by day during the campaign to maximize the media impact. However the Liberal party, as part of their rebuilding effort after their defeats in the 1984 and 1988 elections, devoted considerable attention to developing the Liberal platform. This was published and circulated as the 112-page "Red Book" at the start of the 1993 campaign. The PC party scrambled to produce a smaller "Blue Book" in response. With the development of the internet, the parties have been able to make their platforms easily accessible to anyone who goes to their website. In addition, to fend off criticism about how much the promises cost, parties now usually provide an analysis of the cost of their promises and proposals, although controversies frequently arise as to whether the cost estimates are accurate or misleading.

The publication of party platforms can be useful to journalists and to diligent voters. However, from the point of view of party strategists, the release of the platform may only provide the party with one day of media coverage; whereas releasing party promises one at a time provides a daily stream of newsworthy stories, and sabotages the ability of the other parties to effectively scrutinize and criticize the platform. This may explain why the Conservative party did not release their full platform until six days before the 2008 election.

CAMPAIGN PROMISES

Party platforms and the speeches of the leaders often contain an array of promises. Some promises are vague, and thus it is hard to tell how successfully the governing party has fulfilled them. Although governing parties usually claim to have fulfilled most of their promises by the time of the next election, they frequently have ignored or broken some major promises (see Box 9-4 Promise Made, Promise Broken). Undoubtedly some promises are made simply to gain votes and may not represent a real commitment. However, sometimes circumstances change so that acting on a promise may no longer be in the public interest. Nevertheless, the failure of governments to live up to high-profile election promises may contribute to the disillusionment Canadians feel toward politicians and governments.

Promise Made, Promise Broken

The 1993 Liberal Red Book promised to replace the goods and services tax that the PC party had introduced over the strenuous objections of the Liberals. Liberal leader Jean Chrétien quipped that God would strike him with lightning if he failed to keep all of the promises in the Red Book. For her part, prominent Liberal candidate Sheila Copps promised voters in her Hamilton riding that she would resign her seat if a Liberal government did not eliminate the tax.

Despite the campaign promises, the Liberal government that was elected in 1993 decided to retain the tax. Cabinet minister Sheila Copps initially refused to live up to her promise to resign if the tax was not eliminated. However after considerable public criticism, she resigned but was quickly re-elected in a by-election. A television commercial produced for the PC party in the 2000 election campaign showed a bolt of lightning hitting the Red Book, which then burst into flames (Woolstencroft, 2001).

After their election victory in 2006, Conservative cabinet ministers liked to say, "Promise made, promise kept" to distinguish their record of keeping promises from that of previous Liberal governments.

However a major Conservative promise made by Stephen Harper in the fall 2008 election campaign that "we're not going to run deficits" was quickly broken when the budget his government presented in January 2009 created a large government deficit by increasing spending.

In some cases, the need for good government policies may justify the breaking of campaign promises. Replacing the goods and services tax would likely have been an unwise policy decision, as the alternatives might have proven worse. Keeping the promise not to run a government deficit would have had serious consequences at a time when increased government spending was needed to deal with a global financial crisis.

Perhaps the wisest comment about campaign promises was made by a judge who threw out a lawsuit against the Liberal government of Ontario for breaking a written campaign promise that it would not increase taxes or impose any new ones. In his ruling the judge stated that "anyone who believes a campaign promise is naive about the democratic system"; voters should apply the ancient legal maxim "buyer beware" to campaign promises (Makin, 2006a).

ADVERTISEMENTS

The *Canada Elections Act* requires that broadcasting time for campaign advertisements be allocated on an "equitable basis." Representatives of the registered political parties meet to decide on the distribution of time, but if agreement cannot be reached the Broadcasting Arbitrator, an official connected to Elections Canada, can decide on the allocation. For the 2008 campaign, each broadcaster had to make 396 minutes available during prime time to the parties at their lowest rates. The Conservatives received 95.5 minutes; the Liberal party, 82.5; the NDP, 45; the Bloc, 37.5; the Green party, 22.5; and the other fourteen parties, between 6 and 10 minutes each. Broadcasters could sell additional time, but if they sold it to one party they could not refuse it to other parties. In addition, some radio and television networks are required to provide free time to the parties, allocated in about the same proportion as the paid commercials.

Unlike some other countries, Canada imposes no minimum length for campaign advertisements. As a result, thirty-second television advertisements have become the standard. Although short advertisements can catch the attention of viewers who might be unwilling to listen to a lengthy explanation of a party's views and positions, they provide scant information on which to base a vote.

Some advertisements are designed to try to change perceptions of the party leader. For example, in an effort to soften their leader's harsh and stiff image, a series of Conservative party advertisements in the 2008 election showed a relaxed Stephen Harper casually dressed in a sweater, calmly engaged in a conversation with gentle music playing in the background. Sometimes parties use brief endorsements of the leader or party by what appear to be "ordinary" Canadians interviewed on the street. A simple slogan to sum up the party's basic message is typically featured in a party's ads. For example, in the 2008 campaign the Conservatives ended most of their advertisements with "Canada. We're better off with Harper"; the Liberal ads proclaimed, "We're always there for you"; and the NDP ads asserted, "Leadership and fairness for working families." Most campaign ads focus heavily on the party leaders by presenting their own leader positively or by portraying an opposing party leader in an unflattering light.

Campaign advertisements do not only include brief statements of the promises, goals, values, or priorities of a party and its leader; many advertisements also target another party or its leader. Although the use of "negative" or "attack" advertising has often been criticized, a distinction should be made between critical advertising and advertising based on "dirty politics" that uses such techniques as deception, fear-mongering, and mudslinging (Jamieson, 1992). Advertisements that reveal how one party's position differs from another may help voters in deciding how to vote. Indeed, such advertisements may be more helpful than those that simply indicate that a party, if elected, will look after everyone, make the country strong, or protect the environment. Likewise, if voters are to hold the governing party accountable for its actions, it is useful for the opposition parties to point out the government's failures and broken promises. It would, however, be more helpful if an opposition party indicated how they would fix the problems or govern differently.

Negative or attack ads have quite frequently gone beyond useful criticism to make unfair attacks on another party or its leader. In the 2008 campaign, for example, Conservative ads attacking the Liberal party's "green shift" (carbon tax proposal) were deceptive in their portrayal of the Liberal proposal. The Liberals engaged in fear-mongering in the 2004 election with an ad that quoted Stephen Harper out of context, saying, "When we're through with Canada, you won't recognize it," while the backdrop showed a Canadian flag disintegrating. Similarly, Liberal ads in the 2006 election claimed that Harper had a "hidden agenda" to dismantle the public health care system (Clarke, Kornberg, & Scotto, 2009a).

Although strongly negative ads may grab the attention of potential voters, they can sometimes backfire on the party that sponsored them. For example, in the 1993 campaign, the PC party ran ads that featured a very unflattering image of Liberal leader Jean Chrétien, accompanied by lines such as "Is this a Prime Minister?" and "I would be very embarrassed if he became Prime Minister of Canada." An outpouring of sympathy for Chrétien (who has a facial deformity caused by Bell's palsy) forced the PC party to quickly withdraw the ads. In the 2006 campaign, the Liberal party prepared an attack ad featuring close-ups of Harper accompanied by the sound of beating war drums, with text claiming that Harper wanted "soldiers with guns" in our cities. Although the ad was never aired and only made a fleeting appearance on the Liberal party's website, it was strongly criticized. Indeed it provided the Conservative party with ammunition for their own attack ad—one criticizing the Liberal party's negative advertising, with a clip showing Liberal leader Paul Martin saying that "I approved the ad, there is no doubt about it" (quoted by Clarkson, 2006, p. 51).

The internet offers a newer medium for campaign appeals and is becoming a significant avenue for each party's efforts to influence voters, particularly younger ones. Unlike the broadcast media, the internet has no restrictions on its use. Along with their campaign platforms, parties have included their advertisements (including some specially designed for the internet), announcements, and other campaign materials such as their leader's speeches on their websites. In the 2008 election campaign, the Conservative party set up a separate website, "notaleader.ca," specifically designed to criticize Liberal leader Stéphane Dion. A notorious video on the site featured a puffin flying around and pooping on Dion's shoulder. The parties and their supporters have also made use of YouTube in recent elections. Blogs have been set up by supporters of the different parties, and in 2008 the major party leaders used Twitter to convey brief campaign messages. Emails to supporters are often used to try to raise funds. Each of the major party leaders created a profile on Facebook, and they managed to attract a total of 65 053 "friends" by election day in 2008, with Jack Layton having the most "friends." However, unlike Barack Obama, Canadian politicians have, thus far, not made effective use of social networking. For example, Stephen Harper's Facebook profile did not provide a wall for comments by his "friends" (Small, 2008).

The Mass Media and the Campaign

The mass media provide extensive coverage of the election campaign, with a focus on the leaders of the major parties. Unless there appears to be a difference between the leader of a party and other notable party figures, the national media devote very little attention to the speeches and activities of cabinet ministers and prominent party candidates.

Media coverage of election campaigns has often been criticized. The media tend to highlight what is termed the "horse race" aspect of the campaign. That is, they are often fixated on who is leading or falling back in the race for electoral victory, rather than providing informed analysis of the issues in the campaign. Likewise, campaign debates are often discussed in terms of whether one leader scored a "knockout punch" on another leader. Moreover, considerable attention is paid to any gaffes made by the parties during the campaign. For example, in the 2000 campaign the media devoted considerable attention to a statement made by Canadian Alliance leader Stockwell Day at a Niagara Falls photo op. "Just as Lake Erie drains from north to south, there is an ongoing [brain] drain in terms of our young people," stated Day. The media were quick to point out that Lake Erie actually drains from south to north. Similarly, much was made of a critical comment by Scott Reid, the Liberal communications director, during the 2006 campaign about the Conservative promise to give $1200 a year to parents with young children. His comment? "Don't give people twenty-five bucks a week to blow on beer and popcorn."

In reaction to criticism of their campaign coverage, some media have included "reality checks" that involve a critical analysis of campaign statements. As well, a number of newspapers have provided useful comparisons of party positions. Nevertheless, campaign coverage tends to be dominated by the attacks and counterattacks that leaders aim at each other. As Christopher Waddell (2009) pointed out in his analysis of the 2008 election, newspapers spent "vast amounts of column and news space endlessly chewing over strategy, analyzing poll results, and focusing on the party leaders. Issues, beyond the economy . . . were virtually ignored" (p. 233). The record of the Conservative government on climate change was not examined, Dion's carbon tax plan was deemed too complicated to explain, and Canada's war in Afghanistan was ignored, along with a host of other important issues. In all, the newspapers (and other media) failed "to go beyond what leaders' campaigns feed reporters on their tours" (Waddell, 2009, p. 234).

ELECTION AND PARTY FINANCE

In the past, a very large proportion of the funds the Liberal and Progressive Conservative parties needed for their election campaigns (as well as the operations of their party organization) came from large corporations, as well as from those seeking to gain government contracts. This pattern of election and party finance often led to criticism that the leading political parties were biased in favour of the interests of large corporations. Fuelling this argument were various scandals that arose from time to time concerning government favours to major donors. Not all parties relied on funding from corporate sources. The NDP raised the largest proportion of its funding from its members, although it received, in addition, a significant proportion of its funding from labour unions. The unregulated system of party and election finance also raised questions about whether those parties that were able to raise large sums of money for their campaigns enjoyed an unfair advantage.

Amendments to the *Canada Elections Act* in 1974, 2003, and 2007 have made party financing more transparent by requiring that donations of $200 or more to parties and candidates be publicly reported. Cash donations of over $20 cannot be accepted. To encourage small individual donations rather than large corporate ones, a generous system of tax credits for donations was established (a 75 percent tax credit for donations up to $400 with a lower credit for contributions in excess of $400).

The most radical change has been the ending of corporate donations and the placement of strict limits on individual contributions. Beginning in 2007, only individuals (who are Canadian citizens or permanent residents) were allowed to contribute to political parties, leadership contenders, candidates in an electoral district, and those seeking nomination as candidates. These donations are limited to a maximum of $1100 per year to each registered political party, a total of $1100 per year to the various entities of each registered party (associations, nomination contestants, and election candidates), $1100 in total to candidates for the leadership of a party, and $1100 to independent candidates in an election.[7] Contributions by corporations, unions, and unincorporated associations are illegal.

In addition, people or groups other than candidates, registered political parties, and the district associations of registered parties (termed "third parties") cannot spend more than $183 300 on election-related advertising expenses and not more than $3666[8] to promote or oppose one or more candidates in each electoral district. Stephen Harper, when he was president of the National Citizens Coalition, challenged this provision as a violation of the *Charter of Rights and Freedoms*. However, the provision was upheld by the Supreme Court of Canada as a "reasonable limit" on freedom of expression needed to ensure fairness in elections.

To create some degree of equity, limits have also been placed on the campaign spending of parties and candidates. In the 2008 election, for example, the spending limit of the parties that ran candidates in all, or almost all, districts was about $20 million. As Table 9-3 indicates, only the Conservative party (and the Bloc in Quebec) spent near their limit. This allowed the Conservatives to outspend the Liberal party on advertising by a substantial margin. Individual candidates can spend between about $75 000 and $100 000 depending on the number of voters in their electoral district.

Rebates of campaign expenditures are provided to parties and candidates that receive a significant proportion of votes. Specifically, candidates that receive at least 10 percent of votes can receive a reimbursement of 60 percent of their eligible campaign expenses. Political parties are reimbursed for 50 percent

---

[7]The original limit of $5000 was lowered in 2007. The limits will be adjusted to take account of inflation.
[8]These amounts are as of March 2009 and are adjusted annually for inflation.

TABLE 9-3
**CAMPAIGN SPENDING,
2008 CANADIAN ELECTION**

PARTY	SPENDING	PERCENTAGE OF SPENDING LIMIT	RADIO/TV ADS
Conservative	$19 418 579	97.1	$10 266 343
Liberal	$14 530 294	72.6	$5 827 650
NDP	$16 813 890	83.8	$7 071 205
Bloc	$4 879 603	96.3	$2 377 417
Green	$2 795 412	14.2	$1 579 103

Source: *Compiled and calculated from Elections Canada, 2009, Registered Party Financial Transactions Returns, Contributions and Expenses Database. Retrieved from www.elections.ca*

of their eligible campaign expenses if their party receives at least 2 percent of the valid votes nationally or 5 percent of the valid votes in those electoral districts in which the party ran a candidate.

Beginning in 2007, registered political parties became entitled to an annual allowance of $1.75 (adjusted for inflation) for each vote received by the party in the previous election, provided that candidates endorsed by the party received at least 2 percent of valid votes cast nationally or 5 percent of the votes cast in electoral districts in which the party ran a candidate. The Conservative government's economic update of November 2008 proposed the elimination of this subsidy. This would have seriously hurt the finances of their opponents, particularly the Liberal party, which was struggling with a substantial debt. It was likely no coincidence that the Conservative party is the least dependent on the subsidy of the five largest parties (Flanigan & Jansen, 2009). The Conservatives dropped this proposal when faced with defeat in the House of Commons.

Although there are various loopholes and enforcement problems, the election (and party) financing legislation has become quite rigorous. The five major political parties have come to rely fairly heavily on public subsidies, although the Conservative party has succeeded in building a larger base of individual donors than the Liberal party and thus depends less on these subsidies (see Table 9-4).

TABLE 9-4
**CONTRIBUTIONS TO
POLITICAL PARTIES, 2008**

PARTY	CONTRIBUTIONS	NUMBER OF CONTRIBUTORS
Conservative	$21 179 482	112 184
Liberal	$5 811 491	30 890
NDP	$5 412 939	29 732
Bloc	$713 085	7 444
Green	$1 621 532	17 288

Source: *Elections Canada, 2009, Registered Party Financial Transactions Returns, Contributions and Expenses Database. Retrieved from www.elections.ca*

VOTER CHOICE

In this age of skepticism surrounding politicians, voters may struggle harder than ever to find a candidate or party that expresses their point of view. What explains the choices voters make in casting their ballots in an election? Undoubtedly, the choice made by voters will reflect their thoughts about which candidate, party, and party leader are best. In turn these preferences for candidates, parties, and leaders will be shaped, to a considerable extent, by the long-term perceptions that voters have of the political parties, by the general political values that voters hold, and by the interests related to the groups to which voters belong or with which they identify.

Canadian Election Study:
www.ces-eec.mcgill.ca/ces.html

Long-Term Influences on Voting Behaviour

SOCIAL CHARACTERISTICS   Our social characteristics can have an impact on how we vote. People with the same social characteristics may have similar interests at stake in politics. For example, students may be inclined to vote for the political party that seems most favourable to reducing the cost of education. Those who have similar social characteristics may also tend to have similar values that affect their choice of party. As well, we are more likely to come into contact with people of similar social characteristics, which may lead to having similar views about which party is best. If most of your friends or most of the people in your neighbourhood favour a particular party, that tendency may somewhat influence your voting choice. Further, our social characteristics are often associated with our sense of identity. Even if we as individuals do not stand to benefit materially by voting for a particular party, we may be inclined to vote for a party that we perceive as respecting and recognizing our identity. For example, some French Quebecers support the Bloc Québécois to express their Québécois identity, even if they do not fully support that party's platform.

In national politics, there is a complex relationship between social characteristics and voting because of Canada's great diversity. A variety of social divisions are apparent, with no one division having a dominant influence on voting. Nevertheless, there are some persistent patterns in which people with certain social characteristics show a tendency to support a particular party. As discussed in Chapter 8, important provincial and regional differences affect the support for different political parties—differences that are highlighted and exaggerated by the nature of the Canadian electoral system. For example, support for the Liberal party has been weak in Western Canada for the past half century. Except for the 1984 and 1988 elections, Quebecers have provided little support for Conservative parties. The Liberals have also tended to gain the support of voters in Canada's largest cities, while the Conservatives have done better in the rural areas and towns in most English-speaking areas of the country.

There have also been long-standing and substantial differences in vote choice among those with different religious ties. For instance, Catholics are more likely than Protestants to support the Liberal party.[9] However, the Liberal lead among Catholic voters has dropped sharply since 2000. In the 2008 election, more Catholics voted for the Conservative party than for the Liberal party. Nevertheless, Catholics were still slightly more likely than Protestants to vote Liberal in the 2006 and 2008 elections. The Conservative party has developed particularly strong support from fundamentalist and evangelical ("born again") Christians (Gidengil et al., 2006a; Gidengil et al., 2009).

Ethnic ancestry is also linked to voting patterns. Support for the Liberal party has been quite strong among many of those who identify with ethnic groups that are neither British nor French in ancestry. In particular, voters of non-European ancestry have shown a strong tendency to support the Liberal party. However, the Conservatives made substantial inroads into this base of Liberal support in the 2008 election, leaving the Liberal party with only a slight lead among this diverse grouping. The Liberal party has also been the leading party of French Canadians for over a century. However, the Progressive Conservatives were able to gain the support of Quebecers in 1984 and 1988. Subsequently, the Bloc Québécois has won the support of many French Quebecers. English-speaking and immigrant Quebecers have tended to give the Liberal party strong support. Traditionally, the Conservative party has enjoyed strong support among those of British ancestry. Since the 1950s the Conservatives have increased their support among various groups of people of continental European ancestry.

Differences in voting among those of different social classes have never been strong at the national level, although class-based trends are evident in some provinces such as British Columbia. The NDP and Bloc tend to draw more of their support from unionized workers and, at least in some elections, from those with lower incomes. Gender differences in voting choice have been minimal (with the Liberals doing only slightly better among women than men and the Conservatives doing slightly better among men than women). In recent elections, however, the NDP has gained significantly more votes from women than men. Indeed, in the 2008 election more young women voted for the NDP than for any other party (Strategic Counsel, 2008). The Green party (as well as the NDP) tends to draw more of their support from younger rather than older voters.

VALUES   The basic values and ideological perspectives held by Canadians help to shape their party preferences. Voters who support the values of the

---

[9]In Newfoundland and Labrador, Catholics have been more likely to vote Conservative and Protestants, Liberal.

free-enterprise system are more likely to vote for the Conservative party and less likely to vote for the NDP. Those who hold socially conservative values (for example, those who oppose same-sex marriage and have traditional views on the role of women) are more likely to vote Conservative and less likely to vote for the Liberals or NDP (Gidengil et al., 2006b). In Quebec, however, the key political perspectives affecting the choices of voters differ starkly from those in the rest of Canada. Individuals who support Quebec sovereignty are much more likely to vote for the Bloc Québécois, while those opposed to Quebec independence are much more likely to vote for the Liberal party (Blais, Gidengil, Nadeau, & Nevitte, 2002). Because a person's basic values and ideological perspective tend to persist over time and because parties may find it challenging to change their basic image and perspective, values and perspectives can be considered an important long-term influence on the vote.

PARTY IDENTIFICATION   Most voters have at least a limited sense of attachment to a particular political party. That is, they will tend to view one party as "their party," even if they are not a member of that party and have never participated in any of its activities. For some people, **party identification** starts at an early age and may be transmitted from parents to children. For others it may develop over time as voters see a particular party as reflecting their preferred values, interests, and policy positions, or as having the best record when it forms the government.

PARTY IDENTIFICATION
A sense of attachment to a particular political party.

Those who identify with a particular party will tend to evaluate their party's current leader, candidates, and issue positions in a favourable light. However, this does not mean that they will always vote for their party. An unpopular leader or candidate, the adoption of issue positions that the voter disagrees with, or a poor performance by a party in government may result in a party identifier voting for a different party in a particular election. This is especially the case for voters who do not have a strong party identification. Nevertheless, unless there is a major change in the party system, we may expect many voters to retain their party identification even if they do not vote in line with that identification in a given election.

By examining the distribution of party identification, we can get a sense of the competitive position of different political parties. A survey conducted after the 2006 election found that 30.6 percent of Canadians identified with the Liberal party, 26.8 percent with the Conservative party, 10.1 percent with the NDP, 8.3 percent with the Bloc, and 1.0 percent with other parties. No party identification was reported by 22.2 percent, and 1.2 percent responded "don't know" (Gidengil et al., 2006b).[10] Although the Liberal party had a

---

[10]Party identification was determined from the following question: "In federal politics, do you usually think of yourself as a: Liberal, Conservative, NDP, Bloc Québécois, or none of these?" For one-half of the sample, "another party or no party" was used instead of "none of these."

small lead in terms of party identification, it was not enough to ensure victory. In the 2006 election, for example, about one-third of Liberal party identifiers did not vote according to their Liberal identification, in part because of the Liberal government's "sponsorship scandal" and the perceived weak performance of the Liberal prime minister. A very high proportion of Conservative identifiers voted for "their" party, which, combined with support from some Liberals and those without party identification, was sufficient to give the Conservative party a modest lead in the vote and win a plurality of seats (Gidengil et al., 2006b). This enabled the Conservatives to form a **minority government** (that is, a government formed by a single party that does not have a majority of members in the House of Commons). One survey done at the time of the 2008 election found that the Conservatives had a fairly substantial lead in party identification, particularly because of a decline in Liberal identification (Gidengil et al., 2009). A different survey, however, found little difference between the Liberal and Conservative parties in terms of the proportion of people identifying with each party around the time of the 2008 election (Clarke, Kornberg, & Scotto, 2009b).

A person's party identification tends to persist over time. However, a significant proportion of the electorate does change its party identification either in the sense of identifying with a different party or in changing to or from identifying with no political party (Clarke et al., 2009a).[11] Indeed, the rise of new parties (Reform and Bloc Québécois) and the sharp decline in support for older parties (PC and NDP) in the 1990s suggests that, at times, there can be major shifts in attachments to political parties. Because party identification in the electorate as a whole is not particularly strong and subject to change, political campaigns and other political events can have important effects on voters and election outcomes.

Short-Term Influences on Voting Behaviour

Increasingly voters say they make up their mind as to who to vote for during the election campaign. Indeed, many voters decide at the last minute—just before election day. This can mean that the leaders and candidates themselves, and the issues raised during a campaign, become significant factors in the choices of the electorate.

Many voters say that it is the issue positions of the parties, leaders, and candidates that matter most to their voting decisions (Pammett, 2008). However, since the leading parties often do not take markedly different positions

MINORITY GOVERNMENT
A single party forms the government, but does not have a majority of members in the House of Commons.

---

[11]Because the nature of party competition often differs between the national level and the provincial level, a substantial proportion of the electorate identifies with different political parties in the two political arenas.

A Mandate for Free Trade? The 1988 Election

In 1988, the House of Commons passed the controversial Canada–United States Free Trade Agreement that the Conservative government had negotiated. However, Liberal leader John Turner argued that the Canadian people should go to the polls to decide this important issue. He asked Liberal senators who had the majority in that body to prevent the passage of the legislation. Finally, frustrated by the obstruction of the unelected senators, Prime Minister Brian Mulroney called an election to resolve the issue. The free trade issue dominated the election campaign, with the PC party arguing passionately for the agreement and the Liberals and New Democratic Party vehemently opposing it.

Researchers found that most voters saw free trade as the most important issue and had an opinion on it by the time of the election. In addition, most voters could identify the position on the issue taken by the major parties and voted for the party that took the position they preferred (Johnston, Blais, Brady, & Crête, 1992).

The election decided the outcome of the free trade controversy, as the PC party won the election with their candidates victorious in 169 of the 295 seats in the House of Commons. Liberal senators allowed the free trade agreement to pass. However, the PC party had obtained only 43.0 percent of the vote in the election while 52.3 percent of voters supported the Liberal and New Democratic parties that opposed the agreement. Thus, despite the unusual referendum-like focus on a single crucial issue by the political parties and the voters, the 1988 election did not allow the democratic will of the majority to prevail. The single-member plurality electoral system and the vote split between the leading opposition parties resulted in a tainted mandate for the governing party to proceed with the free trade agreement.

on key issues in an election campaign and voters are often unclear about the differences in party positions, voters may have trouble expressing their views on important issues through their voting choice. Only occasionally does an issue on which the parties take different positions have a strong impact on voters (See Box 9-5, A Mandate for Free Trade? The 1988 Election). Instead, voters are often more likely to be affected by their perceptions of which party they feel is best able to handle a crucial problem (such as reducing unemployment and inflation, providing accessible health care, and protecting the environment) than by issues on which the parties take different positions, such as being for or against same-sex marriage or gun control (Clarke et al., 2009a). This perception can vary by the type of issue. For example, a survey carried out at the time of the 2008 election found that the Conservative party was more likely than any of the other parties to be viewed as best able to deal with crime, the economy, and, to a lesser extent, jobs. The NDP was viewed as best able to address social welfare and health care needs. The Green party was viewed as the best party to handle environmental issues. The Liberal party did not have a lead on any of the issue areas covered in the survey (Gidengil et al., 2009). Somewhat similar results were found in another survey that asked which party was closest on the issue each voter considered as most important in the 2008 election (Clarke et al., 2009b). As well, issues linked to perceptions of the competence or corruption of the governing party can affect voters. For example, the sponsorship scandal contributed to the substantial decline in Liberal party support in the 2004 and 2006 elections (Gidengil et al., 2009).

With the focus on the party leaders in an election campaign and in politics generally, it is not surprising that the party leaders can play a key role in voting choice. For example, a study of elections from 1968 to 2000 found that evaluations of the leaders had a significant independent effect on voters. On average, 6.3 percent of voters "would probably have voted differently were it not for the party leaders" (Gidengil & Blais, 2007, p. 48). However, the overall impact of party leaders should not be exaggerated. For example, in the 2006 election NDP leader Jack Layton tended to be viewed positively while Liberal leader Paul Martin and Conservative leader Stephen Harper tended to be viewed negatively (Clarke et al., 2009a). The relatively positive rating of Layton likely contributed to the rise in NDP support from 15.7 percent in the 2004 election to 17.5 percent in the 2006 election, but was still not enough to make the NDP a contender to form the government. Similarly, the tendency of voters to have negative feelings toward Stephen Harper did not prevent his party from slightly improving their results in the 2008 election,[12] although this result may have been aided by even more negative feelings toward the Liberal leader (Clarke et al., 2009b).

Voting involves choosing among the candidates in an electoral district. Generally, political scientists have found that the local candidates scarcely affect the outcome of the election in their district (Clarke, LeDuc, Jenson, & Pammett, 1979), although the incumbent (current MP) benefits from a small advantage over challengers (Krasinsky & Milne, 1986). However, a study done at the time of the 2000 election found that 44 percent of voters had developed a preference for a local candidate. This preference for the local candidate was a decisive factor in the voting choice of 5 percent of Canadians independent of the effects of their feelings about the parties and their leaders. Thus, although preferences for local candidates are generally less important than preferences for parties and party leaders in affecting voting choice, the local candidates are not irrelevant (Blais et al., 2003).

---

[12]Harper was viewed by a somewhat higher proportion of people as being the best leader to manage the economy in the 2008 election, in which the economy was, by far, the most important issue for voters (Clarke, Kornberg, & Scotto, 2009b).

Summary and Conclusion

Canadian elections in recent decades have been carried out fairly and impartially with the right to vote available to citizens who are at least eighteen years old. Elections and the governments they produce are, therefore, generally accepted as legitimate. There is, however, considerable controversy concerning Canada's single-member plurality electoral system. While the system provides a simple voting mechanism and a connection between voters and their elected representative, it causes distortions in the translation of the votes for a party into the proportion of the seats that party obtains. This can result in the election of a government with a majority of seats that is supported by a minority of voters and, in some cases, in a government to which the majority of voters objects. Questions have, therefore, been raised concerning whether the single-member plurality system is consistent with democratic principles. Furthermore, the electoral system tends to exaggerate regional differences and can prevent or discourage the representation of diverse minority perspectives and interests that are not geographically concentrated.

Supporters of the single-member plurality system argue that it is more likely than other electoral systems to result in good government because it increases the chances that a majority government will be formed. Others argue that the virtues of majority government are overrated: minority or coalition governments can also provide good government if politicians from different political parties are willing to negotiate with each other in good faith.

Concerns have been raised about whether campaign practices, such as negative advertising, mislead voters and foster cynicism concerning politicians and government. As well, questions often arise as to whether the media coverage of election campaigns provides the information and analysis needed by the average voter to make an intelligent choice. Although elections are often considered to be the cornerstone of a democracy, election campaigns might be viewed as involving the manipulation of voters by the contending parties rather than promoting a dialogue about the direction of the country.

The rules for financing election campaigns and political parties have changed considerably in recent times. In particular, donations by business and labour organizations have been banned, and strict limits have been placed on the amounts that individuals can donate. This can be viewed as a democratic advance, as it has reduced the dependence of political parties on a small number of corporations and wealthy donors. Instead, in addition to encouraging parties to seek small donations from large numbers of people, the new rules provide for substantial public funding for parties that are able to gain a minimal proportion of the vote.

Studies of voting behaviour have found that the long-term factors of social characteristics, basic political values, and party identification are associated with the choices that voters make. The regional, ethnocultural, and religious diversity of Canada is reflected, to some extent, in voting choices. Differences based on class, gender, and age generally have a weaker effect on voting choices. However, voting behaviour also reveals considerable flexibility. Short-term factors, including perceptions of which party leader and candidate is best and which party is most competent to deal with important issues, also play an important role when voters go to the polls.

Discussion Questions

1. Should the voting age be lowered?
2. Should every electoral district have about the same number of people?
3. Are fixed election dates desirable? Under what circumstances, if any, should an election be held earlier than four years?

4. Should Canada change its single-member plurality electoral system?

5. Should donations to political parties be strictly limited? Should public funds be used to subsidize political parties?

6. How will you decide who to vote for in the next election?

Further Reading

Blais, A., Gidengil, E., Nadeau, R., & Nevitte, N. (2002). *Anatomy of a Liberal victory. Making sense of the vote in the 2000 Canadian election.* Peterborough, ON: Broadview Press.

Clarke, H. D., Jenson, J., LeDuc, L., and Pammett, J. (1996). *Absent mandate: Canadian electoral politics in an era of restructuring* (3rd ed.). Toronto, ON: Gage.

Clarke, H. D., Kornberg, A., & Scotto, T. S. (2009). *Making political choices: Canada and the United States.* Toronto, ON: University of Toronto Press.

Courtney, J. C. (2004). *Elections.* Vancouver: UBC Press.

Milner, H. (Ed.). (2004). *Steps toward making every vote count: Electoral system reform in Canada and its provinces.* Peterborough, ON: Broadview.

Pammett, J. H., & Dornan, C. (Eds.). (2009). *The Canadian federal election of 2008.* Toronto, ON: Dundurn. (See also similarly titled books for earlier elections.)

Pilon, D. (2007). *The politics of voting. Reforming Canada's electoral system.* Toronto, ON: Edmond Montgomery.

THE CONSTITUTION, THE FEDERAL SYSTEM, AND ABORIGINAL PEOPLES

Part IV

Chapter 10

THE CONSTITUTION AND CONSTITUTIONAL CHANGE

PHOTO ABOVE: Elijah Harper, holds an eagle feather for spiritual strength just as he did in the Manitoba legislature during his filibuster to delay the debate on the Meech Lake Accord, June, 1990. Harper objected to the fact that the proposed accord had been negotiated in 1987 without the input of Canada's Aboriginal peoples.

CHAPTER OBJECTIVES

After reading this chapter, you should be able to

1. Outline the basic elements of the Canadian constitution.
2. Discuss the procedures for changing the constitution.

3. Examine the reasons that formal constitutional change has been difficult to achieve.
4. Discuss the extent to which the various demands for constitutional change have been met.

On June 12, 1990, Elijah Harper stood in the Manitoba legislature holding up an eagle feather to indicate his opposition to the Meech Lake Accord, an important package of constitutional changes that had been agreed to by the prime minister and premiers. While hundreds of Aboriginals beat their drums in support, Harper, a member of the Red Sucker First Nation, prevented the legislature from voting on the accord by refusing to give the unanimous consent needed to bring it to an immediate vote. Frustrated that the accord did not address Aboriginal concerns, Harper raised the feather every day until the accord went down to defeat when it failed to be passed by the June 23 deadline.

The Meech Lake Accord was drafted in 1987 at a closed door, all-night meeting of Prime Minister Brian Mulroney and the ten premiers. It was primarily a response to Quebec's demands for constitutional change and included a controversial clause recognizing Quebec as a "distinct society." Despite the unanimous agreement of the eleven leaders at the Meech Lake meeting, three provincial legislatures (Manitoba, New Brunswick, and Newfoundland) had not approved the accord a few weeks before the three-year deadline. On June 3, 1990, Mulroney invited the premiers to a dinner meeting in Ottawa to try to secure passage of the accord. They ended up staying for seven days and nights of intense meetings. An Ottawa clothing store donated clean shirts and underwear for the premiers who had come unprepared.

The media badgered the prime minister and premiers as they entered and exited the closed-door meetings, and pundits claimed that this was "Canada's last chance"—the country would break up if no deal was reached. In the end, the prime minister and premiers left smiling from the meetings. An agreement had been struck: The accord would remain unchanged, but there would be another document outlining issues to be dealt with in future constitutional negotiations. Despite the apparent agreement, Newfoundland Premier Clyde Wells added an asterisk to his signature, stating that he would submit the accord "for appropriate legislative or public consideration" prior to the

deadline. Mulroney boasted that he had "rolled the dice" (by waiting until the last minute) and won.

With the deadline for passage just hours away, members of the Newfoundland House of Assembly stated their views in support of or in opposition to the accord. At the end, Premier Wells announced that he was cancelling the vote, thereby ensuring that the accord, which required the approval of all provincial legislatures, would fail. Wells was particularly annoyed that he was not informed about last-minute manoeuvring by the Canadian government to ask the Supreme Court for a ruling about whether the deadline could be extended for three months in order to obtain Manitoba's agreement, provided that Newfoundland approved the accord by June 23 (Russell, 2004).

Constitutional issues have aroused intense controversy and raised doubts about the future of Canada. As discussed in this chapter, it was only after decades of constitutional negotiations that the Constitution was finally made a strictly Canadian document in 1982. The opposition by the Quebec government to the provisions of the *Constitution* Act, 1982, led to the Meech Lake and Charlottetown Accords, both of which failed to be passed. The difficulty in gaining approval for major constitutional changes and the conflicts that have accompanied attempts at important constitutional changes have made politicians very reluctant to reopen the constitutional "can of worms."

THE CANADIAN CONSTITUTION

A **constitution** sets the fundamental rules by which a country is governed. In particular, a constitution provides the organizational framework within which various governing institutions operate, and the legitimate processes by which governments can act and laws can be passed. In addition, constitutions may limit the authority of governments by establishing various rights and freedoms for the population of the country. Finally, some constitutions clearly state the general goals and values of the country (see Box 10-1, The Quest for Constitutional Values).

The word "constitution" may conjure up an image of a formal, legal document that establishes all the rules for governing a country. For example, the Constitution of the United States of America, ratified in 1788, along with subsequent amendments to that document, provides the supreme law for governing that country. There is no single document that contains all aspects of the Canadian constitution. Instead, we can think of the constitution as consisting of four basic elements:

1. Formal constitutional documents
2. Ordinary acts of the Canadian Parliament and provincial legislatures that are of a constitutional nature
3. Constitutional conventions
4. Judicial decisions that interpret the constitution

Formal Constitutional Documents

A number of formal documents, including the *Constitution Act, 1867*, the *Constitution Act, 1982*, amendments to these acts, and sundry other documents, are listed in a schedule attached to the *Constitution Act, 1982*. Together, these documents are described as the Constitution of Canada,[1] which is "the supreme law of Canada, and any law that is inconsistent with the provisions of the Constitution is, to the extent of the inconsistency, of no force or effect" (*Constitution Act, 1982*, section 52).

THE CONSTITUTION ACT, 1867   The **Constitution Act, 1867** (originally termed the *British North America Act, 1867*), is an act of the Parliament of the United Kingdom that established Canada as a federal union of just four provinces: Ontario, Quebec, Nova Scotia, and New Brunswick. Among its provisions were the establishment of the Canadian Parliament consisting of the House of Commons and Senate, a division of the authority to pass legislation between the Canadian Parliament and provincial legislatures, and various provisions concerning the executive and the judiciary.

---

[1]Throughout this textbook, we use Constitution with a capital "C" to refer to the formal Constitution, and constitution with a small "c" to refer to the constitution as a whole.

The Quest for Constitutional Values

The *Constitution Act, 1867*—the foundation in law of the new country—does not contain a statement of basic Canadian values. Indeed, the act's preamble is more pragmatic than rousing: It simply states that the provinces "have expressed their Desire to be federally united . . . with a Constitution similar in Principle to that of the United Kingdom" and that "such a Union would conduce to the Welfare of the provinces and promote the Interests of the British Empire." One phrase in the act, however, stands out from the rest—"Peace, Order, and Good Government." Commentators have often cited this phrase in the *Constitution Act, 1867*, as representing Canadian values. Moreover, "Peace, Order, and Good Government" are often contrasted with the values of "life, liberty, and the pursuit of happiness" in the American Declaration of Independence. However, the "Peace, Order, and Good Government" phrase falls under section 91, which lists the legislative powers of the Canadian Parliament, and thus is not a general statement of values.

More than a century later, in negotiations between the Canadian government and provincial governments that eventually resulted in the *Constitution Act, 1982*, the authors attempted to draft a new preamble to the Constitution. However no consensus could be reached. The Canadian government proposed that the preamble open with the words "We, the people of Canada . . .," echoing the preamble to the American Constitution. However, Quebec Premier René Lévesque argued that the term "people" implied that Canada was a single nation and thus did not recognize the existence of the Quebec nation. Compromise proposals followed. The Canadian government suggested stating a commitment "to the distinct French-speaking society centred in though not confined to Quebec," whereas the Quebec government wanted to recognize the "distinctive character of Quebec society with its French-speaking majority." In the end, all of the proposals were unsuccessful (Romanow, Whyte, & Leeson, 1984, pp. 85–86). The mundane phrasing of the 1867 preamble survives, and Canadian values, whether within or beyond the Constitution, are as hard to pin down as ever.

The formation of Canada in 1867 did not create an independent country—the country remained a British colony with a degree of self-government. Therefore, the act is not a comprehensive constitutional document (Hogg, 2006). The governing system stayed basically true to the British model, except for the adoption of the federal system.

Following are some of the key provisions of the *Constitution Act, 1867*:

- Establishing the Canadian Parliament, consisting of the House of Commons and the Senate, along with legislatures for Ontario and Quebec and the continuation of the legislatures of Nova Scotia and New Brunswick.
- Distributing the power to make laws between Parliament and provincial legislatures.
- Protecting the rights and privileges of Roman Catholic schools in Ontario and Protestant and Roman Catholic schools in Quebec.

- Allowing either English or French to be used in Parliament and the Quebec legislature, with both languages used in the records, journals, and the printed acts of those bodies. Either English or French also may be used in Canadian and Quebec courts.

Although it has sometimes been argued (particularly by Quebec governments) that Canada was formed as a compact between two founding peoples (English and French), the *Constitution Act, 1867*, reflected this view only to a limited extent. By making "property and civil rights" an exclusively provincial matter, Quebec was able to maintain its system of civil law, which differs from the common law system of other provinces (as discussed in Chapter 17). Provision was made for the use of French in Parliament and Canadian courts. The importance of English Quebecers was reflected in provisions concerning language and Protestant schools in Quebec, as well as in the geographical underpinnings for selecting senators from the regions of Quebec.

THE CONSTITUTION ACT, 1982   Although Canada had become an independent country by the *Statute of Westminster, 1931* (and, in practice by 1926), Canada's Constitution was not fully a Canadian document until 1982. In particular, some aspects of the Constitution could only be amended (changed) by the Parliament of the United Kingdom, although in practice it only acted on the recommendation of the Canadian Parliament. By adopting procedures to ensure that all aspects of the Constitution could only be amended in Canada, the Constitution was "patriated," that is, it became a wholly Canadian document, in 1982. In addition to establishing amending formulas, the **Constitution Act, 1982**,[2] added the *Charter of Rights and Freedoms* (discussed in Chapter 11), recognition of the rights of Aboriginal peoples (discussed in Chapter 12), and a commitment to the principle of making equalization payments to the poorer provinces (see Chapter 13). As well, the *Constitution Act, 1982*, amended the *Constitution Act, 1867*, to give provinces greater legislative authority over non-renewable natural resources, forestry resources, and electrical energy.

OTHER FORMAL DOCUMENTS   The other formal documents that make up the Constitution include the *Statute of Westminster* (1931), an act of the Parliament of the United Kingdom that formalized the independence of Canada, and some other British statutes and orders-in-council, including those that added British Columbia (1871), Prince Edward Island (1873), Newfoundland (1949), and other territories to Canada. The acts of the Canadian Parliament establishing Manitoba (1870), Alberta (1905), and Saskatchewan (1905) are also part of the formal Constitution.

Constitution Acts, 1867 to 1982:
http://laws.justice.gc.ca/en/Const/index.html

CONSTITUTION ACT, 1982
This act patriated the Constitution, established a formula for amending the Constitution, added the *Charter of Rights and Freedoms,* recognized the rights of Aboriginal peoples, and made a commitment to the principle of equalization payments.

---

[2]Technically, the *Constitution Act, 1982*, is a schedule attached to the *Canada Act, 1982*, which was passed by the Parliament of the United Kingdom. The *Canada Act* simply terminates any power of the United Kingdom to legislate for Canada.

Acts of a Constitutional Nature

Various acts can be considered part of the constitution, even though they are not included in the list of documents that form the Constitution of Canada. Such important laws as the *Canada Elections Act,* the act establishing the Supreme Court of Canada, and the *Clarity Act* that sets up the provisions by which a province could separate from Canada could be included. However, such acts (sometimes termed "quasi-constitutional") are not part of the supreme law and thus do not have priority over other laws. No formal list of such acts exists, and they do not differ from other laws passed by Parliament or provincial legislatures in the method by which they are approved or changed.

Constitutional Conventions

Constitutional conventions are widely accepted informal constitutional rules. Some reflect the basic principles underlying Canada's system of government. For example, the convention that the prime minister and cabinet must maintain the confidence (support) of the House of Commons reflects the principle of responsible government that underlies our system of democratic government. Canadian courts have recognized the existence of conventions and have provided opinions describing particular conventions (as, for example, with the convention concerning constitutional amendments in the *Patriation Reference* discussed later in this chapter). As well, the courts may consider conventions in cases involving interpretations of the Constitution (Heard, 1991). Conventions are deeply embedded in the ways that many people think about the governing system. A government that violated an important convention would likely be viewed as acting illegitimately by a significant part of the population. Nevertheless, despite their importance, conventions are not legally enforceable by the courts.

Constitutional conventions are important because the formal constitutional documents do not fully describe how government is to operate. Indeed, the prime minister and cabinet are absent from the Constitution acts—they receive no mention at all. Similarly, even though the Constitution appears to grant great authority to the monarch, there is an important convention that the governor general (acting on behalf of the monarch) follows the advice of the prime minister and cabinet. Earlier in this chapter, we were introduced to the statement in the preamble to the *Constitution Act,* 1867, that Canada is to have "a Constitution similar in Principle to that of the United Kingdom." Based on that statement, the constitutional conventions that had developed in the United Kingdom also apply to Canada, except as modified by the Constitution acts.

Judicial Decisions That Interpret the Constitution

Judicial decisions have played a major role in interpreting the provisions of the Constitution. In effect, important judicial interpretations of the Constitution

CONSTITUTIONAL CONVENTIONS
Widely accepted informal constitutional rules.

have become an essential part of the constitution. To fully understand the provisions of the Constitution, it would be necessary to review the multitude of court decisions that have added to the very sparse wording of many provisions of the Constitution acts. The Supreme Court of Canada has drawn on its view of the "unwritten principles" of the constitution, such as democracy, federalism, minority protection, and judicial independence, to go beyond the "literal language" of the Constitution acts in its judgments (Hogg, 2006, p. 16).

The *Constitution Act, 1867*, did not explicitly authorize the courts to overturn laws passed by Parliament or provincial legislatures that they deemed to be in violation of the Constitution (a power known as **judicial review**). However, because of Canada's colonial status, the United Kingdom's *Colonial Laws Validity Act* meant that Canadian laws could be struck down as invalid if they conflicted with British laws (including the *Constitution Act, 1867*). The **Judicial Committee of the Privy Council**, a panel of judges primarily from the British House of Lords that acted as the highest court of appeal for Canada until 1949, used the power of judicial review to strike down a number of laws that it viewed as violating the division of powers between Parliament and provincial legislatures. Its judgments were important in clarifying the constitutional division of powers between the Canadian Parliament and provincial legislatures. In 1949, the **Supreme Court of Canada** took over as the country's highest judicial body. The adoption of the *Charter of Rights and Freedoms* in 1982 has considerably expanded the scope of judicial review, as discussed in Chapter 11.

JUDICIAL REVIEW
The authority of the courts to invalidate laws passed by Parliament or provincial legislatures that they deem to be in violation of the Constitution.

JUDICIAL COMMITTEE OF THE PRIVY COUNCIL
The highest court of appeal for Canada until 1949.

SUPREME COURT OF CANADA
The highest judicial body in Canada since 1949.

CONSTITUTIONAL CHANGE

Because a constitution sets the fundamental rules for governing a country, the provisions of a constitution are expected to be stable features of the political scene. However, some flexibility is needed in a constitution. Not surprisingly, Canada today is a very different country from what it was in 1867. Democratic values are much more important than they were at Canada's founding, and Canada's population is much more diverse in terms of ethnic ancestry. Changes in the constitution are necessary from time to time because of changing circumstances and changing values, as well as difficulties with the constitution that no one foresaw when it was first adopted.

Constitutional conventions generally evolve gradually as new situations arise or different understandings of the conventions develop. Likewise, judicial interpretations of the provisions of the Constitution change as rulings in new cases sometimes modify interpretations in previous cases. Laws that are of a fundamental nature, but that are not in the formal Constitution, can be changed by a majority in Parliament or a provincial legislature. For example, election laws have changed so as to award women, those who do not own property, and Aboriginal peoples the right to vote.

Formal Amendments to the Constitution

The *Constitution Act, 1982*, sets out the requirement that one of the following four formulas, determined by the subject matter, has to be used to amend the formal Constitution:

1. *A majority in the House of Commons (and in the Senate) plus a majority in each provincial legislature.* This is needed for amendments that change the office of the Queen, the governor general, and the lieutenant governor; the requirement that a province have at least as many seats in the House of Commons as it has in the Senate; certain constitutional provisions concerning the use of English and French; the composition of the Supreme Court of Canada; and the amending formulas.

2. *A majority in the House of Commons (and in the Senate) and a majority in at least two-thirds of the provincial legislatures that represent at least one-half of the population of all the provinces.* This applies to many aspects of the Constitution acts, including the powers, method of selection, and representative nature of the Senate; the establishment of new provinces; and the division of legislative powers between Parliament and provincial legislatures. However, provincial legislatures can "opt out" of any constitutional changes that reduce their rights or powers. If the change is related to education and other cultural matters that are under provincial control, the provincial government that opted out is guaranteed "reasonable" financial compensation from the Canadian government, so the province can continue to run its own programs.

3. *A majority in the House of Commons (and in the Senate) as well as a majority in the legislature of the province or provinces that are affected by the change.* For example, a change in the boundaries of a province would require only the approval of Parliament, plus the affected provinces.

4. *Parliament or provincial legislatures operating alone.* Except for matters covered in the first formula, Parliament or provincial legislatures can change the operating procedures and institutions of their own government.

The first formula that requires Parliament and all provincial legislatures to agree on certain changes safeguards some basic features of the governing system. The requirement of unanimity makes it difficult to change these features and, as discussed later in this chapter, has made it challenging to achieve a comprehensive package of major constitutional changes.

The second formula (often referred to as the "general formula") can be viewed as a compromise between the principle that each province should be treated the same regardless of its population and the reality that Canadian provinces vary dramatically in population and importance. However, if Quebec is viewed as one of the two founding "nations," then it is not surprising that the formula is controversial. The possibility exists that Quebec could be forced to surrender some of its powers if most of the other provinces agreed to

FIGURE 10-1
CONSTITUTIONAL TIMELINE

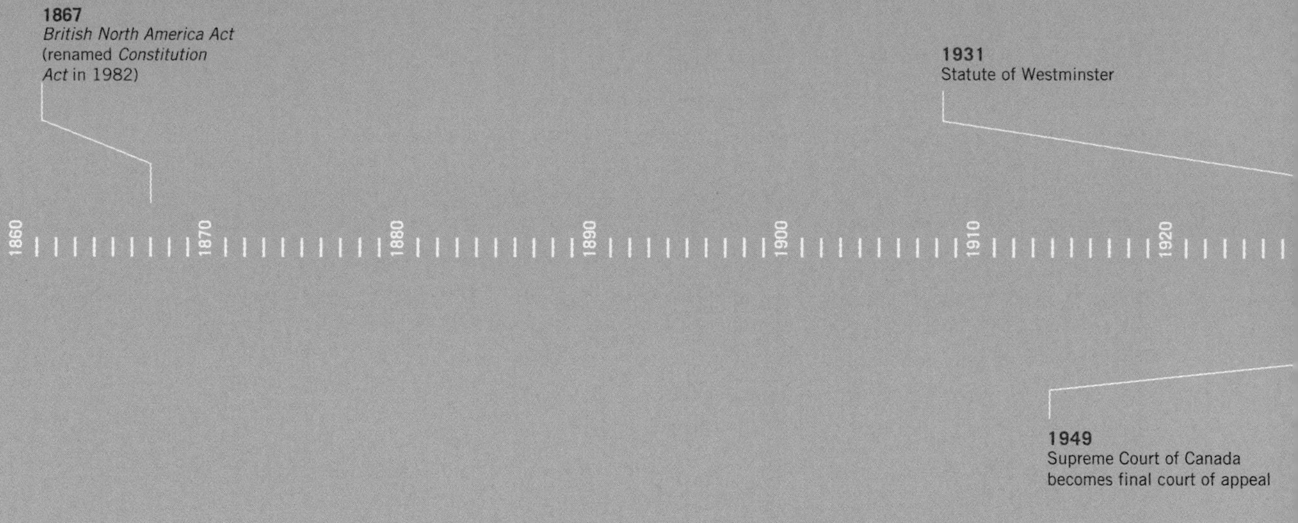

1867
British North America Act
(renamed *Constitution
Act* in 1982)

1931
Statute of Westminster

1860 | 1870 | 1880 | 1890 | 1900 | 1910 | 1920

1949
Supreme Court of Canada
becomes final court of appeal

hand over specific provincial powers to Ottawa. To reduce the impact of that possibility, the second formula allows a province to "opt out" of any constitutional changes that reduce its own rights or powers. To ensure that opting out is not unrealistic given the costs involved in a province exercising a power, the formula guarantees "reasonable" financial compensation if related to education or other cultural matters. Although education and culture are highly prized in Quebec, Quebec governments have argued that compensation should not be limited to those areas.

Almost all formal constitutional amendments normally need to be passed by majorities in both the House of Commons and the Senate. However, the House of Commons can override objections by the Senate by passing a constitutional resolution a second time after a delay of 180 days. This provision ensures that the Senate cannot indefinitely prevent constitutional changes that would change the Senate itself—a major topic of constitutional reform discussions.

The *Constitution Act*, 1982, does not mention the use of a referendum to gain the approval of Canadian citizens for a constitutional amendment. However, in 1992 the public voted on a major package of constitutional changes (the Charlottetown Accord) in a referendum.[3] It may well be that there is a political expectation that significant changes to the Constitution require the approval of a majority of those voting in a referendum. Indeed, British

---

[3]Newfoundland and Labrador held two referendums to gain public support for its proposal to change its constitutionally protected denominational school system. However, Quebec did not hold a referendum to change its denominational school system.

Early 1960s
Quebec's Quiet
Revolution

1970s–1980s
Western provinces and
Newfoundland seek
constitutional changes

1982
Constitution Act, 1982

1987–1990
Meech Lake Accord

1995
Quebec sovereignty
referendum defeated

2000
Clarity Act

1971
Victoria Charter

1976
Election of
Parti Québécois

1980
Quebec referendum on
sovereignty-association
defeated

1981
Supreme Court
ruling on proposed
constitutional changes

1992
Charlottetown
Accord

1996
*Constitutional
Amendments Act*

1998
*Reference re:
Secession*

Columbia and Alberta have adopted laws requiring that a referendum be held before their legislatures will approve a constitutional amendment.

Finally, although the procedure for approving constitutional amendments established in the *Constitution Act,* 1982, has not changed, an act of Parliament, the **Constitutional Amendments Act, 1996,** requires that proposed constitutional changes cannot be presented to Parliament by the Canadian Cabinet unless it has the support of the following:

- Quebec;
- Ontario;
- British Columbia;
- a majority of the Prairie provinces having at least one-half of the population of the Prairie provinces (in effect, Alberta plus either Saskatchewan or Manitoba); and
- at least two of the four Atlantic provinces containing a majority of the region's population.[4]

CONSTITUTIONAL CONTROVERSIES

Constitutional issues have, to a considerable extent, been at the heart of Canadian politics (see Figure 10-1). Much discussion and controversy has surrounded not only changes to specific provisions in the Constitution, but also

CONSTITUTIONAL
AMENDMENTS ACT, 1996
An act of Parliament that sets out the combination of provinces and regions whose support is needed before the Canadian Cabinet presents proposed constitutional changes to Parliament.

Constitutional Amendments Act:
http://www.constitutional-law.net/
conamact.html

---

[4]The *Constitutional Amendments Act* does not specify whether the approval of provincial legislatures is needed or whether some other mechanism such as a referendum could be used to gain the necessary support.

major changes to the Constitution that have been proposed. Key issues have included Quebec's place in Canada, Aboriginal rights, the powers of provincial governments, constitutional protection of rights and freedoms, and provincial representation in the Senate.

Quebec governments have long promoted the view that Canada is based on "two founding peoples"—English and French. Quebec governments have seen themselves as the principal custodians of the French "fact" in Canada, and thus have rebuffed attempts by the Canadian government to encroach upon the powers of the Quebec government.

As discussed in Chapter 4, Quebec underwent major social and political changes in the early 1960s. The "Quiet Revolution" involved the modernization of Quebec society and politics, and resulted in the Quebec government's appeal for more constitutional powers to lead social and economic development. Quebec governments also argued for greater constitutional powers to protect and promote language and culture. As well, they have asked to retain what they consider Quebec's traditional right to veto any constitutional changes that could result in a loss of their province's powers. And finally, Quebec governments have fought for constitutional recognition of the province's distinctiveness. The challenges inherent in achieving such constitutional changes helped to fuel the creation of the Parti Québécois, led by Réne Lévesque, whose goal was to pursue some form of sovereignty for Quebec. The Parti Québécois was in power at the provincial level from 1976 to 1985 and from 1994 to 2003. Referendums were held in 1980 and 1995 in the effort to win a mandate to pursue independence. The prospect of Quebec independence has created, at times, a sense of urgency about constitutional change, but has also presented obstacles to achieving it.

Western Canadian governments, particularly the government of Alberta, also began lobbying for major constitutional changes in the 1970s based on Western Canadian resentment of the domination of Canadian politics by Ontario and Quebec. Not long after, Canada's National Energy Policy (1980) was seen as robbing Alberta of the benefits of high oil prices in order to satisfy the industries of central Canada. Thus the Alberta government, bolstered by other Western Canadian governments and by the Newfoundland government of Brian Peckford, pressed for constitutional changes to enhance provincial government control of natural resources and natural resource revenues. The Alberta and Newfoundland governments also fought to give the smaller provinces a stronger voice in Parliament by advocating a "**Triple-E Senate**"; that is, an elected and effective Senate based on equal representation from each province regardless of population.

Aboriginals have also demanded basic constitutional changes so as to recognize what they view as their inherent right to self-government, to establish Aboriginal governments with wide-ranging powers, and to have guaranteed representation in national political institutions. Aboriginal leaders have

TRIPLE-E SENATE
A proposal that the Senate be reformed to be elected and effective based on equal representation from each province regardless of population size.

also sought to secure a place in constitutional negotiations for Aboriginal representatives.

Finally, the Canadian government, especially the government of Prime Minister Pierre Trudeau, has wanted to enhance the Canadian political community to counter the forces of Quebec nationalism and provincialism. In particular, a major goal of the Trudeau Government was to entrench a Charter of Rights and Freedoms that included expanded French- and English-language rights in the Constitution. Some provincial governments opposed a constitutional Charter, fearing that a uniform set of rights would undermine the diversity of Canada and erode the power of provincial governments. The Canadian government has also wanted to safeguard its ability to establish national standards in social programs and to remove provincial barriers to trade and mobility within Canada.

Constitutional Negotiations

THE VICTORIA CHARTER, 1971   A major series of constitutional negotiations from 1968 to 1971 culminated in a tentative deal known as the **Victoria Charter**, 1971. Among other provisions, it set out the following requirements for approving constitutional changes:

VICTORIA CHARTER
A tentative deal for constitutional change reached in 1971.

- approval by Quebec;
- approval by Ontario;
- approval by at least two of the four Western provinces having at least half of the population of the region; and
- approval by at least two of the four Atlantic provinces.

However, the Quebec Liberal government of Robert Bourassa decided not to sign the deal when strong opposition developed in Quebec. In particular, many Quebecers were critical of the lack of significant gains in Quebec's constitutional powers, especially over social policy. Negotiations from 1977 to 1979 were also unsuccessful. Only after an extremely difficult series of events was the *Constitution Act*, 1982, adopted.

THE RUN-UP TO THE CONSTITUTION ACT, 1982   Pierre Trudeau returned from retirement in 1979 to lead the Liberal party to victory in the 1980 Canadian election, including winning seventy-four of Quebec's seventy-five seats. A few months later, the Parti Québécois government held a referendum, hoping to win a mandate from Quebecers to negotiate sovereignty-association—that is, political sovereignty (independence) for Quebec while retaining an economic association with the rest of Canada. In urging Quebecers to reject this proposal, Prime Minister Trudeau and other political leaders promised Quebecers that a no vote would lead to a "renewed federalism." Although Trudeau's promise of "renewed federalism" was vague, the provincial Liberal party during the referendum campaign presented a detailed proposal that would have given the Quebec government substantially greater powers.

The referendum battle concluded with a no vote—"non" to sovereignty-association. With a second chance to unify the country, Trudeau was determined to reassert the leadership role of the Canadian government and achieve his goals of patriating the constitution and entrenching a Charter of Rights and Freedoms in the Constitution. However, three months of negotiations failed, and a lengthy list of proposals for constitutional changes, presented by the premiers to Trudeau, was rejected. Trudeau felt that the proposals transferred massive powers to the provinces. Instead, he presented a proposal to Parliament that included a Charter, a commitment to the principle of equalization payments to the poorer provinces, and an amending formula that would have allowed Parliament to bypass provincial government opposition to constitutional changes through the use of a referendum. By presenting the plan before the Canadian Parliament with the intention of sending it to the Parliament of the United Kingdom for final approval, Trudeau avoided the established practice that included provincial government approval of constitutional changes that affect provincial governments.

Not surprisingly, most provincial governments were outraged by the Trudeau Government's plan to unilaterally request major changes to the Constitution. After some unsuccessful attempts by the federal government to come up with compromises that would satisfy a few provinces (particularly Saskatchewan), eight provincial governments (labelled the "Gang of Eight") formed a united front to challenge the Canadian government's proposal. Reinvigorated by a provincial election victory in 1981, the Parti Québécois government was determined to quash the Trudeau Government's initiative. To form a united front with the other seven dissenting provincial governments, it accepted a proposal for an amending formula originally developed by the Alberta government, even though it meant dropping Quebec's traditional demand for a veto over constitutional changes. Support for the Canadian government's proposal came from only two provinces—Ontario and New Brunswick. The Ontario government, which favoured the Canadian government's controversial National Energy Program, was concerned that various provincial proposals, particularly those regarding natural resources, would undermine the national economy. The New Brunswick government was won over by the Trudeau Government's proposals for official bilingualism.

In the Manitoba, Quebec, and Newfoundland courts, provincial governments launched reference cases[5] challenging the Canadian government's unilateral plan with mixed results. In September 1981, the Supreme Court of Canada ruled in the *Patriation Reference* that Trudeau's plan for adopting constitutional

---

[5]*References* are questions posed by the federal or a provincial government asking for an advisory opinion. Only the Canadian government can present a reference to the Supreme Court of Canada, but provincial governments can present a reference to their province's court of appeal.

BOX 10-2

The "Night of Long Knives"

The stakes were high in November 1981 as Prime Minister Trudeau and the provincial premiers met for one final effort to reach an agreement on constitutional change. Little progress occurred over several days as attempts were made to find a compromise between the position taken by the "Gang of Eight" (the eight premiers who, for various reasons, opposed the federal proposal) and the prime minister, who continued to threaten to take his proposal to the British Parliament where its fate was uncertain. Faced with an impasse, Pierre Trudeau challenged René Lévesque to agree to a referendum to let the people decide on the outstanding issues: "You the great democrat," he is reported to have said to Lévesque, "don't tell me you're afraid to fight" (Lévesque, 1986). Distrustful of his fellow premiers, Lévesque took the bait and accepted the idea, confident that he could convince Quebecers to defeat Trudeau's proposals. The other members of the "Gang of Eight" felt betrayed by Lévesque's agreement with Trudeau and shuddered at the idea of publicly campaigning against a Charter of Rights and Freedoms. With the unity of the "Gang of Eight" broken, renewed efforts were made to find a compromise. As René Lévesque and his staff left for their hotel rooms across the river in Hull, Quebec, he wrote in his memoirs that he called out, "If anything new comes up, don't forget to call us" (Lévesque, 1986).

In a kitchen in Ottawa, Minister of Justice Jean Chrétien worked with Attorneys General Roy Romanow (Saskatchewan) and Roy McMurtry (Ontario) to hammer out a compromise. Other premiers and members of their delegations were consulted throughout the night, and Newfoundland Premier Brian Peckford put together a draft proposal. Ontario Premier Bill Davis took the final version of the proposal to Pierre Trudeau, who reluctantly agreed to it after Davis threatened to withdraw his support for a request to the British Parliament if Trudeau rejected a compromise (Trudeau, 1993). No call was made to Lévesque and the Quebec delegation.

At a breakfast meeting the next morning, Premier Lévesque was informed of the agreement that had been reached during the night. Angrily he denounced what he termed a "betrayal": "I have been stabbed in the back during the night by a bunch of carpetbaggers" (Lévesque, 1986). Quebec nationalists to this day refer to the time when the *Constitution Act,* 1982, was drafted as the "Night of Long Knives"—a reference to a similarly named night in 1934 when Hitler ordered the purge of his Brownshirt supporters, many of whom were executed.

changes without the approval of provincial legislatures was *legal,* but that it violated the *constitutional convention* that required provincial legislative approval for changes affecting their powers. However, although the Canadian government had obtained *unanimous* provincial approval in the past for changes affecting the powers of the provinces, the Supreme Court of Canada ruled that only *substantial* provincial approval was needed to satisfy the constitutional conventional (with the definition of "substantial" left unclear). With some British Members of Parliament indicating their uneasiness with passing the unilateral constitutional proposal and the Supreme Court ruling that the process violated constitutional convention, pressure mounted in November 1981 for another attempt by the prime minister and the premiers to reach an agreement (See Box 10-2, The "Night of Long Knives").

▶ In 1983, Peter Greyson entered Ottawa's National Archives (known today as Library and Archives Canada) and poured red paint over the Constitution. The Toronto artist was displeased with U.S. missile testing in Canada and wanted to "graphically illustrate" how wrong he thought this was. Specialists opted to leave most of the paint stain intact, fearing attempts at removing it would only do further damage.

The compromise agreed to on November 5, 1991 (with Premier Lévesque refusing to sign[6]), involved two basic elements: The amending formula proposed by the dissenting provinces was accepted but without the provisions to financially compensate provinces that "opted out" of constitutional changes.[7] The *Charter of Rights and Freedoms* proposed by the Trudeau Government was also accepted, but a "notwithstanding clause" was added to allow a legislative body to override the Charter on certain matters (see Chapter 13). The women's movement successfully mounted pressure to prevent the male–female equality clause in the Charter from being subject to the notwithstanding override.

THE PASSAGE OF THE CONSTITUTION ACT, 1982, AND ITS AFTERMATH   Despite the opposition of the Quebec National Assembly, the *Canada Act* that included the *Constitution Act, 1982*, was passed by the Parliament of the United Kingdom. While Queen Elizabeth II signed the official documents making the Constitution fully Canadian at a ceremony in Ottawa, Premier Lévesque ordered flags in Quebec to fly at half-mast.

However, fundamental political questions remained. Should the major constitutional changes have been pushed through without the approval of the Quebec legislature? Trudeau pointed out that almost all the members of the Canadian Parliament from Quebec supported the constitutional changes. In

---

[6]Lévesque's specific objections are listed in Chapter 4.
[7]The final version restored compensation for opting out of education and other cultural matters.

contrast, a substantial majority of the members of the Quebec legislature passed a motion rejecting the *Constitution Act*, 1982. In their view, the act was illegitimate because the agreement of the Quebec government had not been obtained.

The Aboriginal Position   Aboriginal leaders were not invited to participate in the negotiations that led to the *Constitution Act*, 1982, and the patriation of the Constitution was carried out over the vigorous objections of many Aboriginal groups. In their view, the treaties their peoples had signed with the British Crown could not be transferred to Canada without their consent. Aboriginal groups launched a lawsuit in Britain to prevent passage of the constitutional changes. Ultimately, their efforts failed.[8] When Canadian Parliamentary hearings were held on the proposed *Constitution Act*, the National Indian Brotherhood (NIB) eventually succeeded in negotiating the addition of the clause recognizing and affirming the "existing aboriginal and treaty rights of the aboriginal peoples of Canada." However, other Aboriginal groups rejected the NIB's support for the *Constitution Act*, and the NIB leadership was forced to reverse its support for the constitutional proposal. Aboriginal groups wanted the Constitution to include an explicit recognition of their inherent right to self-government, as well as a provision that future amendments to the Constitution affecting their rights would require Aboriginal agreement (Sanders, 1983).

The *Constitution Act*, 1982, did include a requirement for future constitutional negotiations concerning Aboriginal issues. A series of three constitutional conferences on Aboriginal issues took place, but they ended in failure in March 1987, when the British Columbia, Alberta, Saskatchewan, and Newfoundland governments rejected proposed constitutional provisions concerning Aboriginal self-government. In their view, the details of self-government needed to be determined before establishing a general right to self-government in the Constitution. Nevertheless, a constitutional amendment adopted in 1983 clarified that the rights acquired by land claims agreements or new treaties are constitutionally recognized. Thus, as discussed in Chapter 12, Aboriginal groups that have signed agreements or treaties in recent years (and in the future) providing for self-government and other rights now have these rights constitutionally guaranteed.

Further Efforts at Constitutional Change

The Progressive Conservative party led by Brian Mulroney won the 1984 Canadian election on a platform that included a promise to bring Quebec back into the Constitution "with honour."[9] Likewise, the death of Premier

---

[8]A lawsuit by the Quebec government to invalidate the *Constitution Act*, 1982, also did not succeed.
[9]Although the Quebec government did not agree to the *Constitution Act*, 1982, it is nevertheless bound by it. "Bringing Quebec back in" thus refers to gaining the support of Quebec for the Constitution.

Lévesque and the subsequent election victory of the Quebec Liberal Party led by Robert Bourassa provided an opportunity to reach a settlement. However, the Mulroney Government's two attempts to make major changes to the Constitution would end in failure.

THE MEECH LAKE ACCORD   In 1986, the government of Quebec laid out the five conditions that would have to be met in order for Quebec to sign the *Constitution Act, 1982*:

- Constitutional recognition of Quebec as a distinct society.
- A role for Quebec in making appointments for the three Quebec judges on the Supreme Court of Canada.
- Increasing Quebec's role in selecting immigrants to the province.
- Full financial compensation for opting out of new federal programs in areas of provincial jurisdiction.
- A veto over constitutional amendments affecting Quebec (Russell, 2004).

With all the premiers agreeing that these conditions were an acceptable basis for renewed constitutional talks, Brian Mulroney called them to a private meeting at the government's Meech Lake retreat on April 30, 1987.

The prime minister and premiers were able to reach a unanimous agreement known as the **Meech Lake Accord**. The accord basically met Quebec's five conditions while extending the powers granted to Quebec to all provinces. The accord included a controversial **distinct society clause**—that the constitution should be interpreted in a manner consistent with "the recognition that Quebec constitutes within Canada a distinct society."[10] Quebec's role in preserving and promoting its distinct identity would be affirmed, but no specific new powers were attached to this role.

Other provisions would have enhanced the powers of all provincial governments to some extent by giving them a role in nominating Supreme Court of Canada judges and senators, establishing their right to opt out of national social programs while receiving reasonable financial compensation to set up their own programs, and increasing jurisdiction over immigration. As well, the Meech Lake Accord proposed changing the general amending formula for the Constitution so as to require the agreement of every provincial legislature (as well as Parliament) for changes to the Constitution.

Strong opposition developed to the accord. Many English-speaking Canadians complained about the recognition of Quebec as a distinct society. Former Prime Minister Pierre Trudeau bitterly denounced the accord, saying that by giving the premiers what they wanted, the accord would "render the Canadian state totally impotent . . . to eventually be governed by eunuchs." The decision

MEECH LAKE ACCORD
An agreement on constitutional change reached by the prime minister and premiers in 1987 that failed to be ratified by all provincial legislatures. The accord satisfied the conditions laid out by Quebec for signing the *Constitution Act, 1982*, while extending the powers granted to Quebec to all provinces.

The Meech Lake Accord:
http://home.cc.umanitoba.ca/
~sprague/meech.htm

DISTINCT SOCIETY CLAUSE
A clause in the Meech Lake Accord that the constitution should be interpreted in a manner consistent with the recognition of Quebec as a distinct society.

---

[10]The clause also recognized "that the existence of French-speaking Canadians, centered in Quebec but also present elsewhere in Canada, and English-speaking Canadians, concentrated outside Quebec but also present in Quebec, constitutes a fundamental characteristic of Canada."

of the Bourassa government in 1988 to use the notwithstanding clause in the *Charter of Rights and Freedoms* to pass legislation requiring that only French be permitted on signs outside stores (discussed in Chapter 4) infuriated many English-speaking Canadians, adding to the opposition to the distinct society clause. Aboriginal groups were upset by what they perceived to be preferential treatment for Quebec; that province's demands had been dealt with in the accord, but Aboriginal demands for their inherent right to self-government to be recognized had not been considered. Those in the territories (along with Aboriginals) complained that they had not been represented in the Meech Lake discussions. In particular, they objected to provisions that would make it difficult for the territories to eventually gain provincial status. As well, many Western Canadians felt irked that Senate reform to create a Triple-E Senate was not included. Women's groups in English Canada campaigned strongly against the accord, claiming that recognizing Quebec as distinct could allow that province to undermine the male–female equality that was guaranteed in the *Charter of Rights and Freedoms*. Multicultural groups were concerned the accord recognized French- and English-speaking Canadians as "a fundamental characteristic of Canada." And finally, there was considerable criticism of the process of constitutional change by those who felt that deal-making by eleven heads of government (all white males) in closed meetings hardly made for a model of democracy at work.

Because the package of constitutional proposals in the Meech Lake Accord included changes to the amending formula and the Supreme Court, the accord required the approval of Parliament and all provincial legislatures. Despite the support of all First Ministers for the Meech Lake Accord and the ratification of the agreement by the legislatures of most provinces including Quebec, elections brought new governments to power in Newfoundland and New Brunswick that were critical of the accord. In particular, although the Newfoundland House of Assembly had ratified the accord, this was reversed when the Liberal party, led by Clyde Wells, was elected in 1989. Wells campaigned vigorously across the country against the accord, which he viewed as undermining the equality of the provinces. As discussed in the opening vignette, a last-minute effort to win the approval of all provincial legislatures failed.

Many Quebecers were deeply troubled by the defeat of the accord, which they viewed as the minimum set of changes that their province could accept. Support for independence rose sharply. To step up the pressure for change, Quebec Premier Robert Bourassa arranged for a referendum on Quebec sovereignty to be held in 1992 if the rest of Canada had not put forward an acceptable binding constitutional proposal. As political scientist Léon Dion graphically put it, Quebec was holding "a knife at the throat" of English Canada (quoted in Bothwell, 1998, p. 219).

THE CHARLOTTETOWN ACCORD   Faced with the threat of a referendum on Quebec independence, politicians resumed efforts to develop a package of

▶ Robert Bourassa, premier of Quebec from 1970–76 and 1985–94, tried hard to achieve constitutional changes that would increase support for the Canadian federal system in his province, but he was ultimately unsuccessful.

constitutional changes acceptable to all the diverse elements of Canadian society. Unprecedented and lengthy efforts were made to involve Canadians in the public discussion of constitutional issues before formal negotiations began. About 400 000 people participated in the Citizens' Forum that travelled across the country (Russell, 2004). Unlike the Meech Lake Accord, which was described as the "Quebec Round" of constitutional reform, these discussions led to the "Canada Round" of negotiations, with the goal of satisfying constitutional demands raised by a wide variety of groups and interests.

Formal negotiations on constitutional change involving representation of the Canadian government and all provincial governments (except Quebec), the territorial governments, and four national Aboriginal organizations began in March 1992. After agreement was reached on a draft package of constitutional changes, the Quebec government, fearing that the package would be unacceptable to the majority of Quebecers, decided to join the negotiations in late July. After intense negotiations resulted in some modifications to the proposal, all the participants finalized their agreement at a meeting in Charlottetown on August 28, 1992.

The **Charlottetown Accord** reached beyond the more limited provisions of the Meech Lake Accord. Its provisions included:

- *Constitutional recognition of the inherent right of Aboriginals to self-government within Canada.* Aboriginal governments would constitute a "third order" of government with powers to be defined that might be similar to those of provincial governments.

- *An elected Senate with six senators from each province, one from each territory, and representation of Aboriginals to be determined at a later date.* The Senate would no longer have a power to veto legislation (except on natural resource laws), with disagreements between the House of Commons and Senate to be decided by a majority vote at a joint sitting of the two bodies.

- *Extra seats for Ontario and Quebec.* In return for losing Senate representation, Ontario and Quebec would gain some additional seats in the House of Commons, and Quebec would be guaranteed to have at least one-quarter of the seats in the House of Commons.

- *A "Canada clause."* The clause would require that the Constitution be "interpreted in a manner consistent with a number of fundamental characteristics": democracy; a parliamentary and federal system of government, and the rule of law; Aboriginal rights; Quebec's distinct society; official language minority communities; racial and ethnic equality; individual and collective rights and freedoms; equality of female and male persons; and equality of the provinces.

- *A commitment to establish a social and economic union.* The union would include such objectives as reasonable access of all people to housing, food, and other basic necessities, as well as access to post-secondary education; protection of the rights of workers to organize and bargain collectively; protection of the integrity of the environment; the goal of full employment; and the free movement of people, goods, services, and capital.

- *Greater powers for provincial governments.* Provincial governments would have increased powers in a number of fields of jurisdiction and the right to opt out of new national shared-cost programs in areas of provincial jurisdiction and to receive full financial compensation.

- *Changed procedure for appointing justices.* Supreme Court of Canada justices would be appointed by the Canadian government from lists of nominees prepared by the provinces and territories.

Because British Columbia and Alberta had adopted requirements that constitutional changes had to be approved by a referendum, it was decided to hold a national referendum. In Quebec, a referendum on the Charlottetown Accord replaced the planned referendum on Quebec sovereignty.

Consensus Report on the Constitution:
www.solon.org/Constitutions/Canada/English/Proposals/CharlottetownConsensus.html

CHARLOTTETOWN ACCORD
An agreement in 1992 on a broad package of constitutional changes, including Aboriginal self-government, Senate reform, and a statement of the characteristics of Canada. The agreement, which had the support of the prime minister, all premiers and territorial leaders, and four national Aboriginal leaders, was defeated in a referendum.

TABLE 10-1

RESULTS OF THE REFERENDUM ON THE CHARLOTTETOWN ACCORD, 1992, BY PROVINCE AND TERRITORY (PERCENTAGE)

Referendum question: "Do you agree that the constitution of Canada should be renewed on the basis of the agreement reached on August 28th, 1992?"

	YES	NO	TURNOUT
Newfoundland	63.2	36.8	53.3
Prince Edward Island	73.9	26.1	70.5
Nova Scotia	48.8	51.2	67.8
New Brunswick	61.8	38.2	72.2
Quebec	43.3	56.7	82.7
Ontario	50.1	49.9	71.9
Manitoba	38.4	61.6	70.6
Saskatchewan	44.7	55.3	68.7
Alberta	39.8	60.2	72.6
British Columbia	31.7	68.3	76.7
Northwest Territory	61.3	38.7	70.4
Yukon	43.7	56.3	70.0
Canada	45.0	55.0	74.7

Source: *McRoberts & Monahan, 1993, Appendix 3.*

The referendum question took the following form: "Do you agree that the constitution of Canada should be renewed on the basis of the agreement reached on August 28th, 1992?" A full 55 percent of voters replied in the negative, including a majority of Quebecers, non-Quebecers, and Aboriginals living on reserves (see Table 10-1). Like the Meech Lake Accord before it, the Charlottetown Accord had to be scrapped.

Many English-speaking Canadians, particularly in the West, felt the Charlottetown Accord still went too far in appeasing Quebec. Many Quebecers felt that the Accord provided less for Quebec than the Meech Lake Accord (see Box 10-3, Mind Your Words: Quebec's Indiscretion). Although the leadership of the Assembly of First Nations approved the accord, First Nations chiefs voted to oppose the accord, fearing that the right to self-government would be unduly limited by the *Charter of Rights and Freedoms*. The Native Women's Association of Canada, which was not represented at the negotiations,[11] fought against the accord despite its guarantees of equal rights for Aboriginal women and men. Their concern was that too much power would be placed in the hands of male Aboriginal leaders. Still other groups, such as gays and lesbians and people with disabilities, were incensed because they were not recognized in the Canada clause. Women's groups argued that wording of the accord created a hierarchy of rights in which male–female equality was not awarded the same priority as the rights of some other groups. Former Prime Minister Trudeau publicly opposed the accord particularly because, like the Meech Lake Accord, it weakened the power of the Canadian government and

[11]However, the Inuit delegation was headed by its leader, Mary Simon, and women were part of the other Aboriginal delegations. The Native Women's challenge to the exclusion of their organization was upheld by the Federal Court of Canada (Russell, 2004).

Mind Your Words: Quebec's Indiscretion

At first glance, the Charlottetown Accord gave the appearance of a possible face-saving solution for the Quebec government. Although Premier Bourassa, a supporter of the Canadian federal system, had committed his province to hold a referendum on independence if no acceptable constitutional offer was received, the threat proved hollow when the draft proposal offered less to Quebec than the Meech Lake Accord. Rejecting the proposal might have resulted in an outcome Bourassa did not want: a majority vote for independence. Bourassa thus decided to join the final negotiations to push for changes that would make the proposal more appealing to Quebecers. Although Bourassa was successful in gaining some changes that benefited Quebec, critics argued that he had not fought hard enough to promote Quebec's constitutional positions. The scandal that broke out shortly afterward seemed to confirm the view of Bourassa's critics.

As luck would have it, a person in Quebec City was illegally scanning private cellphone conversations at the time of the negotiations leading to the accord. This person recorded a conversation between Quebec's deputy minister of intergovernmental affairs and Premier Bourassa's constitutional adviser concerning the negotiations that one of them had been unable to attend because of illness. In the conversation, Bourassa was portrayed as having caved in to pressure from other participants, resulting in an agreement that was a disgrace to Quebec. When the Quebec government heard about the leak, they tried to prevent a Quebec newspaper from publishing a transcript of the conversation. Their efforts only served to heighten interest in the conversation, which was eventually published. Furthermore, British Columbia's constitutional affairs minister, in promoting the accord to a B.C. audience, claimed that Bourassa had lost in the negotiations. This lent further credence to the views expressed in the recorded conversation.

Although these events undoubtedly reinforced the decision of a majority of Quebecers to reject the accord, public opinion polls indicated that the decline in the support of Quebecers for the accord had begun before these damaging comments were publicized (Johnston, Blais, Gidengil, & Nevitte, 1996).

Robert Bourassa announced his decision to retire from politics in September 1993 after unsuccessful treatment for skin cancer. The Parti Québécois defeated the Quebec Liberals in 1994, leading to the referendum on independence that Bourassa had tried to avoid.

---

promoted collective rights (that is, the rights of particular groups) rather than the rights of all individual Canadians. Finally, there was uncertainty about the provisions of the Charlottetown Accord because the legal text of the accord was not prepared until shortly before the referendum date. Even so, the legal text left many provisions open to further negotiations.

The 1995 Referendum

The failure of the Charlottetown Accord shut down the process of seeking major changes to the Constitution. The Progressive Conservative party that held power while both the accords were negotiated was reduced to just two seats in the House of Commons. Instead, the Liberal party led by Jean Chrétien promised that constitutional issues should not be reopened for "a long, long time," and won the 1993 Canadian election. The Liberal plan to avoid constitutional issues was, however, upended by political events in Quebec. The Parti Québécois was elected in 1994 and wasted no time in holding a referendum in 1995. On this occasion, the question was whether or not "Quebec should become sovereign after making an offer of economic and political partnership to Canada." When it appeared that a majority might vote yes, Prime Minister Chrétien made a last-minute television appeal to Quebecers. He vowed to recognize Quebec as a distinct society, to ensure that constitutional changes that affect the powers of Quebec should only be made with the consent of Quebecers, and to work toward greater decentralization of power from the Canadian government to provincial governments. Quebecers responded to Chrétien's promises—but just barely. The referendum result was extremely close: 49.4 percent voted yes and 50.6 percent, no.

As discussed in Chapter 4, a challenge to Quebec's referendum led to an opinion by the Supreme Court of Canada (*Secession Reference,* 1998) that a province could not unilaterally secede from Canada. However, if a clear majority in a province voted in favour of independence on a clear question in a referendum, then Canada as a whole would have a duty to negotiate the terms of independence in good faith. This became the basis for the *Clarity Act* (2000), which set out the procedures by which a province could pursue independence. The Canadian House of Commons would determine whether a clear majority of the population of a province voted on a clear question regarding independence. An amendment to the Constitution agreed to by all provincial legislatures would then be needed for a province to secede.

Finding too little support from provincial governments for a constitutional amendment to recognize Quebec as a distinct society, the Chrétien government created a fallback solution: It encouraged the House of Commons to pass a symbolic resolution recognizing Quebec as a distinct society. The *Constitutional Amendments Act* (discussed earlier in this chapter) gave Quebec and various other provinces a veto over constitutional changes. As well, provincial powers were expanded by providing financial assistance to any provincial government that wanted to take control of labour market training. Thus, to some extent, the promises made in 1995 were met without formal changes to the Constitution.

Future Constitutional Change?

It is often argued that the defeat of the Meech Lake and Charlottetown Accords indicates that seeking major changes to the formal Constitution is undesirable and nearly impossible to achieve. Restarting constitutional talks is often described as "opening a can of worms." It would be difficult to get everyone to agree to change even one major aspect of the Constitution, as various groups would insist on having their key issues addressed.

Although the Liberal governments of Jean Chrétien and Paul Martin avoided formal constitutional negotiations, Conservative Prime Minister Stephen Harper, after being elected in 2006, showed a willingness to reopen constitutional talks. However, at the time this chapter was written, his government had shied away from that initiative. Instead, the Harper Government took various non-constitutional measures to try to beef up the support of Quebecers for the Canadian federal system. These included increasing the financial capabilities of provincial governments, allowing Quebec to take a formal role at the United Nations Educational, Scientific and Cultural Organization (UNESCO), and introducing a motion that the House of Commons "recognize that the Québécois form a nation within a united Canada" (a motion that passed by a 266 to 16 margin).

Summary and Conclusion

Canada's constitution is not to be found in a single document, but rather consists of a variety of elements. The Constitution acts that form the cornerstone of the Constitution are the supreme law of the country and can be used by the courts to invalidate laws that are inconsistent with the Constitution. Ordinary laws of a constitutional nature, constitutional conventions, and judicial interpretations of the Constitution acts are also key elements of the constitution.

Canada's formal Constitution is difficult to change. This has meant that Canada's unelected Senate continues to be, in the view of many, an undemocratic relic of Canada's past. Nevertheless, despite the challenges involved in making major changes to the Constitution, governments have been able to work around the provisions of the Constitution to adjust to changing circumstances. As well, the evolution of constitutional conventions and changing patterns of judicial interpretation of the Constitution have allowed for flexibility in Canada's constitution. Thus the impasse concerning formal constitutional change has not been a major obstacle to good government. Nevertheless,

the preoccupation of governments with constitutional change since the early 1960s reduced their ability to deal with other important problems.

Disagreements about major changes to the Constitution have created severe political crises on several occasions, and even raised concerns about the future of Canada. Developing a consensus about major changes in the Constitution is difficult because there is no shared vision of Canada. In particular, it is challenging to reconcile the different views of Canada. Should Canada be considered primarily as a country of equal provinces, two founding peoples, a partnership between Aboriginals and settlers, or a diverse collection of ethnocultural groups?

Despite their differences, political elites were able to agree on the major constitutional changes proposed in the Meech Lake and Charlottetown Accords. However, these compromises proved to be unacceptable to a variety of groups and to the public at large. Constitutional change is thus no longer a matter that can be resolved exclusively through bargaining among political elites. Instead, a strong expectation has developed that major constitutional changes should be achieved more democratically, through citizen engagement in the process of deliberation and through the use of a referendum to approve changes. As well, the importance of Canadian diversity is evident. No longer is constitutional change primarily about the powers of the Canadian and provincial governments, but also about groups representing different segments of the population that seek recognition and various rights in the Constitution. Further, it has become accepted practice that Aboriginal organizations and territorial governments will participate in constitutional negotiations, at least on matters that affect them.

Although the defeat of the Charlottetown Accord in 1992 ended the focus of Canadian politics on major constitutional changes, some basic constitutional issues will not likely fade away. The rejection of the *Constitution Act,* 1982, by the government of Quebec, Aboriginal demands for recognition of their inherent right to self-government, calls for substantial reform to the Senate, demands by various provincial governments for further limits to the power of the Canadian government and, likely in the future, the desire of major cities for constitutional status—all of these will serve to keep constitutional change on the political agenda.

Discussion Questions

1. Should Canada try to gain the support of the Quebec government for the *Constitution Act,* 1982?

2. Should Canada's formal Constitution include a statement of Canadian values? If so, what values are important?

3. Why is it difficult to change Canada's formal Constitution?

4. Did the Meech Lake and Charlottetown Accords contain useful provisions for future constitutional change?

5. Should major constitutional changes require approval in a referendum? If so, should a majority of Canadian voters suffice or should a majority in all provinces or regions be required for approval?

Further Reading

Banting, K., & Simeon, R. (Eds.). (1983). *And no one cheered: Federalism, democracy and the Constitution Act.* Toronto, ON: Methuen.

Behiels, M. D. (Ed.). (1988). *The Meech Lake primer: Conflicting views of the 1987 Constitutional Accord.* Ottawa, ON: University of Ottawa Press.

Coyne, D. (1992). *Roll of the dice.* Toronto, ON: Lorimer.

Heard, A. (1991). *Canadian constitutional conventions: The marriage of law and politics.* Toronto, ON: Oxford University Press.

Johnston, R., Blais, A., Gidengil, E., & Nevitte, N. (1996). *The challenge of direct democracy: The 1992 Canadian referendum.* Montreal, QC: McGill-Queen's University Press.

McRoberts, K. (1997). *Misconceiving Canada: The struggle for national unity.* Toronto, ON: Oxford University Press.

McRoberts, K., & Monahan, P. (Eds.). (1993). *The Charlottetown Accord, the referendum, and the future of Canada.* Toronto, ON: University of Toronto Press.

Monahan, P. (1991). *Meech Lake: The inside story.* Toronto, ON: University of Toronto Press.

Romanow, R., Whyte, J., & Leeson, H. (1984). *Canada . . . Notwithstanding: The making of the constitution 1976–1982.* Toronto, ON: Methuen.

Russell, P. (2004). *Constitutional odyssey* (3rd ed.). Toronto, ON: University of Toronto Press.

Chapter 11

THE CHARTER OF RIGHTS AND FREEDOMS

PHOTO ABOVE: Governor General Michaëlle Jean stands with abortion rights activist Henry Morgentaler after decorating him as a member of the Order of Canada on October 10, 2008, at the Citadelle in Quebec City.

CHAPTER OBJECTIVES

After reading this chapter, you should be able to

1. Explain the limitations of the *Canadian Bill of Rights*.
2. Outline the major provisions of the *Charter of Rights and Freedoms*.
3. Explain the importance of the "reasonable limits" clause.
4. Discuss the significance of the "notwithstanding" clause.
5. Assess the argument that the Charter has made the courts too powerful.

Henry Morgentaler, born in Poland in 1923, weighed 32 kg when he was liberated from a Nazi concentration camp where his parents and sister had been murdered. Determined to help people, he came to Canada, studied medicine, and opened a practice in the poor east end of Montreal. After testifying before a House of Commons Committee in 1967 that women should have the right to a safe abortion, he found his practice deluged with women desperately seeking the procedure. Although performing an abortion could, at the time, result in a life sentence, Dr. Morgentaler, a father of four, opened a clinic where he performed abortions using a safe technique that he developed. He openly defied the abortion law—even performing an abortion on Mother's Day for CTV's nation-wide program, *W5*.

In 1973, Dr. Morgentaler was charged with performing an illegal abortion. Although a Montreal jury refused to convict him, an appeal to a higher court resulted in a conviction. Morgentaler tried to defend his actions in terms of the *Canadian Bill of Rights*. However, the Supreme Court of Canada ruled that the Bill of Rights did not provide the courts with the ability to overturn legislation or deal with the uneven application of the law. Morgentaler spent ten months in jail, but did not give up. He was acquitted twice more by Quebec juries. Morgentaler opened a Toronto clinic and invited the police chief to visit the clinic. A Toronto jury acquitted him on charges of performing illegal abortions, but the Ontario Court of Appeal set aside the acquittal and a new trial was ordered. Finally, in 1988 Morgentaler was successful at the Supreme Court of Canada. In a 5–2 decision, the Court struck down the abortion law particularly because the delay in treatment caused by the law increased the risk to a woman's health and thus violated section 7 of the *Charter of Rights and Freedoms* protecting the security of the person. One justice, Bertha Wilson, took the position that "the Charter gives a woman the right to decide for herself whether or not to terminate her pregnancy" although not necessarily in the later stages of pregnancy (quoted in Russell, Knopff, Bateman, & Hiebert, 2008, p. 235).

The Supreme Court decision left it open to Parliament to pass a new abortion law that would be consistent with the Charter by providing a fairer procedure (than the system of authorization by a committee that relatively few hospitals established) for determining when abortions should be permitted. However, after the House of Commons passed a bill regulating abortion, the bill was defeated in the Senate as a result of a tie vote. With no further attempts to deal with this controversial issue, Canada has remained without a law limiting the circumstances in which an abortion may be performed.

In 2008, despite strenuous objections from anti-abortionists, Dr. Morgentaler was awarded the Order of Canada "for his commitment to increased health care options for women, his determined efforts to influence Canadian public policy and his leadership in humanist and civil liberties organizations."

THE CHALLENGE OF DEFENDING RIGHTS AND FREEDOMS

Most Canadians take great pride in this country's traditions of freedom and democracy. On Remembrance Day, we acknowledge the sacrifices made by so many to promote those ideals. We are shocked when we hear about the brutal suppression of freedoms by dictatorships. And we take pride, too, in the leading role some Canadians have played in promoting human rights at the United Nations: Louise Arbour, Philippe Kirsch, and Steven Lewis, in their quests to better the well-being of the world's peoples, have increased Canada's profile as a defender of freedom and democracy.

The terrorist attacks on the United States on September 11, 2001 (along with subsequent bombings in London and Madrid), jolted the world and had consequences far beyond the human carnage—in the longer term, they resulted in laws and actions by many democratic countries that suspended or violated various long-standing rights and freedoms. In Canada, the *Anti-Terrorism Act* (2001) was the legal response to the attacks. It

- included severe penalties for those who provide any support to a terrorist organization;
- allowed police to arrest suspects without a warrant;
- provided for secret investigative hearings at which an individual may be compelled to testify; and
- broadened surveillance powers for police and national security agencies.[1]

Some viewed these measures as necessary to deal with the threat of terrorism and protect public safety. Others argued that giving up rights and freedoms meant the loss of something valuable and opened the door to arbitrary and oppressive government actions.

A key problem with defending rights and freedoms is that unpopular individuals or groups typically are the first targets of actions to limit rights and freedoms. There is often little public outrage if suspected terrorists are held for long periods without being charged with an offence, if police officers harass minority youth, or if fascists are denied the right to free speech. A danger exists, however, that if some people are stripped of their rights and freedoms, this may lead to a greater erosion of rights and freedoms for us all. Indeed, in today's world, there is a risk that the books we borrow from the library, the websites we visit, and the phone conversations we initiate may be monitored by a government agency.

How, then, can we balance individual rights and freedoms against the interests of society as a whole? For example, although most of us value freedom of

---

[1]Some measures expired in 2007, and the government's attempt to renew these provisions failed to pass in the House of Commons. The courts eventually struck down some other measures (such as indefinite prison terms for non-citizens).

expression, difficult questions often arise when we apply this abstract value to particular situations. Should someone be free to publish an article that promotes hatred against a particular ethnic or racial group? What if a political party calls for the revolutionary overthrow of an elected government? Should an artist be arrested for painting a nude picture of a child? Some people hold the libertarian position that rights and freedoms should not be tampered with unless there is decisive proof of serious harm to others, while others believe that the interests of society deserve priority over the rights and freedoms of individuals.

HISTORICAL DEVELOPMENT

PARLIAMENTARY SUPREMACY
The principle that Parliament is the supreme law-making body whose ability to legislate has not been restricted by a superior constitutional document.

COMMON LAW
A body of law developed through the accumulation of court decisions that become binding precedents for similar future cases.

The British political system is based on the principle of **parliamentary supremacy**. Parliament is the supreme law-making body whose ability to legislate has not been restricted by a superior constitutional document. Unlike the United States where rights and freedoms are protected by the constitutional Bill of Rights, which can be used by the courts to invalidate legislation, the British courts cannot overturn an act of Parliament.[2] Nevertheless, the protection of individual freedom is an important part of the British political culture. The English system of **common law** (the accumulation of court decisions) reflects and reinforces this orientation to individual freedom.

Canada inherited many aspects of the British system of law and governing, including English common law (except for Quebec's system of civil law). However, unlike the United Kingdom, Canada has had a written constitution since 1867 that places some limits on the supremacy of Parliament. In particular, the *Constitution Act, 1867,* divides legislative authority between Parliament and provincial legislatures. This has given judicial bodies the power of judicial review—that is, the power to declare a law invalid because it violates the Constitution.

The *Constitution Act, 1867,* outlined only a narrow set of rights. The right to use either English or French in the Canadian Parliament, the Quebec legislature, and in federal and Quebec courts was protected, along with the existing rights and privileges of denominational schools. However, by including in the preamble to the *Constitution Act, 1867,* that Canada would have a "constitution similar in principle to that of the United Kingdom," it was assumed that traditional British liberties would continue to be respected in Canada.

The record of protecting rights and freedoms before the adoption of the *Charter of Rights and Freedoms* was far from exemplary. Although many traditional rights based on the English common-law system were respected, at times various minorities were stripped of their rights by the federal or provincial governments. For example, a variety of ethnic and religious groups had their

---

[2]The British system has been modified somewhat by the United Kingdom's membership in the European Union and the adoption of the *Human Rights Act* (1998).

right to vote taken away, Aboriginals living on reserves were denied basic human rights, and Japanese Canadians were arrested, interned, and deprived of their property during World War II.[3]

Canadian courts and the Judicial Committee of the Privy Council (JCPC)—the final court of appeal until 1949—did, on occasion, invalidate laws that interfered with rights and freedoms on the grounds that the legislative body that passed the law did not have the authority to do so under the *Constitution Act*, 1867. Less frequently, some justices used the concept of an **"implied bill of rights"** in the Constitution derived from the preamble to the *Constitution Act, 1867* (see Box 11-1, Media Accountability: The Alberta Press Case and the "Implied Bill of Rights").

The Canadian Bill of Rights

In 1960, Parliament passed the **Canadian Bill of Rights**. The Bill of Rights was quite limited in its significance. It was an ordinary statute (law), and did not clearly specify that the courts had the power to invalidate legislation that violated rights and freedoms. Nor did it fully challenge the traditional principle of the supremacy of Parliament. Rather, it contained a clause that allowed Parliament to pass a law infringing upon rights and freedoms, provided that the law made an express declaration to that effect. As well, the *War Measures Act* was excluded from the provisions of the Bill of Rights. This allowed the Canadian Cabinet, after the kidnappings of the British trade commissioner and Quebec's minister of Labour by the Front de Libération du Québec in 1970, to declare a state of apprehended insurrection and jail people without explanation and without bail. In addition, the *Canadian Bill of Rights* only applied to matters within the legislative authority of the Canadian Parliament, although most provincial governments adopted their own bills of rights (beginning with Saskatchewan in 1947).

The courts were very reluctant to use the Bill of Rights to invalidate federal legislation. For example in *Robertson and Rosetanni* (1963), the Supreme Court of Canada upheld a conviction under the *Lord's Day Act* for operating a bowling alley on Sunday. The majority opinion implied that the Bill of Rights could not be used to invalidate existing legislation (Russell et al., 2008). In the *Lavell and Bédard* case (1974), two women who had lost their Indian status for marrying non-Indians challenged the *Indian Act* as discriminatory because Indian men did not lose their status for marrying non-Indian women. In the majority opinion, it was argued that the Bill of Rights should not render "Parliament powerless" to enact "legislation which treats Indians living on Reserves differently from other Canadians in relation to their property and

IMPLIED BILL OF RIGHTS
The judicial theory that rights are implied by the preamble to the *Constitution Act,* 1867, and therefore could not be infringed by ordinary legislation.

CANADIAN BILL OF RIGHTS
An act of Parliament passed in 1960 establishing various rights and freedoms that only applied to matters under federal jurisdiction.

---

[3]The existence of a constitutional Bill of Rights did not prevent similar violations of rights in the United States.

BOX 11-1

Media Accountability:
The Alberta Press Case and the
"Implied Bill of Rights"

When the Alberta Social Credit government was elected in 1935, it decried the unflattering coverage it received in the province's newspapers. Newspapers, Premier Aberhart claimed, were filled with the propaganda of political parties that opposed the social credit philosophy. The government retaliated by directing the Alberta legislature to pass the *Accurate News and Information Act* (1937)—legislation that required newspapers to publish the government's official responses to criticisms and to disclose the names and addresses of the sources and names and addresses of those the government considered to be providing bogus news (Gibson, 2005). The Alberta press launched a legal appeal, and the Supreme Court of Canada unanimously found the act (and two other related pieces of legislation) ultra vires—that is, beyond the legislative authority of the provincial legislature.

In his comments on the case, Chief Justice Lyman Duff noted that the parliamentary institutions established by the Constitution "derive their efficacy from the free public discussion of affairs, from criticism and answer and counter-criticism, from attack upon policy and administration and defence and counter-attack; from the freest and fullest analysis and examination from every point of view of political proposals." Curtailing or suppressing debate in public meetings or through the press would be "repugnant to the provisions of the British North America Act" (quoted in Russell et al., 2008, p. 163).

Duff's view has come to be known as the "implied bill of rights." It was based on the preamble to the Constitution and was supported by another two of the six justices. Although the implied bill of rights was considered a radical change of thinking that only had a limited effect on subsequent cases, some Supreme Court justices used it to strike down a series of Quebec laws in the 1950s that interfered with political and religious freedoms (Gibson, 2005). For example, some of the Supreme Court justices referred to fundamental freedoms in striking down Quebec's *Act to Protect the Province against Communistic Propaganda* (commonly known as the "Padlock Law") that had been used to lock someone who had been distributing communist literature out of his apartment. Generally, however, the courts relied on the argument that provincial laws that restricted rights and freedoms were unconstitutional because criminal law was a responsibility of the Canadian Parliament.

The death knell to the implied bill of rights was sounded by the majority opinion of the Supreme Court of Canada in the Dupont case (1978), which stated that "none of the freedoms (speech, assembly, and association, press, and religion) is enshrined in the constitution so as to be above the reach of competent legislation" (quoted in Russell et al., 2008, p. 169). Nevertheless, the Supreme Court of Canada has come to accept unwritten constitutional values and principles as a guide to interpreting the Constitution (Gibson, 2005). In its view, the underlying constitutional principles of federalism, democracy, the rule of law, and respect for minorities "are binding on both courts and government," as "it would be impossible to conceive of our constitutional structure without them" (*Secession Reference,* 1998).

civil rights" (quoted in Russell et al., 2008, p. 186). Furthermore, the require-ment of "equality before the law" in the Bill of Rights was claimed to mean only equality in the administration and enforcement of the law. Because the *Indian Act* applied equally to all women affected by the discriminatory provi-sion, it did not violate equality before the law. In his dissent from the judgment, Justice Bora Laskin argued that upholding Parliament's ability to discriminate against Indian women under the *Indian Act* would "compound racial inequal-ity with sexual inequality" (quoted in Russell et al., 2008, p. 183).

The only case in which the Canadian Bill of Rights was used to invalidate legislation that infringed rights and freedoms involved a Status Indian who had been convicted under the provisions of the *Indian Act* for being intoxi-cated in Yellowknife while not on a reserve (although there were no reserves in the Northwest Territories). In a 6–3 decision on *Drybones,* the Supreme Court of Canada upheld the acquittal on the grounds that a provision of the *Indian Act* was discriminatory by providing a more severe penalty on the basis of race than would apply to a non-Indian. Although the judgments in *Drybones* and *Lavell and Bédard* appear contradictory, the Supreme Court viewed the policy implications of *Lavell and Bédard* as more serious; they believed that striking down the discriminatory provision would allow a large increase in the number of people who would be eligible for benefits under the *Indian Act.* In addition, the Supreme Court may have considered the political implications of challenging the provisions of the *Indian Act* at a time when First Nations were opposed to the federal government's White Paper propos-als (discussed in Chapter 12) that could end the special rights of Status Indians[4] (Russell et al., 2008).

THE CHARTER OF RIGHTS AND FREEDOMS

Liberal Prime Minister Pierre Trudeau passionately advocated the adoption of the **Charter of Rights and Freedoms.** Trudeau viewed constitutional protec-tion of rights and freedoms as necessary to prevent government from tamper-ing arbitrarily with the rights and freedoms of individuals. In the face of growing nationalism and separatism in Quebec, he also saw the protection of French and English language rights of people throughout Canada as being crucial to promoting national unity. Accordingly, in constitutional negotia-tions he pushed hard for the entrenchment of the Charter in the constitution despite the opposition of some premiers. In particular, the premiers of Mani-toba and Saskatchewan were concerned that the Charter would undermine the principle of parliamentary supremacy—the foundation of much of the

CHARTER OF RIGHTS AND FREEDOMS
As part of the *Constitution Act,* 1982, the Charter is superior to ordinary legislation, allows the courts to invalidate legislation, and applies to the actions of all governments and organizations under the control of government.

---

[4]Most organizations representing Status Indians intervened in the case to oppose the granting of Indian status to Lavell and Bédard. This discriminatory provision in the *Indian Act* was changed in 1985.

Canadian governing system. René Lévesque, the premier of Quebec, was also critical of the Charter, viewing it as imposing a centralist, uniform view of Canada.

When televised Parliamentary hearings on the proposed Charter were held, many groups supported the idea of the Charter while lobbying for various additions to it. In particular, women's groups and various ethnic groups mobilized supporters to successfully press for the adoption of provisions to provide for strong protections of women's rights and the recognition of the multicultural nature of Canada. In the end, as discussed in Chapter 10, all the premiers, except Lévesque, agreed to the inclusion of the Charter in the *Constitution Act* (with a modification to keep an element of parliamentary supremacy).

The Charter is a much more powerful tool for protecting rights and freedoms than is the *Canadian Bill of Rights*. For example, the Supreme Court of Canada used the Charter to strike down the federal *Lord's Day Act* as a violation of freedom of religion,[5] unlike its earlier decision to uphold the act using the *Canadian Bill of Rights*. The Supreme Court's judgment stated that, "the *Charter* is intended to set a standard upon which present as well as future legislation is to be tested" (*Big Drug Mart Ltd.*, 1985).

The *Constitution Act,* 1982, of which the Charter is an important part, states that the Constitution is "the supreme law of Canada, and any law that is inconsistent with the provisions of the Constitution is, to the extent of the inconsistency, of no force or effect" (section 52). Thus the Charter is clearly superior to ordinary legislation. Further, the Charter provides that anyone whose Charter rights or freedoms "have been infringed or denied may apply to a court of competent jurisdiction to obtain such remedy as the court considers appropriate and just in the circumstances" (section 24). Thus, unlike the Bill of Rights, the Charter clearly empowers the courts to invalidate legislation that is inconsistent with the Charter. Further, the Charter does not only apply to legislation passed by the Canadian Parliament and provincial legislatures, but also to the actions and policies of the Canadian, provincial, territorial, and municipal governments, as well as to agencies under the control of government or carrying out government policies. The Charter does not apply to businesses, private organizations, or the relations among individuals. The human rights codes adopted by the Canadian and provincial governments apply to situations where, for example, a business or a landlord discriminated against a person based on such characteristics as age, gender, or race. Such codes are expected to be consistent with the provisions of the Charter.

---

[5]Striking down the *Lord's Day Act* did not necessarily make provincial Sunday closing laws invalid. In *R. v. Edwards Books and Art Ltd.* (1986), Ontario's *Retail Business Holiday Act* was upheld because it was framed in secular rather than religious terms, and because it had an exemption for those small business owners who have a religious duty to close on Saturdays.

Provisions of the Charter

The Charter is more comprehensive than the *Canadian Bill of Rights* in establishing rights and freedoms. Indeed, its scope is wider than the U.S. Bill of Rights to which it is often compared (for example, by establishing language rights and equality rights). The Charter establishes seven basic categories of rights and freedoms:

The Canadian Charter of Rights and Freedoms:
http://laws.justice.gc.ca/en/charter/

- *Fundamental freedoms,* consisting of "freedom of conscience and religion; freedom of thought, belief, opinion and expression, including freedom of the press and other media of communication; freedom of peaceful assembly: and freedom of association" (sec. 2).
- *Democratic freedoms,* including the right of all citizens to vote and hold elected office as well as limiting the maximum term of the House of Commons and provincial legislatures to five years. (Parliament and several legislatures have adopted legislation setting a maximum term of four years.)
- *Mobility rights,* including the right to move and to pursue a livelihood in any province.
- *Legal rights,* including the right to life, liberty, and security of the person, the right to a trial within a reasonable period of time if charged with an offence, the right to be secure against unreasonable search or seizure, and the right to be presumed innocent until proven guilty by an independent and impartial tribunal.
- *Equality rights,* including the provision that every person is equal under the law and has the right to the equal protection and equal benefit of the law without discrimination on such grounds as race, national or ethnic origin, colour, religion, sex, age, or disability. This does not preclude laws, programs, or activities designed to improve the conditions of disadvantaged individuals or groups. The equality rights clause was at the centre of the issue of same-sex marriage (as discussed in Box 11-2, Same-Sex Marriage: Kevin and Joe, Elaine and Anne, and the Charter of Rights).
- *Language rights,* including the right to communicate with and receive services in English or French from Canadian government offices where there is sufficient demand. New Brunswick is the only province that has established the same right in the Charter.
- *Minority language education rights,* including the right of Canadian citizens whose mother tongue is either English or French to have their children educated in that language where numbers warrant. In Quebec this right only applies to parents who received their primary schooling in English in Canada.

Other provisions of the Charter require that "the Charter shall be interpreted in a manner consistent with the preservation and enhancement of the multicultural heritage of Canada," and that the rights and freedoms in the

BOX 11-2

Same-Sex Marriage:
Kevin and Joe, Elaine and Anne,
and the Charter of Rights

On January 14, 2001, two couples, Kevin Bourassa and Joe Varnell and Elaine and Anne Vautour, exchanged wedding vows in Toronto's Metropolitan Community Church. They were in love and ready to commit but the Ontario government refused to register the wedding licences of the two same-sex couples. The couples undertook legal actions challenging the 1866 common law definition of marriage: "as understood in Christendom . . . the voluntary union for life of one man and one woman, to the exclusion of all others" (quoted in Russell et al., 2008, p. 364). The definition was, argued the challengers, a violation of equality rights provisions of the Charter. In fact, courts in a number of provinces ruled that the prohibition on same-sex marriage was unconstitutional, and the Ontario government registered the marriages in 2003.

The Canadian government did not appeal the rulings of the provincial courts of appeal, but instead drafted its own legislation: "Marriage, for

▲ Recognition of same-sex equality rights in Canada came after much struggle. Couples Kevin Bourassa (left, glasses) and Joe Varnell and Anne Vautour and Elaine Vautour (right) may have exchanged wedding vows in front of Reverend Brent Hawkes in January 2001, but their marriages were not officially registered until 2003.

civil purposes, is the lawful union of two persons to the exclusion of all others in terms of the union of two persons." The Liberal government anticipated stormy opposition to the legalization of same-sex marriage and therefore asked the Supreme Court of Canada for a reference opinion on four questions related to the proposed legislation. The Supreme Court confirmed that Parliament has the legislative authority to decide who may marry, that extending the capacity to marry to persons of the same sex is consistent with the Charter, and that the Charter's guarantee of freedom of religion protects religious officials from being forced to perform same-sex marriages contrary to their religious beliefs. The Supreme Court refused to answer the fourth question— whether an opposite-sex requirement for marriage is consistent with the Charter—since the government had not pursued an appeal to the ruling of the lower courts on this issue. Already, thousands of same-sex couples had been legally married as a result of the lower court decisions.

In upholding same-sex marriage, the courts followed the Supreme Court of Canada's ruling in *M. v. H.* (1999); in that case, the Court ruled that two women who had been in a same-sex relationship for at least five years were not being treated equally by being denied access to the same support system as married spouses upon the breakup of their relationship. Furthermore, the Court stated, "the human dignity of individuals in same-sex relationships is violated by the definition of 'spouse' in terms of opposite sex relationships in Ontario's Family Law Act" (quoted in Russell et al., 2008, p. 339).

To the cheers of the gay and lesbian community and the jeers of Catholic bishops, Canada became one of the world's first countries to officially recognize same-sex marriages.

Charter "are guaranteed equally to male and female persons." In addition, the rights and freedoms specified in the Charter do not affect any treaty or other rights or freedoms of Aboriginal peoples (see Chapter 12).

However, the Charter does not contain provisions for all of the rights and freedoms that some people would like. Some were disappointed that **social rights** such as the right to education, housing, or employment are not mentioned. Such rights (which are articulated in some of the international treaties Canada has signed) require government action, including government spending, to provide the rights. Others were disappointed that property rights were not explicitly protected.

The rights and freedoms listed in the Charter are quite broadly written and can even be considered somewhat vague. The courts have to interpret these rights as they apply to the particular cases that come before them. Judges are expected to examine precedents—that is, how the courts have interpreted a particular clause in similar cases. In particular, the lower courts are expected to follow the interpretations of the Supreme Court of Canada. However the Supreme Court has not always felt bound by its previous rulings. For example, in 1987 the Supreme Court rejected the idea that collective bargaining is protected by the Charter. In *Health Services and Support,* 2007, the Supreme Court stated that its earlier decision did not "withstand principled scrutiny," and ruled that the Charter's freedom of association provision protected the process of collective bargaining (quoted in Russell et al., 2008, p. 396).

Limitations on Rights and Freedoms

The Charter does not provide absolute guarantees of listed rights and freedoms. In particular, the Charter allows "reasonable limits" on rights and freedoms. As well, through the "notwithstanding" clause, Parliament and provincial legislatures can pass laws that contradict some of the Charter's provisions.

THE "REASONABLE LIMITS" CLAUSE   Clause 1 of the Charter guarantees that the rights and freedoms in the Charter are "subject only to such reasonable limits prescribed by law as can be demonstrably justified in a free and democratic society." If in ruling on a particular case a court decides that a particular law or government action violates the Charter, the **reasonable limits clause** places the onus on the government to provide evidence to demonstrate that the law or action is a reasonable limit on rights and freedoms. It is, however, a matter of judgment as to what reasonable limit is justified in a free and democratic society. How much and what kind of evidence is needed to "demonstrably" justify the limit on rights and freedoms is also often hotly debated.

In developing the "**Oakes test**," the Supreme Court of Canada laid out the basic principles to apply in determining whether a limit on rights and freedoms is justified in a particular case (see Box 11-3, Innocent Until Proven Guilty? David Oakes and the *Narcotics Control Act*).

SOCIAL RIGHTS
Rights that require government action, such as the right to education, housing, or employment.

REASONABLE LIMITS CLAUSE
A clause of the *Charter of Rights and Freedoms* that allows for reasonable limits on rights and freedoms, provided the limits can be demonstrably justified in a free and democratic society.

OAKES TEST
A Supreme Court of Canada ruling setting out basic principles in applying the reasonable limits clause.

BOX 11-3

Innocent Until Proven Guilty? David Oakes and the *Narcotics Control Act*

David Edwin Oakes was arrested outside an Ontario tavern in 1981 and was found to be in possession of $619.45 and eight one-gram vials of hashish oil. He was charged with trafficking under the *Narcotics Control Act,* which carries a much more severe penalty (potentially life imprisonment) than for simple possession. The act required that the accused had to prove they were not engaged in trafficking if they claimed they were only in possession.

The lawyer for Mr. Oakes challenged the *Narcotics Control Act,* arguing that it violated the right to be considered innocent until proven guilty that is guaranteed in the Charter—it was therefore up to the Crown prosecutor to prove that David Oakes was guilty of trafficking, not up to the defendant to prove his innocence. After the court hearing the case struck down the provision in the act concerning trafficking, the Supreme Court of Canada was eventually called upon to decide if the act's provision was a reasonable limit on a guaranteed legal right.

In their ruling, the judges laid out two criteria that together could help determine when "reasonable limits" could be used to uphold a law that interfered with the rights and freedoms in the Charter:

1. The objective of the law "must be sufficiently important to warrant overriding a constitutionally protected right or freedom." That is, the objective must at least "relate to societal concerns which are pressing and substantial in a free and democratic society."

2. The interests of society must be balanced against the rights and freedoms of individuals and groups. Specifically,

   - the measures contained in the law "must be carefully designed to achieve the objective in question" and "rationally connected to the objective,"
   - the measures "should impair as little as possible the right or freedom in question," and

   - the more harmful the effects of the measures are in limiting rights and freedoms, the more important the objective must be.

Applying these criteria to the Oakes case, the judges agreed that drug trafficking was a "substantial and pressing" concern, thus meeting the first criterion. However, the second criterion was not fulfilled, since there was "no rational connection" between the possession of a small amount of hashish oil and the presumption that the possession was for the purpose of trafficking. Therefore the judges concluded that section 8 of the *Narcotics Control Act* was of "no force and effect," and the appeal of the acquittal of Oakes was dismissed (*Oakes,* 1986).

The "Oakes test" has been used in a large number of cases since 1986, although not always resulting in an acquittal of the accused. For example, in *Keegstra* (1990), the Supreme Court of Canada upheld the conviction of a high school teacher under the "hate speech" provision of the Criminal Code for his wilful promotion of hatred against Jews in his classes. The justices found that the "hate speech" provision infringed upon the Charter's guarantee of freedom of speech. However the majority of justices upheld the provision, finding that hate propaganda was a "pressing and substantial concern," that there was a rational connection between the law and the objective of the law, that freedom of expression was impaired as little as possible, and that the limitation of hate speech is "only tenuously connected with the values underlying the guarantee of freedom of speech" (quoted in Russell et al., 2008, p. 282).

Although David Oakes succeeded in avoiding a lengthy jail term, the "test" that bears his name has not always been vigorously applied by the courts to invalidate laws that the government claims place "reasonable limits" on rights and freedoms (MacIvor, 2006).

THE "NOTWITHSTANDING" CLAUSE   The Charter allows Parliament or provincial legislatures to override some provisions of the Charter by using the **notwithstanding clause**. This involves a legislative body explicitly declaring that a particular law shall operate *notwithstanding* the provisions of the Charter. Such a declaration is effective for only five years, although it can be re-enacted as often as is desired.

The notwithstanding clause applies to three types of rights:

1. fundamental freedoms,
2. legal rights, and
3. equality rights (other than male–female equality).

Democratic rights, mobility rights, and language rights cannot be overridden.

The requirement that legislation has to explicitly state that the Charter is being overridden makes it politically risky for a government to use the notwithstanding clause, as the government may be accused of trampling on individual rights (as discussed in Box 11-4, No Kids but Compensation: Sexual Sterilization and the Notwithstanding Clause). Thus far, the notwithstanding clause has not been frequently used. The most widely publicized and significant use of the clause was by the Quebec government in 1988. As discussed in Chapter 4, the Quebec National Assembly passed a law banning languages other than French on signs outside businesses and invoked the notwithstanding clause to protect the law from being challenged as a violation of the right to freedom of expression. However, the Quebec government did not seek to renew its use of the notwithstanding clause when the five-year limit ran out and instead passed less restrictive legislation.

The Quebec government also included the clause in all legislation between 1982 and 1985 as a protest against the passage of the *Constitution Act, 1982*.

NOTWITHSTANDING CLAUSE
A provision in the *Charter of Rights and Freedoms* that allows a Parliament or a provincial legislature to explicitly declare that a particular law (related to some sections of the Charter) shall operate notwithstanding the provisions of the Charter.

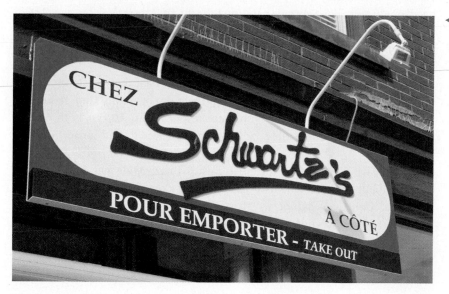

◄ When the Quebec National Assembly banned languages other than French from signs outside businesses in 1988, it invoked the notwithstanding clause to protect the law from a Charter challenge. Although French must still dominate, the language restrictions have loosened since 2003, as seen in this sign outside the venerable Schwartz's deli in Montreal.

No Kids but Compensation: Sexual Sterilization and the Notwithstanding Clause

In 1928, the Alberta legislature passed the *Sexual Sterilization Act* to prevent those deemed to be mentally incompetent or unsuitable as parents from having children. About 2800 were sterilized, many without their consent or even knowledge, before the law was repealed in 1972. Fifty-eight percent of those sterilized were women. Teenagers, the poor, Aboriginals and other minorities, and those with a history of alcoholism or other problems in their family were also singled out. As Margaret Gunn, president of the United Farm Women, a group that actively campaigned for the legislation, argued, sterilization will "achieve racial betterment through the weeding out of undesirables" (quoted in Grekul, 2008, p. 250).

Faced with claims for compensation by the victims, the Alberta government introduced legislation in 1998 (the *Institutional Confinement and Sexual Sterilization Compensation Act*) to limit compensation to a maximum of $150 000 per person. The proposed act included the notwithstanding clause. Immediately there was a public outcry against the proposed legislation, with the *Edmonton Journal* running the front-page headline, "Province Revokes Rights." Within twenty-four hours the government withdrew the proposed legislation. Eventually the claims were settled for a total of about $142 million (McLachlin, 2005).

Although governments have contemplated invoking the notwithstanding clause on a number of occasions, they have usually decided to avoid its use, fearing that, as in the case of the Compensation Act, there will be serious political consequences.

There have been only a very small number of other uses, none of which have been significant. For example, an amendment to Alberta's *Marriage Act* to define marriage as involving only opposite-sex couples turned out to be irrelevant when the Supreme Court of Canada ruled that defining marriage is a federal responsibility.

The notwithstanding clause is highly controversial. For some, the clause potentially undermines the Charter's protection of rights and freedoms. Others argue that it allows the ultimate responsibility to rest with elected representatives of the people rather than unelected and unaccountable judges.

Progressive Conservative Prime Minister Brian Mulroney criticized the clause, claiming that "any constitution that does not protect . . . the rights of individual Canadians is not worth the paper it is written on" (quoted in Manfredi, 2003). In contrast, during the 2004 Canadian election campaign, Conservative leader Stephen Harper said that he would use the clause to strengthen child pornography laws and perhaps to deny same-sex couples the right to marry. Liberal leader Paul Martin strongly criticized Harper, saying that a Liberal government would never use the clause.[6] The issue surfaced again in the 2006 election. Martin accused Harper of wanting to use the clause to take away the rights of minorities and women. Instead, Martin promised to amend the constitution to remove the ability of Parliament to use the clause. Harper countered the criticism by promising not to use the clause to overturn the law allowing same-sex marriages.

The Significance of the Charter

The *Charter of Rights and Freedoms* is not simply a statement of principles that governments are expected to follow. Rather, the courts are expected to uphold the Charter, and can choose from a variety of possible remedies when deciding on cases where rights and freedoms have been denied. Peter Hogg (2006) lists six types of remedies:

- Strike down (nullify) a law that is inconsistent with the Charter.
- Postpone the nullification of a law for a given period in order to give a legislative body time to correct the legislation.
- Strike down the offending parts of a law without nullifying the entire law.
- "Read in" additional words to make the law more inclusive. (For an example of "reading in," see Box 11-5, Is Honesty the Best Policy? Human Rights Legislation and Sexual Orientation.)
- "Read down" a law, meaning that the courts can choose a narrower rather than a broader interpretation of a law to make it conform to the Charter.
- Grant an exemption to individuals or groups from legislation that would violate the Charter if it applied to them. For example, a Sunday store-closing law could exempt those who observe a different day of rest to protect their freedom of religion.

The Supreme Court has only occasionally used the "read in," "read down," or exemption-granting remedies, wishing to avoid, in effect, writing legislation. As well, the Supreme Court of Canada has often preferred to give a legislative body a chance to change a law rather than simply striking it down. Generally, the courts have accepted the rewritten version of the law, even when the law uses a different approach to resolving the conflict with the Charter than the strategy suggested by the Supreme Court (MacIvor, 2006).

HAS THE CHARTER MADE THE COURTS TOO POWERFUL? The *Charter of Rights and Freedoms* has increased the importance of the courts in the governing of Canada. Many important public policies have been affected or determined by Supreme Court decisions based on their interpretation of the

---

[6]Earlier, however, Martin had said he might use the clause if needed to protect churches that refused to perform same-sex marriages (MacIvor, 2006).

Is Honesty the Best Policy? Human Rights Legislation and Sexual Orientation

In 1991, Delwin Vriend was fired from the position he had held for three years as laboratory coordinator and instructor at the King's College, Edmonton, after he disclosed that he was gay. Vriend was raised as a member of the evangelical Christian Reformed Church (which was involved in the founding of King's College).

The Alberta Human Rights Commission turned down his complaint of discrimination because Alberta's *Individual Rights Protection Act* did not include sexual orientation in its list of prohibited grounds for discrimination. Vriend then challenged the act in court on the grounds that it violated the equality rights provisions of the Canadian Charter.

In the Supreme Court of Canada's opinion, even though sexual orientation is not specifically mentioned in the equality rights clause of the Charter, it is comparable to the other categories of prohibited discrimination (such as race and sex). By excluding gays and lesbians who suffer from discrimination, the act implicitly sent a message that they are not equal in dignity and rights—a message that offends the principle of the equality provision. Further, the act could not be saved by the "reasonable limits" clause because the exclusion of sexual orientation contradicts the objective of the act, which is to protect and promote human rights. Rather than striking down the act, which would strip all Albertans of human rights protection, the Court chose the remedy of "reading in" (adding) sexual orientation to the sections of the act covering prohibited grounds of discrimination (*Vriend v. Alberta,* 1998).

Several members of the Alberta legislative assembly tried to persuade Premier Ralph Klein to introduce legislation to overturn the Supreme Court's decision. Their proposed weapon? The notwithstanding clause! Klein initially considered this strategy, but in the end decided not to pursue it. As for Vriend, he later found a position at the University of Alberta, but eventually left Canada because he could not escape the media spotlight. His was one of the rare cases in which the Supreme Court resorted to a "read in" solution to correct a perceived injustice.

Charter. For example, the Supreme Court ruled that the government needed to amend the *Unemployment Insurance Act* because it did not provide benefits to biological fathers that were given to fathers of adopted children (*Schachter,* 1992).

Does this mean that the tradition of parliamentary supremacy has been replaced by judicial supremacy (Morton, 2003)? Those who argue that we now have a system of judicial supremacy point out that the courts have gone beyond the wording of the Charter to impose their own views about rights and freedoms. Others argue that Canada has moved toward a system of "constitutional supremacy" rather than "judicial supremacy," as the courts are simply ensuring that the laws and government actions conform to the provisions of the Charter and other constitutional provisions that were approved by Parliament and almost all provincial legislatures (Kelly & Murphy, 2001).

Although the power of the courts to strike down legislation using the Charter might be viewed as undemocratic, Peter Hogg and Allison Thornton (1997, 1999) have argued that the Charter has created a "dialogue" between the Supreme Court of Canada and legislative bodies. They point out that striking down legislation seldom stops a legislative body from pursuing a particular objective. A legislative body can use the notwithstanding clause to override a Charter-based decision it does not want to accept (for some aspects of the Charter). Second, it can modify the legislation so that it satisfies the "reasonable limits" provision, particularly by ensuring that it does not damage the right or freedom more than necessary. Third, a legislative body can make use of the qualifications of rights in the Charter. For example, when some of the provisions of the *Anti-Combines Act* were struck down by the Supreme Court on the grounds that they violated "the right to be secure from unreasonable search and seizure" of section 8 of the Charter, Parliament changed the provision to require a warrant issued by a judge to authorize these actions (Hogg & Thornton, 1999, pp. 21–22).

The "**Charter dialogue**" that Hogg and Thornton refer to does not involve a tête-à-tête over coffee or an exchange of memos. Rather, they point out that the decisions of Supreme Court justices often contain suggestions as to how to modify a law to make it acceptable. Critics have argued that this does not really constitute a "dialogue" among equals because the legislative body will tend to change a law to reflect the Supreme Court's wishes. For example, F. L. Morton (1999) contends that what is described "as a dialogue is usually a monologue, with judges doing most of the talking and legislatures most of the listening" (p. 26). Furthermore, the notwithstanding clause has rarely been used because the public does not view it as legitimate, and so it is not a very useful tool for limiting "judicial supremacy."

The claim that the Charter had created "judicial supremacy" was most persuasive in the years following its adoption, when the courts were most active in striking down legislation. In recent years fewer laws have been invalidated (MacIvor, 2006). To some extent this is a result of the more careful drafting of legislation to avoid a Charter challenge. Indirectly, the Supreme Court may be considered to be powerful as legislators try to anticipate how the Court will react to their legislative proposals. Nevertheless, the courts seem to be generally more deferential to the wishes of legislative bodies than was the case in the earlier years of the Charter (see Box 11-6, Empty Coffers, Hollow Justice? Pay Equity and the Charter). Overall, in analyzing a variety of key rulings, Ian Greene (2006) concluded that "the Supreme Court of Canada's approach to the Charter could, at best, be described as mildly activist" (p. 148).

CHARTER DIALOGUE
The view that the Charter has created a dialogue between the courts and legislatures.

BOX 11-6

Empty Coffers, Hollow Justice?
Pay Equity and the Charter

In 1988 the government of Newfoundland signed a pay equity agreement to improve the wages of public employees in female-dominated occupations in the health care field who were paid less than those in male-dominated occupations but who performed work of equal value. The health care workers (both female and male), whose salaries would have increased by several thousand dollars per year, were jubilant. Then in 1991, the provincial government passed the *Public Sector Restraint Act*, which nixed the increases for the previous three years, saving the government about $24 million.

The Newfoundland Association of Public Employees challenged the act. In 2004 the Supreme Court of Canada handed down its ruling: The act involved gender discrimination and thus violated the equality clause of the Charter. However, to the dismay of the workers who stood to benefit, the Supreme Court accepted the provincial government's argument that it was a "reasonable limit." The Court's rationale was simple—the province of Newfoundland was facing a severe financial crisis* (*Newfoundland [Treasury Board] v. N.A.P.E*, 2004).

The willingness of the Supreme Court to consider the financial implications of its decision contrasts with some of its earlier rulings that had, in effect, imposed financial burdens on the Canadian government. For example, to comply with a Supreme Court decision in 1985 requiring a mandatory oral hearing for those seeking refugee status, the Canadian government set up a program costing nearly $200 million and provided an amnesty for 15 000 claimants (Knopff & Morton, 1992).

---

*In 2006, the government of Newfoundland and Labrador decided to give $24 million in back pay to those who had been deprived of the promised increase from 1988 to 1991.

Whether or not we view the courts as too powerful, clearly the Charter has given them an expanded role in the policy process. While judges are skilled at carefully analyzing the wording of legislation and constitutional provisions, the courts are not well equipped to deal with complex matters of public policy. The training and legalistic orientation of judges does not necessarily prepare them to consider the impact of their judgments on society and the economy—for example, how overturning a ban on private heath insurance for basic medical services (*Chaoulli*, 2005) might affect Canada's system of universal public health care. Unlike government, they do not have the staff to weigh the possible consequences of their rulings. In fact, the courts rarely oversee the implementation of the rulings they hand down. Thus they do not have the opportunity to learn from observing how well their rulings work in practice.

EFFECTS ON THE POLITICAL PROCESS   The Charter has affected the political process. Because of the importance of some of the decisions made by the courts in applying the Charter, many groups and individuals find it useful or necessary to use the courts to advance or defend their interests. The courts have encouraged this development by allowing a variety of groups to have intervener status so that they can present their positions in court. The Charter has thus provided another avenue for groups and individuals to engage in the political process. This is particularly helpful for groups that have trouble making their voices heard by government, legislators, and political parties. From a different perspective, conservative critics of the courts have argued that feminists, civil liberties groups, those seeking greater social equality, and other "special interests" have succeeded in advancing causes that would not garner support from a majority of the public (Morton & Knopff, 2000). However, while groups seeking social change have gained considerable attention through their Charter cases, business interests have also made extensive use of the Charter (Hein, 2000).

A problem with using the courts to advance political interests is that it is very expensive. Taking a case to the Supreme Court of Canada can cost hundreds of thousands of dollars in legal fees. Governments have helped some groups with the legal costs of Charter cases. However, as discussed in Chapter 7, funding for the Court Challenges Program was eliminated in 2006. Not only is legal action costly, it can also be a very slow process. It often takes many years before a case makes it to the Supreme Court. Thus individuals may find their rights and freedoms limited for many years while their case works its way through the court system.

It has also been argued that the Charter in "legalizing politics" does little to invigorate democracy. By shifting the focus of political action to legal abstractions, it can muddy political issues and divert energies away from a political struggle for change (Mandel, 1994).

DOES THE CHARTER HELP TO FOSTER NATIONAL UNITY? The Charter defines a set of national values and may help to create a common sense of being Canadian based on our common possession of rights and freedoms. The Charter focuses attention on the rights of national groups, including women, ethnic minorities, and people with disabilities, and on national issues (such as abortion and same-sex marriage) rather than on the concerns and grievances of particular provinces or regions (Cairns, 1992). And a national institution (the Supreme Court of Canada) has gained in power and visibility as a result of the Charter.

However, the Charter may also be responsible for creating an atmosphere in which individuals and groups aggressively assert and demand their rights. In making decisions that support the rights of one group, the courts may stir up conflicts between groups. Politicians often try to make decisions that balance the views or interests of different groups. Yet judges tend to make their decisions based on principles that clearly distinguish winners and losers. In this respect, the ability of the Charter to foster national unity may be limited.

Summary and Conclusion

The *Charter of Rights and Freedoms*, incorporated into the Constitution in 1982, has become a key aspect of the Canadian political system. It has increased the power of the courts by providing them with extensive grounds on which to overturn laws and government actions. With the addition of the Charter, many Canadians feel that the constitution is something relevant to the people, rather than just governments.

The ability of the courts to invalidate legislation is sometimes viewed as undemocratic. One concern is that elected representatives have little or no involvement in the selection of judges. And once appointed, judges are not accountable for their decisions. However, even though court decisions may not reflect the views of the majority of citizens, the ability of the courts to invalidate legislation that strips individuals and minority groups of their rights and freedoms is consistent with liberal democratic values. Indeed, the courts have used the Charter to expand the scope of rights and freedoms on controversial topics such as gay and lesbian rights, which politicians have often hesitated to address. Overall, the Charter, as interpreted by the courts, has protected the diversity of Canadian society.

Although the entrenchment of the Charter in the constitution gives considerable potential power to the courts, the notwithstanding clause may be viewed as a partial reaffirmation of the principle of parliamentary supremacy. However, with governments reluctant to use the notwithstanding clause, this remaining element of parliamentary supremacy has played a limited role. Instead, the "reasonable limits" clause provides an opportunity for government to defend legislation that places limits on rights and freedoms, provided it can convince the courts that such limits are necessary and compatible with a free and democratic society.

The existence of the Charter does not fully guarantee that rights and freedoms will be protected. Governments, police, and security forces do sometimes infringe upon rights and freedoms. It often takes many years before laws that violate rights and freedoms are successfully challenged, and the oversight of police and security forces is often inadequate to ensure that they operate in keeping with the Charter.

Some of those who hoped that the Charter would usher in a new era of much greater social and economic equality have been disappointed. Although discriminatory laws have been struck down, the lack of an explicit set of social and economic rights in the Charter has meant that the courts have generally been reluctant to require governments to adopt policies to reduce social and economic inequalities.

Nevertheless, by providing a check on the arbitrary actions of government, protecting rights and freedoms, and challenging laws that do not provide equal benefits, the Charter (as applied by the courts) plays an important part in moving Canada further in the direction of good government that can benefit us all.

Discussion Questions

1. Should the notwithstanding clause be removed from the *Charter of Rights and Freedoms*?

2. Should additional rights such as the right to an education, health care, and housing be added to the *Charter of Rights and Freedoms*? What about property rights?

3. Has the Charter made the courts too powerful?

4. Should the *Charter of Rights and Freedoms* be suspended when there is a threat of terrorism?

5. Do you think there is a proper balance in Canada between the rights and freedoms of individuals and the good of the country as a whole?

Further Reading

Hiebert, J. (2002). *Charter conflicts: What is Parliament's role?* Montreal, QC: McGill-Queen's University Press.

Howe, P., & Russell, P. (Eds.). (2001). *Judicial power and Canadian democracy.* Montreal, QC: McGill-Queen's University Press.

Kelly, J. P. (2005). *Governing with the Charter.* Vancouver: UBC Press.

MacIvor, H. (2006). *Canadian politics and government in the Charter era.* Toronto, ON: Thomson Nelson.

Mandel, M. (1994). *The Charter of Rights and the legalization of politics in Canada* (rev. ed.). Toronto, ON: Wall and Thompson.

Manfredi, C. (2003). *Judicial power and the Charter: Canada and the paradox of liberal constitutionalism* (2nd ed.). Don Mills, ON: Oxford University Press.

Morton, F. L., & Knopff, R. (2000). *The Charter revolution and the court party.* Peterborough, ON: Broadview Press.

Roach, K. (2001). *The Supreme Court on trial: Judicial activism or democratic dialogue.* Toronto, ON: Irwin Law.

Sharpe, R. J., & Roach, K. (2005). *The Charter of Rights and Freedoms* (3rd ed.). Toronto: Irwin.

Chapter 12

ABORIGINAL RIGHTS AND GOVERNANCE

PHOTO ABOVE: Under the gaze of then Assembly of First Nations Chief Phil Fontaine (right, wearing headdress), Prime Minister Stephen Harper stands in the House of Commons on June 11, 2008, to officially apologize on behalf of all Canadians to former students of Native residential schools for more than a century of abuse and cultural loss involving the schools and their programs.

CHAPTER OBJECTIVES

After reading this chapter, you should be able to

1. Outline the historical background of the relations between Aboriginal peoples and the Canadian government.
2. Explain the significance of constitutional changes and court cases in establishing Aboriginal rights.
3. Examine the key features of recent land claims settlements.
4. Describe the changes to government policy concerning Aboriginal peoples in recent times.
5. Discuss alternative approaches to the position of Aboriginal peoples in Canada.

Phil Fontaine, then head of the Assembly of Manitoba Chiefs, shocked Canadians in 1990 when he revealed in a national television interview that he had been subjected to ten years of physical and sexual abuse at the Fort Alexander Indian Residential School. Although he was reluctant to provide the details of the abuse that the children at his school had experienced, he did say that his aunt had been stripped and whipped by a priest in front of a class (Fontaine, 1990). In the following years, other Aboriginals across Canada came forward with similar stories of abuse in residential schools.

The residential schools funded by the Canadian government and run primarily by the Catholic, Anglican, United, and Presbyterian churches reflected the persistent view that Aboriginals were primitive, should give up their native customs, and needed to be taught European values. The first residential school was established in 1883, and in 1920 education was made mandatory for Aboriginal children aged seven to fifteen. From 1883 until the last school was closed in 1998, about 160 000 First Nations, Inuit, and Métis children were enrolled in the residential school system.

Children were forcibly removed from their parents to attend schools that were often distant from their homes. They were not allowed to speak their native languages during and outside class hours, and many were beaten for violating this rule. They were taught that their culture was inferior and were required to adopt the Christian religion. Physical and sexual abuse by those in authority was common, and there was a high death rate as a result of malnutrition and tuberculosis in the more crowded schools. Many students tried to run away, and some committed suicide to escape their horrific treatment. The residential school experience had the effect of making many Aboriginals ashamed of their ancestry and heritage, and disrupted the transmission of language and culture from parents and other family and community members to children.

While some who went through the residential school system turned to alcohol, drugs, and prostitution, Phil Fontaine pursued his education, receiving a degree in political studies at the University of Manitoba. As National Chief of the Assembly of First Nations from 1997 to 2000 and 2003 to 2009, he worked to achieve reconciliation by seeking an apology for past injustices at the residential schools and compensation for the victims of abuse.

Faced with the threat of lawsuits on behalf of thousands of victims, the Canadian government eventually accepted responsibility and paid about $1.9 billion in compensation for the victims of residential schools. The religious denominations that ran most of the schools apologized to the victims. Finally, in June 2008, in the presence of Fontaine and other Aboriginal leaders, Prime Minister Harper issued a formal apology in the House of Commons and asked the forgiveness of Aboriginal peoples for the great harm caused by the policy of assimilation and the abuse of helpless children who were separated from their "powerless families and communities" (Harper, 2008).

THE ABORIGINAL PEOPLES OF CANADA

Nearly 1.2 million Canadians (3.8 percent of Canada's total population) consider themselves as having an Aboriginal identity according to the 2006 census (see Table 12-1). Moreover, the Aboriginal population (North American Indian or First Nation, Inuit, and Métis) is growing rapidly, increasing 45 percent between 1996 and 2006 compared with just 8 percent for the non-Aboriginal population (Statistics Canada, 2009). In addition to a higher birth rate, a greater number of those with Aboriginal ancestry are now willing to describe themselves as having an Aboriginal identity.

Although Aboriginals are taking greater pride in their identity and enjoying some improvements in their living conditions, they are still much worse off than other Canadians. The average lifespan of Aboriginals is several years less than other Canadians. There is an exceptionally high rate of suicide among Aboriginals (see Box 12-1, Undue Hardship: The Innu of Davis Inlet). Average incomes are substantially lower than those of other Canadians, and unemployment rates are higher. As well, many Aboriginals live in crowded accommodations and in houses requiring major repairs. Aboriginal youth are more likely than other Canadians to drop out of school and less likely to attend university or college. The rates of violent crime and alcohol and drug abuse among

TABLE 12-1
ABORIGINAL IDENTITY POPULATION (PERCENTAGE)

*The total Aboriginal identity population includes the Aboriginal groups (North American Indian, Métis and Inuit), multiple Aboriginal responses, and Aboriginal responses not included elsewhere.

	TOTAL ABORIGINAL IDENTITY POPULATION*	NORTH AMERICAN INDIAN	MÉTIS	INUIT	NON-ABORIGINAL IDENTITY POPULATION
Canada	**3.8**	**2.2**	**1.2**	**0.2**	**96.2**
Newfoundland and Labrador	4.7	1.6	1.3	0.9	95.3
Prince Edward Island	1.3	0.9	0.3	0.0	98.7
Nova Scotia	2.7	1.7	0.9	0.0	97.3
New Brunswick	2.5	1.7	0.6	0.0	97.5
Quebec	1.5	0.9	0.4	0.1	98.5
Ontario	2.0	1.3	0.6	0.0	98.0
Manitoba	15.5	8.9	6.3	0.0	84.5
Saskatchewan	14.9	9.6	5.0	0.0	85.1
Alberta	5.8	3.0	2.6	0.0	94.2
British Columbia	4.8	3.2	1.5	0.0	95.2
Yukon Territory	25.1	20.8	2.6	0.8	74.9
Northwest Territories	50.3	30.8	8.7	10.1	49.7
Nunavut	85.0	0.3	0.4	84.0	15.0

Source: *Statistics Canada, 2008,* Aboriginal identity population by age groups, median age and sex, percentage distribution (2006), for Canada, provinces and territories - 20% sample data *(table);* Aboriginal Peoples Highlight Tables, 2006 Census, *Catalogue no. 97-558-XWE2006002, Statistics Canada. Retrieved from http://www12.statcan.ca/english/census06/data/highlights/aboriginal/index.cfm?Lang=E.*

BOX 12-1

Undue Hardship:
The Innu of Davis Inlet

In February 1993, the Innu (First Nation) community of Davis Inlet, located on a remote island off the Labrador coast with a population of about 500, attracted worldwide attention. A video broadcast internationally showed six children from Davis Inlet inhaling gasoline fumes and screaming that they wanted to die. Equally alarming was a disaster that had taken place the previous year, when six unattended children between six months and nine years old had died in a house fire while their parents were drinking at a Valentine's Day dance.

Tragically, these were not isolated events. Many adults in Davis Inlet were alcoholics, and about one-quarter of all adults in the community had attempted suicide in the previous year. More shockingly, many children in the community, some as young as five years old, were chronic abusers of gasoline and other solvents ("Davis Inlet," 2005).

The problems the Innu face can be traced back to the change from their nomadic life hunting caribou in the interior of Labrador to their settlement around Davis Inlet on the coast, close to a Hudson's Bay trading post and a Catholic priest. They became dependent on a cash economy and were cut off from Innu spirituality because of the pressure to adopt Christianity. In 1948, the Newfoundland government closed the government depot at Davis Inlet and moved the Innu to Nutak on the barren north coast of Labrador. Two years later, intent on returning home, they walked back to Davis Inlet.

In 1967, government officials, a priest, and the unelected leader of the Innu persuaded the Innu to move the Davis Inlet community to Iluikoyak Island, eleven kilometres off the Labrador coast (Press, 1995). The island location made it difficult to continue the hunting that had been their primary source of food and the key aspect of their lifestyle. The promises that modern facilities would be provided were not kept; the island is solid rock, and installing water and sewage facilities proved too expensive. Most residents lived in small, uninsulated houses in one of the harshest climates to be found anywhere. Indeed, reporters compared Davis Inlet to communities in the impoverished Third World. Beset with hardships, the Innu people received no benefits from the huge iron mines and massive hydroelectric generation that took hold on the lands they once occupied.

Shamed by negative publicity in 1993, the Canadian government agreed to relocate the Innu to Natuashish (Shango Bay) on the mainland of Labrador at a cost of nearly $200 million. Nevertheless, the problems of suicide, violence, alcoholism, and drug usage continued to plague the community. In 2008 the community voted by a very narrow margin to ban alcohol. Fortunately, the level of violence and crime in the community has declined and, for the first time, students are completing their high school education.

Although Davis Inlet may be an extreme case, many Aboriginal communities in Canada suffer from harrowing social problems. To a considerable extent, these problems can be traced to the destruction of traditional ways of life, inappropriate government policies, discrimination, and the lack of economic and social opportunities. The plight of this country's Aboriginal peoples continues to trouble many Canadians who believe in equal opportunity and social justice.

Aboriginals are substantially higher than the Canadian average, and a dispro-portionate number of prison inmates are of Aboriginal ancestry. Despite Canada's general prosperity, many Aboriginal communities lack the basic necessities of life, such as safe drinking water and proper sewage facilities. Moreover, resource developments, such as Alberta's oil sands, often destroy the environment of Aboriginal communities and harm the health of their inhabitants.

The relationship of Aboriginal peoples to the Canadian state and its governing structures often poses difficult, but important, challenges. While many Canadians believe that all Canadians should be treated as equal citizens with the same rights, many Aboriginals argue that they have special rights due to their prior occupancy of land that was often taken away from them illegally or improperly. First Nations frequently expect to relate to Canadian governments on a "nation to nation" basis. Indeed, some First Nations claim that they never gave up their sovereignty (independence) and thus argue that they should not be subject to Canadian law.

In this chapter we examine the constitutional status of Aboriginals, the variety of court cases that have increasingly recognized Aboriginal rights, the slow process of settling Aboriginal land claims, and the movement toward self-government for Aboriginal peoples.

HISTORICAL BACKGROUND

Unlike many other indigenous peoples in the Americas, Aboriginals in Canada were never conquered by the European powers. Instead, military alliances were often formed between various tribes and the competing European powers. The Royal Proclamation of 1763 that formalized British control over the former French colonies in Canada declared that "the several Nations or Tribes of Indians with whom we are connected and who live under our protection shall not be molested or disturbed in the possession of such parts of our dominions and territories as, not having been ceded or purchased by Us, are reserved to them, or any of them, as their hunting grounds." To protect against exploitation from non-Aboriginal settlers, private individuals were prohibited from buying land reserved for Indians.[1] Instead, the governing authorities negotiated treaties to take possession of traditionally occupied land in exchange for some compensation.

Although First Nations played an important role in the defence of the British North American colonies by fighting alongside British troops in the War of 1812, they were not represented in colonial legislatures and were not involved or consulted in the discussions that led to the formation of Canada in 1867. The *Constitution Act*, 1867, gave exclusive jurisdiction to

---

[1]Although the term "Indian" is a misnomer, it continues to be used to distinguish people who have a distinct legal status (sometimes referred to as "Status Indians") from the Inuit, Métis, and non-status Indians. In recent decades, North American Indians have preferred to be termed "First Nations."

the Parliament of Canada to make laws concerning "Indians, and Lands reserved for the Indians" (sec. 91 [24]).[2] However the *Constitution Act* did not include any provisions concerning the rights of Aboriginals.

As the Canadian government opened large areas of land for settlers and immigrants to farm, many First Nations were moved to reserves, often in remote areas that were not suitable for farming. As a result of the decline of the fur trade, the encroachment of settlements on hunting grounds, the commercialization of resources such as the fishery, and the devastating diseases brought by Europeans, many Aboriginals came to depend on the Canadian government and the supplies provided by treaties for sustenance. Others found work, generally as low-paid labourers.

Indian Acts

Under the *Indian Acts* passed by Parliament beginning in 1876, the Canadian government tried to strictly control the lives of First Nations people and their communities. The Canadian government placed an official (the "Indian agent") in charge of each reservation. The people of First Nations were considered "wards" of the state, rather than citizens. Efforts were made to destroy First Nations culture. For example, some First Nations cultural practices were declared illegal, including the potlatch, a feasting ceremony of the peoples of northwestern North America in which the host gains prestige by giving gifts or, sometimes, by destroying personal wealth. As well, many bands were required to elect band councils in keeping with Canadian models of governance rather than the traditional First Nations models of governance that relied on the wisdom of tribal elders. The overall effect of control by the Canadian government, according to a House of Commons committee report (the Penner Report, 1973), was to turn "previously free self-sustaining First Nations communities" into a state of "dependency and social disorganization" (quoted in Prince & Abele, 2005, p. 243). In effect, Canada could be said to have acted as an imperial power in its treatment of Aboriginal peoples (see Box 12-2, Canada: An Imperial Power?).

The system of reserves tended to isolate the First Nations from the Canadian mainstream. However, the Canadian government tried to encourage **Status Indians** (those of Indian ancestry who are listed in the official government registry and are entitled to certain benefits, including exemption from taxation on property or income earned on the reserve) to give up their Indian

STATUS INDIANS
Those of Indian ancestry who are listed in the official government registry and are entitled to certain benefits, including exemption from taxation on property or income earned on the reserve.

---

[2]This provision is usually viewed by the Canadian government as applying primarily to the members of the more than 600 First Nations bands living on reserves. The Inuit, as a result of a 1939 Supreme Court of Canada decision, are also the responsibility of the Canadian government but are not covered by the *Indian Act* (Hunter, 2006). Provincial laws and programs can also apply to First Nations, but the federal *Indian Act* is considered superior to provincial legislation. Generally, the Canadian government has provided services such as education, health care, and housing to those living on reserves while provincial governments have provided services to other Aboriginals.

BOX 12-2

Canada:
An Imperial Power?

In the nineteenth and early twentieth centuries, the racist belief in the superiority of those of European ancestry was used to try to justify the subjection of non-whites around the world. Submitting to European rule and culture would lead to the advancement of indigenous peoples—or so the argument went (Cairns, 2000). Likewise, the Canadian government viewed Aboriginal people as inferior to those of European ancestry. Because they were deemed to be incapable of governing their own affairs, it was thought that Aboriginals needed to remain under the tutelage of the Canadian government and had to be encouraged to adopt the values and practices of the more "advanced" or "superior" civilization. So invasive was the traditional relationship of the Canadian government to Aboriginals that it is sometimes compared to that of the European imperial powers to the indigenous people of their colonies.

The idea that First Nations could give up their "Indianness" and enter the mainstream of Canadian society more often than not proved unrealistic. The displacement of Aboriginals by white settlers and the location of many reserves in remote, unproductive areas meant that Aboriginal peoples did not have the opportunity to develop and use modern skills. Likewise, being viewed as "primitive," Aboriginals often found it difficult to gain regular employment. Further, many Aboriginals did not want to give up their traditional way of life,

adopt an alien culture, and live in communities that did not treat them with respect.

In the twentieth century, imperialism was challenged as people in Africa and Asia fought for independence (or, as in South Africa and Zimbabwe, struggled against rule by the minority of European ancestry). The United Nations Charter (1945) and the International Covenants on Civil and Political Rights and on Economic, Social, and Cultural Rights (1966), ratified by the governments of most countries (including Canada), recognize the right of all peoples to "self-determination"—that is, the right to "freely determine their political status and freely pursue their economic, social and cultural development." However, in 2007, Canada was one of the few countries to vote against the United Nations Declaration of the Rights of Indigenous Peoples, which included the right of indigenous peoples to self-government and the right to the lands they traditionally owned or occupied.

Various Aboriginal groups have different relationships with the federal and provincial governments and differing views about self-determination and self-government. Nevertheless, like other indigenous peoples around the world, they are trying to forge new relationships that do not hark back to their experiences as subjects of governments that often acted imperialistically, not to mention imperiously (Papillon, 2009).

status and assimilate into the general population. For example, those who accepted a government offer of money and land, voted, owned property, or served in the Armed Forces were often required to give up their Indian status (a process termed "enfranchisement").[3] As Duncan Campbell Scott, Deputy Superintendent General of Indian Affairs, stated in 1920, "I want to get rid of

[3]In 1985 those who had been enfranchised, as well as women (and their offspring) who had lost their Indian status by marrying non-Indian men, were allowed to recover their Indian status.

the Indian problem. . . . Our object is to continue until there is not a single Indian in Canada that has not been absorbed into the body politic and there is no Indian question, and no Indian Department" (quoted in Cairns, 2004, p. 351).

PROPOSALS FOR CHANGE

The Hawthorn Report

In 1963, the Canadian government commissioned a major study of the condition of Indians under the direction of anthropologist Henry Hawthorn. The **Hawthorn Report** was critical of the Canadian government's policy of treating Indians as wards rather than as citizens, and recommended that Indians be regarded as **"citizens plus"** (Cairns, 2000). That is, "in addition to the normal rights and duties of citizenship, Indians possess certain additional rights as charter members of the Canadian community" (quoted in Cairns, 2000, pp. 161–162). The Hawthorn Report was also critical of the long-standing government policy of assimilation and recommended that Indians should not be forced to acquire the values of the majority society (Dickason, 2009).

The White Paper on Indians

Prime Minister Pierre Trudeau rejected the Hawthorn Report's key recommendation. Trudeau's view (consistent with his rejection of a "special status" for Quebec) was that all Canadians should be treated as individual citizens, with each person having exactly the same rights. Trudeau's view was reflected in the Canadian government's **White Paper on Indians** (1969), which argued that "the separate legal status of Indians and the policies which have flowed from it have kept the Indian people apart from and behind other Canadians." Instead, Indian people should have the fundamental right "to full and equal participation in the cultural, social, economic and political life of Canada" (Indian and Northern Affairs, 1969). To achieve this, the White Paper proposed ending the different legal status of Indians and the separate provision of services to them. Specifically, the special responsibility of the Canadian Parliament to legislate for Indians would be ended, the federal Indian Affairs Department would be phased out, and provincial governments would be responsible for providing the same services (such as health, education, and welfare) as provided to other provincial residents. Control of Indian lands would be transferred from the government to Indian bands, with each band deciding whether to manage the lands itself or to transfer title to individuals. Although "lawful obligations" would be recognized, the White Paper viewed treaties as providing minimal benefits to Indians, and thus called for a review to see how the treaties could be "equitably ended."

The White Paper held out the promise that Aboriginal identities could be strengthened and their distinctive culture preserved while Aboriginals would play a full role in Canadian society. However, in a bestselling book, *The Unjust*

HAWTHORN REPORT
A Canadian government report that recommended that Indians should have rights in addition to those of other citizens and not be forced to assimilate into the majority society.

CITIZENS PLUS
The idea that Indians possess certain rights in addition to the normal rights and duties of citizens.

WHITE PAPER ON INDIANS
A 1969 Canadian government discussion paper that proposed to end the different legal status of Indians.

Society, Alberta Cree leader Harold Cardinal (1969) condemned the White Paper as "a thinly disguised programme of extermination through assimilation" (p. 1). Many First Nations leaders mobilized strong opposition to the proposals in the White Paper (which was withdrawn in 1971) because they wanted to maintain their distinctive status and collective rights. This mobilization fuelled the development of politically active Aboriginal organizations and the willingness and determination of Aboriginal peoples to take political actions to pursue their rights.

Initially some First Nations leaders who opposed the White Paper advocated the "citizens plus" concept of the Hawthorn Report. However, within a short time, the developing Aboriginal movement turned to gaining recognition of what they viewed as their **inherent right to self-government**—that is, the right to govern themselves based on their independence before European colonization. They view this right as *inherent* in that it was not ceded by First Nations and thus does not depend on the Canadian Constitution or Canadian law (McNeil, 2007).

INHERENT RIGHT TO SELF-GOVERNMENT
The perspective that First Nations have the right to govern themselves based on their independence before European colonization, a right that was never ceded.

The Royal Commission on Aboriginal Peoples

In 1991, the Canadian government established the **Royal Commission on Aboriginal Peoples** headed by four Aboriginal commissioners and three non-Aboriginal commissioners. Its 4000-page report published in 1996 detailed the ill-treatment and injustices suffered by Aboriginals, and called for a fundamental restructuring of the relationship between Aboriginal and settler societies based on the recognition of Aboriginal nationhood. Canada should be viewed as a partnership of Aboriginal and non-Aboriginal nations, with the details of the relationship worked out on a nation-to-nation basis. The hundreds of specific recommendations of the Royal Commission included the following:

ROYAL COMMISSION ON ABORIGINAL PEOPLES
A Royal Commission established by the Canadian government that recommended a fundamental restructuring of the relationship between Aboriginal and settler societies based on the recognition of Aboriginal nationhood.

- A new Royal Proclamation acknowledging past injustices and recognizing the inherent right of Aboriginals to self-government.
- A Lands and Treaties Tribunal to speed up the process of settling land claims, with the authority to impose binding orders if negotiations fail.
- Consolidation of the more than six hundred Indian bands into sixty to eighty self-governing nations with an average population of five to seven thousand people and an enlarged land base.
- Recognition of Aboriginal governments as a "third order" of government in Canada (federal, provincial/territorial, and Aboriginal), each autonomous with its own spheres of jurisdiction and sharing the sovereignty of Canada as a whole. Aboriginal governments would be subject to the *Charter of Rights and Freedoms.*
- Establishment of an Aboriginal House of First Peoples to provide advice to the House of Commons and Senate and eventually empowered to initiate and pass legislation crucial to Aboriginal peoples.

- A very substantial increase in funding by the Canadian government to deal with Aboriginal problems, and the adoption of an equalization formula to ensure Aboriginal governments had the financial capacity to provide services to their peoples equivalent to the services provided by other governments.
- Aboriginals would be citizens of the First Nation community to which they belonged, as well as citizens of Canada.

Aboriginal leaders generally responded quite positively to the report and demanded the implementation of its recommendations. Some Inuit leaders, however, felt that the report did not give sufficient attention to the problems faced by their people.

CONSTITUTIONAL PROPOSALS AND CHANGES

Constitution Act, 1982

Aboriginal organizations did not participate directly in the negotiations between the prime minister and premiers that led to the *Constitution Act, 1982* (discussed in Chapter 10). Nevertheless, Aboriginal groups pressed for constitutional recognition of their rights. The act included a provision that "the existing aboriginal and treaty rights of the aboriginal peoples of Canada are hereby recognized and affirmed." These constitutionally enshrined rights are not limited to Status Indians but apply to all Aboriginal peoples, including Indian, Inuit, and Métis peoples, and apply equally to males and females. Although the word "existing" could be viewed as freezing rights, a later constitutional amendment in 1983 clarified that "'treaty rights' includes rights that now exist by way of land claims agreements or may be so acquired." In other words, new rights are constitutionally protected.

The *Constitution Act,* 1982, did not spell out the rights held by Aboriginal peoples but instead required the holding of constitutional conferences, with Aboriginal representatives, to deal with constitutional matters relating to Aboriginal peoples. However, a proposal to entrench the right to self-government in the constitution failed in 1987, when four provincial governments opposed the proposal on the grounds that its implications were unclear.

The Charlottetown Accord

The Charlottetown Accord (1992)—agreed to by national, provincial, and territorial governments as well as the leaders of Aboriginal organizations representing Status Indians, non-status Indians, Inuit, and Métis—would have recognized the inherent right of self-government of Aboriginal peoples. This included the authority of Aboriginal governments "to safeguard and develop their languages, cultures, economies, identities, institutions, and traditions and to develop, maintain and strengthen their relationship with their lands, waters and environment, so as to determine and control their development as peoples according to their own values and priorities and to ensure the integrity of their societies" (*Consensus Report on the Constitution,* 1992, pp. 37–38). Aboriginal governments would be established as a "third order" of government alongside the Canadian and provincial orders of government. The details of Aboriginal self-government and its implementation would have been left to a five-year period of negotiation before legal action could have been taken if the negotiations had proved unsuccessful.

The Charlottetown Accord was defeated by a majority of Canadians voting in a national referendum, including a majority of First Nations voting on reserves. Among First Nations there were concerns that self-government would be limited by subjecting Aboriginal governments to the *Charter of Rights and Freedoms,* as well as to the residual powers of Canadian Parliament. The Native Women's Association mounted a strong opposition campaign based, in part, on concerns that Aboriginal governments would be male dominated (Turpel, 1993).

The defeat of the Charlottetown Accord ended efforts to entrench the inherent right to Aboriginal self-government in the Constitution. Instead, important changes in Aboriginal rights and governance have occurred through other means—court cases, settlement of comprehensive land claims, and changes in government policy.

ABORIGINAL RIGHTS AND THE COURTS

In recent decades, Aboriginal groups have launched legal actions as they energetically pursued recognition of their rights and title to traditional lands. In several important decisions (see Table 12-2), the Supreme Court of Canada has recognized Aboriginal rights and, since 1982, expanded upon the meaning of the constitutional affirmation of "existing aboriginal and treaty rights."

Land Claims and the Nisga'a Tribal Council

A Supreme Court of Canada decision in 1973 regarding the claim by the Nisga'a Tribal Council in British Columbia that "their aboriginal title to

TABLE 12-2
IMPORTANT COURT DECISIONS REGARDING ABORIGINAL RIGHTS

CASE	YEAR	MAJOR ISSUE
Calder	1973	Aboriginal title to land
Sparrow	1990	Aboriginal rights (fishing)
Van der Peet	1996	Aboriginal rights (fishing)
Pamajewon	1996	Self-government
Delgamuukw	1997	Aboriginal title; oral evidence
Marshall	1999	Treaty rights (fishing)
Campbell et al.	2000	Self-government
Haida Nation	2004	Duty to consult

their ancient tribal territory . . . has never been lawfully extinguished" opened the door to recognition of land claims (*Calder,* 1973). The Nisga'a claim was dismissed by four of the seven judges on the technicality that the tribal council had not received the required permission to sue the government. Three of the judges who voted for dismissal went on to say that the governor of British Columbia, when the province was a colony of the United Kingdom, had acted within his powers to take possession of all lands in the colony and that the Royal Proclamation of 1763 did not apply to British Columbia. The "right of occupancy" that the Nisga'a "might have had" was ended when "the sovereign authority elected to exercise complete dominion over the lands in question."

The three judges who dissented argued that the claim should have been upheld because the actions of the B.C. governor to remove the Nisga'a's Aboriginal title were beyond the scope of his powers. The Nisga'a had a legal right that could only be extinguished "by surrender to the Crown or by competent legislative authority,[4] and then only by specific legislation" (*Calder,* 1973). Significantly, then, the court recognized that Aboriginal title to land could exist through occupancy before European settlement, although the court was divided on whether that right had been extinguished in this case. Similarly, a Supreme Court of Canada decision in 1984 (*Guerin*) recognized Aboriginal title as "a legal right derived from the Indians' historic occupation and possession of their tribal lands" (quoted in Hogg, 2006, p. 634). These decisions helped to persuade the Canadian government to negotiate treaties in areas of the country where none existed.

Fishing Rights and the Musqueam Band

The question of the extent to which Aboriginal rights to fish and hunt are protected by the *Constitution Act,* 1982, has been at the heart of a number of cases. In particular, the *Sparrow* case (1990) involved a member of British Columbia's Musqueam Band charged with fishing with a larger net than allowed by the band's food fishery licence issued under the federal *Fisheries Act* regulations. The Supreme Court found that the right of the members of the band to fish was an existing Aboriginal right, and thus protected by the Constitution. The government's argument that *Fisheries Act* regulations had extinguished the right to fish was rejected. The Court ruled that the regulations controlled the fisheries, but did not extinguish underlying rights. Further, the Supreme Court judgment stated that the phrase "existing aboriginal rights" in the *Constitution Act*, 1982 "must be interpreted flexibly so as to permit their evolution over time" (*Sparrow,* 1990). In other words, the traditional rights of Aboriginals to fish and hunt were not limited to the use of spears and

---

[4]The power of Parliament to extinguish Aboriginal and treaty rights through legislation no longer exists as a result of the *Constitution Act,* 1982.

bows and arrows that were used by their ancestors. However, in another case the Supreme Court ruled that an existing Aboriginal right "must be an element of a practice, custom or tradition integral to the distinctive culture of the aboriginal group" that developed "before the arrival of Europeans in North America"[5] (Van der Peet, 1996, cited in Hogg, 2006, p. 636).

Fishing rights were also at issue in the *Marshall* case. This case was particularly important because of issues linked to the interpretation of a historic treaty signed by a people that relied on their understanding of oral negotiations rather than a document they were unable to read (as discussed in Box 12-3, Standoff at Burnt Church: The Marshall Cases).

Land Claims and Treaty Rights: The Gitksan and Wet'suwet'en

A claim by the Gitksan and Wet'suwet'en for ownership and jurisdiction of 58 000 square kilometres of land in British Columbia resulted in a Supreme Court of Canada ruling that oral histories can be admissible as evidence concerning Aboriginal traditional occupancy of lands. In support of this view, the Court argued that the standard rules of evidence should be adapted so that the Aboriginal perspective on their practices, customs, and traditions, and on their relationship with the land, are given due weight by the courts. In this case, the Supreme Court also clarified the meaning of Aboriginal title. Aboriginal title to land is distinct in that it can only be transferred to the Crown, it derives from possession before the British declaration of sovereignty, and it is held collectively by the band members and cannot be held by individual Aboriginals. It also grants the right to engage in a variety of activities on the land even if they were not traditional practices, as long as they are consistent with the nature of the traditional attachment to the land. The title can only be infringed by the Canadian or provincial governments "in furtherance of a legislative objective that is compelling and substantial" and ordinarily requires fair compensation for the infringement (*Delgamuukw*, 1997).

Situations also occur where treaty rights have not been established but are being seriously pursued. In such cases, the Supreme Court has ruled that the government has the duty to consult and negotiate with, and may have to significantly accommodate, the Aboriginal nation that could be affected by actions that have a bearing on the land and rights they are claiming. In particular, the Court upheld the action by the Haida Nation against the British Columbia government concerning logging that could have potentially denuded the area

---

[5]However in *Powley* (2003), the Aboriginal right of Métis to hunt was upheld because it had existed before "the time of effective European control" (around 1850 in this case) rather than before the time of European arrival in North America (quoted in Hogg, 2006, p. 638).

BOX 12-3

Standoff at Burnt Church: The Marshall Cases

On October 3, 1999, violence occurred at Burnt Church, New Brunswick, after non-Aboriginal fishers destroyed Mi'kmaq lobster traps. The traps had been set out during the closed season by Mi'kmaq fishers who maintained that a Supreme Court ruling based on a treaty dating back to 1760 authorized them to fish out of season. In the midst of allegations and retaliatory actions, one thing was not disputed—the direct origins of the incident at Burnt Church began with the case of Donald Marshall, Jr.

The Marshall case involved a Mi'kmaq who had been charged with fishing and selling eels without a licence, and fishing during the closed season with illegal nets. Lawyers for Donald Marshall, Jr., claimed that he had a right to catch and sell fish under the 1760 Mi'kmaq peace and friendship treaty with the British governor of Nova Scotia. During the negotiations for the 1760 treaty, the Aboriginal leaders asked for "truckhouses" (trading posts) "for the furnishing them with necessaries, in Exchange for their Peltry." However, the treaty itself did not contain any provisions linked to this request. Nevertheless, the Supreme Court of Canada in September 1999 ruled that the minutes of the negotiations over the treaty should not be excluded as evidence given "the difficulties of proof confronted by aboriginal people" (*Marshall,* 1999). The court defined "necessaries" as the right to a "moderate livelihood," which could be obtained through fishing and hunting, and trading such products subject to "justifiable" regulations by the government. Since the prosecution had not provided justification for the regulations, Marshall was acquitted.

The Supreme Court ruling provoked an uproar. Non-aboriginal fishers complained that Aboriginals would have "unlimited and unregulated access" to the Atlantic fishery, depriving them of their livelihood (quoted in Russell et al., 2008, p. 453). Aboriginal statements that the ruling would allow them rights to the region's timber and mineral resources caused further concern. The Supreme Court of Canada refused a request for a re-hearing of the Marshall case. However, in a very unusual move, the Supreme Court decided to elaborate on their ruling.

In their second judgment on November 17, 2007, the Supreme Court reaffirmed that the treaty rights involved the right to a "moderate livelihood" by hunting, fishing, and berry picking, but did "not extend to the open-ended accumulation of wealth." The Canadian and provincial governments could regulate Aboriginal fishing for conservation or "other compelling and substantial public objectives," including fishing by non-Aboriginal groups, provided there was consultation with Aboriginals about limitations on their rights (quoted in Russell et al., 2008, pp. 458–459).

The Supreme Court's clarification of their first ruling did not end the tension between Aboriginal and non-Aboriginal fishers and between Aboriginals and the Department of Fisheries and Oceans. Eventually, however, all First Nations in the area gave up their right to fish for a "moderate livelihood" in return for the boats, equipment, training, licences, and quotas needed for a commercial fishery, subject to the same regulations as non-Aboriginal fishers. Thus the Marshall decision did not result in the restoration of a traditional way of life (Bedford, in press).

the Haida were claiming, and would have made worthless their claim to the right to harvest timber. In the view of the Supreme Court, "in all its dealings with Aboriginal peoples, from the assertion of sovereignty to the resolution of claims and the implementation of treaties, the Crown must act honourably" (*Haida Nation*, 2004).

The Right to Self-Government and the Shawanaga and Eagle Lake First Nations

The Supreme Court has generally avoided ruling on the right to self-government, arguing that this is best achieved through negotiations between Aboriginals and the federal and provincial governments. In the *Pamajewon* case, 1996, the Shawanaga and Eagle Lake First Nations argued that the gambling law they had passed was a valid exercise of their right to self-government, and thus band members conducting gambling operations should not be charged under the Canadian Criminal Code. In the Supreme Court's view, "Aboriginal rights, including any asserted right to self-government, must be looked at in light of the specific circumstances of each case and, in particular, in light of the specific history and culture of the aboriginal group claiming the right. . . . claims to self-government are no different from other claims to the enjoyment of aboriginal rights and must, as such, be measured against the same standard." (*Pamajewon,* 1996). Even though the Ojibwa had a history of informal, small-scale gambling, the Supreme Court concluded that it had not been central to their way of life. Therefore, the Criminal Code rather than the Aboriginal law applied to the case.

The Supreme Court's Interpretation of Aboriginal Rights

Overall, as the cases in the preceding pages illustrate, the Supreme Court of Canada has played a significant role in determining Aboriginal and treaty rights by taking into account the circumstances of Aboriginal peoples rather than applying a narrow legal interpretation of those rights. Nevertheless, the Supreme Court has indicated that these rights are not absolute, but rather some limitations can be placed on them. For example, government regulations for the conservation of resources may be justified, and Aboriginal rights to fish and hunt for food do not necessarily give Aboriginals an exclusive right to commercial use of these resources.

LEGAL CLAIMS

In most of British Columbia, Quebec, Newfoundland and Labrador, and the three territories, governments took over the land without signing treaties with Aboriginals. In the Maritimes, peace and friendship treaties were signed in the eighteenth century, in which Aboriginals agreed not to interfere with settlers and, in some cases, to accept the British Crown's jurisdiction in the region

(Dickason, 2009). In return, the British authorities guaranteed that the tribes that signed the treaties were free to hunt and fish; would be given some provisions such as bread, flour, blankets, and tobacco once or twice a year; and would be able to use the courts. Unlike treaties in other parts of Canada, the peace and friendship treaties did not involve Aboriginals giving up their right to land and resources, although in the nineteenth century reserves were established in the region.

Comprehensive Land Claims

As a result of the *Calder* ruling (discussed above), the Canadian government in 1973 began to negotiate comprehensive land claims with First Nations that had not signed treaties in the past. In negotiating **comprehensive land claims agreements** (which are also referred to as modern treaties), the Canadian government has insisted that the settlement of land claims provide a full and final settlement of Aboriginal rights. Most Aboriginal groups have made the establishment of the right to self-government an essential component of any settlement. The process of reaching land claims settlements has been drawn out and fraught with difficulties. For example, negotiations with the Nisga'a (whose chiefs had canoed to Victoria in 1887 to demand a treaty) began in 1976. An agreement was not reached until 1998.

> COMPREHENSIVE LAND
> CLAIMS AGREEMENTS
> Agreements involving First
> Nations that had not signed
> treaties giving up their land.

The agreements that have been reached generally involve removing the group from the provisions and benefits of the *Indian Act*. In return, the agreements have awarded Aboriginal groups specific rights and benefits (such as a cash settlement) and provisions for self-government (Papillon, 2008). Recent agreements have allowed for the establishment of Aboriginal governments that can provide potentially quite a range of services and can take part in managing natural resources in their region. The powers of Aboriginal governments set out in recent agreements are constitutionally protected and therefore cannot be changed without the approval of the Aboriginal government.[6]

The first agreements in the James Bay area and northern and northeastern Quebec (1975 and 1978) were negotiated to avoid the possibility that the Supreme Court of Canada might grant the Cree and Inuit an injunction to block the development of a large hydroelectric project that would flood lands claimed by these groups. An agreement between the Canadian government and the Yukon First Nations in 1993 provided the basis for modern treaties with eleven of Yukon's fourteen Indian bands (as of 2009). The agreements establish considerable legislative authority for Yukon's Aboriginal governments, which have been developing collaborative governance arrangements with the

---

[6]This constitutional protection does not require a formal constitutional amendment, since section 35 of the *Constitution Act*, 1982, provides for recognition of rights that may be acquired through land claims agreements.

Nisga'a Self-Government Sparks a Public Outcry

In 1998, the final agreement on the Nisga'a comprehensive claims caused a public outcry in British Columbia. Open-line radio shows and letters to the editor were filled with scathing comments. Critics argued that the treaty discriminated against non-Aboriginals, and fears were raised that claims by various Aboriginal groups could result in all the land in B.C. being returned to Aboriginals.

Opponents of the agreement demanded political action. They lobbied for a province-wide referendum on the treaty, and B.C. Liberal opposition leader Gordon Campbell mounted a thirty-day filibuster in the B.C. legislature. Similarly, the Reform Party of Canada proposed 471 amendments to the treaty in the House of Commons to try to delay its passage. The B.C. Liberals challenged the treaty in court, arguing that it was unconstitutional because it infringed upon federal and provincial legislative powers. However the B.C. Supreme Court ruled that the distribution of legislative powers between Parliament and provincial legislatures in the *Constitution Act,* 1867, did not preclude the right of the Nisga'a government to exercise legislative powers and that the treaty was compatible with the sovereignty of the Canadian state (Campbell et. al., 2000).

Campbell's B.C. Liberals gained power in a landslide victory in the 2001 election because of general dissatisfaction with the previous government. They decided not to appeal the loss of their legal challenge to the Nisga'a treaty. Instead, the B.C. government held a non-binding referendum in 2002 to address the controversy (although the treaty was already in effect). Voters were asked whether they agreed with eight statements that criticized various elements of the treaty such as "private property should not be expropriated for treaty settlements." Voters agreed with such statements by large margins, but only 35 percent of the electorate bothered to fill out the mail-in ballot (Lochead, 2004).

Although votes of the members of First Nations have been held in B.C. and elsewhere to approve modern treaties, governments have shied away from referendums to win the approval of the broader population.

Yukon government that has jurisdiction over similar matters (Mason, 2008). Other agreements establishing Aboriginal self-government through land claims settlements include the Tlicho in the Northwest Territories, the Tsawwassen in the greater Vancouver area, and the Inuit in Labrador.

After intense controversy, the British Columbia and Canadian governments ratified the landmark treaty establishing self-government for the Nisga'a in northwest British Columbia (see Box 12-4, Nisga'a Self-Government Sparks a Public Outcry). The treaty provides the Nisga'a government with the authority to make laws concerning such matters as culture and language, public works, regulation of traffic and transportation, land use, solemnization of marriages, health, child welfare, and education services. The authority of the Nisga'a government is not exclusive in these areas, but on some subjects

B.C. Premier Glen Clark and Nisga'a Tribal Council President Joe Gosnell shake hands after signing the Nisga'a Final Agreement in Terrace, B.C., April 27, 1999. The historic ratification of the Nisga'a treaty and Nisga'a constitution won a majority vote by the Nisga'a Nation on November 6, 1998, 113 years after Nisga'a chiefs first sought a treaty.

Nisga'a law prevails if in conflict with federal or provincial law, while on other subjects federal or provincial law prevails to the extent of the conflict. The Nisga'a government received the authority to levy direct taxes and collect royalties on their resources on their land. They were also given ownership of about 2000 square kilometres of land, with the authority to manage forest resources provided they meet or exceed provincial forest standards. In addition, the agreement included a phasing out of the exemption from paying income tax for those on the reserve. Instead the Nisga'a received a payment of $190 million spread over fifteen years, along with fiscal arrangements that would allow the Nisga'a government to provide equivalent services to those enjoyed by other people in the region. They were also given a share of the total allowable salmon catch in the region. Although some Nisga'a argued that their negotiators had given up too much to reach agreement (by, for example, gaining less than 10 percent of traditional lands), 61.2 percent of Nisga'a voters approved the treaty (Lochead, 2004).

Nisga'a treaty:
www.gov.bc.ca/arr/firstnation/nisgaa/default.html

Specific Claims

Comprehensive land claims agreements in areas where no treaties were signed are not the only category of claims that need negotiating. As well, a large number of **specific claims** exist based on allegations that treaties and other legal obligations of the Canadian government have not been fulfilled, or that the Canadian government has not properly administered Aboriginal lands and other assets. The negotiation process established in 1973 to settle specific claims was extremely slow, with claims taking an average of thirteen years to

SPECIFIC CLAIMS
Claims by Aboriginal groups based on allegations that treaties and other legal obligations of the Canadian government have not been fulfilled or that the Canadian government has not properly administered Aboriginal lands and other assets.

be settled. A more streamlined process created in 2008 allows Aboriginal First Nations to use the Specific Claims Tribunal, consisting of judges, if their claim has not been resolved within a specified period of time or has not been accepted for negotiation. The tribunal has the power to make binding decisions and provide monetary compensation of up to $150 million. The specific claims process does not establish rights to self-government.

CHANGES IN GOVERNMENT POLICY

INHERENT RIGHT OF SELF-GOVERNMENT POLICY
A Canadian government policy adopted in 1995 recognizing an inherent right to Aboriginal self-government.

In 1995 the Canadian government announced its **Inherent Right of Self Government Policy**, which recognized an inherent right to Aboriginal self-government. Specifically, Aboriginal peoples would "have the right to govern themselves in relation to matters that are internal to their communities, integral to their unique cultures, identities, traditions, languages and institutions and with respect to their special relationship to their land and their resources" (quoted in Abele & Prince, 2007, p. 178). This right would be exercised under the existing Constitution, with the *Charter of Rights and Freedoms* applying to Aboriginal governments. Laws of overriding federal and provincial importance would prevail over laws passed by Aboriginal governments. The Canadian government would maintain its exclusive authority in areas such as defence and external relations, management of the national economy, maintenance of national law and order and criminal law, and protection of the health and safety of Canadians.

Since then, the *Indian Act* has been amended to give band councils greater powers. Aboriginal governing authorities are now largely responsible for administering most programs and services that used to be administered by the Department of Indian Affairs and Northern Development. However, Aboriginal delivery of services does not create full self-government. Band councils still have only delegated power that is limited to specified local matters, and can have their bylaws overturned by the Minister of Indian Affairs (Bakvis, Baier, & Brown, 2009). Further, with a very high proportion of band revenues coming from the Canadian government, often with conditions attached, band councils still depend heavily on government support (Prince & Abele, 2005). Aboriginal authorities are accountable to the Canadian government for the funds allocated for the programs, and the Canadian government can unilaterally change or cancel most programs (Papillon, 2008). Nevertheless, Aboriginal authorities generally have some flexibility in shaping programs to suit the particular circumstances of their community.

In 2002, the Chrétien government introduced the *First Nations Governance Act*. This act proposed to amend the *Indian Act* to give greater independence to bands to manage their own affairs "on an interim basis pending . . . self-government." Among the specific provisions to provide for "effective governance" were the setting of minimum standards for Aboriginal leadership selection and the administration of band governments. Because of allegations that band funds have, in some cases, been misused, minimum standards would be established for band financial management and accountability, including publicly available audited financial statements. The minister of Indian Affairs would have the authority to assess the financial position of a band and take remedial action in some circumstances. A mechanism would be established so that band members could take up grievances related to the administration of their band, and the *Canadian Human Rights Act* would apply to certain band actions.

The Assembly of First Nations strongly objected to the act, arguing that it violated the inherent right to self-government, imposed more bureaucratic controls on Aboriginal governments, and added to the cost of governing First Nations (Hurley, 2003). Although various amendments were proposed in the House of Commons, the act was never presented for final reading in the House and thus died on the Order Paper.[7]

The controversy over the *First Nations Governance Act* raised fundamental questions about the nature of self-government envisioned by the Inherent Right to Self-Government Policy. Should Aboriginal governments be equivalent to provincial governments that are fully autonomous and do not generally have to account for the money that is transferred to them by the Canadian government? Or should they remain as subordinate governments that are ultimately accountable to the Canadian government that provides most of their funding?

Public Government

In 1992, voters in the Northwest Territories agreed to a division of the territory so as to create the new territory of Nunavut, where about 85 percent of the population is of Inuit ancestry. Unlike self-government arrangements for Aboriginals elsewhere in Canada, the Nunavut government, which came into being in 1999, is a public government involving all residents of the territory—in other words, it is not a government based exclusively on people of Aboriginal ancestry. With Inuit forming the overwhelming majority of the population, the territorial government will almost certainly succeed in representing the interests of the Inuit. The governing practices of Nunavut (and the Northwest Territories) follow the Aboriginal tradition of consensus. Political parties do not feature in territorial elections or in the legislative assembly. Members of the assembly elect the premier and cabinet by secret ballot. The Canadian government has committed to providing training so that Inuit could

---

[7]In 2009, secret Canadian government documents were leaked revealing plans for a new accountability policy (rather than a law) somewhat similar to the abandoned *First Nations Governance Act* (Curry, 2009).

► The nineteen independent members of the Nunavut legislative assembly govern using the consensus model, a system inherited from the Northwest Territories. Without the need for a division between government and opposition benches, the legislature chambers in Iqaluit were designed in the round and members of the legislative assembly meet in a circle.

eventually fill 85 percent of Nunavut's public service positions, although this goal has not yet been achieved (Mifflin, 2008).

At the same time as the public government of Nunavut was established, the Inuit agreed to a land claims settlement entitling them to $1.148 billion over fourteen years and 355 842 square kilometres of land and water (about 19 percent of the territory), including mineral rights on 35 257 square kilometres and a share of royalties on Crown land. They were awarded the right to harvest wildlife and the right to equal representation with government on wildlife, resource, and environmental management boards. Management of $1.148 billion was handed over to an Inuit corporation (Nunavut Tunngavik Incorporated) to which all Inuit belong. However this arrangement has left the territorial government highly dependent on the Canadian government to provide the funding needed to finance its inadequate public services and deal with Nunavut's serious social problems (Mifflin, 2009).

The creation of a public form of Aboriginal self-government that includes non-Aboriginals is only feasible in those areas of northern Canada where an Aboriginal First Nation makes up a large majority of residents. An Agreement in Principle has been reached with the Inuit to set up a public regional government in the part of Quebec north of the fifty-fifth parallel that is inhabited primarily by Inuit.

SELF-GOVERNMENT ISSUES

Aboriginal governments face many challenges. Most First Nations are small, with the majority having only a few hundred people. Establishing a substantial government responsible for developing and administering various programs and services equivalent, in some cases, to those provided by provincial governments is a daunting task. A sizeable expert staff is also needed to coordinate the laws, regulations, and programs of Aboriginal governments with those of the federal and provincial governments.

The Royal Commission on Aboriginal Peoples pointed out that the division of Indians into numerous small bands was primarily the result of past federal government policy designed to weaken and assimilate Indians. It recommended that Indians bands be consolidated into sixty to eighty nations based on similarities in language and culture. However, merging existing First Nations bands might not be acceptable because these bands have developed separate identities and governing structures. And even with consolidation, Aboriginal nations would still have small populations.

Most First Nations have a limited economic basis. Inevitably, they depend heavily on federal government funding, which, in effect, limits their autonomy. A few exceptions exist—bands that are wealthy because they occupy valuable land or have precious resources. Generally, however, the lack of opportunities on remote reserves and in tribal areas has meant that an increasing proportion of the Aboriginal population has migrated to cities. According to the 2006 census, 60 percent of First Nations members lived off-reserve and 54 percent of Aboriginals in 2006 lived in urban areas. Some First Nations (such as the Nisga'a) provide for representation of members who live in urban areas, and First Nations can provide services and programs to those not living in the territory being governed. However, tensions can surface between those who remain on traditional lands and those who have left; the interests of these two groups can diverge, particularly when land claims agreements result in substantial payments to the First Nation.

Self-government agreements give First Nations governments the authority to determine who their citizens are, and thereby restrict who can vote for those in governing positions. Nevertheless, self-government agreements require the Aboriginal government to consult with those who are not citizens of the First Nation but who live on Aboriginal land about decisions that significantly affect them. Non-citizens have the right to participate in non-governmental public institutions such as school boards. Typically, the number of non-citizens living on Aboriginal land is small (about 100 in the case of the Nisga'a). Yet the issue of the democratic rights of non-citizens living on Aboriginal lands may become more significant if Aboriginal governments are established on lands with more diverse populations.

Self-government agreements require that Aboriginal governments operate democratically with a constitution that Aboriginal laws and governing procedures must follow (as well as being subject to the *Charter of Rights and Freedoms* and other provisions of the Canadian constitution). However, putting a meaningful democracy into practice can be challenging. Many Aboriginal communities face governing problems resulting from factionalism, nepotism, and corruption. With soaring levels of poverty and unemployment, and an inadequate supply of housing, it is not surprising that politics in some Aboriginal communities is very contentious when leaders are accused of rewarding their family, clan, and supporters with scarce resources such as jobs and housing. Effective governing requires that Aboriginal citizens be able and willing to hold their government accountable for its actions. This can be difficult in small communities, particularly where a high proportion of people depend upon the chief and band council for employment, housing, and other benefits (Bedford, in press).

Although Aboriginal governance faces an array of problems and challenges, there is a positive side to self-government. Establishing effective self-government can help change attitudes of despair and dependence. Some Aboriginal communities that have gained self-government have become active in economic and community development. For example, the Inuit of Nunavik (Quebec) used some of the money provided by their self-governing agreement to establish the Makivik Corporation, owned by all members of the Inuit community. The corporation operates various businesses, including the major northern airline, First Air.

Overall, there is, and will likely continue to be, great diversity in self-government arrangements for reasons including the following:

1. The wide diversity among First Nations results in contrasting provisions in self-government agreements and differences in the capability and desire of First Nations to take up the powers established by these agreements.

2. Although there are some standard features in the recent agreements that have settled comprehensive land claims, it is unclear whether and to what extent such provisions will in the future apply to those covered by older treaties.

3. The self-government arrangements that have been reached with First Nations that have a specific land base will necessarily be different for non-status Indians, Métis, and other Aboriginals who have dispersed populations and, with the exception of some Alberta Métis settlement areas, have no collective land base.

Intergovernmental Relations

As autonomous Aboriginal governments become more established, relations between these governments and the Canadian and provincial governments will assume greater importance. Since 2004, national Aboriginal organizations have met with provincial and territorial premiers before the annual meeting of the Council of the Federation. However, they have not generally been invited to participate in federal–provincial meetings, except on matters that directly affect Aboriginals.

National Aboriginal organizations[8] did participate in the negotiations and the First Ministers Meetings that resulted in the **Kelowna Accord** (officially known as "Strengthening Relationships and Closing the Gap") in 2005, which promised $5.085 billion over five years to improve the socio-economic conditions of Aboriginals. The accord proposed that annual multilateral forums be held so that First Nations, Inuit, and Métis leaders could meet with federal and provincial cabinet ministers. However, the federal Conservative government has not implemented the terms of the accord, which were agreed to just before the defeat of the Liberal government.[9]

KELOWNA ACCORD
An agreement reached between First Nations and federal and provincial governments in 2005 to improve the socio-economic conditions of Aboriginals.

Aboriginal Representation in Canadian Political Institutions

There have been several proposals to give Aboriginals a greater voice in the governing of Canada as a whole. The Lortie Royal Commission on Electoral Reform and Party Financing (1991) proposed that one or more Aboriginal electoral districts for the House of Commons be established in provinces where a sufficient number of Aboriginals registered to vote in such districts. Adhering to the principle of equality of representation, this would create about six to eight Aboriginal seats in the House of Commons.[10] The Charlottetown Accord proposed that Aboriginals have guaranteed representation in the Senate, with the possibility that the Aboriginal senators, as well as the Senate as a whole, would have to approve some legislation relating to Aboriginals. However, there has been little serious consideration given to direct Aboriginal representation in national political institutions since then.

ABORIGINAL SOVEREIGNTY AND TREATY FEDERALISM

Some First Nations have refused to enter into negotiations to establish self-government arrangements, arguing that they are sovereign nations. In their view, the early treaties that were signed with the British Crown involved an agreement between independent nations to share territory. First Nations retained their sovereignty while delegating some specific powers to the Crown. The Six Nations Confederacy, for example, has a long history of asserting its independence[11]

---

[8]Unlike the negotiations leading to the Charlottetown Accord, the Native Women's Association of Canada was represented in the Kelowna Accord negotiations, along with the Assembly of First Nations, Inuit Tapiriit Kanatami, Métis National Council, and Congress of Aboriginal Peoples.

[9]The increased government spending announced in 2009 to deal with the recession may, however, provide substantial money for projects in Aboriginal communities.

[10]This approach is similar to that used for Maori representation in the New Zealand Parliament.

[11]The Six Nations Confederacy, located in the Grand River area of southern Ontario, has never accepted Canadian sovereignty. Indeed, in 1923 they unsuccessfully applied for membership in the League of Nations, the predecessor of the United Nations (Woo, 2003).

BOX 12-5

Sovereign Powers: The Two-Row Wampum Belt

The *Haudenosaunee* (Six Nations Confederacy) in northeastern North America had developed a democratic political system long before European colonization. In their treaties with the European powers, they used the traditional symbolism of two rows of beads (wampum) to describe and document a relationship of peace and friendship with Europeans. The beads represented the relationship in terms of a canoe and a ship travelling side by side down a river. Each vessel avoided interference with the other and neither crew tried to steer the other's vessel.

In the eyes of the Confederacy, the concept of the two vessels is the basis for the early treaties signed by the Six Nations with other nations, including France and Britain. From this perspective, the goal to be pursued by First Nations should not consist of self-government under the conditions set by the Canadian government within the Canadian Constitution. Rather, in keeping with the two-row wampum belt tradition, First Nations should reassert their sovereignty and share territory with the Canadian government, which they view as the representative of non-Aboriginal peoples.

The two-row wampum concept goes beyond the Inherent Right to Self-Government Policy of the Canadian government. Instead of viewing Aboriginal self-government as enhancing participation in Canada, the two-row wampum tradition looks to the parallel, but separate, development of sovereign Aboriginal and Canadian societies.

Is the ideal of an equal partnership between sovereign First Nations governments and the Canadian government a suitable basis for re-creating Canada in a "postcolonial" world—a world where it is no longer considered acceptable for one nation to exercise control over other nations?

(as discussed in Box 12-5, Sovereign Powers: The Two-Row Wampum Belt). However, Tom Flanagan (2000) has challenged the assertion that First Nations have retained their sovereignty. His argument is that Canadian sovereignty has been acquired, in keeping with international law, by long-term continued possession and effective control of the whole country.

Based on the view that the treaties agreed to by First Nations are "nation-to-nation agreements that enable nations to co-exist peacefully as autonomous entities within the same territory," Kiera Ladner (1993, p. 180) has advocated **"treaty federalism."** This would involve "a renewed nation-to-nation relationship, and a re-constitution of Indigenous polities as sovereigns with their own spheres of influence and jurisdiction and as co-sovereigns with their traditional territories." Unlike self-government, treaty federalism involves restoring the ability of First Nations to govern themselves entirely as they see fit. Members of the First Nations would not be citizens of Canada, but rather First Nations governments would interact with the Canadian government (representing the "newcomers" to Canada) as equal partners (Ladner, 2003).

TREATY FEDERALISM
The view that First Nations and the Canadian government representing later settlers should establish nation-to-nation agreements that enable the nations as co-sovereigns to coexist peacefully as autonomous entities within Canada.

Summary and Conclusion

Aboriginal peoples played a major role in Canada's early development. However, as settlement by those of European ancestry increased, First Nations were pushed to the margins of society and treaty promises were often ignored. In recent decades, Aboriginal peoples have actively pursued their rights and sought to change their relationship with Canadian governments through legal and political action. Nevertheless, many Aboriginal communities continue to suffer from poor housing, inadequate services, poverty, and serious social and health problems. Aboriginals are less likely than non-Aboriginals to participate in Canada's democratic processes, in part because of their historic exclusion or marginalization from the political process and because of the inequalities they continue to face. In addition, the nature of Canadian democracy reflects the political culture of the non-Aboriginal majority rather than that of First Nations peoples.

First Nations have fought for the recognition of their inherent right to self-government. Although Aboriginal and treaty rights were added to the Constitution in 1982, attempts to add the inherent right to self-government to the Constitution did not succeed. Nevertheless, the Canadian government has declared its commitment to the "inherent right to self-government" principle. In those areas of the country where First Nations did not sign treaties, a few recent comprehensive land claims agreements have included self-government provisions, and have removed First Nations from the provisions of the *Indian Act.* For most First Nations, powers have been delegated from the Canadian government to band councils. However, these communities are still under the control of the *Indian Act* and generally lack the financial resources to be truly self-governing. Furthermore, the small and impoverished populations of most First Nations raise questions about the capacity of the more than six hundred First Nations to exercise a wide range of governing responsibilities. Developing good government is a difficult challenge in these circumstances.

The circumstances of the Métis and non-status Indians often receive much less attention than those of Status Indians who are members of First Nations. Nevertheless, these diverse groups represent a substantial proportion of the Aboriginal population and can claim constitutional rights, even though who qualifies as a Métis or a non-status Indian is often unclear and their rights are largely undefined. Likewise, inadequate attention has been paid to the majority of Aboriginals who now live in urban areas. Although some urban Aboriginals have succeeded in pursuing middle-class lifestyles and professions, and have made important contributions to Canadian life, others suffer from poverty and a variety of social problems.

Overall, Aboriginal peoples are a key part of the character of Canada (Saul, 2008). The problems Aboriginals faced were, until relatively recently, largely hidden from view. Through numerous political and legal actions, Aboriginals have increased awareness of the need to address Aboriginal issues. However, both Aboriginals and non-Aboriginals continue to debate how best to resolve governing relationships among Canada's diverse peoples.

Discussion Questions

1. Should Aboriginals have special rights because of their occupancy of the land before European contact?

2. Is the Nisga'a treaty a suitable model for other First Nations?

3. Should Aboriginals be encouraged to integrate into Canadian society?

4. Should Canada be viewed as an equal partnership between Aboriginal nations and Canadian governments?

5. Should Aboriginal governments be subject to the Canadian *Charter of Rights and Freedoms*?

Further Reading

Alfred, T. (1999). *Peace, power, righteousness: An indigenous manifesto*. Don Mills, ON: Oxford University Press.

Alfred, T. (2005). *Wasáse: Indigenous pathways of action and freedom*. Peterborough, ON: Broadview Press.

Belanger, Y. (Ed.). (2008) *Aboriginal self-government in Canada. Current trends and issues* (3rd ed.). Saskatoon, SK: Purich.

Cairns, A.C. (2000). *Citizens plus: Aboriginal peoples and the Canadian state*. Vancouver: UBC Press.

Dickason, O. P., with McNab, D. T. (2009). *Canada's first nations: A history of founding peoples from earliest times* (4th ed.). Don Mills, ON: Oxford University Press.

Flanagan, T. (2000). *First nations? Second thoughts*. Montreal, QC: McGill-Queen's University Press.

Frideres, J. S., & Gadacz, R. R. (2008). *Aboriginal peoples in Canada* (8th ed.). Toronto, ON: Pearson Prentice Hall.

Macklem, P. (2001). *Indigenous difference and the constitution of Canada*. Toronto, ON: University of Toronto Press.

Miller, J. R. (2009). *Compact, contract, covenant: Aboriginal treaty-making in Canada*. Toronto, ON: University of Toronto Press.

Murphy, M. (Ed.). (2005). *Canada: The state of the federation 2003: Reconfiguring aboriginal-state relations*. Kingston, ON: Institute of Intergovernmental Relations, Queen's University.

Schouls, T. (2003). *Shifting boundaries. Aboriginal identity, pluralist theory, and the politics of self-government*. Vancouver: UBC Press.

THE FEDERAL SYSTEM

PHOTO ABOVE: Danny Williams, premier of Newfoundland and Labrador, demonstrated his ire when he ordered Canadian flags struck from provincial buildings in 2004—but he also guaranteed federal government attention for his issues. Balancing national and provincial interests is an ongoing challenge of the federal system.

1. Define a federal system and explain its significance for politics and government in Canada.
2. Discuss the constitutional provisions concerning the federal system and how they have been affected by judicial interpretations.
3. Outline how the federal system has evolved in terms of centralization and decentralization and

the level of interaction of the Canadian and provincial governments.

4. Explain how post-secondary education, health care, and welfare are funded.
5. Describe the system of equalization payments and discuss why it has been controversial.
6. Evaluate the Canadian federal system.

On December 23, 2004, the premier of Newfoundland and Labrador, Danny Williams, ordered the Canadian flag removed from all provincial buildings. Williams was upset that Prime Minister Paul Martin had reneged on a written promise made during the 2004 election campaign. This promise guaranteed that the Newfoundland and Labrador government would receive 100 percent of the royalties from its offshore oil resources without a reduction in the equalization payments the government received as a "have not" province. In Williams's view, a federal offer to solve the dispute was a "slap in the face" that would leave the province $1 billion short of what was promised. The Canadian government, he argued, "was not treating us as a proper partner in Confederation."

A month later, a deal was reached that allowed the provincial government to continue to receive all its offshore resource revenues. The Canadian government would give an "offset payment" for a number of years to fully compensate for the cuts in equalization payments resulting from those revenues. The deal satisfied Williams, and the Canadian flag was hoisted once again in Newfoundland and Labrador.

Premier Williams's satisfaction was short-lived. During the 2006 election campaign, Stephen Harper promised that non-renewable natural resource revenues would not be included in the calculation of a new equalization formula and that there would be no cap on equalization payments. However, the formula adopted by the Harper Government in 2007 included 50 percent of natural resource revenues and placed a cap on equalization payments. The result—the end of equalization payments to the government of Newfoundland and Labrador. Economics professor Wade Locke presented an analysis estimating that the broken promise would mean a total of about $11 billion less for the provincial government over the following thirteen years than it would have received if the promise had been kept ("$11-Billion Rift," 2007).

Danny Williams was livid: "Yesterday, Prime Minister Harper told the people of Newfoundland and Labrador and essentially the people of Canada that his promises

do not matter. His promises do not count, and they most certainly cannot be relied upon" (Newfoundland and Labrador Executive Council, 2007). This time, he did not order the flags lowered. Instead Williams, a Progressive Conservative, announced that he would actively campaign to elect "anything but Conservatives" in the next federal election. In addition to speeches denouncing Harper, a popular website (anythingbutconservative.ca) was set up, and a large billboard carrying the message greeted motorists on the Gardiner Expressway in Toronto. Support for the Conservative party plummeted in Newfoundland and Labrador, and no Conservatives were elected in that province in the 2008 federal election. Williams claimed, "We've sent a very strong message to the Harper Conservatives." However, with no representatives from the province in Harper's Cabinet or in the Conservative caucus to promote the message, the new equalization formula remained unchanged.

Ensuring that all Canadians can receive an equitable level of services from their governments while each province feels that it is being treated fairly is one of the challenges facing the Canadian federal system. An important challenge is finding a balance between having a robust national government able to look after the interests of the country as a whole and strong provincial governments able to respond to the diverse interests of different areas of the country.

WHAT IS A FEDERAL SYSTEM?

A **federal system** is a system of governing in which authority is divided and shared between the central government (in Canada often termed the federal government) and provincial governments, with each deriving its authority from the constitution. The Canadian arrangement differs from a unitary system in which the central government may hand over some authority and administrative responsibilities to lower levels of government (as, for example, in the United Kingdom and France). Instead, in Canada's federal system (like those of the United States and Australia), provincial governments are not legally subordinate to the Canadian government. Provincial legislatures do not need the approval of the Canadian government to act on matters within the exclusive law-making authority that the constitution has granted them. Neither does the Canadian Parliament need the approval of provincial governments for matters under its constitutional authority.

In practice, as discussed in this chapter, the contemporary federal system involves quite a high level of interaction between the federal and provincial governments in the development and implementation of many policies. The Canadian federal system is not only a matter of divided legislative powers, but also requires close cooperation in making and implementing the decisions that affect our lives.

As discussed in Chapter 2, the adoption of a federal system in 1867 was necessary to unite the British North American colonies. Uniting in one country with a central government made it easier to develop the economy and provide for military defence. By adopting a federal system, provincial governments could maintain and nurture their distinctive cultures, traditions, and identities. In other words, the federal system embraces the challenging goal of bringing together unity and diversity (Bakvis & Skogstad, 2008).

FEDERAL SYSTEM
A system of governing in which authority is divided and shared between the central government and provincial governments, with each deriving its authority from the constitution.

THE CONSTITUTION AND THE FEDERAL SYSTEM

Sir John A. Macdonald, a leading proponent of the union of the British North American colonies, wanted a strong central government with the capability to build and unite the new country. The United States, whose constitution greatly limited the scope of the American government, had just gone through a devastating civil war. Macdonald's idea of a vigorous central government was reflected, to a considerable extent, in the *Constitution Act, 1867*.

The Constitution Act, 1867

The *Constitution Act, 1867*, divides most government activity into two categories—those that fall under the exclusive legislative authority of the Canadian Parliament and those that fall under the exclusive legislative responsibility of provincial legislatures.

TABLE 13-1
THE DIVISION OF LEGISLATIVE POWERS IN THE CONSTITUTION ACT, 1867

Note: See the *Constitution Act, 1867* (sections 91–95, 109, and 132) for the complete list and the precise wording.

EXCLUSIVE POWERS OF PARLIAMENT	EXCLUSIVE POWERS OF PROVINCIAL LEGISLATURES	POWERS OF BOTH
Regulation of trade and commerce	Direct taxation for provincial purposes	Agriculture
Raising money by any mode of taxation	Management and sale of public lands	Immigration
Postal service	Hospitals and asylums	
Census and statistics	Municipal institutions	
Military and defence	Shop, saloon, and other licences	
Navigation and shipping	Local works and undertakings	
Fisheries	Incorporation of provincial companies	
Currency and coinage	Solemnization of marriage	
Banking and incorporation of banks	Property and civil rights	
Weights and measures	Administration of justice	
Bankruptcy and insolvency	Education	
Patents and copyrights	Lands, mines, minerals, and royalties	
Indians and lands reserved for Indians		
Marriage and divorce		
Criminal law		

In particular, this document lists many areas of government activity where the Canadian Parliament has exclusive legislative jurisdiction and somewhat fewer areas of exclusive provincial jurisdiction (see Table 13-1). In two policy areas, agriculture and immigration, both Parliament and provincial legislatures received legislative authority,[1] although Canadian laws take precedence if Canadian and provincial laws in these areas conflict.

The *Constitution Act,* 1867, gave Parliament legislative authority over many, but not all, of the important areas of governing in the nineteenth century. However, the provinces retained legislative authority in areas such as education, health, and welfare, which were often the responsibility of religious and charitable organizations in the nineteenth century, as well as municipal government. These responsibilities entrusted to the provinces have evolved into major governmental activities in modern times.

A constitutional document cannot anticipate all matters about which governments might want to legislate. The **residual power** (the power over matters not listed in the *Constitution Act*) was basically given to the national level of

RESIDUAL POWER
Legislative power over matters not listed in the Constitution.

---

[1]In the case of criminal law, Parliament makes the laws while provincial governments are responsible for enforcing them (Bakvis & Skogstad, 2008).

governing, as the *Constitution Act* in section 91 provides that Parliament can make laws for the "peace, order and good government of Canada" in relation to all matters not assigned exclusively to the provincial legislatures. Some residual power was also handed to provincial legislatures, which have the authority to legislate on "generally all matters of a merely local or private nature in the province" (section 92).

Constitutional Amendments

The provisions of the *Constitution Act, 1867,* concerning the division of legislative powers have not changed much. Constitutional amendments have given the Canadian Parliament the authority to pass laws concerning unemployment insurance (1940). As well, Parliament received the authority to pass legislation regarding old-age pensions (1951) and disability benefits (1964), provided those laws do not conflict with provincial laws. Constitutional amendments in 1982 gave the provinces some extra authority related to the control and taxation of natural resources.

Judicial Interpretations

Judicial interpretations of the Constitution have significantly affected the division of legislative powers between the federal and provincial governments. Until 1949 the Judicial Committee of the Privy Council (JCPC) in Britain was the final court of appeal, except for criminal cases. Its decisions frequently overturned the rulings of the Supreme Court of Canada and other Canadian courts. Appeals to the Judicial Committee were abolished in 1949, making the Supreme Court of Canada the country's highest court.

THE JUDICIAL COMMITTEE OF THE PRIVY COUNCIL   In a number of important rulings (particularly from about the mid-1890s), the Judicial Committee declared various laws passed by Parliament invalid because they overstepped the authority granted to the Canadian Parliament. This helped to shift Canada away from a highly centralized federal system.

Of particular importance has been the interpretation of the "peace, order, and good government" clause. This clause might be interpreted as giving Parliament very broad powers to override the specified provincial powers. An early case involved the *Temperance Act* passed by Parliament in 1878, which allowed local governments to ban the sale of alcohol if voters supported the ban in a plebiscite. With his livelihood at stake, pub owner Charles Russell challenged his conviction for selling alcohol in the "dry" city of Fredericton, New Brunswick. In *Russell v. The Queen* (1882), the Judicial Committee upheld the constitutionality of the *Temperance Act* on the basis that provincial jurisdiction over property and civil rights did not prevent Parliament from passing laws "designed for the promotion of public order, safety, or morals, and which subject those who contravene them to criminal procedure and punishment" (quoted in Russell et al., 2008, p. 41).

In later decisions, the Judicial Committee proved less inclined to support a general power for the Canadian Parliament. In the *Local Prohibition* case (1896), the JCPC was asked whether a province could set up its own system of local prohibition. In the JCPC's opinion, the peace, order, and good government clause did not exclude provinces from enacting their own prohibition laws. To safeguard provincial autonomy, the peace, order, and good government clause could not be used to overrule the powers of the provinces enumerated in the Constitution. "Parliament has not the authority to encroach upon any class of subjects which is exclusively assigned to provincial legislatures" (quoted in Russell et al., 2008, p. 49).

The Judicial Committee, particularly after Viscount Haldane became a member in 1911, generally viewed the peace, order, and good government clause as applying only to temporary emergencies (Hogg, 2006). For example, in the *Fort Frances* case (1923), the JCPC upheld the system of price controls that was created during World War I. The "sufficiently great emergency" of the war justified federal action, even though the regulations fell within the normal competence of the provinces (quoted in Hogg, 2006, p. 475). In the *Board of Commerce* case (1922), the JCPC struck down laws passed by the Canadian Parliament after World War I to deal with the serious problems of profiteering, monopolies, and hoarding. In their ruling the JCPC argued that the emergency power could only be used in "highly exceptional circumstances" to override the exclusive provincial power over property and civil rights. Similarly, the JCPC struck down several Canadian laws to tackle the problems of the Great Depression of the 1930s (including unemployment insurance), arguing that only an emergency would justify the use of the peace, order, and good government clause. In the eyes of the JCPC, the Great Depression did not rate as an emergency. The possibility that these measures might become permanent rather than temporary may have also influenced the JCPC decision (Hogg, 2006).

In addition to viewing the peace, order, and good government clause as providing an "emergency" power to Parliament, the Judicial Committee saw the clause as granting residual legislative power to Parliament to deal with subjects not included in the lists of enumerated powers. For example, the *Constitution Act*, 1867, gave Parliament "all powers necessary or proper for performing the obligations of Canada or of any province thereof, as part of the British Empire, towards foreign countries, arising under treaties between the Empire and such foreign countries" (section 132). In 1935, the Canadian Parliament ratified the Draft Conventions of the International Labour Organization and passed three acts dealing with hours of work, minimum wages, and weekly rest to fulfill the obligations of the conventions. The Canadian Cabinet subsequently requested a judicial reference concerning the validity of these acts. The JCPC in the

Labour Conventions case (1937) upheld the power of the Canadian government to sign the conventions (an international treaty), because Canadian treaty-making power was not specifically included in the list of enumerated powers. However, because the labour conventions dealt with the class of subjects under provincial jurisdiction, the legislative power to implement the conventions rested with provincial legislatures rather than Parliament.[2] In the view of the JCPC, "While the ship of state now sails on larger ventures and into foreign waters she still retains the water-tight compartments which are an essential part of her original structure" (quoted in Russell et al., 2008, p. 74). In other words, the JCPC thought the federal system should be based on autonomous federal and provincial governments, each with its own specific areas of responsibility—a view often described as "**classical federalism.**"

When there was a "national dimension" or a "national concern" involved, the Judicial Committee, at times, used the peace, order, and good government clause to uphold legislation passed by Parliament that might be viewed as infringing on provincial powers. For example, in the *Canada Temperance Federation* case (1946), the JCPC gave the opinion that if the subject matter of the legislation "goes beyond local or provincial concern or interests and must from its inherent nature be the concern of the Dominion as a whole [. . .] then it will fall within the competence of the Dominion Parliament as a matter affecting the peace, order and good government of Canada, though it may in another aspect touch on matters specially reserved to the provincial legislatures" (quoted in Hogg, 2006, p. 462).

The national government's authority over the regulation of trade and commerce was interpreted narrowly by the Judicial Committee as granting the legislative authority only over international and interprovincial trade. Trade and commerce within a province has been deemed a matter for provincial legislatures because of their "property and civil rights" power. For example, in the *Insurance Reference* (1916), the JCPC ruled that the federal *Insurance Act* establishing a licensing system for insurance companies operating across Canada was not justified by the trade and commerce power. Likewise, a federal prohibition on the manufacture, sale, or possession of margarine (designed to assist dairy farmers) was struck down on the grounds that the trade and commerce power could not be used to prohibit transactions within a province (Hogg, 2006).

THE SUPREME COURT OF CANADA   The Supreme Court of Canada has taken a somewhat different approach from the Judicial Committee, showing itself less inclined to limit the Canadian government's powers. For example,

CLASSICAL FEDERALISM
The view that a federal system should be based on autonomous federal and provincial governments, each with its own specific areas of responsibility.

---

[2] In the *Radio Reference* (1932), the JCPC ruled Canada could regulate radio transmission in accordance with international agreements Canada had signed because radio was a new matter not mentioned in the *Constitution Act*, 1867.

the *Anti-Inflation Act* passed by Parliament in 1975 instituted controls on wages, prices, and profits for up to three years (with the possibility of an extension). In the *Anti-Inflation Reference* (1976) the Supreme Court of Canada in a 7–2 decision upheld the act using the emergency powers interpretation of the peace, order, and good government clause, even though the *Anti-Inflation Act* involved legislating on provincial matters (for example, by limiting wages of provincial government employees). Indeed, the majority ruled that the government did not need to prove there was an emergency; the burden of proof that an emergency did not exist rested with the opponents of the legislation (Hogg, 2006).

The Supreme Court of Canada has been divided on the use of the "national concern" interpretation of the peace, order, and good government clause to uphold national environmental laws. In 1980, Crown Zellerbach, a forest products company, dredged logging debris, including bark and wood from its shoreline water lot, and dumped it in deeper water off Vancouver Island. The company was charged with an offence under the federal *Ocean Dumping Control Act,* which prohibits dumping at sea, including dumping substances without a permit in provincial territorial waters (other than fresh water). In a 4–3 judgment, the Supreme Court upheld the provision, arguing, "marine pollution, because of its predominantly extra-provincial as well as international character and implications, is clearly a matter of concern to Canada as a whole." In particular the majority noted that in deciding what distinguishes a matter of national concern, "it is relevant to consider what would be the effect on extra-provincial interests of a provincial failure to deal effectively with control or regulation of the intra-provincial aspects of the matter" (quoted in Russell et al., 2008, pp. 132–33).

In 1990, Hydro-Québec was charged with dumping polychlorinated biphenyls (PCBs)—a highly toxic substance that carries serious health risks to both animals and humans—into the St. Maurice River in violation of the *Canadian Environmental Protection Act,* 1985. The Supreme Court of Canada pointed out the environment is a broad subject that the *Constitution Act,* 1867, did not assign exclusively to either level of government. Both national and provincial governments have legislative authority in this area and should cooperate to safeguard the environment. The Supreme Court unanimously agreed that the act was too broad to meet the peace, order, and good government criteria of "national concern" used in the *Crown Zellerbach* case. However in a 5–4 decision, the Supreme Court ruled that "Parliament may validly enact prohibitions under its criminal law power against specific acts for the purpose of preventing pollution . . ." (quoted in Russell et al., 2008, p. 152).

Overall, even though its justices are appointed on the recommendation of the prime minister, the Supreme Court of Canada has not drastically altered the interpretations of the division of powers developed in the JCPC decisions.

Is "Lite Beer" Light?: The Supreme Court Verdict

In 1977, Labatt's introduced Special Lite (now known as Labatt's Lite). With many Canadians becoming diet conscious, this first low-calorie beer was an instant success. However, Labatt's came into conflict with the Canadian government, which has a long history of regulating brewing.

Regulations under Canada's *Food and Drugs Act,* 1970, provide that light beer has to meet certain standards, including an alcohol content of between 1.2 and 2.5 percent. Federal inspectors seized Special Lite, which has an alcohol content of 4 percent. Labatt's sought a court declaration that "Special Lite is not likely to be mistaken for a light beer" (quoted in Russell et al., 2008, p. 121).

The Supreme Court of Canada ruled that Special Lite could be mistaken for "light beer," even though the 4 percent alcohol content was on the beer's label. However, the Supreme Court in a 6–3 decision struck down the standards for the composition of light beer, arguing that the federal trade and commerce power did not apply to the brewing process, even though the sale of beer involved interprovincial trade.

Like the Judicial Committee, the Supreme Court has been reluctant to accept a broad interpretation of the federal government's constitutional powers over trade and commerce. Nevertheless, federal laws concerning "false, misleading or deceptive" packaging and labelling do allow for the indirect enforcement of national standards for consumer products (Russell et al., 2008).

In particular, the Supreme Court of Canada has indicated that it does not view the "peace, order and good government" clause as a sweeping power that can be used to undermine provincial jurisdiction (Kennett, 2000; Lucas & Shawitt, 2000). The Supreme Court of Canada has also hesitated to interpret the federal trade and commerce power as giving the Canadian government a general power to regulate trade by, for example, introducing legislation for national business practices or consumer protection (see Box 13-1, Is "Lite Beer" Light?: The Supreme Court Verdict). The *Anti-Inflation Reference* did, however, raise some provincial government concerns about the broad use of the emergency doctrine in peacetime.

Disallowance, Reservation, and the Declaratory Power

Some political scientists have questioned whether the *Constitution Act,* 1867, established a purely federal system, in part because the act authorized the Canadian government to override the decisions of provincial governments. Specifically, the **disallowance power** gave the Governor General in Council (meaning the Canadian Cabinet) the right to disallow provincial legislation within one year of its passage. In turn, the **reservation power** gave provincial lieutenant governors (who are appointed on the recommendation

DISALLOWANCE POWER
The right of the Canadian Cabinet to disallow provincial legislation within one year of its passage.

RESERVATION POWER
The right of a lieutenant governor to reserve the passage of provincial legislation until that legislation is approved by the Canadian Cabinet.

of the prime minister) the authority to reserve the passage of provincial legislation until the Canadian Cabinet had approved it. In addition, with the **declaratory power,** the Canadian Parliament could declare any "local works or undertakings" within a province to be "for the general Advantage of Canada or for the Advantage of Two or more of the Provinces" and then legislate on that matter.

The Canadian government quite frequently used the disallowance power and the reservation power until World War II. However, these powers have not been used since 1943.[3] Likewise, the Canadian Parliament often took advantage of the declaratory power to legislate on such matters as railways, grain elevators, telephones, and atomic energy, but that power has not been used since 1961. Generally, these powers are viewed as obsolete, and various constitutional reform packages have proposed getting rid of them.

A DECENTRALIZED FEDERAL SYSTEM

How much a federal system leans in a centralist direction (power concentrated in the central government) or a decentralized direction (power dispersed among provincial governments) does not depend only on the constitutional division of legislative authority and the interpretation of the constitution by judicial bodies. An array of social, economic, political, and institutional factors also play an important role in determining the distribution of power.

The diversity of Canada helps to explain the development of a decentralized federal system. Provinces differ markedly in their histories, geographical characteristics, economies, ethnic compositions, languages, and cultures. Provincial governments have tried to defend and promote the particular interests, values, cultures, and identities of those they represent. The concentration of the French minority in Quebec and the determination of Quebec governments to protect their language and culture have been key to ensuring that the federal system does not become highly centralized. To varying degrees, other provincial governments have sought to maintain or expand provincial powers, fearful that their interests would not be looked after in a more centralized system. As provincial governments developed their capabilities, they often tried to promote the distinct identity of their provinces and to rally their residents around specific provincial interests (Cairns, 1977). The growth of provincial governments in recent decades has allowed them (particularly those with greater financial resources) to match the Canadian government in terms of the ability to develop and assess new policy proposals.

---

[3]One hundred and twelve provincial laws were vetoed from 1867 to 1943 and sixty-nine bills were reserved until 1937. In 1961 the lieutenant governor of Saskatchewan reserved a bill, even though the prime minister did not want it reserved. The bill was quickly approved (Heard, 1991).

The development of strong and assertive provincial governments has played an important role in the evolution of Canadian federalism. During his lengthy time in office (1872–96), Ontario Liberal Premier Oliver Mowat fiercely defended the interests of Ontario and promoted the idea of "provincial rights," which clashed with the centralist views of Conservative Prime Minister Macdonald. In the 1880s, Mowat found an ally in Quebec nationalist Premier Honoré Mercier. Ever since, most Quebec governments have energetically defended provincial autonomy based on the view that the Quebec government represents one of the two "founding peoples" or "nations" that agreed to form Canada. In the 1960s, Quebec governments became more activist—instead of defending Quebec from "intrusions" on its constitutional powers by the Canadian government, they demanded additional powers so as to lead Quebec's social and economic development. In the 1970s and 1980s, Alberta, Saskatchewan, and Newfoundland pushed for greater provincial control of natural resources.

Provincial electorates have often supported efforts by their provincial government to take on "Ottawa." For example, Newfoundland and Labrador Premier Williams's battles with the Canadian government, discussed at the beginning of this chapter, undoubtedly contributed to his party's win of almost 70 percent of the vote in the 2007 provincial election and the unprecedented 87 percent approval rating of his government in 2008 ("87 Percent Approve of Williams," 2008).

The federal and provincial party systems have contributed to the independence of provincial governments. Most political parties are not highly integrated in the sense of being unified organizations that work closely together at the provincial and national levels to pursue common goals (Smiley, 1987). The positions taken by a provincial party will often differ from the positions taken by a national party that goes by the same name. Thus even when the same political party is in office provincially and nationally, the provincial premier will not necessarily follow the prime minister's lead. Further, it is common for voters to elect different parties at the two levels of government.[4] Interestingly, in 1980, Quebec voters gave a resounding mandate to the Liberal party, led by Pierre Trudeau, who sought to strengthen the Canadian identity. A year later, they re-elected the separatist Parti Québécois led by René Lévesque.

The careers of provincial and federal politicians also tend to follow separate paths. Relatively few politicians use provincial political experience as a stepping stone to national politics. For this reason, provincial politicians do not have strong incentives to be concerned about the national interest or their national image to advance their careers.

---

[4]Unlike the United States, national and provincial elections are never held on the same day, thereby facilitating different voting patterns at the two levels.

The ability of a number of provincial governments to pursue provincial rights and powers and challenge centralizing initiatives of the Canadian government has been enhanced by the institutional structures of government. Unlike almost all other federal systems,[5] Canada's upper chamber of Parliament, the Senate, does not represent provincial interests to any significant degree because the appointment of its members is on the recommendation of the prime minister. Although Canadian Cabinets have included members from all, or almost all, provinces, the conventions of Cabinet solidarity and secrecy, along with the ever-greater concentration of power in the hands of the prime minister, limit the effectiveness of Cabinet in representing provincial interests. Furthermore, because Parliament features tight party discipline, Members of Parliament are expected to vote along party lines even if this conflicts with the interests of their province. Thus provincial interests are often not effectively taken into account within national-level institutions. Instead, provincial governments may be able to gain support for seeking greater powers or maintaining provincial autonomy because of their ability to act as advocates for the interests of their province. In other words, it has frequently been argued that the weakness of **intrastate federalism** (provincial representation and involvement in national political institutions) has led to a more conflict-prone focus on **interstate federalism,** in which provincial governments are the primary representatives of provincial interests (Smiley, 1987).

INTERGOVERNMENTAL RELATIONS

The federal system since the 1940s has featured a high level of interaction between the national and provincial governments. This has made intergovernmental relations of great importance to politics in Canada and to the policies and programs that affect our lives.

The growing role of government in the period after World War II included the development of many programs involving both levels of government that we now take for granted—the Trans-Canada Highway (construction began in 1950), universal hospital insurance (1957), the Canada Pension Plan (1964),[6] the Canada Assistance Plan (1966), and universal medical insurance (fully implemented in 1971), among others. As governments grew more active, the need to coordinate federal and provincial policies became increasingly evident. For example, the effectiveness of the policies adopted by the Canadian government to improve the competitiveness of the country's economy depends, in part, on the education policies implemented by provincial governments (Smith, 2004). As well, both levels of government are often active in the

INTRASTATE FEDERALISM
A federal system in which provincial interests are represented in national political institutions.

INTERSTATE FEDERALISM
A federal system in which provincial interests are represented primarily by provincial governments.

---

[5]Although the elected U.S. Senate does not directly represent the interests of American states, the relative looseness of party discipline in Congress has resulted in members of Congress representing the interests of their state and district.

[6]Quebec developed and administers its own plan, the Quebec Pension Plan, that is congruent with the Canadian plan.

same policy area. For example, permits for the development of a new bridge or mine may require not only a provincial environmental assessment but also a federal one because of the potential effects on fisheries (a federal responsibility). Thus, instead of the "watertight compartments" of federal and provincial jurisdiction characteristic of classical federalism, the modern federal system features a high level of interdependence between governments. Developing effective and efficient policies requires much cooperation, coordination, and collaboration between the levels of government (Bakvis & Skogstad, 2008).

Cooperative Federalism

In the two decades following World War II, the Canadian government generally took a leadership role in developing and funding many projects, with provincial governments responsible for administering health and social programs according to national guidelines.[7] Since the federal and provincial governments generally cooperated in developing the welfare state, this period is typically referred to as one of "**cooperative federalism.**"

Competitive and Collaborative Federalism

Although considerable intergovernmental cooperation continues, provincial governments have become more reluctant to accept the leadership of the Canadian government. The development of a dynamic and assertive form of nationalism in Quebec, the standoffs between the resource-rich provinces and the Canadian government over energy policy, and the highly charged controversies over constitutional change have made conflict a key aspect of federal–provincial relations, particularly between the early 1960s and 1984. This has resulted in what some term "**competitive federalism,**" in which "provincial and national governments inevitably butt heads as each seeks to maximize its autonomy, jurisdiction, and standing with the voters" (Bakvis & Skogstad, 2008, pp. 7–8).

There has been a general trend toward a more decentralized federal system since the early 1960s, despite Prime Minister Trudeau's attempts to maintain a strong central government. To some extent, federal–provincial relations, particularly since the late 1990s, have involved collaboration more than conflict between the two levels. That is, in what has been termed **collaborative federalism,** both levels of government try to work together as equals in deciding some major policies (Cameron & Simeon, 2002). After the Meech Lake and Charlottetown Accords failed to achieve formal constitutional changes that would have enhanced provincial government powers, a new strategy was needed. Ever since, changes to the workings of the federal system have often

COOPERATIVE FEDERALISM
The feature of Canadian federalism in the two decades following World War II in which federal and provincial governments generally cooperated under federal leadership in developing the welfare state.

COMPETITIVE FEDERALISM
A feature of Canadian federalism, particularly between the early 1960s and 1984, in which provincial and national governments competed to maximize their autonomy, power, and popularity with the voters.

COLLABORATIVE FEDERALISM
A trend in contemporary federalism in which both levels of government try to work together as equals in deciding some major policies

---

[7]In the case of hospital and medical insurance, it was the Saskatchewan government that pioneered the programs that were eventually adopted nationwide.

taken the form of negotiating agreements between the levels of government. However, these agreements (including the Agreement on Internal Trade, 1994; the Canada-wide Agreement on Environmental Harmonization, 1998; the Social Union Framework Agreement, 1999; and the 2003 and 2004 Health Accords) are not legally enforceable and have typically been limited in their scope and effectiveness.

Despite a general trend toward decentralization and greater federal consultation and collaboration with provincial governments, Canadian governments have sometimes continued to act single-handedly and controversially in matters affecting provincial governments. For example, as discussed in Chapter 10, Prime Minister Trudeau pursued major constitutional reforms amid protests from eight provincial governments (although he was pressured to reach a compromise in the end). Likewise, Prime Minister Chrétien ignored an agreement with provincial governments and committed Canada to major cuts in greenhouse gas emissions in the Kyoto Protocol. However, the lack of an effective federal plan to lower emissions, and fierce opposition from several provincial governments, led to Canada's breaking its Kyoto commitments—instead of cutting back on greenhouse gas emissions, Canada has continued to increase them.

OPEN FEDERALISM
The Harper Government's approach to federalism involving such measures as transferring more money to provincial governments, respecting the constitutional division of powers and provincial autonomy, and limiting the use of the federal spending power.

OPEN FEDERALISM   Stephen Harper, a strong advocate of decentralization and provincial autonomy, proclaimed during the 2006 election campaign a commitment to what he termed "**open federalism.**" As defined by Harper, this involved a new relationship with provincial governments, including

- fixing the "fiscal imbalance" by transferring more money to provincial governments;
- respecting the constitutional division of powers and provincial autonomy;
- limiting the use of the federal spending power (explained below);
- allowing provincial governments to opt out of new or modified joint federal–provincial programs with full compensation; and
- giving the Quebec government a role in international affairs related to its constitutional responsibilities through a seat at the United Nations Educational, Scientific, and Cultural Organization (UNESCO).

Despite its label, "open federalism" has not meant that federal–provincial relations have become more open to public scrutiny or more open to participation by non-governmental groups (Bakvis, Baier, & Brown, 2009). Further, like previous governments, the Harper Government has some centralizing goals, including strengthening the Canadian "economic union" and developing plans (over the objections of some provincial governments) to take control of securities regulations (that is, regulations concerning stocks, bonds, and other instruments used by companies to raise money). Overall, the Harper Government's approach to federal–provincial relations is "consistent with the evolution of Canadian federalism in recent decades" (Simeon & Robinson, 2009, p. 174).

Executive Federalism

The basic nature of federal–provincial interaction since the 1940s is often described as **executive federalism;** that is, the interaction of the executives (prime minister and premiers, cabinet ministers, and government officials) of the two levels of government determine many of the policies that affect our lives.

At the peak of executive federalism are the prime minister and premiers (termed "First Ministers").[8] Only three formal meetings of the First Ministers were held before the 1930s. To deal with problems stemming from the Great Depression, four Dominion–Provincial Conferences took place in the 1930s. Since 1945, the First Ministers have met frequently. Numerous **First Ministers Conferences** were held at various times from 1967 to 1992 concerning constitutional changes. These conferences involved large delegations in support of the First Ministers, along with much media attention and, at times, public confrontations between the prime minister and certain premiers. In recent years, the First Ministers Conferences have given way to more informal, private **First Ministers Meetings**. Proposals in the Victoria Charter and Charlottetown Accord that regular annual meetings of First Ministers be held have not been adopted. Instead First Ministers Meetings are called when desired by the prime minister, who chairs the meetings. Prime Minister Harper showed little interest in First Ministers Meetings during his first term in office, holding only two brief meetings. However, with the onset of the recession, he met twice with premiers—in November 2008 and January 2009 (including a session with Aboriginal leaders)—and indicated that further meetings would take place. Prime ministers have also often found it useful to hold meetings and work out deals with individual premiers rather than trying to strike a consensus with all the premiers, who may have conflicting agendas.

Meetings of ministers responsible for particular policy areas are typically held regularly, with support from a full-time secretariat. Some of the Councils of Ministers invite non-governmental groups with an interest in the policy area to participate (Bakvis, Baier, & Brown, 2009). Further, government officials hold numerous meetings (as well as having informal contacts). In part, such meetings, particularly among deputy ministers, lay the groundwork for ministerial meetings. Officials who implement and administer programs find it useful to meet with others who have similar responsibilities. Generally, relationships among officials of different governments and, to a considerable extent, ministers, are friendlier and more cooperative than relationships among First Ministers. However, intergovernmental agreements are usually finalized by the First Ministers.

Not surprisingly, critics have pointed out that executive federalism is undemocratic. The negotiations between the executives of the two levels of government are often secretive and not open to scrutiny by Parliament and

EXECUTIVE FEDERALISM
The basic nature of federal–provincial interaction since the 1940s, involving the interaction of the executives of the federal and provincial governments.

FIRST MINISTERS CONFERENCES
Formal meetings of the prime minister and premiers, along with large supporting delegations of ministers, aides, and officials.

FIRST MINISTERS MEETINGS
Informal private meetings of the prime minister and premiers.

---

[8]Territorial premiers have been regular participants since 1992.

▶ Prime Minister Harper and the thirteen provincial and territorial premiers deep in discussion at their First Ministers Meeting on November 10, 2008, in Ottawa.

Canadian Intergovernmental Conference Secretariat:
www.scics.gc.ca

provincial legislatures. Many agreements reached at intergovernmental relations (such as the Social Union Framework Agreement discussed later in this chapter) either do not need legislative approval or are considered a "done deal" and not subject to much scrutiny and debate before legislative passage (Smith, 2004).

Executive federalism has also been criticized for its tendency to lead to confrontation and conflict between federal and provincial governments. In particular, the departments or branches within governments specifically devoted to intergovernmental affairs are often focused on maintaining or enlarging the power of their government. As well, prime ministers and premiers have usually taken a "hands-on" approach to intergovernmental relations, making the relations highly politicized. Thus, although federal and provincial departmental officials dealing with particular issues are often able to work cooperatively, they may be overruled by those more concerned about the power and autonomy of their government.

Alternatively, executive federalism could be viewed as a practical response that has developed out of a need to coordinate federal and provincial policies. Because of Canada's great regional and cultural diversity, the Canadian government is "unable to forge a national consensus unilaterally" (Hueglin, 2008, p. 153). Instead, through bargaining and negotiations, flexible compromises can be worked out. Further, it has been argued that a quiet process of working out compromises among national and provincial leaders (termed "elite accommodation") is more likely to succeed than processes that involve public debate and scrutiny. In particular, some argue that political elites are more likely to grasp the need for the differential treatment of Quebec than the majority of Canadians (Bakvis, Baier, & Brown, 2009).

Interprovincial Cooperation

Provincial governments have tried to develop a united front to be in a better position to bargain with or make demands on the Canadian government. This strategy can be traced back to 1887 when some premiers met to demand a reduction in the powers of the Canadian government based on the view that Canada was a compact (agreement) among provinces. As well, the premiers aired a variety of provincial grievances. However, it was not until 1960 that annual meetings of the premiers were established. And interprovincial cooperation was not institutionalized until 2003 with the creation of the **Council of the Federation,** which includes a permanent secretariat. Despite its name and its commitment to developing greater collaboration with the Canadian government, the Council of the Federation has not invited the Canadian government to join in its discussions.

The premiers hoped that the council would give them a stronger, more united voice. However, reaching a consensus on some key issues has proven challenging. For example, at their annual meeting in 2006, the premiers failed to strike an agreement on the equalization formula. Similarly, their 2007 meeting did not result in a meaningful agreement on how to deal with climate change. The 2008 meeting succeeded better—the premiers agreed that workers whose qualifications were accredited in one province should automatically be accepted as having that qualification in any other province (with some exceptions). Their 2009 meeting featured disagreement on whether or not the same qualifying period for employment insurance benefits should apply across the country (as preferred by Ontario). However, there was agreement to work alongside Ottawa in seeking an exemption from "Buy American" policies.

In addition to the Council of the Federation, there is also a Council of Atlantic Premiers that promotes regional cooperation and a less formalized Western Premiers' Conference that includes the three territorial leaders. The premiers of Ontario and Quebec also meet occasionally to cooperate on certain issues. These regional forums have had some success in developing common positions and programs. For example, a meeting of the Ontario and Quebec premiers in 2008 resulted in an agreement to establish a "cap and trade" system to reduce greenhouse gas emissions. In 2009, the Western premiers agreed on a joint proposal to present to the Canadian government for reform of Canada's employment insurance system.

FEDERAL–PROVINCIAL FINANCIAL ARRANGEMENTS

The power and reach of any government depends not only on the authority granted to it by the Constitution but also to a considerable extent on its financial capabilities. A government with inadequate revenues may be unable to exercise

COUNCIL OF THE FEDERATION
An organization established by the premiers to enable cooperation among the provinces.

Council of the Federation:
www.councilofthefederation.ca

Council of Atlantic Premiers:
www.cap-cpma.ca

its full constitutional powers. In contrast, a government that has more revenues than it needs to carry out its own constitutional powers may use its extra resources to pursue matters that are within the legislative authority of the other level of government. In other words, a government with abundant revenues may find ways to promote its interests that exceed its legislative powers.

Taxes

As Table 13-2 indicates, the Canadian and provincial governments raise their revenues from some of the same sources. Until 2000, there was a high level of coordination in the income tax system (the largest source of government revenue), as the Canadian government set out the basic formula used by both levels of government for calculating taxable income. Since then, each province can determine its own basis for provincial income tax. The Canada Revenue Agency collects personal income taxes on behalf of both levels of government (except in Quebec).[9] The Canada Revenue Agency also collects corporate income taxes for all provinces except Quebec and Alberta.

Another major source of revenue for both levels of government, the sales tax, features federal–provincial coordination in some provinces but not in others. Newfoundland and Labrador, Nova Scotia, New Brunswick, and Quebec use the harmonized sales tax (a value-added tax on a common tax base collected by a single agency).[10] The other provinces (except Alberta) levy and collect their own retail sales tax, while the Canadian government collects the goods and services tax using a different system. In 2009, the governments of Ontario and British Columbia announced plans to adopt the harmonized

TABLE 13-2
FEDERAL, PROVINCIAL, AND MUNICIPAL TAX REVENUES

	FEDERAL	PROVINCIAL	MUNICIPAL
Personal income tax	yes	yes	
Corporate income tax	yes	yes	
Natural resource revenues		yes	
Property tax			yes
Payroll taxes	yes	yes	
Customs duties	yes		
Lotteries and gaming		yes	
Excise taxes (alcohol, tobacco, gasoline)	yes		
Alcohol sales		yes	

Source: *Based on Bakvis, Baier, & Brown, 2009, p. 141.*

[9]The Canada Revenue Agency is an agency of the Canadian government with a management board that has a majority nominated by provincial and territorial governments.

[10]In Quebec, the tax is collected on behalf of the Canadian government by the provincial government rather than by the Canada Revenue Agency.

sales tax to take effect July 1, 2010. Considerable public opposition developed in both provinces because the harmonized tax is levied on a broader range of goods than their provincial sales tax.

Transfer Payments

Looking at government revenues in total, the Canadian government has more revenue than it needs to carry out its own activities. Although provincial governments collectively raise more money than the Canadian government, they have legislative responsibility for some of the most expensive government activities, including health, education, and social services. To try to ensure that provincial governments have the financial resources to carry out their responsibilities, the Canadian government transfers considerable amounts of money that it has raised itself to provincial governments. In the 2008–09 fiscal year, for example, the Canadian government transferred over $53 billion to provincial governments (as detailed in Table 13-3). Nevertheless some provincial governments have argued that the Canadian federal system suffers from a **fiscal imbalance,** as discussed in Box 13-2, The Canadian Federal System: A Fiscal Imbalance? Overall, provincial governments receive on average about one-fifth of their revenue from the federal government, although the poorer provinces, as well as the territories, receive a higher proportion of their revenues from the Canadian government than the richer provinces (see Figure 13-1).

The *Constitution Act, 1867,* required that the Canadian government provide a grant in aid of each provincial government. However, these small sums

FISCAL IMBALANCE
The view that provincial governments do not have a proper share of revenue to carry out their responsibilities.

MAJOR TRANSFERS	($ BILLIONS)
Canada Health Transfer	22.629
Canada Social Transfer	10.559
Children	1.100
Post-secondary education	3.235
Social programs	6.202
Equalization	13.462
Offshore accords	0.663
Territorial formula financing	2.313
Total	49.626
Targeted transfers	
Labour market training	0.500
Infrastructure	1.625
Wait time reductions (hospital)	0.600
Total	2.725
Trust funds	1.534
Total transfers	**53.885**

TABLE 13-3
FEDERAL TRANSFER PAYMENTS TO PROVINCIAL AND TERRITORIAL GOVERNMENTS

Note: Transfer payments do not include the transfer of tax points. The breakdown of the Canada Social Transfer is notional and does not include a small amount for transitional protection. Trust funds include funds for clean air, patient wait times, community development, and public transit.

Source: *Department of Finance Canada, 2009.*

BOX 13-2

The Canadian Federal System: A Fiscal Imbalance?

In recent years, an important controversy in federal–provincial relations has centred on whether a fiscal balance or imbalance characterizes the federal system. Provincial governments have claimed that they suffer from a fiscal imbalance—they do not have sufficient revenue to carry out their constitutional responsibilities for very costly programs in such fields as health, education, and welfare. The Canadian government, they argue, takes advantage of its excess revenues to meddle in provincial matters (Advisory Committee on Fiscal Imbalance, 2006).

The federal Liberal government disagreed. Backed by the federal Department of Finance, the Liberal government claimed that there was a fiscal balance, noting that it had restored the major cuts in transfer payments to provincial governments made in the 1990s because of the sizeable federal deficit. As well, they argued that almost all provincial governments no longer had budgetary deficits and that provincial debt loads were proportionately smaller than the federal debt. Moreover, they noted that provincial and territorial governments account for a greater proportion of total government spending than the Canadian government and that the Canadian government's share of total government spending is the lowest among the developed countries with a federal system (Department of Finance Canada, 2006). In their view, the Canadian government needs to have considerable control over the revenue capabilities of government in order to manage the Canadian economy. In addition, the Canadian government needs enough financial resources to develop and fund programs that they view to be in the national interest or to try to ensure that provincial governments deliver comparable programs that meet national standards or objectives.

The Conservative party, which favours greater provincial autonomy, made fixing the fiscal imbalance an important issue in the 2006 Canadian election campaign. The Conservatives claimed in their 2007 federal budget that they would end the fiscal imbalance by providing an additional $39.4 billion to provincial governments over seven years.

Discussions of the fiscal imbalance have often focused on whether there is a *vertical* imbalance between the financial capabilities of the Canadian and provincial governments. Yet we should also assess the extent to which a *horizontal* imbalance exists among the provinces and territories. That is, do the governments of the poorer provinces and territories have the financial means to provide services to the public that are of the same quality as services provided by the richer provinces?

were inadequate to help provincial governments deal with the problems caused by massive unemployment during the Great Depression of the 1930s. After World War II, government greatly expanded its role in providing services such as health care, social welfare, and post-secondary education. However, provincial governments that had the legislative authority for many of these services did not have the deep pockets to fund them—their responsibilities outstripped their financial resources.

CONDITIONAL GRANTS To establish national programs in areas in which the provinces have legislative authority, the Canadian government

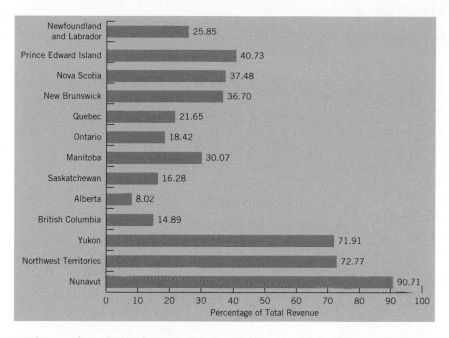

FIGURE 13-1

FEDERAL CASH TRANSFERS TO PROVINCES AND TERRITORIES, 2007–2008

Source: Compiled and calculated from Department of Finance Canada, 2009, Fiscal Reference Tables 2008, Tables 4 and 5. Retrieved from http://www.fin.gc.ca

made use of **conditional grants.** Provincial governments administered the programs that were often developed at the initiative of the Canadian government and had to meet conditions set by the Canadian government to receive money for the programs. By taking the lead in developing national social programs, the Canadian government could ensure that everyone was able to receive a similar basic set of social services wherever they lived. Generally, the Canadian government paid half of the costs of the programs, so these are often called **shared-cost programs.**

The Quebec government and, at times, the governments of some other provinces objected to conditional grants, arguing that health, post-secondary education, and welfare fall exclusively within provincial jurisdiction according to the Constitution. As well, some provincial governments (notably Ontario) argued that the conditional grant programs distorted provincial government priorities by encouraging provincial governments to spend their money on the programs (because they had to pay only half the cost) instead of on provincial government priorities.

The Canadian government has asserted its right to spend the money it raises as it sees fit, even on matters under provincial jurisdiction. Interestingly, this **spending power** of the Canadian government is not explicitly provided for in the Constitution. However some judicial decisions have indicated that the Canadian government can grant or withhold money to any government, institution, or individual and attach conditions to its use. For example, the Supreme Court of Canada upheld the right of the Canadian government to place conditions on money granted to provincial governments for social assistance (Hogg, 2006). Discussions of possible limits on the federal spending power have featured prominently in constitutional negotiations, with both the Meech Lake and

CONDITIONAL GRANTS
Federal grants to provincial governments for specific programs that have to meet conditions set by the Canadian government.

SHARED-COST PROGRAMS
Provincial programs in which the Canadian government generally paid half the costs.

SPENDING POWER
The ability of the Canadian government to spend money as it sees fit, even on matters under provincial jurisdiction.

BOX 13-3

9-1-1 Federalism:
The Social Union Framework Agreement

After the failure of constitutional reform efforts in 1990 and 1992 and the very close vote on Quebec independence in 1995, Prime Minister Jean Chrétien wanted to demonstrate that problems in Canada's federal system could be resolved without formal constitutional change. In his view, the federal government should retain a substantial involvement in social policy (thus the term "social union"), while allowing provincial governments an important role in defining national standards for social programs. Some provincial governments had quite different ideas, however. A proposal prepared for the Ontario government by economist Tom Courchene suggested that "full responsibility for the design and delivery of health care, welfare, and education would devolve to the provinces" (quoted in Fortin, 2009, p. 318). Reflecting this perspective, Progressive Conservative Premiers Ralph Klein (Alberta) and Mike Harris (Ontario) took the lead in demanding that provincial governments determine national standards for social programs through interprovincial agreements (Fortin, 2009).

The Social Union Framework Agreement reached in 1999 between the Canadian government and all provincial governments (except Quebec) was a compromise that included the following provisions:

- A majority of provincial governments would have to agree before the Canadian government launched any new joint federal–provincial social programs. Provincial governments could design their own programs and receive funding provided they met "national objectives."

- The Canadian government could use its spending power without seeking the agreement of provincial governments for programs that direct money straight to individuals, provided three months' notice was given.
- The Canadian government would give a year's notice of changes to its funding of provincial social programs.

While the agreement did not go nearly as far as Alberta and Ontario had initially proposed, nine provinces were willing to accept the compromise that provided a framework for the use of the federal government's spending power. Their agreement was facilitated by the decision of the Canadian government to increase the money it transferred to provincial governments. The Quebec government refused to sign, as the agreement did not guarantee the right of a province to opt out of new social programs with full compensation.

Nevertheless, behind the scenes, the federal government quietly worked out an understanding with Quebec as to how the principles of the agreement would apply there. This pattern of working out a bilateral understanding between the Canadian and Quebec governments similar to an agreement with the other provinces has also been applied in the Canada-wide Accord on Environmental Harmonization (1998) and the Health Accord (2004). Roger Gibbins (1999) has described this process that, in effect, recognizes the distinctiveness of Quebec as "9-1-1 federalism."

Charlottetown Accords proposing certain restrictions on this power. In 1999 a non-binding agreement, termed the Social Union Framework Agreement, was reached that set out some general guidelines for federal spending power and social programs (as discussed in Box 13-3, 9-1-1 Federalism: The Social Union Framework Agreement).

BLOCK GRANTS In 1977, the Canadian government changed its cash transfers for health care and post-secondary education from a shared-cost basis to a single **block grant**—that is, a basically unconditional grant of a block of money to provincial governments. In 1996, the Canada Assistance Plan, which provides welfare and some other social programs, was added to the block grant. In 2004 the grant was divided into two blocks, the **Canada Health Transfer** (for medicare and hospital insurance) and the **Canada Social Transfer** (for post-secondary education, social assistance, early childhood education, and child-care programs). The Canadian government notionally divides the Social Transfer into funding for three categories: social programs, post-secondary education, and child-related programs. However, each provincial government is free to decide how the Social Transfer is to be used.

Block grants are calculated for each province on what is essentially a per capita basis (although with smaller per capita grants to the richest provinces)[11] and flow into the general revenues of a provincial government. Unlike shared-cost grants, they are not based on the costs of provincial programs. Since the Canadian government is no longer committed to provide 50 percent of the costs of the programs, it has managed to unilaterally reduce its share of the costs. In particular, the Canadian government slashed the transfer for health, welfare, and post-secondary education by about one-third in its 1996–97 budget to deal with a serious deficit problem.

Although the Health and Social Transfers are described as block grants, they are not funds transferred to provincial governments with no strings attached. The *Canada Health Act* (1984) allows the Canadian government to cut back on payments to any province that does not respect the principles of public administration, comprehensiveness, universality, portability, and accessibility in its public health care system. The Canadian government has used this act to withhold some money from provincial governments that allowed extra billing of patients and user charges for basic (core) health care services. From 1984 to 2008 the money withheld totalled just over $9 million (Health Canada, 2008). The only condition attached to the Canada Social Transfer is that provincial governments cannot impose a residency requirement for the receipt of social assistance.

Because of the soaring costs of providing health care, provincial governments have lobbied for greater funding from the Canadian government and guarantees that block funding not be subject to unilateral cuts by the federal government. In turn, the Canadian government has wanted some accountability for the funds it transfers to the provinces for health care, as well as kudos from the public for helping to address the problems facing the health care system. As a result of the federal–provincial Health Accord in 2004, the

BLOCK GRANT
The unconditional transfer of a block of money from the federal government to a provincial government.

CANADA HEALTH TRANSFER
A block grant intended to fund medicare and hospital insurance, although some conditions are involved.

CANADA SOCIAL TRANSFER
A block grant intended to fund post-secondary education, social assistance, early childhood education, and child-care programs.

---

[11]Beginning in 1990, a limit was placed on the increase that the richest provinces (Ontario, Alberta, and British Columbia) received for certain transfer payments. This cap is being phased out such that the Canada Social Transfer has provided equal per capita payments since the 2007–08 fiscal year, and the Canada Health Transfer is scheduled to be fully equal per capita by 2014–15.

▶ "It's going to be a long wait." Health care services and funding are perpetual concerns for voters, which makes them a perennial issue for federal–provincial discussion as well.

Canadian government committed to increase the Canada Health Transfer by 6 percent per year for the following ten years.[12] In addition, federal–provincial health agreements in 2003 and 2004 provided special funds for provincial governments that were earmarked for specific purposes, such as reducing waiting times for certain operations and purchasing medical equipment. To improve accountability to the public, the Health Council of Canada was set up to monitor and report on the performance of the health care systems.[13]

EQUALIZATION PAYMENTS   Because provinces differ widely in their economic resources and their ability to raise funds through taxation, some provincial governments are better equipped to provide services to their populations than others. Since 1957, the Canadian government has directed **equalization payments** to the governments of the poorer provinces. A commitment to the principle of equalization, defined as ensuring that "provincial governments have sufficient resources to provide reasonably comparable

EQUALIZATION PAYMENTS
Unconditional grants from the Canadian government to the governments of the poorer provinces to bring their revenue-raising capabilities up to a national standard.

---

[12]The 2007 Canadian budget included a commitment to increase the Canada Social Transfer by 3 percent per year for four years from 2009.

[13]The Health Council is composed of representatives of the Canadian, provincial, and territorial governments, as well as independent members to represent the public. Quebec and Alberta have declined to participate in the council, with Quebec establishing its own Council on Health and Well-Being.

levels of public services at reasonably comparable levels of taxation," was included in the *Constitution Act*, 1982.

Basically, equalization payments are unconditional grants by the Canadian government to the governments of the poorer provinces to bring their revenue-raising capabilities up to a national standard. In the 2009–10 fiscal year, the three Maritime provinces, along with Quebec, Ontario, and Manitoba, received equalization payments totalling $14.2 billion. Equalization does not involve taking money from the governments of the richer provinces, but rather comes out of the general revenues of the Canadian government. Unlike equalization in the Australian federal system, the Canadian equalization method does not take into account the costs of providing services in different provinces or the contrasting needs of the provinces.

The method for calculating equalization payments has varied over time. The system adopted in 2007 involved setting the national standard as the average revenue capacity of all ten provinces in terms of how much each province can raise from its personal income tax, corporate income tax, sales tax, property tax, and 50 percent of its natural resource revenues. There is, however, a cap to ensure that no provincial government receiving equalization will have greater revenue-raising capacity than any provincial government that does not benefit from equalization. As noted in the introductory vignette, the equalization formula adopted in 2007 was strongly condemned by the government of Newfoundland and Labrador. From Newfoundland's perspective, royalties from the province's offshore oil are only a temporary source of wealth, allowing this traditionally poor province a chance to pay down its large provincial debt and to work on developing its economy. However, from the point of view of Ontario Premier Dalton McGuinty, allowing provinces that are no longer needy to keep receiving equalization payments would be grossly unfair. With Ontario residents paying $20 billion more in taxes to the Canadian government than the province receives in transfers and services, McGuinty called upon Ontario residents to fight to change the equalization system that transfers billions of federal tax dollars paid by Ontarians to other provinces ("Ontario Must Fight," 2008). However, because of a nosedive in its economy, Ontario received equalization payments ($347 million) for the first time in the 2009–10 fiscal year.

EVALUATING THE FEDERAL SYSTEM

The federal system is sometimes thought to limit the application of democracy. It restricts the ability of a Canada-wide majority to adopt preferred policies. By increasing the complexity of governing, it makes it harder for citizens to hold their governments accountable. Because both levels of government are active in many policy areas, a government can try to shift blame to the other level of government if the public is dissatisfied with the handling of a particular problem. For example, the federal and provincial governments have blamed each other for the cutbacks in post-secondary education funding (and resulting increases in tuition fees in most provinces) that have occurred over the past few decades.

The complexities in the federal system make it more challenging for citizens to participate effectively in trying to influence public policies. Indeed, many people do not know which level (or levels) of government is responsible for particular policy areas. In addition, governments are not often held accountable to their legislative bodies concerning intergovernmental relations and agreements. The federal system also tends to focus politics on federal–provincial disputes rather than on responding to the needs and wishes of the population. Further, intense disagreements can make building a consensus among governments difficult. Thus it is often a struggle to forge effective policies involving both levels of government. Conflicts among governments can also create or reinforce divisive tendencies within Canada as particular provincial governments voice their dissatisfaction and grievances (Smith, 2004).

On the positive side, provincial governments are more likely to be aware of the needs of their people and are more easily accessible and responsive to the public than would be the case with a single government in a vast country or in a more centralized federal system. The Canadian federal system allows provinces to enjoy a high degree of self-government and enables them to develop their own societies and economies. Citizens may find it easier to participate in politics at the provincial level than at the national one, particularly in the smaller provinces. Although executive federalism in Canada tends to involve bargaining behind closed doors, the competition and confrontations between the two levels of government can help to keep the public in the know about policy issues. As federal and provincial governments vie to mobilize public opinion to their position, issues and alternatives may be brought to public attention. However, the complexity of some issues (for example, issues linked to federal–provincial finances) means that even those who follow politics closely may struggle to make sense of the contradictory and often misleading arguments of the competing governments.

The Canadian federal system can also be viewed positively in terms of protecting and encouraging diversity within the country. This is particularly the case for minorities that are concentrated within a province. The vitality of the French language and culture in Canada is undoubtedly a product, in large part, of the ability of the French majority in Quebec to control their provincial government. However, groups that are not concentrated geographically and in a position to control or strongly influence a provincial government are less likely to see a particular benefit from the federal system.

Quebec has always had, to some degree, a special position within the federal system. The Quiet Revolution of the 1960s and the later development of a separatist movement in the province have often put the question of Quebec's position in Canada at the forefront of discussions of the federal system. Although Prime Minister Trudeau strongly opposed treating Quebec differently from any other province, the federal system since the 1960s has, to some extent, accommodated the distinctiveness of Quebec. This has moved Canada somewhat further in the direction of an **asymmetrical federal system**—that is, a system in which one or more provinces have a different relationship with the federal government, including different powers, from other provincial governments (Milne, 2005). Indeed, the 2004 federal–provincial Health Accord, in establishing some provisions that were different but comparable for Quebec, included a statement explicitly recognizing the idea of asymmetrical federalism. Asymmetry can be viewed as promoting greater flexibility in the federal system by allowing for different arrangements to suit the circumstances and wishes of the various provinces. However, the opposition to the Meech Lake and Charlottetown Accords underlined how the idea that one province might enjoy a different or special status is highly controversial. Nevertheless, Canadian governments have found it useful to try to negotiate bilateral agreements with the governments of individual provinces (not just Quebec), rather than coming to a standard agreement with all provinces.

ASYMMETRICAL FEDERAL SYSTEM
A federal system in which different provinces have a different relationship with the federal government, including different powers from other provincial governments.

Summary and Conclusion

The *Constitution Act,* 1867, provided a strict division of legislative authority between Parliament and provincial legislatures, combined with a broad general power for Parliament to legislate for the "peace, order, and good government" of Canada and provisions that allowed the Canadian government some control over provincial governments. Over time, the federal system has evolved into one of the world's most decentralized federal systems (Simeon & Robinson, 2009). Provincial governments exercise considerable power, have become recognized as the equals of the Canadian government, and have substantial financial independence.

The expansion of the role of government since the 1940s has resulted in much interaction between the federal and provincial governments. Intergovernmental cooperation under federal leadership was generally successful in developing the "welfare state." However, Canadian government involvement in provincial areas of jurisdiction has been challenged and the federal system has moved toward decentralization.

Canada's decentralized federal system mirrors, and to some extent reinforces, the country's provincial diversity and the distinctiveness of Quebec. Although decentralization may be a necessary response to provincialism and Quebec nationalism, it may limit the ability of the Canadian government to forge a stronger sense of national unity and national identity. Nevertheless, equalization payments (along with some other federal programs) have allowed Canadians to enjoy a relatively equal level of services from their governments, no matter where in Canada they live.

The system of executive federalism, which often involves compromises worked out behind closed doors by the prime minister and premiers without the involvement of representative legislative bodies or public participation, may be viewed as undemocratic. Many people in "English Canada" object to the somewhat different provisions for Quebec than for the other provinces, although these measures are often needed to gain the support of the Quebec government. These individuals prefer uniform Canada-wide policies, arguing against "special status" for Quebec. Thus some degree of "elite accommodation" may be needed to hold the country together, even though it conflicts with democratic values (Bakvis, Baier, & Brown, 2009). Furthermore, the complexity of the modern federal system makes it challenging for the public and their elected representatives to hold governments accountable for their actions.

The bargaining and negotiating characteristic of executive federalism has allowed governments to overcome the rigidity of the Constitution and the hurdle of achieving formal constitutional change. Despite the much-publicized conflicts between the Canadian and provincial governments, cooperation and collaboration have led to agreement on various policies. At times, though, a tug-of-war between the Canadian government and various provincial governments has endangered national unity and made it difficult to deal with national problems. Some tension in the federal system is inevitable as Canadian federal governments pursue national objectives and address the concerns of the population as a whole, while each provincial government has its eye on its own interests. Overall, the Canadian federal system features an ever-changing blend of centralization and decentralization, collaboration, cooperation, federal unilateral actions, provincial autonomy, and symmetrical and asymmetrical arrangements.

Discussion Questions

1. What are the advantages and disadvantages of Canada's federal system?

2. Is Canada's federal system a help or a hindrance to democracy?

3. Is the Canadian federal system too centralized or decentralized?

4. Is an asymmetrical federal system a threat to national unity?

5. Should there be greater provincial representation within Canadian governing institutions?

6. Does Canada's equalization system need to be changed?

7. Does the Canadian federal system provide an appropriate balance between unity and diversity?

Further Reading

Bakvis, H., & Skogstad, G. (Eds.). (2008). *Canadian federalism: Performance, effectiveness, and legitimacy* (2nd ed.). Don Mills, ON: Oxford University Press.

Bakvis, H., Baier, G., & Brown, D.M. (2009). *Contested federalism: Certainty and ambiguity in the Canadian federation*. Don Mills, ON: Oxford University Press.

Gagnon, A.-G. (Ed.). (2009). *Contemporary Canadian federalism: Foundations, traditions, institutions*. Toronto, ON: University of Toronto Press.

Peach, I. (Ed.). (2007). *Constructing tomorrow's federalism: New perspectives on Canadian governance*. Winnipeg: University of Manitoba Press.

Rocher, F., & Smith, M. (Eds.). (2003). *New trends in Canadian federalism* (2nd ed.). Peterborough, ON: Broadview Press.

Simeon, R. (2006). *Federal-provincial diplomacy: The making of recent policy in Canada*. Toronto, ON: University of Toronto Press. (Original work published 1972.)

Smith, J. (2004). *Federalism*. Vancouver: UBC Press.

Stevenson, G. (2004). *Unfulfilled union: Canadian federalism and national unity* (4th ed.). Montreal, QC: McGill-Queen's University Press.

Watts, R. L. (1999). *Comparing federal systems* (2nd ed.). Kingston, ON: Institute of Intergovernmental Relations.

THE INSTITUTIONS OF GOVERNMENT

Part V

Chapter 14

THE EXECUTIVE

PHOTO ABOVE: The decision that Canada would not participate in the U.S.-led attack on Iraq in 2003 was made by Prime Minister Jean Chrétien. Eddie Goldenberg (right), then senior policy adviser in the Prime Minister's Office, briefed the prime minister on the issue.

After reading this chapter, you should be able to

1. Explain what it means to have a "constitutional monarchy."
2. Examine the powers of the governor general.
3. Outline the bases of prime ministerial and cabinet power.
4. Discuss whether the prime minister is too powerful.
5. Examine how the policy process works.

It was 9:15 on March 17, 2003, and Eddie Goldenberg had no way of knowing what was coming next.* As senior policy adviser to Prime Minister Jean Chrétien, he had been preparing in his Wellington Street Langevin Block office for a meeting on Chrétien's landmark legislation prohibiting corporate and union financing of political parties. Instead, Chrétien phoned him and said something far more urgent had come up. Indeed it had.

Chrétien told Goldenberg that the British government had contacted the Canadian Foreign Affairs Department and asked for an urgent response to four questions: Would Canada politically support military action against the regime of Saddam Hussein in Iraq? What military capabilities would it bring to the venture? Would it make its position public? What humanitarian assistance and reconstruction aid could it provide? Furthermore, the Blair Government in Britain and the Bush Administration in the U.S. wanted a response to these questions by noon that day!

Chrétien instructed Goldenberg to work on the file right away and draft a set of recommendations. Goldenberg headed to the office of Claude Laverdure, head of the Foreign Policy and Defence Secretariat in the Privy Council Office and the point man on this issue. Before meeting with Chrétien, they reviewed the recent history of military intervention in Iraq: Chrétien had said several times that Canada would not engage Iraq militarily without United Nations approval. Canada's ambassador to the UN, Paul Heinbecker, told Goldenberg and Laverdure that the UN Security Council was not going to authorize force. Moreover, Parliament was in session, and although "the prime minister would have to make the final decision," and "there is no constitutional requirement to inform Parliament first," Chrétien agreed that

the Commons should be the forum for an announcement at 2:15 that afternoon. Goldenberg drafted a statement for question period, which would undoubtedly home in on the issue.

Sure enough, Iraq was the first matter to come up. Chrétien was ready with his reply. If the Security Council did not approve military action against Iraq, Canada would not participate in it. All parties but the Opposition Canadian Alliance cheered.

Here was the Canadian executive in a nutshell. As Goldenberg would put it later in his book *The Way It Works*, there were several factors affecting major public policy decisions, and several participants, but some decisions have to be funnelled and made quickly. "That," he said, "is what heads of government are elected to do." The incident also highlighted aspects other than the prime minister's dominance: the important policy role played by central executive agencies (notably the Privy Council Office), the executive's primary role in international affairs and conflicts, and the ambiguous role of Parliament in the decisions about wars and conflicts. But this just touches the surface of what the executive can do in this country.

---

*This vignette is based on Edward Goldenberg, *The Way It Works: Inside Ottawa*. Toronto: McClelland & Stewart, 2006, pp. 1–3 and 8–9.

ORIGINS AND POWERS

Before there were legislatures and courts of justice, there were kings and their advisers. Of all the branches of government, the executive is the oldest. Executives carry with them a long historical memory of pre-eminence and dominance—and they act accordingly. Yet legislatures and courts have the will of the people and the rule of law to challenge this pre-eminence. Modern history is one of attempting to bind political executives to democratic impulses, as mediated by parliaments, and to various refinements of the rule of law.

As with any entity that has grown over centuries, the executive has taken on differences in form that follow from specializations in function. Where once the monarch and his advisers were unchallenged, later came the prime minister whose job it was to manage a parliament for the monarch, his Cabinet (who in the British tradition doubled as advisers to the monarch and the prime minister), and a burgeoning bureaucracy. In the British tradition, the evolution happened particularly slowly and peacefully for the most part, creating a wealth of precedent, convention, and common law. These we still refer to today as Westminster systems; that is, those fashioned after the "**Westminster Model.**"

In this model, named after the area of London where the Houses of Parliament are situated, voters cast votes for party candidates, and the leader of the party with the majority of candidates elected to the House of Commons is called upon to form the government. The leader, the **prime minister**, nominates the Cabinet and therefore the government. There is a fusion of legislative and executive power in the Cabinet. That is, the political executive (the prime minister and Cabinet) is responsible for the day-to-day functioning of government ("executing" the laws), and can usually expect to have its legislative and budgetary proposals successfully passed because the majority in the House will support its initiatives. Normally, the prime minister and almost all of the members of Cabinet are members of the House of Commons and are expected to answer for the actions of the government in the House.

One result of the evolutionary aspect of executive growth is the existence of formal and informal parts of the executive. The formal executive is expected to be non-partisan and avoid political controversies. By "informal" we refer to the political executive (prime minister and Cabinet), whose far-reaching powers derive largely from custom and convention, but also from their political resources.

THE FORMAL EXECUTIVE

The Queen, the Governor General, and the Privy Council

Sections 9 to 11 of the *Constitution Act*, 1867, outline the **formal executive** and aspects of their authority. Executive government and authority is "vested in the Queen."[1] However, as established by the *Letters Patent*,

---

WESTMINSTER MODEL
The model of representative and responsible government used in the United Kingdom and in other countries that emulate it.

PRIME MINISTER
The head of government, meaning the person chosen by the governor general to form a government able to retain the confidence of a majority of the elected house of Parliament, the Commons.

FORMAL EXECUTIVE
That part of the executive consisting of the Queen, the governor general, and the queen's Privy Council for Canada, which possesses formal constitutional authority and by convention acts on the advice of the political executive.

---

[1]If a king takes the throne, the wording changes accordingly.

1947, the governor general permanently exercises virtually all of the monarch's powers and authorities. Thus the Queen performs only ceremonial duties for Canada.

The governor general, appointed by the Queen on the recommendation of the prime minister, is entrusted with "carrying on the Government of Canada on behalf of and in the name of the Queen," in other words being her representative.[2] Thus the Queen remains Canada's formal head of state, even though some governors general have occasionally referred to themselves as such.

The formal duties of the governor general include summoning people to membership in the Senate, appointing judges, summoning Parliament, dissolving Parliament (which results in an election), and giving royal assent to legislation. By convention, the governor general normally performs these duties on the advice of the Cabinet or, in some cases, the prime minister alone. The governor general also has the duty of choosing a new prime minister upon the resignation or death of a prime minister. However, because the prime minister is the leader of the party that controls the House of Commons, the choice of prime minister normally falls to that political party.

The mandate of the Queen's Privy Council for Canada is "to aid and advise in the Government of Canada." It is the governor general who appoints, and also may remove, members of the Privy Council. The Privy Council consists of all those who have ever been federal cabinet ministers, plus a limited number of honorific appointments. The *Constitution Act, 1867*, establishes that the Privy Council is the main source of advice to the governor general (section 13). Nevertheless, the Privy Council seldom meets, let alone offers advice to the governor general. By convention the **Cabinet** is the only active part of the Council. However, when acting officially, the Cabinet will rely on the formal authority of the Council.

Overall, then, the formal executive is the legal mask for the informal executive. By adopting a "Constitution similar in Principle to that of the United Kingdom," Canada took on the customs and conventions that had developed in the United Kingdom. Specifically, the monarch's representatives only act upon the legally and constitutionally tendered advice of the government of the day. Thus, the prime minister and Cabinet direct the business of government in the name of **the Crown**. Canada, like the United Kingdom, can thus be described as a constitutional monarchy or as a parliamentary democracy.

The Crown, Monarchy, and Prerogative

The best way to discuss the formal executive is to differentiate among the Crown, monarchy, and prerogative. In turn, the best way to investigate the Crown is to review its many meanings and the various sources of its powers.

CABINET
The active part of the Queen's Privy Council for Canada. Composed of the prime minister and ministers, it controls most of the executive and legislative powers of government.

THE CROWN
The Crown is the repository of all of the executive powers of the state and is the supreme authority for government.

---

[2]The lieutenant governor of each province, appointed by the governor general on the recommendation of the prime minister, is the counterpart of the governor general.

The Crown is most generally understood to be the repository of all of the executive powers of the state. Government is carried on in the name of the monarch, the Queen, but the Crown remains the supreme authority. The authority of government thus comes not from Parliament but from the Crown. The Crown is also a term that is used in a looser sense in many circumstances: as a symbol of what belongs to the Canadian public (for example, Crown corporations), as the body that prosecutes in criminal cases, and as government acting as a trustee in specific instances (for instance, regarding the interests of some of the Aboriginal peoples of Canada).

The powers of the Crown come from statute (legislation) and common law (the accumulation of judicial decisions). Parliament grants the Crown statutory powers, which give the Crown both executive power (the power to implement the laws) and legislative power (the power to make law of a delegated or subordinate nature, in the form of regulations or orders-in-council). In the ancient past, the common law allowed the monarch to legislate and act as well. These powers were called the prerogative power. A **prerogative power**, as Dicey (1965) says, is "the residue of discretionary authority, which at any given time is left in the hands of the Crown" (p. 424). This means that the ancient powers the monarch once uniquely possessed that have not been taken away by Parliament are still intact.

PREROGATIVE POWER
The powers the monarch once uniquely possessed that have not been taken away by Parliament.

DISCRETIONARY PREROGATIVE POWERS
Powers that the monarch's representative may exercise upon his or her own personal discretion. Also called *personal prerogatives* or *reserve powers*.

DISCRETIONARY PREROGATIVE POWERS   There are a few **discretionary prerogative powers** (also known as *personal prerogatives* or *reserve powers*)—those that the monarch's representative "may exercise upon his or her own personal discretion" (Hogg, 2006, p. 284). These include the appointment and dismissal of the prime minister, and the dissolution of Parliament. The governor general may also use personal discretion if the government is violating the constitution or does not have the confidence of the House of Commons.

The governor general has used discretionary prerogative powers in only a few instances. In 1896, Conservative Prime Minister Charles Tupper recommended the appointment of a number of his party's supporters to the Senate and the courts after his party was defeated in a general election. Governor General Lord Aberdeen rejected the recommendations. Since the prime minister did not have the confidence of the Commons (and the electorate) and the appointments would have been irrevocable, few would question the use of the discretionary power in this situation. In 1926, however, the use of the discretionary power to refuse the prime minister's request to grant the dissolution of Parliament and call an election was highly controversial (see Box 14-1, A Governor General Stirs Up Controversy: The King-Byng Affair). In more recent times, Governor General Edward Schreyer later revealed that he had been prepared on his own to call an election if Prime Minister Trudeau had pressed on with the unilateral amendment of the Constitution after the Supreme Court in 1981 declared this action a violation of constitutional

BOX 14-1

A Governor General Stirs Up Controversy: The King-Byng Affair

Prime Minister William Lyon Mackenzie King, whose grandfather led the Upper Canada Rebellion in 1837, had a great interest in the occult and regularly communicated with the spirits of his dead mother (whom he consulted for advice) and his beloved dog. Politically, he is still remembered for his challenge to the discretionary power of the governor general in 1926.

King earned a doctorate in political economy at Harvard, served as Canada's first deputy minister of Labour, and headed up the Rockefeller Foundation's industrial research department. In 1919, King won the Liberal party's first leadership convention. Two years later, he became prime minister as head of a minority government that relied on the support of the Progressive party.

The next election, in 1925, returned 101 Liberals, 116 Conservatives, 24 Progressives, 2 Labour, and 2 Independents. Despite the second-place finish, King did not resign and governed for a year with the support of the Progressives, Labour, and Independents. In June 1926, facing a vote of censure over a customs bribery scandal, and with his support in the minor parties deserting him, he asked Governor General Lord Byng to dissolve the House and call an election. Byng refused, noting that the Progressives were now ready to support Arthur Meighen's Conservatives, less than a year had passed since the last general election, and the motives of King—to avoid the will of the House to express censure—were evident.

King resigned, and Meighen accepted the governor general's request to form a government. However, three days later the government was defeated by a single vote. This time, the governor general had no alternative but to grant dissolution. King used the situation to his advantage. As he fought the 1926 election, he argued that the governor general should not have used the prerogative power to deny his request for an election, and was treating Canada like a British colony (Beck, 1968). King's Liberals won a majority government in the 1926 election and he went on to become Canada's longest-serving prime minister.

convention (as discussed in Chapter 10). Governor General Adrienne Clarkson has stated that she would not have granted Prime Minister Paul Martin a request for dissolution and an election if he had requested it within the first six months after the 2004 election that resulted in a minority government (Levy, 2009).

Finally, Governor General Michaëlle Jean generated considerable controversy when, on December 4, 2008, she granted Prime Minister Harper his request to prorogue (end the session of) Parliament (for the background see Chapter 8). In this case, Parliament had sat for only thirteen days since the October 14 election that had returned a minority Conservative government. In addition, a vote on the budget, which the government was certain to lose, was imminent; and the Liberal and New Democratic parties had signed a formal agreement to form a coalition government, which the Bloc Québécois had pledged to support for at least a year and a half.

Critics of the prime minister's request to prorogue Parliament argued that the situation was comparable to Prime Minister Mackenzie King's request for dissolution in 1926 when his government was facing censure in the Commons. Proroguing Parliament, like dissolving Parliament, would prevent the House of Commons from expressing its will. Further, it is a primary responsibility of the governor general to ensure there is a government in place that has the support of the majority in the House of Commons. In this case, an alternative government that clearly would have the support of the majority of the House was ready to assume office. Thus the governor general should have rejected the request for prorogation.

Those who supported the governor general's decision to prorogue Parliament argued that a change of government without an election would be undemocratic and tantamount to a "coup." Further, they claimed that the reliance of the proposed coalition on the support of the Bloc Québécois posed a threat to Canadian unity because of that party's advocacy of Quebec's independence. They also pointed out that the Liberals had promised during the election campaign that they would not form a coalition government (Flanagan, 2009). Further, they were critical of the coalition agreement that would see Stéphane Dion (who had led the Liberals to one of its worst defeats) as prime minister and "socialists" (the New Democratic Party) given six of the eighteen Cabinet positions.

Byng's use of the discretionary power and Jean's decision to accept the request of the prime minister both generated controversy. However, in both cases it was the prime minister who put the governor general in a difficult spot by trying to avoid the will of the majority in the House of Commons.

PREROGATIVE POWERS DEVOLVED TO MINISTERS   Other prerogative powers have devolved from the monarch to ministers who act in the name of the Crown. For example, the large field of foreign policy, including making treaties, declaring war, deploying the armed services in international conflicts, appointing ambassadors, recognizing states, and accrediting diplomats, is largely governed by prerogative power. In the more humdrum areas like issuing passports, granting honours, appointing Queen's Counsel, and clemency, ministers enjoy the exercise of all these powers without necessarily having to involve Parliament. In fact, throughout history, Parliament was bypassed in the decisions to grant this ministerial "prerogative power." Some would argue that in a democracy, the democratically elected representatives ought to be the ones who have the right to declare war, end a war, and determine how a war should be conducted.

THE POLITICAL EXECUTIVE

The Prime Minister, Cabinet, and Ministers of State

POLITICAL EXECUTIVE
The prime minister, Cabinet, and ministers of state.

The **political executive** is made up of the prime minister, cabinet ministers, and ministers of state. The prime minister is sometimes referred to as the "first minister" to indicate his or her leadership role in the Cabinet.

The political executive is the most powerful part of the political system, but surprisingly the formal Constitution is silent on its existence and operation. It operates mostly under the cloak of custom and constitutional convention (binding practices), and occasionally under usages of the constitution (non-binding practices). Silence opens the way for flexibility, and the executive has made full use of flexibility to extend its reach. Thus, the political executive takes much of its direction from convention rather than statute.

In particular, convention dictates that only the active part of the Privy Council—the "Government," or cabinet of the day—can exercise governmental power. Nevertheless, the Cabinet adopts the garb of the Privy Council. This is reflected in the language of government decision making. For example, the *Governor General in Council* (usually referred to as the **Governor in Council**) is the formal name of Cabinet, a *minute of council* is a decision of Cabinet, and an *order-in-council* is a decision taken by virtue of power delegated to the Cabinet. The term "Governor in Council" does not imply that the governor general actually presides over the Cabinet—a practice that ended in the nineteenth century—or even attends Cabinet meetings, but that the governor general acts on the advice of the Cabinet.

Many of the executive functions of the Cabinet are undertaken in the name of the governor general or the Governor in Council. These include some aspects of the prerogative power delegated to the Cabinet collectively: the appointment of privy councillors, judges, and senators; involvement in international affairs; and the power of clemency, or pardon, given to federal offenders.

GOVERNOR IN COUNCIL
The formal name given to Cabinet in order to cloak its decisions with constitutional authority. The phrase means that the governor general is acting on the advice of the Queen's Privy Council for Canada, the active part of which is the Cabinet.

THE FLEXIBILITY OF THE WESTMINSTER SYSTEM
Canadians sometimes take their form of government, and especially cabinet government, for granted, thinking that only one variety exists. This is not the case; parliamentary systems come in a surprising number of guises. The legislatures of Nunavut and the Northwest Territories make for fascinating examples. They do not have political parties, candidates run as independents, all members of the legislative assembly elect the premier and cabinet in secret ballot, and the cabinet as permanent minority[3] often sees its policy and budget decisions subject to change by the legislature. The major similarities to other legislatures in Canada are that the premier chooses the portfolios that cabinet members hold, and certain Westminster principles such as confidence votes and cabinet solidarity apply (White, 2006).

Interesting examples of the variety of the Westminster system can be gleaned from outside Canada as well. For instance, the parliamentary caucuses of the United Kingdom Conservative party and of the Australian Labour party can choose and remove the prime minister. In Australia and New

---

[3]It is a permanent minority because it cannot depend on a party to marshal a majority in the legislature to support its program.

Zealand, the parliamentary caucuses of the Labour parties select members of the ministry. Also in the United Kingdom, the "Government," which can number as many as a hundred members, encompasses many different types of ministers: the twenty to twenty-five or so senior cabinet ministers who run Whitehall departments (sometimes called the "inner cabinet"), and junior ministers and Parliamentary private secretaries.

The Canadian ministry follows few of these characteristics and furthermore has not varied much over the years. The governing party's caucus does not choose the prime minister. Instead, the prime minister is the leader of a political party who is normally chosen, in recent times, by a direct vote of all party members (see Chapter 8). The prime minister advises the governor general on the appointment of all ministers, and the caucus has little role to play other than that of a sounding board for the prime minister and Cabinet. The government does not swell to the size of that of the United Kingdom, and with the exception of an experiment with the short-lived Clark Government (1979–80), recourse to an inner cabinet is unknown.[4]

Categories of Office in the Ministry Canadian practice differentiates between categories of office in the ministry. The following are the most common.

The first category is the *prime minister*. The prime minister is the most powerful of the ministers by virtue of method of appointment, electoral base, and various prerogatives.

Second are the *ministers* who head departments of government. Specific departmental acts, and the *Interpretation Act*, set out the responsibilities of most ministers. However, in special cases, comprehensive statutes such as the *Financial Administration Act* create certain ministerial portfolios and departments. Some ministers—termed line ministers—head departments that are primarily involved in providing services to the public or a segment of society (such as the ministers of Agriculture and Health). Others are responsible for departments that are more concerned with policy coordination (such as the ministers of International Trade and Finance).

Third are *ministers of state* (also termed *secretaries of state*). Many of these people have been assigned to assist ministers in specific areas of their portfolios. The Martin Government (2003–06) created a distinction between the Cabinet and the ministry; in the former were the traditional cabinet ministers, and in the latter were secretaries of state, who were members of the Privy Council but not of the Cabinet. Like cabinet ministers, secretaries of state were bound by the convention of collective responsibility (discussed below). They earned three-quarters of the salary of cabinet ministers. Secretaries of

---

[4]The term "inner cabinet" has a variety of meanings, most of them referring to an elite committee within Cabinet that is the most influential or sets broad policy directions for the rest of Cabinet. However, the sense in which we use the term here is that of the Clark Government (1979). Clark had an inner committee of ministers with final decision-making power, and the full Cabinet was simply a forum for discussion and coordination.

Line ministers lead government departments that deliver services directly to the public at large or segments of the public. After a January 2010 cabinet shuffle, four of these six were line ministers (l–r): Gerry Ritz (back middle) (Agriculture), Jason Kenney (Citizenship, Immigration and Multiculturalism), Chuck Strahl (front left) (Indian Affairs and Northern Development), Peter MacKay (National Defence). Two were not: Peter Van Loan (back right) (International Trade) shares responsibility with the Minister of Foreign Affairs for a department that is more concerned with policy coordination than service delivery. Stockwell Day (front right) (Treasury Board) leads a central agency and is responsible for the translating the policies and programs approved by Cabinet into operational reality and for providing departments with the resources and the administrative environment they need to do their work.

state were able to attend Cabinet on a rotational basis in the Chrétien years, and in Martin's interlude they were expected to attend all Cabinet meetings. *Ministers without portfolio* were the forerunners to this post in the last century and have very occasionally been appointed in more recent times; they were valuable to the setting of collective policy in Cabinet but were not given a department to manage.

Stephen Harper maintained the distinction between "ministry" and "cabinet" but called the officials "ministers of state." Ministers of state can attend the cabinet committee meetings relevant to their areas of responsibility. Ministers of state represent ministers at events, stakeholder meetings, parliamentary committees, and question period, and demonstrate policy leadership in areas specified by the prime minister or minister. Among the ministers of state (as of 2009) are those dealing with sport, the status of women, small business and tourism, and transport. Unlike ministers, however, they do not oversee any area of the public service.

Parliamentary secretaries are government party members chosen by the prime minister to assist a minister, or occasionally more than one minister. Their major function is to act as intermediaries or liaisons among the minister, the Commons and its committees, the caucus, and the general public.

However, parliamentary secretaries are not considered to be part of the ministry and do not have access to Cabinet documents. Their status may vary according to the prime minister in question. Paul Martin had his parliamentary secretaries sworn in as members of the Privy Council, and they were thus bound by the requirements of cabinet solidarity and secrecy. No matter which government they serve, parliamentary secretaries are subject to the *Conflict of Interest Act* and to the Conflict of Interest Code for Members of the House of Commons.

The Political Executive in Action

Whereas conventions govern the relationship between the formal and political executive, other conventions are intended to guide the operation of the political executive itself. The most important ones involve recognizing responsible government and ministerial responsibility.

RESPONSIBLE GOVERNMENT   Responsible government is the central convention of the Canadian constitution. It maintains that the Cabinet needs the continued support of the majority of the elected House to stay in office. This is also known as "collective responsibility." Responsible government is a British heritage because Britain was the model for our struggles for democracy in Canada.

Responsible government still matters, and involves two related aspects: **individual ministerial responsibility**, and the **collective responsibility** of the whole Cabinet.

INDIVIDUAL MINISTERIAL RESPONSIBILITY
The responsibility of individual cabinet ministers to the House of Commons for the decisions and actions of the department they administer.

COLLECTIVE RESPONSIBILITY
The convention that the Cabinet as a group is responsible to the House of Commons for the decisions and actions of the government.

Individual Ministerial Responsibility   Individual responsibility is essentially the duty to submit, to defend, and to resign, if necessary. A minister has to submit his or her department's budgets and plans to the House, to defend them there, and to answer questions about these and related aspects of the department's operations. The minister may be expected to resign if guilty of improper behaviour or of failure to offer correctives to problems in the running of the department. Members of the House may direct questions to a minister about official duties relating to the minister's present portfolio. According to parliamentary rules, the minister does not have to answer questions directed at him or her, but public opinion creates pressure for the minister to complete this ring of ministerial responsibility.

In addition, individual ministerial responsibility includes political culpability or blame that may taint a minister's reputation and reflect badly on the government as a whole. The classic approach holds that the minister is responsible (culpable) for every action that takes place in the department, whether or not the minister knew of it. This approach seems to have had currency up until the mid-twentieth century. However, the enormous job of monitoring increasingly large and complex bureaucracies has led to questioning of the doctrine, although parliamentary opposition members still occasionally refer to it in the hope of making a minister resign for some bureaucratic indiscretion.

The modern realist version of the doctrine recognizes a distinction between official acts of which the minister can reasonably be expected to be aware, and those incompetent or illegal actions the minister could not have known about. To be sure, once having become aware of such incompetence or illegality, the minister may be held culpable before Parliament for failing to take remedial administrative measures or appropriate corrective action. In the House, a minister may be called upon to resign in certain other obvious cases: misleading Parliament, authorizing unreasonable use of executive power, or engaging in immoral conduct or conduct unbecoming a minister of the Crown. "Conduct unbecoming" has been the undoing of several ministers in recent decades. For example, Solicitor General Francis Fox resigned in 1978 after forging the signature of his mistress's husband so she could get an abortion. He returned to Cabinet two years later. Defence Minister Maxime Bernier was forced to resign in 2008 because he broke rules regarding government classified documents; specifically, he left NATO documents for five weeks at the apartment of his girlfriend, who had connections to biker gangs.

Ultimately, the prime minister determines the fate of a minister under attack in the Commons. The calculus that the first minister considers when deciding whether or not the minister is to go is complex. It can include such considerations as whether the minister is only trying to administer a policy that Cabinet decided on collectively, whether the fate of the whole ministry is at stake if the minister does not go, whether the government will appear weak if the prime minister bows to demands from the opposition for the minister's resignation, and, of course, whether public opinion is a threat to the government. Ordering a minister to resign is one of the most painful decisions a prime minister has to take.

Collective Responsibility   Collective responsibility is the second major part of the doctrine of responsible government. As Heard (1991) notes, there are three interrelated aspects of collective responsibility: the responsibility of the Cabinet to the monarch, the responsibility of the Cabinet to itself, and the responsibility of the Cabinet to the House. The first gives rise to the oaths that new members of the Privy Council take, the second to the doctrines of cabinet solidarity and cabinet secrecy, and the third to the confidence convention (the requirement that the Cabinet retain the confidence of the majority in the House of Commons).

The responsibility of the minister to the monarch is reflected in the oaths the new privy councillors take after they receive a commission from the governor general, summoning them to the Privy Council. The oath carries with it the duty to honour the right of the monarch's representative to be consulted, to encourage, and to warn—that is, to be kept up to date on government business and to be consulted on it—and the duty to resign upon refusal of dissolution if the governor decides to use the reserve power.

CABINET SOLIDARITY
The basic principle that ministers must avoid public disagreements over policy once Cabinet decides on it, and that they must vote in unison in the House on government business.

Cabinet is responsible to itself in a number of ways. **Cabinet solidarity** is an important fact of life for Westminster-type governments. Basically, it means that ministers must avoid public disagreements over policy, even if they have already clashed in their opinions in the Cabinet room, and that they must vote in unison in the House on government business. Forsey and Eglington (1985), in a frequently quoted section of their work on responsible government, noted the range of consequences that flow from cabinet solidarity:

1. Government advice to the Crown must be unanimous, even if arrived at after considerations of strongly held but opposed views.

2. A minister (i) must loyally support and defend any cabinet decisions and not quaver by suggestion he was compromised or was reluctantly persuaded; (ii) must be prepared not only to refrain from publicly criticizing other ministers but also to defend them publicly; (iii) must not announce a new policy or change in policy without prior cabinet consent—if he does so cabinet may adopt the policy and save him from resignation, but if it does not, he must resign; (iv) must not express private views on government policies; (v) must not speak about or otherwise become involved in a colleague's portfolio without first consulting him and gaining his approval and probably that of the prime minister; (vi) must not make speeches or do acts which may appear to implicate the government, and must not express personal opinions about future policy except after consultation; (vii) must carry out the policy decided upon by cabinet so far as it affects his own portfolio; (viii) must vote with the government, whether it is in danger or not; (ix) must speak in defence of the government and any of its policies if the prime minister insists. (pp. 147–148)

Cabinet solidarity is important not just because it is a historical practice, but because of its strategic value. The opposition and the media will take advantage of division in the Cabinet, potentially leading to the defeat of the government in the House of Commons, especially if a revolt in the caucus is a factor. Prime Minister Harper has adopted a strict version of cabinet solidarity, directing the Privy Council Office to vet public appearances and interviews by cabinet ministers, as well as approving departmental information sent out to journalists.

As in the case of ministerial resignations, the prime minister decides the degree to which the words or actions of ministers count as a breach of cabinet solidarity and a threat to the stability of the government. However, occasionally the first minister does not have to judge a minister who resists discipline; instead the minister may decide that the disagreement with the Cabinet is so fundamental that it is necessary to withdraw from the government. For example, Lucien Bouchard withdrew from Mulroney's Cabinet in 1990 because he was unable to accept changes to the Meech Lake Accord. Michael Chong resigned from Harper's Cabinet in 2006 because he did not support the government's motion recognizing the "Québécois as a nation within a united Canada." However, resignations from Cabinet on matters of principled disagreement are few and far between.

There may also be instances when the prime minister does not enforce solidarity over issues of conscience. Such was the case with several votes over capital punishment. By a free vote in 1976, Parliament abolished the death penalty, except for certain offences under the *National Defence Act*. Another free vote in 1987 kept the abolition in place. In 1998 Parliament removed the last exceptions under the *National Defence Act*.

Cabinet Secrecy   **Cabinet secrecy** protects the expression of views by ministers in the setting of Cabinet and cabinet committee discussions, in order to encourage frankness. All ministers take an oath committing them to secrecy in their cabinet deliberations. D'Ombrain (2006) notes that "cabinet secrecy is widely assumed to be akin to executive privilege, shielding all that is internal to the Cabinet. The cabinet secrecy convention does not protect the substantive secrets of the cabinet; rather it protects the processes whereby ministers arrive at decisions. That is all it protects" (pp. 334–335). Cabinet secrecy is the reason that cabinet ministers will go to great lengths not to divulge to the incoming administration (of a different party) the cabinet minutes of the previous administration. They will, however, pass along to the new administration the records of decision, which are necessary for the functioning of the state.

Cabinet secrecy also safeguards cabinet ministers from having their opinions made public and having to defend them in the public realm. It complements cabinet solidarity, which is a lynchpin of the cabinet-parliamentary system. It protects the anonymity of public servants: their advice to ministers is kept in confidence and intended to stay that way. Otherwise the public would identify public servants with a certain course of action when they are duty-bound only to serve the will of the government in office. Cabinet secrecy also provides the forum in which brokerage of regional interests can take place. Canadians have come to expect that the political executive is the venue for bargaining between regions rather than the legislative arena, as is the case in the United States.

CABINET SECRECY
A convention that forbids the disclosure of the views expressed by particular ministers in the setting of cabinet (and cabinet committee) discussions, in order to encourage frankness.

EXECUTIVE DOMINANCE

Canadians live in a system marked by executive dominance. This means that the prime minister and Cabinet dominate the legislative branch—they direct its business and are the main originators of policy change and innovation. Some would say that this fact is due to cultural traits that predispose Canadians to "deference to authority" (Friedenberg, 1980). Others have noted a tendency for the executive to gather power around itself over time, especially through the prime minister (Savoie, 2008). Still others will see in executive dominance a holdover of British practices of government inherited from colonial times.

Whatever the broad reasons, the power structure itself contributes to the executive being the pre-eminent body in the political system. The power structure promotes executive dominance through constitutional authority and organizational factors. As we have seen, the Constitution is heavily biased toward the formal executive. In fact the informal executive is the beneficiary of this constitutional windfall, and expresses its will through legislation that refers to the governor general, the Governor in Council, or individual ministers. As well, only about 4000 staff work for the Canadian Parliament compared with approximately 240 000 departmental positions in the federal public service (Axworthy, 2008). Accordingly, the ability of Parliament to scrutinize the executive and hold it accountable is very limited.

However, executive dominance is sometimes weakened. Occasionally the tables turn and Parliament is able, in a limited way, to set the agenda for the government. This is particularly the case in minority government situations. In some cases, the minority government has been toppled by a vote on a matter of confidence, while in other cases (such as in 2008) the prime minister has requested an election in hopes of gaining a majority. Nevertheless, the threat of defeat by vote of non-confidence is often enough to convince the government of the day to adopt some policies promoted by the opposition. The minority Pearson Government in the 1960s was coaxed into developing medicare by its dependence on NDP support. The minority Trudeau Government of 1972–74 took on many initiatives that the NDP had promoted, such as the creation of Petro-Canada and electoral funding legislation. Somewhat similarly, the threat of a Liberal–NDP coalition government replacing the Conservative minority in 2008 spurred the government to action. In November 2008, the government's economic statement had done little to respond to the severe worldwide recession, despite calls for economic stimulus from the opposition parties. After the coalition emerged, the Conservative government quickly changed its tune to announce a major economic stimulus package.

The Prime Minister

THE POWERS AND FUNCTIONS OF THE PRIME MINISTER   Both the prime minister and Cabinet have special powers and functions in the Canadian version of the Westminster Model. First of all, the prime minister in the Canadian system enjoys the "five Ps of power": parliamentary leader, party leader, patronage, policy-maker, and public face. The prime minister leads the Cabinet, which sets the priorities for Parliament, and is influential in allocating Parliament's time, along with the government House leader. The prime minister is a party leader elected by the broad membership of the party. The prime minister also holds the power of rewarding or thwarting ambition, because of the office's control over the levers of patronage. There are thousands of non-public service-related positions in the public sector to be handed out. As well, the prime minister is the chief policy-maker for government, overshadowing in recent years the plenary (full) Cabinet and inviting a kind of "court government," an undemocratic, almost aristocratic approach to governing (Savoie, 2008). Finally, the prime minister is the public face of government; when the prime minister is popular, the governing party is popular and the prime minister needs to expend relatively little political capital to maintain support within the party.

The prime minister is also powerful as a result of being the principal communicator with the Crown. Instruments of Advice are one mechanism the prime minister can use to intercede in, or affect, matters of governance. These are letters informing the governor general of the prime minister's views on matters involving the Royal Prerogative; since 1953, the principal ones have been the summoning of Parliament, recommending the dissolution of Parliament and requesting an election, nominating the Cabinet, summoning qualified people to the Senate, and changing the Crown's prerogative. Other uses of Instruments of Advice are to designate a cabinet minister as deputy prime minister, to accept resignations of ministers, and to change the Table of Precedence for Canada (the list of seniority and rank of government officials). Appointment of the governor general of Canada is done by an Instrument of Advice submitted to the Queen.

The prime minister's powers include the ability to intercede in most procedural and policy areas of government. These run the gamut of public policy but usually apply to foreign affairs, national unity strategy, and intergovernmental affairs—some of the highest-profile issues that can affect a government. In fact, in recent years, ministers filling portfolios for external affairs (the Foreign Affairs minister) and intergovernmental affairs have understood that the policy direction in these areas ultimately comes from the prime minister. Sometimes reminders of the prime minister's dominance take the form of surprise announcements that enable the prime minister to assert authority over Cabinet, knowing that members will seldom raise their voices in objection, at least not publicly. For example, Trudeau's announcement of a major financial restraint program in the mid-1970s surprised even his own finance minister.

Power also originates in the prime minister's role as the principal architect of government. The prime minister can shift the attention of ministers and officials by simply focusing attention on organizational matters. Early in the twentieth century, the prime minister chose personnel for a cabinet that stayed relatively stable in size and configuration. In the intervening years, it became this and more: now added was a general responsibility for the design of government. The first minister can thwart the ambition of both ministers and bureaucrats by forming small cabinets; can control ministers by having a large and powerful planning and policy-oriented central agency; and can position certain ministers above others by assigning the most important departments to them, such as Health, Finance, and Industry. In addition, the prime minister can turn to the Royal Commissions and commissions of inquiry to energize or change the basic direction of government, as was the case with the reports of the Rowell-Sirois Commission (1940), the Gordon Commission (1957), and the Macdonald Royal Commission (1985).

The appointment power is significant, as the prime minister is able to choose the personnel of crucial institutions and agencies of the Canadian state. These include the following:

- Senate vacancies
- The governor general and all the provincial lieutenant governors
- The Justices of the Supreme Court of Canada
- The Chief Justices and Associate Chief Justices of the superior courts of the provinces
- All of the deputy ministers in the government of Canada
- Most of the deputy minister equivalents in agencies, boards, and commissions at the federal level (see Chapter 16)
- All ambassadors who represent the country abroad
- All appointees to international organizations, including the United Nations and the International Monetary Fund
- The head of the RCMP
- The governor of the Bank of Canada and its board
- Several of the officers of Parliament

An additional aspect of prime ministerial power is that elected representatives do not carry out meaningful reviews of these appointments. In this respect, the Canadian system differs considerably from that of the United States. Although the Canadian Public Appointments Commission (not yet implemented as of November 2009) promises an element of control, its input does not amount to a system of checks and balances in the executive government appointment process similar to that practised by the U.S. Senate.

▶ Stephen Harper exercised his prime ministerial power to appoint ambassadors in August 2009 when he named former Manitoba Premier Gary Doer as the next Canadian ambassador to the United States.

In many ways, the prime minister has power because he is a leader and has leadership qualities. Leadership power comes through the official roles that the prime minister is expected to play: symbolic leader, cabinet leader, parliamentary leader, and national leader. Beyond these roles, the prime minister is sometimes seen as the embodiment of the country, reflected in the statesman-like utterances he or she is called upon to make in the appropriate context, like a natural disaster, the deaths of soldiers in conflicts abroad, or in international contexts. Indeed, like American presidents, prime ministers, along with their families, have in modern times been treated as celebrities by the media.

The job of leader of Cabinet involves a number of tasks that enhance the authority of the first minister. The prime minister determines the agenda of cabinet meetings. The leader voices the consensus of Cabinet, which can range from a true consensus to a consensus of one—the prime minister—in unusual cases. Of course, if this minority consensus style becomes the rule rather than the exception, cabinet discord can arise, but this style may often be necessary to move the Cabinet along. Moreover, the prime minister is the only member of the Cabinet who is focused on the overall direction of the government, whereas other ministers tend to develop what is called "portfolio loyalties," which limit their ability to see more broadly. The prime minister also determines the way that cabinet business is handled; for example, whether or not cabinet committees will have effective sign-off on some policy matters as has been the case in recent years. Another leadership power is to determine the relative balance between cabinet material generated by departmental staff on the one hand and central agencies (notably the Privy Council Office, which is under the direction of the prime minister, as discussed in Chapter 16) on the other. In the early days of cabinet operation, there was only a vertical orientation to policy advice, with departments as the main source of information to cabinet. In modern cabinets this vertical axis remains, but there is also a horizontal axis: the provision of policy and financial management counsel by central agencies and central departments (including the Department of Finance and the Treasury Board Secretariat). To the extent that the centre grows stronger, the departments grow weaker.

Parliamentary leadership is another in the list of seemingly endless aspects of power of the first minister. Prime ministers choose a special member of Cabinet called the Government House Leader, and therefore directly affect many aspects of parliamentary operations as discussed in Chapter 15. The prime minister is usually the focus of the daily question period in the House of Commons and therefore is in a position to influence public opinion. The timetable contrasts sharply with that of the U.K. prime minister, who appears only once a week, and for a mere half-hour. As well, the prime minister, acting through the House Leader and others, is able to allocate the time of Parliament to government bills, which typically take up a substantial majority of the time of the lower house.

LIMITS ON THE PRIME MINISTER'S POWER Although journalist Jeffrey Simpson (2001) once described Canada as a "friendly dictatorship" because of the great power of the prime minister, there are some limits to the power of those who hold this position. It is the nature of power to be met, ultimately, with power. In Canada, the federal system provides an important limit to what a prime minister can do. Federal politicians have to tread lightly when it comes to matters that fall within provincial jurisdiction, such as resource taxation, social programs, and education.

Public opinion can sometimes act as a potent counter to the prime minister. The Mulroney Government shelved its plans for partial de-indexation of the old-age pension in 1984 after an old-age pensioner predicted "Goodbye Charlie Brown" to the prime minister in a TV scrum on Parliament Hill, stirring up public opinion (Savoie, 1999). Circumstances await an unwary prime minister; as ex-Prime Minister Harold Macmillan of Britain allegedly replied when asked what he thought was the greatest threat a statesman might face, "Events, dear boy, events." For example, Prime Minister Pearson faced a blizzard of scandals in his first term: individual cabinet ministers were accused of helping the escape from prison of a notorious drug dealer, buying furniture on favourable terms, and accepting a bribe. Prime Minister Paul Martin's short term of office was disrupted by the "sponsorship scandal," which involved a number of government contracts that had been improperly awarded to advertising agencies that produced little or no work on the contracts, with some of the money ending up as donations to Liberal party officials.

Finally, the Cabinet can provide an important limitation to prime ministerial power. Even with the support of the Privy Council Office and the Prime Minister's Office, the prime minister necessarily relies on cabinet ministers for advice. Inevitably, the prime minister cannot know about and participate in all of the deliberations and decisions of modern governments. As noted above, prime ministers tend to focus their attention on selected important policy areas and on setting the overall direction and political strategy of the government. For other matters, ministers, supported by the expertise of their department, usually wield considerable influence. Furthermore, the minister of Finance with responsibility for the budget will typically have a strong impact on what the government can or cannot do. In addition, some cabinet ministers are powerful political figures in their own right because of their support within a particular region of the country or among powerful interests, or because of their following within the caucus or the party as a whole. For example, Paul Martin had considerable power through most of the years that Jean Chrétien was prime minister not only because of Martin's position as Finance minister, but also because of his support within the Liberal party.

Cabinet

The Cabinet carries out a variety of legislative and executive functions. Cabinet introduces most of the legislation that Parliament deals with, not only because

Canadians expect this, but also because the government party arranges the timetable to accommodate this. By virtue of section 54 of the *Constitution Act, 1867*, Cabinet introduces all financial legislation, including Ways and Means bills, which affect taxation; Appropriation bills, which authorize the withdrawal of funds from the Consolidated Revenue Fund; and Borrowing Authority bills, which seek authority to borrow money. It is therefore unconstitutional for the legislature to introduce financial measures as Congress, its counterpart, can do in the United States.[5]

Traditionally parliaments have recognized the limitations of their legislative role and have chosen to share this role with the executive. The executive is better placed to address the specifics of policy areas than is the legislature, and regular legislation involves an extensive planning cycle that is not always convenient, quick, and efficient. Parliament often delegates to the executive the power to pass legislation and regulations to flesh out the details of legislation passed by Parliament. This power to pass **subordinate or delegated legislation** is held either by the full Cabinet (and expressed as being passed by the Governor in Council), by a minister of the Crown, or by an administrative agency vested with delegated legislative authority. It takes a variety of forms: orders-in-council, minutes of council, regulations, and other statutory instruments, such as rules, warrants, and proclamations. The reach of delegated legislation is extensive.

SUBORDINATE (DELEGATED) LEGISLATION
Authority for subordinate legislation that comes from a primary piece of legislation passed by Parliament and takes the form of orders-in-council or regulations made by a minister or agency.

CABINET'S EXECUTIVE FUNCTIONS   The Cabinet is responsible for several executive functions. First, it plays a leadership role for the whole political system. Individual ministers have responsibility for the management and direction of their department. Second, the Cabinet is expected to be the main source of policy generation in the political system. Third, it performs certain measures collectively in the name of the governor general and usually upon the initiative of the prime minister, as discussed earlier in this chapter. Finally, the Cabinet as a great crossroads of information and strategy setting has to provide coordination for all the activities and decisions of government. This places a heavy burden on the prime minister.

CONSIDERATIONS IN CABINET CONSTRUCTION   The prime minister chooses cabinet ministers from among the governing party's Members of Parliament (see Box 14-2, Tradition with a Twist: Building the Harper Cabinet). Almost all cabinet ministers are selected from the House of Commons, although the leader of the government in the Senate (and occasionally other senators) is usually appointed to the Cabinet in order to defend government policies in that chamber.

In constructing the Cabinet, the prime minister is aware of precedent. In particular, a very strong norm dictates that the prime minister should choose

---

[5]The Commons can affect expenditures by moving for the reduction in a vote, but this is a rare occurrence.

BOX 14-2

Tradition with a Twist: Building the Harper Cabinet

Sir John A. Macdonald was fond of describing his occupation as "cabinet-maker," and indeed most other prime ministers have construed this as one of their major tasks. It is, however, a lonely job. Speaking of Mr. Harper's process of choosing the Cabinet after the 2008 election, one (unnamed) Conservative source said, "The only three people who really know what's going to happen are Harper, [his wife] Laureen and [his Chief of Staff] Guy Giorno" ("Harper Gears Up," 2008).

The leader usually goes into retreat (to escape supplicants) and mulls over the demographics he wants to attract to his party and what potential cabinet ministers in the governing caucus can do to win their support. Re-election rather than revenge also seems to be a cabinet-making theme. Referring to Harper's making up his 2006 Cabinet, *Maclean's* observed, "It's intriguing that Harper, along with [Jim] Prentice, his unofficial chief operating officer [soon to be in Cabinet], has been reading historian Doris Kearns Goodwin's *Team of Rivals*, which explores how Abraham Lincoln elevated into his Cabinet former adversaries who had once disdained him, and then let them do their jobs" (Geddes, 2006). It turned out that Harper took his cue from Lincoln.

A look at the construction of the Harper Cabinet in October 2008 shows that some of the traditional guidelines applied. Gail Shea from Prince Edward Island got Fisheries and Oceans, Christian Paradis from Quebec got Public Works, and Agriculture went to Gerry Ritz from Saskatchewan. Paradis was in because businessman Michel Fortier, Harper's hand-picked candidate, had failed to get elected. Contrary to tradition, however, Justice continued under Rob Nicholson from Ontario, most likely based on the scant members—ten—elected from Quebec in 2008. Because of this low number, the usual rough parity between Quebec and Ontario ministers was dropped. Thirteen from the key political region of Ontario (including one senator) received Cabinet appointments, but only five from Quebec. British Columbia and Alberta also had five ministers each (not including the prime minister from Alberta). The Atlantic provinces, a powerful part of cabinets in past centuries, continued their slide in percentage and numbers, totalling just four in Cabinet.

Other customs continued. Every province except Newfoundland and Labrador received its base of at least one minister. Even here, there were extenuating circumstances: the province's premier, Danny Williams, had succeeded in his 2008 "ABC" campaign ("Anything But Conservative"), convincing Newfoundlanders to shut out the Conservatives from receiving even one seat. The important role of lawyers in Cabinet also continued: they amounted to twelve of the thirty-eight-member Cabinet. Eight of the twenty-seven ministers with departmental responsibilities were female (the same proportion as a decade earlier in Chrétien's Cabinet). Of these, Bev Oda, Minister of International Cooperation, is from a visible minority and Health Minister Leona Aglukkaq is Canada's first Inuit minister.

Although Stephen Harper was a strong critic of "big government" before he became prime minister, like other prime ministers he found it useful to increase the size of his Cabinet. A larger cabinet can provide more representation for different groups, as well as helping to avoid the dissatisfaction within the caucus of those who feel they deserve to be in Cabinet.

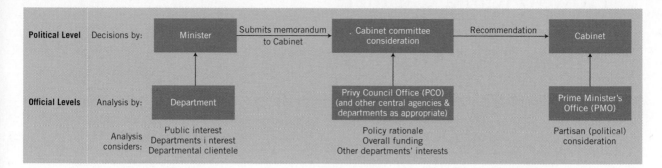

Political Level	Decisions by:	Minister	Submits memorandum to Cabinet →	Cabinet committee consideration	Recommendation →	Cabinet
Official Levels	Analysis by:	Department		Privy Council Office (PCO) (and other central agencies & departments as appropriate)		Prime Minister's Office (PMO)
	Analysis considers:	Public interest Departments i nterest Departmental clientele		Policy rationale Overall funding Other departments' interests		Partisan (political) consideration

FIGURE 14-1
THE ROUTING OF MEMORANDA TO CABINET

CABINET COMMITTEES:
Groups of cabinet ministers who examine policy proposals from related policy fields and recommend to the plenary (full) Cabinet what action should be taken. Their recommendations generally are accepted.

Cabinet Committees

Cabinet committees are relatively recent, but important, actors in the Ottawa policy scene. They were sparsely used before the 1960s for a number of reasons, one being a perception that collective responsibility would be weakened if cabinet decision making was subdivided. Another was that some prime ministers, such as Mackenzie King, felt that they could not adequately exercise power over other ministers if the ministers were out of sight of the prime minister (see Box 14-3, How to Run a Cabinet: The Master Himself, William Lyon Mackenzie King). Others, like John Diefenbaker, the self-proclaimed outsider to the federal scene, distrusted their fellow ministers and felt more comfortable in a full Cabinet situation. One important consideration was that government was still relatively small and its business manageable by full Cabinet.

Later on, committees became progressively more central to the cabinet decision-making process. Lester B. Pearson had made use of cabinet committees, but they had modest mandates and could not make final decisions. Pierre Trudeau formalized the committee process and allowed committees to make more decisions by themselves. With the Policy and Expenditure Management System (PEMS), which spanned three prime ministers—Clark, Trudeau, and Mulroney (1979–89)—committees even began to make budgetary decisions to dovetail with their policy recommendations. This system ended with the 1980s. Yet after this, it was still a cabinet committee, the Expenditure Review Committee chaired by Don Mazankowski, that made most of the important budgetary decisions. Today the committees make many final decisions in government but, in keeping with the convention of collective responsibility, ministers have a right—not often exercised—to challenge the committee recommendation before Cabinet reaches its final decision.

One of the powers of the prime minister is to design the decision-making apparatus. In doing so, the prime minister personally assesses what will work most efficiently and what will most effectively use that rarest of things, ministerial time. The net effect is that the design of government at the centre changes from prime minister to prime minister. Some have numerous cabinet committees, others fewer; some have more ministers and portfolios, others fewer. As well, over time, the prime minister's apparatus tends to become larger and more

How to Run a Cabinet: The Master Himself, William Lyon Mackenzie King

One of the major challenges for a prime minister is how to run a Cabinet. The associated tasks are daunting: managing the immense egos of the politicians involved, preventing ministers from taking over power and prerogatives that belong to the first minister, fostering and giving effect to a common will, destroying one's political enemies—and all this while presenting a pleasing image to the public and seeing the "long picture." One of the masters of the game was Liberal politician William Lyon Mackenzie King (1874–1950).

King used a range of strategies to keep Cabinet on course. Ministers were not made aware of the agenda for Cabinet meetings nor were they supplied with Cabinet papers. Moreover, no minutes were kept of discussions of Cabinet before 1940. As a further tactic, King encouraged rivalries between his ministers to prevent them uniting against him. He delayed action until it was absolutely necessary and often seemed to support both sides in a controversy, like conscription. His reforms of cabinet operations were similarly late in coming and self-serving: for example, he created a small War Committee that he dominated and that centralized decision making throughout the Second World War.

King was ruthless when he had to be, firing several ministers without regret because he never got too close to them in the first place. In fact, he shifted power to trusted top senior civil servants. He trusted only a few ministers, such as C. D. Howe, whom he judged as unselfish and not likely to turn against him. Perhaps most importantly, King concealed his real self from the public, electing to appear bland and inactive, knowing Canadians would prefer a lacklustre leader to an arrogant one.

Although King was supremely successful in holding on to the reins of power, times have changed. The public and the media expect to know about the private life of the prime minister and insist that the prime minister be active and dynamic. Control of the Cabinet and the direction of government present more complex challenges than in King's time.

detailed. The Harper Government, for example, had a ministry of thirty-one in 2006 (twenty-five ministers and six ministers of state) and thirty-eight in 2009 (twenty-seven ministers and eleven ministers of state). It had seven cabinet committees in 2006 and eight in 2009 (one added on Afghanistan), as detailed in Table 14-1. Before Harper, Prime Minister Martin had had a sizeable Cabinet at thirty-nine ministers, including eight ministers of state, and nine cabinet committees. These both contrast significantly with the four cabinet committees Prime Minister Chrétien relied on for most of his tenure (although his initially small cabinet swelled to twenty-eight ministers and eleven ministers of state).

Yet in some ways the first ministers show consensus on the nature of the central executive. Since Chrétien, they have distinguished between the ministry—the collection of ministers who are sworn in as members of the Queen's Privy Council for Canada—and the Cabinet—those privy councillors who have received departmental portfolios or the equivalent. They have seen fit to distinguish between senior and junior ministers, with ministers

TABLE 14-1
**CABINET COMMITTEES
IN THE HARPER
GOVERNMENT, 2009**

CABINET COMMITTEE	MANDATE
Priorities and Planning	Sets government priorities, coordinates expenditure management, ratifies committee recommendations and approves appointments.
Operations	Coordinates the government's issues agenda and legislative management.
Treasury Board	Responsible for financial, personnel, and administrative management; ethics; comptrollership; and approving regulations and most orders-in-council.
Social Affairs	Considers policy issues relating to health, training and skills development, justice, culture, and other aspects of social policy.
Economic Growth and Long-term Prosperity	Considers sectoral issues applying to economic departments of government and to regional development, as well as longer-term matters concerning Canada's economic growth and prosperity, and multi-year infrastructure plans.
Foreign Affairs and Security	Considers foreign affairs, international development, public and national security, and defence policy issues.
Environment and Energy Security	Considers environment and energy security policy issues.
Afghanistan	Considers issues related to Canada's mission in Afghanistan.

of state forming the latter. The majority of prime ministers in the last half-century—excluding Chrétien but including Harper—have seen the need for a Priorities and Planning Committee. This amounts to a kind of "inner cabinet"—a group of the more influential ministers who set priorities for government and coordinate the work of the other committees. The prime minister chairs this important cabinet committee, which can be considered another basis of the prime minister's power.

The Budgetary Process

The minister of Finance presents the budget to Parliament. This crucial document outlines the government's spending priorities for the coming year and often beyond, and explains how the government will collect and spend the taxes of Canadians. It simultaneously tables the Estimates, which are more detailed spending plans. Parts I and II of the Estimates outline the expenditures

FIGURE 14-2
THE BUDGETARY PROCESS

Source: Treasury Board of Canada,
2006, "The Reporting Cycle," *Tools
and Resources for Parliamentarians.*
Retrieved from http://www.tbs-sct.gc.
ca/tbs-sct/audience-auditoire/
parliamentarian-parlementaire-
eng.asp

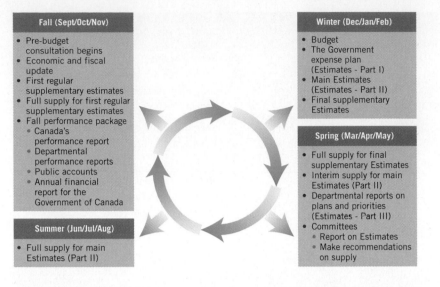

Fall (Sept/Oct/Nov)
- Pre-budget consultation begins
- Economic and fiscal update
- First regular supplementary estimates
- Full supply for first regular supplementary estimates
- Fall performance package
  - Canada's performance report
  - Departmental performance reports
  - Public accounts
  - Annual financial report for the Government of Canada

Summer (Jun/Jul/Aug)
- Full supply for main Estimates (Part II)

Winter (Dec/Jan/Feb)
- Budget
- The Government expense plan (Estimates - Part I)
- Main Estimates (Estimates - Part II)
- Final supplementary Estimates

Spring (Mar/Apr/May)
- Full supply for final supplementary Estimates
- Interim supply for main Estimates (Part II)
- Departmental reports on plans and priorities (Estimates - Part III)
- Committees
  - Report on Estimates
  - Make recommendations on supply

of departments and agencies, both voted and statutory. Part III of the Estimates is composed of two parts, Departmental Reports on Plans and Priorities (RPPs) and Departmental Performance Reports (DPRs). The budgeting process is outlined in Figure 14-2.

The minister of Finance, the president of the Treasury Board, and the prime minister are the major players for most of the process, and the full Cabinet is brought in only at the end of the budget cycle. However, individual ministers are involved in presenting wish lists of new programs, and the Cabinet will have made its general approach known in Cabinet retreats that generally take place the summer before the process starts.

REFORM AND THE PRIME MINISTER AND CABINET

No political system is immutable. Changes always can be brought to the decision-making structure. Over time, reforms have been suggested that would whittle away some of the prerogatives and powers of both the prime minister and Cabinet.

With regard to the prime minister, many ideas have been advanced. Aucoin, Smith, and Dinsdale (2004) analyze some in their report on responsible government in Canada. One idea is to lessen the prime minister's appointment power by reducing the number of appointments that the prime minister can make. Another is to enable the parliamentary party caucuses to remove party leaders, regardless of whether their party leader is currently the prime minister.[6] Yet

---

[6]The Liberal caucus was able to persuade Chrétien to retire earlier than planned, in 2003, and the Liberal caucus was instrumental in removing Dion in 2008, although not provided for in Liberal party procedures. However, the authors no doubt mean arranging for clear policies within party constitutions rather than recourse to these exceptional practices.

another is to have members of the governing party's caucus select the members of the ministry. Other analysts have suggested that the way to control the overwhelming power of the prime minister and the Cabinet is to put into statute what are now prerogative powers, and to subject their decisions to democratic debate. This might include, for example, a law requiring that Parliament approve any foreign combat mission. It would also be possible to put into statute the right of the ordinary public servant to resist political directives that are improper or indicate bad management practices (Savoie, 2008). As well, many of the standard reforms suggested by critics in the eras of constitutional and non-constitutional reform hold the possibility of reduced dominance by the central executive. These include the Triple-E Senate, electoral reform that would tilt the system toward more minority or coalition government scenarios, and provincial input into judicial appointments.

Of course, the context is important. Canadians now live in a world where the reigning idea is not government as such, but governance. More and more, public, private, and non-governmental organizations (NGOs) are sharing power to effect change for public purposes. To some extent, the drifting away of the centralized power of the executive is a natural event and does not have to be planned. Cultural context is also important. A better-educated Canadian public is going to insist on more dialogue surrounding public policy—to take place in more venues.

Summary and Conclusion

The executive has many faces to it and involves many issues. It has a formal face, that which is presented to us in the *Constitution Act*—that of the Queen, governor general, and Queen's Privy Council for Canada. It has its informal but powerful face—the prime minister, Cabinet, and bureaucracy. The formal face carries with it the still-powerful elements of the distant past: prerogative and convention mark it even today and regulate its relations with the informal executive. Although issues arise from the formal side—the validity of monarchy in Canada and the pros and cons of having an elected head of state—by far the most pressing issues are in the political executive's ballpark. The reach of the prime minister's power seems to become more exten-

sive with every new administration, and the recommendation of reforms more urgent.

The concentration of power in the hands of the prime minister and some influential advisers, particularly in the Privy Council Office and the Prime Minister's Office, raises important questions about the quality of democracy in Canada. Even if assertions that we have "prime ministerial government" or "court government" are exaggerated, the decline in the importance of most departments means that interest groups will likely find it more difficult to have input into the major decisions of government. Nevertheless, Cabinet and cabinet committees continue to be a highly important part of the policy-making process, while the Finance minister and the Finance Department play the key role in the budgetary process.

Furthermore, particularly in a majority government situation, the ability of the House of Commons to provide an effective check on the power of the prime minister and Cabinet is limited. The concentration of power could be viewed as resulting in effective government that is able to pursue a particular course of action. On the other hand, if good government is judged in terms of responsiveness, accountability, and transparency, then the concentration of power has to be viewed negatively.

In terms of representativeness, contemporary Cabinets do not fully represent the diversity of Canadian society. Nevertheless, they are more diverse than Cabinets before 1957, which included no women, ethnic or visible minorities, Aboriginals, or non-Christians. At the apex of power, only one woman, Kim Campbell, has held the office of prime minister. Her prime ministership lasted for only a few months in 1993 before her Progressive Conservative party suffered a catastrophic election defeat. As well, with the exception of John Diefenbaker, all prime ministers have been of British or French ancestry.

Discussion Questions

1. Should Canada retain the monarchy?
2. Should the governor general always act on the advice of cabinet?
3. Did the governor general make the right decision in proroguing Parliament in 2008?

4. Is the prime minister too powerful?
5. Is it important to have a representative Cabinet?

Further Readings

Aucoin, P., Smith, J., & Dinsdale, G. (2004). *Responsible government: Clarifying essentials, dispelling myths and exploring change.* Ottawa, ON: Canadian Centre for Management Development.

D'Ombrain, N. (2007). Cabinet secrecy. *Canadian Public Administration, 47,* 332–359.

Dunn, C. (2002). The central executive in Canadian government: Searching for the Holy Grail. In C. Dunn (Ed.), *The handbook of Canadian public administration.* Don Mills, ON: Oxford University Press.

Goldenberg, E. (2006). *The way it works: Inside Ottawa.* Toronto, ON: McClelland & Stewart.

Good, D. A. (2007). *The politics of public money: Spenders, guardians, priority setters, and financial watchdogs in the Canadian government.* Toronto, ON: University of Toronto Press.

Mallory, J. R. (1984). *The structure of Canadian government.* Toronto, ON: Gage.

Savoie, D. (1999). *Governing from the centre: The concentration of power in Canadian politics.* Toronto, ON: University of Toronto Press.

Savoie, D. (2008). *Court government and the collapse of accountability in Canada and the United Kingdom.* Toronto, ON: University of Toronto Press.

Simpson, G. (2001). *The friendly dictatorship.* Toronto, ON: McClelland & Stewart.

Ward, N. (1987). *Dawson's The Government of Canada.* Toronto, ON: University of Toronto Press.

White, G. (2005). *Cabinets and first ministers.* Vancouver: UBC Press.

Chapter 15

PARLIAMENT

PHOTO ABOVE: Although he was never childish about his duties, Pierre Trudeau was as capable of parliamentary antics as the next MP. Here he is as a first-term MP, sliding down a banister at Ottawa's Chateau Laurier in 1968, a week before he became leader of the federal Liberal party.

CHAPTER OBJECTIVES

After reading this chapter, you should be able to

1. Explain the origins and evolution of parliaments in Britain and Canada.
2. Describe the general functions of parliaments, as well as the specific functions of the House of Commons and the Senate of Canada.
3. Explain the functions of parliamentary committees and what forms they take.
4. Assess the effectiveness of the House of Commons.
5. Evaluate possible reforms to the Senate.

Pierre Trudeau once said that Liberal backbenchers were "trained seals" who did the bidding of the government without thinking for themselves, and later described Opposition MPs as "nobodies once they found themselves fifty yards from Parliament Hill." Although Canadians often look to the House of Commons as the centre of representative democracy, many observers point out that political power has shifted from Parliament to the executive. Does this mean the House of Commons is an irrelevant sideshow that only provides the illusion of democracy? Without a doubt, some of the representatives we elect can and do make a difference to the laws and policies that affect us.

Charles Caccia, Liberal MP for Davenport (Toronto), showed that a representative could be a loyal party member while standing up for his beliefs in environmental protection and social justice. Caccia was born in Milan, Italy, in 1930. After graduating from the University of Vienna in 1954, he immigrated to Canada and took a position as a forestry professor at the University of Toronto. He began his political career as a Toronto city councillor and was first elected to the House of Commons in 1968. Although he served in the Trudeau Cabinets, Caccia was relegated to the backbenches when the Liberals returned to power under the leadership of Jean Chrétien. Nevertheless, as chair of the House of Commons Committee on the Environment and Sustainable Development, he worked hard to improve Canada's environmental legislation and was not afraid to challenge his party's policies when they fell short (May, 2008).

Caccia's committee proved especially rigorous in reviewing the government's Species at Risk bill, proposing over one hundred amendments. When the government rejected most of these, Caccia, along with Liberal MPs Karen Kraft Sloan and Clifford Lincoln, publicly threatened to vote against the bill. The government backed down and made important changes, including provisions that the listing of endangered species by a scientific committee would become law unless vetoed by Cabinet, and that the protection of critical habitat would be mandatory for all species on federal lands (Illical & Harrison, 2007). The *Species at Risk Act* received Royal Assent in 2002—more than twenty years after Caccia had presented four private members' bills on that issue.

Under Caccia's leadership, the Environment Committee also suggested many amendments to improve the government's proposed *Canadian Environmental Protection Act*. However, when the government backed down and weakened the proposal after intense industry lobbying, Caccia stuck to his principles and voted against the act (Benevides, 2008). Even though Caccia did not always succeed in pursuing his legislative goals, he forged a lasting influence by educating committee members, MPs, and the public about the importance of protecting the environment. He also strongly supported and encouraged the activities of environmentalists.

Caccia's decision to support Sheila Copps in her unsuccessful bid in 2003 to lead the Liberal party triggered the end of his political career. After winning the leadership contest, Paul Martin backed Mario Silva for the Liberal nomination in Caccia's district. Knowing that Silva had signed up enough voters to win the nomination, Caccia decided to retire. Nevertheless, he tirelessly promoted environmental causes until his death in 2008.

The work of MPs on House of Commons committees often goes unnoticed. And yet, with determination and a principled commitment to improving the world, Members of Parliament can make a difference.

THE GENERAL FUNCTIONS OF PARLIAMENTS

Parliaments are expected to carry out a variety of functions, many of which are of great importance in a democracy:

- *Representation.* Members of Parliament can voice the concerns and promote the interests of their constituents.
- *Conferring legitimacy.* Legitimation means that we feel obligated to obey laws that are fairly considered and duly passed. To ensure that laws are widely accepted as legitimate they must be passed properly: widely accepted rules and procedures must be followed, a majority of each House votes for the act, and the laws should reflect the basic values of society.
- *Scrutiny.* Members of Parliament examine the proposals and actions of the executive.
- *Recruitment.* The prime minister chooses the Cabinet from among the governing party's Members of Parliament (almost all from the House of Commons).[1]
- *Law making.* Although the government presents most legislative proposals to Parliament, Members of Parliament can play a role in law making by carefully examining legislative proposals and developing modifications to improve the proposals.
- *Financing government.* All bills for the raising and spending of public monies (which have to be recommended by the Cabinet) must originate in the House of Commons and must be approved in both Houses. An officer of Parliament, the Auditor General, verifies the accuracy of public financial statements and the legitimacy of expenditures.
- *Political education.* Parliament raises and debates issues, and informs the public, using such instruments as question period, committee hearings and reports, and budget debates.
- *Accountability.* The government is obligated to submit its program to Parliament, defend it, and resign if the House of Commons lacks confidence in it.

This is not to suggest that the Canadian Parliament does a satisfactory job in tackling all of these functions. In this chapter we will consider how successfully Parliament fulfills these functions, as well as examining the organization and operations of Parliament.

THE CANADIAN PARLIAMENT

Canada's Parliament consists of three elements: the House of Commons, the Senate, and the Queen. The citizens of each electoral district elect the members of the House of Commons (often referred to as Members of Parliament, or MPs).

---

[1]Very occasionally, a Canadian prime minister has chosen a cabinet minister who does not hold a seat in Parliament, but this has been quickly followed by the person being elected to the Commons or appointed to the Senate.

In contrast, senators are appointed on the recommendation of the prime minister and hold office until their retirement at age seventy-five. The governor general (representing the Queen) follows the advice of the prime minister and Cabinet in approving legislation passed by Parliament. The governor general does not participate in the deliberations of the two Houses of Parliament.

Parliament can be described as a **bicameral legislature**. That is, it has two chambers, each of which meets separately.[2] Both the House of Commons and the Senate must adopt legislation in identical form before it can be submitted to the governor general for Royal Assent. Each chamber has the authority to initiate most legislation; however, financial legislation has to be introduced by the government in the House of Commons.

BICAMERAL LEGISLATURE
A legislature with two chambers or houses.

Parliament of Canada:
www2.parl.gc.ca/parlinfo/
default.aspx?Menu=Home

British Roots

The British Parliament is called the "Mother of Parliaments" because of its age, having started in the thirteenth century, although some attribute this honour to proto-legislatures earlier in history. In 930, the first legislature, a one-house arrangement called the *Althing*, met in Iceland. There was also the example of the *Witan*, or *Witangemot* ("the assembly of the wise"), the council of the Anglo-Saxon kings. However, the British parliamentary model has proved to be the most exportable and flexible of the early models, so much so that it serves as the primary example in the literature of "parliamentary government."

There are three parts to parliament because over time three great estates—the Crown, the nobility, and the common people—vied for power. The evolution of Parliament can be traced to the rise and fall of each estate. In British history, effective power has passed from the Crown, to the Lords, to the Commons, and from the Commons to the executive.

The rise of the Crown in the modern era began with the Norman Conquest in 1066. The king was the holder of all land in the kingdom, and therefore was the great unifying force. In 1086 William the Conqueror exacted an oath of allegiance from all landholders, thus solidifying his authority. Law making was the prerogative of the king, who received advice from his chief tenants. By the time of Henry II (1154–89), the advisers had become a formal private council (*curia regis*, or Great Council) to the king, with only the major landholders, or barons, in attendance. The latter were the origins of the lords, who had below them a class of tenants; the lords became the intermediaries between the king and the nation. The lords would be assembled to grant monies to the king for the launching of wars and other emergencies; otherwise he would be expected to finance regular expenditures from his own revenue. The Magna Carta, issued during the time of King John (1199–1216), was the origin of statute law and the rule of law.

---

[2]Although some provinces once had bicameral legislatures, all provincial legislatures are now unicameral.

At various times in the thirteenth century, as the financing needs of the monarch became more pressing, the meetings of the Great Council became more inclusive. In 1254 two knights from every shire attended, and in 1265, local leaders from each city and borough were present, as well as the knights. Together, the knights and local leaders represented the "communes," or "commons." Such was the origin of the two houses of parliament: the barons and bishops meeting in one place, and the commoners, the knights from the shires, and the burgesses—the leading citizens from the boroughs—meeting in another. However, the commons was not invited to every such meeting; much depended on how self-financing the king was. By the sixteenth century, a permanent meeting place had been appointed.

In 1275 the first of what might be called the modern form of parliament met, assembled by Edward I (1272–1307). He called together a parliament of bishops, peers, knights, citizens, and burgesses. By 1295, the foundation of the modern parliament was reflected in the writ of summons for the parliament, which declared, "That which touches all should be approved by all" (Pollard, Parpworth, & Hughes, 2001, p. 4). The approval of legislation by both houses, the Lords and Commons, had developed into a firm convention by 1322. Legislation had its origins in the thirteenth century in collective petitions that the Commons presented to the monarch hoping for redress by him.

Over time the balance of power shifted to the Commons, but it was not an easy transition. As the junior chamber, the Commons was expected to act on the will of the king. The subordinate status of the early Commons is evident in today's rituals, in which the Speech from the Throne is read in the upper house, with the Commons assembled silently at the bar. In the fifteenth century, the Commons achieved more law-making power as the convention grew that taxation bills had to originate there before going to the Lords, and bills for redress were granted only after supply (expenditure) was granted. Still, legislation was divided in two: one area passed by Parliament, but another significant area in which the king often exercised his prerogative power.

Growing hostility toward the prerogative power sparked conflict and civil war in the mid-seventeenth century. After the execution of Charles I in 1649, the short-lived abolition of the monarchy and the House of Lords, and the rule of Cromwell,[3] Charles II returned to the restored monarchy in 1660. His successor, James II, tried to restore monarchical rights but was forced from

---

[3]Oliver Cromwell (1599–1658) was a powerful military figure who became a political leader and military dictator following rule by the Council of State, which was elected by the "Rump Parliament" formed after the execution of Charles I. He became the Lord Protector of the Realm in 1653, even ruling for a time without Parliament, and died in 1658, but the Protectorate could not survive his death. Though the monarchy was abolished for a time, Cromwell enjoyed most of the powers that the kings had.

GLORIOUS REVOLUTION
The series of events that led to the removal of James II from the throne in 1688, his replacement by William and Mary, and their acceptance of the Bill of Rights, 1689.

BILL OF RIGHTS, 1689
The bill that followed the Glorious Revolution of 1688, which added protections for parliamentary free speech, regular sessions, and other protections, and is generally regarded as the stage of British history when the Crown accepted the supremacy of Parliament.

the throne after a religious struggle in the "**Glorious Revolution**" of 1688, and was replaced by William and Mary. The **Bill of Rights of 1689** declared freedom of speech for Parliament and insisted that the levying of money for the use of the Crown without grant of Parliament was illegal. Not long after, the authority of Parliament was boosted by its successful claims to regulate the succession to the Crown and to describe the supreme authority as the "King in Parliament." The Lords came to accept that they could not amend financial legislation initiated by the Commons.

The authority grew further still by the expansion of the franchise in the nineteenth century, and the so-called Golden Age of Parliament, characterized by the ability of the Commons to defeat legislation and dismiss ministers on the floor of the House. In the twentieth century, the legislative and financial power of the Lords was curtailed further by the *Parliament Acts* of 1911 and 1949, which reduced to a month the Lords' delaying power for financial bills and, in 1949, one year for other bills. Most of those who held hereditary positions in the House of Lords were removed in 1999. However, by the twentieth century, the executive government had become dominant, so the Commons had won against the Crown and the Lords but faced an even more formidable rival.

The Evolution of Parliament in Canada

Canada's Parliament has evolved as well, but in a more compressed time frame. In 1840, the *Act of Union* established an elected Legislative Assembly for the United Province of Canada, but the increase in parliamentary influence did not come until 1848 after the adoption of the system of responsible government. At least nine ministries (governments) after 1848 had to resign, advise dissolution, or change their leadership and other personnel when they faced the possible loss of support of the Assembly. No ministry in the Province of Canada survived for what would now be called the government's normal life. Despite the existence of some firm factions and alignments, the ministries were overwhelmed by the more politically fickle "loose fish" and "ministerialists," who were faithful only to whichever government could supply them and their ridings with favours.

This pattern continued for about a decade in the new country of Canada, at which time the growth of disciplined parliamentary parties began to change the political dynamics considerably. Gradually parliamentary influence became more restricted. It amounted to the right of the opposition to demand answers from the government and significant time allowed by the rules of the House for the opposition to criticize the government. Over the post-Confederation history of Parliament, only one government (that of Mackenzie King in 1926) has changed hands without an election held.

Overall, there are some differences between the contemporary Canadian and British Parliaments (including important differences between the House

Canadian and American Legislatures: A Study in Contrast

Canadians are sometimes baffled by the workings of Parliament because so much of our news and popular entertainment highlights the U.S. Congress. Despite some similarities, there are fundamental differences between the two.

Both Canada and the United States share the tradition of bicameral legislatures. In both countries the upper house is called the Senate, although the American Senate is elected (with two senators from each state) while the Canadian Senate is appointed on the recommendation of the prime minister. In practice, the U.S. Senate is much more powerful than the Canadian Senate. The elected lower house is the House of Representatives in the United States and the House of Commons in Canada. Both legislatures have elaborate committee systems, although the committees are more influential and independent in the American system. Both Parliament and Congress have faced charges of losing influence in the face of encroaching executive power: in the United States, in the context of "the imperial presidency," and in Canada, in relation to "prime ministerial government."

One marked difference between the two systems is that the executive and legislature are constitutionally separate in the United States, whereas in Canada the executive and the legislature are connected. The American president is elected by the people and holds office for four years whether or not Congress supports the president's policies. Neither the president nor cabinet can be members of Congress, nor do they participate in Congressional discussion.

The Canadian prime minister and Cabinet are Members of Parliament and must hold on to the continued support of the majority of the elected House. Further, since the U.S. executive does not exercise rigid control over the legislative branch, individual members of Congress (with the support of a sizeable staff) actively develop and propose policy, including budgetary measures. In Canada, Parliament's policy role is primarily to ratify policy and budgetary initiatives that come from the executive. Finally, although Congress, like Parliament, is organized along party lines, party discipline is not as tight in Congress. Individual members of Congress do not usually rely heavily on financial support from their party to be elected, and often some members of the Democratic and Republican parties work together to promote or oppose particular policies.

Overall, legislation is easier to pass in Parliament, particularly when one party has a majority of members in the House of Commons, because of the dominant position of the executive. In contrast, members of Congress are more independent and more likely to represent the interests of their state or district. The passage of legislation therefore requires much more bargaining and compromise both among the members of the two Houses of Congress and between Congress and the president. Although Canadians identify in many ways with Americans and share aspects of a North American culture, the political systems of the two countries are a study in contrast.

of Lords and the Senate, and in the practice of party discipline). However, the U.S. Congress (and its governing system in general) differs much more dramatically from the Canadian Parliament and the parliamentary system (see Box 15-1, Canadian and American Legislatures: A Study in Contrast).

THE HOUSE OF COMMONS

Although the House of Commons is often termed the "lower house" and the Senate, the "upper house," the House of Commons is clearly the more important of the two houses:

- First, the House of Commons is a **confidence chamber**, meaning that the life of the government of the day rests on the continued support of a majority of the members of the Commons. Defeat of government measures in the Senate is of no consequence for the Cabinet's continuance.
- Second, the Commons, whose members are elected, offers representative government. Unelected senators have trouble claiming that they represent the people of Canada.
- Third, it is primarily the House that holds the government accountable for its actions. It is in the House that the government is expected to answer questions and respond to the criticism of the opposition parties, which have opportunities to scrutinize government management and expenditures.
- Fourth, the House is where grievances and problems are usually raised and brought to the attention of the public and the media.

Representation in the House of Commons

The House of Commons hinges primarily on the concept of representation by population. Each province is entitled to a share of the seats in the House of Commons that is nearly proportionate to its share of the population. As discussed in Chapter 9, there are some qualifications to this principle, particularly to protect the representation of the smaller provinces. Nevertheless, the central Canadian provinces still dominate numerically. Together, Ontario and Quebec, with 62 percent of the population of Canada, comprise about 59 percent of the Commons membership, with Ontario itself amounting to close to 35 percent of the Commons (see Table 15-1). The Western provinces, with 31 percent of the population, currently have 30 percent of the seats. The Atlantic provinces, with 7 percent of the population, have 10 percent of the seats in the Commons. The Territories, with 0.3 percent of the population, get 1 percent of the seats. Those in Western and Atlantic Canada, therefore, tend to view the House of Commons as dominated by representatives of the two central Canadian provinces. Although representation by population is usually considered a key democratic principle, it means that the regional diversity of Canada is not fully reflected in the House of Commons, given the small number of members from some of the remote areas of the country.

STYLES OF REPRESENTATION   Political scientists have often analyzed three different styles of representation that an elected member might adopt. Members who view themselves as *delegates* will try to act according to the

TABLE 15-1
CHANGES IN PROVINCIAL REPRESENTATION IN THE HOUSE OF COMMONS SINCE 1867

YEAR	CANADA	ONT.	QUE.	N.S.	N.B.	MAN.	B.C.	P.E.I.	SASK.	ALTA.	NFLD.	N.W.T.	Y.T.	NUNA-VUT
1867	181	82	65	19	15									
1870	185	82	65	19	15	4								
1871	191	82	65	19	15	4	6							
1872	200	88	65	21	16	4	6							
1873	206	88	65	21	16	4	6	6						
1882	211	92	65	21	16	5	6	6						
1886	215	92	65	21	16	5	6	6				4		
1892	213	92	65	20	14	7	6	5				4		
1902	214	92	65	20	14	7	6	5				4	1	
1903	214	86	65	18	13	10	7	4				10	1	
1905	221	86	65	18	13	10	7	4	10	7			1	
1914	234	82	65	16	11	15	13	3	16	12			1	
1915	235	82	65	16	11	15	13	4	16	12			1	
1924	245	82	65	14	11	17	14	4	21	16			1	
1933	245	82	65	12	10	17	16	4	21	17			1	
1947	255	83	73	13	10	16	18	4	20	17			1	
1949	262	83	73	13	10	16	18	4	20	17	7		1	
1952	265	85	75	12	10	14	22	4	17	17	7		1	
1966	264	88	74	11	10	13	23	4	13	19	7	1	1	
1975	265	88	74	11	10	13	23	4	13	19	7	1	1	
1976	282	95	75	11	10	14	28	4	14	21	7	2	1	
1987	295	99	75	11	10	14	32	4	14	26	7	2	1	
1997	301	103	75	11	10	14	34	4	14	26	7	2	1	
1999	301	103	75	11	10	14	34	4	14	26	7	1	1	1
2004	308	106	75	11	10	14	36	4	14	28	7	1	1	1

Source: *Adapted from R. Marleau & C. Montpetit, 2000.*

wishes of their constituents. *Trustees* will use their own judgment in acting in what they view as the best interests of their constituents and the country. *Politicos* combine these delegate and trustee roles (Docherty, 2005; Eulau, 1978). However, this analysis of representation is of limited usefulness in understanding the House of Commons.

Individual members of the House of Commons do spend considerable time putting forward the interests of the people of their electoral district. Opposition members, in particular, may raise concerns of their constituents in question period (Soroka, Penner, & Blidook, 2009). As well, MPs and their small staffs try to help constituents with the problems they face with government—such as getting a passport in a hurry, determining eligibility for an old-age pension, or helping family members immigrate to Canada. Further, in the closed-door meetings of their party's **caucus**, MPs may alert their colleagues to the interests and viewpoints of people in their district, and try to persuade their caucus to adopt certain policies and positions. To achieve this objective,

CAUCUS
Parliamentary members who belong to a particular party.

they may meet regularly with other members of their own party from their province or with their party's members who have similar interests to make a stronger case. However, in the governing party, caucus often receives the legislative proposals of the government with little notice, which may not lead to much discussion before the legislation is presented to Parliament.

PARTY DISCIPLINE

The expectation that parliamentary members will vote in keeping with the position that their party has adopted in caucus.

PARTY DISCIPLINE Party discipline is very strict in the House of Commons. Once a party has decided on its position on a particular issue, its MPs are expected to vote in keeping with that position even if it clashes with the views and interests of their constituents. Therefore, all of the members of the governing party almost always support legislation proposed by the Cabinet. Those who vote against government legislation that is considered a matter of confidence may find themselves ousted from their party's caucus and denied their party's nomination. For example, two Progressive Conservative MPs were expelled from the party for voting against the goods and services tax, which was highly unpopular among their constituents. Likewise, Bill Casey was expelled from the Conservative caucus for voting against the Conservative government's budget because the changes to the equalization formula would hurt his home province of Nova Scotia. Criticisms of the Conservative government in his blog may have caused Garth Turner's expulsion from the Conservative caucus in 2006. Breaking party discipline can also have consequences for members of the opposition parties, as Liberal MP Joe Comuzzi found when he supported the Conservatives' 2007 budget, which contained benefits for his district. As a result, he was expelled from the Liberal caucus. With the exception of the very few "free votes" (where MPs are freed from party discipline) that have been held on matters of conscience, such as abortion and capital punishment, MPs rarely vote against the position taken by their party caucus. It is also rare for members of different parties from the same province or region to work together to advance the common interests of those they represent.

Thus, although the individual representative is not irrelevant, representation is primarily by political parties rather than by individuals acting as delegates or trustees of their constituents. Not surprisingly, this can create problems for MPs, who may be accused of acting against the interests or wishes of their constituents. However, party discipline does have advantages: the positions of each party are clearer, individual MPs are not pressured to act according to the wishes of powerful special interests, and each national party can try to develop a position on what it views as being in the interests of the country as a whole.

DIVERSITY AND REPRESENTATION Representation can also be viewed in terms of the personal characteristics of the members of the House of Commons. With the proportion of women, Aboriginals, and visible minorities in the House being much smaller than their proportion of the population (see Chapter 8),

OCCUPATION	NUMBER SINCE 1867	NUMBER IN 2009*
Lawyer	1009	51
Farmer	596	21
Merchant	461	0
Businessperson	460	71
Teacher	324	36
Physician	211	4
Manager	207	30
Professor	165	19
Journalist	150	12
Consultant	140	46
Administrator	119	24
Director	62	20
Political Assistant	23	17

TABLE 15-2

LEADING OCCUPATIONAL BACKGROUNDS OF MEMBERS OF THE HOUSE OF COMMONS

*Some of the 308 MPs have more than one identified occupation.

Source: *Data constructed from the Parliament of Canada website, 2009.*

observers often note that the House is unrepresentative of the diversity of the country. In addition, as Table 15-2 reveals, lawyers and businesspeople have been prominent among the Members of Parliament. Only a small proportion of MPs can be considered to be members of the working class, although farmers have made up a significant proportion of MPs.

Executive Domination

Executive domination is a fact of life for most legislatures in the world. Legislatures often do not have significant influence in policy- and budget-making, and parties and members of the legislature may not have enough funding to perform their roles effectively. In addition, legislative committees may lack independence and support staff, and opposition parties often have a limited ability to hold the government to account.

A significant degree of executive domination characterizes the Canadian Parliament. Four factors encourage executive domination. One is the high rate of turnover in the national legislature (see Table 15-3). Some elections result in new members making up more than a third of the Commons, which means that the executive may be able to exploit the inexperience of many members. A second reason for executive dominance is the workload: relatively short sessions are the hallmark of the House of Commons, with one result being that part-time legislators confront full-time governments. A third reason is the selectivity of the parliamentary press gallery. The focus of media coverage tends to be on governments rather than on oppositions and on government policy announcements rather than on debates—tendencies that are enhanced by the shortness of legislative sessions. A fourth reason is the tendency toward "executive federalism" (discussed in Chapter 13). Parliament has often found

TABLE 15-3
**TURNOVER IN PARLIAMENT:
NUMBER AND PERCENTAGE
OF NEW ELECTED MEMBERS
IN HOUSE OF COMMONS,
BY GENERAL ELECTION
1968–2008**

GENERAL ELECTION DATE	NEW MPS	% OF TOTAL
1968.06.25	97 of 264	37
1972.10.30	95 of 282	34
1974.07.08	50 of 282	18
1979.05.22	98 of 282	35
1980.02.18	43 of 282	15
1984.09.04	133 of 295	45
1988.11.21	116 of 295	39
1993.10.25	199 of 301	66
1997.06.02	84 of 301	28
2000.11.27	45 of 301	15
2004.06.28	101 of 308	33
2006.01.23	65 of 308	21
2008.10.14	65 of 308	21

Source: *Data constructed from the Parliament of Canada website, 2009.*

itself having to debate important decisions reached at federal– provincial conferences, which cannot easily be modified and often cannot be retracted without considerable embarrassment.

Executive dominance is often seen as a challenge to representative and responsible government. Citizens elect members to *represent* them in the legislature, and the executive (cabinet) is directly *responsible* to the legislature (and thus indirectly to the public). If the House loses confidence in the executive, so the theory goes, the legislature can support a new ministry or a general election can be imposed, as decided by the governor general. Generally, however, responsible government makes itself evident in less dramatic ways. It has also been interpreted as the necessity for the government to allow enough legislative opportunities for scrutiny and debate, to respond to criticism, and to disclose enough information to keep legislators and the public informed about the actions and decisions of government. When the government tries to thwart the will of the House by proroguing it (ending a session) in the face of a sure defeat in the Commons (as occurred in 2008), or when it avoids scrutiny and disclosure, the responsible government system is undermined.

However, executive dominance offers some positive features. Many of the policies that are today regarded as central to Canadian life came not from parliamentary initiative but from the executive—and more often than not from a prime minister willing to drive through an initiative over the objections of parliamentarians and even cabinets. This was the case with the Maple Leaf flag, the *Constitution Act* of 1982, free trade, and many others. The fact of centring so much power in the hands of a few individuals makes for decisive, purposeful action on pressing policy issues. It also allows for relatively swift action and quick responses to emergencies. As well, it should be noted that the

Constitution mandates a certain kind of executive domination in taxation and spending matters, placing fiscal initiative and direction plainly in the hands of the federal Cabinet. Having fiscal planning in the hands of both the legislature and the executive might promote irresponsibility and lack of accountability. Governments would not have to take responsibility for finances, since Parliament would be involved in deciding them, and consequently there would be no clear set of individuals to accept praise or blame.

Furthermore, it can be argued that in a diverse country with distinct cultures and a limited sense of national identity, executive dominance at the federal and provincial level can bolster national unity. Prime ministers and premiers or other federal and provincial executives may be able to reach agreements or understandings through elite accommodation—that is, a process of bargaining and compromise—that allows the country to function. In the more public and adversarial environment of legislatures, it may be more difficult to gain acceptance for unpopular compromises. Nevertheless, as discussed in Chapter 13, the process of elite accommodation has been challenged as being undemocratic.

MINORITY AND MAJORITY GOVERNMENT Executive dominance is particularly strong when one party holds a majority of seats in the House of Commons—that is, *a majority government*. By imposing party discipline on its members, the prime minister and Cabinet can be almost certain that the House will pass the legislation and financial measures they propose. In addition, the government does not have to worry about losing the confidence of the House, and thus can govern for a full four-year term without an election.

If the governing party does not hold a majority of seats in the House and forms a *minority government,* the ability of the prime minister and Cabinet to dominate Parliament is more limited. In this case, the prime minister normally has to bargain and negotiate with one (or more) of the other parties in the House for support or risk losing power on a vote of non-confidence (see Box 15-2, A Minority Government Hangs in the Balance). Alternatively, the Cabinet could introduce proposals that opposition parties are unwilling to defeat. If opposition parties are reluctant to force an election, the Cabinet may be able to pass its key proposals with one or more opposition parties abstaining from those votes as has occurred during the Harper Conservative minority governments.

The Organization and Operations of the House

PRESIDING OFFICERS OF THE HOUSE A variety of members and officials are necessary to help the House of Commons work (see Figure 15-1). The **Speaker** acts as the presiding officer for the Commons, which means applying the rules and procedures that have been devised by the chamber itself. The Speaker also has the responsibility to see that parliamentary privilege is protected, that the rights and prerogatives of both the majority and the minority are recognized and upheld, and that order in debate is maintained.

SPEAKER

The presiding officer of the House of Commons, who is responsible for applying the rules and procedures, maintaining order in debate, and overseeing the administration of the Commons.

BOX 15-2

A Minority Government Hangs in the Balance

It was the afternoon of Thursday, May 19, 2005, and the atmosphere in the House of Commons was electric. The fate of the minority government of Paul Martin, in office only a year, hung in the balance.

To prevent being defeated on its budget, the Liberal government had agreed to a demand by the New Democratic Party for an amendment that added an additional $4.6 billion in the budget for social programs. Even with the support of the NDP, the Liberals needed additional votes to stave off defeat by the combined forces of the Conservative party and the Bloc Québécois.

Conservative star Belinda Stronach had recently crossed the floor of the House to join the Liberals and was rewarded with a Cabinet position (in advancing her political fortunes, she lost her boyfriend, Conservative MP Peter McKay). Independent MP Carolyn Parrish (who had been expelled from the Liberal caucus after a TV appearance in which she stomped on a doll representing President George W. Bush) decided to support the Liberals. Likewise, independent MP David Kilgour opted to vote with the Liberals. With the government still having one vote less than those determined to bring it down, attention became focused on another independent MP, Chuck Cadman.

Cadman was first elected as a Reform party MP in 1987, and represented Surrey North (B.C.) as an independent after losing the Conservative party nomination in 2004. The independent MP, whose decision could topple the government, did not make up his mind until a half hour before the vote. To add to the drama, Cadman had malignant melanoma and did not have long to live. He literally raised himself up from his sickbed to attend the vote. Suffering was etched in Cadman's face, but he knew his vote was important. When Cadman voted for the amendment, he said the deciding factor was a poll he had taken in his district, where a sizeable majority made it clear that they did not want an election. His vote created a tie: 152 to 152. Citing convention, the Speaker, Peter Milliken, voted for the amendment, which passed by one vote.

Chuck Cadman died on July 9, 2005. His widow, Dona Cadman (elected as a Conservative in the 2008 election), said her husband told her that he had turned down an offer from two Conservative party officials of a one-million-dollar life insurance policy in exchange for his vote. However, the RCMP claimed they found no evidence to support a charge of bribing an MP. When Cadman died, the story of the bribe was buried with him, and the minority government of Paul Martin survived for another eight months. Then the NDP, influenced by the intensifying Liberal sponsorship scandal, decided to vote with the Conservatives and the Bloc to defeat the government and force an election, which resulted in a Conservative minority government.

He or she is expected to be impartial in the exercise of the position's duties. As well, the Speaker is responsible for overseeing the administration of the House of Commons, although the Clerk of the House of Commons, a permanent official, looks after the day-to-day administration of the House and advises the Speaker. The Board of Internal Economy, which approves the expenditures of the House, is chaired by the Speaker.

FIGURE 15-1
THE HOUSE OF COMMONS

1 Speaker
2 Pages
3 Government Members*
4 Opposition Members*
5 Prime Minister
6 Leader of the Official Opposition
7 Leader of the Second Largest Party in Opposition
8 Clerk and Table Officers
9 Mace
10 Hansard Reporters
11 Sergeant-at-Arms
12 The Bar
13 Interpreters
14 Press Gallery
15 Public Gallery
16 Official Gallery

*Depending on the number of MPs elected from each political party, some government Members may be seated on the opposite side of the Chamber with opposition Members (or vice versa).

Source: Parliament of Canada, 2008, "Find Out More About Canada's Members of Parliament," *House of Commons Report to Canadians 2008.* Retrieved from http://www.parl.gc.ca/information/about/process/house/RTC2008/rtc2008_03-e.html

As we saw in Box 15-2, by convention the Speaker (who is an elected MP usually representing a particular party) does not cast a vote unless it is to break a tie, and that is usually done to maintain the status quo. In the past the prime minister chose this key parliamentary presiding officer, usually from the governing party and alternating between English- and French-speaking Speakers. Since 1986, however, the Speaker has been chosen by a secret ballot of the members of the House of Commons. This reform was designed to try to ensure that the Speaker would enjoy the respect of the House and not be viewed as a representative of the prime minister and the governing party. As of 2009, Peter Milliken, Liberal MP for Kingston and the Islands, had been elected Speaker four times; he has served while both Liberals and Conservatives have been the governing party.

The Leader of Her Majesty's Loyal Opposition is more than a consolation prize; it is a key position in Canada's parliamentary system. This is the person who leads the (usually but not always) second-largest party in the House and who is considered the most likely to be prime minister in the event of a change in government. Thus it is the duty of the Leader of the Opposition to be familiar with the actions and policies of the government, to appoint opposition party members as critics to "shadow" all government portfolios (sometimes referred to as the "shadow cabinet"), and to go about preparing an alternative program by which to govern. The leaders of the other opposition parties also appoint their members as critics to scrutinize the activities of particular ministers and their departments and to develop positions on certain issue areas.

The **House Leaders** are members of each party in the Commons who are tasked by their party leaders (in the case of the Government House Leader, the prime minister) to be the chief strategists for their party. This means negotiating with the other House Leaders on a parliamentary timetable and seeking out broad plans for getting the message of the party onto the floor of the House and in committees. The **party whips** are similarly members of each parliamentary party, whose job is to maintain party discipline, make sure that members attend for crucial votes, and hand out crucial favours such as good offices, parliamentary trips, and placement on the list of speakers in question period.

THE PARLIAMENTARY SCHEDULE   "A parliament" is the term used to denote the life of the legislature between elections. For example, the thirty-ninth Parliament was elected in 2006 and continued until it was dissolved and an election was called in 2008. A parliament begins with its summoning and calling together by the governor general and ends with its dissolution or termination by proclamation of the governor general. The life of a parliament is subdivided into smaller periods: sessions, sittings, adjournments, and prorogations. *Sessions* are the periods into which parliaments are split; they do not necessarily correspond to calendar years and can be of any length, and there is no set number per parliament. A session is composed of many *sittings*. Sittings are meetings of the House, as directed by the Standing Orders of the House, and do not necessarily have to correspond to days. Sittings are ended by *adjournments*, which are the periods, generally short (a few hours or weeks), between sittings. A session of parliament is ended by a *prorogation*, and the period of time between sessions is referred to as a *recess*. Prorogations have the effect of ending the work of committees and official duties of individual members. If the next session should see fit, these may be resumed at the will of the House; but this is not guaranteed.

The first session of a new parliament sees some events that are not repeated in subsequent sessions: the summoning of the parliament, the swearing in of new members, and the election of the Speaker. Each session opens with the governor general reading the **Speech from the Throne**. The Speech from the Throne (written under the direction of the prime minister) is the government's indication of what it considers to be the state of the country, together with a general outline of the kinds of legislation that it has planned for the session. Speeches from the Throne are generally regarded as lacking in any meaningful detail, sometimes derisively referred to as containing nothing but "governor generalities." However, in recent years, with a tendency toward minority parliaments developing, the speech has taken on greater strategic importance with more pointed appeals designed to prevent a defeat on a confidence vote. The January 2009 Throne Speech, for example, adopted a conciliatory tone because a short-lived Liberal–NDP coalition had been set in motion by the Conservatives'

◀ Each parliamentary session opens with the reading of the Speech from the Throne, in which the government describes the state of the country and a general outline of the kinds of legislation planned for the session.

combative economic statement, which included a proposal to end public subsidies for political parties. The Throne Speech is followed by six days allotted for the Throne Speech Debate—a wide-ranging opportunity for all parties to score political points. The Standing Orders provide for a vote of confidence at the end of the Throne Speech Debate.

The **budget** (often scheduled for February) is one of the highlights of the session. The budget's main task is to deliver news of tax increases or decreases, as well as other revenue and borrowing measures, and to outline the state of the economy and government finances in general. The budget speech is always delivered by the minister of Finance and is the government's major policy statement of the session. In fact, in recent years the Finance minister has even begun to monopolize the announcement of new programs in budget speeches and economic statements. The budget is followed by a four-day debate, at the end of which is the next scheduled opportunity for the opposition parties to introduce a vote of non-confidence. Although the budget occurs only once during a session, governments often provide economic and fiscal updates or statements in the fall to adjust the projections made in the budget and, sometimes, to announce new taxing and spending proposals.

The tabling of the **Estimates** follows very closely on the budget and is the next major matter of business for the House for a very good reason. Financial matters were historically the major power that the Commons had to assert its will versus the executive, and there are still elements of that authority today. The House asserts its control not only by insisting on its right to determine how the government may raise money, but also what it can spend it on. The government must submit all of its expenditures to the House for approval, and it does not have the right to spend money that has not been approved by Parliament and, more importantly, by the House. Parliament does not offer

BUDGET

Government statement that proposes tax increases or decreases as well as other revenue and borrowing measures, outlines the state of the economy and government finances in general, and often includes announcements of major new programs.

ESTIMATES

The money the government says is needed by government departments and agencies for the next fiscal year.

A typical day in the House:
www.parl.gc.ca/compendium/web-
content/c_g_typicalsittingday-e.
htm#11

extra revenue or extra expenditure to the government on its own because this would provide the executive with extra room for manoeuvre and defeat the purpose for which Parliament came into being centuries ago.

The degree to which the House can still perform its function of controlling government expenditures is a matter of debate. In 1965 experimentally, and again in 1968 permanently, the House decided to leave the detailed examination of departmental estimates to standing committees and to have them report back by a strict deadline. If they do not finish estimates review by the deadline, they are considered to have reported back anyway and the estimates proceed to the House for approval. The common consensus among academics and parliamentarians alike is that the committees have not done a particularly good job at estimates review. The committees do not take the job seriously and are overly partisan in their work. They also lack the mechanisms that could force the government's hand, particularly the ability to delay the passage of spending programs.

THE PASSAGE OF BILLS   The rest of the session of the House of Commons is devoted primarily to the consideration of bills (proposed laws). Bills can be classified in terms of two major types: public bills and private bills. **Public bills** have an impact on the whole of society or are designed to promote the general welfare. Most of the bills passed are government public bills that a minister introduces on behalf of the Cabinet. **Private members' bills** are public bills put forward by a Member of Parliament who is not a cabinet minister. Private members' bills cannot involve the imposition of taxes or the spending of public money for a new and distinct purpose without the approval of Cabinet. Although a large number of private members' bills are put forward every session, only a very small number are passed. To allow the possibility of a private member's bill to be passed in the limited time available for private members' business, a lottery system is used to select thirty bills, from which a House of Commons committee chooses five to be debated and voted on. **Private bills** are those of concern to a limited group, such as an individual, a corporation, or a charity. For example, the incorporation of a chartered bank requires approval by a private bill. Private bills are generally introduced first in the Senate and examined most closely by that chamber.

The Canadian Parliament (like other legislatures that follow the British model) requires that bills be approved on three separate occasions, or "readings," in the House of Commons and three times in the Senate, as well as being subject to a detailed committee examination (see Figure 15-2). The first reading in the House is basically a formality to introduce the bill. The second reading typically features considerable debate in the House and can result in the approval of the bill in principle. The bill then normally goes to one of the standing committees of the House for detailed "clause-by-clause" analysis. Amendments to the proposed legislation are often made at the committee stage. These amendments cannot, however, change the basic principles of the bill. The bill and the amendments agreed to by the committee are then reported back to the Commons ("report stage"). Any member of the House can also

PUBLIC BILLS
Proposed laws that have an impact on the whole of society or are designed to promote the general welfare.

PRIVATE MEMBERS' BILLS
A public bill put forward by a Member of Parliament who is not in the Cabinet.

PRIVATE BILLS
Proposed laws that are of concern to a limited group.

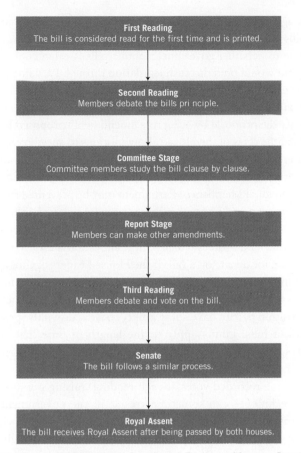

FIGURE 15-2
**STAGES IN THE PASSAGE
OF BILLS, PARLIAMENT
OF CANADA**

Source: Parliament of Canada, 2008, "At Work in Committees," *The House of Commons Report to Canadians 2008*. Retrieved from http://www.parl.gc.ca/information/about/process/house/RTC2008/rtc2008_06-e.html

propose amendments at this stage, although the Speaker decides which amendments are debatable. The Commons votes to accept or reject the amendments. The bill then proceeds to third reading for final approval by the House. If, as is usually the case, the bill was first introduced in the House of Commons, the bill then proceeds to the Senate, where it undergoes a similar process. If the Senate passes the bill in identical wording, the bill can proceed to Royal Assent (approval by the governor general on the advice of the prime minister and Cabinet). If the Senate has amended or rejected the bill, it goes back to the House and cannot be passed until both Houses of Parliament are in agreement. Finally, the government can decide when (or if) the new law (an act of Parliament, also known as a statute) is proclaimed (that is, comes into effect).

Reforms designed to enhance the importance of the House of Commons have created the possibility for bills to be sent to a special legislative committee after first reading rather than the normal second reading to allow for review of the proposed legislation without being limited by the bill's approval in principle. A special legislative committee can, therefore, propose substantial changes to bills. To date, however, only a few bills have followed this procedure.

CLOSURE
A motion in the House of Commons to limit debate on a bill.

TIME ALLOCATION
A motion in the House of Commons that allocates the time that can be spent debating a bill.

The passage of legislation is time-consuming. Since the government typically has many bills it would like to be passed during a parliamentary session, the allocation of time to debating government public bills is often contentious. While the government would prefer to rush legislation through Parliament, the opposition parties want to voice their criticism of legislation, often in the hope that public pressure will lead the government to back down and withdraw the bill, or at least to modify the proposal by accepting amendments proposed by the opposition. However, the rules of the House allow motions to speed passage of legislation. **Closure** can be invoked to limit debate to one day after the motion is passed. Historically, this was considered an extreme, undemocratic measure as it means that individual Members of Parliament may be prevented from discussing the proposed legislation. However, in recent decades closure has been used to cut off debate on some important issues such as the free trade agreements and the goods and services tax. More frequently, **time allocation** is used to set the amount of time provided for debate on a bill. If the House Leaders cannot agree on time allocation, a minister may introduce a motion allocating the time for the stage of the bill that is being debated, provided that at least one day is allocated.

The opposition parties have some ability to slow down the process of passing government bills. Limits apply to the length of time that an individual member can speak, but if each member uses the full allotment of time, this can slow down the passage of legislation. Similarly, proposing numerous amendments, requesting recorded votes at each reading, raising points of order, and using other techniques can sometimes result in the government bargaining with the opposition to modify the legislation or occasionally to withdraw controversial legislation that the government does not view as a high priority.

ACCOUNTABILITY   Although the House devotes much of its time to the passage of legislation and other government business, it also sets aside time for the opposition parties to try to hold the government accountable for its actions. Of particular importance is the daily forty-five minute oral question period in which members, particularly from the opposition, can question the ministers and the ministers can respond. Question period is the highlight of the day in the House of Commons—it receives almost all of the media attention as the opposition raises criticisms of the government on hot-button issues and the ministers defend the government, often by launching a counter-attack on the opposition. Four days a week, a half-hour debate on adjournment (known as the "late show") also provides an opportunity for a few members to discuss further an issue raised in question period. In addition, although most of the session of the House is devoted primarily to government's business, twenty "opposition days" are provided (in addition to the days allotted to debate on the Throne Speech and the budget), in which motions by the opposition (including motions of non-confidence) receive priority.[4]

---

[4]However, the government determines when these days will be held and thus can delay a non-confidence motion that might result in the defeat of the government.

HOUSE OF COMMONS COMMITTEES Visitors to the House of Commons or those who watch the parliamentary channel are often surprised when, except during question period, they see only a small number of MPs in the House. What they may not realize is that much of the work of the Commons is done in committee, and thus members are often busy with committee meetings that typically run simultaneously with meetings of the House. Committees are very useful because they can examine witnesses, question leading bureaucrats, hold public hearings (including hearings in different parts of the country), engage in detailed consideration of legislation and estimates, and provide oversight of government. Ordinary Members of Parliament often view their work in committees as the most satisfying part of their job, as committees are often less partisan than the strongly adversarial nature of the House. This can provide an opportunity for MPs to work with committee members from other parties to help shape laws and policies.

There are five different types of committees: standing committees, legislative committees, special committees, committees of the whole, and joint committees.

Standing committees are permanent committees whose terms of reference are established by the Standing Orders of the House. Many of the standing committees parallel equivalent departments of government, such as the committees on fisheries and oceans, health, and national defence. Others deal with special topics such as access to information, privacy, and ethics; procedure and house affairs; and public accounts. Most bills go to the appropriate standing committee after second reading in the House. Likewise, a standing committee will review the estimates of the particular department that they parallel. In addition, committees can review relevant department-specific statute law, policy objectives, program effectiveness, and regulations. They also are able to launch independent investigations as they see fit on the mandate, management, organization, and operation of the department(s) assigned to them by the House. Committees are no longer as large as they once were; instead of having twenty to thirty members, as was the case before 1984, all of the standing committees as of 2009 had either eleven or twelve members. As a result, committees have tended to become more businesslike, and a degree of cooperation can develop that softens rigid loyalty to party. However, partisan political considerations still influence the workings of committees (as discussed in Box 15-3, Stick-Handling Committees: The Government's Secret Guidebook).

As of November 2009, there were twenty-four standing committees in the Commons. The members of each committee are chosen so as to approximately reflect the proportion of each party's members in the House. The committee members elect the committee chairs and vice-chairs.[5] Members of the governing party chair most committees, with the vice-chairs representing the opposition parties. However, members of the Official Opposition party chair

House of Commons Committees:
**www2.parl.gc.ca/
CommitteeBusiness/Default.aspx**

STANDING COMMITTEES
Permanent committees of the House whose responsibilities include detailed examination of proposed legislation and review of departmental estimates.

---

[5]In 2002, fifty-six Liberals broke ranks with their party to support a motion by the opposition parties for a secret ballot to elect committee chairs. This reduced the ability of the government to control committees (Docherty, 2005).

BOX 15-3

Stick-Handling Committees:
The Government's Secret Guidebook

In May 2007, *Calgary Herald* journalist Don Martin obtained a copy of a two-hundred-page binder that had been distributed to the Conservative chairs of House of Commons committees. The Conservatives were in a tight spot—because of the minority government situation, the majority of members on committees came from the opposition parties. To offset this disadvantage, the guidebook provided advice on how the government could move forward with its agenda by disrupting the work of the committees. The advice included cancelling meetings, stalling the holding of committee votes, and allowing Conservatives to speak as long as they wanted. In addition, the chairs were advised to have the Conservative party help choose the witnesses invited to appear before their committee (to ensure that the witnesses favoured the government) and to help them prepare their testimony and responses to the questions they would likely face (Thompson, 2007).

Conservative House Leader Peter Van Loan did not deny that the binder had been distributed (although refusing to make it public) and ordered its return. He blamed the opposition for sabotaging the work of the committees and delaying the passage of the government's agenda. Indeed, government attempts to control committees are nothing new. As NDP MP Libby Davis claimed, "We thought the Grits [Liberals] were bad. But these guys were taking the gutter stuff to a new level. They've codified it" (quoted in Martin, 2008).

The increasingly destructive partisanship of the committees in minority situations drew the attention of Speaker Peter Milliken, who told the House of Commons, "I do not think it is overly dramatic to say that many of our committees are suffering from a dysfunctional virus that, if allowed to propagate unchecked, risks preventing members from fulfilling the mandate given to them by their constituents . . . [The committee system] is teetering dangerously close to the precipice at the moment" (quoted in Axworthy, 2008).

Unfortunately, excessive partisanship has reduced the ability of committees to function effectively.

LEGISLATIVE COMMITTEES
Temporary committees of the House established primarily to review a specific bill.

SPECIAL COMMITTEES
Committees of the House established to study a particular issue.

COMMITTEES OF THE WHOLE
The members of the House using relaxed rules of debate and procedure to deal with supply motions or other topics.

five committees, including the Public Accounts Committee, which deals with the Report of the Auditor General. There are also two standing joint committees of the House and Senate: one deals with the Library of Parliament and the other with the scrutiny of regulations.

Legislative committees are appointed by the House to review specific bills or, occasionally, to prepare and bring in a bill. They cease to exist with the submission of their report. The Speaker appoints the chair of a legislative committee. **Special committees** are chosen to study an issue, with their existence limited to the duration of the study or to the end of the session. Their terms of reference end with prorogation, but they may be continued into a new session with the agreement of the Commons. As of September 2009, the only special committee in operation concerned the Canadian mission in Afghanistan.

Committees of the Whole are composed of the membership of the entire House, and were once used extensively for consideration of financial bills and legislation. Supply (spending) motions are the only bills regularly referred to Committees of the Whole, although the House may go into the Whole on other matters if it wishes. The incentive for moving to such a committee is informality. The Speaker is not in the chair and the rules of debate and procedure are relaxed. "Take notice" proceedings, where the government gauges the will of the Commons on a non-binding vote, are also conducted in the Committee of the Whole.

House of Commons Effectiveness

Many observers have commented on the "decline of legislatures" around the world. Some Canadian observers have advanced similar arguments about the House of Commons:

- The growth of power in the hands of the prime minister and central agencies means less power in the hands of legislators.
- The growing disparity between the research capabilities available to the Commons and those available to the executive results in an increasingly weaker Commons.
- The high turnover of MPs between some elections has often made for a repetitive pattern of a group of amateur legislators facing a more experienced government.
- The growth of subordinate legislation has exploded in recent decades, leaving effective power to flesh out skeleton legislative proposals in the hands of ministers and departmental officials. Those who are supposed to be implementing laws are increasingly making them.
- Despite the growth of technologies that theoretically make transparency and openness more possible, the executive is becoming more and more reluctant to share information with legislators. Information is the mother's milk of politics, and without it, legislatures suffer.
- Committees are not very effective in their oversight of the executive.
- Parliamentary reforms have taken away some elements of parliamentary influence, such as the ability to delay supply and to speak at length in the House.

These are very serious allegations. However, there are some ways in which the House of Commons has also grown in importance, including the five outlined below.

STANDING COMMITTEE INDEPENDENCE A measure of independence for standing committees is desirable if legislatures are to be stronger and more accountable. Indices of committee independence include the degree of flexibility in the committees' terms of reference and the resources allowed to fulfill these terms of reference.

The 1986 alterations to the federal House of Commons Standing Orders significantly aided committee independence. As noted above, standing committees can now begin independent investigations regarding the mandate, management, organization, or operation of the department(s) assigned to them by the House. The government must table a comprehensive response to the report of a standing or special committee within 120 days. To further aid independence, committee members have a degree of tenure, with membership to continue from session to session within a Parliament during a given year (but ending in the last sitting day of the year). Standing, special, and legislative committees may obtain expert staff as deemed necessary, and the Board of Internal Economy will approve budgets for committee expenses.

ECONOMIC AND FISCAL OVERVIEW   A legislative focus for review of broad economic and fiscal matters is also useful in modifying executive dominance. Despite the importance of such matters, little opportunity exists for legislators to tap public input and both governmental and non-governmental expert opinion on economic and fiscal issues. Two major federal reports—the Lambert Report of 1979 and the Macdonald Commission of 1989—called for committees of the House of Commons to be set up to conduct pre-budget consultations and broad investigations of economic policy. Ultimately a Commons Committee on Finance was established, which follows this general purpose. The Parliamentary Budget Officer took over another purpose for the proposed committee: the assessment of the accuracy of the government's revenue and expenditure projections. However, issues have been raised concerning the independence of this officer and the budget of this office has been cut back.

COMMITTEE SCRUTINY OF APPOINTMENTS   The Standing Orders of the House of Commons now require that order-in-council appointments (other than appointment of judges) and, at the discretion of the government, a nominee for appointment, be referred to a standing committee of the House. The committee can examine the individual's qualifications and competence for the position and can call the individual to appear before the committee. However, the appointment or nomination cannot be vetoed by the committee.

INCREASING THE NUMBER OF OFFICERS OF THE LEGISLATURE AND THEIR STRUCTURAL INDEPENDENCE   Officers of the legislature are neutral officials who fulfill roles central to the operation of the legislature as a collective body in a way that is above politics. In recent years their number and independence of status have increased. These officers are discussed in Chapter 16.

RECOGNITION OF PARTIES IN PARLIAMENT[6]   Some resources are provided for Commons party organization and research purposes, and this strengthens the role of Parliament, giving its driving forces some influence. However, the research capacity of parliamentary parties could be increased so

---

[6]Parties are officially recognized only if they have at least twelve members in the House of Commons.

that parties could be more effective in holding government accountable and better able to analyze and develop legislative proposals.

Despite some moves to increase the independence of the House of Commons and enhance its effectiveness, party discipline remains tight, thereby limiting the independence of the Commons. For decades, party leaders have promised to loosen party discipline, but those promises have rarely been carried out. Prime Minister Paul Martin did introduce a system of reduced party discipline in February 2004 as part of a plan for democratic reforms. Specifically, he adopted the modern British system of one-, two-, and three-line votes. A three-line vote would impose party discipline on all members but would apply only to votes of confidence in the government and a limited number of matters of fundamental importance to the government. Two-line votes would bind cabinet ministers and relevant parliamentary secretaries to support the government position; other members would be encouraged, but not required, to vote in the way preferred by the government. Finally, one-line votes would leave all MPs free to vote as they saw fit. Many votes during Martin's brief term of office were designated as two-line, and a small number of government bills were defeated. The system was not continued when Stephen Harper became prime minister despite Conservative commitments to greatly diminish party discipline. Instead, most votes have been declared to be matters of confidence, so that a failure to pass a bill would trigger an election.

THE SENATE

Parliament's upper house, the Senate, has attracted criticism and ridicule for over a century. It has been described as composed of "greedy, greying, old geezers" or as the late Senator Ernest Manning, once said, "It runs on protocol, Geritol, and alcohol" (quoted in Hermanson, 1995). Proposals for reform abound, and some critics, including the NDP and Premier Dalton McGuinty of Ontario, call for the outright abolition of the upper house. But is the Senate really just a comfortable retirement home for aging politicians? Can it be reformed to play a useful role in the political system and gain the respect of Canadians?

Reasons for Establishment

The Senate was established (along with the House of Commons) by the *Constitution Act, 1867,* at a time when upper houses were meant to serve as bulwarks against unfettered democracy. John A. Macdonald viewed the Senate as a body that would provide "sober second thought" and thus a check on possible rash decisions by the Commons. His Quebec partner in the Confederation project, George-Étienne Cartier, made it clear that second-guessing the Commons would balance democracy and protect private property. In the Confederation Debates (1865), Cartier noted it was important to "give the country a Constitution which might reconcile the conservative with the democratic element; for the weak point in democratic institutions is the leaving of all the power in the hands of the democratic element" (p. 571). In order to protect property, appointees to the Senate had to possess the then-significant amount of $4000 worth of real and personal property over and above debts and liabilities (a requirement that still exists). By establishing a body to represent the interests of the propertied elite, Canadians were trying to copy the House of Lords in the United Kingdom, which had long served such a purpose. In the past, the Senate—especially its Banking, Trade and Commerce Committee—often acted as a lobby for the interests of big business (Campbell, 1978). However this role has become less important, as business interests find it more useful to focus on the policy-makers in government, and fewer senators come from a big-business background.

The Senate was also established to protect regional and provincial interests. French Canadians viewed this protection as the lynchpin to the whole Confederation agreement, which provided equality in the Senate between Ontario and Quebec. New Brunswick and Nova Scotia saw the Senate as protection against domination by central Canada. To achieve these goals, the Senate was established with equal regional ("division") representation. The provinces of Ontario and Quebec qualified as divisions, with twenty-four senators each, and the two Maritime provinces formed the third division, with twenty-four senators in all. The expansion of Canada led to the establishment of a fourth division, Western Canada, as well as representation for Prince Edward Island (within the Maritime division), Newfoundland, and the Territories (see Table 15-4).

TABLE 15-4
PROVINCIAL AND TERRITORIAL REPRESENTATION IN THE SENATE

PROVINCE AND TERRITORY	NUMBER OF REPRESENTATIVES
Ontario	24
Quebec	24
Maritimes, consisting of	24
Nova Scotia	10
New Brunswick	10
Prince Edward Island	4
Western Canada, consisting of	24
Manitoba	6
Saskatchewan	6
Alberta	6
British Columbia	6
Newfoundland and Labrador	6
Yukon	1
Northwest Territories	1
Nunavut	1
Total	105

Source: *Based on the Constitution Act, 1867 (as amended)*. Retrieved from: www.laws.justice.gc.ca/en/const/index.html

◀ The Senate makes an important contribution to the review of legislation, often catching technical errors and suggesting improvements. Many memorable reports on public policy issues have come from Senate committees, including discussions of poverty, the mass media, aging, unemployment, science policy, Canadian–American relations, CSIS, national defence, and airport security. Here, fellow Saskatchewan Senator David Tkachuk stands in the Senate chamber with Pamela Wallin during her swearing-in ceremony on January 26, 2009.

Appointments to the Senate

The governor general appoints senators on the recommendation of the prime minister. With some notable exceptions, prime ministers have filled the Senate with loyal party members. Senators have to be at least thirty years old and can serve only until age seventy-five.[7] They can be removed from their secure positions only if they fail to attend two consecutive sessions of Parliament, become bankrupt, or are convicted of treason, a felony, or other "infamous" crime. Because senators are not elected, the Senate has a legitimacy problem, meaning that public acceptance of its right to affect public policy is limited. It also has an accountability problem, which stems from the fact that there is no real audience to whom the senator can relate and be held accountable.

The method of appointment and lengthy tenure of senators greatly undermine their claim to represent regional and provincial interests. Since the recommendation for their appointment comes solely from the prime minister, neither the people nor the provincial government has a say in who is chosen. Indeed, some senators have only a tenuous connection to the province they "represent." Likewise, since they are secure in their position, they do not have to worry about maintaining the support of people in their province. Unlike other federal systems, therefore, the upper chamber is not relevant in representing provincial interests in the national legislative body.

---

[7]Until 1965, senators were appointed for life.

In a limited way, the Senate is more representative of the characteristics of Canadians than the House of Commons. For example, as of January 2010, one-third of senators were female compared with 22 percent of Commons members. Ten of the thirty-three senators appointed on Prime Minister Harper's recommendation have been female. To some extent, the Senate also reflects Canada's ethnic and racial diversity.

The Significance of the Senate

The House of Commons and the Senate are nearly equal in their legislative powers. All legislation must be passed in exactly the same words by both bodies. Financial bills involving government spending and taxing must be introduced first in the House of Commons and approved by the Senate, although governments typically view Senate amendments to or rejection of financial bills as exceeding the Senate's authority. In effect, the Senate can potentially check the power of the government by rejecting government bills that the House of Commons has passed. Indeed, before 1943, the Senate vetoed 143 government bills, including a bill to establish an old-age pension in 1927 (Schneiderman, 1991). In modern times, the Senate has generally been reluctant to reject government bills outright, preferring to propose amendments for the House (and government) to consider. For example, senators proposed one hundred and fifty amendments to the Harper Government's important *Accountability Act,* ninety of which were incorporated in the final version of the act.

Nevertheless when a new party comes to power, it will typically confront a Senate dominated by the party it defeated. Until the new party can fill enough vacancies with its own supporters to give it a majority, it may find that its legislative proposals face obstacles in the Senate. This occurred particularly in the 1980s, when the Progressive Conservative government led by Brian Mulroney engaged in a number of confrontations with a dynamic Liberal majority in the Senate. The Senate rejected important legislative proposals, including the government's spending plans, drug patent legislation, and changes to unemployment insurance, although the Senate eventually gave in after the House re-passed the bills for a second or third time. While Liberal senators generally accepted that they did not have the legitimacy needed to kill legislation approved by the House, they were effective in informing the public about their criticisms of the legislation. However, when Liberal senators stalled the passage of the unpopular goods and services tax, the government took highly controversial action (see Box 15-4, Pandemonium in the Senate).

More common than the occasional dramatic confrontations between the Senate and the government is the Senate's important contribution to the "technical review" of legislative proposals. Some senators are very diligent in their review of legislation that has been passed by the House of Commons.

Pandemonium in the Senate

Cartoonists typically depict the Senate as a traditional gentlemen's club with elderly senators relaxing in comfortable chairs sipping brandy and smoking cigars. It is seen as a quiet, sedate chamber that differs dramatically from the House of Commons, where catcalls and jeers often interrupt debate.

However, events in 1990 contradicted the sedate image of the Senate. Liberal senators had prevented a major piece of government legislation, the imposition of the goods and services tax (GST), from coming to a vote. Prime Minister Mulroney asserted that unelected senators were undermining democracy and challenging the supremacy of the House of Commons. To overcome the opposition of the Liberals, who had the majority in the Senate, the Mulroney Government drew upon an obscure, never-before-used provision of the Constitution that allowed the Queen to expand the Senate by either four or eight members on the recommendation of the governor general (in effect, the prime minister). Not surprisingly, the prime minister recommended eight people committed to supporting the GST for appointment to the Senate.

The Liberals were incensed. They broke protocol by inviting the media onto the floor of the Senate. Then, blowing kazoos, they approached the Speaker to demand more time to debate the GST. A hasty compromise was reached to allow the Liberals some additional time to voice their criticisms of the proposed tax. With the support of the eight additional senators, the Senate passed the unpopular GST legislation.

Since then, the Senate has returned to its more sedate ways, although a few bills have been rejected by the Senate.

Senators have often caught technical errors that the House did not notice and have suggested many improvements in the details of legislation. Senators have also been active members of the Joint Standing Committee on Regulations, which reviews subordinate or delegated legislation. Although most senators continue their affiliation with a political party after their appointment and attend their party's caucus meetings, the Senate tends to be somewhat less partisan than the Commons, and has usually followed the tradition of being independent of the House of Commons.

The Senate has been especially good at policy work. Most of the memorable parliamentary reports on public policy issues have come from Senate committees. With its more relaxed, less partisan atmosphere, the Senate can engage in the more long-term investigatory work that is usually within the scope of Royal Commissions. It has produced important reports on such topics as poverty, the mass media, aging, unemployment, science policy, Canadian–American relations, security, and national defence. Despite the "establishment" image of the institution, some Senate committee reports have been surprisingly critical of the government. The Senate has also been effective in serving as an early warning mechanism for some national issues. For example, the Senate Standing Committee on National

Senate Committees:
www.parl.gc.ca/common/
Committee_senlist.asp?Language=E

Security and Defence was sounding the alarm about the decline of defence preparedness of the Canadian Forces and airport security a decade before they became issues.

Despite some positive achievements, the Senate has often disappointed Canadians. Some senators simply do not devote much time to their job. Attendance is generally far lower than it is in the Commons, although the Senate workweek is less taxing.

However some senators are very active and dedicated to improving the lives of Canadians. For example, Senator Jack Marshall, a hard-working and highly respected member of the House of Commons from 1968 to 1978, did not take it easy when appointed to the Senate. As chair of the Senate Subcommittee on Veterans Affairs, he campaigned tirelessly to gain full rights and benefits for the merchant marine seamen who had played a crucial role during the Second World War in taking troops and supplies across the Atlantic. Despite suffering the highest proportion of casualties of any of the services in the war, the merchant marine veterans found that the Canadian government ignored their contribution. In 1992, Marshall finally succeeded in gaining the same benefits for those who served in the merchant marine as other veterans received.

Senate Reform

While some believe that the Senate should be scrapped as a relic of the undemocratic past, many see promise in a reformed upper house and have suggested a whole variety of possible functions for it, some old (and modified) and some new.

REGIONAL AND PROVINCIAL REPRESENTATION   There have been many proposals that reflect the need to counterbalance the power of the more populous areas of Canada by creating a new Senate with more meaningful regional or provincial representation. With the growth of the West, the six seats allotted to each of the provinces in this region are often viewed as inadequate. As well, representation in the Senate does not reflect the principle of the equality of the provinces that many people hold. However, reducing Quebec from nearly one-quarter of the seats in the Senate to slightly less than one-tenth would not go over well in that province. Likewise, people often have criticized the notion that tiny Prince Edward Island should have the same number of representatives as Ontario.

Meaningful representation of regions or provinces requires that the power to recommend appointments to the Senate be removed from the hands of the prime minister. In the 1970s, those seeking reform of the Senate often looked to provincial governments or provincial legislatures to nominate senators. Since then, most reformers have adopted the more democratic idea that the population of the province should elect senators to represent their province, with senators required to seek re-election at regular intervals.

LEGISLATIVE REVIEW   Reformers sometimes stress the idea that review of proposed legislation should continue to be an important role for the Senate, but that it must be a review with a clearly subordinate and supportive role. In this perspective, the Senate would exist not to challenge the principle of the legislation but to make it better. This subordinate role would be highlighted by including a suspensive veto (the ability to suspend the passage of legislation for a specified period of time), rather than an absolute veto over legislation passed by the Commons.

Redefining the powers of the Senate would be particularly important if it were to become an elected body. An elected Senate would likely result in a more active and more partisan upper house more willing to challenge legislation passed by the Commons. If the Senate were elected on the basis of equal provincial representation, this would likely often result in different parties controlling the Senate and the Commons. A suspensive veto would help to ensure that a deadlock did not occur between the House and the Senate.

INTERGOVERNMENTAL RELATIONS   A reformed Senate could serve as a chamber for the coordination of federal–provincial relations. It could also provide protection against federal policies that might hurt provincial interests by, for example, requiring that provincial government representatives approve federal legislation that affects the interests of the provinces (as is the case for Germany's *Bundesrat*). Alternatively, it could act as an intermediary between the federal and provincial governments and thus help to reduce federal–provincial conflict.

REPRESENTATION OF MINORITIES   The original *Constitution Act, 1867*, gave limited recognition to the minority protector role of the Senate. Representation for Quebec is divided into twenty-four districts, thereby providing representation for the English-speaking enclaves in the Eastern Townships of the province. Some suggest that the diversity of Canada should be more fully recognized in the Senate by, for example, providing guaranteed representation for Aboriginal peoples, women, and various minorities. The Charlottetown Accord proposed that both a majority of francophone senators and a majority of the Senate as a whole should have to pass bills affecting the French language and culture.

PROTECTION OF DEMOCRACY AND REPRESENTATIVENESS   One common theme of many Senate reformers is that Canada has too many centralizing elements, and not enough countervailing or counterbalancing elements. One way the power of the prime minister could be held in check is by giving the Senate a role in ratifying appointments to the Supreme Court and various agencies, boards, and commissions. As well, enhancing the legitimacy of the Senate by electing its members would allow it a more equal say in Parliament's policy role, thereby limiting the ability of the prime minister and those at the centre of government to dominate Parliament.

ATTEMPTS TO REFORM THE SENATE As discussed in Chapter 10, Senate reform has been one important part of the discussions of comprehensive changes to the Canadian Constitution. Reflecting the development of a movement for a "Triple-E" Senate (one that is equal, elected, and effective) in Western Canada, Alberta premier Don Getty, supported by several other premiers, pushed hard for major Senate reforms that require constitutional amendments. The Meech Lake Accord proposed that senators be chosen from a list of nominees put forward by the government of the province for which there was a vacancy. The Charlottetown Accord proposed that the Senate consist of six persons from each province and one from each territory. Senators would be elected either by the population or by the legislature of the provinces and territories. Although these Accords failed, Alberta has held elections to choose "senators-in-waiting" since 1989.[8] Although Prime Minister Martin refused to recommend the appointment of elected senators, Prime Minister Harper recommended the appointment of Bert Brown, a leader of the Triple-E Senate movement who had won two senatorial elections in Alberta, to the Senate in 2007.

Stephen Harper, an advocate of an elected Senate, promised in the 2006 election campaign to recommend for appointment to the Senate only those who had been elected. Within days of becoming prime minister, however, Harper recommended the appointment of Michel Fortier, who had failed to win a seat in the Commons, to the Senate. Part of Harper's motivation was that he wanted to have a cabinet minister from the Montreal area. Nevertheless, Harper has tried to bring some changes to the Senate. In its first term in office, the Harper Government presented two bills to Parliament concerning Senate reform. One would have limited senators to an eight-year term of office. The other would have provided for senatorial elections. Liberal senators opposed the first bill, demanding that it be referred to Supreme Court for a ruling on its constitutionality. The second bill did not proceed past first reading in the House of Commons. The Senate Term Limits bill was reintroduced in the House of Commons in May 2009.

Between January 2009 and January 2010, thirty-two senators, most of whom were Conservative party insiders, were appointed on the advice of the prime minister, indicating that Harper would no longer wait for an elected Senate to fill vacancies. For the time being, the Senate faces the prospect of a daunting mixture of lack of legitimacy and a perceived but frustrated need for change.

---

[8]Saskatchewan also proposes to hold senatorial elections.

Summary and Conclusion

The House of Commons is at the centre of Canada's system of representative democracy and responsible government. The prime minister and Cabinet can only govern as long as they retain the support of the majority of our elected representatives. Not only can the Commons make or unmake governments, but it is also the key institution for scrutinizing the activities of government and holding government accountable for its actions—a role that is crucial to achieving good government.

Although the House of Commons and the Senate do not usually play a major role in developing new laws and policies, their detailed examination of proposed legislation often results in significant modifications and improvements in government's legislative proposals. Debate in the House helps to inform the public about major political issues and alternatives. Individual Members of Parliament bring the problems, concerns, and viewpoints of those they represent to the attention of government, other legislators, and, to some extent, to people across the country.

A key feature of the House of Commons is its adversarial nature. Party politics dominates the work of the House. Question period, in particular, highlights the extreme partisanship that characterizes the visible face of the Commons, with members on one side defending the government and attacking the opposition, and members on the other side attacking the prime minister and the Cabinet. The rowdy behaviour of MPs during question period, the focus of media coverage, creates a negative impression of the workings of this democratic institution.

The tight party discipline that characterizes the Commons limits the representational capabilities of individual MPs. However, party discipline helps to clarify the positions taken by the opposing parties, thus making it easier for the public to know where each party stands. It also makes individual MPs less likely to be pressured by powerful lobbyists. When one party has a majority in the House, party discipline ensures that the government will have its way and be able to enact the policies in its election platform. A majority also allows the government to get Parliament to pass unpopular measures that the government believes are necessary or desirable. Through party discipline, a majority government can usually take the support of the Commons for granted, and thus does not need to respond to other points of view.

In a minority government situation, the House of Commons assumes greater importance, as the positions and strategies of the parliamentary parties determine the fate of the government. Sometimes this leads to a degree of cooperation between the governing party and one or more of the opposition parties and responsiveness to the views expressed by different parties in the House. Other times it results in a dysfunctional House, in which party competition is especially intense and the constant threat of an election overshadows all of the activities of the members. Unlike many continental European countries, Canada has seen little support for coalition governments, which could allow for a more cooperative power-sharing arrangement between parties and avoid the instability that tends to be associated with minority governments.

The Senate, as currently constituted, is often criticized as being an undemocratic institution. Even though the Senate performs some useful tasks, most observers agree that Senate reform is long overdue. However changes to the powers of the Senate, the method of selecting senators, and the number of senators for each province require a constitutional amendment. Making the Senate an elected body would increase its legitimacy, and thus would make it more likely to use its powers to reject the government's legislative proposals that have been passed by the Commons. The distribution of seats in the Senate would undoubtedly be a major bone of contention if it became a more powerful body. Not only are there strong advocates for equal representation for each province, but also demands for guarantees of representation for women, Aboriginals, and various minority groups would likely be made. A Senate that represented the diversity of Canada would likely have a different view of legislative proposals than the House of Commons. More generally, Senate reform has to address questions about what functions the upper house should perform and how deadlocks between the House and the Senate should be resolved. Achieving agreement to amend the Constitution to institute major reforms of the Senate would not be easy, given the implications for the distribution of political power.

Discussion Questions

1. How well do the House of Commons and the Senate perform their functions?

2. How do the national legislatures of the United States and Canada differ? Can they learn anything from each other?

3. Are reforms of the House of Commons and the Senate needed?

4. Should party discipline in the House of Commons be loosened?

5. Should the Senate be abolished?

Further Reading

Axworthy, T. S. (2008). *Everything old is new again: Observations on parliamentary reform.* Kingston, ON: Centre for the Study of Democracy, Queen's University.

Campbell, C. (1978). *The Canadian Senate: A lobby from within.* Toronto, ON: Macmillan.

Canada, Library of Parliament. (2003). *The Parliament we want: Parliamentarians' views on parliamentary reform.* Ottawa, ON: Author.

Docherty, D. C. (2005). *Legislatures.* Vancouver: UBC Press.

Franks, C. E. S. (1987). *The Parliament of Canada.* Toronto, ON: University of Toronto Press.

Joyal, S. (Ed.). (2005). *Protecting Canadian democracy: The Senate you never knew.* Ottawa, ON: Canadian Centre for Management Development.

Russell, P. H., & Sossin, L. (Eds.). (2009). *Parliamentary democracy in crisis.* Toronto, ON: University of Toronto Press.

Smith, D. E. (2007). *The people's House of Commons. Theories of democracy in contention.* Toronto, ON: University of Toronto Press.

Smith, J. (Ed.). 2009. *The democratic dilemma: Reforming the Canadian Senate.* Montreal, QC: McGill-Queen's University Press.

Thomas, P. G. (2002). Parliament and the public service. In C. Dunn (Ed.), *The handbook of Canadian public administration.* Don Mills, ON: Oxford University Press.

Chapter 16

THE PUBLIC BUREAUCRACY

PHOTO ABOVE: Privacy Commissioner Jennifer Stoddart laughs as she listens to a question during an August 27, 2009, news conference about changes to the popular social networking site Facebook to ensure its future practices would conform to Canadian privacy laws. The work of the commissioner and her staff resulted in changes for Facebook users worldwide.

1. Outline the characteristics of the public, private, and third sectors.
2. Discuss the origins of the public bureaucracy in Canada.
3. Provide a general overview of the staff who work for the three branches of government.

4. Describe the three types of executive department.
5. Discuss the adoption of businesslike approaches in providing public services.

When the twenty-three-year-old billionaire and founder of Facebook, Mark Zuckerberg, entered a Sao Paulo auditorium to give a speech in 2009, he was accompanied by the song "Hotel California." The lyric describing how you can leave whenever you choose to but never truly get away was very appropriate (Ehrman, 2009). Facebook users who had cancelled their accounts were shocked to learn that the personal information they had supplied could still be used by nearly a million software developers in over 180 countries.

Law students at the University of Ottawa working for the Canadian Internet Policy and Public Interest Clinic found twenty-four violations of Canadian privacy law, the *Personal Information Protection and Electronic Documents Act,* when they reviewed Facebook's policy on personal data. In July 2009, Canada's Privacy Commissioner, Jennifer Stoddart, took up their complaint and launched an investigation, which found twenty of their allegations valid. When Facebook denied they had breached Canadian privacy law, the Privacy Commissioner threatened possible prosecution. Confronted with public pressure and a deadline of thirty days imposed by the Privacy Commissioner, Facebook agreed to make changes to conform to Canadian law within one year. Specifically, Facebook (in which the U.S. Central Intelligence Agency and a leading Russian internet tycoon have invested substantial sums of money) agreed to stop sharing member information with third-party developers and to make the language in its user agreement less confusing. Stoddart's success in battling Facebook was hailed around the world, as the changes agreed to will benefit all Facebook users, not just Canadians or those in Canada.

Jennifer Stoddart is a member of the Quebec bar who has held senior positions in the Canadian and Quebec Human Rights Commissions and been president of the Commission d'accès à l'information du Québec. In 2003 she was appointed Privacy Commissioner for a seven-year term, based on unanimous recommendations by the House of Commons and the Senate.

Stoddart is one type of public official that we will examine in this chapter. As an Officer of Parliament, her job is to serve the Parliament of Canada, rather than a cabinet minister, and thus is independent of the wishes of the government. For example, Stoddart, along with provincial and territorial privacy commissioners, went public with criticisms of legislation proposed by the Canadian government in June 2009 to expand the powers of "law enforcement and national security agencies to acquire digital data." This would give these authorities "unprecedented access to Canadians' personal information" by allowing online eavesdropping without judicial authorization (quoted in Office of the Privacy Commission of Canada, 2009). If Stoddart has her way, governments will not win the right to eavesdrop on Canadians' personal digital data.

BUREAUCRACY

The word **bureaucracy** was first used in 1764 by the French philosopher Baron de Grimm to describe what he considered to be a new, and undesirable, form of government: rule by offices and officials (Albrow, 1991). In the classic view of German sociologist Max Weber, the development of bureaucracy reflected the focus of modern society on rationality and efficiency. For Weber, a bureaucratic organization featured a hierarchical chain of command; work that is organized in terms of specialized positions; detailed, impersonal rules; and a system of hiring and promotion based on qualifications and merit. Although Weber thought that the bureaucratization of society was inevitable, he worried that powerful bureaucratic organizations controlled by senior officials would dominate government and sabotage the democratic ideal (Heywood, 2002).

Although the terms "bureaucracy" and "bureaucrat" conjure up very negative images, we prefer to use the terms more neutrally. In this chapter, the term **public bureaucracy** is used to refer to the staffs of a variety of governing institutions. Governing institutions require sizeable staffs in order to be effective. Although bureaucracies are important and influential, the claim that bureaucracies "rule" is an exaggeration. The prime minister and Cabinet play a leading role in the Canadian governing system, although top public servants help them in setting the direction of government. The negative perception of bureaucrats is also misleading. Although many public servants carry out their tasks using well-worn routines, rules, and regulations, crusading public officials have spearheaded many of the advances in social progress in Canada. As the example of Jennifer Stoddart in the opening vignette suggests, public officials can make a positive difference.

The organization of the large number of public servants who work primarily in the departments of government could be viewed, to a considerable extent, as matching Weber's model of bureaucratic organization. Yet even here, the image of employees carrying out routine, detailed administrative tasks can be misleading. Some public servants are heavily involved in developing policy proposals that are eventually decided upon by Cabinet and passed by Parliament. Putting laws and policies into effect can involve a substantial degree of creativity and thought in designing effective programs and dealing with changing circumstances.

Beyond the public service, a wide variety of organizations can be found whose staffs also support the workings of the political executive (prime minister and Cabinet). In addition, legislative and judicial institutions receive support from their own bureaucratic organizations and officials. In other words, bureaucracies take on many differing forms.

BUREAUCRACY
Rule by offices and officials.

PUBLIC BUREAUCRACY
The staffs of a variety of governing institutions.

THE THREE SECTORS OF CANADIAN SOCIETY

Public bureaucracies exist in a specific context, namely a tripartite division of Canadian society. It is common to talk of the **private** (or market) **sector**, the **public** (or governmental) **sector**, and the **third** (or voluntary non-profit) **sector**. The private sector exists in a competitive environment and strives to maximize profit for private owners, be they corporations, family-owned businesses, or self-employed individuals. The public sector, which consists of the institutions and agencies of the state, is concerned, ideally, with acting in the public interest. The third sector consists of voluntary non-profit organizations that contribute to the general good of the public. This sector includes charitable organizations, religious and cultural institutions, and non-profit child-care facilities and nursing homes (Evans & Shields, 2002).

Those in the private sector frequently argue that the public sector has grown too large and is crowding out the private sector, jeopardizing its resources and mission. Those in the public sector may feel that they provide services more fairly and equitably than does the private sector. Nevertheless, those in the public sector may also justify many of their actions by arguing that their role is to promote the health of the market. As former U.S. President Calvin Coolidge once said, "The business of government is business." Canadian politicians have often offered much the same rationale for their actions. For example, in announcing a four billion dollar bailout for the Canadian subsidiaries of U.S. manufacturers Chrysler and General Motors in December of 2008, Prime Minister Harper stipulated that "Canadian taxpayers expect their money will be used to restructure and renew the automotive industry in this country" ("Canada, Ontario Announce," 2008).

There is also a tendency for one sector to influence another sector's administrative practices. In the last quarter century, the public sector has been deeply influenced by something called the New Public Management, a school of public administration that modelled itself on private sector precepts. The financial practices of the public sector (such as the accounting systems and planning and budgeting tools) more and more resemble approaches in the private sector.

For its part, the third sector depends increasingly on the public sector for funding. One implication of this trend is that non-profit organizations have begun spending more of their time and resources on meeting the reporting and accountability requirements that come with such dependence on public financing. Some non-profit organizations even complain that such efforts sidetrack them from their core missions. As well, the third sector tends to mimic the private sector in its financial management practices: "Many voluntary organizations operate as if they were profit-and-loss entities, with cash flows (from fundraising, endowments, or fees charged for services) that dictate the scope of their activities in a similar way to [private sector] firms that are fully revenue-dependent. While their objectives are public in a broad sense, they can act like private organizations from a money-management perspective" (Graham, 2007, p. 8).

However, public sector practices can also influence private ones. It might even be said that the management practices in the private sector are falling more under the public model, which became more stringent in the aftermath of the financial crisis of 2008–09. For example, as governments became one of the partners in the auto industry, government's more rigorous regulations may make their way into the private system.

THE COMPOSITION OF THE PUBLIC BUREAUCRACY

The federal bureaucracy is just one among many in this country. As Table 16-1 indicates, nearly three and a half million Canadians are employed in the many different public organizations. Indeed, the federal government bureaucracy accounts for only a small proportion of total public sector employment.

TABLE 16-1
PUBLIC SECTOR EMPLOYMENT, CANADA, 2004–2008

	EMPLOYMENT (NUMBER OF PERSONS)				
	2004	2005	2006	2007	2008
Public sector	**3 193 390**	**3 241 011**	**3 310 14**	**3 382 323**	**3 490 747**
Government	2 906 402	2 954 785	3 021 726	3 088 736	3 180 501
Federal general government	366 733	370 463	386 765	387 656	400 732
Provincial and territorial general government	330 215	340 051	344 127	350 898	358 644
Health and social service institutions, provincial and territorial	745 542	749 124	764 568	783 142	800 200
Universities, colleges, vocational and trade institutions, provincial and territorial	334 440	338 228	347 527	358 138	365 137
Local general government	498 997	516 842	529 846	548 298	581 221
Local school boards	630 475	640 077	648 892	660 603	674 568
Government business enterprises	286 987	286 227	288 489	293 587	310 246
Federal government business enterprises	94 634	95 436	96 310	99 121	104 864
Provincial and territorial government business enterprises	139 293	136 074	135 621	135 876	144 755
Local government business enterprises	53 060	54 717	56 558	58 589	60 627

Notes:
- Employment data are not in full-time equivalent and do not distinguish between full-time and part-time employees. Includes employees both in and outside of Canada.
- As at December 31 of each year.
- Federal general government data includes reservists and full-time military personnel.

Source: Statistics Canada, 2009.

BOX 16-1

Of Clerics and Kings:
The Surprise Origins of Today's Bureaucrats

When we think of bureaucrats today, images of grey-suited individuals shuffling papers in drab government office blocks are foremost. Yet the forerunners of modern bureaucrats rubbed shoulders with kings and were often at the hub of political life. Theirs is a colourful and unexpected history.

The first recognizable bureaucracy began in the Middle Ages in England with the service of clerics in the royal administration, usually in bishoprics. Clerics—those enrolled in minor religious orders—were chosen because of their educated status. But they had another appeal—as unmarried individuals, they could be trusted to serve without building up a dynasty and threatening that of the monarch. As the Middle Ages progressed, the clerics, or clerks as they came to be known, set their sights less on the religious life and more on a career in a bishopric as an administrator. Their ambition was no longer to become priests. In the sixteenth century, when the Protestant Reformation (the revolt against the religious, cultural, and political domination of the Roman Catholic Church) took hold, many churchmen left the service of the monarchy at the same time as Church properties were seized. This created a need for a whole new class of administrators to fill their old roles, as well as to manage newly acquired ecclesiastical properties and revenues (Pilkington, 1999).

The development of the modern departmental approach to government came with the appointment of Thomas Cromwell as the Principal Secretary of State to Henry VIII in 1534. Six departments were formed, all of them busying themselves with raising revenue in one form or another. It was Cromwell's successor who transformed his office into the Privy Council Office. As well, the separation of the legislative, judicial, and executive functions of governing took place around this time.

Under Henry VII, executive and judicial functions were carried out in the same location as the legislative function—in the Palace of Westminster. But in an about-face, Henry VIII moved the executive powers of the Privy Council to the royal household at Whitehall (the former residence of the Archbishop of York in London). From that time, the legislative and judicial functions of government would become increasingly separated. The legislature would come to be known as "Westminster" and the civil service and government as "Whitehall"—terms that are still in use today, nearly five centuries later. Ultimately the term "Whitehall" would be assigned to the senior civil service and the government administration, rather than to a specific place. Even though many of the British government departments today remain in the traditional Whitehall location, others have shifted elsewhere.

Although the ties of Canada's bureaucrats to clerics and kings are not self-evident, the British style of public administration deeply affected the operation of the colonial administration in British North America. In the early stage of Canada's existence, the same traditions shaped the administration of the new country. Ministerial responsibility was taken seriously and contributed to the hierarchical management style typical of Canadian departments of government. The British installed a formal merit system in the mid-nineteenth century, and Canadians copied the British example in the early twentieth century. Later, British-style public service neutrality and secrecy were so deeply entrenched in the Canadian system that the Canadian government delayed the introduction of the political rights of public servants and adoption of access to information laws.

Some Canadians think of government as a collection of minister-directed departments, but this is only part of the picture. Andrew Graham (2007) insists it is necessary to define government expansively, given the extensive reach of the public sector in modern times. For example, he points out that there is a "shadow government": people working for the private sector under government grants or grants to non-profit organizations. As well, government often achieves its aims by using a variety of "governing instruments," some of which are practices that depend on the private sector for their implementation, such as regulations, inducements, and persuasion designed to change private sector behaviour.

The Origins of the Public Bureaucracy in Canada

The public bureaucracy in Canada, especially the public service bureaucracy, owes its origins to British and American sources and to the Canadian nation-building ethos, which carried with it some aura of patronage and doing what was necessary. (See Box 16-1, Of Clerics and Kings: The Surprise Origins of Today's Bureaucrats, for an account of the British influence.)

BRITISH INFLUENCE   The traditional British style of public administration, modified by Canadian practice and convention, came to be known as the **Whitehall Model**. It would consist of a number of interrelated principles (see Table 16-2).

The British model was a subject of both pride and consternation to Canadians. It offered at the same time a familiar and relatively workable set of principles that could be passed from generation to generation, but as well proved to resist easy change.

AMERICAN INFLUENCE   American influences have also left a lasting mark in Canada. In the late nineteenth century, the **Progressive movement,**

WHITEHALL MODEL
The traditional British style of public administration with such features as ministerial responsibility, public service anonymity and neutrality, secrecy, and the merit principle.

PROGRESSIVE MOVEMENT
A late-nineteenth-century movement that sought to break the "spoils system" in government by making the public sector at all levels more businesslike and shielding it from the political realm.

TABLE 16-2
THE TRADITIONAL WHITEHALL MODEL AND ITS CANADIAN APPLICATION

TRADITIONAL WHITEHALL MODEL	MODIFICATIONS BY CANADIAN PRACTICE AND CONVENTION
Parliamentary supremacy	Subordinate (delegated) legislation
Ministerial responsibility	Answerability and accountability
Public service anonymity	Accounting officers
	Boards of Crown corporations and commissions
	Media access to public servants
Public service neutrality	Rights to engage in various forms of political activity
The secrecy norm	Access to information or freedom of information
The rule of law	Canadian *Charter of Rights and Freedoms*
The merit principle	Employment equity
	Representative bureaucracy

spearheaded by individuals like Woodrow Wilson, sought to break the "spoils system," in which the winning political party gave government jobs to its supporters, by making the public sector at all levels more businesslike and shielding it from the political realm. The Progressive movement had its strongest effect at the local and state levels, where the patronage-ridden political "machines," the target of the Progressives, had their greatest hold.

In Canada's first half century, government jobs were given to political supporters; public contracts went to friends of the government; political figures enriched themselves at public expense, often by padding construction projects; and recent immigrant communities received special "favours" in exchange for voting support at the polls. Among the Progressive movement's effects in Canada were the creation of city managers for urban governance, the foundation of special-purpose bodies to manage some politically sensitive services, and reforms in public budgeting.

SCIENTIFIC MANAGEMENT
A complex system of management of the production process, often associated with time and motion studies, that maintains that there is one best way to increase output.

Around the turn of the century, the second American influence, the **scientific management** school, first set in motion by Frederick Taylor (1856–1915), gained in popularity.[1] Frederick Taylor was a member of the New England upper class who was accepted to Harvard but instead chose to become immersed in the burgeoning American manufacturing sector, first as an ordinary worker, then as an engineer, then as what would be called today a "management consultant." Tireless study of the nature of work and management led him to publish his immediately popular work, *The Principles of Scientific Management,* in 1911.

Although Taylor's ideas on the organization of work found many expressions throughout his career, practitioners have tended to seize on discrete elements of his thought and use them as they see fit. Taylor tried to promote what today would be called "knowledge transfer." He reckoned that the job of managers was to acquire the knowledge of work that traditionally belonged to workers and to organize it so as to make it available to current and future managers. He rather optimistically referred to this as "scientific management," by which he simply meant the organization and quantification of such knowledge, as well as finding "the one best way" to perform tasks. By measuring various aspects of work tasks, the manager could figure out the time it should take for the average worker to perform tasks, the suitability of certain types of workers to specific tasks, and the relative contribution to efficiency offered by various reformulations of tools and workplaces.

Scientific management principles influenced the federal public administration for the better part of the twentieth century. In particular, the Civil Service Commission (established in 1908) adopted an extensive employee classification system based on a report by American consultants (Dawson, 1929).

---

[1]The term "scientific management" was coined by lawyer Louis D. Brandeis in hearings before the Interstate Commerce Commission.

TABLE 16-3
**PRINCIPLES OF NPM
VERSUS BUREAUCRATIC
GOVERNMENT**

PRINCIPLES OF NEW PUBLIC MANAGEMENT (NPM)	TRADITIONAL BUREAUCRATIC GOVERNMENT
Entrepreneurial government	Emphasis on spending
Steering rather than rowing	Concentration on one or a few governing instruments (or means)
Competition	Monopoly
Performance measurement	Rule-driven
Customer-driven government	Ministerial responsibility
Decentralization	Centralization
Market orientation	Command and control
Empowerment	Service

NEW PUBLIC MANAGEMENT   In the final decades of the twentieth century, ideas and practices from Britain, the United States, and New Zealand influenced thinking about public administration. The **New Public Management (NPM)**, the adoption of the practices of private business in the administrative activities of government, emerged as the result of two overlapping influences: rational choice theory and principal-agent theory. As discussed in Chapter 7, rational choice theory (also known as public choice theory) assumes all individuals, including bureaucrats, are self-interested. **Principal-agent theory** is based on the idea that the bureaucrat (the nominal agent, or "servant") who is supposed to follow the will of the principals (the minister or the legislature) often uses specialized knowledge to thwart this arrangement (see Table 16-3). Other factors were at play as well. Ideologues such as British Conservative Prime Minister Margaret Thatcher and U.S. Republican President Ronald Reagan convinced many people that behind poorly performing governments were self-serving bureaucrats who in some areas had scaled the heights of power and needed to be checked. The book *Reinventing Government* by David Osborne and Ted Gaebler (1992) was key to popularizing entrepreneurial government in Canada. In particular, Osborne and Gaebler argued that governing should involve "steering"—setting the policy direction—rather than "rowing," the delivery of services that should be contracted out to private business as much as possible. NPM was seen as the opposite of the traditional bureaucratic form of government. In fact, it was hailed as an antidote to bureaucratic ills, which, it was claimed, resulted in inefficient governing.

CANADIAN DEVELOPMENT   Although influenced by British and American ideas, the Canadian public bureaucracy has developed, to some extent, in its own way. Until 1917, there was only nominal attention to the merit principle (the right person for a specific job) and more to patronage (a public service job seen as a political favour to be bestowed on those who supported the governing party). For the next fifty years (1918–67), the Whitehall Model largely

NEW PUBLIC MANAGEMENT
The adoption of the practices of private business in the administrative activities of government.

PRINCIPAL-AGENT THEORY
A theory based on the idea that the bureaucrat who is supposed to follow the will of the minister or the legislature often uses specialized knowledge to thwart this arrangement.

dominated. Since 1967, collective bargaining by public service unions and the adoption of the *Charter of Rights and Freedom*s have modified the Whitehall Model. For example, strict restrictions on the political activities of public servants to maintain their political neutrality were struck down by the Supreme Court as a violation of the freedoms protected by the Charter. New Public Management also had an effect—although not to the same extent as in some other countries. The long-term effect of these developments is the current blend of rights-based, bargaining-based, and entrepreneurial-based management.

PARLIAMENTARY, EXECUTIVE, AND JUDICIAL BUREAUCRACIES

People often think of bureaucracy as involving the public service, with the employees in each department answering to a cabinet minister. However, there are many kinds of bureaucracies, and only one kind answers to ministers. Parliament, the executive (prime minister and Cabinet), and the judiciary each have their own bureaucracies with a variety of specific aspects.

Executive Institutions

Executive institutions fall into three categories:

1. executive departments headed by cabinet ministers;
2. semi-independent public agencies: Crown corporations and assorted agencies, boards and commissions); and
3. alternative service delivery (ASD), a variety of different methods for delivering public services.

EXECUTIVE DEPARTMENTS HEADED BY CABINET MINISTERS

EXECUTIVE DEPARTMENT
An organization headed by a cabinet minister.

Ministers preside over **executive departments**. Executive departments are those listed in Schedule I of the *Financial Administration Act* (FAA), a list that may only be amended by Parliament and not at the discretion of the minister or Cabinet. Departments are financed through parliamentary appropriations. As of November 2009, there were twenty-one departments. Ministers, in the language of most of the acts creating departments, have "direction and management" of the department. According to convention, ministers are individually responsible to Parliament for implementing the mandate that is conferred upon them in the act.

A minister may have personal responsibility to Parliament for personnel management, staffing, and finances of the department, but does not in fact exercise direct responsibility over the employees or finances of the department. The Public Service Commission is given exclusive responsibility for the staffing of departments under the *Public Service Employment Act,* which came into effect in 2005. This power is often delegated, but it is delegated to the deputy minister, not to the minister of the department. Personnel management other than staffing is the responsibility of the Treasury Board

Auditor General Sheila Fraser and her staff provide Parliament with the information and analysis needed to hold the government accountable for its use of public funds.

and the department's deputy minister, not the minister. Similarly, control over financial administration is shared between the Treasury Board and the department's deputy minister under the *Financial Administration Act,* and the minister is excluded. The reason for these exclusions is historical: In the past, ministers enjoyed much greater powers, but they abused them, aggrandizing the power of their departments, their parties, and themselves.

SEMI-INDEPENDENT PUBLIC AGENCIES   The **semi-independent public agency**, the second type of executive institution, differs from its departmental counterpart in important ways. Although both have a designated minister, Parliament does not usually scrutinize the agency's affairs to the same extent. Ministers will generally submit less readily to questioning in the House of Commons on matters related to boards, commissions, or Crown corporations. These agencies generally have more freedom from central controls in their budgeting and staffing practices. Some are advisory agencies, some perform regulatory functions, and some engage in commercial or business activities, all activities that are rare for departments to perform.

SEMI-INDEPENDENT PUBLIC AGENCY
A government organization that has a degree of independence from executive controls and parliamentary scrutiny.

Crown Corporations   Crown corporations are legal entities set up by the government to pursue commercial or other public policy objectives. The type of Crown corporation most Canadians are familiar with is called a parent Crown corporation (see Figure 16-1). Some of these affect Canadians directly every day, like the Canadian Broadcasting Corporation (CBC), Marine Atlantic, or the Bank of Canada, whereas others have a more indirect impact, like the Business Development Bank of Canada, Atomic Energy of Canada, and the International Development Research Centre (IRDC). A parent Crown corporation is a

FIGURE 16-1
**PARENT CROWN
CORPORATIONS GROUPED BY
MINISTERIAL PORTFOLIO***

*as at July 31, 2008

Agriculture and Agri-Food

- Canadian Dairy Commission
- Farm Credit Canada

**Atlantic Canada
Opportunities Agency**

- Enterprise Cape Breton
  Corporation

Canadian Heritage

- Canada Council for the Arts
- Canadian Broadcasting
  Corporation
- Canadian Museum of
  Civilization
- Canadian Museum of Nature
- Canadian Race Relations
  Foundation
- National Arts Centre
  Corporation
- National Gallery of Canada
- National Museum of Science
  and Technology
- Telefilm Canada

Finance

- Bank of Canada
- Canada Deposit Insurance
  Corporation
- Canada Development
  Investment Corporation
- Canada Pension Plan
  Investment Board
- PPP Canada Inc.[1]

Fisheries and Oceans

- Freshwater Fish Marketing
  Corporation

Foreign Affairs

- International Development
- Research Centre

Industry

- Business Development Bank
  of Canada
- Canadian Tourism Commission
- Corporation for the Mitigation
  of Mackenzie Gas Project
  Impacts
- Standards Council of Canada

**Human Resources and
Social Development**

- Canada Employment Insurance
  Financing Board[2]
- Canada Mortgage and Housing
  Corporation

**Indian Affairs and
Northern Development**

- First Nations Statistical
  Institute

International Trade

- Canadian Commercial
  Corporation
- Export Development Canada

Natural Resources

- Atomic Energy of Canada
  Limited
- Cape Breton Development
  Corporation

**Public Works and
Government Services**

- Defence Construction (1951)
  Limited

**Transport, Infrastructure
and Communities**

- Atlantic Pilotage Authority
- Blue Water Bridge Authority
- Canada Lands Company
  Limited
- Canada Post Corporation
- Canadian Air Transport
  Security Authority
- Federal Bridge Corporation
  Limited, The
- Great Lakes Pilotage
  Authority
- Laurentian Pilotage Authority
- Marine Atlantic Inc.
- National Capital Commission
- Old Port of Montréal
  Corporation Inc.[3]
- Pacific Pilotage Authority
- Parc Downsview Park Inc.[4]
- Ridley Terminals Inc.
- Royal Canadian Mint
- VIA Rail Canada Inc.

Treasury Board

- Public Sector Pension
  Investment Board

[1]P3C, a wholly owned subsidiary of CDIC, has been directed by Order in Council (P.C. 2008-0855) to
report as if it were a Crown corporation.
[2]CEIFB was created by the *Canada Employment Insurance Financing Board Act* on June 20, 2008.
[3]OPMC, a wholly owned subsidiary of CLCL, has been directed by Order in Council (P.C. 1987-86) to
report as if it were a parent Crown corporation.
[4]PDP, a wholly owned subsidiary of CLCL, has been directed by Order in Council (P.C. 2003-1304) to
report as if it were a parent Crown corporation.

Source: *Treasury Board Secretariat, 2008, Annual Report to Parliament—Crown Corporations and Other
Corporate Interests of Canada 2008. Retrieved from http://www.tbs-sct.gc.ca/reports-rapports/cc-se/2008/
cc-se05-eng.asp*

legally distinct entity wholly owned by the Crown and managed by a board of
directors. The mandate, powers, and objectives of the corporation are set out in
two ways. Either there is special legislation constituting the parent Crown corporation, or the mandate, powers, and objectives are set out in the "articles of
incorporation" under the *Canada Business Corporations Act*. As of July 31,
2008, there were forty-five Crown corporations, excluding subsidiaries
(Treasury Board Secretariat, 2008). Three more were created in 2008–09.

Crown corporations report through specific ministers to Parliament, but
the relationship between corporation and minister is not as close or direct as

is the case with ministers and departments. The reason the Crown corporations came into existence in the first place was to free them from the rules and political control that are evident in the regular bureaucracy. However, the arm's-length relationship raises difficulties for those used to thinking in terms of the orthodox doctrine of ministerial responsibility, where the minister is responsible for all matters administrative and political.

For the most part, however, a compromise solution has been settled upon distinguishing between "general" and "day-to-day" policy. This theoretically provides a measure of independence to the boards of semi-independent agencies, in response to the perceived needs of the various professionals involved, but attempts to provide for significant formal accountability. The minister responsible publicly outlines the agency's general role and policy, appoints the board members, and may approve investments and borrowings as well as corporate plans and budgets. For some Crown corporations, the minister may direct the board of directors to follow a particular course of action (Gray, 2006). The minister also answers in Parliament for the corporation. The board of the corporation manages day-to-day operations within the minister's guidelines. To some extent, Parliament exercises its scrutiny role.

There have been three major versions of accountability frameworks for Crown corporations, namely, the amendments to the *Financial Administration Acts* of 1951, 1984, and 2006. They outline other mechanisms for oversight and accountability for the Crown corporations. All Crown corporations have to prepare financial statements and most of them are subject to annual audits of their financial statements by the Auditor General of Canada. Since 1984 most have been required to submit at least once every five years to value-for-money audits known as "special examinations."

The *Federal Accountability Act* of 2006 anticipated the establishment of a "Public Appointments Commission," to assure merit-based appointments to government boards, commissions, and agencies. However, as of September 2009, the Harper Government had not established this commission and continued to make a number of appointments on a patronage basis. The act also extended the *Access to Information Act* to cover all Crown corporations, officers of Parliament, and foundations. However, some Crown corporations, such as the Canadian Broadcasting Corporation, have been reluctant to fully comply with the *Access to Information Act*. The act also removed the government's power to exempt Crown corporations from the *Public Servants Disclosure Protection Act*, its "whistleblower" legislation.

ABCs   A wide variety of agencies, boards, and commissions (ABCs) serve a number of functions, which may overlap to a large extent. They may have adjudicative roles, such as the role played by the Canadian Human Rights Tribunal, which decides cases arising from the *Canadian Human Rights Act*. Some regulate particular industries (see Box 16-2, Dodging the Financial Crisis: The Regulation of Canada's Financial Institutions). For example, the

BOX 16-2

Dodging the Financial Crisis: The Regulation of Canada's Financial Institutions

In 2008, the world was hard hit by a financial crisis that began in the United States with the bankruptcy of Lehman Brothers, one the world's leading financial institutions. Within weeks, long-standing major banks and other financial institutions around the world faced bankruptcy, and either failed or had to be bailed out by government. In many countries, the wave of deregulation of the financial industry in the 1980s and 1990s allowed major financial institutions to make complex, highly speculative investments that collapsed like a house of cards in 2008.

Fortunately, Canadian banks came out of the 2008–09 financial crisis intact. Indeed, Canada has not had a bank failure since 1985. Although Canada also engaged in deregulation, Canadian banks have been encouraged to be cautious by maintaining substantial capital reserves.

The primary agent for regulating financial institutions is the Office of the Superintendent of Financial Institutions (OSFI), led since 2007 by Julie Dickson. The OSFI, an independent agency of the Canadian government that reports to Parliament through the minister of Finance, regulates federally chartered financial institutions. This means all banks and federally incorporated or registered trust and loan companies, cooperative credit associations, and insurance companies fall under its purview. The agency also regulates federally administered pension plans. Its mandate is to protect the policyholders, depositors, and pension plan members from financial loss.

The OSFI often takes a tough-love approach. Dickson discusses best practices with the banks and they usually take the hint. However, if they don't, the OSFI can discipline a bank by requiring it to change its business plan, or acquire more capital, or by taking control of its assets.

The OSFI does not act in a vacuum. Its mandate is financial institutions, but the management of the larger financial sector falls to a group composed of the Finance minister, an associate deputy minister in Finance, the chief executive officers of Canada's largest financial institutions, and the Superintendent of Financial Institutions. Each of these members represents different facets of financial policy. But much of the credit for the strong financial reserves that allowed the banks to weather the crisis of 2008–09 goes to Dickson, according to the *Report on Business* magazine (Perkins, 2009).

Others, however, see the situation differently. Although Canada avoided the collapse of banks experienced by other countries, the Canadian government assisted the banks by purchasing about $75 billion of the mortgage loans they held. As Russell Williams (2009) points out, there is a huge gap in the regulatory framework for activities of Canadian financial institutions engaged in securities trading. No regulations are in place to prevent Canadian banks from investing heavily, as did American financial institutions, in highly risky investments. It was "simply lucky they did not," as monitoring of the banks' holdings is insufficient (p. 50). Unless securities regulations are tightened, Canada's financial institutions might face serious trouble in a future financial crisis.

Canadian Radio-Television and Telecommunications Commission (CRTC) determines which companies can have broadcasting licences and sets requirements for Canadian content in the broadcast media. Some of the CRTC's decisions have been controversial, such as refusing to renew the licence of Quebec City's popular CHOI-FM in 2004 over failure to comply with radio regulations governing offensive language. Also controversial was the licensing in 2005 of two satellite radio services, Canadian Satellite Radio and Sirius Canada, without the normal Canadian content controls. Other agencies have operating responsibilities, like those undertaken by the Canadian Food Inspection Agency, whose mandate is to safeguard food, animals, and plants and overall to provide consumer protection. Some federal agencies have research responsibilities. For example, the National Research Council (NRC) conducts scientific research and development. Others combine research and funding responsibilities. For example, the Canada Council for the Arts, the federal government's arm's-length arts funding agency, provides funding to artists, endowments, and arts organizations and performs research, communications, and arts promotion activities.

Various rationales have been offered for the use of the agencies, boards, and commissions that generally operate at arm's-length from government. One common rationale for the non-departmental form has been the alleged inability of departments to undertake business functions, or similar activities, and the need for the organizational flexibility that these independent agencies provide. Some agencies have been set up in part to allow for freedom in personnel and wage policy that supposedly would not have been possible with directions by the Public Service Commission or the Treasury Board. As well, businesspeople and certain researchers may feel uneasy in highly organized departmental structures and prefer to join organizations that are less foreign to their experience, and more open to expressions of opinion.

A second reason cited is the need to take away some functions from the controversial political arena. Some functions might be inefficient if too much political interference were allowed. It is argued that pricing policies, monetary policy, capital installation locations, and extension of services should be decided in a non-partisan environment.

A third related justification is to remove quasi-judicial functions from the political realm so that a specialized impartial body with no particular interest in the outcome can make the decisions after holding hearings in a court-like manner.

Other reasons for adopting the non-departmental form include the desire to have an "umbrella organization" to deliver services that involve different government departments or different levels of government. For example, the Canada Revenue Agency was transformed from a department (Revenue Canada) to agency status in 1999. This agency administers federal, provincial, and territorial tax programs and other services. It is managed by a Board of Management with fifteen members appointed by the Cabinet, eleven of which are nominated by the provinces and territories.

ALTERNATIVE SERVICE DELIVERY (ASD)   The third kind of executive organization, termed **alternative service delivery** (ASD), is aimed particularly at improving the delivery of government services, reducing the role of government, increasing flexibility, improving coordination among government departments and programs, and generally making government more businesslike and responsive to the needs of the recipients of services. This approach may include establishing new organizational forms within departments or outside traditional departmental structures, termed special operating agencies (such as the self-financing Passport Canada). Alternative service delivery may also involve setting up partnerships with business and voluntary non-governmental organizations, commercializing the provision of services, or contracting out services to private business or to former government employees (Inwood, 2009). Overall, ASD can mean turning to unusual organizational forms and instruments that do not fit the traditional view of government instruments.

THE THREE TYPES OF EXECUTIVE DEPARTMENTS

Three types of executive government departments exist:

1. central agencies and central departments;
2. central coordinating departments; and
3. line departments.

Central Agencies and Central Departments

CENTRAL AGENCIES   **Central agencies**, the Privy Council Office (PCO) and the Prime Minister's Office (PMO), are headed by the prime minister and perform service-wide policy, facilitative, and control functions. Their authority comes from the statutory and conventional authority of Cabinet itself, and their roles are to assist the prime minister directly and to help with the setting of objectives by Cabinet. They have a formal or informal right to intervene in, or otherwise influence, the activities of departments. The **central departments** (Department of Finance and the Treasury Board Secretariat) also perform these functions, but they are headed by ministers rather than by the prime minister, and their objectives are usually collectively set or influenced by Cabinet. They also have the right to intervene in, or otherwise influence, the activities of other departments. The term "central agency" is often used to refer to both types of structures. However, differentiating between the two can be

ALTERNATIVE SERVICE DELIVERY
Methods of delivering government services apart from the use of traditional departments and agencies, with the goal of making government more businesslike and responsive to the needs of the recipients of services.

CENTRAL AGENCIES
The Prime Minister's Office and the Privy Council Office, which provide direct assistance to the prime minister and facilitate the setting of objectives by Cabinet.

CENTRAL DEPARTMENTS
The Department of Finance and the Treasury Board Secretariat, which, along with the central agencies, advise Cabinet and its committees and influence the direction and policies of the government.

TABLE 16-4
**STAFF AND BUDGETS
OF FEDERAL CENTRAL
AGENCIES AND CENTRAL
DEPARTMENTS, 2009–2010**

AGENCY	STAFF NUMBERS	BUDGET
PMO	80	$7.6 million
PCO	978	$133 million
Finance	765	$83 million
Treasury Board	1714	$2.3 billion, but most is for centrally administered funds; $212 million for Treasury Board Secretariat operations

Note: Figures for the PMO are for 2007–08.

Source: *Figures extracted from Smith, 2009.*

useful, since one type, central agencies, provides a venue for direct prime ministerial power and the other, central departments, does not. In fact, one of the central departments, Finance, occasionally jockeys with the prime minister and the central agencies for relative influence.

In contrast, **line departments** are charged with delivery of the basic services of government, such as Health and Defence. Line departments do not have a mandate to intervene in the affairs of other departments. Although the central agencies and central departments exert great influence over government policies and actions, they do not have as large a staff or budget as most government departments do (see Table 16-4). Despite their importance, the central agencies and departments are the organs of government that parliamentarians, and most Canadians, know least about and whose workings are the least transparent, compared with the others.

LINE DEPARTMENTS
Departments that deliver the basic programs and services of government.

PRIME MINISTER'S OFFICE
Provides partisan political advice to the prime minister and is staffed by supporters of the party in power.

Prime Minister's Office:
www.pm.gc.ca

The Prime Minister's Office   The **Prime Minister's Office** (PMO) gives partisan political advice to the prime minister and is staffed by supporters of the party in power, although they are hired under the *Public Service Employment Act* (PSEA). They are classified as "exempt staff" or "ministerial staff" in order to free them from normal public service hiring practices.[2] The reasoning behind this is that the prime minister's government was elected to set a certain political direction for the country. The prime minister thus needs a loyal group to monitor conformity to the program. The PMO has the following functions, among others:

1. advising on political strategy and the political implications of new policy initiatives;
2. advising on senior appointments;

---

[2]Each cabinet minister also has a small political staff separate from the public servants in the department.

3. organizing the prime minister's correspondence, media relations, speeches and timetable; and
4. liaising with ministers, members of caucus, and national party officials.

The Privy Council Office   The **Privy Council Office** (PCO) is the central agency that provides non-partisan policy advice to the prime minister and Cabinet.[3] It serves as the secretariat for the Cabinet and its committees, and provides specialized public policy advice to the prime minister. It is responsible for ensuring that the Cabinet decision-making process runs smoothly and that the government's agenda is implemented. It is also the main designer and adviser for machinery-of-government issues (meaning the design of major structures like departments and agencies) and tries to "foster a high-performing and accountable Public Service" (PCO, 2008). The head of the PCO advises the prime minister on the appointment of **deputy ministers**, who function as the administrative heads of departments, and provide the link between the ministers who are politically responsible for the departments and the non-partisan public servants in the departments. Finally, the PCO coordinates the federal government's strategy in federal–provincial and territorial relations.

The head of the Privy Council is the Clerk of the Privy Council, who serves as the prime minister's deputy minister, the secretary to the Cabinet, and the head of the public service (see Box 16-3, Master Multi-Tasker: The Duties of the Clerk of the Privy Council). The designation "head of the public service" has been in place since the early 1990s in order to provide leadership for the public service of Canada. As head of the public service, the clerk is responsible for matters relating to public service renewal, for representing the public service to the politicians and to the public, and for issuing an annual report on the status of the public service. The "public service" means the core public administration—the employees of the departments as well as some agencies such as the Canada Revenue Agency, the Parks Canada Agency, the Canadian Food Inspection Agency, and the National Research Council of Canada (PCO, 2008).

CENTRAL DEPARTMENTS

Treasury Board Secretariat   The Treasury Board Secretariat (TBS) is a central department that serves as the central management board for the public service, the Treasury Board. The Treasury Board establishment and mandate is outlined in the *Financial Administration Act,* which gives the department responsibility for general administrative policy, financial management, human resources management, internal audit, and public service pensions and benefit

---

[3]The PCO's name comes from the Queen's Privy Council for Canada, which is discussed in Chapter 14.

Master Multi-Tasker:
The Duties of the Clerk of the Privy Council

The Clerk of the Privy Council is arguably the most important public servant in the government of Canada. It falls to the clerk to set the "tone at the top" for the public service and to rally it behind the efforts of the current government.

Kevin G. Lynch is a good example of what an individual clerk is relied upon to do. He was appointed in February 2006 in the new Harper Government. Even though new prime ministers often appoint new clerks when they come to office, the latter are expected to be non-partisan, and to "speak truth to power." This was the case with Kevin Lynch, say Ottawa insiders. He, as most good clerks have to do, balanced the wants of the government with the needs of the public administration that served it.

Few clerks have had to operate in such a turbulent public policy environment. As the world reeled from an international financial crisis in 2008, the worst since the Depression of the 1930s, Lynch worked with the prime minister and the Finance department, where he had previously been deputy minister, to design and implement a wide-ranging stimulus package. The year before, he had worked with the same people to manage a crisis in asset-backed commercial paper, and to help design the tax reductions that had played a key role in the new government's program.

Lynch also took responsibility for overseeing Canada's involvement in the Afghanistan war, the most intense military conflict the country had seen in a half century. In addition, he is often identified with changing the "foreign affairs focus from Africa and Europe to the Americas . . . pushing strengthened ties to the U.S. and [focusing] on rebuilding Canada's Arctic infrastructure" (Laghi, 2009).

One area closely monitored by clerks of the Privy Council Office is the health of the nation's public service. Lynch was no exception. He launched a public service renewal exercise, convinced his political masters to boost federal recruitment efforts, and reorganized the human resources function with the help of outside advisers.

If this seems like an exercise in multi-tasking, that's exactly what it is. Clerks know that the longest they will be in their position is about three or four years, the average length of service for the office. Like his forerunners, Lynch worked tirelessly to make a difference. When he retired in 2009, after thirty-three years in the public service, his legacy was secure. Although the media speculated about possible causes for his stepping down as head of the Privy Council Office, Kevin Lynch said simply that "the time was ripe" and "he wanted to go out on a high" (Laghi, 2009).

programs. It also has responsibilities under a number of other acts, such as the *Public Service Employment Act*, the *Official Languages Act*, the *Access to Information Act*, and *the Employment Equity Act*. In general, the responsibilities of the TBS are

1. setting management policies and monitoring performance;
2. directing expenditure management and performance information systems; and
3. serving as principal employer of the public service.

Treasury Board Secretariat:
www.tbs-sct.gc.ca

However, in recent years the Treasury Board Secretariat has had a more difficult time carving out a distinct role for itself in the central executive. David Good (2007) reveals that of all the central bodies, the TBS has struggled most for a meaningful role after having decentralized most of its management roles to departments in the last few decades.

The establishment in 2009 of the Office of the Chief Human Resources Officer (OCHRO) within the Treasury Board Secretariat centralizes human resources policy (hiring and managing people in the public service), which had been scattered across different organizations for several decades. The OCHRO represents the Canadian government as the "employer" in relations with public service employees and deals with all aspects of salaries and benefits. It also develops broad performance indicator framework policies, analyzes basic data on the public service, and provides leadership in human resources management. Within the policy framework of legislation and the OCHRO, the deputy ministers take responsibility for human resources management in their own departments. (See Figure 16-2.)

The Department of Finance   Finance is often considered the most influential department in the government. It directly and indirectly affects everything that happens in government. It is Finance that helps prepare the annual federal budget, which dictates whether government expenditure in general will be expansionary, stay-the-course, or restrictive. Finance is also instrumental in

- developing taxes and tariffs;
- arranging federal borrowing;
- advising on and managing transfer payments to provincial and territorial governments;
- representing Canada within international financial institutions such as the International Monetary Fund, World Trade Organization, and the World Bank; and
- acting as the government's analytic think tank with regard to major economic issues.

The Finance minister has responsibilities that touch many areas. Although each of these responsibilities is of great significance, the annual federal budget is undoubtedly the one that matters most to the majority of ordinary Canadians. The pre-eminent role of Finance is evident in the construction of the budget. David Good says that outsiders view the budget as one item, but federal insiders view it as comprising five separate parts, four of which are the direct responsibility of Finance: major transfer payments to individuals (for example, benefits to the elderly and employment insurance); major transfer payments to provincial and territorial governments (the Canada Health Transfer, the Canada Social Transfer, and equalization payments); public debt charges; and tax expenditures (tax breaks, such as the Registered Education Savings

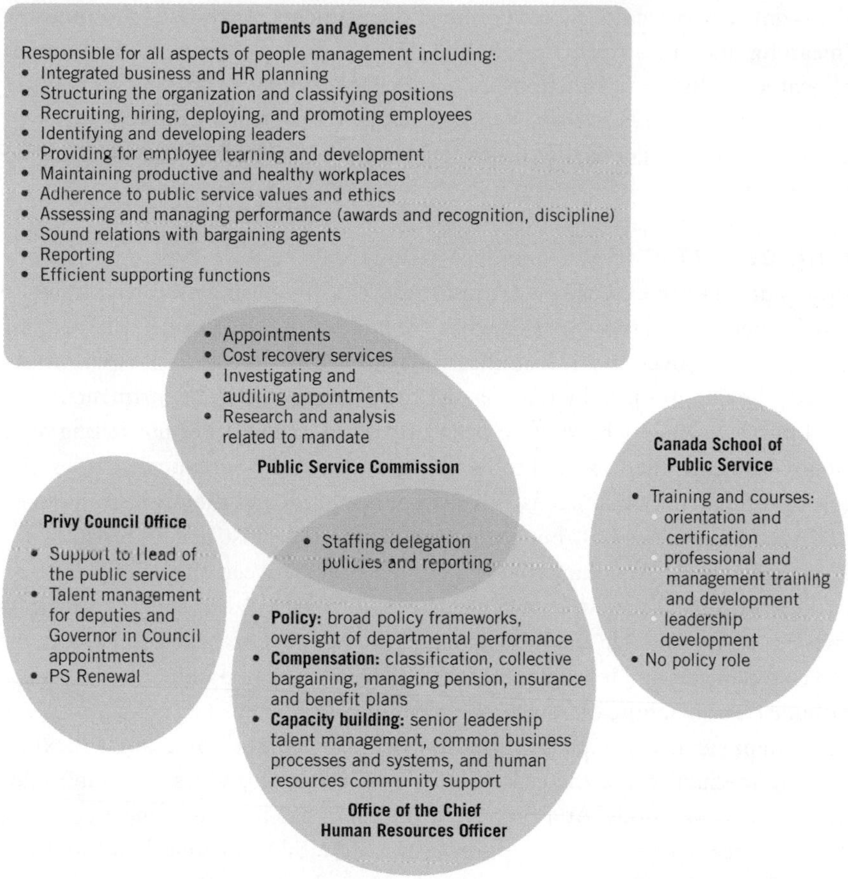

FIGURE 16-2
**NEW HUMAN RESOURCES
GOVERNANCE STRUCTURE**

Departments and Agencies

Responsible for all aspects of people management including:
- Integrated business and HR planning
- Structuring the organization and classifying positions
- Recruiting, hiring, deploying, and promoting employees
- Identifying and developing leaders
- Providing for employee learning and development
- Maintaining productive and healthy workplaces
- Adherence to public service values and ethics
- Assessing and managing performance (awards and recognition, discipline)
- Sound relations with bargaining agents
- Reporting
- Efficient supporting functions

- Appointments
- Cost recovery services
- Investigating and auditing appointments
- Research and analysis related to mandate

Public Service Commission

Canada School of Public Service
- Training and courses: orientation and certification professional and management training and development leadership development
- No policy role

Privy Council Office
- Support to Head of the public service
- Talent management for deputies and Governor in Council appointments
- PS Renewal

- Staffing delegation policies and reporting

- **Policy:** broad policy frameworks, oversight of departmental performance
- **Compensation:** classification, collective bargaining, managing pension, insurance and benefit plans
- **Capacity building:** senior leadership talent management, common business processes and systems, and human resources community support

Office of the Chief Human Resources Officer

Source: PCO, 2009, "Annex B: Human Resources Governance Changes," *Sixteenth Annual Report to the Prime Minister on the Public Service of Canada*. Retrieved from http://www.pco-bcp.gc.ca/index.asp?lang=eng&Page=information&Sub=publications&Doc=ar-ra/16-2009/annex-b-eng.htm

Plan, designed to achieve a policy objective). The Treasury Board Secretariat oversees operating and other expenditures, but "in the words of a senior official, these operating and other expenditures are 'really a residual category' and are what officials refer to as the 'small p' programs of government" (Good, 2007, p. 46). So it is Finance that has the lion's share of some of the most important transfer and economic programs, as well as playing an important budgeting role.

In addition to the central agencies and central departments that are key actors in virtually all policy decisions (Smith, 2009) and play a major role in coordinating government decisions, other government departments also have a coordinating role. For example, the Department of Justice has been responsible for "Charter-proofing" federal legislative proposals (that is, trying to ensure that they will not be struck down by the courts as a violation of the *Charter of Rights and Freedoms*) either by itself or by providing guidelines to the legal services units in government departments. Likewise, the minister (meaning the department) of Public Works and Government Services is allocated exclusive jurisdiction under the *Department of Public Works and Government Services Act* of 1996 and under the *Defence Production Act* of 1985 to procure goods for other departments, as well as for the Armed Forces.

LINE DEPARTMENTS   Line departments are the third type of organization found in the executive government. They function as the backbone of government, delivering most of what we have come to expect in the way of services from government, from the military to the protection of aviation. As noted, they do not usually intervene in the affairs of other departments.

Line departments have often been portrayed as the drab, unexciting area of government. They are said to be the most driven by bureaucratic rules, the most dominated by politicians—their own ministers and the prime minister—and the most in need of, but at the same time the most deeply resistant to, basic reform. A. W. Johnson (1992) noted that between the 1960s and the early 1990s, there was at least "one new major push for reform every three to five years" (p. 7). Even the Privy Council (2002) felt compelled to note, in an internal paper, that a few perennial themes seem to have dominated the public administration landscape since the early 1960s. From a human resources (HR) management perspective, frustrations over cumbersome and inflexible staffing mechanisms or the lack of integrated HR and business planning echo across the generations. At a broader level, there has been an almost constant tension between the need for rigorous accountability on one hand and the desire for creative and flexible management on the other (PCO, 2007).

Some academics have contributed to this view of the federal line bureaucracy as overwhelmed with paperwork and rules. Savoie (2008) describes it thus:

> *Reports of one kind or another, performance measurement schemes, management targets, horizontal government, oversight bodies, major developments in IT (information technology), political crises (often caused by information obtained through access to information legislation), a much more aggressive media, whistle-blowing legislation, an emphasis on managing publicly not privately, constantly changing priorities, collective bargaining, and unionized workers operating in a world with no bottom line. . . . [no wonder] Front-line managers and workers firmly believe that getting things done is much more difficult today than it was forty years ago. (p. 223)*

However, others consider the line bureaucracy as a more independent and a more challenging place to work. Some theorists of the rational choice school, or those who are attracted by the "principal-agent" theory, see the average bureaucrat as a significant power-seeking agent, one whose nominal superiors do not under normal circumstances have enough information or resources to control their employees. The move to the New Public Management approach to public sector organization and management is a sign of just how much politicians fear the power of the bureaucracy in Canada and Britain (Aucoin, 1995).

Recent writing about the federal bureaucracy views some federal deputy ministers as having great success in achieving the departmentally driven agendas. As noted in Chapter 14, David Good (2007) says that departments can be effective if they follow three elemental rules: link the department's proposals to the priorities of government, do your homework, and have a constituency. Linking to government priorities means cultivating close ties with Finance, the PMO, and PCO, and convincing the prime minister that it is "the prime minister's issue," not Cabinet's, and that the prime minister will garner personal credit for the issue and be able to resolve any division in Cabinet on the side of the department. Doing one's homework means doing the policy work surrounding the issue and knowing the issue better than Finance; linking to the concerns of Finance; and thinking like a "guardian," that is, like Finance or the Treasury Board would. Having a constituency means developing support both inside and outside of government, including regional ministers, key sectoral ministers, and important interest groups; and distributing benefits and pain equitably across the whole range of provinces (Good, 2007).

The Three Levels of Bureaucratic Elite in Departments

Three levels of bureaucratic elite characterize departments:

1. the deputy minister (DM) level (and in some departments, associate deputy ministers);
2. the assistant deputy minister (ADM) appointments; and
3. director-level appointments.

Deputy and associate deputy ministers are called Governor in Council (GIC) appointments because they are made by the governor general upon the advice of the Cabinet (acting in the name of the Privy Council). In practice, it is the prerogative of the prime minister, not the minister of the department, to appoint these individuals. In doing so, the prime minister takes into account the need to ensure that the appointees can be trusted to carry out his or her will and see to the needs of the government of the day. The Clerk of the Privy Council provides advice to the prime minister on these appointments.

Despite being chosen by the prime minister and closely associated with the policies of the government, most deputy ministers are retained even when a new government is elected. The deputy minister is expected to be politically neutral and impartial—neither for the government nor against it, but rather the guardian of the administrative order. The task at hand is to advise, to speak truth to power, and to supply the government with the best and most cautious information in spite of how unpalatable this may be politically. The deputy minister controls the management of the department. Although traditionally it is the minister, rather than the deputy minister, that is responsible to Parliament for the actions of the department, the *Financial Administration Act* (2007) has modified this tradition. Specifically, the deputy minister is the accounting officer for the department and, as such, is legally obliged to appear before parliamentary committees to report on conformity to that act (Inwood, 2009).

More generally, the thinking about the role of the deputy minister has evolved in recent years. The public sector has lost its image both as an employer for life and as protector of the public interest. Many young entrants to the public service have an "in and out" mentality; government is only one alternative in the menu of career opportunities. This changed image has meant that the role of deputy minister has to take on added hues. Now the deputy minister needs to pay great attention to succession planning, corporate human resources planning, and employee engagement levels, and generally needs to be sensitive to the issue of government as "employer of choice" (Dunn & Bierling, 2009).

Assistant deputy ministers generally manage branches within a department. They are merit-based positions competitively chosen in recent years by the Office of the Chief Human Resources Officer.

Directors general and directors are the third level of the administrative elite. These are also merit-based appointments. Several hundred individuals operate at this level. For example, reporting to the assistant deputy minister for Science and Technology at Environment Canada are five directors general (Water, Atmospheric, Wildlife and Landscape, Science and Risk Assessment, and Strategies) as well as a director of the Environmental Science and Technology Centre.

PUBLIC SECTOR RENEWAL IN PERSPECTIVE

One matter has not been dealt with yet in this chapter and can only be mentioned in passing: public sector renewal. Canada has been engaged in an almost-constant search for an optimal design for public administration.

Consistency has not been a notable characteristic of the process. The Glassco Commission (Royal Commission on Government Organization) in the early 1960s introduced the notion of decentralization with its "let the managers manage" slogan. In contrast, the Lambert Commission of 1979 (the Royal Commission on Financial Management and Accountability) reintroduced centralization as an option for the public service. Then in the 1990s, the *PS 2000 Report* emphasized the importance of managers in the federal administration.

Public service renewal has faced challenges over the years in figuring out how best to arrange balance in market, government, and non-governmental sectors. Observers of the executive have seen the government struggling to loosen the rigidity of traditional administration by having it bolstered first by Crown corporations, ABCs, and then the wide menu of alternative service delivery arrangements, all the time questioning whether such measures are tenable in the long term. Even within government, the role of the central agencies and the departments remains an issue. The patterns outlined in this chapter suggest that these tensions will be around for a long time to come.

DIVERSITY AND A REPRESENTATIVE BUREAUCRACY

To develop a competent, professional public service based on permanent employees, the hiring of public servants since the early twentieth century has been guided by the merit principle. That is, instead of hiring the supporters of the governing party, the public service focuses on the qualifications of candidates and uses competitive examinations in its hiring practices. However, appointments made strictly on merit do not necessarily result in a public service that represents the diversity of society. In fact, the public service until the 1970s consisted largely of English-speaking males of British ancestry. Since the late 1960s, efforts have been made to create a more bilingual public service able to provide government services in both English and French. As well, supporters of national unity hoped the greater presence of French-speakers in the Canadian government would help to offset the growing separatist movement in Quebec. Today, about 29 percent of public servants speak French as their first language and about two-fifths of positions in the public service require knowledge of both official languages (Treasury Board of Canada Secretariat, 2007).

In recent decades, efforts have continued to develop a *representative bureaucracy* that reflects the diversity of various aspects of Canadian society. Employment equity targets and timetables have been set up to increase the proportion of women, people with disabilities, Aboriginals, and visible minorities in the public service, particularly in the higher ranks. Some people have raised concerns that efforts to develop a representative bureaucracy will weaken the merit principle. However, those hired and promoted still have to meet the appropriate criteria of competence for their positions. Nevertheless, the requirement to hire the person "best qualified" for a position no longer exists. Instead, managers have to justify their hiring decisions in terms of the "right fit" for the job among applicants meeting the essential merit criteria. Furthermore, a deputy minister

TABLE 16-5

DIVERSITY IN THE PUBLIC SERVICE, 2007–2008 (PERCENTAGE)

Notes: The proportion of people (other than women) is based on self-identification. The figures for the available workforce are based on the 2001 Canadian census.

	EXECUTIVE	SCIENTIFIC AND PROFESSIONAL	TOTAL PUBLIC SERVICE	AVAILABLE WORKFORCE
Women	41.7	45.3	54.4	52.2
Aboriginals	3.4	2.5	4.4	2.5
Persons with disabilities	5.7	4.0	5.9	3.6
Visible minorities	6.7	13.4	9.2	10.4

Source: *Compiled from the figures in Treasury Board of Canada Secretariat, 2009.*

of a department has the authority to restrict the selection of hiring for a position to the members of a designated group and to include employment equity objectives as a criterion of merit (Public Service Commission, 2007).

As Table 16-5 indicates, the public service as a whole is quite representative of the available workforce. However, visible minorities are slightly under-represented, particularly when the increase of this grouping in the available workforce since the 2001 census is taken into account. Women are still under-represented in executive and scientific and professional positions. Nevertheless, the public service bureaucracy has become much more representative than in the past.

Parliamentary Institutions

In the Canadian Parliament, three sets of institutional players keep the institution running: political officers, officers of parliament, and procedural officers.

POLITICAL OFFICERS   Political officers are not bureaucratic officers in the normal sense, but because they do some routine administrative work—administering rules, scheduling, monitoring, rendering accountability, and so forth—they might be considered part of the bureaucracy of Parliament. The political officers of the House of Commons, including parliamentary party officials such as the Speaker, the Deputy Speaker, the party House Leaders, and the party whips, have come to be known as **"House Officers."** These individuals are at once politicians and administrators, in the sense of making the routine machinery of Parliament work. It should also be added that many of them have individuals working for them as well. The Speakers, for example, have legal and financial officers attached to their offices, who assist in deciding on matters of parliamentary law and in administering the precincts of parliament.

HOUSE OFFICERS
Political officers of the House of Commons.

OFFICERS OF PARLIAMENT
Independent officials that assist Parliament in holding government accountable and protecting various rights of Canadians.

OFFICERS OF PARLIAMENT   Officers of Parliament such as the Auditor General and the Chief Electoral Officer, along with the offices they head, have sometimes been called "servants of Parliament," "parliamentary watchdogs," or the "parliamentary control bureaucracy." Paul Thomas (2002) has described them as "independent accountability agencies created first to assist Parliament in holding ministers and the bureaucracy accountable and, second, to protect various kinds of rights of individual Canadians" (p. 288). As "servants of Parliament," these are offices that serve and are responsible to the legislative branch rather than the executive, and to that end have been freed from the normal constraints that bind the executive government.

Over time, the category of officers has tended to expand, as have some of their powers. In 2007 the Harper Government created a number of new officers: the Conflict of Interest and Ethics Commissioner, the Commissioner of Lobbying, and the Public Sector Integrity Commissioner.

The Harper Government also created another official, who is like an Officer of Parliament but not designated one, called the Parliamentary Budget Officer (PBO). The PBO is an independent officer of the Library of Parliament who reports to the Parliamentary Librarian who, in turn, reports to Speakers of both chambers. The Office of the Parliamentary Budget Officer provides non-partisan financial and economic analysis to support Parliament's oversight role and to provide budget transparency. For example, in 2009, Kevin Page, the Parliamentary Budget Officer, issued a report detailing the high cost of Canada's involvement in Afghanistan. As well, his office's estimate of the government's likely deficit was far greater than the official government estimate. However,

◄ As they accompany the Speaker during the ceremonial walk to start the daily session, the procedural officers and staff of the House of Commons—the Sergeant-at-Arms, the Clerk, the Law Clerk, and even the page—represent the bureaucracy that supports the Speaker and the House.

because the Parliamentary Budget Officer reports directly to the Parliamentary Librarian, some people have expressed concerns that he may be constrained by the Parliamentary Library's desire to avoid political controversy.

PROCEDURAL OFFICERS OF PARLIAMENT   Procedural officers of Parliament are essentially the public servants of Parliament, providing the equivalent of department-like services to the House of Commons and the Senate. The key figures in the House who furnish these services are the Clerk of the House, the Deputy Clerk, the Clerk Assistant, the Law Clerk and Parliamentary Counsel, and the Sergeant-at-Arms. In the Senate there are similar procedural officers.

The Clerk of the House is the senior permanent official responsible for advice on the procedural aspects of the plenary (whole) House, and looks after the ongoing administration of the House of Commons. The Clerk of the Senate performs the same role for the Senate. The Clerks' role is comparable to the role of deputy ministers in the executive departments. In the Commons, the Clerk is the permanent head responsible for the management of staff and daily operational affairs. The Clerk takes direction from the Speaker in relation to policy matters. In turn, the Speaker takes overall direction in management from the Internal Economy Commission (IEC), an all-party committee statutorily charged with administering the House. In parliamentary matters, within the House itself, the Speaker is supreme and takes direction from no one in particular, except the will of the House.

Judicial Institutions

The Supreme Court of Canada, the Federal Court, the Federal Court of Appeal, the Tax Court, and the Court Martial Appeal Court are administered federally. Reflecting the principle of judicial independence, the administration of these courts operates at arm's-length from the executive government.

The staff of the Supreme Court of Canada is headed by the Registrar who is responsible to the Chief Justice of the Court. The Registrar and Deputy Registrar are Governor-in-Council appointees who oversee a staff of nearly two hundred public servants who manage cases and hearings; provide legal support to the judges; edit, translate, and publish judgments; manage the flow of documents; and perform a variety of other essential tasks.

Support for the four other federally administered courts is provided by the Courts Administrative Service. The Chief Administrator, a Governor-in-Council appointee, is responsible for the overall operations of these four courts and their staff of about six hundred public servants. The Chief Justice of any of the four courts may issue binding directives to the Chief Administrator. In addition, each Chief Justice has authority over such matters as determining workloads and court sittings and assigning cases to judges, and may appoint a judicial administrator from among the employees of the service for such duties as establishing the time and place of court hearings.

Summary and Conclusion

Public officials work in a multiplicity of organizational forms. The majority of government employees work in departments under the political direction of a cabinet minister and the administrative direction of the deputy minister. However, central agencies and central departments have developed a considerable influence over the direction of government departments. Further, a variety of Crown corporations and semi-independent agencies, boards, and commissions do not operate according to the traditional departmental model of public administration. When we think of the staff of the various governing institutions, we often ignore those who work for Parliament and the courts. Of particular importance has been the establishment of various Officers of Parliament who, with their staffs, help Parliament in trying to hold the executive accountable for its actions and assist people who have complaints about government.

Bureaucratic organizations are necessary for the achievement of good government. A large, professional staff is required to administer the multitude of government programs. Many government officials play a major role in developing new policies and in evaluating existing policies and programs. While politicians concerned about re-election tend to focus on short-term popularity, career public servants may be more likely to take a long-term perspective on what is in the public interest. Furthermore, through their experience and knowledge, public servants are able to be an important source of non-partisan advice for cabinet ministers. Through their interactions with interest groups in developing policy proposals, public servants can make government more responsive to societal concerns. Moreover, by speaking "truth to power," public servants can play a vital role in the pursuit of good government.

The adoption of businesslike approaches in providing some public services, including New Public Management and alternative service delivery, may increase the efficiency of government. However, because government is, ideally, concerned with the general public interest, the adoption of business practices focused on profitability does not necessarily support good government, which involves achieving a broader set of societal goals.

The public service bureaucracy in the executive departments has been the subject of considerable criticism. Some argue that the bureaucracy is too rule-bound and inflexible, and not oriented to providing good service to people and businesses. Those who use the rational choice theory view bureaucrats as self-interested individuals seeking to expand government so that they can gain more status, privileges, and power. Indeed, some critics argue that senior bureaucrats wield excessive undemocratic power by influencing cabinet ministers who rely on them for advice.

However, there are limits to the power of bureaucrats. The prime minister and Cabinet working with the central agencies and central departments are able to set the direction of government policy. As well, the prime minister and Cabinet increasingly rely on alternative sources of advice from partisan political advisers, consultants, and think tanks. Furthermore, the various Officers of Parliament such as the Auditor General, Information Commissioner, and Privacy Commissioner provide some checks on the power of the executive bureaucracy. Although the convention of ministerial responsibility for the actions of government can shield the bureaucracy from public scrutiny, access to information legislation (even though imperfect in its application) and other reforms have brought some transparency and accountability to the activities of the bureaucracy.

Employment equity programs that include preferential treatment in hiring and promotion for members of disadvantaged and under-represented groups have increased the diversity of the bureaucracy. This has led to some resentment among individuals who feel adversely affected. Nevertheless, the greater presence of francophones in the public service and the improved ability of public service employees to operate in both official languages can be viewed as contributing to national unity. Although women are still somewhat under-represented in executive positions in the public service, the growing number of women in senior positions makes for a positive contrast to the relatively small proportion of women elected to the House of Commons.

Discussion Questions

1. Is bureaucracy a threat to democracy?

2. Is it important to have a non-partisan bureaucracy, or would it be better to have senior officials committed to carrying out the political direction of the government?

3. If you were to envisage yourself as a future public servant, what branch of government, and what level, would strike you as being the most interesting? The most challenging?

4. If you were to lead a program of public service reform in the government of Canada, what would it focus on?

5. Is it important to have a representative bureaucracy?

Further Reading

Aucoin, P. (1995). *The new public management: Canada in comparative perspective* Montreal, QC: Institute for Research on Public Policy.

Evans, B., & Shields, J. (2002). The third sector: Neo-liberal restructuring, governance, and the remaking of state-civil society relationships. In C. Dunn (Ed.), *The handbook of Canadian public administration*. Toronto, ON: Oxford University Press.

Good, D. A. (2007). *The politics of public money: Spenders, guardians, priority setters and financial watchdogs inside the Canadian government*. Toronto, ON: University of Toronto Press.

Graham, Andrew. (2007). *Canadian public sector financial management*. Montreal, QC: McGill-Queen's University Press.

Inwood, G. J. (2009). *Understanding Canadian public administration: An introduction to theory and practice* (3rd ed.). Toronto, ON: Pearson Prentice Hall.

Savoie, D. J. (2003). *Breaking the bargain: Public servants, ministers and Parliament*. Toronto, ON: University of Toronto Press.

Chapter 17

THE JUDICIAL SYSTEM:
LAW AND THE COURTS

PHOTO ABOVE: The statue of the "Famous Five" on Parliament Hill depicts the reactions of Emily Ferguson Murphy, Irene Marryat Parlby, Nellie Mooney McClung, Louise Crummy McKinney, and Henrietta Muir Edwards on hearing the news of the 1929 judgment of the Judicial Committee of the Privy Council in Great Britain declaring women "persons," and eligible to sit in the Senate.

CHAPTER OBJECTIVES

After reading this chapter, you should be able to

1. Explain the basic difference between the legal system in Quebec and the legal system in other provinces.
2. Discuss the methods used for appointing judges.

3. Examine the significance of the rule of law.
4. Outline the structure of the court system.
5. Discuss the significance of the independence of the judiciary.

Emily Murphy was born in 1868 into a family of prominent lawyers and politicians. After moving with her husband and three daughters to Alberta, she became a prominent campaigner for women's rights, as well as a popular writer using the pen name "Janey Canuck."

In 1916 Emily Murphy was appointed the first female magistrate in the British Empire. Earlier that year, women had won the right to vote in Alberta and were soon elected to the provincial legislature. Murphy had greater ambitions: she wanted to be appointed to the Canadian Senate. Unfortunately, she had to confront a formidable legal obstacle before she could enter this male bastion of privilege. The *British North America Act,* 1867, specified that "persons" with certain qualifications were eligible to be appointed to the Senate. Although Murphy met these qualifications, under the common law women were not considered "persons" with rights and privileges. She was hostage to her gender.

Murphy decided to challenge this interpretation. Together with four other women's rights advocates— Henrietta Muir Edwards, Louise Crummy McKinney, Irene Marryat Parlby, and Nellie Mooney McClung— known as the "Famous Five," Murphy submitted a petition to the Supreme Court of Canada in 1927 asking for an advisory opinion as to whether "persons" included women.

In their judgment, the majority of judges cited English common law rulings, including one that claimed, "chiefly out of respect to women, and a sense of decorum, and not from their want of intellect, or their being for any other such reason unfit to take part in the government of the country," women have "been excused" from taking part in public affairs. Given this legal context, Parliament in passing the act in 1867 should have expressly indicated that women could be appointed to the Senate, if that was their intention (*Edwards,* 1928).

Prime Minister Mackenzie King agreed to ask the Judicial Committee of the Privy Council in Great Britain, which was at the time the highest appeal body, for its opinion on the issue. In a unanimous ruling in 1929, the Judicial Committee concluded that women were eligible to be appointed to the Senate, as "persons." Excluding women from public office was a "relic of days more barbarous than ours."

In explaining their ruling, the Judicial Committee argued that the Constitution should not be interpreted in a "narrow and technical" manner, but rather as a "living tree capable of growth and expansion within its natural limits" (*Edwards,* 1930). The law should evolve in response to the changing values and circumstances of society. By applying the "living tree" concept, the courts can have an important political role in affecting the course of public policy rather than, as some would prefer, sticking to the precise wording of the law, the express intention of those who wrote the laws, and past precedents of interpreting the law.

The Persons case (as it has come to be known) is celebrated as a major victory for the rights of women. In 1930, Cairine Reay Wilson was the first woman to be appointed to the Senate. As for Emily Murphy, she died in 1933 without receiving the Senate appointment she so cherished. Her role in the Famous Five assures her place in history, but she also finally has a place in the upper chamber: In October 2009, the Senate voted for Murphy and the other members of the Famous Five to be named honorary senators.

THE RULE OF LAW AND THE JUDICIARY

A basic feature of the Canadian political system is the **rule of law**—the principle that individuals should be subject only to known, predictable, and impartial rules, rather than to the arbitrary orders of those in governing positions. This does not mean only that we are expected to abide by the many thousands of laws that control our behaviour and our relationships with others. Crucially, it also means that those people with authority, including those responsible for making, implementing, and enforcing laws, are expected to act in keeping with the law, including the legal and constitutional procedures for passing and changing laws. In particular, the rule of law protects the people against arbitrary actions by government and those empowered to act for the state, including police and security services.

The rule of law is a key feature of liberal democracy, distinguishing it from various forms of dictatorial rule. The rule of law includes the principle that all individuals are equal before and under the law, regardless of their wealth, social status, or political position—it is blind to the differences between a homeless person sheltering under a bridge and a CEO living in a mansion with a lakeside view. The rule of law also requires that the courts be independent, so that judges can be impartial in settling disputes without interference from government.

The judiciary (the court system) is important in the governing process. Not only do courts administer justice by applying laws and penalizing those who break the law, but also they are essential in interpreting the law and the constitution. As well, the courts have the authority to review laws to determine their validity (that is, the power of judicial review). Further, the courts play an important role in resolving disputes involving individuals and businesses.

In this chapter, we discuss the fundamental nature of Canada's legal systems, the structure of the court system, the procedures for selecting judges, and the relationship between the judicial system and the government.

LAWS

Laws can be thought of as rules of behaviour concerning the relationships and disputes involving individuals, businesses, groups, and the state (Hausegger, Hennigar, & Riddell, 2009). The laws governing human behaviour strive to maintain an orderly society by establishing a set of rules for disputes and by enabling the state to take actions against those who break those rules.

Laws can be considered to fall primarily into two basic categories: public and private, each of which involves various specific areas of law (see Table 17-1). Laws concerning the relationship of the state to individuals and laws concerning the authority and operations of the state are referred to as **public law**. There are four major types of public law:

1. *Criminal law* deals with behaviour that is an offence against the public of sufficient importance that the state (the Crown) is responsible for prosecuting the alleged offender.

RULE OF LAW
The principle that individuals should be subject only to known, predictable, and impartial rules, rather than to the arbitrary orders of those in governing positions.

PUBLIC LAW
Laws concerning the relationship of the state to individuals and laws concerning the authority and operations of the state.

TABLE 17-1
TYPES OF LAWS

PUBLIC LAW	PRIVATE LAW
Criminal law	Contract law
Constitutional law	Property law
Administrative law	Family law
Tax law	Torts
	Various others (e.g., intellectual property rights, wills and trusts, business organization, real estate, and consumer rights)

2. *Constitutional law* deals with the rules concerning those aspects of governing that are set out in the Constitution, including the division of authority between the national and provincial governments and the rights and freedoms of individuals.

3. *Administrative law* concerns the standards that government and its agencies are required to follow in their administrative and regulatory activities.

4. *Tax law* refers to the rules for the collection of revenue from individuals and businesses.

PRIVATE LAW

Areas of law dealing with the relationships among individuals, groups, and businesses that are primarily of private interest rather than general public interest.

TORT

Harmful actions, negligence, or words that allow the injured party to sue for damages.

Private law (often termed civil law) deals with issues in the relationships among individuals, groups, and businesses that are primarily of private interest rather than general public interest. Various types of private law exist. For instance, contract law establishes rules for enforceable agreements; property law concerns the rights linked to owning and possessing property; family law deals with domestic relations, including rules related to consequences of the break-up of a marriage; and the law of **torts** establishes rules for the remedies available to an injured party as a result of the actions, negligence, or words of another party. Other areas of private law relate to such topics as intellectual property rights, wills and trusts, business organization, real estate transactions, and the rights of consumers. Disputes in the area of private law involve one side (the plaintiff) initiating action against the other side (the defendant).[1]

The Sources of Law

As discussed in Chapter 10, the Canadian Constitution divides the authority to pass laws between Parliament and provincial legislatures, with only a small number of areas in which both Parliament and provincial legislatures have legislative power. For example, the Canadian Parliament is responsible for criminal law while provincial legislatures are responsible for many subjects related to private law. However, some areas of private law, such as marriage

---

[1]Some legal actions can involve both public and private law. For example, if one person attacks another causing injury, criminal proceedings on the charge of assault may be launched by the Crown, while the injured person may sue the attacker for damages under the law of torts.

and divorce, and patents and copyrights, fall under the legislative authority of the Canadian Parliament.

Laws that have been passed by an act of Parliament or a provincial legislature are known as **statutory laws**. Legislative bodies often delegate the ability to pass subordinate legislation to other institutions. For example, Parliament can delegate to Cabinet the authority to make regulations in keeping with the general principles of an act of Parliament. Provincial governments delegate authority to municipal governments to make bylaws, provided the bylaws are consistent with provincial legislation.

Many laws are not set out in statutes, but rather are based on common law and codified civil law. Public law throughout Canada, along with private law in all provinces other than Quebec, is based on the English system of **common law**. This system started in the twelfth century as the increasingly powerful king's courts began to use the "common customs" of the country as the basis for their decisions rather than the traditions of different localities used by the courts of various nobles (Hausegger et al., 2009, p. 12). The practice that developed was for judges to use precedents (that is, to examine decisions in previous similar cases) to guide their decisions.[2] Common law thus consists of court judgments in many centuries of cases, first in England and then in Canada, that have never been brought together in a single document. In court, lawyers present a variety of precedent cases that they consider relevant to the case being decided. The judge has to decide which precedents are most relevant, keeping in mind that precedents set in cases before superior courts are binding on lower courts.

The common law system is used in most of the English-speaking Commonwealth and in the United States (other than Louisiana). It has sometimes been criticized for preserving rules that are outdated and no longer reflect the changing values of society. However, the common law can evolve over time as judges find features in the cases before them that differ from precedent cases, and thus interpret the principles underlying common law somewhat differently. Further, the Supreme Court of Canada has occasionally overturned its own precedents. More importantly, legislatures have been active in passing laws that, in effect, replace the provisions of common law.

Quebec uses the *Code Civil du Québec* as the basis of its private law. This system of **codified civil law** traces its origins back to the sixth century, when the Byzantine Emperor Justinian I created a code of laws out of the laws of the Roman Empire, along with the commentaries of legal scholars (Hausegger et al., 2009). The French emperor Napoleon commissioned a codified system of law in 1804 (that has become known as the Napoleonic Code) based on Roman and French sources. This code has become the foundation of the private law systems of many continental European and Latin American countries. Under

STATUTORY LAW
A law that has been passed by an act of Parliament or a provincial legislature.

COMMON LAW
Law based on the accumulation of court decisions.

CODE CIVIL DU QUÉBEC
A codified system of law that is the basis of private law in Quebec.

CODIFIED CIVIL LAW
A system of private law used in Quebec based on a comprehensive set of legal principles.

---

[2]This is known as the doctrine of *stare decisis*, a Latin term meaning "to stand by decided matters."

BOX 17-1

The Protection of Privacy:
The *Civil Code* and the Common Law

In 1957, a Mr. Robbins sued the Canadian Broadcasting Corporation. Robbins had written a letter criticizing a television program. In response, the television program displayed his address and telephone number and invited the viewing audience to phone or write Robbins to "cheer him up." Robbins received many abusive and annoying letters and telephone calls. A Quebec court ordered the CBC to pay damages to Robbins. Under Quebec's *Civil Code,* there had been a wilful and wrongful invasion of Robbins's privacy.

Under the common law, the protection of privacy is not as straightforward. In the United Kingdom and Australia, the courts have denied that a tort of privacy exists, while in the United States courts have generally recognized a common law tort of privacy. Judges outside Quebec have gradually become willing to provide a remedy for the invasion of privacy without recognizing it as a specific tort (Craig, 1997). For example, in an often-cited case involving harassing telephone calls, the Alberta Court of Appeal (*Motherwell v. Motherwell,* 1976) awarded damages to the victim on the grounds of property rights rather than on the invasion of privacy.

Because the right to privacy is not well protected by the common law, several provinces have adopted privacy legislation. In addition, the Canadian Parliament has used its legislative authority over criminal law to identify new offences: electronic eavesdropping without the target's consent, as well as voyeurism for a sexual purpose, now are criminal offences punishable by law. Nevertheless, as electronic technology raises a host of new concerns about privacy, the slowly evolving common law may be inadequate to fully protect individual privacy. Legislation that established a tort of privacy equivalent to that provided by Quebec's civil law would make it easier to claim damages for the suffering that can be caused by an invasion of privacy (Craig, 1997).

French rule, the *Coutume de Paris* was used in Quebec from 1664 until Quebec came under British rule in 1763 and English criminal and private law was imposed. The *Quebec Act* (1774) restored the use of French private law. In 1866 Quebec established a system of codified civil law based, in part, on the Napoleonic Code. This was replaced by the *Code Civil du Québec,* which came into effect in 1994. Because civil code systems provide a full set of legal principles for resolving disputes, judges can apply these principles to reach their decisions in particular cases (Hausegger et al., 2009).[3]

Common law and Quebec's civil code continue to be important sources of law, resulting in differences in the private law between Quebec and the rest of Canada.[4] (For an example see Box 17-1, The Protection of Privacy: The *Civil Code* and the Common Law.) However, the doctrine of parliamentary

---

[3]Quebec judges also increasingly use precedents to help in applying laws (Hausegger et al., 2009).
[4]Because of these differences, most lawyers are educated, and can practise, in only one of the two legal systems. However, a few universities offer law students the opportunity to qualify in both systems.

supremacy that Canada inherited from Britain means that statutory law has modified or replaced a considerable proportion of common law or the civil code provisions.

Judicial Review

In the British system of government, Parliament is the supreme law-making authority, and thus the courts cannot review or invalidate legislation to decide its validity or desirability. They can, however, play a role in interpreting vague or ambiguous provisions in laws based on established principles of interpretation.

In Canada, in contrast, the door has always been left open for judicial review of legislation. That is, the courts have the authority to invalidate laws or government actions that they consider to be in violation of the Constitution. Because the Constitution divides legislative authority between the national Parliament and provincial legislatures, the courts can be called upon (by a government, individuals, or businesses) to determine whether a piece of legislation passed by Parliament or a provincial legislature is within the constitutional authority of that legislative body. The *Charter of Rights and Freedoms* in the Constitution (1982) has greatly increased the political significance of the courts, as legislation and government actions can be struck down if they are deemed by the courts to have violated the Charter. As discussed in Chapter 11, governments have hesitated to use the notwithstanding clause, which allows a legislative body to prevent a court challenge of laws that violate some aspects of the Charter.

COURTS

The Structure of the Court System

Essentially, Canada has a unified court system that hears most cases involving both national and provincial laws (see Figure 17-1). The Supreme Court of Canada, whose members are appointed by the Canadian government, sits atop the hierarchy of the court system. The provincial **superior courts** are also appointed and paid by the Canadian government. The provincial superior courts[5] include both trial and appeal courts. In addition, some provinces have created specialized superior courts, such as family courts. At the bottom of the hierarchy are provincial (or territorial) courts, whose judges are appointed and paid by each provincial government. **Provincial courts** are exclusively trial courts, with appeals from judgments going to superior courts. Some provinces have established specialized provincial courts, such as

SUPERIOR COURTS
Courts in each province whose judges are appointed and paid by the Canadian government.

PROVINCIAL COURTS
Trial courts whose judges are appointed and paid by the provincial government.

---

[5]In British Columbia, Prince Edward Island, Nova Scotia, Newfoundland and Labrador, the Yukon, and the Northwest Territories, the superior court is labelled the Supreme Court of the province or territory while in Alberta, Manitoba, New Brunswick, and Saskatchewan, it is known as the Court of Queen's Bench. Ontario and Quebec use the term Superior Court. Nunavut has a single Court of Justice combining the superior and territorial courts.

FIGURE 17-1
OUTLINE OF CANADA'S COURT SYSTEM

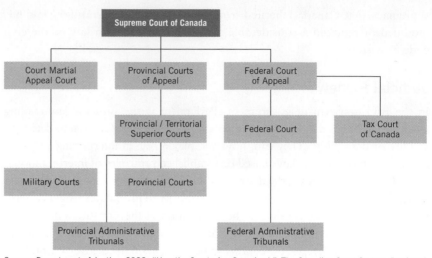

Source: Department of Justice, 2009, "How the Courts Are Organized," *The Canadian Court System*. Retrieved from http://justicecanada.ca/eng/dept-min/pub/ccs-ajc/page3.html

traffic, youth, and small claims courts. In some provinces, justices of the peace, who may issue search warrants and subpoenas and hear some cases involving violations of provincial laws, assist the work of the provincial courts. Generally, justices of the peace are not members of the legal profession (Hausegger et al., 2009).

Although the Canadian government appoints provincial superior court judges, provincial governments are responsible for setting up and administering the court system in their province. A superior court judge must hear certain serious criminal offences, such as murder, treason, and piracy. For other indictable offences[6] (serious offences such as arson and robbery), the person accused can choose to be tried in a superior or a provincial court. Petitions for divorce and a variety of private law cases are heard in superior court. Most offences against federal and provincial laws (including all summary offences; that is, less serious offences such as causing a disturbance) are heard in a provincial court.

FEDERAL COURT OF CANADA
A court that hears cases related to certain acts of Parliament, such as laws concerning copyright and patents, citizenship and immigration, and access to information and privacy. As well it hears appeals against the rulings of national administrative bodies.

An exception to the unified court system is the **Federal Court of Canada,** which tries cases related to certain acts of Parliament (including laws concerning copyright and patents, citizenship and immigration, and access to information and privacy). It also hears appeals against the rulings of national administrative bodies (for example, appeals by those denied benefits by the Canada Employment Insurance Commission). Likewise, the Tax Court of Canada and military courts deal only with cases related to those Canadian government responsibilities.

---

[6]Many offences in the Criminal Code, such as impaired driving, are "hybrid offences" where the Crown attorney may charge the accused with either an indictable or a summary offence. The penalties when convicted of a summary offence are less severe (a maximum of a $5000 fine and six months in jail) than when convicted of an indictable offence.

The Supreme Court of Canada was created by an act of Parliament in 1875. Although intended primarily to have a nationalizing effect on Canadian laws, the Supreme Court was unable to fulfill this purpose because appeals from provincial superior courts could go directly to the Judicial Committee of the Privy Council in the United Kingdom; the Judicial Committee, for its part, favoured limiting the powers of the Canadian government (Bazowski, 2004). Since 1949 the Supreme Court of Canada has acted as the final court of appeal for all cases. The Court consists of nine judges appointed on the recommendation of the prime minister, three of whom must come from Quebec so as to be familiar with Quebec's distinctive legal system. Informally, there is a longstanding tradition that three Supreme Court judges are from Ontario, two from Western Canada, and one from Atlantic Canada. Appeals are often heard by panels of seven judges selected by the chief justice of the Supreme Court.

Since 1985, the right to appeal to the Supreme Court of Canada has been limited to a few specific circumstances (such as when a provincial court of appeal has overturned an acquittal). Instead the Supreme Court grants "leave" to hear appeals only in cases that it considers to raise issues of public importance (usually less than one-fifth of the applications for appeal). These cases include those involving constitutional issues, the interpretation of important laws, the definition of Aboriginal rights, and the possible unfair conviction of a defendant (Hausegger et al., 2009). The Supreme Court of Canada can also hear **references**, questions asked by the Canadian government seeking an opinion on matters of law or constitutional interpretation, as well as appeals of references requested by a provincial government that are first heard in a provincial court of appeal.

Characteristics of the Court System

The court system is by nature adversarial. That is, both the Crown prosecutor and the lawyer for the accused (or the lawyers for the plaintiff and the defendant in private law cases) make as strong a case as possible by providing evidence and arguments that support their position. Witnesses do not only give evidence for one side, but are also cross-examined by the other side to try to pinpoint flaws in their testimony. The trial judge is expected to uphold the rules governing proceedings, but generally leaves it up to the opposing sides to present their case without involvement in the questioning of witnesses.

Trial courts, presided over by a single judge, deal primarily with ascertaining the facts of the case, particularly by assessing the credibility of witnesses. Appellate (appeal) courts usually involve a panel of three judges. Generally, they take the facts presented at the trial as given, and focus instead on questions to do with the trial judge's interpretation of the law.

The *Charter of Rights and Freedoms* provides the right to choose trial by jury for offences where the maximum punishment is at least five years' imprisonment (except for offences under military law). In addition, the right to trial

REFERENCE
The opinion of the courts on a question asked by the federal or provincial government.

by jury is allowed for many other indictable offences. Juries are also occasionally used, at the discretion of the judge, in certain types of private law cases if requested by the parties to the dispute.[7]

JURY DUTY   Most people will from time to time receive a summons to report for jury duty. Jury duty is considered an important obligation for all citizens. A refusal to report can result in a fine or even imprisonment.

To ensure that a jury represents a cross-section of the community, potential jurors are randomly selected from among adult citizens in a given area. Some people are shut out of jury duty because of their occupation (including lawyers, police officers, and employees of government agencies related to the justice system) or other characteristics (such as being elderly or physically weak, mentally incompetent, or unfamiliar with the language of the trial). Also, people can be excused from jury duty if serving on a jury would cause extreme hardship. In some provinces full-time students are automatically exempted.[8]

Being summoned for jury duty involves being part of a group from which a jury is selected. A few questions are asked of each potential juror to gauge whether that person would be able to consider the case fairly. The judge has the right to dismiss a potential juror for cause (such as potential bias). As well, lawyers for the prosecution and the defendant are entitled to a certain number of pre-emptory challenges (the number depends upon the offence), which can be used to dismiss a potential juror without explanation.

After the prosecution and the defence present their case, the judge instructs the jury about the legal issues involved in the case. In particular, in a criminal case, the jury will be reminded that a guilty verdict has to be proved "beyond a reasonable doubt." In a private law dispute, the defendant is liable "on a balance of probabilities"—a lower level of proof. The jury then meets to discuss the case and reach a verdict. For criminal cases, the verdict has to be unanimous. In private law cases, in most provinces five of the six jurors have to agree on the verdict. In spite of the temptation many jurors may feel to share details of a case with friends or family, they are strictly forbidden to tell other people what occurred in the jury room.

The jury system is not without critics. Some people argue that jurors generally lack the expertise to assess the often complicated issues that arise in a trial. In high-profile cases, the jury may be influenced by public opinion and media coverage despite instructions from the judge to consider the case only as it was presented in court. In the *Morgentaler* case discussed in the introductory vignette of Chapter 11, juries acquitted Dr. Morgentaler even though he admitted that he had broken the law by performing illegal abortions. Although the

---

[7] Juries are not used for private law cases in Quebec and in cases heard in federal courts.
[8] Employers are required to give time off for jury duty, although in some provinces they do not have to pay their employees for the time spent. Some provinces provide daily payment for serving on a jury.

judge instructed the jury that they could not ignore the law, the jury likely concluded that they should not convict a person who felt the need to challenge a law that many considered unjust and harmful.

JUDICIAL INDEPENDENCE

An important principle of liberal democracy is that of **judicial independence**. To ensure that all people receive a fair trial, the courts are expected to be independent of government and its agencies, legislative bodies, and other influences. Without an independent judicial system, governments, police, and security services could use their power to intimidate individuals with impunity. The independence of the judiciary thus serves as an important tool in helping to protect the rule of law.

To protect judicial independence, the *Constitution Act*, 1867, provides that federally appointed judges hold office assuming "good behaviour" until age seventy-five and can only be removed by a joint resolution passed by both the House of Commons and the Senate. In 1971, the **Canadian Judicial Council**, composed of provincial chief and associate chief justices, was set up to review complaints about federally appointed judges. Although the council cannot dismiss a judge, it can hold an inquiry to decide whether to recommend dismissal, and can also issue a statement expressing disapproval of a judge's behaviour (see Box 17-2, Tom Berger's Indiscretion). No superior court judge has ever been removed by a parliamentary resolution,[9] although several judges facing dismissal resigned when removal was recommended. For example, in 2009, Ontario Supreme Court Justice Paul Cosgrove was recommended for dismissal by the Canadian Judicial Council for "pervasive incompetence" and "abuse of judicial power" in presiding over a murder case in 1998. Two days later, he resigned just nine months before his retirement date. Provincial judicial councils can reprimand, suspend, or recommend the dismissal of provincially appointed judges. In most provinces, the attorney general and cabinet can choose to remove a judge after the judicial council's recommendation.[10] Only Ontario requires a vote by the provincial legislature to remove a judge (Hausegger et al., 2009).

The independence of the judiciary is also maintained by the convention that cabinet ministers, elected representatives, and government officials are not supposed to contact judges about particular cases. As well, independent processes that recommend compensation for judges have been set up to ensure that government cannot try to intimidate judges through control of their salaries.

JUDICIAL INDEPENDENCE
The principle that the courts are expected to be independent of government and its agencies, legislative bodies, and other influences.

CANADIAN JUDICIAL COUNCIL
A body of senior judges established to review complaints about federally appointed judges.

---

[9]Four federally appointed county or district court judges were removed by joint resolutions (Greene, 2006). County and district courts no longer exist.

[10]In Manitoba and British Columbia, the council's recommendation is binding on the government.

BOX 17-2

Tom Berger's Indiscretion

Like many of his peers on the bench, Judge Tom Berger had been politically active before being appointed in 1971 to the Supreme Court of British Columbia. One of his most high-profile cases had involved representation of the Nisga'a people in their landmark case to gain recognition of Aboriginal rights. Berger had also been active in national and provincial politics, including a brief stint as leader of the provincial NDP.

As a Supreme Court judge, Berger was appointed to head the Mackenzie Valley Pipeline Inquiry, which recommended that a natural gas pipeline not be built until Aboriginal land claims in the region were settled. In 1981, Berger made a move that would later haunt him—he publicly supported the effort to get Aboriginal rights included in the Constitution. As a result, another judge complained to the Canadian Judicial Council that Berger had violated judicial independence by criticizing the constitutional deal.

In commenting on the case in a speech to the Canadian Bar Association, Bora Laskin, chief justice of the Supreme Court of Canada, stated,

"A judge has no freedom of speech to address political issues which have nothing to do with his judicial duties. His abstention from political involvement is one of the guarantees of his impartiality, his integrity, his independence" (quoted in Van Loon & Whittington, 1987, p. 218). Nevertheless, higher court judges have been speaking out more and more on public issues. Indeed, the practice of appointing judges to public inquiries and Royal Commissions can result in reports that are critical of government or in judges becoming entangled in political controversies. The line between the generally accepted practice of a judge discussing a legal issue in a scholarly journal or in a speech to a law society and commenting on a controversial issue in a more public forum can sometimes be difficult to draw.

Tom Berger apparently crossed the line in openly supporting a public cause. He resigned after an inquiry by the Canadian Judicial Council ruled that he had been "indiscreet" in criticizing the government, although they did not recommend his removal (Greene, 2006).

The Appointment of Judges

The prime minister takes responsibility for recommending the appointment of Supreme Court of Canada judges and the chief justices and associate chief justices of each of the provincial superior courts. The federal minister of Justice makes recommendations to the Canadian Cabinet for other federally appointed judges. In turn, the attorney general of a province makes recommendations to the provincial cabinet for appointments to the provincial courts.

All federally appointed judges and, in most cases, provincially appointed judges have to be members of their provincial bar association and have at least ten years of experience as a lawyer or a judge. Unlike the practice in a number of continental European countries, judges are not given extensive training and do not follow a separate career path from lawyers. There is no requirement that judges take any formal training, although the Canadian

Institute for the Administration of Justice puts on a one-week seminar for new judges, and the National Judicial Institute offers voluntary educational seminars (Greene, 2006).

THE APPOINTMENT OF SUPERIOR COURT JUDGES   In the past, most judges were appointed, at least in part, because of their party affiliation. Many lawyers were active in party politics in the hopes of a judgeship (or of gaining legal business from the governing party). This patronage-based system, however, could be perceived as undermining the principle of judicial independence. As well, this system did not ensure that the best individuals were chosen as judges.

The traditional system started to change in 1967, with the minister of Justice establishing a committee of the Canadian Bar Association to rate candidates being considered by the minister as "qualified" or "unqualified." This system was later extended as judicial advisory committees for each province were established, with the mandate of advertising for people interested in appointments and screening applicants (including the possibility of interviewing them). In addition, the responsibility for creating a list of potential applicants was moved from the office of the minister of Justice to a commissioner for federal judicial affairs (Greene, 2006).

As of 2009, the system for appointing superior court judges (other than Supreme Court of Canada judges) involves an eight-member **Judicial Advisory Committee** in each region. Each committee is composed of three people selected by the federal minister of Justice, who are intended to represent the general public, and one person selected by the federal minister of Justice from each short list of three names submitted by the following groups and individuals:

JUDICIAL ADVISORY COMMITTEE
A committee that assesses candidates for appointment as a superior court judge.

- the provincial or territorial law society;
- the provincial or territorial branch of the Canadian Bar Association;
- a judge nominated by the chief justice or senior judge of the province or territory;
- the law enforcement community; and
- the provincial attorney general or territorial minister of justice.

The Advisory Committee provides an assessment of applicants as "recommended" or "unable to recommend."[11] The federal justice minister (or the prime minister, for the appointment of provincial chief justices and associate chief justices) can engage in further consultations before making a recommendation to the federal Cabinet. The entire process is strictly confidential and applicants do not have to be interviewed by the Committee.

---

[11]For provincial or territorial judges who are seeking to be appointed to a superior court, comments are provided rather than recommendations. Decisions concerning the promotion of superior court trial judges to provincial appeals courts are made by the minister of Justice and the naming of chief justices of superior courts is done by the prime minister without the involvement of a judicial advisory committee.

When Justice Minister Vic Toews announced this modified system of appointing superior court judges in 2006, the chief justice of the Supreme Court of Canada criticized the minister for introducing the changes without consulting the Canadian Judicial Council and the bar societies. Critics argued that the number of federal government appointees might compromise the independence of the advisory process, and were concerned about the inclusion of a police representative (Schmitz, 2006).

THE APPOINTMENT OF SUPREME COURT OF CANADA JUDGES   The *Supreme Court of Canada Act* places the authority to appoint Supreme Court judges in the hands of the "Governor in Council"—in effect, the Canadian Cabinet. In practice, in the past, the prime minister recommended appointments after the minister of Justice consulted informally with provincial attorneys general, chief justices, and leading members of the legal community.

The government of Paul Martin in 2004 and 2005 made the process somewhat more formal and slightly more transparent. The minister of Justice prepared an initial list of five to eight candidates after consulting informally with provincial attorneys general, chief justices, and leading members of the legal community. Then an advisory committee (consisting of a Member of Parliament from each political party, a retired judge from the region, a nominee of provincial attorneys general, a nominee of the law societies, and two prominent Canadians who were neither judges nor lawyers) provided the minister of Justice with a confidential unranked short list of three candidates (Hogg, 2009). The prime minister continued to take responsibility for the final decision of whom to recommend for the Supreme Court position. The minister of Justice appeared before the Standing Committee on Justice of the House of Commons to answer questions about the search process and the qualifications of the selected candidate.

The Harper Government slightly changed this procedure in 2006. In a three-hour televised hearing, the candidate, Marshall Rothstein, answered questions before an ad hoc parliamentary committee chaired by the Justice minister and a former law school dean. The members of the parliamentary committee were asked to be civil and respectful. In addition, the committee was told that it would be inappropriate for the nominee to answer questions about his views on controversial issues, his views on cases that might come before the court, and the rationale for his decisions in past cases. Although some committee members asked questions about hotly debated issues such as gun control, Rothstein avoided stating his views on particular issues (Hogg, 2009). The committee did not have the power to confirm or reject the nominee and did not prepare a report or make a recommendation. After the hearing, the prime minister recommended the appointment of Rothstein.

In 2008 the Harper Government changed the composition of the advisory committee so that it consisted of five Members of Parliament, including one from each of the opposition political parties and two cabinet ministers from the governing party. The opposition parties argued that the presence of the two cabinet ministers compromised the independence of the committee. As well, they complained that one of the ministers faced potential charges for allegedly violating the *Canada Elections Act*. Prime Minister Harper cancelled the work of the advisory committee, claiming that the opposition members were not cooperating. Instead, his solution was to recommend the appointment of Thomas Cromwell to the Supreme Court without holding a public hearing. Although the legal community generally viewed Justice Cromwell as an appropriate choice, the process for choosing Supreme Court judges still seems to be fraught with problems as political considerations potentially taint the process.

Because the choice of Supreme Court of Canada judges ultimately rests in the hands of the prime minister, some argue that the court system does not provide a fully independent check on the power of the prime minister (Russell, 2008). Although most people appointed to the Supreme Court have been well qualified and independent-minded, there is a risk that a prime minister could, over time, try to stack the Court with people eager to promote the prime minister's agenda or ideological perspective. It could also be argued that the largely secretive process for choosing Supreme Court judges does not reflect democratic principles.

Others, however, argue that the Canadian system for choosing Supreme Court judges is preferable to the more open U.S. system, where the Senate can veto the president's selection of Supreme Court judges. Public hearings conducted by the Senate Judiciary Committee have sometimes involved detailed, aggressive, and partisan questioning of nominees about their views on contentious issues, such as abortion, that might come before the Court, their past judgments, and their personal lives. The politicization of the process of selecting judges in the United States can undermine the principle of judicial independence and reduce the respect for the fairness of the judges and their decisions. Even though Supreme Court judges are inevitably involved in making important decisions with political implications, separating the process of appointing judges as much as possible from the political process may be necessary to ensure that the courts operate so that justice is done (and is seen as being done) in accordance with the rule of law. However, there is no guarantee that political considerations will not feature in the prime minister's selection of Canadian Supreme Court judges.

The appointment of judges of the Supreme Court of Canada on the recommendation of the prime minister also raises questions of whether the Supreme Court of Canada as currently appointed is an appropriate body to rule on constitutional issues that often involve disputes between national and provincial governments. Both the Meech Lake and Charlottetown Accords proposed that Supreme Court judges be nominated by provincial governments and selected from among the nominees by the national government. Critics of the accords argued that this would further politicize the appointment procedure.

► Canada's Supreme Court judges in February 2009. Back row: The Honourable Mr. Justice Marshall Rothstein, the Honourable Madam Justice Rosalie Silberman Abella, the Honourable Madam Justice Louise Charron, and the Honourable Mr. Justice Thomas A. Cromwell. Front row: The Honourable Madam Justice Marie Deschamps, the Honourable Mr. Justice William Ian Corneil Binnie, the Right Honourable Beverley McLachlin, P.C., Chief Justice of Canada, the Honourable Mr. Justice Louis LeBel, and the Honourable Mr. Justice Morris J. Fish.

Diversity and the Selection of Judges

There have been some efforts in recent years to make the courts better representative of the diversity of Canada. The members of the Judicial Advisory Committees that consider applicants seeking federal judicial appointments are supposed to reflect relevant factors, including geographical, gender, language, and multicultural characteristics (Greene, 2006). Recent prime ministers have made efforts to appoint women to the Supreme Court of Canada. As of 2009, four of the nine Supreme Court judges were women, including Beverley McLachlin, the first woman ever to serve as Chief Justice. However, to date, no Aboriginals have been appointed to the Supreme Court of Canada and very few have been appointed as judges to other courts.

JUDICIAL DECISION MAKING

LEGAL MODEL OF JUDICIAL DECISION MAKING
The view that judges base their decisions on a careful reading of the relevant law.

How do judges decide on the cases before them? In the **legal model of judicial decision making,** it is assumed that judges base their decisions on a careful reading of the relevant law using precedents, or in the case of Quebec the principles of the *Civil Code,* to aid them in applying the law to particular cases. If a statutory law is ambiguous, judges turn to the discussion of the law by those who developed it; for example, they can examine legislative debates. But do legal factors fully explain the decisions made by judges, particularly those at the highest level of the judicial system? The **strategic model of judicial decision making** assumes that a bargaining process among the judges takes place for them to reach a majority or a unanimous decision. Thus the wording of decisions often reflects compromises among judges with differing opinions. Finally, the **attitudinal model of judicial decision making** postulates that judges pursue their own policy preferences in interpreting the law, as well as being influenced by their attitudes toward the facts of the case (Ostberg & Wetstein, 2007).

The attitudinal and strategic models were developed in studies of the Supreme Court of the United States, where individual judges are often quite consistent in taking liberal or conservative ideological positions on many cases before the Court. A study of the decisions taken by the Supreme Court of Canada between 1984 and 2003 in criminal, economic, and fundamental freedom cases (Ostberg & Wetstein, 2007) found that ideological differences among the judges along liberal–conservative lines were significant. Even so, the attitudinal model is less applicable in Canada; that is, it "is less definitive and more subtle in the Canadian context than in the US Supreme Court" (p. 11). For equality and civil rights cases, gender rather than liberal or conservative ideological orientation was particularly important. Female judges "speak in distinctively different voices," particularly to protect women and vulnerable minorities (p. 152).

Overall, the study concluded that many of the Supreme Court judges tend to be ideologically consistent in how they vote. However, this did not mean that they took consistent liberal or conservative positions across the three areas examined. Chief Justice McLachlin, for example, took a "hard line" on the criminal cases (a conservative position) while taking a liberal approach favourable to civil liberties when ruling on other cases (Ostberg & Wetstein, 2007). The finding that the judges' gender is linked to certain types of judicial decisions suggests that the attitudinal model may need to factor in the personal characteristics of judges (Songer & Johnson, 2007).

Furthermore, the attitudinal model struggles to explain why a high proportion of Supreme Court of Canada cases results in unanimous decisions, even though the judges vary in their political attitudes. Research on unanimous decisions (Songer & Siripurapu, 2009) suggests that judges are sometimes willing to compromise in order to reach a unanimous decision, that they are open to persuasion by their colleagues on the Court, and that the law and precedents may lead the judges to a common position. However, unanimity is less likely in cases where the most important political issues are at stake, particularly if the issue has a high public profile (Songer & Siripurapu, 2009).

Even if the Canadian Supreme Court judges do not fit the attitudinal model as consistently as U.S. Supreme Court judges, Canadian Supreme Court judges have indicated that they do not strictly follow the legal model of decision making. They have made it clear that in interpreting the Constitution, they will not be bound by the original wording. Rather, they will adjust

STRATEGIC MODEL OF JUDICIAL DECISION MAKING The view that a bargaining process among the judges takes place for them to reach a majority or a unanimous decision.

ATTITUDINAL MODEL OF JUDICIAL DECISION MAKING The view that judges pursue their own policy preferences in interpreting the law, as well as being influenced by their attitudes toward the facts of the case.

the interpretation in response to changes in society and social values. Further, in interpreting statutes, Supreme Court of Canada judges do not rely heavily on the record of legislative discussion to determine the intent of those who developed the legislation (Hausegger et al., 2009).

PROBLEMS OF THE JUDICIAL SYSTEM

There are several problems in entrusting justice to the court system. First, it can take a long time for a case to go to trial. Most courts have a lengthy backlog of cases due, in part, to a shortage of judges. As well, lawyers will frequently engage in delaying tactics or are too busy to prepare their cases in a reasonable time. It may take years for an innocent person to clear his or her name. As well, the backlog of cases also encourages plea bargaining—that is, accepting a guilty plea to a lesser charge.

A Supreme Court of Canada decision (*Ashov*) found that a delay of nearly three years between a criminal charge and trial, caused by the underfunding of the Ontario court system, violated the Charter right "to be tried in a reasonable time." This led to 50 000 criminal charges being stayed or withdrawn (MacIvor, 2005).

Second, the costs of using courts can be prohibitive. It can take lawyers a long time to adequately prepare for a court case, and can involve many days, if not weeks or even months of court time. With lawyers' fees ranging from $200 to $800 dollars per hour, along with a variety of extra costs, going to court can be a severe financial hardship for the average person. For example, a teacher in Richmond, B.C., who was charged with the sexual abuse of two students in 1992 spent over $500 000 in legal fees before being found not guilty in 1997 (Matas, 1998). It is hardly surprising that a growing number of people are turning up in court without a lawyer—a practice that creates problems for judges, who may have to explain the rules of procedure to those without that expert knowledge.

Legal aid is available to low-income people with limited assets. However, legal aid programs have been chronically underfunded. Although the government of Canada pays one-half of the costs of provincial legal aid systems, it has capped the amount that it will share with provincial governments. It can also be challenging to find lawyers willing to take legal aid cases, as the hourly rates paid by the system are typically lower than the normal rates charged by private lawyers. In addition, legal aid may not provide enough hours for adequate representation in complex cases. Legal aid generally covers criminal cases, serious family disputes, and immigration problems. Legal aid coverage for other private law cases varies from province to province, but tends to be spotty. Unlike in other countries, legal insurance is not widely available in Canada, meaning that only a small proportion of Canadians has purchased coverage. Some legal assistance is available through law clinics and the pro bono services of law students and some lawyers.

Sham Justice: Wrongful Convictions

In 1984, Guy Paul Morin was convicted in the first-degree murder of his nine-year-old next-door neighbour. Christine Jessop had been found fifty-six kilometres from home with multiple stab wounds. A police dog given a scent of her clothing pawed at the window of Morin's car.

Although Morin had been acquitted in his first trial in 1986, the Ontario Court of Appeal ordered a new trial because of an error by the judge. Six years later, in 1992, Morin was convicted in his second trial. Already lengthy, his experience of the legal system did not end there. Eventually Morin underwent DNA testing that proved his innocence, and in 1995, a full eleven years after he was first convicted, he was acquitted on appeal.

A commission of inquiry into the Morin affair found evidence of misconduct by the police and the prosecution, and a misrepresentation of evidence by the Ontario Centre for Forensic Science. The problems were many: A forensic analyst did not adequately communicate the limitations of hair analysis to the police and prosecution. Information about the contamination of the fibre evidence at the centre was withheld. In addition, the jailhouse informant who claimed to have overheard a confession had lied in the past and had been diagnosed as a pathological liar. Further, the police had conducted a flawed and inadequate investigation, including failure to preserve evidence.

Similarly, a commission of inquiry into three wrongful murder convictions in Newfoundland and Labrador headed by retired Supreme Court of Canada Chief Justice Antonio Lamer found that the police were overly impressed by "junk" evidence, and that the Crown prosecutors were overaggressive in pursuit of legal victories, had tunnel vision, lacked objectivity, and were wedded to police theories (Makin, 2006b).

Fortunately for Guy Paul Morin, capital punishment for murder had been abolished in 1976. As for Christine Jessop, her murderer has never been found.

Third, a number of cases have come to light in which those accused of serious crimes have been wrongfully convicted (see Box 17-3, Sham Justice: Wrongful Convictions). In particular, the development of DNA testing has resulted in the overturning of a number of convictions after innocent people have spent many years behind bars. For example, sixteen-year-old David Milgaard was convicted of the rape and murder of Gail Miller and spent twenty-three years in prison until determined efforts by his mother led to an overturning of his conviction by the Supreme Court. Several years later he was exonerated by DNA evidence and received $10 million in compensation for his ordeal. Although we cannot expect the courts to be right all of the time, some of the cases of wrongful conviction have resulted from serious and avoidable mistakes by the police and Crown prosecutors. In particular, those wrongly convicted have often been people of lower class status, which suggests that the judicial system may suffer from class bias.

► David Milgaard and Solange Dumont (seated), wife of wrongfully convicted Quebecer Michel Dumont, wait in Saskatoon for a 2005 news conference to begin detailing Milgaard's support of the wrongfully convicted. The table banner quotes William Gladstone: "Justice delayed is justice denied."

IS JUSTICE DENIED

ABORIGINALS AND THE CANADIAN JUDICIAL SYSTEM

Compared with non-Aboriginals, a disproportionate number of Aboriginals find themselves in prison, not least because of the serious social problems plaguing their communities, including high levels of violence and substance abuse. Moreover, Aboriginals have endured a long history of insensitivity and injustices by the Canadian legal system, and they have faced problems in dealing with a judicial system that is based on the culture of the non-Aboriginal majority. A growing awareness of these inequities has led to proposals that an Aboriginal justice system be established. For example, the Royal Commission on Aboriginal Peoples, noting what it viewed as the fundamentally different world views of Aboriginal and non-Aboriginal peoples, recommended that the inherent right of Aboriginals to self-government should include the right to establish and administer their own justice system.

It is often argued that the adversarial judicial system that Canada inherited from Britain does not mesh with Aboriginal traditions that focus on conflict resolution. Further, where the Canadian legal system emphasizes the punishment of offenders, along with often inadequate and unsuccessful efforts to rehabilitate those in jail, Aboriginal traditions focus on **restorative justice**—that is, taking responsibility for one's actions, repairing the harm that has been caused, and reconciling the offender, the victim, and the community. The concept of restorative justice has been applied in some cases through the use of **sentencing circles**. These circles may include the guilty individual, the victim, their families, elders, and other interested members of the Aboriginal community, along with the prosecutor,

RESTORATIVE JUSTICE
The perspective that justice should focus on offenders taking responsibility for their actions, repairing the harm that has been caused, and reconciling the offender, the victim, and the community.

SENTENCING CIRCLE
A group that may include the guilty individual, the victim, their families, elders, and other interested members of the community, along with the prosecutor, defence lawyer, and police officers. The goal is to reach a consensus about what measures are needed to reintegrate the offender as a responsible member of the community and to assist the victim.

The Pauchay Case:
The Sentencing Circle Sidelined

On January 29, 2008, the frozen bodies of two girls aged one and three were found on Saskatchewan's Yellow Quill First Nation reserve. Their father, Christopher Pauchay, had been drinking heavily. Because his house did not have a phone and his wife had left after a fight, he decided to carry the girls (who were not properly dressed) to his sister's house 400 metres away to get help when one of the girls took sick. He got lost in a bitterly cold winter storm, dropped the girls, and was found on a neighbour's doorstep four and a half hours later. The girls were later found frozen to death in a snowbank. Pauchay pleaded guilty to a charge of criminal negligence causing death. The judge arranged for a sentencing circle, which recommended that Pauchay not go to prison. Instead, the participants suggested that he should receive treatment for his drug and alcohol problems, assist elders in their ceremonial duties for the rest of his life, and reunite with his wife and newly born daughter ("Father of Girls," 2009). However, the trial judge rejected the recommendations, sentencing Pauchay (who had fifty-two prior convictions, most for failing to comply with court orders) to three years in prison.

Pauchay's case attracted much media attention. Many people were outraged at the possibility that he might avoid serving time in prison. Others argued that serving time in prison would not help him overcome his problems and become a better member of his community. Further, some argued that Pauchay had suffered enough from the death of his daughters and that the deplorable conditions on the reserve, including soaring unemployment and lack of adequate housing, were the underlying cause of the high level of alcoholism and other problems faced by individuals in the community. Pauchay indicated his willingness to participate in rehabilitative programs in prison, and he may be eligible for early parole.

defence lawyer, and police officers. The goal is to reach a consensus about what measures are needed to reintegrate the offender as a responsible member of the community and to assist the victim. Measures may involve addiction treatment, counselling, community service, and reparations to the victim. Sentencing circles occasionally have also recommended the traditional Aboriginal penalty of banishment from the community for a length of time, as well as the conventional penalties of jail and probation. Normally, provincial courts use sentencing circles only for offences for which the maximum penalty is less than two years in jail (see Box 17-4, The Pauchay Case: The Sentencing Circle Sidelined).

The use of sentencing circles in some cases is supported by a provision in the Criminal Code (section 718.2). This provision states that one of the principles a court should take into consideration when imposing a sentence is that "all available sanctions other than imprisonment that are reasonable in the circumstances should be considered for all offenders, with particular attention to the circumstances of aboriginal offenders." In the *Gladue* case (1999), the Supreme Court of Canada elaborated on this provision, stating that for Aboriginal offenders, "the judge must consider: (A) The unique systemic or background

BOX 17-5

The Controversy over Sharia Law in Ontario

In 1991, Ontario's family courts were hopelessly backlogged. At the request of several religious groups, Ontario amended its *Arbitration Act* (1991) to allow "faith-based arbitration." This meant that individuals from a particular religion could agree to use a person or a panel of people to apply the laws of their faith to settle family disputes, including disputes over divorces and, in some cases, disputes of a commercial nature. Such tribunals could provide either mediation or legally binding arbitration that could be enforced in court. No proposal generated more controversy than that put forward by the president of the Canadian Society of Muslims, when in 2003 he suggested setting up arbitration tribunals that would apply sharia law to family disputes. Sharia (Islamic law) is based on the Qur'an and the rulings of the Prophet Mohammed. It varies considerably from country to country and is often interpreted on the basis of patriarchal traditions and customs that oppress women.

Faced with considerable public outcry over the introduction of sharia into Canada, the Ontario government commissioned former Ontario Attorney General Marion Boyd to review the *Arbitration Act.* Her report noted that although arbitration is conducted by mutual consent, women might feel pressured to accept arbitration out of a sense of religious or community duty and the impact that isolation from their community might have on

them and their children. Further, immigrant women were often vulnerable because of "perceived immigration sponsorship debt, disabilities, issues of class and race, violence and abuse" (Boyd, 2004, p.107). However, Boyd also found a positive side to religious tribunals—they were efficient and saved the government money. Her report concluded that Ontario should continue to allow binding, enforceable arbitration subject to a variety of conditions to try to protect the rights of women.

Boyd's report stirred up much controversy. The Canadian Council of Muslim Women argued that arbitration under religious law would mean unequal treatment for women. Other Muslims worried that it would ghettoize new Muslim immigrants. Some people (both Muslim and non-Muslim) feared that this would be the ""foot in the door" to the more general application of sharia in Canada. On the other side, an editorial in *The Globe and Mail* argued that "the report struck a proper balance between allowing for the religious practices and the protection of rights" (quoted in Hausegger et al., 2009, p. 92). Further, some Muslims argued that they should have the same rights as religious Jews and Christians to use faith-based arbitration, and denied that it would oppress women. In the end, Premier McGuinty chose to ban all forms of religious arbitration in the province of Ontario.

factors which may have played a part in bringing the particular Aboriginal offender before the courts; and (B) The types of sentencing procedures and sanctions which may be appropriate in the circumstances for the offender because of his or her particular Aboriginal heritage or connection."

Overall, although the possibility of some differential treatment in the judicial system exists for Aboriginals, Canada has not yet moved to adopt separate legal or judicial systems for Aboriginals (unlike the tribal courts in the United States). Where self-government agreements have been reached, First Nations governments are able to pass laws on some topics and some First Nations have taken responsibility for policing.

ALTERNATIVE DISPUTE RESOLUTION

Alternative dispute resolution involves the disputing parties choosing a third party (rather than a judge) to try to resolve the dispute. There are two basic types of alternative dispute resolution. The first, mediation, involves a mediator actively working with the parties, most often informally, to try to find a solution to the problems that led to the dispute. The second, arbitration, is a more formal process in which the arbitrator listens to the positions put forward by the two parties and makes a binding decision (if the parties have already agreed to accept whatever decision the arbitrator makes). In some cases, arbitration is chosen after attempts at mediation have failed. Mediation and arbitration are commonly used in collective bargaining and in some disputes between businesses and between businesses and consumers. Alternative dispute resolution is gaining popularity as a way of settling family disputes, such as those linked to divorce (see Box 17-5, The Controversy over Sharia Law in Ontario).

Alternative dispute resolution may allow some common ground to be found between the parties to a dispute, and thus lead to a more amicable solution than is likely in the adversarial format of a court. With Canadian courts often facing a severe backlog of cases, alternative dispute resolution allows for a faster outcome. It is also usually much less costly than using the courts. Furthermore, alternative dispute resolution is often preferred because it is done in private.

ALTERNATIVE DISPUTE RESOLUTION
A process where disputing parties choose a third party (rather than a judge) to try to resolve the dispute.

Summary and Conclusion

The rule of law is a fundamental principle of Canada's liberal democracy. Although there are instances when agencies of the state have not acted in accordance with the rule of law, for the most part Canadians have been protected from arbitrary orders by those in positions of authority.

Canada's legal system reflects, to some extent, the diversity of the country. Quebec's system of codified civil law is an important element in the maintenance of Quebec's distinctiveness. Other provinces and territories have maintained the common law system inherited from the United Kingdom. Both Parliament and provincial or territorial legislatures can pass laws (consistent with their constitutional authority) that supersede the provisions of common law or Quebec's civil code. Aboriginal First Nations are likely to continue to look for the development of an Aboriginal system of

justice to better reflect their culture and world view. On the other hand, many Canadians are concerned about the possible introduction of different legal systems based on different cultures and religions. Consider, for example, the outcry sparked by the introduction of sharia into the arbitration of family disputes.

Despite the federal nature of the governing system, Canada has a basically unified court system that (with certain exceptions) is responsible for hearing cases involving both national and provincial laws. The courts are expected to be independent of governments, legislatures, and public officials in order to uphold the rule of law and ensure that those accused of violating the law receive a fair and impartial trial.

The courts are involved not only in applying laws, but also in interpreting them and deciding on their validity. Through its decisions, the Supreme Court of

Canada, in particular, significantly affects the lives of Canadians and the governing of the country.

The importance of judicial decisions for the good government of Canada makes the selection of judges of great significance. At present, the prime minister and the minister of Justice have the primary responsibility for the selection of most judges, although some processes of consultation are involved. From a democratic perspective, greater transparency and the involvement of the public or of legislative bodies in the process of selecting judges, particularly Supreme Court judges, would be desirable. However, there is a risk that greater politicization of the appointment processes could endanger the principle of judicial independence and undermine the perception of the courts as impartial.

An independent court system does not necessarily ensure a fair and impartial hearing for all people, as the costs of using the courts, delays in cases being heard, and problems with the investigation of crimes can lead to unfair results, particularly for the less advantaged members of society.

Discussion Questions

1. Should Parliament and provincial legislatures be involved in the selection and appointment of Supreme Court of Canada judges?

2. Should judges be selected so as to reflect the social diversity of Canada?

3. Should the use of juries be eliminated?

4. Would it be desirable to establish an Aboriginal system of justice for Aboriginal peoples?

5. Should faith-based tribunals be permitted to provide legally enforceable arbitrations if both parties to the dispute agree to abide by the decision of the arbitrator?

Further Reading

Gall, G. (2004. *The Canadian legal system* (5th ed.) Toronto, ON: Thomson Carswell.

Greene, I. (2006). *The courts.* Vancouver: UBC Press.

Hausegger, L., Hennigar, M., & Riddell, T. (2009). *Canadian courts: Law, politics, and process.* Toronto, ON: Oxford University Press.

Manfredi, C., & Rush, M. (2008). *Judging democracy.* Peterborough, ON: Broadview Press.

McCormick, P. (1994). *Canada's Courts.* Toronto, ON: James Lorimer.

Mellon, H., & Westmacott, M. (Eds.). (2000). *Political dispute and judicial review: Assessing the work of the Supreme Court of Canada.* Scarborough, ON: Nelson.

Morton, F. L. (Ed.). (2002). *Law, politics and the judicial process in Canada.* Calgary, AB: University of Calgary Press.

Ostberg, C. L., & Wetstein, M. E. (2007). *Attitudinal decision making in the Supreme Court of Canada.* Vancouver: UBC Press.

Russell, P. (2001). *Judicial power and Canadian democracy.* Montreal, QC: McGill-Queen's University Press.

Russell, P. (1987). *The judiciary in Canada: The third branch of government.* Toronto, ON: McGraw-Hill Ryerson.

Sharpe, R. J., & McMahon, P. I. (2008). *The Persons case: The origins and legacy of the fight for legal personhood.* Toronto, ON: University of Toronto Press.

FOREIGN POLICY

Part VI

Chapter 18

CANADA'S PLACE IN THE WORLD

PHOTO ABOVE: Prime Minister Lester B. Pearson continues to watch over Parliament Hill through this statue that honours his lifetime accomplishments, nationally and internationally.

CHAPTER OBJECTIVES

After reading this chapter, you should be able to

1. Outline the development of Canadian independence in international affairs.
2. Explain the significance of the Cold War and the "war on terror" for Canadian foreign policy.
3. Discuss Canada's involvement in peacekeeping.
4. Examine and evaluate Canada's role in promoting human security.
5. Discuss the significance of the United States in affecting Canada's place in the world.

Canada's peacekeeping activities have been a source of pride for many Canadians. In fact, Lester B. Pearson was responsible for creating the United Nations' first peacekeeping force when he was Canada's External Affairs minister in 1956. For this remarkable accomplishment, Pearson was awarded the Nobel Peace Prize in 1957.

Pearson was born in 1897 in Newtonbrook, Ontario, the son of a Methodist minister. He experienced first-hand the horrors of war as a stretcher-bearer and a fighter pilot in the First World War. After receiving his M.A. at Oxford, he taught modern history at the University of Toronto and coached football and hockey. When recruited for the fledgling Canadian Foreign Service in 1928, Pearson eagerly took up the challenge of pursuing his vision of Canada's place in the world.

During his diplomatic career, Pearson held a variety of important posts, participated in the founding of the United Nations, and in 1946 became the top official in the Department of External Affairs. Two years later, he began a political career as External Affairs minister in the Liberal government of Louis St. Laurent, where he played a major role in the formation of the North Atlantic Treaty Organization and served a term as president of the General Assembly of the United Nations. Not least among his accomplishments was serving as prime minister of Canada from 1963 to 1968. Pearson believed that Canada as a "middle power" could play a key role in the world by mediating disputes, helping to forge peaceful compromises, and encouraging the establishment of international institutions to foster cooperative relationships. The Suez Canal Crisis presented him with an opportunity to put his ideas into practice.

On July 26, 1956, the government of Egypt nationalized the Suez Canal Company owned by British and French investors, including the British government. The canal, which runs through Egypt, provides a strategically and economically important shipping link between Europe and Asia. As part of a secret plan to allow Britain and France to seize control of the Canal Zone, Israel (which had been prevented from using the canal) invaded Egypt on October 29. As Israeli troops fought their way toward the canal, the British Royal Air Force started bombing Egypt and on November 6, British and French troops invaded Egypt and quickly captured the canal. The United States government opposed the invasion and called for a ceasefire and the withdrawal of British and French troops.

At the beginning of November, Pearson went to the United Nations with a proposal that the UN set up its first peacekeeping force to resolve the conflict. Previously, the United Nations had only sent observers to oversee ceasefire agreements. The United Nations General Assembly voted to accept the proposal for a United Nations Emergency Force and on November 15, the first UN contingent, including Canadian troops, arrived in Egypt to set up a buffer zone in the canal area between Egyptian and Israeli troops. As part of a ceasefire agreement, Israel withdrew from the Sinai Peninsula and UN peacekeepers were stationed on the Egyptian side of the country's border with Israel.

Pearson's peacekeeping efforts came in for considerable criticism at home, particularly by the Progressive Conservatives, who denounced Pearson and St. Laurent for betraying Britain by criticizing its invasion of Egypt. Nonetheless, Pearson's efforts helped to ensure that the sharp disagreement between the United States and Britain did not threaten the unity of the Western allies during the Cold War. It also helped to save the Commonwealth, as many former British colonies were enraged by the imperialist action of Britain in Egypt.

Canada's contribution to United Nations–led peacekeeping forces has declined sharply in recent times. Nevertheless, Canada has continued to play an important role in world affairs, searching for new ways to match Pearson's international contribution.

GENERAL PERSPECTIVES ON CANADA'S PLACE IN THE WORLD

Throughout much of the world, Canada enjoys a reputation as a country that promotes international harmony, peace, and global order. This role of Canada in the world has often been analyzed in terms of the **liberal internationalist perspective**. In this perspective, growing interaction and interdependence among the peoples, economies, and countries of the globe make possible a peaceful and orderly world in which the aggressive pursuit of national interests is no longer desirable. Canada as a "middle power" tries to constrain the great powers by encouraging (particularly in cooperation with other middle powers) the development of international law and multilateral organizations such as the United Nations (Kirton, 2007). Through such organizations, the great powers can be encouraged to respect rules and laws that less powerful countries like Canada have a hand in shaping.

Canada, particularly during the time Pearson served as External Affairs minister, became known as a "helpful fixer" of international problems through the use of quiet diplomacy. Nevertheless, despite the emphasis on promoting peaceful cooperation, advocates of the liberal internationalist approach, such as Pearson, saw the Soviet Union as a threat to world peace and supported maintaining the military strength of the **North Atlantic Treaty Organization** (NATO) to prevent the spread of communism.

Those with a more negative view of Canada's place in the world, termed the **peripheral dependence perspective** (Kirton, 2007), argue that Canada is unable or unwilling to develop independent foreign policies because of constraints imposed by the United States—the dominant partner in Canada–U.S. relations. This perspective views the various international institutions and laws that Canada has tried to create as largely reflecting the interests of the world's superpower, the United States. In some versions of this perspective, Canada is viewed as a mere satellite of its neighbour to the south, carrying out U.S. bidding on the international stage.

Many of those who hold this perspective favour nationalist measures to try to limit American economic and cultural penetration of Canada by, for example, placing limits on American investment and avoiding agreements that result in Canadian integration into a U.S.-dominated economic system. Likewise, during the **Cold War**, they argued that Canada should adopt a position of neutrality in world affairs rather than membership in U.S.-dominated alliances.

The **realist perspective** on international relations argues that in a world without a central authority able to impose order, each country is concerned primarily with survival and security. Because international institutions cannot be relied upon to provide security, each country strives to promote its

LIBERAL INTERNATIONALIST PERSPECTIVE
The view that growing international interaction and interdependence make possible a peaceful and orderly world, particularly through the development of international law and multilateral organizations such as the United Nations.

NORTH ATLANTIC TREATY ORGANIZATION
A military alliance of the United States, Canada, and democratic European countries.

NATO:
www.nato.int

PERIPHERAL DEPENDENCE PERSPECTIVE
The view that Canada is unable or unwilling to develop independent foreign policies because of constraints imposed by the United States.

COLD WAR
The severe tensions between the Western countries, led by the United States, and communist countries, led by the Soviet Union, that developed after the end of the Second World War and ended with the collapse of the Soviet Union in 1991.

REALIST PERSPECTIVE
The view that in a world without a central authority able to impose order, each country is concerned primarily with survival and security.

◀ Participation in international institutions is important to Canada's place in the contemporary world. Here, the heads of state and government are shown at the G8 in Heiligendamm, Germany, June 2007, representing (l–r) Japan, Canada, France, Russia, Germany, the United States, the United Kingdom, Italy, and the European Union.

own national interests. A variation on this perspective, termed the **complex neo-realism perspective**, has been advanced by John Kirton (2007) to explain Canada's place in the contemporary world. In this perspective, the major powers act together to maintain an orderly world while promoting their own national interests and values. However, changes in the international system, notably the end of the Cold War and the reduced stature and capabilities of the United States, have resulted, according to Kirton, in Canada becoming a "principal power"—a country that is able to independently assert its national values and interests in its foreign policy. Specifically, Canada has joined "plurilateral" international institutions (that is, organizations that have an exclusive membership) in which Canada can play a major role, such as the G8, a group of powerful, economically developed countries. In recent times Canada has paid somewhat less attention to participation in multilateral, inclusive institutions, notably the United Nations. As well, Kirton argues that Canada has shifted away from its peacekeeping role to pursue its own interests and values through the use of military force.

COMPLEX NEO-REALISM PERSPECTIVE
The view that changes in the international system have resulted in Canada becoming a "principal power," able to independently assert its national values and interests in international politics.

HISTORICAL BACKGROUND

Confederation and the Early Years

At its founding in 1867, Canada was part of the British Empire. Although Canada was basically self-governing in domestic matters, Britain directed the country's external relations. Only gradually was Canada able to take control of its foreign policy and establish its own place in the world.

In 1871, Canada's prime minister, Sir John A. Macdonald, was part of the British delegation that negotiated the Treaty of Washington, which laid the groundwork for friendly relations between Britain and the United States and dealt with a variety of issues affecting Canada–United States relations. As it turned out, Macdonald was unhappy with the concessions made by Britain at Canada's expense. In 1880, Canada took a step toward representing itself by appointing a high commissioner to London to voice Canadian interests related to immigration and trade. In 1893 Canada negotiated a tariff agreement with France, although the British ambassador in Paris had to sign the treaty on behalf of Britain, as the Canadian government did not have treaty-making power. In 1909, a tiny Department of External Affairs was set up, although foreign policy remained a British responsibility. To begin with, Canada's newborn Department of External Affairs was housed above an Ottawa barbershop.

The First World War and Its Aftermath

In 1914, Canada was automatically at war with Germany when Britain issued its declaration of war. The Canadian government decided to participate heavily in the First World War, including sending over 600 000 soldiers to fight in Europe.[1] Nevertheless, the government complained that Canada had no voice in the conduct of the war (and was not even consulted or informed about the progress of the war) despite its major contribution to the war effort. Eventually, in 1917, after a change in the British government and the growing dependence of Britain on troops from Canada and other British dominions, an Imperial War Cabinet was established. With a mandate to consult with the dominions on the conduct of the war, the War Cabinet included representation from Canada. As well, an Imperial War Conference was set up to deal with other matters linked to the Empire and its relations with the dominions. One of the resolutions of the conference was as follows: the dominions must be recognized as "autonomous nations of an Imperial Commonwealth" with a right to "an adequate voice in policy and in foreign relations," and arrangements must be made "for continuous consultation in all important matters of common Imperial concern, and for such necessary concerted action, founded on consultation, as the several Governments may determine" (quoted in Department of Foreign Affairs and International Trade, n.d.).

Canada's major contribution to the successful battles in World War I,[2] along with its heavy casualties, earned the country a place at the negotiating table that set the terms of peace. Canada also became a member of the League of Nations, an organization created after the war to try to prevent future

---

[1]As discussed in Chapter 2, the imposition of conscription in 1917 was very unpopular among French Quebecers.

[2]Canada also sent 4197 troops to Siberia after the end of WWI in 1918–19 as part of an allied force opposing the Bolshevik (Communist) revolutionary government. French-Canadian conscripts (apparently influenced by B.C. socialists) mutinied in Victoria while being marched to the troop carrier (Isitt, 2006).

conflicts. In fact, the country was a signatory to the treaty establishing the League, although with an indication that Canada was still part of the British Empire. In 1923, despite British objections, Canada negotiated and signed a treaty with the United States about the protection of Pacific halibut.

In 1922, Turkish forces threatened to attack British and French troops stationed near Chanak in Turkey to protect a demilitarized neutral zone in the Dardanelles that had been established after the defeat of the Ottoman Empire in World War I. The British government asked for military assistance from Canada and the other dominions, but Liberal Prime Minister Mackenzie King had not been consulted about the issue and responded that the Canadian Parliament would decide on Canada's course of action. Although Conservative party leader Arthur Meighen stated that Canada should have replied "ready, aye, ready" to the British request, the incident laid down the principle that Canada would not automatically take part in British wars.

At an Imperial Conference a resolution, known as the **Balfour Declaration (1926)**, was adopted. It stated that Britain and the dominions are "autonomous Communities within the British Empire, equal in status, in no way subordinate one to another in any aspect of their domestic or external affairs, though united by a common allegiance to the Crown, and freely associated as members of the British Commonwealth of Nations."[3] Later, the principles of the declaration were confirmed by the British *Statute of Westminster* (1931), which ended the ability of the British Parliament to legislate for Canada. To reflect its new control over its own foreign policy, Canada appointed ambassadors to the United States (1927), France (1928), and Japan (1929).

BALFOUR DECLARATION (1926)
A resolution of the Imperial Conference that declared that Britain and the dominions are autonomous and equal communities in no way subordinate one to another.

The Second World War

In a departure from the First World War, the Canadian government did not view itself as automatically at war with Germany as soon as Britain declared war. Instead, Canada entered the war a week later after a vote in the Parliament. Overall, about 1.1 million Canadians served in the Armed Forces during the Second World War—a high proportion of Canada's population of about 11.5 million.

The Second World War marked the beginning of a close military relationship with the United States. With the real possibility that most of Canada's armed forces would be lost if Nazi Germany successfully invaded Britain, President Roosevelt promised to defend Canada. The Ogdensburg Agreement in 1940 included the creation of a Permanent Joint Board on Defence to plan for

---

[3]Since 1949, the term "British" has been dropped from the name of the Commonwealth, which now consists of fifty-three independent states. Although the British monarch is recognized as the ceremonial head of the Commonwealth, members are no longer required to have the British monarch as their head of state.

the defence of North America. This was followed by the Hyde Park agreement in 1941, in which the United States (still officially neutral in the war) provided Canada with components for the production of munitions to be sent to Britain, and increased its purchase of Canadian goods to offset the large trade deficit that Canada was experiencing because of the war.

The Cold War

The end of the Second World War brought a major change to the international system. With the other major powers devastated by the war, the United States and the Soviet Union emerged as the "superpowers." This created a "bipolar system" in which two superpowers competed with one another, and most lesser powers become either allies or satellites of one or the other of the superpowers (Mintz, Close, & Croci, 2009).

The establishment of the United Nations (UN) in 1945 led to hopes that this body would prove more effective than the League of Nations in encouraging the development of a more peaceful world. In addition to promoting human rights, decolonization, and development, the United Nations provided the basis for the collective security of countries by empowering the **Security Council** to take action, including military action if necessary, "to maintain or restore international peace and security" (*Charter of the United Nations*, Article 42). Although Canada emerged from World War II with a powerful military and a vigorous economy, the country was not included among the five permanent members of the Security Council (the United States, Soviet Union, Britain, France, and China), each of which continues to have a veto over the actions of the Council. Several times, however, the UN General Assembly has elected Canada to serve a two-year term on the fifteen-member Council.

The hopes for world peace in the aftermath of the Second World War were dashed by the Cold War. A communist coup in Czechoslovakia in 1948 and the blockade of Berlin by Soviet forces from 1948 to 1949 encouraged Canada and the United States to form a military alliance (NATO) with a number of European countries. This collective security agreement included the provision that an armed attack against any of the member countries in Europe or North America would be considered an attack against all of them. Each member would be required to take "such action that it deems necessary, including the use of armed force" in such circumstances.

The Cold War resulted in large numbers of NATO troops and weaponry being stationed in central Europe in order to respond to a possible attack by the Soviet army. Canada sent about 10 000 troops, stationed mainly in Germany. However, it was in other parts of the world that Cold War hostilities led to warfare. The invasion of South Korea by communist North Korea in 1950 was countered by forces from a number of countries led by the United States and

SECURITY COUNCIL
A key body of the United Nations responsible for maintaining international peace and security. It consists of five permanent members who each have a veto and ten members elected by the UN General Assembly for two-year terms.

"You Pissed on My Rug!"

In a speech delivered at Temple University in Philadelphia on April 2, 1965, Prime Minister Lester B. Pearson criticized Democratic President Lyndon Baines Johnson's decision to begin bombing North Vietnam. The next day at a luncheon meeting, Johnson berated Pearson for more than an hour. Then, according to journalist Lawrence Martin, "He moved beyond the realm of words. Having pinned the much smaller Pearson against the rail, the president of the United States grabbed him by the shirt collar, twisted it and lifted the shaken prime minister by the neck. The verbal abuse continued in a venomous torrent. 'You pissed on my rug!' he thundered." At a later meeting with the press, Johnson reported that it had been a friendly discussion and Pearson said, "It has been a very pleasant couple of hours" (quoted in Martin, 1982, p. 2).

Whether or not Martin's depiction is entirely accurate, relations between prime ministers and presidents have varied between the cozy relationship of Brian Mulroney and Ronald Reagan to the frosty relationship between Richard Nixon and Pierre Trudeau. Indeed, because of the close relationship between the two countries, Pearson may have felt free to mildly criticize American policy while in the United States, and Johnson felt justified in indicating his displeasure in private. Regardless of the personal relationships between prime ministers and presidents, the governments of the two countries will have differences based on their separate interests, values, and power positions.

authorized by a resolution of the Security Council of the United Nations.[4] About 26 000 Canadians fought in the Korean War.

Despite the relatively cozy relationship between Canada and the United States that developed during the Cold War, Canada avoided direct participation in the U.S.-led Vietnam War (1964 to 1973). Not only was there limited public support for the war, but also Canada represented Western democracies on the International Commission for Supervision and Control in Vietnam, set up by the Geneva Accords that ended the French Indochina War in 1954. Nevertheless, Canadian companies produced many of the armaments used by the United States, including the now-notorious Agent Orange (a jungle defoliant), which was tested at Camp Gagetown, New Brunswick. However, Prime Minister Lester Pearson, in a striking departure from "quiet diplomacy," publicly criticized the American bombing of North Vietnam (as discussed in Box 18-1, "You Pissed on My Rug!").

The Cold War, along with innovations in military technology, also ended Canada's isolation from the potential theatres of war. In the 1950s, the Soviet Union deployed long-range bombers carrying nuclear weapons that could

---

[4]The Soviet Union did not exercise its veto because it was boycotting the Security Council at the time to protest that the government of the Republic of China (Taiwan) rather than the communist People's Republic of China was holding China's permanent seat on the Council.

strike targets in the United States and Canada. Canada's position between the Soviet Union and the United States thus became of strategic importance. In the 1950s Canada and the United States cooperated in building three radar systems across Canada, the Pinetree Line, the Mid-Canada Line, and the Distant Early Warning System (the DEW Line), to detect, warn about, and potentially intercept Soviet bombers. Each quickly became out of date, particularly with the development of intercontinental and submarine-launched ballistic missiles.

In 1957, the desire for the coordinated air defence of North America led to the establishment of the North American Air Defence Command (NORAD), an organization based in Colorado with an American commander who reports to the president of the United States and a Canadian deputy commander who reports to the prime minister. As part of Canada's participation in NORAD and NATO, the Canadian government in the 1950s committed to using fighter aircraft, bombers, and anti-aircraft missiles designed to carry nuclear warheads (see Box 18-2, Nukes in Canada? A Government Divided). NORAD was renamed the **North American Aerospace Defense Command** in 1981 to reflect its role in securing the North American airspace through an integrated system including satellites, ground and airborne radar, and fighter aircraft. In 1985, some of the DEW Line stations located mainly in the High Arctic were converted into the North Warning System, which provides aerospace surveillance of the polar region with the ability to detect supersonic bombers and long-range cruise missiles.

NORAD.
www.norad.mil

NORTH AMERICAN AEROSPACE DEFENSE COMMAND
A joint U.S.–Canadian organization that provides for the detection of and response to an attack on North America, particularly by aircraft and missiles.

THE CONTEMPORARY WORLD

With the ending of communist rule in several Eastern European countries in the late 1980s and the dissolution of the Soviet Union in 1991, the Cold War drew to a close. However this did not result in as peaceful a world as many had hoped. For example, a war in the Democratic Republic of the Congo from 1998 to 2003 (sometimes referred to as "Africa's world war") involved eight countries and a variety of armed groups and resulted in millions of deaths. Ethnic and religious tensions have triggered a variety of conflicts, many of which involve civil war within a state. For example, ethnic tensions underlying the breakup of the multinational Federal Republic of Yugoslavia led to war between Serbs, Croats, and Muslims in Bosnia between 1992 and 1995. Some conflicts have involved massive human rights violations, such as the genocide in Rwanda (1994), where Hutu militias massacred as many as a million people: mostly members of the Tutsi minority as well as Hutu moderates.

Terrorist activity has also highlighted the continuing threat of international violence. For example, a bomb placed by Sikh terrorists on an Air India flight that originated in Vancouver in 1996 resulted in 329 deaths, most of them Canadians. The dramatic attack by al-Qaeda on the United States on September 11, 2001, led President George W. Bush to declare a global "war on terror." Among the measures taken was support for the overthrow of the

BOX 18-2

Nukes in Canada? A Government Divided

Many Canadians look back with horror at the 1945 American bombings of Hiroshima and Nagasaki, scenes of devastation and unspeakable suffering. Yet Canada contributed to the development of the nuclear weapons that devastated these cities. Not surprisingly, in the aftermath of World War II, questions about the rightness and wrongness of nuclear warfare did not go away. Indeed, one of the most hotly debated political issues in Canada during the Cold War involved the presence of nuclear weapons on Canadian soil.

After the war, the Canadian government decided not to use its own capability to produce nuclear weapons, although it participated in the development of the nuclear arsenal of the United States and Britain by selling them uranium and plutonium. Moreover, the Progressive Conservative government of John Diefenbaker agreed to deploy Bomarc-B anti-aircraft missiles and CF-101B Voodoo interceptors that were fully effective only with American nuclear warheads. In addition, CF-104 Starfighter bombers designed to be equipped with tactical nuclear weapons would be stationed in Europe as part of Canada's NATO commitment. However, with the Defence minister, Douglas Harkness, strongly supporting nuclear weapons and the External Affairs minister, Howard Green, strongly opposed, the prime minister couldn't decide whether Canada should accept these weapons.

In January 1963, Diefenbaker claimed in the House of Commons that Canada could postpone arming the CF-104s with nuclear warheads because confidential talks between American President John F. Kennedy and British Prime Minister Harold Macmillan had put NATO's nuclear strategy into question. The U.S. State Department strongly criticized Diefenbaker's statement, which it claimed was inaccurate. Harkness (and two other ministers) resigned from the Cabinet, and several other cabinet ministers plotted to remove Diefenbaker as prime minister. Liberal Opposition leader Lester Pearson (who had reversed his position from opposition to support for acquiring tactical nuclear weapons) moved a non-confidence motion in the House of Commons. With the support of the Social Credit and New Democratic parties, the minority PC government was defeated in 1963.

In the election that followed, the Liberals headed by Lester B. Pearson came to power. They quickly proceeded to allow nuclear warheads to be located in Canada and supplied to Canadian forces in Germany. Pierre Trudeau, who had bitterly attacked the Liberals in 1963 for their pro-nuclear policy, was elected as a Liberal MP in 1965 and became prime minister in 1968. During his term in office, Canada phased out the deployment of nuclear warheads (completed in 1984) and was active in promoting the nuclear non-proliferation treaty (1970).

Canada's commitment to the reduction and eventual elimination of nuclear weapons is qualified by its membership in NATO and NORAD, which view nuclear weapons as an essential deterrent to aggression. Indeed, NATO policy continues to accept the potential use of nuclear weapons in a pre-emptive "first strike" against its enemies.

extremist Taliban government, which had allowed Osama bin Laden and his al-Qaeda supporters to operate out of Afghanistan. As well, the war on terror was used as part of the justification for the U.S.-led invasion of Iraq in 2003, although there was no proven connection between al-Qaeda and the Iraq regime.

Although Canadians and Americans have often taken pride in having the world's longest undefended border, the fear of terrorist attacks led the U.S. government to tighten its border with Canada.[5] With Canada heavily reliant on exports to the United States, long delays at border points can seriously harm Canadian businesses. Business interests have therefore pressured the Canadian government to coordinate, collaborate, and share information with the United States on a variety of matters relating to security. Further, concerns about access to American markets have led some associated with the business community to lobby for a close integration of Canada and the United States, including a North American Security Perimeter and closer military ties (Tomlin, Hillmer, & Hampson, 2008). For some, Canada's national interest should be pursued by developing a close partnership with the United States rather than promoting internationalist values (Hart, 2008; Rempel, 2006).

The intense anxiety about terrorism also brought a high level of attention to "homeland security" in the United States. The U.S. North Command (NORTHCOM) was established in 2002 to provide a unified American military command that would coordinate the defence of North America in the event of an attack. Because NORTHCOM's jurisdiction includes all of Canada and Mexico, as well as up to 800 kilometres of adjoining ocean, both Canada and Mexico have voiced concern about the potential threat to their countries' sovereignty.

Because of concern about terrorism (as well as concern about the flow of illegal drugs into the United States), the role of NORAD has grown to include a maritime warning system. Although the government of Paul Martin resisted American pressure to participate in the U.S. ballistic missile defence system, the Canadian government agreed that NORAD's radar and surveillance system could contribute to the operation of such a system (Tomlin et al., 2008).

Change in the International System

The end of the Cold War fundamentally transformed the international system, making it unipolar rather than bipolar. The United States became the lone superpower, whose military capabilities far exceeded those of any other country and, indeed, surpassed those of almost any combination of countries. This has given the United States the capability to launch unilateral actions almost anywhere in the world. Nevertheless, there are limits to the military and financial capabilities of the United States, including its ability to fight more than one war at a time. Therefore the United States has persuaded other countries to join in various military actions, both to reduce its personnel and financial burdens and to try to enhance the legitimacy of its actions. Furthermore, while the United States can wield its military might globally, several regional

---

[5]Many Americans believe that some of the al-Qaeda terrorists entered the United States from Canada. Indeed, in April 2009, Homeland Security Secretary Janet Napolitano repeated this myth.

powers (including Russia, China, India, Iran, and South Africa) are influential in their own parts of the world.

The collapse of the Soviet Union in 1991 has resulted in the expansion of NATO to twenty-eight members, including many Eastern European countries that were members of the Soviet-led Warsaw Pact, as well as the Baltic states that were once part of the Soviet Union.[6] NATO's activities have also moved beyond the collective security of its members and beyond the borders of Europe. In particular, NATO has played an active role in various conflicts arising from the breakup of Yugoslavia and in combating the insurgency in Afghanistan.

PEACEKEEPING, PEACE OPERATIONS, AND COMBAT MISSIONS

Peacekeeping and Peace Operations

As discussed in the introductory vignette, the Canadian government played a leading part in the development of a substantial peacekeeping role for the United Nations and has participated in many of the peacekeeping missions authorized by the United Nations. The nature of peacekeeping has, however, changed over the years. In what Stephen Holloway (2006) describes as **"classic" peacekeeping**, the goal is generally to support a ceasefire between countries in conflict or to supervise the implementation of a peace agreement. This might involve positioning observers to monitor the actions of the conflicting countries or placing peacekeepers in a neutral zone between the combatants to uphold a ceasefire agreement. If the "blue helmeted" UN forces are armed, they are expected to use their weapons only in self-defence. Finally, classic peacekeeping is carried out with the agreement of the countries involved, respects the sovereignty of those states, and is under the control of the United Nations (Holloway, 2006). This form of peacekeeping has proven useful in some situations, but it is not always successful. For example, in the case of the United Nations Emergency Force that was deployed in 1956 as a result of the Suez Canal crisis, the peacekeeping mission did not prevent further warfare. In 1967 the Egyptian president, Gamal Abdel Nasser, ordered the UN Emergency Force out of the country and amassed large numbers of troops and tanks on the Israeli border. Shortly afterwards, Israel launched a pre-emptive strike on Egypt, beginning the Six Day War in the Middle East.

Although classic peacekeeping is still important, it does not lend itself to all circumstances. Many of the situations that have resulted in the use of outside forces under the banner of the United Nations have involved conflicts within a state rather than between states. In fact, since 1998 about 90 percent

CLASSIC PEACEKEEPING
Activities carried out under the United Nations banner to support a ceasefire between countries in conflict or to supervise the implementation of a peace agreement.

Pearson Peacekeeping Centre: **www.peaceoperations.org**

---

[6]As of 2009, two additional countries have been invited to be members, with several more countries under consideration. There are also twenty-two "partner" countries, including Russia.

of UN peacekeeping operations have involved internal conflicts (Pelz & Lehmann, 2007). In failing or failed states (such as Somalia) where the governing authorities are unable to exercise effective control, armed escorts may be needed to ensure humanitarian relief and the safe delivery of development assistance; outside intervention may be needed also to protect human rights, and assistance may be required to provide law and order. To build an effective and legitimate state, failing or failed countries may need help as well in setting up effective governing institutions and monitoring elections to ensure their fairness. To recognize the spectrum of activities that aim to build and enforce peace, the term **"peace operations"** is often used instead of "peacekeeping." This wide range of activities, including the use of military force, tends to blur the line between war and peace.

Peace operations often involve not only troops under UN command but also police and civilians, as well as non-governmental organizations offering development assistance. Furthermore, organizations other than the United Nations, such as NATO and the African Union, have increasingly carried out these operations.

Canada has participated in forty-eight of the sixty-three UN peacekeeping missions since 1948, with Canadians suffering one hundred and fourteen fatalities. However, Canada's contribution to UN peacekeeping operations has shrunk drastically in recent times as Canada has turned down requests to take an active role in some major UN peacekeeping operations, such as the mission in the Democratic Republic of Congo. For example, out of a total of over 93 000 UN military and police peacekeepers in July 2009, only 182 were Canadian—ranking Canada fifty-fourth in terms of number of personnel (United Nations Peacekeeping, 2009).

Combat Missions

Canada is often thought to be a peace-loving country, although it has participated in wars and other military missions (see Table 18-1). From the end of the Korean War in 1953 to the end of the Cold War in 1981, Canada did not directly engage in active combat. Since then, Canada has taken an active role in several conflicts. In particular, Canada participated in 1991, along with thirty-three other countries, in the United States–led Gulf War against Iraq, which was authorized by the UN Security Council after Iraq invaded and annexed Kuwait. Canada's participation in this short war included the use of fighter aircraft to protect American bombing missions, naval vessels to enforce a blockade of Iraq, and a mobile military hospital to treat the wounded. In 1999 Canada and thirteen other NATO countries conducted seventy-eight days of air strikes against Yugoslavia. This devastating attack (discussed later in this chapter) was designed to persuade Serbian forces to stop their assaults on ethnic Albanians in the province of Kosovo and to withdraw their troops from that area.

PEACE OPERATIONS
A wide range of activities with the aim of building and enforcing peace, including peacekeeping, peace building, and peace enforcement.

TABLE 18-1
CANADIAN COMBAT MISSIONS

MISSION	DATES	NUMBER INVOLVED	DEATHS
Nile Expedition (Sudan)	1884	386	16
South Africa (Boer War)	1899–1902	8300	242
World War I	1914–1918	Over 600 000	60 661
Siberian Expedition	1918–1919	4197	19
World War II	1930–1945	About 1.1 million	42 042
Korean War	1950–1953	About 26 000	516
Gulf War (Iraq)	1990–1991	Over 4000	0
Yugoslavia	1999	300	0
Afghanistan	2002–	2500	133

Sources: *Isitt, 2006; Morton, 2007; Veterans Affairs Canada, n.d.*

Notes: Figures for World War II refer to troops sent overseas. Deaths include disease and accidents, as well as those that are combat related, but do not include deaths that occurred after the end of the war related to injuries suffered during war. Different sources provide different figures for the number involved and number of deaths. Deaths of soldiers in Afghanistan are to mid-November 2009. Two aid workers and one diplomat have also been killed in Afghanistan.

THE WAR IN AFGHANISTAN   Canada's lengthiest combat mission has been in Afghanistan—an initiative that began after al-Qaeda's attack on the United States in September 2001. NATO quickly invoked its Article 5, which obliged member states to come to the defence of the United States. Three days later, the United States, along with the United Kingdom, sent troops to Afghanistan to defeat the Taliban, destroy al-Qaeda, and capture or kill its leader, Osama bin Laden. Shortly afterwards, Canada sent military vessels to the region, secretly deployed its elite Joint Task Force 2, and early in 2002 deployed regular troops to fight alongside the Americans in Kandahar for six months—Canada's first ground combat mission since the Korean War.

With the American-led invasion of Iraq looming in 2003, Canada accepted an American request to return Canadian troops to Afghanistan and lead the International Security Assistance Force (ISAF) for six months. This participation assisted the United States, which was redeploying troops to Iraq. The ISAF is a NATO force authorized by the UN Security Council. It was originally intended to ensure security around Kabul to support the establishment of a transitional governing authority, as well as to provide security for humanitarian relief.

In 2005 Canada sent a provincial reconstruction team (PRT) to Kandahar. PRTs are organizations that combine military and civilian personnel; the various NATO countries have established PRTs throughout Afghanistan. The Department of Foreign Affairs, the Department of National Defence, and the Canadian International Development Agency, along with personnel from the RCMP and Corrections Canada, jointly run Canada's 330-member PRT. The idea is to integrate the traditionally separate activities of defence, diplomacy, and development following the "whole of government" approach that was recommended by the Canadian government's International Policy Statement in 2005. Among the goals of the PRT is to develop good governance, build relationships with local and provincial leaders, and undertake various reconstruction projects that meet the needs of the people in the region.

Although the PRT has done some useful work, problems have arisen in coordinating the different departments and agencies contributing to the PRT and working with non-governmental agencies (Cooper, 2009; Stein & Lang, 2007). With the intensification of the Taliban insurgency beginning in 2007, serious problems of security developed and Canadian involvement tended to focus more on combat than reconstruction.

In 2006, Canadian Forces took ISAF responsibility for the troubled southern region based in Kandahar, which is the heartland of the Taliban. As a result, Canada's 2500 troops have taken a disproportionate number of casualties compared with other NATO countries. In spite of the losses, the initial two-year mission was extended to 2009, confirmed by a close vote in the House of Commons in which Conservative MPs, along with the majority of Liberals, supported the extension. Those who opposed the extension were members of the NDP and Bloc, along with thirty Liberals. In 2008 the mission was extended further—this time to 2011—with most Liberals supporting the Conservative decision. Prime Minister Harper promised in the 2008 election that Canada's military commitment would end in 2011.

Canada's involvement in Afghanistan has sparked much debate in recent years. Human rights violations by the Afghan government, serious government corruption, and problems with the 2009 Afghan election resulted in dwindling support from the Canadian public for the counter-insurgency effort. The Afghan government has shown itself unable to exercise effective control over much of the country. Instead, a number of "warlords" preside over large areas of Afghanistan. With the Taliban being able to operate from secure bases in bordering Pakistan, a number of analysts have viewed the war against the Taliban as not "winnable." Indeed, Prime Minister Harper admitted that foreign troops "were not going to ever defeat the insurgency" (Koring, 2009). As of mid-November 2009, 133 Canadian soldiers, as well as two aid workers and one diplomat, had died as a result of the conflict. The Parliamentary Budgetary Officer estimated that the conflict will have cost Canada a total of $18.1 billion by 2011. Many people insist that we should support our troops as they struggle to bring stability and development to this troubled land by defeating the insurgents. Others argue that the presence of foreign troops has proved futile, that negotiations with moderate elements of the insurgency need to be carried out, and that humanitarian and development efforts should be redirected to other countries in need.

IRAQ   The Liberal government of Jean Chrétien refused to take part in the American-led invasion of Iraq in 2003. Although Stephen Harper as leader of the Opposition in the House of Commons at first demanded that Canada participate in the invasion,[7] Prime Minister Chrétien declared that Canada would

---

[7]Michael Ignatieff, then director of Harvard's Carr Center for Human Rights Policy, also publicly supported the invasion of Iraq. As Liberal MP, he recanted his support in 2007.

not join the invasion because it lacked specific UN authorization. A large majority of Canadians opposed the war.

By playing an active role in Afghanistan, the Canadian government was able to satisfy the U.S. government that Canada was participating in the war on terror (Stein & Lang, 2007). Even so, the Canadian government allowed about one hundred Canadian officers who were on exchange with U.S. forces to serve in the Iraq war; among them was Lieutenant General Walter Natynczyk (later to become Canada's Chief of Defence Staff), who served as the Deputy Director of Strategy, Policy and Plans, and subsequently as the Deputy Commanding General of the Multi-National Corps in Iraq (Barker, 2008). In addition, Canadian military vessels took up patrolling duties around Iraq in support of the war. Indeed, senior Canadian officials told their American counterparts that Canada's contribution to the Iraq war went beyond that of nearly all of the countries that directly participated in it (Stein & Lang, 2007).

HUMAN SECURITY

The realist perspective points out that the primary focus of the foreign and defence policies of all countries has typically been **national security**—that is, protecting the country from foreign threats to its population, territory, and independence (Sens & Stoett, 2005). However, building on a growing concern about human rights since World War II, the idea of "security" has been broadened from a focus on the security of the state from foreign aggression to include **human security**. As defined by the United Nations Human Development Report (1994), human security includes economic, food, health, environmental, community, and political security—or more simply, freedom from fear and freedom from want. In an address to the General Assembly of the United Nations in 1996, Canadian foreign affairs minister Lloyd Axworthy argued,

> At a minimum, human security requires that basic needs are met, but it also acknowledges that sustained economic development, human rights and fundamental freedoms, the rule of law, good governance, sustainable development and social equity are as important to global peace as arms control and disarmament. . . . Canada has both the capacity and the credibility to play a leadership role in support of human security in the developing world. (Axworthy, 1997, p. 183)

In Axworthy's view, values rather than national self-interest were coming to the fore in international politics. Canada's success in building a peaceful liberal-democratic state that respected the diversity of its peoples could set a positive example for other countries. Thus even though Canada did not possess a high level of "hard power" (the ability to use coercive force) because its military capabilities were limited, the country could play a key role in international politics by drawing on its "soft power"—that is, leadership by its values and its example. The way for Canada to exert influence was not to rely on the

NATIONAL SECURITY
Protection of a country from foreign threats to its population, territory, and independence.

HUMAN SECURITY
A view of security that focuses on the protection of people from various threats to their well-being.

power of the United States. Instead, Canada could play an independent role in world affairs by working with the growing number of non-governmental organizations that were pursuing peace and development goals, as well as by participating in multilateral forums with other middle powers that shared similar values (Bernard, 2006). Reflecting this view, Canada played an essential role in the effort to ban anti-personnel landmines, which culminated in the 1997 signing of the Convention on the Prohibition of the Use, Stockpiling, Production and Transfer of Anti-Personnel Mines and on their Destruction (known as the "Ottawa Treaty"). As well, Canada played a major role in the creation of the International Criminal Court, which can bring to trial those responsible for genocide and other serious human rights violations. In both these initiatives, international agreements were reached despite the vehement objections of the leading powers (the United States, Russia, and China). Non-governmental organizations and cyberactivism proved important in mobilizing the popular support that led to these agreements.

Canadians have also played an essential part in raising the environmental concerns that seriously threaten human security. Specifically, Canada took centre stage in the UN-sponsored Conference on the Human Environment in 1972, and Canadian Maurice Strong chaired the UN Conference on Environment and Development (better known as the "Earth Summit") in 1992. Canada also played a key role in the development of the Montreal Protocol (1987), a treaty providing for the phasing out of ozone-depleting substances.

However, Canada has been a laggard rather than a leader in efforts to reduce the emission of greenhouse gases, which is potentially the most serious threat to the global environment. In ratifying the Kyoto Protocol on global climate change in 2002, Canada committed to reduce its emissions to 6 percent below the 1990 level by 2008–12. However by 2007, Canada's emissions had soared to 26 percent above the 1990 level—a worse performance than that of almost all the developed countries, including the United States, which did not ratify the Protocol. With ballooning greenhouse gas emissions from production in Alberta's oil sands, threats to Canada's boreal forests (a major carbon "sink"), and little effective government action, Canada will likely continue to hold the dubious distinction of being a world leader in per capita emissions.

HUMANITARIAN INTERVENTION AND THE RESPONSIBILITY TO PROTECT

During the 1990s, UN-backed peacekeeping missions failed to stop horrific human rights abuses in several countries. For example, during the genocide in Rwanda, Roméo Dallaire, the Canadian commander of the UN Assistance Mission, pleaded for more troops. However, the UN Security Council refused and instead severely cut back the number of UN troops in Rwanda. As discussed in Box 18-3, Humanitarian Intervention: Hornet Fighters over Yugoslavia,

BOX 18-3

Humanitarian Intervention: Hornet Fighters over Yugoslavia

On March 24, 1999, Canadian CF-18 Hornet fighter aircraft took off from the United States Air Force base in Aviano, Italy, to participate in the bombing of Yugoslavia. Seventy-eight days later, the mission designed to stop the "ethnic cleansing" of Albanians in the province of Kosovo succeeded in its objective.

Kosovo, at the time, was an autonomous province of Serbia (the primary component of Yugoslavia). It has a population divided along ethnic and religious lines, with a large Albanian Muslim majority and a Serbian Orthodox Christian minority. As Yugoslavia disintegrated in the early 1990s, President Slobodan Milosevic curbed Kosovo's autonomy and took measures against the Albanians. An independence movement erupted in Kosovo, and the Kosovo Liberation Army (KLA) attacked Serbian police and military forces. After a massacre of Albanian civilians by the Serbian police in January 1999, NATO threatened military action unless Yugoslavia agreed to negotiate a peaceful settlement.

Later, peace talks failed as Serbia rejected the proposed Rambouillet Accord that would have established NATO administration of Kosovo and given NATO troops unrestricted access to all of Yugoslavia. NATO began bombing Yugoslavia. Serbian attacks on Albanians accelerated and about 800 000 Albanians fled from Kosovo. Eventually, Milosevic agreed to pull his troops out of Kosovo.

With Serbian forces gone, Albanian refugees flowed back into Kosovo. Some Albanians took revenge on the Serbian minority, murdering Serbian residents and wrecking their businesses and churches. About 200 000 Serbs fled Kosovo. While arguments over its fate persisted, Kosovo became a United Nations protectorate. In 2008, the Kosovo Assembly declared independence. As of 2009, fifty-eight countries, including Canada, have recognized Kosovo as an independent country, while Serbia insists on considering Kosovo as its territory. As for Milosevic—he died before his trial for genocide, crimes against humanity, and war crimes could be completed.

Canada, as part of a NATO force, decided to take military action in Yugoslavia without UN authorization to try to prevent a humanitarian catastrophe.

The attack on Yugoslavia sparked controversy because it involved a foreign military intervention in the affairs of a sovereign state, thereby violating a basic principle of international law. Because the attack by NATO was not in self-defence and was not authorized by the Security Council as is required under the UN Charter, it could be considered an illegal operation. Supporters of the intervention argued that it was necessary on humanitarian grounds to protect the Albanian population that was in imminent danger; Yugoslavia was violating the human rights that it had agreed to respect by signing various international agreements. The United Nations could not effectively resolve the crisis because Russia and China would have likely wielded their veto power to stop the UN Security Council from authorizing military action. As well, the conflict in Kosovo threatened the stability of the region and thus could have seriously jeopardized the well-being of other countries (Ignatieff, 2002).

The Responsibility to Protect

To avoid the controversy often associated with the term "humanitarian intervention," which highlights interference with state sovereignty, Lloyd Axworthy promoted the concept of the **"responsibility to protect,"** which is intended to focus on the responsibility of the government of each country to protect its people. This new terminology was adopted by the Canadian-sponsored International Commission on Intervention and State Sovereignty (ICISS). In its report, the ICISS laid out the basic principles of its view of the responsibility to protect:

> *State sovereignty implies responsibility, and the primary responsibility for the protection of its people lies with the state itself. Where a population is suffering serious harm, as a result of internal war, insurgency, repression or state failure, and the state in question is unwilling or unable to halt or avert it, the principle of non-intervention yields to the international responsibility to protect. (ICISS, 2001, p. xi)*

The responsibility to protect includes preventing crises that put populations at risk and responding with appropriate measures. In extreme cases involving actual or apprehended large-scale loss of life or ethnic cleansing, military intervention could be used as a last resort. The report argued that the UN Security Council was the most appropriate body to authorize military intervention and suggested ways to improve its performance. However, if the Security Council failed in its duty, the report suggested two alternatives—the General Assembly of the UN could recommend that the Security Council take action or regional organizations might take action within their regions and later seek authorization from the Security Council. Finally, the report noted that if the Security Council failed to act, "concerned states may not rule out other means to meet the gravity and urgency of that situation."

At the UN World Summit in 2005, delegates agreed that there is a collective international responsibility to protect if genocide, war crimes, ethnic cleansing, and crimes against humanity are at stake. Timely and decisive action through the Security Council should be taken when "peaceful means prove inadequate and national authorities are manifestly failing to do it." The Security Council unanimously reaffirmed this agreement in 2006. However, the agreement did not authorize intervention without the approval of the United Nations.

Russia, China, and the Group of 77 (as of 2009 consisting of 130 developing countries) have voiced concerns about the responsibility to protect.[8] Basically, critics view the responsibility to protect as new terminology that could be used to justify self-interested interference, particularly by Western countries, in the affairs of other countries. This sets off alarm bells in the

RESPONSIBILITY TO PROTECT The responsibility of a state to protect its population from genocide, war crimes, ethnic cleansing, and crimes against humanity and, as a last resort, the responsibility of the international community, particularly through the United Nations, to intervene if a state is unwilling or unable to protect its population.

International Coalition for the Responsibility to Protect: **www.responsibilitytoprotect.org**

---

[8]However, Russia's foreign minister claimed that Russia was exercising its responsibility to protect when it invaded Georgia in August 2008 after Georgia's attack on Russian forces in South Ossetia (a breakaway region of Georgia).

many former colonies that have suffered from imperialistic conquest and domination. Because of this concern, the right to protect resolution has not been used by the Security Council, even after the High Level Commission of the UN's Human Rights Council reported that the government of Sudan has "manifestly failed to protect the population of Darfur" (Bellamy, 2009).

The Darfur/Sudan Peace Network: **www.sdcanada.org**

Canada's commitment to the responsibility to protect faded after John Manley replaced Lloyd Axworthy as Liberal minister of Foreign Affairs and the concern about terrorism took high priority. The Harper Government has further distanced itself from Axworthy's ideals—going so far as to direct Foreign Affairs personnel not to use terms such as "human security" and the "responsibility to protect" (Davis, 2009).

DEVELOPMENT ASSISTANCE

Development assistance (foreign aid) had its origins in the Cold War, particularly as a tool to try to staunch the spread of communism among the newly decolonized countries. Under Prime Minister Pearson, Canadian policy shifted toward "humane internationalism"—that is, helping those in the poorest countries. However, at times, the focus on the poorest countries has met with challengers: those who feel aid should go to countries that have succeeded in emerging from desperate poverty and are therefore potential markets for Canadian goods and investment. As well, until fairly recently, more than two-thirds of Canada's foreign aid had to be used to purchase Canadian goods and services (World Bank, 2004). This emphasis tends to serve the interests of Canadian businesses rather than assisting entrepreneurs in the recipient countries. In addition, to protect Canadian businesses, the Canadian government has placed quotas and tariffs on some goods from developing countries. The cost to poorer countries of this restriction on their ability to sell their products outweighs the benefits they receive from foreign aid.

UN Millennium Development Goals: **www.un.org/millenniumgoals**

Development assistance has tended to focus on the poorest countries since the United Nations adopted the **Millennium Development Goals** in 2000, to be achieved by 2015. These goals include the following:

MILLENNIUM DEVELOPMENT GOALS
Goals established by the United Nations for the development of poorer countries.

- eradicating extreme poverty and hunger;
- achieving universal primary education;
- promoting gender equality and empowering women; and
- reducing child mortality.

Canada's *Official Development Assistance Accountability Act*, 1998[9] states that "official development assistance may be provided only if the competent minister is of the opinion that it contributes to poverty reduction, takes into account the perspectives of the poor and is consistent with international human rights standards."

Canadian Council for International Co-operation: **www.ccic.ca**

Canadian International Development Agency: **www.acdi-cida.gc.ca**

---

[9]This was a private member's bill introduced by Liberal MP John McKay. It received unanimous approval in Parliament.

▶ In recent years, the Canadian government has stated that development assistance should be used to promote good governance, democracy, sustainability, and political stability in recipient countries. Here, PO2 Stephan Belanger places bags of corn soya blend while HMCS St John's is being loaded with humanitarian supplies by local men and the ship's company, with the collaboration of the Canadian embassy and representatives of the World Food Program (WFP), September 2008 at Port au Prince, Haiti. Acting on a request from the UN WFP and UN International Maritime Organization, the government sent HMCS St John's to the region to provide naval humanitarian aid over several weeks.

In recent years, the Canadian government has stated that development assistance should be used to promote good governance, democracy, sustainability, and political stability in recipient countries. Assistance may be of little benefit to the people in countries plagued by corruption and dictatorial rule. To be effective, development aid also requires that Canada and other donors work closely with recipient countries to set priorities that meet local needs (Tomlin et al., 2008). Achieving all of these goals is, however, far from easy, as the countries most in need of aid are often poorly governed and resentful of

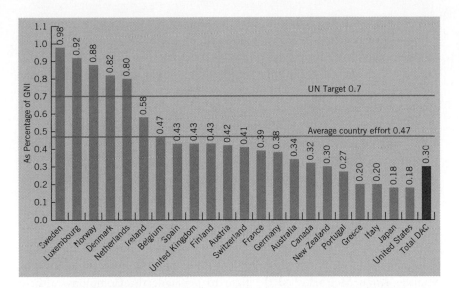

FIGURE 18-1
**OFFICIAL DEVELOPMENT
ASSISTANCE AS A
PERCENTAGE OF GROSS
NATIONAL INCOME**

Source: *Organization of Economic Co-operation and Development, 2009, "Table 1: Net Official Development Assistance in 2008." Retrieved from www.oecd.org/dataoecd/25/42/42472714.pdf*

outside interference in their affairs. Further, Canada's development assistance is often linked to its other foreign policy goals. For example, reflecting a shift in foreign policy priorities toward the Americas, the Canadian government cut its direct aid to Africa from fourteen countries to seven in 2009.

The Commission on International Development (chaired by Lester B. Pearson) recommended that the developed countries dedicate 0.7 percent of their gross national income to assist the development of poorer countries—a goal that the developed countries (including Canada) and the United Nations adopted in 1970. However, Canada has never reached that goal and, in fact, the amount of assistance dropped in the 1990s as the Canadian government struggled to shrink its budgetary deficit and debt. As Figure 18-1 indicates, Canada's official development assistance continues to fall below the average of the donor countries, although Canada has increased its assistance in recent years.

INTERNATIONAL ORGANIZATIONS

In addition to participating in the United Nations, NATO, and NORAD, Canada is an active member of many other international organizations. Some of these, such as the World Bank, the World Trade Organization, and the International Monetary Fund, are of great economic importance, as well as being quite inclusive organizations that involve many or most countries of the world. The G8, on the other hand, is an exclusive club of countries (including Canada) with some of the largest economies.[10] In addition to its highly publicized informal

---

[10]The G8 consists of Canada, France, Germany, Italy, Japan, Russia, the United Kingdom, and the United States, along with a representative of the European Union.

annual meetings of the eight countries' leaders (and invited leaders from other countries, who participate in some sessions), the G8 holds regular meetings of ministers responsible for particular policy areas, such as finance and the environment. Canada is also a member of the G20 that in the past consisted of the Finance ministers and central bank chairs of the major economies (including developing countries such as China, India, and Indonesia). As a result of the global financial crisis, the G20 took on added significance, holding meetings of the heads of government and heads of state of the member countries. At the September 2009 meeting, the government leaders decided that the G20 would supersede the G8 as the major international economic forum. The future role of the G8 is unclear.

As well, Canada is an active participant in two large international organizations that reflect the country's British and French heritage: the Commonwealth and *la Francophonie*. In both these organizations, Canada has, at times, pursued a democracy and human rights agenda. For example, Prime Minister Brian Mulroney led the fight to persuade the Commonwealth to impose economic sanctions on the apartheid regime in South Africa.

L'Organisation internationale de la Francophonie:
www.francophonie.org

The Commonwealth:
www.thecommonwealth.org

In addition, Canada is a member of regional organizations, including the Organization of American States, the Arctic Council, and Asia-Pacific Economic Cooperation. In total, Canada is a member of more than eighty international governmental organizations.

CANADIAN SOVEREIGNTY

Canada faces daunting challenges to its sovereignty in the Arctic. Although Canada claims the Northwest Passage through the territorial waters of the Arctic, American ships have sailed through the passage without informing the Canadian government. Likewise, Russian submarines have entered the Canadian Arctic. As Arctic ice continues to thin due to global climate change, it may not be long before the Northwest Passage becomes a major international shipping route, raising fears of the impact of oil spills on the fragile northern environment. In addition, the potential melting of the polar ice cap has led to competing territorial claims by Russia, Canada, the United States, Denmark, and Norway in order to exploit the huge oil, gas, and mineral resources believed to lie under the seabed of the High Arctic.

In the 2006 Canadian election, the Conservative party promised to build three armed heavy icebreakers to enforce Canadian sovereignty in the Arctic. This was followed up with an announcement in July 2007 that the Canadian navy would be equipped with six to eight lighter ice-capable patrol vessels for nearly year-round operation at a projected cost of $3.1 billion. Such vessels would, however, be unable to cut through the thick ice in the High Arctic. As of June 2009, the Canadian government had not asked shipbuilders for proposals for the patrol vessels, perhaps because of the escalating expected costs ("Navy Waters Down Plans," 2009). Instead, the prime minister continued his practice of making well-publicized visits to the Arctic each summer to "show the flag."

DEMOCRACY, DIVERSITY, GOOD GOVERNMENT, AND FOREIGN POLICY

Democracy

Despite the unquestionable importance of foreign policy and military actions, Parliament's role in decisions concerning this area is generally minimal. Although Parliament did vote to approve the declaration of war against Germany in 1939, no votes were held to approve Canada's involvement in the Korean War and the Gulf War. Nor did Parliament approve the Liberal government's decision to deploy troops to Kandahar in 2005. Instead, the House of Commons held a debate on a motion to "take note of Canada's military mission in Afghanistan." Although the Conservative minority government initially opposed holding a Parliamentary debate or vote on extending the Kandahar mission in 2007, they later relented, agreeing first to hold a "take note" debate and then a formal vote (Bercuson & Carment, 2008). The decision to hold a vote may have been part of a political strategy to highlight the divisions on the issue within the Liberal party. In general, the prime minister has played the biggest role in determining foreign policy, sometimes with the participation of Cabinet, but without effective scrutiny by Parliament (Bercuson & Carment, 2008).

At times, however, there have been significant efforts to engage the public in discussion of foreign policy issues. In particular, Foreign Affairs minister Lloyd Axworthy saw public consultation as crucial to foreign policy development and worked closely with Canadian non-governmental organizations that championed international human rights issues (Tomlin et al., 2008). A variety of non-governmental organizations have increased the awareness and concern of the public about humanitarian issues in many parts of the world. However, it is doubtful that non-governmental organizations can play a major role in influencing the fundamental direction of Canadian foreign policy (Riddell-Dixon, 2008).

Like other Western countries, Canada has been involved in promoting democracy in nations undergoing a transition to democracy or where democracy is fragile. The collapse of communist regimes in Eastern Europe in the late 1980s as a result of civil society (voluntary groups and associations that are distinct from government, business, and family) activity had an impact on governments. Specifically, it encouraged governments to assist in the growth of non-governmental organizations (particularly public interest groups) in less-developed countries in addition to providing economic assistance and election observers. The assumption is that democracy can best be built up by looking to ordinary people and by creating a democratic political culture rather than focusing on a top-down process of adopting formal democratic institutions and procedures. However, changing the political culture and nurturing the development of groups that represent all of the people rather than an educated, urban-based elite is not an easy task. Although promoting democracy has rarely involved assisting political parties, Stephen Fletcher, Minister of State for Democratic Reform, has announced that Canada will help to develop principle-based political parties (Berthiaume, 2009).

Diversity

To what extent does the diversity of Canadian society affect foreign policy? Many Canadians remain engaged in happenings in their ancestral homelands, and new Canadians often retain strong links to the countries where they were born. For example, in 2009, Tamil Canadians mounted large demonstrations to demand that the Canadian government pressure Sri Lanka to agree to a ceasefire in its conflict with Tamil rebels that was endangering the lives of civilians. The concentration of newer Canadians in certain urban electoral districts makes some federal politicians sensitive to issues related to the homelands of their electorate. For example, the Canadian government's active involvement in Haiti, the most destitute country in the Western hemisphere, may be related to the presence of a thriving Haitian population in Montreal, as well as to the desire of the Canadian government to play a greater role in the Caribbean. However, various ethnic communities are unlikely to succeed in shaping the basic features of Canadian foreign policy, such as Canada's close relationship with the United States and the Western world. Nevertheless, as Elizabeth Riddell-Dixon (2008) suggests, the increasing proportion of people from various parts of the world "is likely to result in an incremental reorientation that will have profound effects in the long run" (p. 46). In particular, the growing diversity of Canada's population may encourage heightened concern for the struggles of the developing world, even if it does not shift Canada's basic positions in international politics.

Differences between French- and English-speaking Canadians feed into Canada's international involvements. The issue of conscription deeply divided Canadians in both world wars. Likewise, support for Canada's involvement in Afghanistan has been much lower in Quebec than in the rest of Canada. Given the close cultural ties between English Canada and the United States, it is not surprising that English-speaking Canadians tend to view the United States somewhat more positively than French Quebecers (Potter, 2008). As well, many French Quebecers appear to be less supportive than English Canadians of the strongly pro-Israel position taken by the Harper Government.

In response to the rise of Quebec separatism, French President Charles de Gaulle's infamous "Vive le Quebec Libre" speech in Montreal in 1967, and de Gaulle's encouragement to the small African country of Gabon to invite Quebec rather than Canada to an international conference in 1968, the Canadian government saw the need for action. It has assumed a vigorous role in the International Organization of the Francophonie and in developing strong relationships with French-speaking countries (Kirton, 2007).[11]

Good Government

Good governance has been a priority of Canadian foreign policy since the early 1990s (Keating, 2001). The Canadian International Development Agency defined good governance as "the effective, honest, equitable and accountable exercise of power by governments" (CIDA, 1996). This includes an effective public service; a reliable and independent judiciary; effective mechanisms to deal with corruption, financial accountability, and transparency; and appropriate levels of military expenditures. Canada's 2005 International Policy Statement listed good governance first in its recommendations for a greater focus in development assistance. Specifically five pillars of good governance were identified:

1. democratization;
2. human rights;
3. the rule of law;
4. public sector institution and capacity building; and
5. conflict prevention, peacebuilding, and security-sector reform (CIDA, 2005).[12]

Although good governance is essential to forging meaningful development in poorer countries, it is not easy to achieve. While Canada can draw on its experience in developing good government over more than a century, the country's model of liberal democracy is not necessarily a good fit for countries with different histories, cultures, societies, and economies. Further, insisting that countries receiving aid adopt institutions and practices based on Canadian values may be viewed as a form of neo-colonialism or Western imperialism that can trigger resentment and hostility in the recipient country. To improve the governing of poor countries, the donor country has to have staff in the field that have enough time to understand the local culture and a willingness to listen to the people and focus on their needs (Welsh, 2007).

---

[11]Both Quebec and New Brunswick are considered "participating governments" in the organization. The Francophonie was originally established as the Agency for Cultural and Technical Co-operation in 1970.

[12]This major policy statement was never officially adopted.

Summary and Conclusion

Canada's place in the world has often been viewed from the perspective of liberal internationalism. Over the years, Canada has built a fine international reputation through its role in peacekeeping, its tradition of "quiet diplomacy," its effectiveness as a "helpful fixer," and its commitment to international organizations such as the United Nations, the World Trade Organization, the Commonwealth, and *la Francophonie*. However, Canada is no longer a major player in the United Nations peacekeeping operations, and the country's development assistance is less generous than that of a number of other comparable countries.

Canada's global status is strongly affected by our relationship to the United States. The integration of the economies of the two countries, the close relationship between the Canadian and American militaries, the influence of American media and cultural products, and cross-border family and personal relations make it unlikely that the Canadian government would take a radically different course of action in world affairs from that of the U.S. government. Further, the gulf in power between the two countries means that the relationship will not be one of equals.

Nevertheless, the peripheral dependence perspective does not seem adequate to understand Canada's place in the world. While many leaders of the Canadian business community and the Canadian military would like to see a deeper integration of Canada and the United States, many Canadians are wary of being too closely tied to their neighbour to the south. An element of nationalism and anti-Americanism has persisted in Canadian politics, even though it has not been strong enough to prevent closer economic and military ties between the two countries. Nevertheless, Canadian governments have avoided direct involvement in the Vietnam and Iraq wars and in American ballistic defence systems. And even a strongly pro-American prime minister such as Stephen Harper came to see the virtue in trying to reduce Canadian dependence on the United States by negotiating a number of bilateral trade agreements with other countries and seeking a major trade agreement with the European Union.

Furthermore, the notion that Canada will inevitably be drawn into subordination to the American "empire" ignores some realities in the relationship between the two countries. The security of energy supplies is an important political and strategic concern, and Canada has become the largest single supplier of oil to the United States. As well, despite the global military superiority of the United States, the country relies on support from its allies to try to make the exercise of that power legitimate. The manufacturing and technological dominance of the United States has been challenged by the developing Asian countries, and the government of the United States has been falling deeply into debt. Moreover, the global financial crisis that began in 2008 exposed the weaknesses of American financial institutions and the relative strength of Canada's banks. While it would be misleading to talk about the "decline and fall of the American empire," changes may be happening in the global distribution of power. Canada's place in the world is not only as a good neighbour of the United States, but also Canada can be a significant actor on the larger global stage in a changing world.

Has Canada become a "principal power" in the contemporary international system, as suggested by the complex neo-realism perspective? Canada has successfully taken leadership on some key issues and has enjoyed some success in promoting Canadian interests and values on the international stage. Yet despite being a respected participant in international politics, Canada does not generally wield the same "clout" as the United States and the other members of the Security Council and may be surpassed in importance by such rising powers as India in the future. Indeed, although Canada has taken a leading role in the Afghanistan conflict (at least until the surge of U.S. forces in 2009), the Canadian government has tended to curb its international activism since the beginning of the twenty-first century.

Canada's experiences in meeting the challenges of democracy, diversity, and good government provide an opportunity for the country to take its place in the world as a model for other countries striving to satisfy similar goals and aspirations. Of course, as discussed in various places in this textbook, there are many challenges still confronting Canada, such as conditions faced by Aboriginal peoples. Nevertheless as Jennifer Welsh (2004) argues, defining our values on the international stage (as well as improving the application of these values to domestic problems) can help to foster a distinctive Canadian identity. Others argue that instead of promoting its values worldwide, Canada should focus on pursuing its national interest by building a strong military, acting as a loyal ally to the United States, and working toward a closer integration of the Canadian and American economies.

Should Canada focus on developing a close partnership with the United States in order to protect Canadian prosperity and security? Or should Canada take an internationalist position in the world, demonstrating leadership by grappling with such global problems as climate change, poverty, disease, human rights, and conflict?

Discussion Questions

1. Should Canada end its military involvement in Afghanistan?

2. Should Canada increase its assistance to poor countries?

3. Should Canada develop a closer economic, military, and political relationship with the United States?

4. Should Canada increase its involvement in peace-keeping operations?

5. Should Canada substantially increase the strength and capabilities of its military forces? If so, for what purposes? If not, why not?

6. Should Canada intervene in the internal affairs of other countries to prevent serious human rights abuses?

Further Reading

Axworthy, L. (2003). *Navigating a new world. Canada's global future*. Toronto, ON: Knopf.

Byers, M. (2007). *Intent for a nation*. Vancouver, BC: Douglas & McIntyre.

Carroll, M. K. (2009). *Pearson's peacekeepers: Canada and the United Nations Emergency Force, 1956—67*. Vancouver: UBC Press.

Cohen, A. (2003). *While Canada slept: How we lost our place in the world*. Toronto, ON: McClelland & Stewart.

Dallaire, R. (2003). *Shake hands with the devil: The failure of humanity in Rwanda*. Toronto, ON: Random House.

Holloway, S. K. (2006). *Canadian foreign policy: Defining the national interest*. Peterborough, ON: Broadview Press.

Janes, P., Michaud, N., & O'Reilly, M. J. (Eds.). (2008). *Handbook of Canadian foreign policy*. Lanham, MD: Lexington Books.

Keating, T. (2002). *Canada and the world order: The multilateralist tradition in Canadian foreign policy* (2nd ed.). Don Mills, ON: Oxford University Press.

Kirton, J. (2007). *Canadian foreign policy in a changing world*. Toronto, ON: Thomson Nelson.

Stein, J. S., & Lang, E. (2007). *The unexpected war: Canada in Kandahar*. Toronto, ON: Viking Canada.

Tomlin, B. W., Hillmer, N., & Hampson, F. O. (2008). *Canada's international policies: Agendas, alternatives, and politics*. Don Mills, ON: Oxford University Press.

Welsh, J. (2004). *At home in the world: Canada's global vision for the 21st century*. Toronto, ON: HarperCollins.

GLOSSARY

Alternative dispute resolution A process where disputing parties choose a third party (rather than a judge) to try to resolve the dispute.

Alternative service delivery Methods of delivering government services apart from the use of traditional departments and agencies, with the goal of making government more businesslike and responsive to the needs of the recipients of services.

Anti-dumping duties Duties imposed on imports of a particular product when a foreign producer sells the product in the importing country for less than its "fair value."

Assimilation The process through which groups of individuals with a different culture learn and adopt the values and norms of the host society.

Asymmetrical federal system A federal system in which different provinces have a different relationship with the federal government, including different powers from other provincial governments.

Attitudinal model of judicial decision making The view that judges pursue their own policy preferences in interpreting the law, as well as being influenced by their attitudes toward the facts of the case.

Authority The right to exercise power.

Balanced budget The practice of government spending no more than the revenues it collects annually.

Balfour declaration (1926) A resolution of the Imperial Conference that declared that Britain and the dominions are autonomous and equal communities in no way subordinate one to another.

Bicameral legislature A legislature with two chambers or houses.

Bill of rights, 1689 The bill that followed the Glorious Revolution of 1688, which added protections for parliamentary free speech, regular sessions, and other protections, and is generally regarded as the stage of British history when the Crown accepted the supremacy of Parliament.

Block grant The unconditional transfer of a block of money from the federal government to a provincial government.

Branch plant A term that usually refers to a factory set up by an American company to produce and sell products for the Canadian market similar to the company's plant in the United States.

British north america act, 1867 An act of the Parliament of the United Kingdom establishing the Dominion of Canada. In 1982 it was renamed the Constitution Act, 1867.

Brokerage theory A perspective that maintains that parties do not have clear and coherent ideological programs, and that they act pragmatically in order to appeal to the greatest number of voters at election time.

Budget Government statement that proposes tax increases or decreases as well as other revenue and borrowing measures, outlines the state of the economy and government finances in general, and often includes announcements of major new programs.

Bureaucracy Rule by offices and officials.

Cabinet committees Groups of cabinet ministers who examine policy proposals from related policy fields and recommend to the plenary (full) Cabinet what action should be taken. Their recommendations generally are accepted.

Cabinet secrecy A convention that forbids the disclosure of the views expressed by particular ministers in the setting of cabinet (and cabinet committee) discussions, in order to encourage frankness.

Cabinet solidarity The basic principle that ministers must avoid public disagreements over policy once Cabinet decides on it, and that they must vote in unison in the House on government business.

Cabinet The active part of the Queen's Privy Council for Canada. Composed of the prime minister and ministers, it controls most of the executive and legislative powers of government.

Canada health transfer A block grant intended to fund medicare and hospital insurance, although some conditions are involved.

Canada social transfer A block grant intended to fund post-secondary education, social assistance, early childhood education, and child-care programs.

Canada-united states automotive agreement, 1965 ("auto pact"). An agreement that eliminated tariffs between the two countries on new automobiles, trucks, buses, and original vehicle parts, while providing guarantees about the level of production in Canada.

Canadian bill of rights An act of Parliament passed in 1960 establishing various rights and freedoms that only applied to matters under federal jurisdiction.

Canadian judicial council A body of senior judges established to review complaints about federally appointed judges.

Caucus Parliamentary members who belong to a particular party.

Central agencies The Prime Minister's Office and the Privy Council Office, which provide direct assistance to the prime minister and facilitate the setting of objectives by Cabinet.

Central departments The Department of Finance and the Treasury Board Secretariat, which, along with the central agencies, advise Cabinet and its committees and influence the direction and policies of the government.

Charlottetown accord An agreement in 1992 on a broad package of constitutional changes, including Aboriginal self-government, Senate reform, and a statement of the characteristics of Canada. The agreement, which had the support of the prime minister, all premiers and territorial leaders, and four national Aboriginal leaders, was defeated in a referendum.

Charlottetown conference, 1864 A meeting of the leaders of Canada and the Maritimes at which it was decided to hold further discussions about uniting the British North American colonies.

Charter dialogue The view that the Charter has created a dialogue between the courts and legislatures.

Charter of rights and freedoms As part of the Constitution Act, 1982, the Charter is superior to ordinary legislation, allows the courts to invalidate legislation, and applies to the actions of all governments and organizations under the control of government.

Citizens plus The idea that Indians possess certain rights in addition to the normal rights and duties of citizens.

Civic engagement A set of activities in the community, such as joining a voluntary organization, volunteering for the organization, helping others directly, or giving financial donations to charitable causes.

Civic nation A community based on the common territory in which its members live and are governed.

Civil disobedience The deliberate and public breaking of a law in order to draw attention to injustice.

Civil society The voluntary associations and non-governmental organizations that bring people together to achieve a common goal.

Class consciousness The awareness within a social class of their common interests and a willingness to collectively act on those interests.

Classic peacekeeping Activities carried out under the United Nations banner to support a ceasefire between countries in conflict or to supervise the implementation of a peace agreement.

Classical democratic theory The belief that it is desirable to have a large number of citizens from different backgrounds participating in political affairs.

Classical elite theory The belief that only a small ruling class has the knowledge and skills to decide what is in the public interest, and that mass political participation is undesirable.

Classical federalism The view that a federal system should be based on autonomous federal and provincial governments, each with its own specific areas of responsibility.

Classical liberalism An intellectual tradition based on a belief in a minimal role for government, leaving individuals free to pursue their interests and follow their own beliefs as long as they do not seriously harm others.

Closure A motion in the House of Commons to limit debate on a bill.

Code civil du quÉbec A codified system of law that is the basis of private law in Quebec.

Codified civil law A system of private law used in Quebec based on a comprehensive set of legal principles.

Cold war The severe tensions between the Western countries, led by the United States, and communist countries, led by the Soviet Union, that developed after the end of the Second World War and ended with the collapse of the Soviet Union in 1991.

Collaborative federalism A trend in contemporary federalism in which both levels of government try to work together as equals in deciding some major policies.

Collective benefits Benefits to society as a whole.

Collective responsibility The convention that the Cabinet as a group is responsible to the House of Commons for the decisions and actions of the government.

Committees of the whole The members of the House using relaxed rules of debate and procedure to deal with supply motions or other topics.

Common law A body of law developed through the accumulation of court decisions that become binding precedents for similar future cases.

Common law Law based on the accumulation of court decisions.

Competitive federalism A feature of Canadian federalism, particularly between the early 1960s and 1984, in which provincial and national governments competed to maximize their autonomy, power, and popularity with the voters.

Complex neo-realism perspective The view that changes in the international system have resulted in Canada becoming a "principal power," able to independently assert its national values and interests in international politics.

Comprehensive land claims agreements Agreements involving First Nations that had not signed treaties giving up their land.

Conditional grants Federal grants to provincial governments for specific programs that have to meet conditions set by the Canadian government.

Confidence chamber A legislative body (in Canada, the House of Commons) whose continued majority support is necessary for the government to remain in office.

Conscription crisis The imposition of compulsory military service during the First World War that sharply divided many English and French Canadians.

Conservatism An ideological perspective that generally looks to laws based on traditional (religious) moral values and established institutions to maintain an orderly society.

Constitution act, 1791 Divided Quebec into two separate colonies: Upper Canada and Lower Canada.

Constitution act, 1867 An act of the Parliament of the United Kingdom that established Canada as a federal union of Ontario, Quebec, Nova Scotia, and New Brunswick.

Constitution act, 1982 This act patriated the Constitution, established a formula for amending the Constitution, added the Charter of Rights and Freedoms, recognized the rights of Aboriginal peoples, and made a commitment to the principle of equalization payments.

Constitution The fundamental rules by which a country is governed.

Constitutional amendments act, 1996 An act of Parliament that sets out the combination of provinces and regions whose support is needed before the Canadian Cabinet presents proposed constitutional changes to Parliament.

Constitutional conventions Widely accepted informal constitutional rules.

Constitutional government A government that consistently acts in keeping with established fundamental rules and principles.

Cooperative federalism The feature of Canadian federalism in the two decades following World War II in which federal and provincial governments generally cooperated under federal leadership in developing the welfare state.

Council of the federation An organization established by the premiers to enable cooperation among the provinces.

Countervailing duties Duties imposed on imports of a particular product that have been subsidized by the exporting country in a way that harms the home producers of that same product.

Court Challenges Program A federal government program that provided some money for individuals and groups seeking to challenge Canadian laws and government actions that violate equality rights and minority language rights.

Cyberactivism Political activism that employs online communications tools such as websites, emails, blogs, and social networking services.

Declaratory power The right of the Canadian Parliament to declare any "local works or undertakings" within a province to be "for the general Advantage of Canada or for the Advantage of Two or more of the Provinces" and then legislate on that matter.

Deliberative democracy A form of democracy in which governing decisions are made based on discussion by citizens.

Deliberative democracy A form of democracy in which governing decisions are made based on fair and open discussion by citizens.

Democracy Rule by the people either directly or through the election of representatives.

Departmentalized cabinet A form of cabinet organization that emphasizes ministerial autonomy and relies on the prime minister and full Cabinet to achieve coordination.

Deputy minister The administrative head of a department and the link between the minister who is politically responsible for the department and the non-partisan public servants in the department.

Differentiated citizenship The granting of special group-based legal or constitutional rights to national minorities and ethnic groups.

Direct democracy A form of democracy in which citizens are directly involved in making the governing decisions.

Disallowance power The right of the Canadian Cabinet to disallow provincial legislation within one year of its passage.

Discretionary prerogative powers Powers that the monarch's representative may exercise upon his or her own personal discretion. Also called personal prerogatives or reserve powers.

Distinct society clause A clause in the Meech Lake Accord that the constitution should be interpreted in a manner consistent with the recognition of Quebec as a distinct society.

Durham report A report of the British governor that recommended the union of Upper and Lower Canada and the adoption of responsible government.

Electoral district association An association of members of a political party in a territorial area that is represented by a member in the House of Commons.

Electoral system The system by which the votes that people cast are translated into the representation of political parties in the House of Commons.

Employment equity Programs that encourage or require the hiring and promotion of women (or other groups) for positions in which they are under-represented.

Equalization payments Unconditional grants from the Canadian government to the governments of the poorer provinces to bring their revenue-raising capabilities up to a national standard.

Estimates The money the government says is needed by government departments and agencies for the next fiscal year.

Ethnic groups Groups of immigrants who have left their countries of origin to enter another society, but who do not occupy a separate territory in their new homeland.

Ethnic nation A community with a distinctive culture and history, which operates solely for the benefit of that cultural group. Members of the ethnic nation share common ancestry, language, customs, and traditions.

Executive department An organization headed by a cabinet minister.

Executive federalism The basic nature of federal- provincial interaction since the 1940s, involving the interaction of the executives of the federal and provincial governments.

Federal court of canada A court that hears cases related to certain acts of Parliament, such as laws concerning copyright and patents, citizenship and immigration, and access to information and privacy. As well it hears appeals against the rulings of national administrative bodies.

Federal system A system of governing in which authority is divided and shared between the central government and provincial governments, with each deriving its authority from the constitution.

First ministers conferences Formal meetings of the prime minister and premiers, along with large supporting delegations of ministers, aides, and officials.

First ministers meetings Informal private meetings of the prime minister and premiers.

Fiscal imbalance The view that provincial governments do not have a proper share of revenue to carry out their responsibilities.

Foreign investment review agency (FIRA) A Canadian government agency established in 1973 to review proposals from foreigners to take over Canadian businesses or to set up new businesses.

Formal executive That part of the executive consisting of the Queen, the governor general, and the queen's Privy Council for Canada, which possesses formal constitutional authority and by convention acts on the advice of the political executive.

Formative events theory A theory that emphasizes the importance of a crucial formative event in establishing the basic character of a country's political culture.

Founding fragments theory The theory that in the founding of new societies, only a fragment of the political culture of the "mother country" formed the basis for the political culture of the new society.

Franchise The right to vote.

Free rider An individual who enjoys the benefits of group action without contributing.

Generational replacement The process through which younger-age cohorts enter the electorate and replace their older predecessors.

Gerrymandering The drawing of boundaries for partisan advantage, particularly for the advantage of the governing party.

Glorious revolution The series of events that led to the removal of James II from the throne in 1688, his replacement by William and Mary, and their acceptance of the Bill of Rights, 1689.

Government The set of institutions that have the authority to make executive decisions; present proposed laws, taxes, and expenditures to the appropriate legislative body; and oversee the implementation of laws and policies.

Governor in council The formal name given to Cabinet in order to cloak its decisions with constitutional authority. The phrase means that the governor general is acting on the advice of the Queen's Privy Council for Canada, the active part of which is the Cabinet.

Hawthorn report A Canadian government report that recommended that Indians should have rights in addition to those of other citizens and not be forced to assimilate into the majority society.

Heritage language All languages other than the Aboriginal languages of the First Nations and Inuit peoples and the official languages of English and French.

House leaders Members of each party who are responsible for their party's strategy in the House of Commons, including negotiating the parliamentary timetable with other House Leaders.

House officers Political officers of the House of Commons.

Human security A view of security that focuses on the protection of people from various threats to their well-being.

Identities Individual and group self-understandings of their traits and characteristics.

Implied bill of rights The judicial theory that rights are implied by the preamble to the Constitution Act, 1867, and therefore could not be infringed by ordinary legislation.

Independent immigrants People with specific occupational skills, experience, and personal qualifications who are selected on the basis of criteria that assess their ability to adapt and to contribute to the country.

Individual ministerial responsibility The responsibility of individual cabinet ministers to the House of Commons for the decisions and actions of the department they administer.

Inherent right of self-government policy A Canadian government policy adopted in 1995 recognizing an inherent right to Aboriginal self-government.

Inherent right to self-government The perspective that First Nations have the right to govern themselves based on their independence before European colonization, a right that was never ceded.

Initiative A proposed new law or changes to an existing law drafted by an individual or group rather than by a government or legislature. The proposal is put to a vote by the people after enough signatures have been collected.

Institutionalized cabinet A form of cabinet organization that emphasizes collective decision making and seeks to achieve it by a highly structured system of cabinet committees and central agencies.

Institutionalized interest group A group that has a formal organizational structure, a well-established membership base, paid professional staff, executive officers, permanent offices, and the capability to respond to the interests of its members by developing policy positions and promoting them through regular contact with government policy-makers.

Integration The multidimensional process through which an immigrant becomes a member of the host society.

Interest groups Organizations that pursue the common interests of groups of people, particularly by trying to influence the making and implementation of public policies.

Interstate federalism A federal system in which provincial interests are represented primarily by provincial governments.

Intrastate federalism A federal system in which provincial interests are represented in national political institutions.

Investment canada A Canadian government agency established in 1985 with a mandate to attract foreign investment.

Judicial advisory committee A committee that assesses candidates for appointment as a superior court judge.

Judicial committee of the privy council The highest court of appeal for Canada until 1949.

Judicial independence The principle that the courts are expected to be independent of government and its agencies, legislative bodies, and other influences.

Judicial review The authority of the courts to invalidate laws passed by Parliament or provincial legislatures that they deem to be in violation of the Constitution.

Kelowna accord An agreement reached between First Nations and federal and provincial governments in 2005 to improve the socioeconomic conditions of Aboriginals.

Keynesian economics A perspective on managing the economy through government stimulation of the economy when business investment is weak and cooling the economy when inflation is rampant.

Leadership convention A meeting of party members to select a new leader.

Leadership review The formal process that sets out the procedures for evaluating and possibly replacing a party leader.

Legal model of judicial decision making The view that judges base their decisions on a careful reading of the relevant law.

Legislative committees Temporary committees of the House established primarily to review a specific bill.

Legitimacy The acceptance by the people that those in positions of authority have the right to govern.

Liberal democracy A political system in which the powers of government are limited by law, the rights of the people to freely engage in political activity are well established, and fair elections are held to choose those who make governing decisions.

Liberal democracy A political system that includes the ideas of a free society, tolerance of different viewpoints, competitive elections, limited government, and the rule of law associated with liberalism combined with the democratic ideal that power should ultimately rest with the people, with each citizen being of equal political significance.

Liberal internationalist perspective The view that growing international interaction and interdependence make possible a peaceful and orderly world, particularly through the development of international law and multilateral organizations such as the United Nations.

Liberalism An ideological perspective that emphasizes the value of individual freedom based on a belief that individuals are generally capable of using reason in pursuit of their own interests.

Life-cycle effects The tendency for people to vote at higher rates as they age.

Line departments Departments that deliver the basic programs and services of government.

Lobbying An effort to influence government decisions, particularly through direct personal communication with key government decision makers.

Loyalists Americans who remained loyal to the British Crown at the time of the War of Independence. Subsequently, many Loyalists migrated to the British North American colonies.

Majority government A governing party that has a majority of seats in the House of Commons regardless of whether it received a majority of votes in an election.

Maritime rights movement A political movement in the 1920s that sought better terms for the Maritime provinces within Canada.

Marxist theory The theory that a fundamental feature of capitalist societies is an antagonistic and exploitative relationship between the capitalist class and the working class that leads to class conflict.

Meech lake accord An agreement on constitutional change reached by the prime minister and premiers in 1987 that failed to be ratified by all provincial legislatures. The accord satisfied the conditions laid out by Quebec for signing the Constitution Act, 1982, while extending the powers granted to Quebec to all provinces.

Millennium development goals Goals established by the United Nations for the development of poorer countries.

Minority government A single party forms the government, but does not have a majority of members in the House of Commons.

Mixed economy A combination of public and private ownership and control of the economy.

Mixed member proportional system An electoral system in which voters cast one vote for the party they prefer and one vote for the candidate they prefer. Some legislators represent the district in which they received the most votes, while other legislators are selected based on the proportion of votes received by their party.

Multination state A state that contains more than one nation.

Multi-party system with a dominant party One large party receives about 40 percent of the vote, and the two largest parties together win about two-thirds of voter support.

Multi-party system without a dominant party Competition where there is no dominant party and three or four parties are well- placed to form coalitions.

Nation A historical community with its own institutions, occupying a given territory or homeland, and sharing a distinct language and culture.

National energy program A Canadian government program adopted in 1980 that included keeping oil prices below the international level, increasing the Canadian government's share of oil revenues, establishing a federal Crown corporation to be involved in the oil industry, and encouraging and subsidizing oil exploration on federal lands in the Arctic and offshore Newfoundland.

National minority A culturally distinct and potentially self-governing society that has been incorporated into a larger state.

National policy A Canadian government policy adopted in 1879 that included a high tariff on the import of manufactured products, railway construction, and the encouragement of immigration to Western Canada.

National security Protection of a country from foreign threats to its population, territory, and independence.

Nation-state A state in which the population shares a single ethnic culture.

Neo-liberalism A perspective based on a strong belief in a free market system that advocates such measures as a major reduction in the role of government, including the dismantling of the welfare state, substantial reduction in taxes, and global free trade.

New deal A package of programs adopted by U.S. President Franklin Delano Roosevelt that included relief to those suffering from the Great Depression of the 1930s and reforms of the banking system.

New public management The adoption of the practices of private business in the administrative activities of government.

New social movement theory A theory that in post-industrial society new social movements have developed, particularly among the new middle class that is interested in post-materialist values such as a concern for the quality of life, identity, participation, and individual freedom.

New social movement A social movement concerned particularly with developing a collective sense of identity among those who are deemed to suffer from oppression, along with adopting new cultural values and lifestyles rather than pursuing material interests.

North american aerospace defense command A joint U.S. Canadian organization that provides for the detection of and response to an attack on North America, particularly by aircraft and missiles.

North american free trade agreement A 1992 agreement between Canada, the United States, and Mexico that established a high level of economic integration in North America.

North atlantic treaty organization A military alliance of the United States, Canada, and democratic European countries.

Notwithstanding clause A provision in the Charter of Rights and Freedoms that allows a Parliament or a provincial legislature to explicitly declare that a particular law (related to some sections of the Charter) shall operate notwithstanding the provisions of the Charter.

Oakes test A Supreme Court of Canada ruling setting out basic principles in applying the reasonable limits clause.

Officers of parliament Independent officials that assist Parliament in holding government accountable and protecting various rights of Canadians.

Official multiculturalism A policy introduced in 1971 that encouraged individuals to embrace the culture and tradition of their choice while retaining Canadian citizenship.

Open federalism The Harper Government's approach to federalism involving such measures as transferring more money to provincial governments, respecting the constitutional division of powers and provincial autonomy, and limiting the use of the federal spending power.

Parliamentary supremacy The principle that Parliament is the supreme law-making body whose ability to legislate has not been restricted by a superior constitutional document.

Party conventions Meetings of party members that are held to elect party officials and debate policy and amendments to the party's constitution.

Party discipline The expectation that parliamentary members will vote in keeping with the position that their party has adopted in caucus.

Party identification A sense of attachment to a particular political party.

Party system A pattern of electoral competition that emerges between two or more parties.

Party whips Members of each party who maintain party discipline and ensure that members attend votes.

Pay equity Laws or policies that require that equal pay be given for work of equal value.

Peace operations A wide range of activities with the aim of building and enforcing peace, including peacekeeping, peace building, and peace enforcement.

Peripheral dependence perspective The view that Canada is unable or unwilling to develop independent foreign policies because of constraints imposed by the United States.

Permanent residents Immigrants who are allowed to live in Canada and receive certain rights and privileges, while remaining a citizen of their home country. Permanent residents must pay taxes and respect all Canadian laws.

Philanthropy Charitable giving.

Plebiscitary democracy The use of referendums, initiatives, and recall procedures as an alternative to what some view as the elite-oriented nature of representative democracy.

Pluralist theory The theory that the freedom of individuals to establish and join groups that are not controlled by the government results in a variety of groups having an ability to influence the decisions of government, with no group having a dominant influence.

Policy community Government officials responsible for a particular policy area and relevant institutionalized interest groups that collaborate regularly in developing public policies.

Political culture The fundamental political values, beliefs, and orientations that are widely held within a political community.

Political discourse The ways in which politics is discussed and the rhetoric that is used in political persuasion.

Political efficacy A belief that government is responsive to the people and that they can influence what government does.

Political executive The prime minister, Cabinet, and ministers of state.

Political ideology A set of ideas, values, and beliefs about politics, society, and the economic system based on assumptions about human nature.

Political participation Actions people take to raise awareness about issues, to influence the choice of government personnel, and to shape the content of legislation and public policies.

Political party An organization that endorses one or more of its members as candidates and supports their election.

Political socialization The process by which new generations and immigrants are socialized into the political culture.

Politics Activity related to influencing, making, and implementing collective decisions.

Polyethnic right A group-based right that allows ethnic groups and religious minorities to express their cultural distinctiveness without discrimination.

Polyethnic state A state that contains many ethnic groups.

Post-materialist theory A theory that those who have grown up in relative security and affluence are more likely to give priority to post-materialist values rather than materialist values.

Post-materialist values Values such as self-expression, participation in economic and political decisions, emphasis on the quality of life, tolerance of diversity, and concern for environmental protection.

Power The ability to affect the behaviour of others particularly by getting them to act in ways that they would not otherwise have done.

Prerogative power The powers the monarch once uniquely possessed that have not been taken away by Parliament.

Prime minister The head of government, meaning the person chosen by the governor general to form a government able to retain the confidence of a majority of the elected house of Parliament, the Commons.

Prime minister's office Provides partisan political advice to the prime minister and is staffed by supporters of the party in power.

Prime minister-centred cabinet A form of cabinet organization in which the first minister is so powerful that the nominal mechanisms for collective decision making, such as cabinet committees and central agencies, serve the prime minister's personal agenda.

Principal-agent theory A theory based on the idea that the bureaucrat who is supposed to follow the will of the minister or the legislature often uses specialized knowledge to thwart this arrangement.

Private bills Proposed laws that are of concern to a limited group.

Private law Areas of law dealing with the relationships among individuals, groups, and businesses that are primarily of private interest rather than general public interest.

Private members' bills A public bill put forward by a Member of Parliament who is not in the Cabinet.

Private sector The sector of economic society that exists in a competitive environment and strives to maximize profit for private owners, be they corporations, family-owned businesses, or self-employed individuals.

Privy council office The central agency that provides non-partisan policy advice to the prime minister and Cabinet.

Procedural officers of parliament The staff who provide services to the House of Commons and Senate.

Programmatic parties Parties that articulate distinct, consistent, and coherent ideological agendas.

Progressive movement A late-nineteenth-century movement that sought to break the "spoils system" in government by making the public sector at all levels more businesslike and shielding it from the political realm.

Proportional representation system An electoral system in which the proportion of seats a party receives in the legislative body reflects the proportion of votes the party obtained.

Protest activities Political acts that include non-violent actions such as signing a petition, boycotts, peaceful marches, demonstrations, and strikes. They may sometimes involve the use of violence to damage property or harm the opponents of the cause.

Provincial courts Trial courts whose judges are appointed and paid by the provincial government.

Public bills Proposed laws that have an impact on the whole of society or are designed to promote the general welfare.

Public bureaucracy The staffs of a variety of governing institutions.

Public interest group A group that pursues goals that can be viewed as being for the public good and do not benefit members of the group exclusively.

Public law Laws concerning the relationship of the state to individuals and laws concerning the authority and operations of the state.

Public sector The institutions and agencies of the state, concerned, ideally, with acting in the public interest.

Purposive incentives Incentives to join a group based on the satisfaction that is gained by expressing one's values or promoting a cause in which one believes.

Quebec act, 1774 An act of the British Parliament that guaranteed that Catholics would be able to freely practise their religion, the privileges of the Catholic Church would be maintained, and the French system of civil (private) law would be used alongside British criminal law.

Quiet revolution A series of political, institutional, and social reforms ushered in under the Quebec Liberal leader Jean Lesage beginning in 1960.

Rational choice theory A theory based on the assumption that individuals rationally pursue their own self-interest.

Realist perspective The view that in a world without a central authority able to impose order, each country is concerned primarily with survival and security.

Reasonable limits clause A clause of the Charter of Rights and Freedoms that allows for reasonable limits on rights and freedoms, provided the limits can be demonstrably justified in a free and democratic society.

Recall A procedure that allows citizens to recall their representative and require that a new election be held, provided sufficient names are obtained on a petition.

Reference The opinion of the courts on a question asked by the federal or provincial government.

Referendum A vote by the people on a particular question asked by the government or legislative body.

Refugees People living in or outside Canada who fear persecution in their home country or whose removal from Canada to their country of origin would subject them to torture, a risk to their life, or a risk of cruel and unusual treatment.

Representative democracy A form of democracy in which citizens elect representatives to make governing decisions on their behalf.

Reservation power The right of a lieutenant governor to reserve the passage of provincial legislation until that legislation is approved by the Canadian Cabinet.

Residual power Legislative power over matters not listed in the Constitution.

Responsibility to protect The responsibility of a state to protect its population from genocide, war crimes, ethnic cleansing, and crimes against humanity and, as a last resort, the responsibility of the international community, particularly through the United Nations, to intervene if a state is unwilling or unable to protect its population.

Responsible government A governing system in which the executive is responsible to an elected, representative legislative body and must retain its support to remain in office.

Restorative justice The perspective that justice should focus on offenders taking responsibility for their actions, repairing the harm that has been caused, and reconciling the offender, the victim, and the community.

Royal commission on aboriginal peoples A Royal Commission established by the Canadian government that recommended a fundamental restructuring of the relationship between Aboriginal and settler societies based on the recognition of Aboriginal nationhood.

Royal proclamation, 1763 Established British rule over the former French colonies and placed "Indians" under the protection of the British Crown.

Rule of law The principle that individuals should be subject only to known, predictable, and impartial rules, rather than to the arbitrary orders of those in governing positions.

Scientific management A complex system of management of the production process, often associated with time and motion studies, that maintains that there is one best way to increase output.

Security council A key body of the United Nations responsible for maintaining international peace and security. It consists of five permanent members who each have a veto and ten members elected by the UN General Assembly for two-year terms.

Selective benefit A particular benefit that is made available to the members of an interest group but is not available to the public as a whole.

Self-government right A group-based right that grants a national minority some kind of territorial jurisdiction or autonomy over its political and cultural affairs.

Self-interest groups Interest groups that are primarily concerned with selective benefits that are directed toward their members.

Semi-independent public agency A government organization that has a degree of independence from executive controls and parliamentary scrutiny.

Sentencing circle A group that may include the guilty individual, the victim, their families, elders, and other interested members of the community, along with the prosecutor, defence lawyer, and police officers. The goal is to reach a consensus about what measures are needed to reintegrate the offender as a responsible member of the community and to assist the victim.

Shared-cost programs Provincial programs in which the Canadian government generally paid half the costs.

Single-member plurality electoral system An electoral system in which voters in each district elect a single representative. The candidate with the most votes is elected, regardless of whether that candidate received the majority of votes.

Social capital The networks, norms of generalized reciprocity, and trust that foster coordination and cooperation for mutual benefit.

Social class A large category of people who hold a similar position in the hierarchy of society.

Social conservatism An ideology based on a commitment to traditional ideas about the family and morality.

Social democracy A perspective that government should play an active role in reducing or eliminating inequalities, provide a wide range of public services, and ensure that businesses act in the public interest.

Social movement A network of groups and individuals that seeks major social and political changes, particularly by acting outside of established political institutions.

Social rights Rights that require government action, such as the right to education, housing, or employment.

Socialism An ideological perspective that emphasizes the value of social and economic equality and generally advocates social ownership of the major means of production.

Socio-economic status A combination of income (or wealth), education, and occupational status.

Solidary incentives Incentives to join a group for social reasons, such as the opportunities to attend meetings and interact with others.

Speaker The presiding officer of the House of Commons, who is responsible for applying the rules and procedures, maintaining order in debate, and overseeing the administration of the Commons.

Special committees Committees of the House established to study a particular issue.

Special representation rights The provision of guaranteed representation for particular groups in legislative bodies or other political institutions.

Specific claims Claims by Aboriginal groups based on allegations that treaties and other legal obligations of the Canadian government have not been fulfilled or that the Canadian government has not properly administered Aboriginal lands and other assets.

Speech from the throne Government's indication of what it considers to be the state of the country, together with a general outline of the kinds of legislation that it has planned for the parliamentary session the speech introduces.

Spending power The ability of the Canadian government to spend money as it sees fit, even on matters under provincial jurisdiction.

Standing committees Permanent committees of the House whose responsibilities include detailed examination of proposed legislation and review of departmental estimates.

State An independent self-governing country whose governing institutions are able to make and enforce rules that are binding on the people living within a particular territory.

State-centred theory The theory that the state is largely independent of social forces and thus state actors are relatively free to act on their own values and interests.

Status indians Those of Indian ancestry who are listed in the official government registry and are entitled to certain benefits, including exemption from taxation on property or income earned on the reserve.

Statute of westminster, 1931 An Act of the Parliament of the United Kingdom ending British control of Canada.

Statutory law A law that has been passed by an act of Parliament or a provincial legislature.

Strategic model of judicial decision making The view that a bargaining process among the judges takes place for them to reach a majority or a unanimous decision.

Subcultures Variations on the national political culture.

Subordinate (delegated) legislation Authority for subordinate legislation that comes from a primary piece of legislation passed by Parliament and takes the form of orders-in-council or regulations made by a minister or agency.

Superior courts Courts in each province whose judges are appointed and paid by the Canadian government.

Supply-side economics The perspective that reducing taxes on those who supply goods and services is the most effective way to achieve economic growth.

Supreme court of canada The highest judicial body in Canada since 1949.

Tariff A tax or customs duty on imported goods.

The crown The Crown is the repository of all of the executive powers of the state and is the supreme authority for government.

Third sector Voluntary, non-profit organizations that contribute to the general good of the public.

Time allocation A motion in the House of Commons that allocates the time that can be spent debating a bill.

Tort Harmful actions, negligence, or words that allow the injured party to sue for damages.

Tory touch An element of traditional conservatism that includes the defence of a hierarchical rule by a privileged elite on behalf of the collective good of the nation.

Treaty federalism The view that First Nations and the Canadian government representing later settlers should establish nation-to-nation agreements that enable the nations as co-sovereigns to coexist peacefully as autonomous entities within Canada.

Triple-e senate A proposal that the Senate be reformed to be elected and effective based on equal representation from each province regardless of population size.

Two-and-a-half party system Pattern of competition whereby two major parties win at least three-quarters of the vote, and a third party receives a much smaller share of the vote.

Two-party system A pattern of competition in which there are two, or primarily two, parties.

Victoria charter A tentative deal for constitutional change reached in 1971.

Volunteering Providing unpaid service to help others.

Welfare state A country whose governments ensure that all people have a minimum standard of living and are provided protection from hardships, including those caused by unemployment, sickness, disability, and old age.

Welfare state A state in which government ensures that all people have a minimum standard of living and receive some protection from hardships resulting from unemployment, sickness, disability, and old age.

Westminster model The model of representative and responsible government used in the United Kingdom and in other countries that emulate it.

White paper on indians A 1969 Canadian government discussion paper that proposed to end the different legal status of Indians.

Whitehall model The traditional British style of public administration with such features as ministerial responsibility, public service anonymity and neutrality, secrecy, and the merit principle.

REFERENCES

Abdelal, R., Herrera, Y., Johnston, A., & McDermott, R. (2005, July 22). *Identity as a variable*. Retrieved from http://www.wcfia. harvard.edu/sites/default/files/1076__YH_identityvariable.pdf

Abele, F., & Prince, M. J. (2007). Constructing political spaces for aboriginal communities in Canada. In I. Peach (Ed.), *Constructing tomorrow's federalism: New perspectives on Canadian governance* (pp. 171–200). Winnipeg: University of Manitoba Press.

Abelson, D. E. (2007). Any ideas? Think tanks and policy analysis in Canada. In L. Dobuzinskis, M. Howlett, & D. Laycock (Eds), *Policy analysis in Canada: The state of the art* (pp. 551–573). Toronto, ON: University of Toronto Press.

Adams, M. (2007). *Unlikely utopia: The surprising triumph of Canadian pluralism*. Toronto, ON: Viking Canada.

Albrow, M. (1991). Bureaucracy. In V. Bogdanor (Ed.), *The Blackwell encyclopedia of political science* (pp. 61–64). Oxford: Basil Blackwell.

Almond, G., & Verba, S. (1963). *The civic culture: Political attitudes and democracy in five nations*. Princeton, NJ: Princeton University Press.

Andersen, R., Curtis, J., & Grabb, E. (2006). Trends in civic association activity in four democracies: The special case of women in the United States. *American Sociological Review, 71,* 376–400.

Angus Reid Strategies. (2009, June 9). *Separation from Canada unlikely for a majority of Quebecers*. Montreal, PQ: Angus Reid Strategies.

Anti-Inflation Reference 2 S.C.R. 373 (1976).

Aucoin, P. (1995). *The new public management: Canada in comparative perspective* Montreal, QC: Institute for Research on Public Policy.

Aucoin, P., Smith, J., & Dinsdale, G. (2004). *Responsible government: Clarifying essentials, dispelling myths and exploring change.* Ottawa, ON: Canadian Centre for Management Development.

Axworthy, L. (1997). Canada and human security: The need for leadership. *International Journal, 52*(2), 183–196.

Axworthy, L. (2003). *Navigating a new world. Canada's global future.* Toronto, ON: Knopf.

Axworthy, T. S. (2008). *Everything old is new again: Observations on parliamentary reform.* Kingston, ON: Centre for the Study of Democracy, Queen's University.

Ayers, J. M. (1998). *Defying conventional wisdom: Political movements and popular contention against North American free trade.* Toronto, ON: University of Toronto Press.

Badescu, C. G. (2007). Authorizing humanitarian intervention: Hard choices in saving strangers. *Canadian Journal of Political Science,40,* 51–78.

Bakvis, H., & Skogstad, G. (Eds.). (2008). *Canadian federalism: Performance, effectiveness, and legitimacy* (2nd ed.). Don Mills, ON: Oxford University Press.

Bakvis, H., Baier, G., & Brown, D.M. (2009). *Contested federalism: Certainty and ambiguity in the Canadian federation.* Don Mills, ON: Oxford University Press.

Ball, T., Dagger, R., Christian, W., & Campbell, C. (2010). *Political Ideologies and the democratic ideal* (2nd Canadian ed.). Toronto, ON: Pearson Education Canada.

Bantjes, R. (2007). *Social movements in a global context: Canadian perspectives.* Toronto, ON: Canadian Scholars' Press.

Barker, T. (2008, June 6). Background: Canada's new Chief of Defence Staff Lt.-Gen. Walter T. Natynczyk. *National Post.* Retrieved from http://network.nationalpost.com/np/blogs/posted/ archive/2008/06/06/background-canada-s-new-chief-of-defence-staff-lt-gen-walter-j-natynczyk.aspx

Barney, D. (2000). *Prometheus wired: The hope for democracy in the age of network technology.* Vancouver: UBC Press.

Barsh, R. (1994). Canada's Aboriginal peoples: Social integration or disintegration? *Canadian Journal of Native Studies, 14*(1), 1–46.

Barsh, R., Fraser, M., Bull, F., Provost, T., & Smith, K. (1997). The Prairie Indian vote in Canadian politics 1965–1993: A critical case study from Alberta. *Great Plains Research, 7*(1), 3–26.

Batson, C. D., Jasnoski, M. L., & Hanson, M. (1978). Buying kindness: Effect of an extrinsic incentive for helping on perceived altruism. *Journal of Personality and Social Psychology, 40,* 86–91.

Baum, M. (2002). Sex, lies, and war: How soft news brings foreign policy to the inattentive public. *American Political Science Review, 96,* 91–109.

Bazowski, R. (2004). The judicialization of Canadian politics. In J. Bickerton & A.-G. Gagnon (Eds.), *Canadian politics* (4th ed., pp. 203–223). Peterborough, ON: Broadview Press.

B.C. Ministry of Education. (2008). *Program guide for graduation transitions.* Victoria: Author.

Beck. J. M. (1968). *Pendulum of power:. Canada's general elections.* Scarborough, ON: Prentice-Hall.

Bedford, D. (2003). Aboriginal voter participation in Nova Scotia and New Brunswick. *Electoral Insight, 5*(3), 16–20.

Bedford, D. (in press). Emancipation as oppression: The Marshall Decision and self-government. *Journal of Canadian Studies.*

Belanger, P., Carty, K., & Eagles, M. (2003). The geography of Canadian parties' electoral campaigns: Leaders' tours and constituency election results. *Political Geography, 22,* 439–455.

Belanger, Y. (Ed.). (2008). *Aboriginal self-government in Canada. Current trends and issues* (3rd ed.). Saskatoon, SK: Purich.

Bell, D. V. J. (1992). *The roots of disunity. A study of Canadian political culture* (rev. ed.). Toronto, ON: Oxford University Press.

Bellamy, A. (2009). Realizing the responsibility to protect. *International Studies Perspectives, 10,* 111–128.

Benevides, H. (2008). Tribute to Charles Caccia. Retrieved from the Canadian Environmental Law Association website: http://www.cela.ca/article/canadian-environmental-protection-act-1999-first-cepa-review/tribute-charles-caccia-1930-200

Bercuson D., & Carment, D. (Eds.). (2008). *The world in Canada: Diaspora, demography, and domestic politics.* Montreal, QC: McGill-Queen's University Press.

Bernard, P. (2006). Canada and human security: From the Axworthy doctrine to middle power internationalism. *American Review of Canadian Studies, 36,* 233–261.

Berthiaume, L. (2009, February 18). *Embassy.* Full steam ahead on spreading democracy Retrieved from http://www.embassymag.ca/mobile/story/spreading_democracy-2-18-200

Berton, P. (1994). *Winter.* Toronto, ON: Stoddart.

Bickerton, J., & Gagnon, A.-G. (Eds.). (2004). *Canadian politics* (4th ed.). Peterborough, ON: Broadview Press.

Big Drug Mart Ltd. 1 S.C.R 295 (1985).

Bisoondath, N. (1994). *Selling illusions: The cult of multiculturalism in Canada.* Toronto, ON: Penguin.

Black, J. (2008). The 2006 federal election and visible minority candidates: More of the same? *Canadian Parliamentary Review, 31*(3), 30–36.

Black, J., & Erickson, L. (2006). Ethno-racial origins of Canadians and electoral performance. *Party Politics, 12,* 541–561.

Black, J., & Hicks, B. (2006). Visible minority candidates in the 2004 election. *Canadian Parliamentary Review, 29*(2), 26–31.

Blais, A. (2000). *To vote or not to vote? The merits and limits of rational choice.* Pittsburgh, PA: University of Pittsburgh Press.

Blais, A., & Carty, K. (1990). Does proportional representation foster voter turnout? *European Journal of Political Research, 18*(20), 167–182.

Blais, A., Gidengil, E., Dobryznska, A., Nevitte, N, & Nadeau, R. (2003). Does the local candidate matter? Candidate effects in the Canadian election of 2000. *Canadian Journal of Political Science, 36,* 657–664.

Blais, A., Gidengil, E., Nadeau, R., & Nevitte, N. (2002). *Anatomy of a Liberal victory. Making sense of the vote in the 2000 Canadian election.* Peterborough, ON: Broadview Press.

Blatchford, A. (2007, March 31). FIFA should have overruled hijab ban: Ejected girl's mother says. *The Globe and Mail.* Retrieved from http://www.theglobeandmail.com/news/national/article744823.ece

Bloemraad, I. (2006). *Becoming a citizen: Incorporating immigrants and refugees in the United States and Canada.* Berkeley: University of California Press.

Blondel, J. (1968). Party systems and patterns of government in western democracies. *Canadian Journal of Political Science 1*(2), 180–203. doi:10.1017/S0008423900036507

Blonigen, B. A. (2005). The effects of NAFTA on antidumping and countervailing duty actions. *World Bank Economic Review, 19,* 407–424.

Board of Commerce 1 A.C. 191 (1922).

Boatright, R. G. (2009). Interest group adaptations to campaign finance reform in Canada and the United States. *Canadian Journal of Political Science*, 42, 17–44.

Bothwell, R. (1998). *Canada and Quebec: One country, two histories.* Vancouver: UBC Press

Bothwell, R., Drummond, I., & English, J. (1989). *Canada since 1945:. Politics, power and provincialism* (rev. ed.). Toronto, ON: University of Toronto Press.

Boyd, D. R. (2003). Unnatural law: Rethinking Canadian environmental law and policy. Vancouver: UBC Press.

Boyd, M. (2004). Executive summary. *Dispute resolution in family law: Protecting choice, promoting inclusion.* Retrieved from the Ontario Ministry of the Attorney General website: www.attorneygeneral.jus.gov.on.ca/english/about/pubs/boyd/executivesummary.pdf

Brodie, J., & Jenson, J. (1980). *Crisis, challenge, and change: Party and class in Canada.* Toronto, ON: Methuen.

Brodie, J., & Jenson, J. (1988). *Crisis, challenge and change: Party and class in Canada revisited.* Ottawa, ON: Carleton University Press.

Brown, S. (2009). The green vote in Canada. In D. VanNijnatten & R. Boardman, (Eds.), *Canadian Environmental Policy and Politics* (3rd ed., pp. 14–28). Don Mills, ON: Oxford University Press.

Bumsted, J. M. (2003a). *Canada's diverse peoples: A reference sourcebook.* Santa Barbara, CA: ABC CLIO.

Bumsted, J. M. (2003b). *The peoples of Canada. A pre-Confederation history* (2nd ed.). Don Mills, ON: Oxford University Press.

Bumstead, J. M. (2004). *The peoples of Canada: A post-Confederation history* (2nd ed.). Don Mills, ON: Oxford University Press.

Bumsted, J. M. (2008). *The peoples of Canada. A post-Confederation history* (3rd ed.). Don Mills, ON: Oxford University Press.

Cairns, A. C. (1968). The electoral system and the party system in Canada, 1921–1965. *Canadian Journal of Political Science, 1,* 55–80.

Cairns, A. C. (1977). The governments and societies of Canadian federalism. *Canadian Journal of Political Science, 10,* 695–725.

Cairns, A. C. (1992). *The charter versus federalism: The dilemmas of constitutional reform.* Montreal, QC: McGill-Queen's University Press.

Cairns, A. C. (2000). *Citizens plus: Aboriginal peoples and the Canadian state.* Vancouver: UBC Press.

Cairns, A. C. (2003). Aboriginal people's electoral participation in the Canadian community. *Electoral Insight, 5*(3), 2–9.

Cairns, A. C. (2004). First Nations and the Canadian nation: Colonization and constitutional alienation. In J. Bickerton & A.-G. Gagnon (Eds.), *Canadian politics* (4th ed., pp. 439–455) Peterborough, ON: Broadview Press.

Calder v. Attorney General of British Columbia CanLII 4, (S.C.C., 1973).

Cameron, D., & Simeon, R. (2002). Intergovernmental relations in Canada: The emergence of collaborative federalism. *Publius: The Journal of Federalism, 32*(2):49–72.

Campbell, C. (1978). *The Canadian Senate: A lobby from within.* Toronto, ON: Macmillan.

Campbell et al. v. Nisga'a, BCSC 619 (CanLII, 2000).

Canada, Ontario announce $4B auto aid package. (2008, December 20). *CBC News.* Retrieved from http://www.cbc.ca/canada/story/2008/12/20/auto-package.html

Canadian Broadcasting Corporation. (2004). *CBC/RadioCanada pre-election poll.* Retrieved from http://www.cbc.ca/canadavotes/thepolls/democracypoll.htm

Canadian Election Study. (2004, 2006). *Surveys,* Retrieved from http://ces-eec.mcgill.ca/surveys.html

Canadian Heritage/Decima. (2006). *Official language annual report 2005–2006.* Official Languages Support Programs. Ottawa, ON: Canadian Heritage.

Canadian Human Rights Commission. (2009). *2008 Annual Report.* Ottawa: Author. Retrieved from http://www.chrc-ccdp.ca/publications/ar_2008_ra/ar_08_ra-en.asp

Canadian Parents for French. (2006–2007). National French immersion enrolment. *Enrolment trends 2006–2007.* Retrieved from http://www.cpf.ca/eng/resources-reports-enrolment-0607.html

Cardinal, H. (1969). *The unjust society: The tragedy of Canada's Indians.* Edmonton, AB: Hurtig.

Carrigan, D. O. (1968). *Canadian party platforms 1867–1968.* Urbana: University of Illinois Press.

Carroll, W. K. (2004). *Corporate power in a globalizing world: A study in elite social organization.* Don Mills, ON: Oxford University Press.

Carty, K. (1991). *Canadian political parties in the constituencies.* Toronto, ON: Dundurn Press.

Carty, K. (2006). The shifting place of political parties in Canadian political life. *Choices, 12*(4), 3–13.

Carty, K., Cross, W., & Young, L. (2000). *Rebuilding Canadian party politics.* Vancouver: UBC Press.

Castells, M. (1997). *The power of identity.* Cambridge, MA: Blackwell.

Center for Research and Information on Canada. (2002). *Portraits of Canada, 2002.* Retrieved from http://www.cric.ca/pdf/cahiers/cricpapers_dec2002.pdf

Chaoulli 1 S.C.R. 791 (2005).

Chase, S., & Perkins, T. (2009, October 8). How a scattered army of insurance brokers outmuscled the Big Five. *The Globe and Mail.* Retrieved from http://www.theglobeandmail.com/report-on-business/how-a-scattered-army-of-insurance-brokers-outmuscled-the-big-five/article1317631/

Christian, W., & Campbell, C. (1990). *Political parties and ideologies in Canada* (3rd ed.). Toronto, ON: McGraw-Hill Ryerson.

Chui, T., Tran, K., & Maheux, L. (2007). 2006 census: Immigration in Canada: A Portrait of the Foreign-born Population. *2006 Census: Findings* (Catalogue No. 97-557-XIE2006001). Retrieved from http://www12.statcan.ca/census-recensement/2006/as-sa/97-557/figures/c2-eng.cfm

CIDA. (1996). *Policy for CIDA on human rights, democratization and good governance.* Retrieved from http://www.acdi-cida.gc.ca/CIDAWEB/acdicida.nsf/En/REN-218124821-P93#sec2

CIDA. (2005). Canada's International Policy Statement. Retrieved from http://www.acdi-cida.gc.ca/ips-development#61a

Citizenship and Immigration Canada. (2008). In Canada asylum program. *The refugee system in Canada.* Retrieved from http://www.cic.gc.ca/english/refugees/canada.asp

Citizenship and Immigration Canada. (2009). The Multiculturalism Program. *Application guidelines for funding "Promoting Integration."* Retrieved from http://www.cic.gc.ca/english/multiculturalism/funding/guide/101-eng.asp#a2

Clancy, P. (2008). Business interests and civil society in Canada. In M. Smith (ed.), *Group politics and social movements in Canada.* Peterborough, ON: Broadview Press.

Clark, W. (2003). *Immigrants and the American dream: Remaking the middle class.* New York, NY: Guildford.

Clarke, H.D., Jenson, J., LeDuc, L., & Pammett, J. (1996). *Absent mandate: Canadian electoral politics in an era of restructuring* (3rd ed.). Toronto, ON: Gage.

Clarke, H. D., Kornberg, A, & Scotto, T. J. (2006). *Measuring political efficacy with positive overtones: A survey experiment.* Paper presented to the Midwest Political Science Association. Retrieved from http://allacademic.com/meta/p137157_index.html

Clarke, H. D., Kornberg, A., & Scotto, T. S. (2009a). *Making political choices: Canada and the United States.* Toronto, ON: University of Toronto Press.

Clarke, H. D., Kornberg, A., & Scotto, T. J. (2009b). None of the above: Voters in the 2008 federal election. In J. H. Pammett & C. Dornan (Eds.), *The Canadian federal election of 2008.* Toronto, ON: Dundurn Press.

Clarke, H. D., LeDuc, L.; Jenson, J.; & Pammett, J. (1979). *Political Choice in Canada.* Toronto: McGraw-Hill.

Clarke, H. D., LeDuc, L.; Jenson, J.; & Pammett, J. (1991). *Absent mandate. Interpreting change in Canadian elections* (2nd ed.). Toronto: Gage.

Clarke, H., Jenson, J., LeDuc, L., & Pammett, J. (1979). *Political choice in Canada.* Toronto, ON: McGraw.

Clarke, H., Jenson, J., LeDuc, L., & Pammett, J. (1984). *Absent mandate: The politics of discontent in Canada.* Toronto, ON: Gage.

Clarke, H., Jenson, J., LeDuc, L., & Pammett, J. (1991). *Absent mandate: Interpreting change in Canadian elections* (2nd ed.). Toronto, ON: Gage.

Clarke, H., Jenson, J., LeDuc, L., & Pammett, J. (1996). *Absent mandate: Canadian electoral politics in an era of restructuring* (3rd ed.). Toronto, ON: Gage.

Clarke, H., Kornberg, A., & Wearing, P. (2000). *A Polity on the edge: Canada and the politics of fragmentation.* Peterborough, ON: Broadview Press.

Clarkson, S. (1979). Democracy in the Liberal Party: The experiment with citizen participation under Pierre Trudeau. In H. Thorburn, (Ed.), *Party Politics in Canada* (4th ed.). Scarborough, ON: Prentice-Hall.

Clarkson, S. (2001). The Liberal threepeat: The multi-system party in the multi-party system. In J. Pammett & C. Dornan (Eds.), *The Canadian general election of 2000* (pp. 13–58). Toronto, ON: Dundurn Press.

Clarkson, S. (2006). How the big red machine became the little red machine. In J. H. Pammett & C. Dornan (Eds.), *The Canadian general election of 2006.* Toronto, ON: Dundurn.

Clarkson, S. (2008). *Does North America exist? Governing the continent after NAFTA and 9/11.* Toronto, ON: University of Toronto Press.

Clarkson, S., & McCall, C. (1994). *Trudeau and our times: Vol. 2. The heroic delusion.* Toronto, ON: McClelland & Stewart.

Clement, W. (1977). Continental corporate power: Economic elite linkages between Canada and the United States. Toronto, ON: McClelland & Stewart.

Coleman, W. D., & Skogstad, G. (1990). Policy communities and policy networks in Canada: A structural approach. In W. D. Coleman & G. Skogstad (Eds.), *Policy communities and public policy in Canada: A structural approach* (pp. 14–33). Toronto, ON: Copp Clark Pitman.

Conference Board of Canada. (2008). *How Canada performs.* Retrieved from http://www.conferenceboard.ca/HCP/default.aspx

Connor, W. (1972). *Ethnonationalism: The quest for understanding.* Princeton, NJ: Princeton University Press.

Conrad, M., & Finkel, A. (2007). *Canada: A national history.* Toronto, ON: Pearson.

Cook, R., (with Ricker, J., & Saywell, J). (1977). *Canada: A modern study.* Toronto, ON: Clarke Irwin.

Cooper, A. F. (2009). Redefining the core ingredients of Canadian foreign policy. In J. Bickerton & A.-G. Gagnon (Eds.), *Canadian politics* (5th ed., pp. 359–372). Toronto: University of Toronto Press.

Cooper, B. (1984). Western political consciousness. In S. Brooks (Ed.), *Political thought in Canada: Contemporary perspectives.* Toronto, ON: Irwin.

Corak, M. (2008). Immigration in the long run: The education and earnings mobility of second generation Canadians. *Choices 14*(13).

Corbeil, J., & Blaser, C. (2007). 2006 census: The evolving linguistic portrait, 2006 census: Findings. Statistics Canada (Catalogue no. 97-555-XWE2006001). Retrieved from http://census2006.ca/census-recensement/2006/as-sa/97-555/index-eng.cfm

Córdova Guillén, A. (2008). Social trust, economic inequality, and democracy in the Americas. In M. Seligsen (Ed.) *Challenges to democracy in Latin America and the Caribbean: Evidence from the Americas Barometer 2006–07* (pp. 153–154). Nashville TN: Vanderbilt University.

Council of Canadian Academies. (2009). *Innovation and business strategy: Why Canada falls short: Report of the expert panel on business innovation in Canada.* Retrieved from http://www.scienceadvice.ca/documents/(2009-06-11)%20Innovation% 20Report.pdf

Court Challenges Program of Canada. (2007). *Annual report 2006–2007*. Retrieved from http://www.ccppcj.ca/documents/CCPC-AR2007

Courtney, J. (1973). The selection of national party leaders in Canada. Toronto, ON: Macmillan.

Courtney, J. C. (1995). *Do conventions matter? Choosing national party leaders in Canada*. Montreal, QC: McGill-Queen's University Press.

Courtney, J. C. (2004). *Elections*. Vancouver: UBC Press.

Craig, G. (Ed.) *Lord Durham's Report*. Toronto, ON: Carleton Library.

Craig, J. D. R. (1997). Invasion of privacy and Charter values. *McGill Law Journal, 42*, 355–396.

Crête, J., & Lachapelle, G. (2001). The Bloc Québécois. In H. Thorburn (Ed.), *Party politics in Canada* (8th ed., pp. 292–301) Scarborough, ON: Prentice Hall.

Cross, W. (2004). *Political parties*. Vancouver: UBC Press.

Cross, W., & Young, L. (2002). Policy attitudes of party members in Canada: Evidence of ideological politics. *Canadian Journal of Political Science, 35,* 859–880.

Cross, W., & Young, L. (2004). Contours of party membership in Canada. *Party Politics, 10*(40), 427–444.

Cross, W., & Young, L. (2006). Are Canadian political parties empty vessels? Membership, engagement and policy capacity. *Choices, 12*(4), 14–28.

CTV Inc. (2008, October 3). Canada Votes CTV No. 1 for 2008 Debate Coverage. Retrieved from http://newswire.ca/en/releases/archive/October2008/03/c3225.html

Curry, B. (2009, March 3). Secret documents reveal sweeping new rules for natives. *The Globe and Mail.*

Dahl, R. A. (1998). *On democracy*. New Haven, CT: Yale University Press.

Dalton, R. (2000). The decline of party identifications. In R. Dalton & M. Wattenberg (Eds.), *Parties without partisans: Political change in advanced industrial democracies* (pp. 19–36). Oxford, UK: Oxford University Press.

Dalton, R. J. (2006). *Citizen politics: Public opinion and political parties in advanced industrial democracies* (4th ed.). Washington, DC: CQ Press.

Dalton, R. J., McAllister, I., & Wattenberg, M. P. (2000). The consequences of partisan dealignment. In R. J. Dalton & M. P. Wattenberg (Eds.), *Parties without partisans: Political change in advanced industrial democracies* (pp. 37-63). Oxford, UK: Oxford University Press.

Davis Inlet: Innu Community in Crisis. (2005). *CBC Digital Archives.* Retrieved from http://archives.cbc.ca/society/poverty/topics/1671/

Davis, J. (2009, July 1). Liberal-era diplomatic language killed off. *Embassy.* Retrieved from http://www.embassymag.ca/page/view/diplomatic_language-7-1-2009

Dawson, R. M. (1929). *The civil service of Canada*. London, UK: Oxford University Press.

Deibert, R. (2002). The politics of internet design securing the foundations for global civil society networks. Retrieved from http://www.pinkcandyproductions.com/portfolio/conferences/globalization/pdfs/deibert.pdf

Delgamuukw v. British Columbia CanLII 302 (S.C.C, 1997).

Democracy Watch. (2008). *Summary of the 90 undemocratic and accountability loopholes in Canada's federal government.* Retrieved from http://www.dwatch.ca/camp/SummaryOfLoopholes.html

Department of Canadian Heritage. (2007). *Official languages annual report volume 1: Official languages support programs.* Ottawa, ON: Author.

Department of Citizenship and Immigration Canada. (2009). *Rating guidelines*. Ottawa, ON: Author.

Department of Finance Canada. (2009). *Federal support to provinces and territories*. Retrieved from http://www.fin.gc.ca/fedprov/mtp-eng.asp

Department of Justice. (2009a). *Employment Equity Act* (1995, c. 44). Ottawa, ON: Author. Retrieved from http://laws.justice.gc.ca/en/E-5.401/index.html.

Department of Justice. (2009b). How the courts are organized. *The Canadian Court System.* Retrieved from http://justicecanada.ca/eng/dept-min/pub/ccs-ajc/page3.html

deToqueville, A. (1969). Democracy in America (Rev. ed., trans. H. Reeve). New York, NY: Colonial Press. (Original work published in 1900)

Deutsch, K., & Foltz, W. (Eds.) (1963). *Nation-building*. New York, NY: Atherton Press.

Dewar, E. (1995). *Cloak of green: The links between key environmental groups, government, and big business*. Toronto, ON: Lorimer.

Dewing, M., & Leman, M. (2006). *Canadian multiculturalism.* Library of Parliament. Retrieved from http://www.parl.gc.ca/information/library/PRBpubs/936-e.htm

Dicey, A. V. (1965). *The law of the Constitution* (10th ed.). New York, NY: St. Martin's Press.

Dickason, O. P. (with McNab, D. T.). (2009). *Canada's first nations: A history of founding peoples from earliest times* (4th ed.). Don Mills, ON: Oxford University Press.

Dobrowolsky, A. (2008). The women's movement in flux: Feminism and framing, passion and politics. In M. Smith, (Ed.), *Group politics and social movements in Canada* (pp. 159–180). Peterborough, ON: Broadview Press.

Dobuzinskis, L. (2007). Back to the future? Is there a case for re-establishing the Economic Council and/or the Science Council? In L. Dobuzinskis, M. Howlett, & D. Laycock (Eds.), *Policy analysis in Canada. The state of the art* (pp. 315–350).Toronto, ON: University of Toronto Press.

Docherty, D. C. (2002). Our changing understanding of representation in Canada. In N. Nevitte (Ed.), *Value change and governance in Canada* (pp. 165–206). Toronto, ON: University of Toronto Press.

Docherty, D. C. (2005). *Legislatures*. Vancouver: UBC Press.

Doern, G. B. (2002). Environment Canada as a networked institution. In D. L. VanNijnatten & R. Boardman (Eds.), *Canadian environmental policy: Ecosystems, politics and process* (2nd ed., pp. 107-122). Toronto, ON: Oxford University Press.

Doern, G. B. & Tomlin, B. (1991). *Faith and fear: The free trade story*. Toronto, ON: Stoddart.

D'Ombrain, N. (2007). Cabinet secrecy. *Canadian Public Administration, 47,* 332–359.

Dunn, C. (1995). *The institutionalized cabinet: Governing the western provinces*. Montreal, QC: McGill-Queen's University Press.

Dunn, C., & Bierling G.. (2009). Les sous-ministres des gouvernements provinciax canadiens comme figures archétypales." *Téléscope: Revue d'analyse comparée en administration publique, 15*(1), 65–78. Retrieved from http://www.observatoire.enap.ca/OBSERVATOIRE/docs/Telescope/Volumes12-15/Telv15n1_pouvoir_desAP.pdf

Dupré, J. S. (1985). Reflections on the workability of executive federalism. In R. Simeon (Ed.), *Intergovernmental relations* (pp. 1–32). Toronto, ON: University of Toronto Press.

Duverger, M. (1954). *Political parties*. London, UK: Methuen.

Duverger, M. (1959). *Political parties, their organization and activity in the modern state* (2nd ed., B. & R. North, Trans.). London, UK: Methuen.

Dyck, R. (2008). *Canadian politics. Critical approaches* (5th ed.). Toronto, ON: Thomson Nelson.

Dyer-Witherford, N. (2005). Canadian cyberactivism in the cycle of counterglobalization struggles. In D. Skinner, J. R. Compton, &

M. Gasher (Eds), *Converging media, diverging politics: A political economy of news media in the United States and Canada* (pp. 267–290). Lanham, MD: Lexington Books.

Edwards v. A.G. of Canada S.C.R. 276 (1928).

Edwards v. A.G. of Canada A.C. 124 (1930).

Ehrman, E. (2009, September 8). From Facebook to casebook . . . Privacy violations spark legal action. *The Huffington Post.* Retrieved from http://www.huffingtonpost.com/eric-ehrmann/from-facebook-to-casebook_b_278888.html

87 percent approve of Williams, PCs: poll. (2008, June 5). *CBC News.* Retrieved from http://www.cbc.ca/canada/newfoundland-labrador/story/2008/06/05/williams-poll.html

Elections Canada advocates online voting to increase turnout. (2009, June 27). *CBC News.* Retrieved from: http://www.cbc.ca/canada/story/2009/06/27/online-voting.htm

Elections BC. (2005). *2005 Provincial general election post event review—Executive summary.* Victoria: Author.

Elections Canada. (1997). *36th general election official voting results: Synopsis.* Retrieved from http://www.elections.ca/content.asp?section=gen&document=synopsis03&dir=rep/dec3097&lang=e&textonly=false

Elections Canada. (1997). *A History of the vote in Canada.* Retrieved from http://www.elections.ca

Elections Canada. (2003). *37th general election official voting results: Synopsis.* Retrieved from http://www.elections.ca/content.asp?section=gen&document=synopsis03&dir=rep/37g&lang=e&textonly=false

Elections Canada. (2004). *38th general election official voting results.* Retrieved from http://www.elections.ca/scripts/OVR2004/default.html

Elections Canada. (2006). *Final list of confirmed candidates—39th general election.* Retrieved from http://www.elections.ca/content.asp?section=med&document=jan0506b&dir= pre&lang=e&textonly=false

Elections Canada. (2008a). *Estimation of voter turnout by age group at the 39th federal general election, January 23, 2006.* Retrieved from http://www.elections.ca/loi/res/rep39ge/estimation39ge_e.pdf

Elections Canada. (2008b). *Fortieth general election 2008: Official voting results.* Retrieved from http://www.elections.ca/content.asp?section=pas&document=index&dir=40ge&lang=e

Elections Canada. (2009). *40th general election 2008: Official voting results, 2008.* Retrieved from http://www.elections.ca/scripts/OVR2008/default.html

Elections Canada. (2009). *Third party election advertising reports for the 40th general election.* Retrieved from http://www.elections.ca/content.asp?section=pol&document= index&dir=thi/tp40&lang=e

Elections Canada. (n. d.). *Information from past elections.* Retrieved from http://www.elections.ca/intro.asp?section=pas&document=index&lang=e

Electoral Commission. (2005). *Understanding electoral registration: The extent and nature of non-registration in Britain.* Retrieved from www.electoralcommission.org.uk/templates/search/document.cfm/13545

$11-billion rift found on equalization: economist:. Tougher interpretation could see Atlantic Accord benefits end in 2012. (2007, April 13). *CBC News.* Retrieved from http://www.cbc.ca/canada/newfoundland-labrador/story/2007/04/13/equalization.html

Erickson, L. (1998). Entry to the Commons: Parties, recruitment and the election of women in 1993. In M. Tremblay & C. Andrew (Eds.), *Women and political representation in Canada.* Ottawa, ON: University of Ottawa Press.

Eulau, H. (1978). Changing views of representation. In J. Walkhe and A. Abramowitz (Eds.). *The politics of representation: Continuities in theory and research* (pp. 31–53). Beverly Hills, CA: Sage.

Evans, B., & Shields, J. (2002). The third sector: Neo-liberal restructuring, governance, and the remaking of state-civil society relationships. In C. Dunn (Ed.), *The handbook of Canadian public administration.* Toronto, ON: Oxford University Press.

Farrell, D., & Webb, P. (2000). Political parties as campaign organizations. In R. Dalton & M. Wattenberg (Eds.), *Parties without partisans: Political change in advanced industrial democracies* (pp. 102–128). Oxford, UK: Oxford University Press.

Father of girls who froze to death gets 3 years in prison. (2009, March 6). *CBC News.* Retrieved from http://www.cbc.ca/canada/saskatchewan/story/2009/03/06/sk-pauchay-sentence.html

Fearon, J. (2003). Ethnic and cultural diversity by country. *Journal of Economic Growth, 8,* 195–222.

Feehan, J. (2009) The Churchill Falls contract: What happened and what's to come. *Newfoundland Quarterly, 101*(4), pp. 35–38.

Finding their voice: Aboriginals in Canada. (2008, June 14–20). *The Economist.*

Flanagan, T. (2000). *First nations? Second thoughts.* Montreal, QC: McGill-Queen's University Press.

Flanagan, T. (2001). From Reform to the Canadian Alliance. In H. Thorburn, (Ed.), *Party politics in Canada* (8th ed., (pp. 280–291). Scarborough, ON: Prentice Hall.

Flanagan, T. (2009, January 10). Only voters have the right to decide on the coalition. *The Globe and Mail.* January 10, 2009.

Flanigan, T. & Jansen, H. J. (2009). Election campaigns under Canada's party finance laws. In J. H. Pammett & C. Dornan (Eds.), *The Canadian federal election of 2008.* Toronto, ON: Dundurn Press.

Fleras, A. (2005). *Social problems in Canada: Conditions, constructions and challenges* (4th ed.). Toronto, ON: Pearson.

Focus Canada. (2006). *Canadians' attitudes toward Muslims.* Toronto, ON: Environics.

Fontaine, P. (1990, October 30). Shocking testimony of sexual abuse. *The Journal.* CBC Digital Archives. Retrieved from http://archives.cbc.ca/society/education/clips/11177/

Food Banks Canada. (2008). *Hunger count 2008.* Retrieved on from http://www.foodbankscanada.ca/documents/HungerCount_en_fin.pdf

Forbes, H. D. (1987). Hartz-Horowitz at twenty: Nationalism, toryism, and socialism in Canada and the United States. *Canadian Journal of Political Science, 20*(2), 287–315.

Forsey, E., & Eglinton, G. C. (1985). *The question of confidence in responsible government.* Ottawa, ON: Special Committee on the Reform of the House of Commons.

Fort Frances Pulp and Power Co. v. Manitoba Free Press A.C. 695 (1923).

Fortin, S. (2009). From the Canadian social union to the federal social union of Canada, 1990–2006. In A.-G. Gagnon (Ed.), *Contemporary Canadian federalism: Foundations, traditions, institutions* (pp. 303–329). Toronto, ON: University of Toronto Press.

Frideres, J. (2008). Creating an inclusive society: Promoting social integration in Canada. In J. Biles, M. Burstein, & J, Frideres (Eds), *Immigration and integration in Canada in the twenty-first century* (pp. 77–101). Montreal, QC: McGill-Queen's University Press.

Friedenberg, E. Z. (1980). *Deference to authority: The case of Canada.* White Plains, NY: Sharpe.

Friends of Clayoquot Sound. (2006). *Clayoquot sound not saved.* Retrieved from http://www.focs.ca/news/060801_PRwatershed.pdf

Gagnon, A-G., & Tanguay, A. B. (2007). *Canadian parties in transition* (3rd ed.). Toronto, ON: University of Toronto Press.

Gall, G. (2004. The Canadian legal system (5th ed.) Toronto, ON: Thomson Carswell.

Galt, V. (2007, January 22). Most trusted professionals: The fire-fighters, not the CEO. *The Globe and Mail.*

Garcea, J. (2003). The construction and constitutionalization of Canada's citizenship regime: Reconciliation of diversity and equality. *Canadian Diversity, 2*(1), 59–63

Gay, O. (2003). *Officers of Parliament—A comparative perspective* (Research Paper 03/77). Retrieved from the House of Commons Library website: http://www.parliament.uk/commons/lib/research/rp2003/rp03-077.pdf

Gibbins, R. (1999). Taking stock: Canadian federalism and its constitutional framework. In L. Pal (Ed.), *How Ottawa spends, 1999–2000.* Toronto, ON: Oxford University Press.

Gibbins, R. & Arrison, S. (1995). *Western visions: Perspectives on the west in Canada.* Peterborough, ON: Broadview Press.

Gibson, D. (2005). Bible Bill and the money barons: The social Credit court references and their constitutional consequences. In R. Connors & J. M. Law (Eds.). *Forging Alberta's constitutional framework* (pp. 191–236). Edmonton: University of Alberta Press.

Giddens, A. (1994). *Beyond left and right: The future of radical politics.* London, UK: Polity.

Gidengil, E., & Blais, A. (2007). Are party leaders becoming more important to vote choice in Canada? In H. J. Michelmann, D.C. Story, & J. S. Steeves (Eds.), *Political leadership and representation in Canada: Essays in honour of John C. Courtney.* Toronto, ON: University of Toronto Press.

Gidengil, E., Blais, A., Everitt, J., Fournier, P., & Nevitte, N. (2005). Missing the message: Young *Adults and the Election Issues.Electoral Insight, 7,* 6–11.

Gidengil, E., Blais, A., Everitt, J., Fournier, P., & Nevitte, N. (2006a). Back to the future? Making sense of the 2004 Canadian election outside Quebec. *Canadian Journal of Political Science, 39,* 1–25.

Gidengil, E., Blais, A., Everitt, J., Fournier, P., & Nevitte, N. (2006b). *Long-term predisposition or short-term attitude? A panel-based comparison of party identification measures.* Paper prepared for presentation in the Beyond Party Identification and Beyond Workshop at the Joint Sessions of the European Consortium for Political Research, Nicosia. Available at http://ces-eec.mcgill.ca/documents/Long_Term_Predisposition.pdf

Gidengil, E., Blais, A., Nevitte, N., & Nadeau, R. (2004). *Citizens.* Vancouver, BC: University of British Columbia Press.

Gidengil, E., Fournier, P. Everitt, J., Nevitte, N., & Blais, A. (2009). *The anatomy of a Liberal defeat.* Paper prepared for presentation at the annual meeting of the Canadian Political Science Association, May 2009. Retrieved from http://ces-eec.mcgill.ca/publications.html

Gillmor, D., Menaud, A., & Turgeon, P. (2001). *Canada: A people's history* (Vol. 2). Toronto, ON: McClelland & Stewart.

Gillmor, D., & Turgeon, P. (2000). *Canada: A people's history* (Vol. 1). Toronto, ON: McClelland & Stewart.

Gillmor, D., Michaud, A., & Turgeon, P. (2001). *Canada: A people's history* (Vol. 2). Toronto, ON: McClelland & Stewart.

Gladue. (1999). R. v Gladue 1S.C.R. 688 (1999).

Goldenberg, E. (2006). *The way it works: Inside Ottawa.* Toronto, ON: McClelland & Stewart.

Good, D. A. (2007). *The politics of public money: Spenders, guardians, priority setters, and financial watchdogs in the Canadian government.* Toronto, ON: University of Toronto Press.

Government of Canada. (2000). *Background to the introduction of Bill C-20, the Clarity Bill.* Depository Services Program (PRB 99-42E). Retrieved from http://dsp-psd.pwgsc.gc.ca/Collection-R/LoPBdP/BP/prb9942-e.htm

Government of Canada. (2007). Public consultation on Canada's democratic institutions and practices. Retrieved on July 5, 2009 from http://www.democraticreform.gc.ca

Grabb, E.; & Curtis, J. (2005). Regions apart. *The four societies of Canada and the United States.* Toronto, ON: Oxford University Press.

Graham, A. (2007). *Canadian public sector financial management.* Montreal, QC: McGill-Queen's University Press.

Grant, H., & Sweetman, A. (2004). Introduction to economic and urban issues in Canadian immigration policy. *Canadian Journal of Urban Research/Revue canadienne de recherche urbaine, 13*(1), 1–45.

Gratschew, M. (2002). Compulsory voting. In R. López Pintor & M. Gratschew (Eds.), *Voter turnout since 1945: A global report* (pp. 105–110). Stockholm, SE: International Institute for Electoral Democracy and Assistance.

Gray, T. (2006). *Crown corporation governance and accountability framework: A review of recently proposed reforms* (PRB 05-8-E). Parliamentary Information and Research Service. Retrieved from the Library of Parliament website: http://www.parl.gc.ca/information/library/PRBpubs/prb0580-e.htm

Greene, I. (2006). *The courts.* Vancouver: UBC Press.

Greenpeace stunt disrupts Stelmach fundraising dinner. (2008, April 24). *CBC News.* Retrieved from http://www.cbc.ca/canada/story/2008/04/24/stelmach-dinner.html

Greenspon, E., & Wilson-Smith, A.(1996*). Double vision. The inside story of the Liberals in power.* Toronto, ON: Doubleday Canada.

Grekul, J. (2008). Sterilization in Alberta, 1928–1972: Gender matters. *Canadian Journal of Sociology, 45,* 247–266.

Guerin v. The Queen 2 S.C.R. 335 (1984).

Guérin, D. (2003). Aboriginal participation in Canadian federal elections. In *Electoral Insight, 5*(3), 10–15.

Guillén Córdova, A. B. (2008). Social trust, economic inequality, and democracy in the Americas. In M. Seligsen (Ed.), *Challenges to democracy in Latin America and the Caribbean: Evidence from the Americas Barometer 2006–07* (pp. 153–54). Nashville TN: Vanderbilt University.

Haddow, R. (1990). The poverty policy community in Canada's liberal welfare state. In W. D. Coleman & G. Skogstad (Eds.), *Policy communities and public policy in Canada.* Toronto, ON: Copp Clark Pitman.

Haida Nation v. British Columbia (Minister of Forests) SCC 73 (CanLII, 2004)

Hall, M., Barr, C., Easwaramoorthy, M., Sokolowski, S. W., & Salamon, L. (2005). *The Canadian non-profit and voluntary sector in comparative perspective.* Toronto, ON: Imagine Canada.

Hall, M., Lasby, D., Ayer, S., & Gibbons, W. (2009). *Caring Canadians, involved Canadians: Highlights from the 2007 Canada Survey of Giving, Volunteering and Participating* (Catalogue no. 71-542-X). Ottawa, ON: Ministry of Industry.

Hall, M., Lasby, D., Gumulka, G., & Tryon, C. (2006). *Caring Canadians, involved Canadians: Highlights from the 2004 Canada Survey of Giving, Volunteering and Participating* (Catalogue no. 71-542-XIE). Ottawa, ON: Minister of Industry.

Hall, P. (2002). The role of government and the distribution of social capital. In R. Putnam (Ed.), *Democracies in flux: The evolution of social capital in contemporary society* (pp. 21–58). Oxford, UK: Oxford University Press.

Harada, S. (2006). Great expectations: The Green Party of Canada's 2006 campaign. In C. Dornan, & J. Pammett (eds.), *The Canadian federal election of 2006* (pp. 143–170). Toronto, ON: Dundurn Press.

Harper gears up to build new cabinet. (2008, October 22). *Canada.com.* Retrieved from http://www.canada.com/topics/news/national/story.html?id=4a6b20f2-bf48-4eb3-81e8-6d9ab476550b\

Harper, S. (2009, June 11). Prime Minister Stephen Harper's statement of apology. *CBC News.* Retrieved from www.cbc.ca/canada/story/2008/06/11/pm-statement.html

Harper wants fixed dates for federal elections. (2006, May 27). *CTV News*. Retrieved from http://www.ctv.ca/servlet/ArticleNews/story/CTVNews/20060526/harper_fixed_ elexns_060526

Hart, M. (2008). *From pride to influence: Towards a new Canadian foreign policy*. Vancouver: UBC Press.

Hartz, L. (1955). *The liberal tradition in America*. New York, NY: Harcourt.

Hartz, L., McRae, K. D., et. al. (1964). *The founding of new societies: Studies in the history of the United States, Latin America, South Africa, Canada, and Australia*. New York, NY: Harcourt.

Hausegger, L., Hennigar, M., & Riddell, T. (2009). *Canadian courts: Law, politics, and process*. Toronto, ON: Oxford University Press.

Health Canada. (2008). *Canada Health Act annual report 2007–2008*. Retrieved from http://www.hc-sc.gc.ca/hcs-sss/pubs/cha-lcs/2008-cha-lcs-ar-ra/index-eng.php

Heard, A. (1991). *Canadian constitutional conventions: The marriage of law and politics*. Toronto, ON: Oxford University Press.

Heard, A. (2008). *Canadian election results by party, 1867–2008*. Retrieved from http://www.sfu.ca/~aheard/elections/1867-present.html

Heckmann, F. (1997). *Integration und Integrationspolitik in Deutschland* (Paper No. 11). EFMS. Retrieved from http://www.efms.uni-bamberg.de/pdf/efms_p11.pdf

Hein, G. (2000). Interest group litigation and Canadian democracy. *Choices, 6*(2).

Henderson, A. (2007). *Nunavut: Rethinking political culture*. Vancouver: UBC Press.

Henderson, A., Brown, S., Pancer, S., & Ellis-Hale, K. (2007). Mandated community service in high school and subsequent civic engagement: The case of the "double cohort" in Ontario, Canada. *Journal of Youth and Adolescence, 36,* 849–860.

Hermanson, E. N. (1995). The Senate. In *House of Commons of Canada, 35th Parliament, 2nd Session, Journals no. 69, September 18, 1996*.

Heywood, A.(2002). *Politics* (2nd ed.) Basingstoke, UK: Palgrave.

Hiebert, J. (1991). Interest groups and the Canadian federal elections. In F. L. Seidle (ed.). *Interest groups and elections in Canada*. Ottawa: Ministry of Supply and Services Canada.

Hiebert, D., Schuurman, N., & Smith, H. (2007). Multiculturalism "on the ground": The social geography of immigrant and visible minority populations in Montreal, Toronto and Vancouver, projected to 2017 Metropolis British Columbia (Working paper #07–12). Vancouver: Metropolis British Columbia.

Hogg, P. W. (2006). *Constitutional law of Canada* (Student ed.). Toronto, ON: Carswell.

Hogg, P. W. (2009). Appointment of Justice Marshall Rothstein to the Supreme Court of Canada. In M. Charlton & P. Barker (Eds.), *Crosscurrents. Contemporary political issues*. Toronto, ON: Nelson.

Hogg, P. W. & Thornton, A. A. (1997). The Charter dialogue between courts and legislatures. *Osgoode Hall Law Journal, 35*.

Hogg, P. W. & Thornton, A. A. (1999, April). The Charter dialogue between courts and legislatures. *Policy Options,* 19–22.

Holloway, S. K. (2006). *Canadian foreign policy: Defining the national interest*. Peterborough, ON: Broadview Press.

Horowitz, G. (1966). Conservatism, liberalism, and socialism in Canada: An interpretation. *Canadian Journal of Economics and Political Science, 32,* 143–171.

Howard, R. (1998). "History stalks before it strikes": Tightened identity and the right to self-determination: Essays in honour of Peter Baehr. In M. Castermans-Holleman, F. van Hoof, & J. Smith (Eds.), *The role of the nation-state in the twenty-first century* (pp. 61–78). Cambridge, MA : Kluwer Law International.

Howe, P. (2003). Where have all the voters gone? *Inroads: The Canadian Journal of Opinion, 12*(Winter/Spring), 74–83.

Howe, P. (2006). Political knowledge and electoral participation in the Netherlands: Comparisons with the Canadian case. *International Political Science Review, 27*(2), 137–166. doi:10.1177/0192512106061424

Howe, P. (2007). *The electoral participation of young Canadians*.Ottawa, ON: Elections Canada.

Howe, P., & Bedford, D. (2009). *Electoral participation of Aboriginals in Canada*. Ottawa, ON: Elections Canada. Retrieved from http://www.elections.ca/med/eve/APRC/abo_participation_e.pdf

Howe, P., & Northrup, D. (2000). *Strengthening Canadian democracy: The views of Canadians* (Policy Matters Series vol. 1, no. 5). Ottawa, ON: Institute for Research on Public Policy.

Hueglin, T. O. (2008). Working around the American model: Canadian federalism and the European Union. In L. A. White, R. Simeon, R. Vipond, & J. Wallner (Eds.), *The comparative turn in Canadian political science* (pp. 140–157). Vancouver: UBC Press.

Human Resources and Social Development Canada. (2009). *Monthly seasonally adjusted unemployment rates by Employment Insurance (EI) regions*. Retrieved from http://srv129.services.gc.ca/eiregions/eng/rates.aspx?id=2009#data

Hunter, A. (2006). The politics of aboriginal self-government. In J. Grace, & B. Sheldrick (Eds.), *Canadian politics. democracy and dissent*. Toronto, ON: Pearson.

Hurley, M. C. (2003). *Bill C-7: The First Nations Governance Act*. Library of Parliament. Parliamentary Information and Research Service. Retrieved from http://www2.parl.gc.ca/Sites/LOP/LegislativeSummaries/Bills_ls.asp?Parl=37&Ses=2&ls=c7#35

Hurtig, M. (2008). *The truth about Canada: Some important, some astonishing, and some truly appalling things all Canadians should know about our country*. Toronto, ON: McClelland & Stewart.

Ignatieff,, M. (2002). The war of words: A dialogue on intervention. In M. Charlton & P. Barker (Eds.), *Crosscurrents. Contemporary political issues* (4th ed.). Toronto, ON: Thomson Nelson.

Illical, M. & Harrison, K. 2007 (15) Protecting endangered species in the US and Canada: The role of negative lesson drawing. *Canadian Journal of Political Science, 40,* 367–394.

Indian and Northern Affairs Canada. (1969). *Statement of the Government of Canada on Indian policy*. Retrieved from http://www.ainc-inac.gc.ca/ai/arp/ls/pubs/cp1969/cp1969-eng.asp

Inglehart, R. (1971). The silent revolution in Europe: Intergenerational change in post-industrial societies. *American Political Science Review, 65,* 991–1017.

Inglehart, R. (1977). *Silent revolution: Changing values and political styles among western publics*. Princeton, NJ: Princeton University Press.

Inglehart, R. (1990). *Culture shift in advanced industrial society*. Princeton, NJ: Princeton University Press.

Inglehart, R. I. (2009). Inglehart-Welzel cultural map of the world. Retrieved from http://www.worldvaluessurvey.org

Insurance Reference re Dominion Insurance Act 1 A.C. 588 (1916).

International Commission on Intervention and State Sovereignty (ICISS). (2001). *The responsibility to protect*. Ottawa, ON: International Development Research Centre.

Inwood, G. J. (2009). *Understanding Canadian public administration: An introduction to theory and practice* (3rd ed.). Toronto, ON: Pearson Prentice Hall.

Irving, J. (1959). *The Social Credit movement in Alberta*. Toronto, ON: University of Toronto Press.

Isitt, B. (2006). Mutiny from Victoria to Vladivostok. *Canadian Historical Review, 87,* 223–264.

Jamieson, K. H. (1992). *Dirty politics: Deception, distraction, democracy*. New York, NY: Oxford University Press.

Jantzen, L. (2008, Spring). The relationship between diversity and official language minorities. *Canadian Issues/Thèmes Canadiens,* 9–13.

Jedwab, J. (2005). Neither finding nor losing our way: The debate over Canadian multiculturalism. *Canadian Diversity, 4*(1), 95–102.

Jedwab, J. (2008). Receiving and giving: How does the Canadian public feel about immigration and integration? In J. Biles, M. Burstein, & J. Frideres (Eds), *Immigration and integration in Canada in the twenty-first century* (pp. 211–30) Montreal, QC: McGill-Queen's University Press.

Johnston, R., Blais, A., Brady, H. E., & Crête, J. (1992). *Letting the people decide. Dynamics of a Canadian election.* Montreal, QC: McGill-Queen's University Press.

Johnston, R., Blais, A., Gidengil, E., & Nevitte, N. (1996). The challenge of direct democracy: The 1992 Canadian referendum. Montreal, QC: McGill-Queen's University Press.

Kahn, S., & Saloojee, R. (2003). Muslims and citizenship in Canada. *Canadian Diversity, 2*(1), 52–54.

Keating, M. (1996). *Nations against the state: The new politics of nationalism in Quebec*

Keating, T. (2001). Promoting democracy in Haiti. In R. Irwin (Ed.), *Ethics and security in Canadian foreign policy.* Vancouver: UBC Press.

Kelley, N., & Trebilcock, M. (1998). *The making of the mosaic: A history of Canadian immigration policy.* Toronto, ON: University of Toronto Press.

Kelly, J. B., & Murphy, M. (2001). Confronting judicial supremacy: A defence of judicial activism. *Canadian Journal of Law and Society, 16*(1), 3–27.

Kennett, S. A. (2000). Meeting the intergovernmental challenge of environmental assessment. In P. C. Fafard & K. Harrison (Eds.), *Managing the environmental union: Intergovernmental regulations and environmental policy in Canada.* Montreal, QC: McGill-Queen's University Press.

Kirton, J. (2007). *Canadian foreign policy in a changing world.* Toronto, ON: Thomson Nelson.

Klein, A. (2004, November 23). Credit raters exert international influence. *Washington Post,* p. A01.

Kneebone, R. D., & White, K. G. (2009). Fiscal retrenchment and social assistance. *Canadian Public Policy, 35,* 21–40.

Knopff, R., & Morton, F. L. (1992). *Charter politics.* Scarborough, ON: Nelson.

Knowles, V. (1992). *Strangers at our gates: Canadian immigration and immigration policy 1540–1990.* Toronto, ON: Dundurn Press.

Koring, P. (2009, March 1). Canada, allies will never defeat Taliban, PM says. *The Globe and Mail.* Retrieved from www.globeandmail.com/news/politics/article974793.ece

Krasinsky, M., & Milne, W. (1986). The effect of incumbency in the 1984 federal and 1985 Ontario elections. *Canadian Journal of Political Science, 18,* 155–165.

Kushner, J., Siegel, D., & Stanwick, H. (1997). Ontario municipal elections: Voting trends and determinants of electoral success in a Canadian province. *Canadian Journal of Political Science, 30,* 539–559.

Kymlicka, W. (1995). *Multicultural citizenship: A liberal theory of minority rights.* Oxford, UK: Oxford University Press.

Kymlicka, W. (2009). The current state of multiculturalism in Canada. *Canadian Journal for Social Research 2*(1), 15–34.

Labour Conventions: Attorney General of Canada v. Attorney General of Ontario A.C. 327, III Olmsted 180 (Privy Council; 1937).

Ladner, K. L. (2003). Treaty federalism: An indigenous vision of Canadian federalisms. In F. Rocher, & M. Smith (Eds.), *New trends in Canadian federalism* (2nd ed.). Peterborough, ON: Broadview Press.

Laframboise, H. L. (1971). Administrative reform in the federal public service: Signs of a saturation psychosis. *Canadian Public Administration, 14,* 303–325.

Laghi, B. (2009, August 14). The wizard of Ottawa, behind the curtain. *The Globe and Mail.* Retrieved from http://www.theglobeandmail.com/news/politics/the-wizard-of-ottawa-behind-the-curtain/article1246477/

Lapp, M. (1999). Ethnic group leaders and the mobilization of voter turnout: Evidence from five Montreal communities. *Canadian Ethnic Studies, 31*(2), 17–42.

LaSelva, S. (1996). *The moral foundations of Canadian federalism.* Montreal, QC: McGill-Queen's University Press.

LaSelva, S. V. (2009). Understanding Canada's Origins: Federalism, multiculturalism, and the will to live together. In J. Bickerton & A.-G. Gagnon (Eds.), *Canadian Politics* (5th ed.). Toronto, ON: University of Toronto Press.

LeDuc, L. (1990). Party strategies and the use of televised campaign debates. *European Journal of Political Research,18*(1), 121–141.

LeDuc, L. (2003). *The politics of direct democracy: Referendums in global perspective.* Peterborough, ON: Broadview Press.

LeDuc, L. (2005, January). Making votes count: How well did our electoral system perform? *Electoral Insight.* Retrieved from http://www.elections.ca/eca/eim/article_search/article.asp?id=128&lang=e&frmPageSize=&textonly=false

LeDuc, L., Pammett, J., & Bastedo, H. (2008). *The problem of young voters: A qualitative and quantitative analysis.* Prepared for presentation at the annual meeting of the American Political Science Association Boston MA, August 28–30.

Lemaitre, G. (2005). *The comparability of international migration statistics* (Statistics Brief No. 9). Paris: Organization for Economic Cooperation and Development.

Lévesque, R. (1986) *Memoirs* (P. Stratford, Trans.). Toronto, ON: McClelland & Stewart.

Levy, G. (2009). A crisis not made in a day. In P. H. Russell and L. Sossin (Eds.), *Parliamentary democracy in crisis.* Toronto, ON: University of Toronto Press.

Li, Peter. (1998). *Chinese in Canada* (2nd ed.). Don Mills, ON: Oxford University Press.

Liberal Party of Canada. (2009). *The Liberal Party of Canada Constitution.* Retrieved from http://www.liberal.ca/pdf/docs/lpc-2009-constitution-en.pdf.

Lipset, S. M. (1990). *Continental divide: The values and institutions of the United States and Canada.* New York, NY: Routledge.

Lipset, S. M. (1996). *American exceptionalism: A double-edged sword.* New York, NY: Norton.

Lipset, S., & Rokkan, S. (Eds.). (1967). *Party systems and voter alignments: Cross-national perspectives.* New York: NY: Free Press.

Lochead, K. E. (2004). Whose land is it anyway? The long road to the Nisga'a treaty. In R. M. Campbell, L. A. Pal, & M. Howlett (Eds.), *The real worlds of Canadian politics: Cases in process and policy* (4th ed., pp. 267–334). Peterborough, ON; Broadview Press.

López Pintor, R., Gratschew, M., & Sullivan, K. (2002). Voter turnout rates from a comparative perspective. In R. López Pintor & M. Gratschew (eds.), *Voter Turnout since 1945: A global report* (pp. 75–94). Stockholm, SE: International Institute for Electoral Democracy and Assistance.

Lucas, A. L., & Shawitt, L. (2000). Underlying constraints on intergovernmental cooperation in setting and enforcing environmental standards. In P. C. Fafard & K. Harrison (Eds.), *Managing the environmental union: Intergovernmental regulations and environmental policy in Canada* (pp. 133–162). Montreal, QC: McGill-Queen's University Press.

Lynch. K. G. (2007). *Succeeding in a globalized world: Canada's challenges and opportunities.* Government of Canada Privy Council Office. Retrieved from http://www.pco-bcp.gc.ca

Macdonald, D. (2007). *Business and environmental politics in Canada.* Peterborough, ON: Broadview Press.

MacDonald, L. I. (2007, September). SES-Policy Options exclusive poll: The limits of reasonable accommodation. *Policy Options, 28*(8), 1–5.

MacIvor, H. (2006). *Canadian politics and government in the charter era.* Toronto, ON: Thomson Nelson.

Mackenzie, H. (2009). *Banner year for Canada's CEOs: Record high pay increase.* Retrieved from Canadian Centre for Policy Alternatives website: http://www.policyalternatives.ca/~ASSETS/DOCUMENT/National_Office_Pubs/2008/Banner_Year_For_CEOs.pdf

Macpherson, C. B. (1953). *Democracy in Alberta: The theory and practice of a quasi-party system.* Toronto, ON: University of Toronto Press.

Mahtani, M. (2002). Interrogating the hyphen-nation: Canadian multicultural policy and "mixed race" identities. *Social Identities 8*(1), 67–90. doi:10.1080/13504630220132026

Mair, P. (2002). Comparing party systems. In L. LeDuc, R. Niemi, & P. Norris, (Eds.), *Comparing democracies 2: New challenges in the study of elections and voting* (pp. 88–107). London, UK: Sage.

Makin, K. (2006a, January 29). Politicians promises not set in stone, court says. *The Globe and Mail.*

Makin, K. (2006b, June 22). Prosecutors must share blame for botched cases, report says wrongful convictions in Newfoundland blamed on systemic lack of objectivity. *The Globe and Mail.*

Maloney, W. (2006). Political participation: Beyond the electoral arena. In P. Dunleavy, R. Hefferman, P. Cowley, & C. Hay, (Eds.) *Developments in British politics 8.* Basingstoke, UK: Palgrave.

Mandel, M. (1994). The Charter of Rights and the legalization of politics in Canada (rev. ed.). Toronto, ON: Wall and Thompson, 1994.

Manfredi, C. P. (2003, October). Same-sex marriage and the notwithstanding clause. *Policy Options, 24*(9), 21–24.

Marleau, R., & Montpetit, C. (Eds.). (2000). Composition of the House. In *House of Commons Procedure and Practice.* Retrieved from http://www2.parl.gc.ca/MarleauMontpetit/DocumentViewer.aspx?DocId=1001&Sec=Ch04&Seq=2&Lang=E

Married/Born/Died. (2005). *Eastern Chronicle and Pictou County Advocate* (Nova Scotia). Retrieved from the Library and Archives Canada website: http://www.collectionscanada.gc.ca/confederation/023001-505-e.html (Original work published 1867, July 3)

Martell, L. (1994). *Ecology and society: An introduction.* Amherst, MA: University of Massachusetts Press.

Martin, L. (1982). *The presidents and the prime ministers: Washington and Ottawa face to face: the myth of bilateral bliss, 1867–1982.* Toronto, ON: Doubleday Canada.

Martin, L. (2008, August 15). Cry us a river, Tories, but who wrote the book on chaos? *The Globe and Mail.*

Martin, L. (2009, March 31). Enough of multiculturalism—bring on the melting pot. *The Globe and Mail.* Retrieved from http://v1.theglobeandmail.com/servlet/story/RTGAM.20090330.wcomartin31/BNStory/specialComment/

Mason, G. (2008, July 29). Canada can learn from Yukon's unique partnerships. *Globe and Mail Online.* Retrieved fromhttp://www.theglobeandmail.com/

Matas, R. (1998, January 13). A teacher relives a legal nightmare. *The Globe and Mail.*

McKinney, J. A. (2004). Political economy of the U.S.-Canada softwood lumber dispute. *Canadian-American Public Policy, 57,* 1–53.

Mathieu, E., & Taylor, L. (2009, 12 May). Mobilizing huge crowds starts with a few emails. *Toronto Star,* p. GT5.

May, E. (2008, May 5). A tribute to Charles Caccia [Blog entry]. Retrieved from www.greenparty.ca/en/node/4505

McLachlin, B. (2005). Medicine and the law: The challenge of -mental illness. Retrieved from the Supreme Court of Canada website: http://www.scc-csc.gc.ca/court-cour/ju/spe-dis/bm05-02-17-eng.asp.

McNeil, K. (2007). The jurisdiction of inherent right Aboriginal governments. Research paper for the National Centre for First Nations Governance. Retrieved from http://www.fngovernance.org/pdf/Jurisdiction_of_Inherent_Rights.pdf

McNaught, K. (1969). *The Pelican history of Canada.* Harmondsworth, UK: Penguin Books.

McRoberts, K. (1988). *Quebec: Social change and political crisis* (2nd ed.). Toronto, ON: McClelland & Stewart.

McRoberts, K. (1993). *Quebec: Social change and political crisis* (3rd ed.). Don Mills, ON: Oxford University Press.

McRoberts, K. (1997). *Misconceiving Canada. The struggle for national unity.* Toronto, ON: Oxford University Press.

McRoberts, K., & Monahan, P. (Eds.). (1993). *The Charlottetown Accord, the referendum, and the future of Canada.* Toronto, ON: University of Toronto Press.

Meinhard, A., & Foster, M. (1999). The impact of volunteer community service programs on students in Toronto's secondary schools (Working Paper Series No. 12). Toronto, ON: Centre for Voluntary Sector Studies.

Meinhard, A., & Foster, M. (2000). Structuring student volunteering programs to the benefit of students and the community (Working Paper Series No. 14). Toronto, ON: Centre for Voluntary Sector Studies.

Meisel, J., & Mendelsohn, M. (2001). Meteor? Phoenix? Chameleon? The decline and transformation of party in Canada. In H. Thorburn, (Ed.), *Party politics in Canada* (8th ed., pp. 163–178). Scarborough, ON: Prentice Hall.

Mellon, H., & Westmacott, M. (Eds.). (2000). Political dispute and judicial review: Assessing the work of the Supreme Court of Canada. Scarborough, ON: Nelson.

Mendelsohn, M., & Parkin, A. (2001). Introducing direct democracy in Canada. *Choices, 7*(5), 3–38.

Michels, R. (1915). *Political parties: A sociological study of the oligarchical tendencies of modern democracy* (E. & C. Paul, Trans.). New York, NY: Hearst.

Mifflin, M. (2008, July–August). Canada's Arctic sovereignty and Nunavut's place in the federation. *Policy Options, 29*(7), 86–90.

Mifflin, M. (2009, July–August). The prince and the pauper—the Nunavut Tunngavik Incorporated and the Government of Nunavut. *Policy Options,* 92–96.

Milbrath, L., & Goel, M. L. (1977). How and why do people get involved in politics? (2nd ed.). Lanham, MD: University Press of America.

Mill, J. S. (1872). *Considerations on representative government.* London, UK: Longmans.

Milne, D. (2005). Asymmetry in Canada, past and present. Retrieved from the Queen's University Institute of Intergovernmental Relations website: http://www.queensu.ca/iigr/working/asymmetricfederalism/Milne2005.pdf

Milner, H. (2000). Is Canada really no. 1? The shaky foundations of Canada's welfare state. *Inroads* (9).

Milner, H. (2008). *The informed political participation of young Canadians and Americans.* Maryland, MD: Centre for Information and Research on Civic Learning and Engagement.

Mintz, E. (1985). Election campaign tours in Canada. *Political Geography Quarterly, 4*(1), 47–54.

Mintz, E., Close, D., & Croci, O. (2009). *Politics, power, and the common good. An introduction to political science* (2nd ed.). Toronto, ON: Pearson.

Mishler, W. (1979). *Political participation in Canada: Prospects for democratic citizenship.* Toronto, ON: Macmillan Canada.Pammett,

J. H., & Dornan, C. (Eds.). (2006). *The Canadian federal election of 2006*. Toronto, ON: Dundurn.

Montpetit, E. (2004). *Misplaced distrust. Policy networks and the environment in France, the United States, and Canada*. Vancouver: UBC Press.

Morton, D. (2006). *A short history of Canada* (6th ed.). Toronto, ON: McClelland & Stewart.

Morton, D. (2007). *A military history of Canada* (5th ed.). Toronto, ON: McClelland & Stewart.

Morton, F. L. (1999, April). Dialogue or monologue? *Policy Options, 19*(3), 23–26.

Morton, F. L. (2003, October). Can judicial supremacy be stopped? *Policy Options,24*(9), 25–29.

Morton, F. L. (Ed.). (2002). Law, politics and the judicial process in Canada. Calgary, AB: University of Calgary Press.

Morton, F. L., & Knopff, R. (2000). *The Charter revolution and the court party*. Peterborough, ON: Broadview Press.

Morton, W. L. (1950). *The Progressive Party in Canada*. Toronto, ON: University of Toronto Press.

Mosca, G. (1965). *The ruling class* (A. Livingston, Ed., H. D. Kahn, Trans.). New York, NY: McGraw Hill.

Motherwell v. Motherwell 73 D.L.R. (3d) 62 Alberta Supreme Court (1976).

Municipalité Hérouxville. (n.d). *Publication of standards*. Retrieved January 28, 2009, from http://municipalite.herouxville.qc.ca/Standards.pdf

Murphy, M. (Ed.). (2005). Canada: The state of the federation 2003: Reconfiguring aboriginal-state relations. Kingston, ON: Institute of Intergovernmental Relations, Queen's University.

Nadeau, R. (2002). Satisfaction with democracy: The Canadian paradox. In N. Nevitte (Ed.), *Value change and governance in Canada* (pp. 37–70). Toronto, ON: University of Toronto Press.

Native Women's Association of Canada. (2007). *Aboriginal women and Bill C-31, An issue paper*. Prepared for the National Aboriginal Women's Summit, Corner Brook, NL. Retrieved from www.nwac-hq.org/en/documents/nwac.billc-31.jun2007.pdf

Navy waters down plans. (2009, June 16). *CTV News*. Retrieved from http://www.ctv.ca/servlet/ArticleNews/storyv2/CTVNews/20090616/navy_arctic_090616?s_name=&no_ads=

Nevitte, N. (1996). *The decline of deference: Canadian value change in cross-national perspective*. Peterborough, ON: Broadview Press.

New Democratic Party. (2000). Running and winning with the NDP: A handbook for equity seeking groups. Ottawa, ON: Author.

New Democratic Party. (2001). *Constitution of the New Democratic Party as amended by the Federal Convention, Winnipeg*. Retrieved from http://ottawacentre.org/en/Pages/pdf/ndp-e.pdf

Newfoundland (Treasury Board) v. N.A.P.E., SCC 66, (2004), 3 S.C.R. 381.

Newfoundland and Labrador Executive Council. (2007). Premier Williams says "a promise made is not a promise kept" for Newfoundland and Labrador (News release). Retrieved from http://www.releases.gov.nl.ca/releases/2007/exec/0320n04.htm

Niemi, R., Hepburn, M., & Chapman, C. (2000). Community service by high school students: A cure for civic ills? *Political Behaviour, 22*, 45–69.

O'Neill, B. (2002). Sugar and spice? Political culture and the political behaviour of Canadian women. In J. Everitt & B. O'Neill (Eds.), *Citizen politics. Research and theory in Canadian political behaviour* (pp. 40–55). Don Mills: ON: Oxford University Press.

Office of the Commissioner of Official Languages. (2006). *The evolution of public opinion on official languages in Canada*. Retrieved from http://www.ocol-clo.gc.ca/html/evolution_opinion_section_1_e.php

Office of the Parliamentary Budget Officer. (2008). Fiscal impact of the Canadian mission in Afghanistan. Retrieved from http://www2.parl.gc.ca/Sites/PBO-DPB/documents/Afghanistan_Fiscal_Impact_FINAL_E_WEB.pdf

Office of the Privacy Commissioner of Canada. (2009, September 10). Privacy commissioners urge caution on expanded surveillance plans. Retrieved from http://www.priv.gc.ca/media/nr-c/2009/nr-c_090910_e.cfm

Olsen, D. 1980 (1) *The state elite*. Toronto, ON: McClelland & Stewart

Olson, M. (1965). *The logic of collective action; public goods and the theory of groups*. Cambridge, MA: Harvard University Press.

Ontario Ministry of Education and Training. (1999). *Ontario secondary schools, grades 9 to 12: Program and diploma requirements*. Toronto, ON: Author.

Ontario must fight equalization formula. (2008, May 8). *CBC News*. Retrieved from: http://www.cbc.ca/canada/ottawa/story/2008/05/08/ot-equalization-080508.html

Organization for Economic Cooperation and Development. (2006). *Where immigrants student succeed: A comparative review of performance and engagement in PISA 2003*. OECD Program for International Student Assessment.

Organization for Economic Co-operation and Development. (2008). Country Note: Canada. *Growing unequal: Income distribution and poverty in OECD countries*. Retrieved from http:/www.oecd.org/els/social/inequality

Organization for Economic Cooperation and Development. (2009). *Statistics portal*. Retrieved from http://www.ocde.p4.siteinternet.com

Organization for Economic Co-operation and Development. (2009). Table 1: Net official development assistance in 2008. Retrieved from www.oecd.org/dataoecd/25/42/42472714.pdf

Ornstein, M., & Stevenson, H. M. (1999). *Politics and ideology in Canada: Elite and public opinion in the transformation of a welfare state*. Montreal, QC: McGill-Queen's University Press.

Osborne, D., & Gaebler, T. (1992). *Reinventing government: How the entrepreneurial spirit is transforming the public sector*. New York, NY: Basic Books.

Ostberg, C. L., & Wetstein, M. E. (2007). Attitudinal decision making in the Supreme Court of Canada. Vancouver: UBC Press.

Pal, L. A. (1993). *Interests of state: The politics of language, multiculturalism, and feminism in Canada*. Montreal, QC: McGill-Queen's University Press.

Pammett, J. (2008). Elections. In M. Whittington & G. Williams (Eds.). *Canadian politics in the 21st century* (7th ed., pp. 153–157). Toronto, ON: Nelson.

Pammett, J., & LeDuc, L. (2003). *Explaining the turnout decline in Canadian federal elections: A new survey of non-voters*. Ottawa: Elections Canada.

Pammett, J., & LeDuc, L. (2006). Voter turnout in 2006: More than just the weather. In J. Pammett & C. Dornan (Eds.), *The Canadian federal election of 2006* (pp. 304–326). Toronto, ON: Dundurn Press.

Papillon, M. (2008). Canadian federalism and the emerging mosaic of Aboriginal multilevel governance. In H. Bakvis & G. Skogstad (Eds.), *Canadian federalism: Performance, effectiveness, and legitimacy* (2nd ed., pp.291–313). Don Mills, ON: Oxford University Press.

Papillon, M. (2009). The (re)emergence of Aboriginal governments. In J. Bickerton & A.-G. Gagnon (Eds.), *Canadian politics* (5th ed., pp. 179–196). Toronto, ON: University of Toronto Press.

Parliament of Canada. (2008). *Women candidates in general elections—1921 to date*. Retrieved from http://www2.parl.gc.ca/Sites/LOP/HFER/hfer.asp?Language=E&Search=WomenElection

Parliament of Canada. (2008). Find out more about Canada's Members of Parliament. *House of Commons Report to Canadians 2008*.Retrieved from http://www.parl.gc.ca/information/about/process/house/RTC2008/rtc2008_03-e.html

Parliament of Canada. (2008). At work in committees. *The House of Commons Report to Canadians 2008*. Retrieved from http://www.parl.gc.ca/information/about/process/house/RTC2008/rtc2008_06-e.html

Parliament of Canada. (2009). *Electoral results by party*. Retrieved from http://www2.parl.gc.ca/Parlinfo/compilations/ElectionsAndRidings/ResultsParty.aspx?Language=E

Parliament of Canada. (2009). History of Federal Ridings since 1867. Retrieved from http://www2.parl.gc.ca/Sites/LOP/HFER/HFER.asp

Parliament of Canada. (2009). *Occupations of members of the House of Commons*. Retrieved from http://www2.parl.gc.ca/parlinfo/Lists/Occupation.aspx?Menu=HOC-Bio&Section=03d93c58-f843-49b3-9653-84275c23f3fb&Parliament=8714654b-cdbf-48a2-b1ad-57a3c8ece839&Name=&Party=&Province=&Gender=&CurrentParliamentarian=False&Occupation=&OccupationType=

Parliament of Canada. (n.d.) Women candidates in general elections—1921 to date. *History of Federal Ridings since 1867*. Retrieved from http://www2.parl.gc.ca/Sites/LOP/HFER/hfer.asp?Language=E&Search=WomenElection

Parliament of Canada. (n.d.). Women candidates in general elections—1921 to date *History of federal ridings since 1867*. Retrieved from http://www.parl.gc.ca/information/about/process/house/hfer/hfer.asp?Language=&Search=WomenElection

Pelz, T., & Lehmann, V. (2007). The evolution of UN peacekeeping: Reforming DPKO (Fact sheet). *Dialogue on Globalization*. Retrieved from the ReliefWeb website: http://www.reliefweb.int/rw/lib.nsf/db900sid/PANA-7HRDVG/$file/fes_nov2007.pdf?openelement

Pérez, O.J. (2008). Measuring democratic political cultures in Latin America. In R. Millett, J. S. Holmes, & O. J. Pérez (Eds.), *Latin American democracy: Emerging reality or endangered species* (pp. 21–41). New York, NY: Routledge.

Perkins, T. (2009, April 20). Nobody's saviour. *The Globe and Mail*. Retrieved from www.theglobeandmail.com/report-on-business/article1138040

Perreaux, L. (2009, April 9). For determined re-enactors, the war won't be over until the battle goes on. *The Globe and Mail*. Retrieved from http://www.theglobeandmail.com/news/national/article972336.ece

Philips, S. (2004). Interest groups, social movements, and the voluntary sector: En route to reducing the democratic deficit. In J. Bickerton & A.-G. Gagnon (Eds.), *Canadian Politics* (4th ed., pp. 323–347). Peterborough, ON: Broadview Press.

Pickersgill, J. (1962). *The Liberal Party*. Toronto, ON: McClelland & Stewart.

Picot, G., & Hou, F. (2003). *The rise in low-income rates among immigrants in Canada* (Analytical Studies Branch Research Paper Series No. 198). Ottawa, ON: Statistics Canada.

Pilkington, C. (1999). *The civil service in Britain today*. Manchester, UK: Manchester University Press.

Pollard, D., Parpworth, N., & Hughes, D. (2001). *Constitutional and administrative law*. London, UK: Butterworths.

Porter, J. (1965). *The vertical mosaic: An analysis of social class and power in Canada*. Toronto, ON: University of Toronto Press.

Potter, E. (2008). Public perceptions of Canada-US relations: Regionalism and diversity. In D. Carment & D. Bercuson (Eds.), *The world in Canada. Diaspora, demography, and domestic politics* (pp. 149–168). Montreal, QC: McGill-Queen's University Press.

Press, H. (1995). Davis Inlet in crisis: Will the lessons ever be learned? *Canadian Journal of Native Studies, 15,* 187–209.

Prince, M. (2007). *The electoral participation of people with special needs*. Ottawa, ON: Elections Canada.

Prince, M. J., & Abele, F. (2005). Paying for self-determination: Aboriginal peoples, self-government, and fiscal relations in Canada. In M. Murphy (Ed.), *Canada: the state of the federation 2003. Reconfiguring Aboriginal-state relations*. Montreal, QC: McGill-Queen's University Press.

Privacy Commissioner of Canada. (2009). Report of findings into the complaint filed by the Canadian Internet Policy and Public Interest Clinic (CIPPIC) against Facebook Inc. under the *Personal Information Protection and Electronic Documents Act,* by Elizabeth Denham, Assistant Privacy Commissioner of Canada (PIPEDA Case Summary #2009-008). Retrieved from http://www.priv.gc.ca/cf-dc/2009/2009_008_0716_e.cfm

Pross, A. P. (1992). *Group politics and public policy* (2nd ed.). Toronto, ON: Oxford University Press.

Public Service Commission. (2007). Employment equity. *Appointment policy: Questions and answers*. Retrieved from http://www.psc-cfp.gc.ca/plcy-pltq/qa-qr/appointment-nomination/equity-equite-eng.htm

Putnam, R. (with Leonardi, R.). (1993). *Making democracy work: Civic traditions in modern Italy*. Princeton, NJ: Princeton University Press.

Putnam, R. D. (2000). *Bowling alone: The collapse and revival of American community*. New York, NY: Simon & Schuster.

Putnam, R. D. (Ed.). (2002) *Democracies in flux: The evolution of social capital in contemporary societies*. New York, NY: Oxford University Press.

Radio Reference re Regulation and Control of Radio Communication in Canada, A.C. 304 (1932).

Receiver General for Canada, 2008, *Public accounts of Canada 2008:, Vol. 1. Summary Report and Financial Statements,* Financial Statements Discussion and Analysis Section 1 1.7; retrieved from http://www.tpsgc-pwgsc.gc.ca/recgen/pdf/49-eng.pdf

R. v. Keegstra 3 S.C.R. 697 (1990).

R. v. Marshall CanLII 665 (S.C.C., 1999)

R. v. Oakes, 1 S.C.R 103 (1986).

R. v. Pamajewon CanLII 161 (S.C.C., 1996).

R. v. Sparrow CanLII 104 (S.C.C., 1990).

Reference re Secession of Quebec 2 S.C.R. 217 (1998). Retrieved from http://csc.lexum.umontreal.ca/en/1998/1998rcs2-217/1998rcs2-217.html

Religious accommodation hits the playing field. (2007, March 5). *Maclean's*. Retrieved from http://www.macleans.ca/canada/national/article.jsp?content=20070227_100426_7612

Rempel, R. (2006). *Dreamland: How Canada's pretend foreign policy has undermined sovereignty*. Montreal, QC: McGill-Queen's University Press.

Resnick, P. (2005). *The European roots of Canadian identity*. Toronto, ON: Broadview Press.

Riddell-Dixon, E. (2008). Assessing the impact of recent immigration trends on Canadian foreign policy. In D. Carment & D. Bercuson (Eds.), *The world in Canada: Diaspora, demography, and domestic politics* (pp. 31-49). Montreal, QC: McGill-Queen's University Press.

Roberts, A. (1997). Worrying about misconduct: The control lobby and the PS 2000 reforms. *Canadian Public Administration, 39,* 489–523.

Romanow, R., Whyte, J., & Leeson, H. (1984). *Canada . . . Notwithstanding: The making of the constitution 1976–1982*. Toronto, ON: Methuen.

Royal Commission on Financial Management and Accountabiliy (Lambert Commission). (1979). *Final report.* Ottawa, ON: Supply and Services Canada.

Royal Commission on Government Organization (Glassco Commission). (1962). *Report: Vol. 1. Management of the public service.* Ottawa, ON: Queen's Printer.

Rubenson, D., Blais, A., Fournier, P., Gidengil, E., & Nevitte, N. (2004). Accounting for the age gap in turnout. *Acta Politica, 39,* 407–421.

Ruspini, P. (2005). Public policies and community services for immigrant integration: Italy and the European Union. *Global Migration Perspectives, 45.* Retrieved from http://www.gcim.org/attachements/GMP%20No%2045.pdf

Russell v. The Queen. 7 A.C. 829, (1882).

Russell, P. H. (2004) *Constitutional odyssey: Can Canadians become a sovereign people* (3rd ed.). Toronto, ON: University of Toronto Press

Russell, P. H. (2006). Constitutional politics: In a new era Canada returns to old methods. In H. J. Michelmann & C. DeClercy (Eds.), *Continuity and change in Canadian politics: Essays in honour of David E. Smith* (pp. 19–38). Toronto, ON: University of Toronto Press.

Russell, P. H. (2008). *Two cheers for minority government. The evolution of Canadian parliamentary democracy.* Toronto, ON: Emond Montgomery.

Russell, P. H., Knopff, R., Bateman, M. J., & Hiebert, J. I. (2008*). The court and the constitution. Leading cases.* Toronto: Emond Montgomery.

Ryan, C. (2003). *Quebec and interprovincial discussion and consultation.* Retrieved from the Institute for Research on Public Policy website: http://www.irpp.org/miscpubs/archive/federation/ryan.pdf

Sadik, T. (2009, March). *Aboriginal electoral participation.* Presentation to the Elections Canada 2009 Aboriginal Policy Research Conference, Ottawa, ON.

Sanders, D. E. (1983). The Indian lobby. In K. Banting & R. Simeon (Eds.), *And no one cheered: Federalism, democracy and the Constitution Act* (pp. 301–332). Toronto, ON: Methuen

Sartori, G. (1976). *Parties and party systems.* Cambridge, UK: Cambridge University Press.

Saul, J. R. (2008). *A fair country: Telling truths about Canada.* Toronto, ON: Viking Canada.

Savoie, D. (1999). *Governing from the centre: The concentration of power in Canadian politics.* Toronto, ON: University of Toronto Press.

Savoie, D. (2008). *Court government and the collapse of accountability in Canada and the United Kingdom.* Toronto, ON: University of Toronto Press.

Scarrow, S. (2000). Parties without members? Party organizations in a changing political environment. In R. J. Dalton & M. P. Wattenberg (Eds.), *Parties without partisans: Political change in advanced industrial democracies* (pp. 79–101). Oxford, UK: Oxford University Press.

Schachter 2 S.C.R. 679 (1992).

Schmitz, C. (2006, November 24). Organized Bench and Bar want impartial nominating. *The Lawyers Weekly.* Retrieved from www.lawyersweekly.ca/index.php?section=article&articleid=386

Schneiderman, D. (1991, November). On stacking the Senate. *Policy Options,* 34–35.

Secession Reference of Quebec 2 S.C.R. 217 (1998). Retrieved from http://csc.lexum.umontreal.ca/en/1998/1998rcs2-217/1998rcs2-217.html

Sens, A., & Stoett, P. (2005). Global politics. Origins, currents, directions (3rd ed.). Toronto, ON: Thomson Nelson.

Sharpe, R. J., & McMahon, P. I. (2008). *The Persons case: The origins and legacy of the fight for legal personhood.* Toronto, ON: University of Toronto Press.

Siaroff, A. (2005). *Comparing political regimes: A thematic introduction to comparative politics.* Peterborough, ON: Broadview Press.

Siegfried, A. (1966). *The race question in Canada.* Toronto: McClelland & Stewart.

Simeon, R., & Robinson, I. (2009). The dynamics of Canadian federalism. In J. Bickerton & A.-G. Gagnon (Eds.), *Canadian politics* (5th ed., pp. 155–178). Toronto: University of Toronto Press.

Simpson, G. (2001). *The friendly dictatorship.*Toronto, ON: McClelland & Stewart.

Small, T. A. (2008, November). The Facebook effect? On-line campaigning in the 2008 Canadian and United States elections. *Policy Options, 29*(10), 85–87.

Smiley, D. V.(1987). *The federal condition in Canada.* Toronto, ON: McGraw.

Smith, A. (1976). *Nationalist movements.* London, UK: Macmillan.

Smith, A. (1999). *Myths and memories of the nation.* Oxford, UK: Oxford University Press.

Smith, A. (2009). *The Roles and responsibilities of central agencies (*PRB 09-01E). Retrieved from the Library of Parliament website: http://www.parl.gc.ca/information/library/PRBpubs/prb0901-e.htm#a15

Smith, D. (1971). President and Parliament: The transformation of parliamentary government in Canada. In T. A. Hockin (Ed.), Apex of power: The prime minister and political leadership in Canada. Scarborough, ON: Prentice Hall.

Smith, G. (1891). *Canada and the Canadian question.* Toronto, ON: Hunter, Rose.

Smith, J. (2004). *Federalism.* Vancouver: UBC Press.

Smith, M. (2005). *Group politics and social movements in Canada.* Peterborough, ON: Broadview Press.

Smith, M. (Ed.). (2008). *Group politics and social movements in Canada.* Peterborough, ON: Broadview Press.

Sniderman, P. M., Fletcher, J. F., Russell, P. H., & Tetlock, P. E. (1996). *The clash of rights: Liberty, equality, and legitimacy in pluralist democracy.* New Haven, CT: Yale University Press.

Songer, D. R., & Johnson, S. W. (2007). Judicial decision making in the Supreme Court of Canada: Updating the personal attribute model. *Canadian Journal of Political Science, 40,* 911–934.

Songer, D. R., & Siripuparu, J. (2009). The unanimous decisions of the Supreme Court of Canada as a test of the attitudinal model. *Canadian Journal of Political Science, 42,* 65–92.

Soroka, S., Penner, E., & Blidook, K. (2009). Constituency influence in Parliament. *Canadian Journal of Political Science, 42,* 563–591.

Standing Senate Committee on Foreign Affairs and International Trade. (2007). *The evacuation of Canadians from Lebanon in July 2006: Implications for the Government of Canada.* Ottawa, ON: The Senate of Canada.

Stanford, J. (2008). Staples, deindustrialization and foreign investment: Canada's economic journey back to the future. *Studies in Political Economy, 82,* 7–34.

Statistics Canada. (2003). *Ethnic diversity survey: Portrait of a multicultural society* (Catalogue No. 89-593-XIE). Retrieved from http://www.statcan.gc.ca/bsolc/olc-cel/olc-cel?lang=eng&catno=89-593-X

Statistics Canada. (2005). *Census of population. Population and growth components (1851–2001 censuses).* Retrieved from http://www40.statcan.gc.ca/l01/cst01/demo03-eng.htm?sdi=population

Statistics Canada. (2005, October 25). The socio-economic progress of the children of immigrants. *The Daily.*

Statistics Canada. (2006). Highlight tables, 2006 census. *Canada's ethnocultural mosaic* (Catalogue number 97-562-XWE200602). Retrieved from http://www12.statcan.ca/english/census06/data/highlights/ethnic/pages

Statistics Canada. (2006). *Portrait of the Canadian population in 2006, by age and sex.* Retrieved from http://www12.statcan.ca/english/census06/analysis/agesex/NatlPortrait2.cfm

Statistics Canada. (2008). *Ethnocultural portrait of Canada highlight tables, 2006 census* (Catalogue no. 97-562-XWE2006002). Retrieved from http://www12.statcan.ca/english/census06/data/highlights/ethnic/index.cfm?Lang=E

Statistics Canada. (2008a). *Labour force and participation rates by age and sex, 2007.* Retrieved from http:/www40.statcan.ca/l01/labor05.htm

Statistics Canada. (2008b). *Median total income, in 2005 constant dollars, of economic families, Canada, provinces and territories, 2000 and 2005* (Catalogue no. 97-563-XWE2006002). Retrieved from http:/www12.statcan.ca/english/census06/analysis/income/tables/table12.htm

Statistics Canada. (2009). *Canada's population clock.* Retrieved from http://www.statcan.gc.ca/edu/clock-horloge/edu06f_0001-eng.htmStatistics Canada. (2009). Public sector employment, wages and salaries (employees) (CANSIM table 183-0002). Retrieved from http://www40.statcan.gc.ca/l01/cst01/govt54a-eng.htm

Statistics Canada. (2009a). *Average earnings by sex and work pattern* (CANSIM Table 202-0102). Retrieved from http://www40.statcan.ca/l01/cst01/labor01b-eng.htm

Statistics Canada. (2009b). *Employment by industry* (Catalogue no. 71F0004XCB). Retrieved from http://www40.statcan.gc.ca/l01/cst01/econ40-eng.htm?sdi=industry

Statistics Canada. (2009c). *Export of goods on a balance-of-payments basis, by product.* Retrieved from http://www40.statcan.gc.ca/l01/cst01/gblec04-eng.htm

Statistics Canada. (2009d). *Labour force characteristics, seasonally adjusted, by province* (Catalogue no. 71-001-XIE). Retrieved from http://www40.statcan.gc.ca/l01/cst01/lfss01a-eng.htm and http://www40.statcan.gc.ca/l01/cst01/lfss06-eng.htm?sdi=unemployment%soterritory

Statistics Canada. (2009e) *Population by year, by province and territory.* Retrieved from http://www40.statcan.gc.ca/l01/cst01/demo02d-eng.htm

Statutes of Quebec. (2000). *An act respecting the exercise of the fundamental rights and prerogatives of the Québec people and the Québec state* (ch. 46). Retrieved from http://www2.publicationsduquebec.gouv.qc.ca/dynamicSearch/telecharge.php?type=2&file=/E_20_2/E20_2_A.html

Stein, J. S., & Lang, E. (2007). *The unexpected war: Canada in Kandahar.* Toronto, ON: Viking Canada.

Stewart, I. (2002). Vanishing points: Three paradoxes of political culture research. In J. Everitt & B. O'Neill (Eds.), *Citizen politics: Research and theory in Canadian political behaviour* (pp. 21–39). Don Mills, ON: Oxford University Press.

Strategic Counsel. (2008). *A report to The Globe and Mail and CTV: 2008 federal election pre-election national poll.* Retrieved from: http://www.thestrategiccounsel.com/our_news/polls/2008-10-12%20National%20Poll%20 (reporting%20Oct10-11)f.pdf

Tanguay, A. B., & Kay, B. J. (1998). Third party advertising and the threat to electoral democracy in Canada: The mouse that roared. *International Journal of Canadian Studies, 17,* 57–79.

Taylor, C. (1992). The politics of recognition. In A. Guttman (Ed.), *Multiculturalism: Examining the politics of recognition* (pp. 25–74). Princeton, NJ: Princeton University Press.

Temelini, M. (2008). The Canadian student movement and the January 25, 1995 "National Day of Strike and Action." In M. H. Callaghan & M. Hayday (Eds.), *Mobilizations, protests & engagements: Canadian perspectives on social movements* (pp. 222–243). Halifax, NS: Fernwood.

Thomas, P. G. (2002). Parliament and the public service. In C. Dunn (Ed.), *The handbook of Canadian public administration.* Don Mills, ON: Oxford University Press.

Thompson, D. (1976). *John Stuart Mill and representative government.* Princeton, NJ: Princeton University Press.

Thompson, E. (2007, May 19). Tories dirty little tricks. *Montreal Gazette.*

Thorburn, H. G. (2001). The development of political parties in Canada. In H. G. Thorburn & A. Whitehord (Eds.), *Party politics in Canada* (pp. 1–8). Toronto, ON: Prentice Hall.

Tilly, C. (1975). *The formation of national states in Western Europe.* Princeton, NJ: Princeton University Press.

Timeline: The Quebec kirpan case. (2006, March 2). *CBC News Online.* Retrieved from www.cbc.ca/news/background/kirpan

Tomlin, B. W., Hillmer, N., & Hampson, F. O. (2008). *Canada's international policies: Agendas, alternatives, and politics.* Don Mills, ON: Oxford University Press.

Torrance, J. (1986). *Public violence in Canada, 1867–1982.* Montreal, QC: McGill-Queen's University Press.

Tossutti, L. (2007). *The electoral participation of ethnocultural communities.* Ottawa, ON: Elections Canada.

Tossutti L., & Najem, T. (2002). Minority representation in the fourth party system: Macro and micro constraints and opportunities. *Canadian Ethnic Studies/Études ethniques au Canada,34*(1), 85–111;

Tossutti, L., & Najem, T. (2002). Minorities and elections in Canada's fourth party system. *Canadian Ethnic Studies 34*(1), 85–112.

Treasury Board of Canada. (2006). The reporting cycle. *Tools and resources for parliamentarians.* Retrieved from http://www.tbs-sct.gc.ca/tbs-sct/audience-auditoire/parliamentarian-parlementaire-eng.asp

Treasury Board of Canada Secretariat. (2007). *Quick facts about official languages.* Retrieved from http://www.tbs-sct.gc.ca/faq/fat-eng.asp

Treasury Board Secretariat. (2008). *Annual report to Parliament—Crown corporations and other corporate interests of Canada 2008.* Retrieved from http://www.tbs-sct.gc.ca/reports-rapports/cc-se/2008/cc-se05-eng.asp

Treasury Board of Canada Secretariat. (2009). *Employment equity in the public service of Canada 2006–2007 and 2007–2008.* Retrieved from http://www.tbs-sct.gc.ca/rp/0608ee06-eng.asp

Trudeau, P. E. (1968). *Federalism and the French Canadians.* New York, NY: St. Martin's Press.

Trudeau, P. E. (1993). M*emoirs.* Toronto, ON: McClelland & Stewart

Turnbull, L., & Aucoin, P. (2006). *Fostering Canadians' role in public policy: A strategy for institutionalizing public involvement in policy* (CCRN Research Report P07). Ottawa, ON: Canadian Policy Research Networks.

Turpel, M. E. (1993). The Charlottetown discord and Aboriginal peoples' struggle for fundamental political change. In K. McRoberts & P. Monahan (Eds.), *The Charlottetown Accord, the referendum, and the future of Canada.* Toronto, ON: University of Toronto Press.

Uhr, J. (1998). *Deliberative democracy in Australia: The changing place of Parliament.* Cambridge, UK: Cambridge University Press.

United Nations. (1994). *Human development report 1994.* Retrieved from http://hdr.undp.org/en/reports/global/hdr1994/

United Nations Peacekeeping. (2009). *Monthly summary of contributors of military and civilian police personnel.* Retrieved on August 30, 2009, from http://www.un.org/Depts/dpko/dpko/contributors/index.shtml

Van Loon, R., & Whittington, M. S. (1987). *The Canadian political system. Environment, structure and process* (4th ed.). Toronto, ON: McGraw.

Vegh, S. (2003). Classifying forms of online activism: The case of cyberprotests against the World Bank. In M. McCaughey & M. D. Ayers (Eds.), *Cyberactivism: Online activism in theory and practice* (pp. 71–95). New York, NY: Routledge.

Verba, S., & Nie, N. (1972). *Participation in America: Political democracy and social inequality.* New York, NY: Harper and Row.

Verba, S., Nie, N., & Kim, J. (1971). *The modes of democratic participation: A cross-national comparison.* Beverly Hills, CA: Sage.

Veterans Affairs Canada. (n.d.). *Canada remembers.* Retrieved from: www.vac-acc.gc.ca/remembers

Vriend v. Alberta, 1 S.C.R. 493 (1998).

Waddell, C. (2009). The campaign in the media 2008. In J. H. Pammett & C. Dornan (Eds.), *The Canadian federal election of 2008.* Toronto, ON: Dundurn.

Walzer, M. (1992). Comment. in A. Guttman (Ed.), *Multiculturalism and the "politics of recognition."* Princeton, NJ: Princeton University Press.

Wanner, R. A. (2009). Social mobility in Canada: Concepts, patterns, and trends. In E. Grabb & N. Guppy (Eds.), *Social inequality in Canada: Patterns, problems, and policies.* Toronto, ON: Pearson.

Welsh, J. (2004). *At home and abroad: Canada's global vision for the 21st century.* Toronto, ON: HarperCollins.

Welsh, J. (2007). Challenges and new directions for Canada. In J. Welsh & N. Woods (Eds.), *Exporting good governance: Temptations and challenges in Canada's aid program.* Waterloo, ON: Wilfrid Laurier University Press.

White, G. (2006). *Cabinets and first ministers.* Vancouver: UBC Press.

Whitehorn, A. (2001). Alexa McDonough and NDP gains in Atlantic Canada. In H. Thorburn (Ed.), *Party politics in Canada* (8th ed., pp. 264–279). Scarborough, ON: Prentice Hall.

Whitehorn, A. (2007). Social democracy and the New Democratic Party. In A.-G. Gagnon & B. Tanguay (Eds.), *Canadian parties in transition* (3rd ed.). Toronto, ON: University of Toronto Press.

Williams, R. A. (2004). Mergers if necessary, but not necessarily mergers: Competition and consolidation at Canada's "Big Banks." In R. M. Campbell, L. A. Pal, & M. Howlett. (Eds.), *The real worlds of Canadian politics. Cases in process and policy* (4th ed.). Peterborough, ON: Broadview Press.

Williams, R. A. (2009). Endogenous shocks in subsystem adjustment and policy change: The credit crunch and Canadian banking regulation. *Journal of Public Policy, 29,* 29–53. doi:10.1017/S0143814X09001007

Wilson, J. (2002). Continuity and change in the Canadian environmental movement. In D. L. VanNijnatten & R. Boardman (Eds.), *Canadian environmental policy. Context and Cases.* Don Mills, ON: Oxford University Press.

Winnemore, L., & Biles, J. (2006). Canada's two-way street integration model: Not without its stains, strains and growing pains. *Canadian Diversity 5*(1), 23–29.

Wiseman, N. (2007). *In search of Canadian political culture.* Vancouver: UBC Press.

Woo, G. (2003). Canada's forgotten founders: The modern significance of the Haudenosaunee (Iroquois) application for membership in the League of Nations. *Law, Social Justice & Global Development Journal,*(1). Retrieved from http://www2.warwick.ac.uk/fac/soc/law/elj/lgd/2003_1/woo

Woodward, J., & Roper, E. (1950). Political activity of American citizens. *American Political Science Review, 44,* 872–885.

Woolstencroft, P. (2001). Some battles won, war lost. The campaign of the Progressive Conservative party. In J. H. Pammett & C. Dornan (Eds.), *The Canadian general election of 2000.* Toronto, ON: Dundurn.

World Bank. (2004). *World development report, 2004.* Washington, DC: Author.

World Values Survey. (2001–2009). *World Values Survey 1981–2008 official aggregate* (v.20090901). Aggregate file producer: ASEP/JDS, Madrid. Retrieved from the World Values Survey Association website: http://worldvaluessurvey.org

Worms, J.-P. (2002). Old and new civic ties and social ties in France. In R. Putnam (Ed.). *Democracies in flux: The evolution of social capital in contemporary society* (pp. 137–188). Oxford, UK: Oxford University Press.

Wortley, S., & Tanner, J. (2004). Discrimination or "good" policing? The racial profiling debate in Canada. *Our Diverse Cities 1,* 97–201.

Wyatt, N. (2007, February 26). Rules forbid hijab, says Quebec Soccer Federation. *Toronto Star.* Retrieved from http://www.thestar.com/News/article/185923

Young, I. (1989). Polity and group difference: A critique of the ideal of universal citizenship. *Ethics, 99,* 250–274.

Young, L. (2003). Can feminists transform party politics? The Canadian experience. In M. Tremblay & L. Trimble (Eds.), *Women and electoral politics in Canada* (pp. 76–91). Don Mills, ON: Oxford University Press.

Young, L., & Everitt, J. (2004). *Advocacy groups.* Vancouver: UBC Press.

Young, R. (1999). *The struggle for Quebec.* Montreal. QC: McGill-Queen's University Press.

Zakaras, A. (2007). John Stuart Mill, individuality and participatory democracy. In N. Urbinati & A. Zakaras (Eds.), *J. S. Mill's political thought: A bicentennial reassessment* (pp. 200–220). Cambridge, UK: Cambridge University Press.

CREDITS

Photo Credits

Text Credits

Page 15, Figure 1-1 Compiled from Parliament of Canada (2008). Women Candidates in General Elections -1921 to Date. http://www2.parl.gc.ca/Sites/LOP/HFER/hfer.asp?Language=E&Search=WomenElection Reproduced with the permission of the Library of Parliament, 2009.

Page 69, Figure 3-1 Public Works and Government Services Canada, Public Accounts of Canada 2008. Financial Statements Discussion and Analysis Section 1 1.7 http://www.tpsgc-pwgsc.gc.ca/recgen/pdf/49-eng.pdf Reproduced with the permission of the Minister of Public Works and Government Services Canada, 2009.

Page 103, Figure4-5 Jack Jedwab, 2008, "Receiving and Giving: How Does the Canadian Public Feel about Immigration and Integration?" in J. Biles, M. Burstein, and J. Frideres (Eds.), Immigration and Integration in Canada in the Twenty-first Century (211–230), Montreal, QC, and Kingston, ON: Queens Policy Studies Series, McGill-Queen's University Press

Page 127, Table 5-4 With permission from Harold D. Clarke, Ashbel Smith Professor, University of Texas at Dallas

Page 150, Table 6-1 Printed with permission of the Institute for Research on Public Policy, 2005, p4

Page 166, Table 6-2 Based on: Chart 1.12 Chart 2.6 Chart 2.20 Source: Statistics Canada, Caring Canadians, Involved Canadians: Highlights from the Canada Survey of Giving, Volunteering and Participating, 2007, Catalogue 71-542, June 8, 2009, URL: http://www.statcan.gc.ca/pub/71-542-x/71-542-x2009001-eng.htm

Page 192, Figure 7-1 Printed with permission of the Institute for Research on Public Policy 2000 vol 6 no 2 p. 9

Page 212, Table 8-1 Reproduced with the permission of the Library of Parliament, 2009 http://www2.parl.gc.ca/Parlinfo/compilations/ElectionsAndRidings/ResultsParty.aspx?Language=E

Page 209, Figure 8-1 Reproduced with the permission of the Library of Parliament, 2009 http://www2.parl.gc.ca/Sites/LOP/HFER/HFER.asp http://www2.parl.gc.ca/Parlinfo/compilations/ElectionsAndRidings/ResultsParty.aspx?Language=E

Page 292, Table 10-1 Source: K. McRoberts & P. Monahan, The Charlottetown Accord, the referendum, and the future of Canada. University. of Toronto Press; Elections Canada; Directeur Général des Élections du Québec

Page 362, Table 13-2 Adapted from Bakvis, Baier & Brown, Contested Federalism. Oxford Univ. Press, 2009, p. 141

Page 363, Table 13-3 Source: Department of Finance Canada. Federal Support to Provinces and Territories.

Retrieved June 22, 2009 from http://www.fin.gc.ca/fedprov/mtp-eng.asp Reproduced with the permission of the Minister of Public Works and Government Services, 2009.

Page 363, Figure 13-1 Compiled and calculated from Department of Finance Canada, Fiscal Reference Tables 2008, Tables 4 and 5. Retrieved on June 21, 2009 from http://www.fin.gc.ca Reproduced with the permission of the Minister of Public Works and Government Services Canada, 2009.

Page 375 The Way It Works: Inside Ottawa © 2006 by Edward Goldenberg. Published by McClelland & Stewart Ltd. Used with permission of the publishers.

p.386, E. Forsey and G.C. Eglington, The Question of Confidence in Responsible Government. A Study prepared for the Special Committee of Reform of the House of Commons, 1985

Page 402, Figure 14-2 Source: Government Expenditure Cycle, http://www.tbs-sct.gc.ca, Treasury Board of Canada Secretariat, 2009. Reproduced with the permission of the Minister of Public Works and Government Services Canada, 2009.

Page 413, Table 15-1 adapted from House of Commons Procedure and Practice Edited by Robert Marleau and Camille Montpetit © House of Commons

Page 415, Table 15-2 From http://www2.parl.gc.ca/parlinfo/default.aspx?Menu=Home:Reproduced with the permission of the Library of Parliament, 2009.

Page 419, Figure 15-1 © House of Commons

Page 423, Figure 15-2 © House of Commons

Page 443, Table 16-1 Source:.Statistics Canada http://www40.statcan.gc.ca/l01/cst01/govt54a-eng.htm

Page 450, Figure 16-1 Source: Parent Crown Corporations Grouped by Ministerial Portfolio, http://www.tbs-sct.gc.ca/reports-rapports/cc-se/index-eng.asp, Treasury Board of Canada Secretariat, 2009. Reproduced with the permission of the Minister of Public Works and Government Services Canada, 2009

Page 455, Table 16-4 Alex Smith, Library of Parliament, The Roles and Responsibilities of Central Agencies, April 23, 2009. PRB 09-01E http://www.parl.gc.ca/information/library/PRBpubs/prb0901-e.htm#a15 Reproduced with the permission of the Library of Parliament, 2009.

Page 459, Figure 16-2 Source: Sixteenth Annual Report to the Prime Minister on the Public Service of Canada, Annex B: Human Resources Governance Changes-2009 (New Human Resources Governance Structure figure)

INDEX

Note: Entries for figures and tables are followed by "*f*" and "*t*," respectively.